International Gastronomy

International Gastronomy

Clive F. Finch

and

Harry L. Cracknell

Longman

Addison Wesley Longman

Addison Wesley Longman Limited,
Edinburgh Gate, Harlow,
Essex CM20 2JE, England
and associated companies throughout the world

First published 1997

British Library Cataloguing in Publication Data
A catalogue entry for this title is available from the British Library

ISBN 0-582-29336-7

Library of Congress Cataloging-in-Publication Data
A catalog entry for this title is available from the Library of Congress

Set by 8 in 9.5 on 11.5pt Garamond
Produced by Longman Singapore Publishers (Pte) Ltd.
Printed in Singapore

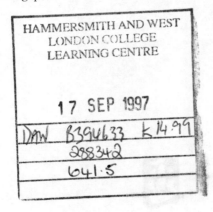

Contents

Introduction

This book is written as a reference book for all grades of staff working in the catering industry and for students studying National Vocational Qualifications GNVQ/GSVQ Level 3, City and Guilds (International) Diploma and Advanced Diploma in Culinary Arts, Higher National Diploma (HND), Ordinary and Honours Degree catering courses, the Hotel and Catering International Management Association (HCIMA) Certificate and Diploma and postgraduate Diploma in Management Studies (DMS) Hotel and Catering programmes. The text will also be of special interest to industrial practitioners, in particular chefs and managers engaged in the food and beverage operation of all kinds of establishments.

The catering industry has moved on from the Anglo-French-Italian dishes by introducing dishes from many other countries. Today's catering students, chefs and managers require a far greater knowledge of international foods and beverages than hitherto was the case, and this book aims to help them to acquire the appropriate knowledge and skills that will enable them to satisfy an ever more discerning, adventurous and knowledgeable clientele.

Consumers are becoming increasingly aware of the nature of the food they are eating and its possible effect on their health, which places increasing pressure on caterers to meet that change. This text provides a catalogue of information that will act as a planning tool and an aide-mémoire to all who are working as caterers as they plan their response to consumers' demands.

International Gastronomy provides over 3000 references divided into 14 chapters. Chapter 1 is concerned with social and cultural aspects of each of the 20 countries reflected in the recipe section; in addition a number of religions and religious sects are discussed within the context of their dietary laws. This section also lists and defines essential commodities such as herbs and spices as used throughout the book. Chapter headings reflect their content, e.g. sauces, soups, egg dishes, farinaceous dishes, etc. Within each section the dishes are aligned to methods of cookery such as baking, boiling, grilling and so on. Each dish is named in English, followed by its ethnic equivalent and country of origin. Repertoire-style descriptions of dishes as given in this book are designed to provide the reader with a brief overview of required ingredients and the practical implications of producing a particular dish; where appropriate, quantities are given for ten average size portions. The Menu Planner in Appendix 1 is designed to give ease of access to the many recipes contained in this book by aligning them to their country of origin and according to menu type, e.g. soup, farinaceous, rice, etc. In Appendix 2, the glossary, all unusual ingredients and unusual terms are listed and defined. Ease of access to information is provided by a comprehensive outline of Contents which is underpinned by details at the beginning of each chapter.

Foreword

On reading this book, I was impressed by its scope and by the professional manner in which it deals with the vast range of dishes from so many different parts of the globe. The breadth of cuisine covered allows the reader to dip into the cookery of many different countries, to experiment with unusual ingredients, and, by following the recipes, create innovative dishes.

International Gastronomy covers a broad spectrum of subjects, making it a cookery book not only for the keen culinary craftsman, but one which gives every reader a glimpse of the culinary heritage of the various areas of the world. Its clear, concise format makes it easy to follow, and it is packed with useful information and advice.

The many influences which affect our eating habits and the frequent changes in our lifestyles are having a significant effect on our eating patterns, so it is vital to keep abreast of the latest culinary developments. This book captures the contemporary spirit of today's catering industry, covering the latest trends such as ethnic cuisines, and other topical influences. I am very sure every reader will enjoy it and I thoroughly recommend it.

Michael Coaker
Executive Chef
The May Fair Hotel
London

Authors' Biographies

Clive F. Finch M.Phil, MHCIMA, DMS, Cert Ed, Dip WTC, CGLI Adv, ACF

Clive Finch worked for many years as a chef in hotels, restaurants and clubs before entering catering education, where he taught preliminary, intermediate and advanced level craft courses and supervisory and management studies. Formerly Head of School of Hotel, Catering and Tourism Management at Middlesex Polytechnic (now Middlesex University), he is Visiting Professor at the School of Hospitality Management, Thames Valley University. His experience in the fields of catering, catering education, food preparation, recipe formulation, product labelling, consultancy and research is considerable. He is a member of the Hotel and Catering International Management Association and of the Association Culinaire Française de Grande Bretagne. He is the author of *Food Preparation*, now a standard text for catering students at all levels.

Harry L. Cracknell FHCIMA, ACF

Harry Cracknell studied his craft at Westminster College, and subsequently worked in some of the foremost kitchens in London and abroad, including The Dorchester, the Park Lane Hotel and at the Colony Club. As a manager he worked at hotels in Padua and Venice, at the Royal Palace Hotel Kensington and the Hôtel de Paris in Paris. After war service in the Middle East he spent six more years in the kitchens of the Savoy, subsequently being appointed Catering Manager at two London hospitals and also at de Havillands Aircraft factory. Moving from industry to education Harry Cracknell was appointed as Lecturer at Battersea Polytechnic, followed by his appointment to Head of Department at Thanet Technical College, at the Oxford College of Technology and then as Food Production Manager at Dorset Institute of Higher Education, now Bournemouth University.

Harry Cracknell is a member of the Association Culinaire Française de Grande Bretagne, an Examiner for City and Guilds of London Institute and a Fellow of the Hotel and Catering International Management Association.

Chapter One

Background Essentials

European Model of Menu Compilation

Religious dietary laws:

✧ Buddhism ✧   ✧ Judaism ✧

✧ Christianity ✧   ✧ Rastafarianism ✧

✧ Hinduism ✧   ✧ Sikhism ✧

✧ Islam ✧

The Cuisines of:

✧ Caribbean islands ✧   ✧ Japan ✧

✧ China ✧   ✧ Mexico ✧

✧ France ✧   ✧ Middle East ✧

✧ Germany ✧   ✧ Portugal ✧

✧ Great Britain ✧   ✧ Russia ✧

✧ Greece and Turkey ✧   ✧ Scandinavia ✧

✧ Hungary ✧   ✧ South Korea ✧

✧ India ✧   ✧ Spain ✧

✧ Indonesia ✧   ✧ Thailand ✧

✧ Israel ✧   ✧ The United States of America ✧

✧ Italy ✧

Within this chapter the cuisines of 28 countries are dealt with in
alphabetical order; this number includes the Caribbean group of islands,
the four Scandinavian countries and four of the Middle Eastern countries
– Egypt, Lebanon, Syria and Iran.

The eating traditions of every country and culture are the result of millennia of history, tempered by political, economic, industrial and social upheavals. Geographic location and climatic conditions naturally play a predominant role in the growing, harvesting and availability of food products and in what the indigenous people eat. Another important factor influencing people's attitude towards food and their likes and dislikes is religion; most religious dietary laws are based upon sound principles of diet and health. Industrialisation and economic movement from a peasant economy to a manufacturing base is yet another key factor that affects lifestyles and fashions in food.

Developments in transportation from earliest times to today's efficient systems mean that fresh fruits, vegetables, fish and meats from all corners of the world are readily available in industrialised countries, normally at a cost most people can afford; foods that until relatively recently were considered exotic are now seen as commonplace. Technological developments, from the early stages of conserving foods by sun-drying, salting, pickling and potting to today's highly commercial factory-produced products, have and will continue to have a direct effect upon the dietary habits and eating trends of nations.

As stated, eating patterns are influenced by social, economic and political changes on one hand, and by changes in personal values and by fashion on the other. Because the public is becoming increasingly nutrition-conscious this must be reflected in menu choice, cooking methods and food availability. Even the casual observer is aware of food trends including the relationship of diet to health and the importance of nutritionally balanced meals of lower fat content, which can lead to less ill-health and obesity.

European Model of Menu Compilation

A typical table d'hôte lunch consists of a first course of hors-d'oeuvre, soup, egg or farinaceous dish, followed by a main course of fish or meat, finishing with a hot or cold sweet. Dinner may comprise a good quality hors-d'oeuvre or soup, followed by a fish, meat, poultry or game dish with vegetables, and a sweet followed by cheese. Coffee and petits fours bring a normal dinner to its logical conclusion.

Menu balance means starting with light foods then moving to slightly more substantial dishes and finishing with light dishes. The visual impact of dishes is considered important, therefore considerable effort is given to the presentation of food. Avoidance of repetition of basic ingredients, methods of cookery, colour, texture, flavour, seasonings, spices, herbs and consistency are guiding principles. Foods in season such as game, vegetables, fruits and meats also need to be considered.

Meals may be preceded by an aperitif, accompanied by a selection of canapés which consists of savoury items, such as smoked salmon, pâté, smoked ham and sausage, asparagus tips and prawns, on small savoury biscuits or toast and glazed with aspic jelly.

Wine and table water may be served throughout the meal. A liqueur or brandy is served with coffee at the end of the meal.

Table layout – cutlery and other table accoutrements should be laid out with military precision according to the requirements of each of the courses on the menu. For an à la carte meal the appropriate cutlery is laid on the table as each course is to be served.

This model of service is used in most western countries with only minor differences, such as in France where the cheese course is served before the sweet.

Religious Dietary Laws

These laws govern the foods that people of certain religions may eat, how they should be prepared, and in what combinations. The traditions of abstinence and the Lenten diet were once governed by strict rules. Many people of several creeds still abide by them. The religions most concerned with dietary laws are Buddhism, Christianity, Islam and Judaism.

Buddhism – These dietary laws are applied personally by each individual according to his or her own conscience. The essence of Buddhism is to abstain from taking life, falsehood, sexual misconduct, theft, and using intoxicants and drugs which will cloud the mind. The central feature is the practice of meditation by concentrating on differing subjects which should lead to transcendental wisdom. Ahimsa, or non-violence and the respect for life, extends to the prohibition of killing animals for food, since every living thing is inhabited by a soul. This means that Buddhists require a vegetarian diet and avoid all strong drink. Zen Buddhism is a Japanese version which arrived by way of China. Its belief lies in the contemplation of a person's essential nature as practised by Buddhist monks, who brought literature, medicine, education and art into China and Japan.

Christianity – Christians believe in and follow Jesus Christ's teachings and example. The Anglican Communion of the United Kingdom includes the episcopal churches of Australia, Canada and many other Commonwealth countries. The Roman Catholic and Eastern Orthodox churches are parts of the Christian church. Fasting is almost universal across many cultures, being either an act of self-denial, a self-administered punishment or to purify the body. Lent is the longest period of fasting in the Christian calendar. The strict rules are kept to by only a minority and most people merely give up a particular item of food and drink for its duration. Catholics have two other Fast Days during the year and donate the money saved on food to Third World charities.

Hinduism – Hindus are vegetarians; eggs are considered to be a source of life and therefore cannot be eaten.

Note: Jain – Jainism, a religion of non-violence, is an ancient Indian religion which has no supreme deity yet recognises some Hindu Gods.

Islam – Muslims must follow certain restrictions on meat. Pork and products derived from pork are prohibited and other meats that are not 'halal' are also unacceptable. Products baked in moulds or tins that have been greased with lard, or items of food fried in bacon fat or containing beef suet, are prohibited. With the exception of prawns, all fish that do not have fins or scales are forbidden. Food that has been in contact with 'unacceptable' foods, for example a salad with the ham removed, is not acceptable. Utensils not washed after 'contaminated' foods have been cooked in them are unacceptable. To some Muslims all foods that have not been prepared in separate pots and with separate utensils are unacceptable. All alcohol is strictly forbidden. Ramadan is the holy ninth month in the Islamic calendar during which Muslims fast from dawn until dusk each day of the month, doing it as an act of purification. It coincides with the Christian weeks of Lent.

For meat to be halal, the name of Allah, the sole deity, must be pronounced over the animal as its throat is cut so that it bleeds to death.

Alevi are a non-orthodox Shiite sect of Muslims. Sunni Muslims are orthodox Muslims.

Judaism – Jewish people fast on the Day of Atonement, which ends Ten Days of Penitence which begin on the Jewish New Year's Day. Dietary laws laid down in the Torah list prohibited foods including the camel, swine, the horse, the hare, eagle, osprey, raven, cuckoo, cormorant, owl, pelican, swan, heron, stork and bat. All molluscs, crustaceans, tortoise and eels are forbidden and only fish with fins and scales may be eaten. Meat and poultry must be ritually slaughtered under Rabbinical supervision. Meat must not be kept or cooked in utensils that have held milk or milk products, and may not be used together with milk in any single meal. Dairy products may not be served after meat foods, and vice versa, until six hours have elapsed. 'Kosher' denotes those foods which comply with Jewish religious laws controlling the selection, preparation and consumption of foods and beverages.

Rastafarianism – Rastafarians follow a West Indian religious movement which encourages them to live a distinctive way of life based on strict dietary rules founded on vegetarianism. Orthodox rastas do not eat fish, flesh, fowl, milk or eggs, or use salt or alcohol. The strict diet and code of conduct are based on Mosaic laws.

Sikhism – this religion is a combination of Hinduism and Islam and was founded in the 16th century as a meditative rather than a ritual religion. Its religious centre is the Golden Temple of Amritsar which is the holy shrine of all Sikhs, who are mainly based in the Punjab which lies between central India and Pakistan. Its followers may not eat beef because cows are considered sacred or pork because pigs are regarded as scavengers. Many Sikhs are vegetarians.

Cuisines of the World

Caribbean Islands (West Indies)

Note: statistical data in this section is for Jamaica, and should not be regarded as representative of the 200 islands of the Caribbean.

Profile (Jamaica)

Land area 10,991 sq km. *Population* 2.47m.
Composition: 74.7% Black, 12.8% Mixed Black, 1.3% East Indian.
Main religions: 60% Protestant, 10% Baptist, 7% Anglican, 7% Adventist, 5% Pentecostal, 5% Roman Catholic.
Economy: based on agriculture, mining and tourism.
Average dietary intake: 83% vegetable products, 17% animal products.

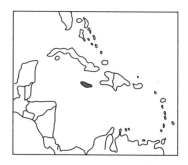

The history of the West Indies shows the many cultural influences brought to these islands over the centuries, which makes it difficult to generalise or to standardise the several types of cuisine that still exist. Many conquerors including Dutch, English, French and Spanish have left their individual traditions, and African, Chinese and Creole immigrants have expanded the repertoire even further.

With ten Commonwealth countries and 11 republics and dependencies, many of them small islands, it is difficult to give a succinct description of what is meant by Caribbean cuisine as there are so many different foodways. Taking an empirical view it is clear there is an abundance of exotic fruits and vegetables, fresh fish and shellfish, pork as the main source of meat, plenty of poultry and dried pulses and cereals, all cooked in interesting combinations. Simplicity is coupled with an emphasis on the intense aroma of spices. The cooking methods are still rather basic but this does not present a problem to the cooks of this area, whose skills can surmount such inconveniences.

Creole and Cajun cookery are two basic cuisines and Rastafarians living in the Caribbean have their own basic cookery laws.

China

Profile

Land area 9,572,900 sq km. *Population* over 1
  bn.
Composition: 92% Chinese, 2% Chuang, 0.87%
  Hui, 0.42% Mongolian, 0.41% Tibetan.
Main religions: no official religion, 12% atheist,
  6% Buddhist, 2.4% Muslim.
Economy: 45% manufacturing, mining, building,
  construction and electricity generation, 40%
  agricultural, fishing, forestry and small manufacturing.
Average dietary intake: 89% vegetable products,
  11% animal products.

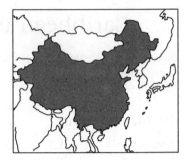

China is composed of 28 provinces and has eight dialects and 60 ethnic minorities, with Mandarin as the common speech. There are four main styles of
Chinese cookery: Canton, Peking, Shanghai and Szechwan, which correspond to
the southern, northern, eastern and western regions respectively.

Chinese gastronomy is recognised as being one of the world's oldest, greatest
and most influential. Certainly the Chinese are concerned with their meals, as
reflected in the extensive repertoire of Chinese dishes, which exists even though
the staple ingredient is rice and almost everything is cooked either in a wok or a
steamer, with the accent on flavour and aroma rather than on presentation.

A Chinese meal is usually served as follows. A number of dishes, generally six or
seven, are laid on the table together. The balance of textures, flavours and ingredients in a typical meal may comprise soup, meat or poultry, fish or shellfish and
vegetables. Sweets are not a feature of a Chinese meal, however, fresh fruits are
sometimes served. For dinner a meal might comprise six different dishes, and for a
celebratory meal the number of dishes would be increased. Jasmine tea, beer and
Chinese wines are served throughout the meal, which can be rounded off with
liqueurs. Meals are generally an informal affair though communal by nature, and this
is reflected by the round table upon which they are served. The use of chopsticks
means that everything is cut small before it is cooked. Spoons are used for liquids.

A resumé of the four regions shows Cantonese cooking as being generally
regarded the best. Rice is most widely used, sweet and sour dishes are favoured
and duck and other foods are given a glossy finish. Many of the dishes are cooked
by steaming. Peking cookery features noodles rather than rice and there are other
farinaceous items such as steamed dumplings and pancake dishes. The dishes are
more substantial and the cookery is more cosmopolitan than elsewhere in the
country. More foods are deep fried and generally there is more crispness of texture,
as exemplified by Peking Duck with its very crisp skin. More use is made of wine
in cooking. Shanghai cookery is more robust with more use of flour and oil,
greater emphasis on garlic, ginger and other spices, and a more peppery result.
Here also it is the tradition to serve noodles instead of rice. The cookery of the
western region of Szechwan bordering on India and Myanmar is noted for its hot
spiciness, including the use of chillies.

Yin and Yang have been a tenet of Chinese medicine since 2700 BC, the Yin being the principle of darkness and coldness or the negative force of life and Yang being the opposite, that of light and warmth and the positive life force. Every item of food is classed as being either yin or yang and illness can be cured by the appropriate diet as advised by the doctor.

Soya beans feature widely in Chinese cookery in the form of soya oil, soya milk, soya bean curd, several kinds of soy sauce and soya bean sprouts. Vegetables are more important than meat, as may be seen in the Chinese recipes included in this book. The egg section does not include the use of thousand-year-old eggs though these are readily available nowadays, being duck eggs that have been treated in ashes, lime and salt and left buried in it for a few months!

France

Profile

Land area 210,068 sq km. *Population* 57.6m.
Composition: 93% French, 2.3% German Alsatian, 1% Breton, 0.4% Catalan, 2.6% Arabic.
Main religions: 76.4% Roman Catholic, 4% other Christian, 3% Muslim.
Economy: leads Europe in agricultural production; fruits, vegetables, wine, iron, steel and motor vehicles. The fourth largest industrialised country in the world.
Average dietary intake: 61% vegetable products, 39% animal products.

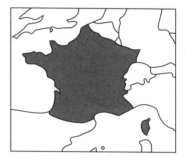

Major developments in French cookery as we know it today are closely associated with Louis XIV and later the Emperor Napoleon Bonaparte, whose opulent and grandiose 18th century courts are legendary.

The fine art of French cookery has been recognised for over three hundred years by emperors, empresses, tzars, tzarinas, kings, queens, the aristocracy of Europe and all other continents and is still considered to be the epitome of gastronomic achievement the world over. French classical cookery is a highly refined form of cookery based on sound cooking principles and dishes of peasant origin. It has been able to suit all prevailing social climates while absorbing any worthwhile influences from other countries without losing its true identity.

To gain an insight into some of the best-known regions which rank high in gastronomic circles, an account of the food of Provence will serve as a guide. The Provençale style of cooking and eating is based entirely on its traditional cuisine, with the accent on the locally produced ingredients of olive oil, garlic and herbs with their aromatic smell of bay, basil, thyme, sage and rosemary. The presence of garlic is not as pronounced as it is further along the Mediterranean coast on the Côte d'Azur but is used quite abundantly in many local specialities. Needless to say, oil and tomatoes are widely featured.

Alpes   A mountainous region which forms the country's eastern border with Switzerland and Italy and embraces the Dauphine and Savoy areas. From its three great lakes comes fish including the rare féra and lavaret, which are best cooked by stuffing and baking or braising, or by grilling. Game features on local gourmet menus, and there is a wide array of items of charcuterie, including air-dried hams, to add extra interest to the culinary repertoire of the region. Local cheeses include such famous names as Reblochon, Beaufort, Saint-Marcellin, some blue-veined varieties and several tommes including Tommes de Savoie with its mouldy appearance and strong aroma but delicious flavour. Some tommes are made from mountain goat's milk. Several of the cheeses add distinction to regional gourmet dishes including the well-known gratin dauphinoise, and are also used with crayfish and with chicken and veal. This region is also noted for the quality of its apricots, peaches and other fine fruits and the Savoy area has long been noted for its contribution to pastry work, including brioches filled with purée of pumpkin, and for nougat de Montélimar.

Alsace and Lorraine   The two départements of Alsace and Lorraine lie along the borders of Germany and Luxembourg and form outstanding meccas of gastronomy, renowned for the richness of their dishes and the distinction of their white wines and eaux-de-vie based on bilberries, blackcurrants and other fruits, not forgetting their beers. Their riches are simple, for example, the wide range of quiches with their savoury filling of eggs and cream that make them universal favourites, or choucroute Alsacienne with its collection of muted and pungent flavours and textures. The matelote and potée are mixtures of soup and fish. Foie gras is produced on a large scale from geese and ducks, and is made into many forms.

Bordeaux   is considered one of the main gastronomic regions, with fish and shellfish from its rivers and the Bay of Biscay and the quality of the baby lambs of Pauillac and the salt marshes. Dishes cooked in the Bordelaise style are discernible by the flavours of the claret and sometimes cognac brandy used in the cooking.

Brittany   This region is ideally situated to benefit from a wide variety of first-class commodities from its farms and market gardens and from the sea and the fishing fleets that use its many fishing ports such as St. Malo. Shellfish are featured on local menus, cooked in many traditional ways including à l'Amoricaine after the ancient name of this region, Amor, the sea country. Artichokes, cauliflowers, garlic and onions enjoy a high reputation. The region's charcuterie is also highly regarded and includes Morlaix smoked hams, pâtés, andouilles, boudins and rillettes. A dish that has become famous everywhere is the gigot de pré-salé Bretonne, a roast leg of marsh lamb served with buttered haricot beans. Pancakes of various kinds, both sweet and savoury, are a great speciality of this region with many different kinds of fillings, and dumplings also are enjoyed by the Bretons. As in Normandy, local cider is the principal drink.

Burgundy and Franche-Comté   This famous wine-growing area has always enjoyed a reputation as an important gastronomic region and there are many dishes in the international repertoire which have become world famous by being cooked à la Bourguignonne, usually with a red or white Burgundy wine to give a special distinction to the dish. Snails are a speciality and meurette and pauchouse are typical of the fish stews, both cooked with local wines. The

Bresse chickens are considered to be the best in France and the Charolais cattle give excellent lean beef. Cream is not as widely used in cookery as it is in other regions but cheese making is an important industry of the Franche-Comté area. The whole region produces Gruyère, bleu de Bresse, Chevrotan, Saint-Florentin and Soumaintrain and other well-known cheeses. Items of charcuterie include brési which is salted, smoked and dried joints of beef and veal for slicing thinly, and smoked saucissons and saucisse de Lyon. Gaudes is a local speciality and is porridge made with coarsely ground maize, served hot with cream or cold in slices. Game from the forests of the Jura area and truffles and morels are also used in local recipes. Dijon mustard is much used in cooking.

Central France   This region has a reputation for serving honest household dishes in large portions, without any pretentiousness of style or presentation. The soups can be eaten as a meal in themselves, well garnished with cabbage or oats. Belly of pork is garnished with haricot beans, and black and white puddings and tripe are cooked in many interesting ways. Alicot is a way of using the giblets of poultry as a succulent stew. Many of the region's cheeses are made of goat's milk, those of national renown being Cantal, Saint-Nectaire, Roquefort and Bleu d'Auvergne. Aligot potatoes is a local way of using Aligot cheese, which is a fresh one similar to Mozzarella, and pommes purée flavoured with garlic, shallow fried as small potato cakes. Cheese cakes are also a feature of the region and fruit tarts are other local specialities.

Corsica   The cooking of Italy and Provence have had an influence on Corsica's own culinary traditions which makes for well-flavoured and substantial dishes with plenty of fish and shellfish including bass, daurade and rascase, anchovies and large crawfish. There are plenty of game animals including wild boar, and birds which are often made into excellent pâtés. Pork products are highly esteemed; possibly they taste different here because chestnuts are added to the pig's diet. Apart from pork, goat and horse meat are used in stews and smoked goat is of some considerable note. Goat's and sheep's milk cheeses are eaten and cooked, all of which puts the island's culinary heritage on a high gastronomic level among all the regions of France.

Languedoc-Roussillon   This vast area of southern France is bordered by the Pyrenees mountains of Spain and the Mediterranean Sea and includes cities such as Toulouse and the towns of Carcassonne, Castelnaudary and Nimes, all names that carry culinary connotations of gourmet fare. Local dishes comprise the entire sequence of courses including such well-known soups as the aigo bouido and ouillarde, fish and shellfish soups which include oysters and mussels from Sète. For the fish course there is brandade de morue from Nimes, tripe from the stomachs of tuna fish braised in white wine with pimento and tomato, fresh anchovies and sardines and crawfish. The extensive and varied list of main dishes includes cassoulet à la Castelnaudary, gigot de mouton à la pistache, daube de boeuf, estofats – which is like a cassoulet – and many dishes based on cow's and lamb's tripe, as in cabassol in which lamb's tripe is cooked with the boned head and trotters and vegetables. Vegetables are cultivated extensively and the globe artichokes, cauliflowers, peas and tomatoes are of excellent quality. Fruits include apples, apricots, cherries, peaches and raspberries. Local dishes of the Roussillon part of this region convey the influence of Catalonia in the abundant use of olive oil and garlic, but there is also some finesse from dried orange peel as a flavourer.

Loire   This region is known as the garden of France because of its production of fruit including reinette apples, apricots, grapes, melons, peaches, william pears, quinces and soft fruits in season; also for its excellent artichokes, asparagus and mushrooms. The fish includes carp, eels, lampreys, pike and shad which are often prepared in the form of matelotes or bouilletures. Feathered and furred game is found in the Sologne forest and made into pâtés and terrines, and the region's lamb and beef enjoy a high reputation for their quality. As in most other regions there is a wide variety of high-class charcuterie items and among the famous cheeses produced in the Loire are Port Salut and Saint-Maure, as well as many goat's cheeses. This area is also renowned for its pastry products, of which pithiviers, tarte Tatin and clafoutis are featured on many high-class menus.

Lyon is universally acknowledged as the gastronomic capital of France and many famous chef-patrons have their establishments in the Lyonnaise region, which is further surrounded by the region of Burgundy. Thus the cuisine is amply supplied with an abundance of fine quality ingredients from the area to be made into dishes fit for the most discerning gourmets and into fine local produce such as a great array of local hams, salamis, saucissons and other items of charcuterie.

Midi-Pyrénées   This département lies along the border with Spain and includes Toulouse, a city of some 400,000 and the headquarters of France's aero industry which is also noted for its choice quality produce and the high standards of local cookery. It is another area for the production of foie gras and is the centre of the French market for truffles, fungi found under the roots of oak trees. This is also the home of magrets of goose and duck as by-products of the foie gras industry and of Armagnac brandy and Roquefort cheese.

Northern France   This heavily industrialised region borders onto Belgium, and the local pattern of eating is as substantial as that of the Belgians. Beer is more likely to be used than wine in cooking and for drinking. Prime vegetables from local market gardens make a significant contribution and include cabbages both red and white, Belgian endive and leeks, which are also used in the substantial soups and in the fish soups-cum-stews which are an interesting feature of the coastal areas and include fish pot-au-feu. Charcuterie products are a strong feature with andouilles and andouillettes and pâtés of all kinds. This area is also noted for its savoury flans called goyères and flamiches.

South-Western France   The Sud-Ouest region adjoins Languedoc-Roussillon and also borders onto Spain and onto the Atlantic Ocean as the Côte d'Argent, reaching to the Bordeaux region. The basic cookery of the region is noted as being of a stalwart peasant standard, based on good quality but ordinary commodities. Goat meat and goat's milk cheese prevail but duck and goose are of more importance with a large production of foie gras in its many forms, as well as magrets and confits. Game animals such as the chamois are hunted in the Pyrenees, and game birds from the forests of the Landes include buntings, wild pigeons, figpeckers, larks and woodcock. From the town of Orthez comes the best-known of all cured hams, the Jambon de Bayonne, which is smoked after curing in a mixture of wine, herbs and spices. Other items of local charcuterie include boudins blanc, loukinka which is a spicy sausage, and black puddings. Piperade, the very popular dish of eggs with pimento, onion and tomato is usually served accompanied with wafer-thin slices of Bayonne ham. Fish and shellfish are in plentiful supply and are often used in interesting fish soups and stews. Beef is cooked en daube and as estouffade; lambs are farmed here and poultry is often combined with meat in pot-au-feu and en compote. Armagnac brandy is produced here and Cahors is the centre of France's truffle trade.

Western France   This region lies in between Brittany and Bordeaux, with a coastline on the Bay of Biscay which provides its culinary repertoire with all the different kinds of fish and shellfish, notably Marennes oysters and Royan sardines, many fish also being landed at the port of La Rochelle. From the salt marshes of the Marais come lambs and many quality vegetables including artichokes, broad beans, courgettes and haricot beans.

The emphasis given here to the culinary traditions of France is because of the great impact it has had on the eating habits of many other countries. Try as we may to release ourselves from its influence it will always be with us as the highest possible standard of culinary refinement. Hybrids of French classical dishes are to be found on the menus of many of the countries featured in this book, and in each case a certain understanding of the basics of French cookery was needed to make them worthy additions. Pseudo-French cooking has no place in any country's menus.

Germany

Profile

Land area 356,733 km. *Population* 81.2m.
Composition: 93.4% German, 2.1% Turkish, 0.8% Yugoslav, 0.7% Italian, 0.4% Greek, 0.4% Polish, 0.2% Spanish.
Main religions: 37% Protestant, 34% Roman Catholic, 2.7% Muslim, 0.1% Jewish.
Economy: mainly an industrially based economy and the second largest trading nation in the world, one of the world's leading economic powers.
Average dietary intake: 65% vegetable products, 35% animal products.

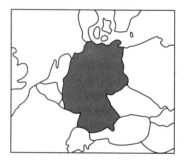

In AD 800 all of Germany and parts of Austria formed part of the Holy Roman Empire ruled by the Emperor Charlemagne. Much later, in 1841 the German Empire was born, created by Bismark, then chancellor to William 1st of Prussia.

The food of Germany has been influenced by its many neighbours: France, Poland, Czechoslovakia and Hungary, and by some of the Balkan countries. Reunited after its separation into two republics, the whole of Germany can now be enjoyed on a long tour of all its centres of gastronomy, which are considerable and match the country's prosperity and the love of food by its population. Large appetites are amply satisfied by a wide diversity of plainly cooked food with no ostentation and as unrefined as it was originally. Flavourings and seasonings help to stimulate the appetite, assisted by contrasts of sour and sweet sensations, matching the contrasting meat with fruit and fruit with vegetables, or chilled foods with hot foods. Colour contrasts are bold and gravies rather than sauces are used. The strong flavour of game is very much appreciated and it would be the wild rather than the reared animal that is chosen. Most commonly used commodities are potatoes, cabbage in its many forms, and pork; favourite dishes include the hundred different kinds of sausages and other items of the pork butcher's art, and many kinds of dumplings and pancakes.

Breakfast is as the continental style with some form of bread and butter and a preserve plus coffee. Lunch is a fairly substantial meal of three or four courses and dinner is of less importance, though it can include fish, meat or sausages and cheese as well as a sweet. Otherwise menu organisation and structure follow the European model.

Great Britain

Profile

Land area 244,110 sq km. *Population* 58m.
Composition 94.2% white, 2.5% Asian Indian,
   0.8% Afro-Caribbean.
Main religions: 79% Christian, 2.5% Muslim,
   0.7% Sikh, 1.5% Hindu, 1.2% Jewish.
Economy: major trade from manufactured products such as motor vehicles and aircraft engines, fabrics and man-made fibres, which together with chemicals and oil production make a significant contribution to the economy.

Average dietary intake: 66% vegetable products, 34% animal products.

Down the centuries British cookery as we know it today has been influenced in turn by the Roman occupation and the period of unprecedented change following the invasion by the Duke of Normandy, William the Conqueror. During the Middle Ages returning Crusaders introduced a Middle Eastern dimension to the food fashions of the day. The spice trade, the tea trade and the entrepreneurial nature of businessmen, seafarers and explorers of the 16th century in turn introduced a whole range of new ingredients to the British larder. The impact of the British Empire, which reached its zenith in Victorian times, gave access to low-cost foods from around the globe and resulted in the adoption of many Indian and Chinese dishes into the British repertoire. The employment of French chefs to run the kitchens of country houses of the nobility and gentry was a feature of food fashion for over two hundred years.

The British have always been rather puritanical about their food and culinary traditions despite the rich store of local and regional recipes. Sound culinary precepts from other countries have always been welcomed and have allowed recipes to be interlaced with foreign influences.

Taking account of the seasons and the weather, of the economic climate and of the prevailing social atmosphere, traditional British dishes are perhaps intended for hearty male appetites – cuts from roast joints of prime meat, succulent beef steaks, mutton chops, boiled beef and dumplings, hot-pots and pies such as steak and kidney, savoury and sweet puddings, tripe and onions, saveloys and pease pudding, jellied eels, fish and chips to name only a few of the extensive list of Britain's culinary delights. The cookery traditions of Northern Ireland, Wales and Scotland are very similar to those of England.

Greece

Profile

Land area 131,957 sq km. *Population* 10.3m.

Composition: 95.5% Greek, 1.5% Macedonian, 1% Turkish, 0.6% Albanian.

Main religions: 98% Christian of which 97% are Greek Orthodox, 0.4% Roman Catholic, 0.1% Protestant; 1.5% Muslim.

Economy: private enterprise-financed economy. Increasing its industrial base yet remains agriculturally centred, producing olive oil, tobacco, citrus fruit, cotton and wine. Tourism is important and there is a large merchant fleet.

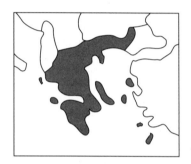

Average dietary intake: 74% vegetable products, 26% animal products.

Greek cuisine is discussed together with Turkish cuisine in the section below.

Turkey (The Republic of Turkey)

Profile

Land area 779,452 sq km. *Population:* 59.8m.

Composition: 85.7% Turkish, 10.6% Kurdish, 1.6% Arab, 0.3% Circassian, 0.3% Turkman, 0.2% Georgian.

Main religions: 90% Sunni Muslim, 9.6% Alevi, 0.4% Christian.

Economy: main agricultural crops are grain and tobacco; tourism is a growth area; oil.

Average dietary intake: 92% vegetable products, 8% animal products.

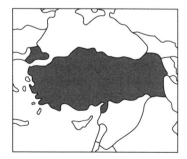

Greek cookery is not recognised for any imaginative dishes and it is very traditional, with little of its erstwhile Byzantine influences; it is simple, down-to-earth cookery. Greek and Turkish cooking are very similar to the extent that a number of dishes overlap and some even have the same names. However, there are variations between the two countries' cooking traditions brought about by historical and religious traditions, Greece being mainly Christian and Turkey an Islamic country. Greece was occupied by the Turks for over 400 years and was therefore part of the Ottoman Empire until its liberation in 1830. It is therefore not too difficult to understand the links that exist between the two cuisines. Greece, the cradle of civilisation, enjoyed a long tradition of fine food and its culture can be traced back to the 5th century BC, when it was noted for its high culinary standards. As the 'Greek Miracle', the culture of Greek cuisine spread to many Mediterranean countries including Italy, Sicily, Turkey and those in the Middle East. Greek cookery has its own distinct identity with its own unique set of gastronomic traditions.

About 90 per cent of the population of Turkey live in the European part and less than 10 per cent in that part of the country which is in Asia. Turkey was formerly known as the Ottoman Empire and so its food has the distinctive taste of the Middle East, brought in by the minority races who dwell within its borders including Armenians, Circassians, Georgians, Greeks, Kurds and Lazes. The food is varied and interesting and many dishes have become popular in the international repertoire.

The styles of Greek and of Turkish cuisine utilise very fresh ingredients, well flavoured with herbs such as thyme and rosemary, with just a hint of spiciness, and cooked as simply as possible, with much emphasis on the use of olive oil, olives, yogurt and lemon juice to enhance the main ingredients. The basic diet comprises fish, lamb, beans, bread, rough cheeses and fresh fruit. Rice and potatoes are featured with most main courses.

Menu organisation and structure generally follow the European model as discussed on page 2. Meals are usually rounded off with a selection of locally grown fresh fruits. There is little or no emphasis on sweet dishes and those that are served lack the richness of French desserts and English puddings. Aperitif may be served before a meal, beer and wine are served throughout, and the meal is rounded off with the distinctive aroma and flavour of Greek or Turkish coffee. Alternatively, a mezze menu may be offered which consists of a selection of up to 18 separate dishes – a meal in itself.

Hungary

Profile

Land area 93,000 sq km. *Population* 10.2m.

Composition: 97.8% Magyar, 1.4% Gypsy, 0.3% German, 0.1% Croatian, 0.1% Romanian, 0.1% Slovac.

Main religions: 89.9% Christian of which 64.1% are Roman Catholic; 0.9% Jewish.

Economy: agriculturally based on fruit, vegetables and meats. Significant industrial development in recent years.

Average dietary intake: 63% vegetable products, 37% animal products.

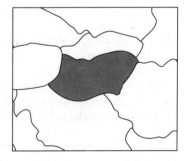

Since the mid-15th century Hungary has undergone continuous turmoil and domination by its neighbours Turkey, Austria, Germany and Italy. In the 1600s Hungary was divided between two of central Europe's major powers, the Hapsburg Empire and the Austro-Hungarian Monarchy, until the revolution of 1848 when Hungary gained a short period of independence. After the First World War, Hungary was partitioned by the Treaty of Trianon among the Balkan states, Rumania, Czechoslovakia and Yugoslavia. In 1949 the communists took the monopoly of power which lasted until 1991.

Hungarian cookery has been greatly influenced by its neighbouring countries as well as adopting French and Italian classical cuisines and borrowing and adapting many specialities from the Slav population who live in Hungary and its neighbouring countries.

The Hungarian repertoire can fairly claim to be very sophisticated, having developed a wide repertoire of national dishes conceived by inventive cooks as well as many dishes from outside influences, these being somewhat more substantial.

Hungarian salamis and foies gras enjoy good reputations; freshwater fish, especially carp, is cooked creatively, and meat is stewed in the form of goulash. Paprika features prominently in Hungarian cookery, as does caraway and soured cream. The pastry section is noted for its strudels.

As is to be expected by its geographical location and past history, menu organisation and structure follow the European model (see page 2).

India (also including Pakistan, Bangladesh and Sri Lanka)

Profile

Land area 3,166,414 sq km. *Population* 1094m.
Main religions: 83% Hindu, 11% Muslim, 2.5% Christian, 1.9% Sikh, 0.71% Buddhist, 0.4% Jain.
Economy: mainly agricultural, including tea, jute and cotton, current industrial development of mineral resources.
Average dietary intake: 93% vegetable products, 7% animal products.

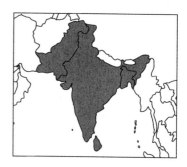

There are no fewer than 25 states in the subcontinent of India, each having its own capital city and its own culinary inheritance. The different religions and sects play important parts in food choice.

There is a tendency to generalise about native dishes and to assume that curry is the one and only national dish, and the hotter it tastes the more authentic it must be. This is not so; there are many different kinds of curry, each having a different blend of spices and herbs, ranging from extremely hot through medium to mild. For example, vindaloo curry of Madras in the south of India is very hot, as is that of Goa.

The richest cookery of India is reckoned to be that of the Mogul dynasty, as now found in and around the Indian capital Delhi and also featured in Pakistan. Apart from a number of regional specialities the overall colours of food are varying shades of yellow, brown and red as is to be expected from the traditional blends of spices that give colour and flavour to most of India's national dishes.

European versions of curry dishes are usually made with proprietary brands of curry powder or paste but chefs and gourmets usually prefer to keep a spice rack and blend the ingredients to suit their own taste.

Pakistan

This is an Islamic country: about 95 per cent of the approximately 85m population are Muslims and follow the tenets of that religion. This is the home of Tandoori cooking – cooking food in specially designed clay ovens – but otherwise the diet is similar to that in India, except perhaps for more detailed presentation with more meat dishes and flour-based foods than rice. Balti cooking is a method and style of cookery of Kashmir in northern Pakistan. Highly spiced curries of fish, meat, poultry and vegetables are cooked in a balti pan to provide dishes of a style which has recently become somewhat of a phenomenon in Great Britain; balti cookery applies similar principles to stir-fried Chinese cookery.

The authentic cookery of Bangladesh is not well known outside its borders and it is therefore assumed that it is no different from the other parts of the subcontinent. Bangladesh, in what was formerly East Pakistan with the provinces of East Bengal and Assam, has a population of some 90 million, with its capital at Dhaka. It produces rice and plenty of prawns from the Bay of Bengal. There is a difference from India in that cheese is used for cooking. Dahls are very important. Mustard seed oil is preferred to ghee and there is a wider use of spices to add their flavour to the locally produced prawns.

Sri Lanka (formerly Ceylon)

European influence has given an added dimension to this island, which is separated from the southern tip of India by only a narrow strip of water. With its Buddhist religion, it was ruled by the Portuguese for 150 years followed by the Dutch East Indies Company and then the British from 1802 until 1948. Here the curry dishes are really hot, though if made with coconut milk, which is used extensively, can be made much milder. Black curries are made using fried spices and the red-coloured curries contain a large quantity of chopped chillies. Many of its curries are of a vegetarian nature to suit public demand.

Menu planning comprises simply compiling a list of dishes to suit the occasion taking into account the range of ingredients and balance of flavour and texture, between protein and carbohydrates, and between richness and spiciness. The number and range of dishes selected for the menu will naturally depend upon economic constraints, a sense of occasion and religious considerations. Muslims and Sikhs tend to eat one or two meat dishes, Hindus favour a large range of vegetarian dishes. Traditionally food is served and eaten on a thali, which can be an elaborately decorated silver tray or a banana leaf; food may also be served in individual bowls. Soft drinks rather than wine would be served during the meal.

Indonesia

Profile

Land area 1,919,317 sq km. *Population* 182m.
Composition: 39% Javanese, 16% Sundanese, 12% Indonesian, 3% Madurese.
Main religions: 87% Muslim, 10% Christian, 2% Hindu, 1% Buddhist.
Economy: agriculturally based, agriculture employing over 55% of the population; developing oil and gas industries.
Average dietary intake: 97% vegetable products, 3% animal products.

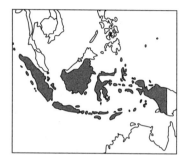

This republic includes Bali, Borneo, Java and Sumatra, and was previously known as the East Indies. The first two cultural and religious influences were the arrival of Buddhists and Hindus from India who were followed by Portuguese settlers then a hundred years later by the Dutch. Immigrants came in large numbers from China, having a great deal of influence on the islands' cookery. Javanese coffee and tea have good reputations for fine taste; Indonesian-brewed beer is considered one of the best; there is a strong wine made from rice and the ubiquitous coconut palm is used for making refreshing drinks as well as for flavouring dishes. Rice is served at nearly every main meal but with only a small amount of fish, meat or chicken. These main ingredients and vegetables are usually cut into small pieces so as to absorb the spicy seasonings and to cook quickly, as well as to make it easy to eat without a need for cutlery, preferably using the fingers. Saté is a very popular national dish usually in the form of barbecued skewers of meat and fish which have been well coated with various spices and are served with peanut sauce. Nasi goreng is also a well-known dish, using rice which is fried with chillies, garlic and spices, mixed with sautéed strips of meat, poultry, shellfish and flat omelette. Many restaurants in Holland feature Indonesian cookery.

The table etiquette is to set the table with a plate, fork and spoon with a bowl for soup, if to be served. When serving a meal everything is placed on the table at the same time, with the exception of sweets or fresh fruits. Rice is taken first followed by other dishes and accompaniments. Finger bowls form part of the formal table setting as an Indonesian meal is eaten with one's fingers; only the tips of the right hand are used. It is of course necessary to use spoons when eating soup and suchlike. Due to religious laws beers and wine are not strictly a feature of an Indonesian meal.

Israel

Profile

Land area 20,700 sq km. *Population* 5.4m.
Composition: 82% Jewish, 18% Arab and other.
Main religions: 82% Jewish, 13% Sunni Muslim,
  2.5% Christian.
Economy: diamond cutting makes a significant
  contribution towards the economy. Agriculture is very important as are manufacturing
  of textiles and clothing and tourism.
Average dietary intake: 79% vegetable products,
  21% animal products.

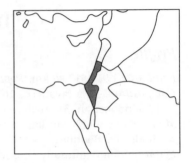

This Middle Eastern country is populated by Jewish and Arab people, who are all
Israelis. The Jewish people in Israel are mainly immigrants from Europe, mainly
from Germany, Poland and Russia. There are also immigrants from Spain and
Portugal, and more recently the Jewish minorities from Ethiopia and other African
countries, Syria and Iran have made their homes in Israel.

   The Jews have adapted available permitted raw commodities to their cooking
methods and made them into Jewish dishes. During the many times they were
banished into ghettos they made a little food go a long way by making it into
stuffed dishes, both savoury and sweet. Many interesting dishes are made expressly
for the many Jewish festivals in the calendar, and only unleavened bread called
Matzos may be eaten during the Feast of the Passover, which commemorates the
night when a destroying angel smote the first-born of the Egyptians but spared
those Jews in the houses where the doorposts and lintels were daubed with blood.

   Many arab dishes have become part of the Israeli way of life and felafel (deep-
fried spiced chickpea balls), houmous (chickpea purée), tahina (paste of sesame
seeds, oil and lemon) and halva (sweetmeat made of semolina, butter, sugar and
nuts) are appreciated. The fruit and vegetables of Israel are of a very high quality,
meat and poultry are of good quality and the wines are equal to those of Europe.
Menu organisation and structure follow the European model (see page 2).

Italy

Profile

Land area 301,302 sq km. *Population* 57.3m.
Composition: 94.1% Italian, 2.7% Sardinian, 1.3%
  Rhaetian.
Main religions: 83.2% Roman Catholic.
Economy: 33% manufacturing, including motor
  vehicles and textiles, and construction; 4%
  agricultural; tourism is a major contributor to
  the economy.
Average dietary intake: 74% vegetable products,
  26% animal products.

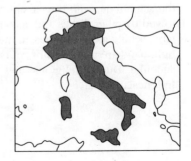

The Italians take their national gastronomy very seriously and are convinced that when Catherine de' Medici left her home in Florence to marry King Henry the Second of France in 1533 the cooks she took with her influenced Henry's own staff, and that they adopted many of the Italians' culinary skills to improve the prevailing French standards. Certainly Italy has helped to civilise the art of dining and table presentation including artistic centrepieces and other ornamentations; delicate embroidered table napery, porcelain, silver and glassware, as well as impeccable service, are part of its heritage.

Basically, Italy's culinary tradition is that of feeding a large family with inexpensive yet wholesome fresh food; the cookery is pure and uncomplicated for leisurely consumption. It is very unprepossessing in presentation and largely unaffected by current international influences, though unwittingly contributing to the worldwide popularity of many Italian dishes. Each of Italy's 17 regions has its own specialities and cooking methods, many of them of medieval if not Roman or Etruscan origin, but in general it can be stated that pork and veal are the country's most widely used meats, with horse meat, goat, lamb, poultry, game and song birds and game animals making a considerable contribution. Italy is almost surrounded by sea and takes delight in the many kinds of fish, cooking them in simple ways by grilling or shallow frying. Italy has become synonymous with high quality pasta dishes, pizzas, smoked hams and its fine quality fruits and vegetables which are available in great variety and abundance. The dessert course on menus contains few purely Italian classic sweet dishes, so cheese plays a major role in rounding off the meal.

Menu organisation and structure follow the European model (see page 2).

Japan

Profile

Land area 377,750 sq km. *Population* 124.5m.
Composition: 99% Japanese, 0.6% Korean 0.1% Chinese.
No official religion, 38% follow Shintoism and Buddhism.
Economy: highly developed and successful export manufacturing base which is dependent upon imports of raw materials.
Average dietary intake: 79% vegetable products, 21% animal products.

Japan comprises a group of four main islands and a number of smaller islands. Buddhist monks of the Kuya sect came to Japan from China during the Heian period 794–1192, bringing with them many of their staple foods. During this period Japan was a strictly religious country and vegetarianism formed the basis of the national diet. During the 16th century Chinese ideas and foods began to influence the Japanese diet.

The national diet is based on fish from the Pacific Ocean that surrounds the islands that form this highly industrialised country. Only one sixth of the country can be cultivated or used for grazing but rice, potatoes, vegetables and wheat are grown and fruits harvested. Vegetables are important to the Japanese diet because many of the people follow a vegetarian regime. Dairy produce does not enter traditional dietary preparations. Some of the most predominant cookery methods associated with Japanese cookery are tempura, a classic batter-coated deep-fried dish of vegetables or shellfish, and Sushi, a delicately flavoured vinegared rice which is presented with a variety of toppings such as raw fish, omelettes and vegetables. Nabemono, one-pot dishes, are a popular form of cookery in which foods, meats, fish and poultry are cooked at table in special earthenware pots on table heaters.

Meals are small, the few and simple ingredients being made sharper to the taste with soy and other seasonings. A typical meal may comprise an aperitif of saké served warm in small cups, rice soup, rice, raw fish known as sashimi marinated with soy sauce and very hot horseradish relish, and vegetables. The entire meal may be served together in individual bowls, plates or dishes to be consumed in no particular order. Selected dishes can be hot, tepid or cold. Rice is omnipresent and there are no desserts afterwards, thus the diet is fairly fat-free. Delicately flavoured green unfermented tea in tiny bowls is served throughout, as are beer and wine. Wines are increasing in popularity as is the proprietary brand of Sappora beer. Emphasis is placed on preparation, which is always expected to be perfect thus showing skill, imagination and creativity. The methods of service are as traditional as the cooking, being based on precise presentation without being marshalled or ordered. Food is enhanced by being served in decorative porcelain dishes with each table setting having a pair of chopsticks laid on a ceramic rest together with a spoon, appropriately aligned.

Mexico

Profile

Land area 1,958,201 sq km. *Population* 89.9m.
Composition: 60% Mestizo, 30% Amerindian, 9% Caucasian.
Main religions: 90% Roman Catholic, 5% Protestant.
Economy: traditionally agriculturally based, major exporter of cotton, currently moving towards a semi-industrialised economy and a developing oil industry.
Average dietary intake: 82% vegetable products, 18% animal products.

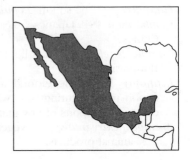

The food of this Spanish-speaking nation has become very popular in many countries and has a special appeal to young people who appreciate its exciting flavours, which are quite intense on the palate and are hot but not too hot. Also it is fairly cheap and substantial and makes good use of low-cost ingredients, yet is nutritionally sound. Mexico has an old established cuisine which stems from the native Indians and the Aztecs and then from the Spanish who arrived here in 1519. There is some French influence too which came with the installation of the Emperor Maximilian, younger brother of the Emperor of Austria, who was married to the daughter of King Leopold 1 of Belgium. The cuisine is based on an abundance of native ingredients made extremely hot by the use of chillies, cooked simply without much roasting or baking, and supported by accompaniments made of maize, which plays a much larger part in the diet than wheat. Everyday maize products include enchiladas, burritos, tacos, tortillas and many others. The diet also includes several different types of dried beans. Mexicans like to eat and drink frequently throughout the day and their menu is graced by the national dish called Mole Poblano, considered to be one of the world's most outstanding Mexican dishes.

Plates of small crisp-fried pork rinds, cubes of cooked pork or chicken accompanied by dips such as guacamole and tortillas may be served as an appetizer. Menu organisation, structure and design generally follow the French model.

Middle East

This section includes Egypt, Lebanon, Syria and Iran. Because of its antiquity a profile of Egypt has been selected as representative of this area.

Profile (Egypt)

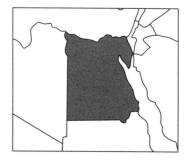

Land area 997,739 sq km. *Population* 57.1m.
Composition: 99% Egyptian.
Main religions: 90% Sunni Muslim, 10% Christian.
Economy: based on cultivation of a strip of
   land 8–25 km wide along the Nile; newly
   developed industrialisation.
Average dietary intake: 92% vegetable products,
   8% animal products.

In 500 BC the Persians conquered Egypt and dethroned its ruler. In 332 BC it fell to the Greek leader Alexander the Great. Thirty years before the birth of Christ, Egypt was conquered by the Romans. With the breakup of the Roman Empire in the 5th century Egypt was under continuous threat, being invaded now and then from the north and the south. In the year 641 Egypt was conquered by the Arabs, who burned the city of Alexandria to the ground. In 1517 Egypt fell to the Turks and the great Ottoman Empire. During the early 1800s it was ruled by France under Napoleon Bonaparte. The building of the Suez Canal left Egypt's economy in a perilous state and in 1882 in an attempt to stabilise the economy the British took temporary occupation, the protectorate being terminated in 1922 when Egypt once again became a sovereign state. In 1952 King Farouk I was forced to abdicate and Egypt became a Republic.

This islamic republic is an arid land. More than half the population depend upon agriculture for a livelihood and tend sheep, goats and cattle and grow wheat, rice and barley. Its culinary inheritance has been influenced by many other countries, especially Greece, Turkey, France and Italy. Popular dishes include morgh polou, a festive dish which demonstrates the use of fruit with meat, being chicken cooked with apricots, raisins and rice with saffron as the flavouring. Kebabs, stuffed vine and cabbage leaves, meat balls and rice dishes are traditional and flavourings include coriander, fenugreek and rose-water. The Egyptians love simple dishes cooked by simple, economic methods yet with certain subtle traditional touches.

Portugal

Profile

Land area 92,389 sq km. *Population* 9.8m.
Composition: 99% Portuguese, Cape Verdean and Brazilian.
Main religions: 94.5% Roman Catholic.
Economy: agriculturally based, wine, olive oil, forestry and cork; commercial fishing makes a significant contribution; tourism is a fast growth area.
Average dietary intake: 76% vegetable products, 24% animal products.

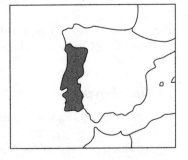

Spain lies close to Portugal and together they make up the Iberian peninsula. They naturally shared many of the early invasions by the Romans, Celts, Teutons, Arabs from Morocco and the Moors in the 8th century. Today the indigenous Portuguese population has grown out of these stock. The island of Madeira belongs to Portugal and for many centuries Brazil came under Portuguese control. In 1850 Spain occupied Portugal and ruled it for a period of 60 years, thus historically the two countries' gastronomies have much in common.

The simple peasant style of Portuguese cooking is straightforward. Pork, especially sucking piglets, goat meat, poultry, fresh fish and bacalhao, the dried salted cod which is prepared in a large number of ways, are all important. Fish stews are also popular including some containing shellfish. Escabeche, the fried then marinated fish dish, is traditional in Portugal. Rice and tomatoes are basic ingredients but neither port nor madeira wines are used for cooking. The main difference between the cooking of Portugal and Spain is that in Spanish cooking there is a greater emphasis on the use of herbs and spices, particularly the use of freshly picked coriander leaves.

Menu organisation and structure follow the European model (see page 2).

Russia

Profile

Land area 17m sq km. *Population* 275m.
Composition: 81% Russian, 4% Tartar, 3% Ukrainian and 1% Shuvash.

Main religions: there is no official religion but predominantly Russian Orthodox, Catholics, Protestants, Muslims, Jews.

Economy: from being essentially an agricultural country Russia has become the world's second largest industrial power with great potential for the future; forests cover over 40 per cent of the land and timber exports are large; its mineral wealth is enormous.

It should be remembered that Russia covers a vast territory equal to one sixth of the area of the world. The range of climatic conditions and the number of different races, cultures and languages is on a scale unequalled in any other country.

Now that market forces have replaced the former socialist ownership of the means of production there is an increase in the availability and choice of goods, so the previous limitations on diet are being expanded.

The westernisation of Russia was begun by Peter the Great (1672–1725) and the 18th and particularly the 19th century was the time when the arts, including poetry, fiction, music and the arts of the table, developed enormously. The awakening of royal and noble families to the pleasures of the table was the time when the social and economic situation helped to develop a truly Russian style of cookery based on traditional ingredients and methods, which was further refined by foreign influences, mainly those of France.

Catherine the Great (1729–1796), who continued to patronise the arts, brought chefs from France to work in her royal households and they helped to enlarge and improve traditional Russian dishes and bring them to gourmet standards. These chefs imported foods from France to widen the culinary repertoire, and other influences came from Scandinavian countries. Felix Urbain-Dubois (1818–1902) worked for the last Czar of Russia, Nicholas II who reigned from 1894 to 1917, and helped advance the standards of Russian cookery and establish it in the international repertoire.

Menu organisation and structure follow the European model (see page 2). A main meal usually begins with a selection of small snacks called zakuski, some made in tartlets or on blinis and topped with caviar, herring, liver and egg, and served with vodka. Vodka was traditionally served with most meals but because of the problems of alcohol abuse and its effect upon society this social trait has been rigorously discouraged. Nowadays light wines or kvass, a low-alcohol drink, are more likely to be served throughout the meal.

Scandinavia (Denmark, Finland, Norway and Sweden)

Note: Statistical data is for Sweden only, being selected as the largest and most populated country in the group. This data is not intended to be representative of the group.

Profile (Sweden)

Land area 449,964 sq km. *Population* 8.7m.
Composition: 90.4% Swedish, 2.4% Finnish.
Main religions: 88.2% Church of Sweden, 1.7% Roman Catholic, 1.1% Pentecostal.
Economy: one of the leading industrial economies in the world, also forestry, paper milling, minerals, car manufacture and mercantile marine.
Average dietary intake: 63% vegetable products, 37% animal products.

The four countries which constitute Scandinavia have a population of 18.2m people and cover 816,936 sq km. Because of their closeness they have much in common as regards gastronomy and each country features fish and game birds and animals plainly cooked, and the use of soft berry fruits as garnishes with all kinds of food. Each Scandinavian country has its own version of the buffet display of food which has become world famous under the title of Smörgasbord, which can be an hors-d'oeuvre, first course or a complete meal.

Denmark enjoys the richest of the Scandinavian cuisines and has overtones of German and French cookery. The Danes are serious gourmets who like to discuss as well as partake of the glories of their cookery, in which sauces play an important part.

The food of Finland has been influenced by two neighbours, a French influence that came via French chefs employed at the Russian Court at St Petersburg and a Swedish influence from Swedish chefs who, although few in number, have always enjoyed a high reputation in many western countries.

A very distinctive part is played by the great variety of soft fruits grown in Finland which give their taste to dishes throughout the menu from soup to sweet, and a recent trend to more artistic presentation is being assisted by their use. Potatoes are of importance in the diet and are served at most meals all through the year, including with the Baltic herrings available fresh, salted, smoked or pickled in a sweet marinade.

Game in season includes wild duck, snow goose, hare, moose and bear, and the hunting season coincides with the harvesting of the many species of wild mushrooms. In Finland, as in other Scandinavian countries, the Smörgasbord or Voileipäpöytä is of great importance as constituting a meal in itself.

Breakfast in Finland usually consists of porridge, eggs, cheese, yogurt, fruit juice and a preserve. Lunch is served at midday and is a fairly light meal but dinner is slightly more elaborate with a few good main courses with a glass or so of the national alcohol aquavit.

Norway calls its smörgasbord a Koldtbord and uses many kinds of fish in its preparation. As in all these countries, fish is very popular and appears in many guises, as a soup, a stew, in its own right, as fish balls, fish pudding, in smoked, salted and dried forms, and in spicy marinated items. Apart from fish, pork, mutton and venison are used, often with a garnish of berries or other soft fruit. Lamb and mutton is cured in the same way as is bacon, being smoked to give added flavour and eating quality.

In Sweden people like to eat little and often and their version of smörgasbord helps them to do this at a very high standard, for this country is a rich leading industrial nation. Gravlax is common to this country and to Norway and is a cured cut of salmon flavoured with dill and aquavit, served with mustard sauce.

Supper, as a family occasion, is the main meal of the day and may consist of soup, meat or fish or other main course then cheese followed by fresh fruit; sweets are reserved for special events. Menu organisation and structure follow the European model (see page 2).

South Korea

Profile

Land area 99,000 sq km. *Population* 22.5m.
Composition: 99% Korean.
Main religions: 54% Buddhist, 19% Protestant, 6% Roman Catholic, 1% Confucian.
Economy: 20% of working population are engaged in agriculture; currently experiencing rapid industrialisation with significant growth in motor vehicle manufacturing and ship building.
Average dietary intake: 87% vegetable products, 13% animal products.

Korea's civilisation is as old as China's and much older than that of Japan. Korea's history has been rather turbulent and in more recent years the country was partitioned on ideological grounds. North Korea was sealed against outside influences whilst South Korea participated in international affairs and has developed one of the world's fastest growing industrial economies. The Korean peninsular is situated just below Manchuria and Siberia, extending between the Yellow Sea and the Sea of Japan. Korea is an East Asian nation which is closely bordered by China and Japan.

Koreans eat three full meals a day, breakfast, lunch and dinner, the number and range of dishes increasing each time. Short-grain rice forms the staple food at each meal, to which barley and millet are sometimes added to improve the nutritional value of the meal. Sliced raw fish, shellfish, oysters, beef, chicken, pork and fresh vegetables are staple foods to which a wide range of fragrant spices and herbs are added. Noodles, buckwheat, soybean and pulses are an important part of Korean

cookery. Side dishes of kimchee, which is vegetables pickled in brine, are considered an integral part of every meal.

The usual Korean meal may consist of rice, soup, chicken, beef, vegetables,
sweet and sour sauces and pickles. The range of food is served all at once and
eaten from individual bowls. Fresh fruit is sometimes served but this is by no
means an everyday occurrence. The meal is served at a formal table setting to be
eaten with chopsticks and spoons.

Spain

Profile

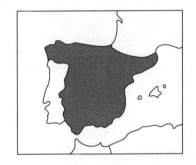

Land area 504,783 sq km. *Population* 39.1m.

Composition: 72% Spanish, 16% Catalan, 8%
   Galician and 2% Basque.

Main religions: 97% Roman Catholic.

Economy: agriculturally based economy; tourism continues to be a major growth area;
   one of Europe's major motor vehicle
   exporters.

Average dietary intake: 68% vegetable products
   and 32% animal products.

Like many other Mediterranean countries Spain's culinary heritage can be traced
back to the Roman times and much later to the Middle East and the Moors. The
Spanish were justifiably proud of themselves when in 1492 the Moorish strong-
hold at Grenada was conquered, which was to be the beginning of a period of
trade and of colonial power. At its zenith the Spanish realms took in all of Spain,
Portugal, the Netherlands, parts of Italy and of North and Central America, most of
the Caribbean islands and all the South American continent, not to mention the
Philippines. Therefore, seen within an historical framework, it is understandable
that Spain has absorbed a whole range of cookery styles to produce its own distinctive style.

This fertile country attracts millions of visitors each year and supplies many of its
European neighbours with high quality fruit and vegetables of all kinds and in all
seasons. It also has Europe's largest fishing fleet and produces many very fine
wines. Its cooking can be rich and distinctive but does not have sufficient tradition
or variety in its ingredients to rank very high among European cuisines, and its
contributions to the international repertoire are few. Many of its popular dishes
are mixtures of fish, shellfish, meat, poultry and game with an assortment of vegetables and cereals.

Menu organisation, structure and design follow the European model (see page
2).

Tapas, normally associated with 'Tapas bars', range from the most simple of
small snacks to the most delicate, and have now developed into an appetizer to be
eaten just before a meal. Tapas may comprise any number and variety of small
items, their content being a reflection of the imagination of those who make them.

Tapas bars have been part of the way of life of the Spanish people since the early part of the 19th century and the Spaniards move leisurely from one bar to the next to partake of a selection of tapas as appetizers together with a glass of sherry or wine.

Tapas are set out in special dishes on the bar counter for customers to choose from while they stand talking, drinking and eating at meal times. Having tasted a few they may decide to stay and eat a plateful as a meal, either at table or still standing and talking. Informality is the key-note of the experience, as it is in the selection on display which includes such popular foods as Gambas com Gabardina – deep-fried prawns in batter, Gambas al Ajello – shallow-fried prawns with garlic, Calamares Fritos – fried rings of squid, Scoldaditos di Pavia – strips of soaked dried cod in batter, Vieiras al Horno – scallops baked in the half shells, Pincho de Morcilla o Chorizo – shallow-fried slices of black pudding or chorizo sausage on toasted French bread, Albondiigas – meatballs, Alcachofas al Montilla – artichokes cooked in oil, montilla wine and garlic. Many kinds of vegetables are used, and olives, pieces of omelette, portions of paella, salads and jamón serrano are all featured.

Thailand

Profile

Land area 513,115 sq km. *Population* 58m.
Composition: 79% Thai of which 52% are Siamese and 27% Lao; 12% Chinese, 4% Malay, 3% Khmer.
Main religions: 94% Buddhist, 4% Muslim.
Economy: agriculturally based economy employing three-quarters of the work force, the fifth largest exporter of food in the world, mainly rice, maize and rubber.
Average dietary intake: 91% vegetable products, 9% animal products.

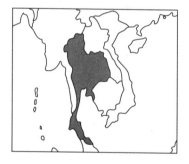

Thai cookery is considered one of the foremost cuisines of Southeast Asia and is recognised for the complexity of its dishes as compared with many of its neighbours. The comprehensive repertoire of dishes has been strongly influenced by Chinese gastronomy and is not dissimilar to those of its neighbours, in particular China, India, Indonesia and Malaysia. Yet the Thais have introduced many subtle flavourings to their dishes to provide a distinct classical cuisine.

Thai meals are generally based on rice, from which an infinite variety of dishes has been created. A typical menu usually begins with a soup, followed by a number of dishes called kaengs, which are dishes with gravy, and as large a number of side dishes as possible, followed by a selection of fresh fruits. There is not the obsessive requirement to serve food hot as in the west. Chopsticks are used but there is now a growing tendency for food to be eaten with spoon and fork.

The classic cookery of Thailand has an ability to enhance the pungency of its simple basic ingredients by means of exotic herbs and spices, often in sweet and sour combinations. Salt is replaced as a seasoning by nam pla, a preserved fish essence or sauce which gives added piquancy to many ethnic dishes in this country. In addition, a selection of spices are served as side dishes at main meals.

United States of America

Profile

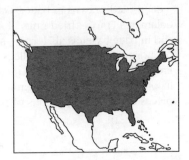

Land area 9,529,063 sq km. *Population* 258.2m.
Composition: 86% Non-Hispanics, 9% Hispanics, 3% Asian and Pacific Islanders and 0.7% American Indian and Eskimo.
Main religions: 86.5% Christian, 1.9% Muslim, 1.8% Jewish.
Economy: self-supporting economy, has vast natural resources and is the world's major economic power.
Average dietary intake: 70% vegetable products, 30% animal products.

It is not easy to encompass all that can be classed as American cookery in a few short sentences since it is an amalgam of all the waves of immigrants who went to America seeking a better way of life than that of their mother country. These people had to adapt their styles of cooking to the conditions which prevailed where they settled and kept their culinary traditions; it is still possible to find communities with what are now regional specialities but which were originally alien.

The major influences may have been Dutch, French, English and Native American but almost every other nationality in the world is now represented in the USA. In addition to Creole and Cajun in the deep south there are Spanish, Mexican, Jewish, German, Swiss, Scandinavian, Chinese, Japanese and many other forms of cookery included in the basic American mode of living, but these are very much more noticeable in the places where these people have congregated.

America is the world's greatest producer of foods thus allowing a very interesting and widely varied menu. Many of its good dishes are accepted as international favourites. The United States of America consists of 50 states and one federal district and these can be grouped into nine main regions, each embracing several states.

The Far West covers California, Oregon and Washington and is a region where things are done on a grand scale bordering on the extravagant, possibly because of its bounteous nature which includes vast orchards of exotic fruits and nuts, abundant valleys giving all kinds of prime vegetables, lakes, rivers and the sea that yield succulent shellfish and fish of all kinds, and the forests abounding with every sort of game. The regional recipes embrace the cultures of American-Indian, plus Chinese, French, Italian, Japanese and Mexican immigrant influences, which lead to what outsiders consider to be rather bizarre combinations.

New England This region covers the states of Connecticut, Maine, Massachusetts, New Hampshire and Vermont on the north Atlantic coast, which is a mountainous region noted for the quality of its shellfish and fish. Its culinary heritage stems from the Puritans who settled there in 1614 to farm the wilderness and cook for their families by the simplest of methods, using local commodities as cultivated by the indigenous Indians. The self-denial practised by these immigrants gave rise to a spartan diet of English puddings and duffs and boiled meats, a diet that was then enriched by other waves of immigrants from Ireland, Italy and Portugal. The tradition of Thanksgiving Day has been held ever since 1621, on the fourth Tuesday in November, to celebrate the first harvest of the Pilgrim Fathers, and is the day when Americans eat roast turkey with mashed turnip and succotash followed by pumpkin pie with cider to drink.

Mid-Atlantic This region covers the states of Delaware, Maryland, New Jersey, New York, Pennsylvania and Virginia, a very fertile region which produces a vast range of different foods with plentiful supplies of fish, corn and pork. These are cooked to a pattern originating from British, Dutch and German settlers and the influence of the Quakers of Philadelphia and all the many nationalities who came into New York before spreading afar. However, the European and particularly the English cookery traditions have been predominant, and even the French aspects arrived via England. Since then many other influences have been inherited from Chinese, Italian, Jewish and Spanish immigrants.

The South covers Alabama, North Carolina, South Carolina, Florida, Georgia and Mississippi, and the diet can be defined as more domesticated or simple and quite mild in taste, making use of local produce from sea and field. Fried dishes are often a feature of meals. First courses include savoury titbits of all kinds served with dips. Bisque soups are made from vegetables as well as shellfish and cold cream, and vegetable soups and fish broths are featured. All kinds of fish are used but mainly cooked by baking and broiling; shellfish is in plentiful supply and alligators, crocodiles and lizards from the salt-water swamps also appear on menus. Beef, lamb, pork, veal, venison and poultry, including Cornish hens, ducks, turkeys, doves and quail as well as most game birds, are regular menu items.

Mountain region Here one will find Soulfood or the cookery of the deep south of black America, which includes Arkansas, Kentucky, Missouri, Tennessee and West Virginia. The mountains are the Appalachians, where isolated communities of hardy settlers lived frugally on wild plants, fish and game, cooked on primitive equipment and without any attempt at fineness. Stews such as Brunswick are based on small game and any available domestic animals such as goat, old hens and squirrels and are served with corn pone, a maize loaf made with molasses. Maize and pork are used in many different ways: pork becomes ham and bacon and all its offals have many culinary uses, as has the razor back wild pig. The Kentucky ham is dry-cured by rubbing with salt and sugar but does not get buried to mature as happens to Virginia hams. Squirrel is cooked as a pie and muskrat as a stew; pot likker or vegetable cooking water is used as a beverage to drink with such dishes.

Midwest America is the continent's heartland, being the most highly developed and populated area of the USA, with a vast extent of agricultural lands, lakes and rivers, including the Mississippi system and its great forests and prairies. Early pioneers arrived from less blessed regions of America and were joined by immigrants from Germany and Scandinavia. They liked food to be simply cooked but substantial to provide the necessary calories to work hard – roasts and grills with plain boiled vegetables and potatoes cooked entirely without any need for sophisticated flavours. One of the traditional meals is the Buffet, which is a help-yourself service of hot and cold items laid out in the form of a Scandinavian smörgasbord; dingle doos is the local name for an hors-d'oeuvre selection. Wild rice grows wild here and is gathered from the banks of the swamps. Many of the fashionable salades tièdes originated in the Midwest and some salads are left to marinate overnight. Aspics of vegetables and of fruits are popular. Frogs grow to a large size in the great lakes of this region and the legs are big enough to treat like chicken. Beef is corn-fed and the armadillo is not disdained in the form of a main dish. Ice-cream parties are social occasions and old-fashioned ice-cream parlours serve traditional richly made flavours in the form of sundaes and glories.

The West is not densely populated and towns and houses are sited in isolation, thus households have become self-supporting on a limited range of commodities that can be kept with no deterioration. The population relies on protein from beef and lamb and carbohydrates from corn; game animals include antelope, elk and moose and contribute much to the diet. Buck stew is made from venison in season and fresh offals are very popular. Mulligan is a campfire venison stew and minced venison is used in making mincemeat for pies and tarts.

Southwest America covers the states of Arizona, New Mexico and Texas. Bordering with Mexico means there is a distinctly Spanish and Mexican accent allied to that of the pioneer settlers who came directly or from other regions to open up this vast area of fruit-growing and cattle-raising country. Undertones of Indian cookery are noticeable. Beef is the most important product and is raised in vast herds to premium standards, providing the king-size steaks that are so much part of the all-American lifestyle. Many dishes bear Mexican names but are usually less highly spiced with chillies than the authentic versions; in fact, here chilli con carne is quite mild to the taste. Spicy sauces of chillies and tomatoes are served with the many local versions of barbecues and spit-roastings; mass barbecues catering for thousands of people are a common source of entertainment. Other normal accompaniments for all barbecues are coleslaw and potato salads, tomato and onion salad and baked beans, followed by apple pie. A chuckwagon meal is really a barbecue of beef steaks and beans. Corn is used in many ways, such as Peshofa where the kernels are ground, allowed to ferment then dried for use in beef stews and in Tamale loaf as a binding agent for the spiced minced beef mixture. Tamales are the outer husks of sweetcorn filled with chicken, cornmeal and pork stuffing.

Menu organisation and structure follow the European model (see page 2).

Chapter Two

Basic Stocks and Sauces

This chapter is divided into seven categories which are as follows:

✧ Basic Stocks ✧

✧ Basic Sauces ✧

✧ Hot Sauces ✧

✧ Relishes ✧

✧ Dips ✧

✧ Cold Sauces ✧

✧ Dressings ✧

For 10 average portions allow: 1 litre of completed sauce or 600 ml for dressings, relishes and dips

Basic Stocks

White Meat or Poultry Stock   Chop or cut bones into small pieces; blanch, refresh, drain and cover with cold water and bring slowly to the boil. Add thyme, bayleaf, parsley stalks and roughly cut onion, carrot, celery and leek. Simmer gently for approx. 2 hr, skimming as necessary. Strain and use.

Brown Meat, Poultry or Game Stock   Chop or cut bones into small pieces and brown them in a hot oven; add roughly cut onion, carrot, celery and leek. Cover with cold water and bring to the boil then add thyme, bayleaf and parsley stalks. Simmer gently for 2–3 hr.

Fish Stock   Sweat sliced onion, chopped fish bones, bayleaf, parsley stalks and peppercorns for 5 min then cover with water, add a little lemon juice and simmer for 20 min.

White Vegetable Stock   Sweat roughly cut onion, carrot, celery, leek and mushroom stalks. Cover with water and simmer for 45 min with thyme, bayleaf, parsley stalks and squashed tomatoes.

Brown Vegetable Stock   Golden fry roughly cut onion, carrot, celery, leek and mushroom stalks. Cover with water and simmer for 45 min with thyme, bayleaf, parsley stalks and squashed tomatoes.

Asian Soup Stocks

First Soup Stock   Place cold water in a pan, add squares of dried kelp previously wiped with a damp cloth; bring to boiling point and remove the kelp. Bring the liquid to boiling point and add bonito flakes, remove from the heat, stand for 3 min, strain and use as required. The kelp and bonito flakes should be kept for making the following second soup stock.

Second Soup Stock   Simmer cold water with the kelp and bonito flakes reserved from first soup stock and simmer for approx. 5 min; strain and use.

Indonesian Soured Stock   To simmering water add fresh or dried chillies, kaffir lime leaves, ginger, galingale, lemon grass, salt and tamarind juice. Allow to infuse, strain and use.

Japanese Soup Stock [*Dashi*]   To simmering water add squares of washed kombu, cook for 2 min then remove the kombu and add katsuobushi. Stir to the boil, remove from the heat and allow the flakes to settle to the bottom of the pan; strain and use.

Noodle Broth   Simmer together dashi, salt, dark and light soy sauces, sugar and mirin.

Basic Sauces

Béchamel Sauce [*France*]   Make a white roux with butter and flour, allow to cool then gradually add boiling milk to form a smooth sauce; add a small studded onion and simmer for 20 min.

Bread Sauce [*GB*]   Infuse milk with a small studded onion, add white bread-crumbs to form a sauce.

Jus lié [*France*]   Boil brown veal stock and lightly thicken with diluted arrowroot then add roughly cut carrot, onion, leek and celery, thyme, bayleaf, garlic, mush-room trimmings, squashed tomatoes and tomato purée. Simmer for 1 hr then strain.

Velouté [*France*]   Make a blond roux with butter and flour then gradually add white stock to form a smooth sauce, and allow to simmer for 1 hr.
  Note: depending upon its use white chicken, veal, fish, mutton or vegetable stock may be used.

Velouté [*Alternative Method*]   Boil stock then thicken with diluted arrowroot and simmer for 10 min; finish by incorporating margarine or butter.

White Sauce [*Alternative*]   Infuse a studded onion in milk then thicken with diluted arrowroot and simmer for 10 min. Finish by incorporating margarine or butter.

Hot Sauces

Chasseur Sauce [*Sauce Chasseur* France]   Sauté sliced button mushrooms, add chopped shallots and tomato concassée and sauté. Moisten with white wine then reduce by half, add jus lié and finish with chopped tarragon.

Cheese Sauce [*Sauce Mornay* France]   Add grated Parmesan cheese to hot béchamel sauce and finish with cream.

Cherry Sauce [*Sauce aux Cerises* France]   Flavour jus lié made with game stock with juniper berries and cinnamon. Add stoned sour black cherries and simmer until the cherries are soft then stir in redcurrant jelly.

Chicken Suprême Sauce [*Sauce Suprême* France]   Flavour chicken velouté with a reduction of chicken stock and mushroom trimmings then reduce to a coating consistency. Finish with butter and cream.

Chilli and Tomato Sauce [*Salsa Rossa* Italy]   Sauté chopped onion, stir in flour and cook to a roux. Moisten with a little stock and cook. Mix in cream, brandy and chopped fresh red chilli. Boil, then add chopped tomato flesh; cook then strain with pressure.

Chilli Sauce [*Salsa de Chile Rojo* Mexico]   Sauté chopped onion and garlic, add soaked chillies and their soaking liquid, tomato sauce, oregano and cumin then simmer and finally liquidise.

Coconut Sauce [*Caribbean*]   Sauté chopped onion, garlic and fresh red chillies in peanut oil then stir in curry powder, sambal ulek and ground ginger. Moisten with thin coconut milk, add desiccated coconut and the zest and juice of lemons then thicken with arrowroot.

Coconut and Fenugreek Sauce [*Kiri Hodhi* India]   Boil 1 part thin coconut milk with soaked fenugreek seeds and the liquid, chopped onion, curry leaves, cinnamon stick, fresh green chillies and turmeric powder and simmer until the onion has become a pulp. Remove the cinnamon and leaves then finish with 1 part coconut milk and lemon juice.

Cream Sauce [*Sauce Crème* France]   Add cream to hot béchamel sauce then season.

Devilled Sauce [*Sauce Diable* France]   Boil white wine, vinegar, chopped shallots, crushed peppercorns, bayleaf and thyme and reduce to a glaze; moisten with jus lié and simmer, strain and finish with knobs of butter.

Dill Sauce [*USA*]   Add chopped dill to white wine fish sauce.

Dill and Soured Cream Sauce [*Kapormàrtàs* Hungary]   Garnish a dill flavoured velouté with chopped dill and finish with soured cream.

Gherkin and Soured Cream Sauce [*Uborkamàrtàs* Hungary]   Add chopped gherkin and sugar to veal velouté and finish with soured cream.

Hazelnut Sauce [*Marakit Bunduk* Midddle East]   Combine soaked and squeezed bread, chopped hazelnuts, garlic, lemon juice and chicken stock to form a sauce consistency then season with paprika.

Hot Pepper Jelly [*USA*]   Cook peeled and quartered apples with strips of lemon peel and water. Pass the apple liquid through a muslin. Heat the liquid, add sugar and reduce until the liquid sets. Boil chopped fresh red and green chillies, chopped onion and cider vinegar for 4 min, add the apple liquid and simmer until it sets when tested.

Lemon Sauce [*GB*]   Flavour jus lié with grated zest and juice of lemon.

Lemon and Coriander Sauce [*Ningmeng Zhi* China]   Sauté chopped onion, garlic and grated root ginger, then add diced green and red pimento. Moisten with lemon juice, saké, light and dark soy sauces, ginger syrup, hoisin sauce, honey and grated zest of lemon, then reduce by one third. Add chicken stock and thicken with arrowroot. Finish with chopped coriander leaves.

Lemon and Egg Sauce [*Avgolemono Saltsa* Greece]   Thicken chicken stock with arrowroot then add a liaison of stiffly beaten egg whites, to which egg yolks and lemon juice have been added.

Lobster Sauce [*GB*]   Quickly sauté crushed cooked lobster shells, then add chopped onion, carrot, celery and garlic and parsley stalks and cook for 5 min. Flambé with brandy then moisten with dry white wine and fish stock. Add tomato purée and tomato concassée and simmer, reducing the liquor by one half. Add fish velouté and reduce by one third. Pass the sauce firmly through a coarse conical strainer then a fine strainer.

Madras Sauce [*Kari* India]   Sauté chopped onion and grated ginger in ghee then stir in chilli powder, ground black pepper, cumin, coriander and turmeric and chopped fresh green chillies. Moisten with chicken stock, thicken with arrowroot and simmer, then add garam masala and lemon juice.

Maltese Sauce [*Malteser Sobe* Germany]   Reduce chopped shallots and white wine vinegar, add egg yolks and cook gently then whisk in softened butter. Strain through a muslin and finish with lemon juice and blanched finely shredded zest of orange.

Mandarin Sauce [*Ging Doh Tsup* China]   Sauté chopped spring onions in sesame oil, add mandarin juice and honey and reduce by one third. Moisten with brown duck stock, thicken with arrowroot and season with five-spice powder, salt and pepper.

Mushroom Sauce [*Sauce Champignons* France] Sweat quartered mushrooms, moisten with stock and simmer, then liquidise. Reboil and finish with cream.

Paprika Sauce [*Sauce Hongroise* France] Sauté chopped shallot then stir in paprika. Moisten with dry white wine and reduce by two-thirds then add chicken velouté. Simmer for a few mins then strain. Finish with butter and cream.

Parsley Sauce [*Sauce Persil* France] Add cream to hot béchamel sauce with the addition of blanched chopped parsley.

Peanut Sauce [*Sauskatyang* Indonesia] Stir-fry crushed dried chillies and chopped onion and garlic in coconut oil then stir in sambal trasi. Add thin coconut milk, peanut butter and sweet soy sauce. When thick finish with lemon juice.

Peanut and Tamarind Sauce [*Kacang* Indonesia] Blend trasi, peanuts, chopped onion, garlic, soft brown sugar and peanut oil to a paste. Shallow fry the paste for 2 min in peanut oil then add tamarind liquid and stock. Simmer for 15 min and season with laos powder, cayenne pepper and salt.

Plum Sauce [*Sumeizhi* China] Boil lemon juice, chopped shallots, ginger syrup, sugar, purée of plums, chilli oil, light and dark soy sauces and saké until reduced to a light sauce consistency.

Plum Sauce [*Bainiku-jöyu* Japan] Combine puréed pickled plums and tosa soy sauce.

Pomegranate Sauce [*Caribbean*] Boil pomegranate juice with water, sugar and grated ginger and thicken with arrowroot.

Reform Club Sauce [*GB*] Reduce crushed peppercorns and vinegar by two-thirds then add jus lié and redcurrant jelly. Simmer, strain and garnish with julienne of beetroot, white of hard-boiled egg, gherkin, mushroom and tongue.

Saté Sauce with Oil [*Bumbu Saté Dengan Minjak* Indonesia] Blend roasted peanuts and fresh chillies to a paste. Fry sliced onion in peanut oil then stir in the peanut mixture, moisten with water, add brown sugar, reduce to a sauce consistency then add soy sauce and lime juice.

Saté Sauce without Oil [*Bumbu Saté Tidak Dengan Minjak* Indonesia] Blend roasted peanuts, garlic, onion, fresh chillies, tamarind liquid, lemon juice and coconut cream to a paste. Add soy sauce and water then simmer until it thickens.

Silver Sauce [*Gin-an* Japan] Lightly thicken dashi, light soy sauce and salt with cornflour.

Sweet and Sour Sauce [*Tim Soen Tsijoen* China] Sauté chopped onion, garlic, fresh chillies and grated ginger in peanut oil. Moisten with vinegar, light soy sauce and saké, sugar and ginger syrup and boil and reduce by one-third. Moisten with chicken stock and Chinese tomato sauce and thicken with arrowroot.

Tarragon and Soured Cream Sauce [*Tàrkonymàrtàs* Hungary] Garnish tarragon flavoured velouté with chopped tarragon and finish with soured cream.

Tempura Sauce [*Japan*] Simmer saké, mirin and light soy sauce for 2 min then add grated daikon and grated ginger and cook out.

Teriyaki Sauce [*Japan*] Simmer equal quantities of saké, mirin and dark soy sauce for 2 min with a little sugar.

Tomato Sauce [*Sauce Tomate* France] Sauté chopped onion and garlic in olive oil then add crushed fresh tomatoes and tomato purée. Moisten with chicken or vegetable stock, add a bouquet garni and simmer. Liquidise, reboil and adjust to a sauce consistency.

Tomato Sauce [*Alternative Method*]   Sauté roughly cut onion, carrot and celery, bacon pieces, garlic, thyme and bayleaf. Stir in flour to form a roux, mix in tomato pureé and moisten with white stock. Simmer, then strain with light pressure.

Tomato Sauce [*Fanquie Zhi* China]   Boil white stock, Chinese tomato sauce, light and dark soy sauce, saké, ginger syrup, hoisin sauce and sugar and reduce by one-third. Thicken to sauce consistency with arrowroot.

White Wine Fish Sauce [*Sauce au Vin Blanc* France]   Boil equal quantities of fish stock, dry white wine and fish velouté and reduce by two-thirds to a coating consistency; strain. Finish by incorporating butter and cream.

Yakitori Sauce [*Japan*]   Boil dark soy sauce, saké, mirin and sugar for 2 min.

Relishes

Application

Relishes should have a very distinctive flavour as they are served as an accompaniment to complement and enhance the flavour of a range of foods.

Blackberry Relish [*GB*]   Combine purée of blackberries with grated apple, onion and horseradish and mayonnaise, flavour with lemon juice and a few drops of Worcester sauce.

Chilli Relish [*Nam Prik Poa* Thailand]   Fry soaked dried red chillies and chopped garlic and shallot in groundnut oil. Blend to a paste with lemon juice and nam pla.

Coconut Relish [*Narial Pachachadi* India]   Fry cooked chickpeas, crushed dried green chillies and curry leaves in ghee then blend to a paste with grated fresh coconut, lemon juice and salt. Fry a pinch of ground asafoetida and mustard seeds in ghee then blend with the paste and chill before serving.

Coriander Relish [*Dhania Pachachadi* India]   Blend coriander leaves and stems, fresh green chillies, grated coconut, ginger, lemon juice and salt to a paste. Fry a pinch of ground asafoetida, mustard seeds and curry leaves in ghee and blend with the paste.

Courgette and Lime Relish [*Calabacitas con Limón y Cilantro* Mexico]   Mix together shredded courgettes, chopped cilantro, lime juice, olive oil, sugar and seasoning.

Ginger Relish [*Adhrak Pachachadi* India]   Blend grated ginger, coconut, garlic, dried green chillies, sugar and salt to a paste then combine with yogurt. Fry curry leaves, mustard seed and crushed dried red chillies then blend into the yogurt mixture and chill.

Horseradish and Beetroot Relish [*Chrain* Israel]   Combine equal amounts of grated cooked beetroot and grated horseradish and season with vinegar and caster sugar.

Hot Tomato Relish [*Sekhoog* Israel]   Blend green chillies, garlic, tomato flesh, coriander leaves, salt, ground cumin and fenugreek seeds to a paste.

Mango Relish [*Caribbean*]   Boil vinegar and soft brown sugar then stir in tamarind liquid and reduce by half. Add chopped fresh red chillies, ground cloves, allspice, seedless raisins, grated ginger, lime juice and diced mango flesh then simmer. Season with salt and ground black peppercorns.

Radish and Cilantro Relish [*Salsa de Rabanitos y Cilantro* Mexico] Mix together sliced radishes, chopped onion and cilantro, lime juice, olive oil and seasoning.

Red Chilli Relish [*Caribbean*] Simmer chopped fresh red chillies and onion with water and salt and allow to cool.

Sweet Beetroot Relish [*Israel*] Simmer grated cooked beetroot with water, sugar, lemon juice and grated ginger. When the mixture thickens, add chopped walnuts and almonds.

Dips

Application

Dips are served hot or cold as an accompaniment for crudités, savoury snacks and a range of hors-d'oeuvre and other savoury menu items.

Anchovy, Garlic and Truffle Dip [*Bagna Cauda* Italy] Cook cloves of garlic in olive oil until soft but not coloured, add anchovy fillets chopped to a paste and finely sliced white truffle. Serve very hot as a dip for crudités.

Apple and Almond Dip [*Charoset* Israel] Blend dessert apples, almonds, walnuts, cashew and pecan nuts, cinnamon, allspice and sweet red wine to a paste.

Avocado Dip and Tomato [*Guacamole* Mexico] Combine diced tomato flesh, chopped coriander leaves, onion and fresh green chillies and macerate in lemon or lime juice. Add puréed flesh of avocado pears and season.

Banana and Yogurt Dip [*Kela Pachchadi* India] Combine yogurt, bananas, lemon juice, grated coconut, sugar and a pinch of chilli powder. Fry mustard and cumin seeds in ghee and add to the yogurt preparation.

Beetroot and Honey Dip [*Israel*] Combine grated cooked beetroots, horseradish, honey, salt and cider vinegar.

Bulkoki Dip [*Bulkoki* Korea] Blend Chinese bean paste, sesame seeds, garlic, spring onions, cayenne, sugar, salt, sesame oil and soy sauce to a paste.

Chickpea and Sesame Dip [*Houmous bi Tahini* Middle East] Combine a purée of cooked chickpeas, tahini paste, lemon juice, garlic and salt.

Chickpea and Tahina Dip [*Falafel and Houmous* Israel] Combine a purée of cooked chickpeas, garlic, lemon juice, olive oil and salt. Serve in individual dishes with a swirl of tahina on top, sprinkle with sieved egg yolk, chopped parsley and cayenne. Serve accompanied by quartered hard-boiled eggs and falafel balls.

Coriander and Yogurt Dip [*Dhania Raita* India] Blend chopped coriander leaves, fresh green chillies and lemon juice to a paste then combine with yogurt and add roasted cumin seeds.

Cucumber, Coconut and Yogurt Dip [*Khira Raita* India] Combine yogurt, grated cucumber, coconut, chopped fresh green chillies and mustard and cumin seeds fried in ghee.

Date, Fig and Walnut Dip [*Charoset* Israel] Blend dates, figs, walnuts, ginger, cayenne pepper, sugar and sweet red wine to a paste.

Eggplant Dip [*Patlican Salatasi* Greece]   Grill eggplants cut in half, peel then blend the flesh to a purée with onion, then slowly add olive oil until of a sauce consistency; finish with lemon juice and seasoning.

Eggplant Dip with Sesame Oil [*Baba Ghannouge* Middle East]   Grill eggplants cut in half, discard the peel then blend the flesh to a purée with garlic, tahina and lemon juice, then slowly add sesame oil until of a sauce consistency. Finish with chopped mint and pomegranate seeds.

Eggplant and Sesame Dip [*Baba Ghannouj* Middle East]   Blend baked eggplant flesh, lemon juice, tahini paste, olive oil and chopped parsley to a paste.

Eggplant and Yogurt Dip [*Baigan Raita* India]   Fry mustard seed in ghee with chopped onion, fresh green chillies, diced eggplant, tomato flesh, garam masala and seasoning. Moisten with water and cook. Blend to a purée and add yogurt and chopped coriander leaves.

Houmous [*Greece*]   Cook chickpeas until grainy then blend with chopped garlic, tahini paste, lemon juice, oil, cumin powder and some of the cooking liquid. Serve sprinkled with olive oil and cayenne pepper.

Olive and Caper Dip [*Tapenade* France]   Blend stoned black olives, capers and anchovy fillets then whisk in olive oil and lemon juice to a paste.

Pawpaw Dip [*Caribbean*]   Barely cover pawpaw flesh with water, add lemon or lime juice, sugar and ground cloves and cook, reducing the liquid to a syrup. Blend to a purée, season and serve hot or chilled.

Sesame Dip [*Tahina* Israel]   Blend sesame seeds, garlic, lemon juice and water to a paste.

Spinach and Yogurt Dip [*Palak Raita* India]   Fry mustard seeds in ghee, add cumin and fenugreek seeds, ground cumin and a pinch of chilli powder. Allow to cool then mix together with yogurt and cooked chopped spinach.

Taramasalata [*Greece*]   Blend together white or brown bread soaked and squeezed, with the crusts removed, smoked cod roe or salted tarama and lemon juice, then gradually add olive oil. Garnish with olives and segments of lemon.

Vinegar Dip [*Chojang* Korea]   Combine soy sauce, rice vinegar or cider vinegar, toasted sesame seeds, chopped ginger, red pepper powder and sugar.

Cold Sauces

Apple and Horseradish Sauce [*Apfelkren* Germany]   Combine grated horseradish or horseradish sauce with grated apple, lemon juice, cream and seasoning.

Andalusian Sauce [*Molho Andaluz* Portugal]   Combine mayonnaise with tomato sauce, chopped red pimento and chopped parsley.

Beirao-Style Sauce [*Molho Beirao* Portugal]   Combine sieved hard-boiled egg, olive oil, wine vinegar, chopped onion and parsley.

Cambridge Sauce [*GB*]   Blend hard-boiled egg, anchovy fillets, capers and chopped parsley, tarragon and chervil to a fine purée, then combine with mayonnaise.

Chilli Mayonnaise [*Caribbean*]   Whisk together soured cream, mayonnaise, mustard and red pepper flakes then thin with beef stock.

Chilli Sauce [*Caribbean*]   Macerate chopped onion in lime juice then simmer for 2 min and add crushed garlic, chopped fresh green and red chillies, olive oil and salt.

Chilli Sauce [***Romescu** Spain*]   Blend tomato flesh, dried red chillies, garlic, toasted almonds, pine and hazelnuts and vinegar to a paste, then whisk in olive oil and seasoning.

Chilli and Eggplant Sauce [***Nam Prik** Thailand*]   Blend dried shrimps, garlic, dried red chillies, sugar, nam pla and lime juice to a paste then combine with chopped eggplant and fresh green chillies and serve.

Chilli and Tamarind Sauce [***Nam Prik Pao** Thailand*]   Blend crisply fried garlic and shallots, shrimp paste, brown sugar, tamarind juice, soaked dried red chillies and their liquid to a thick paste.

Egg and Chilli Sauce [***Nam Prik Kai Kem** Thailand*]   Blend fresh green chillies and shallots to a paste then add sieved hard-boiled yolks of egg, shrimp paste, palm sugar, nam pla and lime juice.

Garlic Mayonnaise [***Aioli** France*]   Blend crushed garlic with salt and raw egg yolks to a paste, then whisk in olive oil, lemon juice and seasoning.

Garlic Sauce [***Skorthaliá** Greece*]   Blend together crushed garlic, white wine vinegar, hot water and soaked and squeezed bread, then gradually add olive oil to form a sauce.

Garlic and Egg Sauce [***Salça Yumurtali** Greece*]   Blend together crushed garlic and sieved hard-boiled egg yolks, olive oil and lemon juice to form a sauce.

Garlic and Tahina Sauce [***Tarator di Tahina** Middle East*]   Blend together tahina paste, warm water, lemon juice and crushed garlic to form a sauce.

Gravlax Sauce [*Scandinavia*]   Blend together French mustard, sugar, cooked egg yolks, vinegar and olive oil, then add chopped dill and season.

Green Mayonnaise [***Sauce Verte** France*]   Blend blanched spinach, watercress, parsley, tarragon, chervil and chives to a paste then add to mayonnaise.

Green Sauce [***Salsa Verde** Spain*]   Blend slices of bread soaked with lemon juice and vinegar and chopped parsley, chives, spring onions and garlic to a paste, then gradually whisk in olive oil and season.

Horseradish Sauce [***Sauce Raifort** France*]   Combine white breadcrumbs previously soaked in milk with grated horseradish, lightly whipped cream, vinegar and seasoning.

Hot Pepper Sauce [***Ixni-Pec** Mexico*]   Blend together chopped onion, tomato flesh, red chillies, orange and lime juices and seasoning.

Lime, Dill and Yogurt Sauce [*Scandinavia*]   Combine yogurt, lime juice, chopped dill and seasoning.

Mayonnaise [***Sauce Mayonnaise** France*]   Whisk together egg yolks, vinegar, lemon or lime juice, English mustard and seasoning, then slowly whisk in a suitable oil.

Mayonnaise with Soured Cream and Dill [*GB*]   Combine equal quantities of mayonnaise and soured cream with lemon juice, chopped dill and seasoning.

Pesto [***Pesto alla Genovese** Italy*]   Blend fresh basil, pine nuts, garlic, salt and olive oil to a fine paste, then whisk in olive oil and grated Parmesan or Sardo cheese.

Pine Nut Sauce [***Tarator Çamfistikli** Greece*]   Blend together pine nuts, crushed garlic, olive oil, and lemon juice to form a sauce.

Red Sauce [*Salsa Roja* Mexico]   Combine diced tomato flesh, chopped jalapeño pepper, coriander, garlic, lime juice and olive oil.

Soured Cream and Tomato Sauce [GB]   Combine soured cream, cider vinegar, crushed garlic, chopped dill, strips of tomato flesh and seasoning.

Sweet Fish Sauce [*Nam Pla Wan* Thailand]   Crisp fry chopped shallots, garlic and dried red chillies in oil. Dissolve palm sugar in tamarind liquid and nam pla, stir in chopped spring onions and coriander leaves then combine with the garlic mixture.

Tartar Sauce [*Sauce Tartare* France]   Combine mayonnaise with chopped capers, gherkin and fresh herbs.

Villain Sauce [*Molho Vilao* Portugal]   Combine sieved hard-boiled egg with chopped onion, garlic, parsley and coriander, wine vinegar and olive oil.

Vinegar Sauce [*Molho de Escabeche* Portugal]   Sauté chopped onion, garlic and diced green pimento in oil then add diced tomato flesh.

Dressings

Almond Dressing [*Picadilla* Spain]   Blend almonds, chopped garlic, olive oil, vinegar, lemon juice and seasoning to a smooth dressing.

Avocado Dressing [Israel]   Blend together avocado flesh, lime juice, cider vinegar, garlic, chopped coriander leaves and olive oil. Whisk the mixture onto egg yolks and cream and add chopped spring onion and seasoning.

Basil and Pine Nut Pesto [*Pesto Genovese* Italy]   Blend basil leaves, garlic, toasted pine nuts and Pecorino and Parmesan cheese to a paste. Whisk in olive oil and add seasoning.

Basil and Wine Dressing [*Agliata* Italy]   Combine breadcrumbs soaked in white wine, crushed garlic and chopped basil and parsley. Blend in olive oil and season.

Black Olive, Tomato and Basil Dressing [*Tapenad* Italy]   Blend capers, anchovy fillets, Dijon mustard, fresh basil, olive oil, red wine vinegar and pitted black olives to a paste. Fold in chopped parsley and chopped sun-dried tomatoes and season well.

Blue Cheese Dressing [USA]   Blend onion, garlic, lemon juice, red wine vinegar, soured cream, mayonnaise and blue cheese to a smooth dressing.

Blue Stilton Dressing [GB]   Combine mashed Blue Stilton cheese with French dressing, lemon juice and seasoning.

Caper and Onion Dressing [*Molho de Vilao* Portugal]   Combine olive oil, wine vinegar, chopped onion, parsley and capers.

Cheese and Herb Dressing [*El Aliño* Spain]   Blend olive oil, vinegar, Dijon mustard, chopped garlic, sugar, basil, thyme, marjoram, grated horseradish, grated Parmesan cheese and seasoning.

Coconut Dressing [Caribbean]   Blend red pimento, garlic, lime juice, sugar, chilli powder, salt, brown sugar and grated coconut to a smooth dressing.

Cream Dressing [Caribbean]   Flavour crème fraîche and yogurt or cream with lemon juice and seasoning.

Dill Dressing [*Dill Sallad Sas* Scandinavia]   Combine sieved hard-boiled egg, chopped dill, tarragon vinegar, olive oil, lemon juice, lightly whipped cream and seasoning.

French Dressing [***Vinaigrette*** *France*]   Combine 1 part vinegar with 2 parts oil and season with salt and pepper.

Green Dressing [***Salsa Verde*** *Italy*]   Combine olive oil, lemon juice, chopped parsley, watercress, capers, anchovy fillets, Dijon mustard and seasoning.

Gribiche Dressing [***Sauce Gribiche*** *France*]   Combine French mustard, vinegar and walnut oil then add chopped gherkins, capers, chives, tarragon and parsley, sieved hard-boiled eggs and seasoning.

Herb Dressing [*GB*]   Combine olive oil, lemon juice, chopped mint, chives and tarragon and seasoning.

Lemon Dressing [***Epanthicen Lathólemono*** *Greece*]   Combine walnut or olive oil with lemon juice, chopped parsley and seasoning.

Lime and Féta Cheese Dressing [***Epanthicen me Fetta Lemonew*** *Greece*]   Combine olive oil with the juice and grated zest of lime, crushed garlic, chopped fresh green chilli and coriander leaves, grated Féta cheese and seasoning.

Mustard Dressing [*GB*]   Combine English mustard, wine vinegar, French dressing, mayonnaise, cream, crushed garlic and seasoning.

Mustard Dressing [*Japan*]   Mix dry mustard to a paste with water, then stir in dashi, miso and light soy sauce.

Mustard and Egg Dressing [*Japan*]   Mix dry mustard with water, whisk in egg yolks and dark soy sauce.

Orange Dressing [*Caribbean*]   Boil zest of oranges in raspberry vinegar, add orange juice, walnut oil, chopped tarragon and parsley and seasoning.

Ponzu Dressing [***Ponzu*** *Japan*]   Mix together lemon juice, rice vinegar, dark soy sauce, tamari sauce, mirin, bonito flakes and 5-mm pieces of kelp.

Red Chilli Dressing [***Rouille*** *Greece*]   Blend soaked dried red chillies, garlic, red pimento and olive oil to a paste then whisk in egg yolks and seasoning.

Roasted Garlic Dressing [*Caribbean*]   Roast garlic until brown and soft. Crush the garlic and blend with one-third balsamic vinegar, two-thirds olive oil and seasoning.

Russian Dressing [***Sous iz Gorchitsey*** *Russia*]   Combine Dijon mustard with wine vinegar and olive oil then whisk onto smetana and season well.

Sea Urchin Dressing [***Uni*** *Japan*]   Blend together puréed sea urchin, beaten eggs, mirin and saké.

Sesame Dressing [***Goma*** *Japan*]   Combine mirin, soy sauce, dashi and toasted and finely ground sesame seeds.

Sweet Vinegar Dressing [***Amazu*** *Japan*]   Boil rice vinegar, mirin, dashi and a little sugar, then cool.

Tarragon Dressing [*GB*]   Combine English mustard, vinegar, oil and chopped tarragon.

Thousand Island Dressing [*USA*]   Combine chopped red and green pimento and parsley, sieved hard-boiled egg, vinegar, olive oil, tabasco and seasoning.

Tomato and Cumin Dressing [***Vinagreta de Tomate*** *Spain*]   Blend together tomato flesh, garlic, cumin, olive oil, vinegar, paprika and seasoning.

Tomato and Chilli Dressing [***Salsa Mexicana*** *Mexico*]   Combine strips of tomato flesh, chopped fresh green chillies, onion, garlic, coriander leaves, lime juice and seasoning.

Three Vinegar Dressing [***Sambaizu*** *Japan*]   Heat mirin, rice vinegar, soy sauce and dashi.

Two Vinegar Dressing [*Nihaizu* Japan]   Whisk together rice vinegar, soy sauce and dashi.

White Miso Dressing [*Tofu* Japan]   Liquidise tofu, sugar, toasted and finely ground sesame seeds, mirin and salt.

Chapter Three

Soups

This chapter is divided into six main categories of soup, which are grouped together as follows:

✦ Vegetable Soups and Broths ✦

✦ Chilled Soups ✦

✦ Clear Soups and Consommés ✦

✦ Creams and Veloutés ✦

✦ Fish Soups ✦

✦ Purée Soups ✦

Allow two litres of completed soup for 10 average portions.

Vegetable Soups and Broths

Baby Corn Soup and Tofu [*Sup Jagung Muda Dengan Tahu* Thailand] Cook baby sweetcorn, cubes of smoked tofu and shredded spinach in vegetable stock flavoured with dried red chillies, ginger and spinach.

Beef Broth [*Gom-Gook* Korea] Boil turnip-flavoured beef stock, flavour with soy sauce and garnish with chopped garlic and spring onions, ground sesame seeds, diced pimento, turnip and beef.

Beef Broth [*Sopa de Caldo de Carne* Portugal] Place bread sippets into soup bowls, fill with rich beef stock and garnish with vermicelli and mint leaves.

Beef Soup [*Sopa de Carne* Portugal] Sweat paysanne of onion, carrot and turnip, moisten with beef stock and add diced potato and shredded cabbage; cook until tender. Garnish with diced beef and slices of chorizo sausage.

Beef and Chicken Broth [*Gilàa* Hungary] Sweat brunoise of carrot, onion, celery, turnip and leek; stir in paprika and tomato purée then moisten with chicken and beef stock; add caraway seeds and diced tomato flesh. Garnish with diced chicken and beef.

Beef and Paprika Soup [*Gulyásleves* Hungary] Golden fry chopped onion in lard, add diced beef, paprika, grated potato, caraway seeds and tomato purée; moisten with beef stock and cook. Add diced potatoes and sliced green pimento and finish cooking.

Beef and Vegetable Broth [*Marhahúsleves* Hungary] Sweat chopped onion, garlic, paysanne of carrot and strips of green pimento; add diced tomato flesh and paprika then moisten with beef stock; add dice of celeriac and parsnip, sliced mushrooms and savoy cabbage and vermicelli. Garnish with golden-fried grated carrot, chopped parsley and semolina dumplings (see page 91).

Beetroot Soup [*Bortsch* Russia] Sweat sliced onion and julienne of carrot and leek and moisten with dill-flavoured beef stock, white wine vinegar and lemon juice, then add shredded cabbage, tomato concassée and diced potato and allow to simmer. Garnish with batons of beetroot and diced breast of duck and serve topped with a spoonful of smetana.

Beetroot Soup Ukrainian Style [*Bortsch* Russia] Simmer chicken stock with diced potato, julienne of carrot and celery, dried lima beans and whole beetroot. When cooked add shredded cabbage and remove the beetroot. Finely grate the beetroot and add to the soup and serve garnished with chopped dill and garlic, topped with a spoonful of smetana.

Beetroot and Potato Soup [Israel] Cook peeled beetroots, finely chopped beetroot tops and onion in water with salt and sugar. Grate the beetroot, return to the soup and finish with lemon juice. Garnish with small boiled potatoes and serve accompanied by soured cream, diced dill cucumber, chopped fresh dill and sliced hard-boiled egg.

Beetroot Top Soup [USA] Cook shredded blanched beetroot tops and diced potato in chicken stock. Thicken with arrowroot, season with salt, allspice and Tabasco sauce and finish with cream.

Black Bean Soup [*USA*]   Cook black beans with sautéed diced salt pork, smoked ham and chopped onion, garlic and oregano in beef stock. Liquidise half the beans and return to the soup, season with cayenne and salt and finish with dry sherry and red wine. Garnish with the remainder of the beans.

Black Bean Soup [*Sopa de Frijoles Negros Mexico*]   Cook black beans in water with a ham bone then add chopped onion, garlic, jalapeño and diced tomato flesh and cook. Garnish with diced ham and chopped coriander.

Borage and Lettuce Soup [*Zuppa alla Genovese Italy*]   Garnish chicken stock with diamonds of four savoury egg custards (royales) each flavoured with borage, lettuce, Parmesan cheese, onion, parsley and mixed spice.

Brown Chicken and Beef Soup [*Königinsuppe Germany*]   Thicken brown beef and chicken stock with arrowroot; finish with a liaison of egg yolks and soured cream and garnish with chopped almonds and diced lamb.

Brown Windsor Soup [*GB*]   Sweat a mirepoix of vegetables, add tomato purée, moisten with brown beef stock and cook. Liquidise, thicken with arrowroot and garnish with boiled rice and diced mixed vegetables.

Cabbage Soup [*Shchi Russia*]   Sweat chopped onion, diced parsnip and celery, julienne of carrot and tomato concassée. Moisten with beef stock then add shredded cabbage and diced potato. Serve topped with a spoonful of smetana and chopped dill.

Cabbage Soup [*Soupe au Chou France*]   Sweat a paysanne of onion, leek and carrot, moisten with chicken stock and add paysanne of cabbage, potato and lardons of bacon.

Cabbage and Bean Soup [*Jota Italy*]   Boil shredded cabbage in water with salt and cumin seeds for 5 min and drain. Stir the cabbage into hot garlic-flavoured butter, add cooked navy beans, lardons of bacon and chicken stock then lightly thicken with cornflour. Finish with chopped fresh herbs.

Cabbage, Bean and Pimento Soup [*Potaje de Coles Verdes Spain*]   Cook kidney beans in water with diced salt pork, add shredded cabbage, sliced onion, garlic, diced potato, red pimento and tomato flesh and cook.

Cabbage and Cheese Soup [*Zuppa di Valpelline Italy*]   Line the bottom of a soup tureen with slices of toast, cover with alternate layers each of boiled Savoy cabbage leaves, lardons of bacon and grated Fontina cheese. Cover with toast, moisten with stock seasoned with cinnamon, sprinkle with melted butter and gratinate.

Cauliflower and Noodle Soup [*Sup Kembang Kol Indonesia*]   Flavour beef stock with ground mace, coriander, cumin and cloves. Garnish with florets of cauliflower and fine egg noodles, cooked in the soup.

Chestnut Soup [*Sopa de Castanhas Portugal*]   Cook peeled and chopped chestnuts and shredded cabbage in water. Serve garnished with stellini pasta.

Chickpea and Chestnut Soup [*Minestra di Ceci e Castagne Italy*]   Cook soaked chickpeas in stock. Golden fry garlic and lardons of bacon in olive oil, add mashed chestnuts and crushed bayleaf and cook. Stir the chestnut mixture into the chickpea soup and serve in soup bowls lined with slices of toasted bread.

Chickpea and Chorizo Soup [*Sopa de Garbanzos y Chorizo Spain*]   Cook chickpeas in water with chopped onion and garlic, a piece of bacon and a bouquet garni. When cooked, cut the bacon into dice, add sliced chorizo sausage, season to taste and serve.

Chicken and Egg Soup [*Dahn Tong* China]   Garnish chicken stock with sliced dried mushrooms, diced cooked chicken, strips of tofu cooked in soy sauce, cider vinegar and chilli oil. Finish by pouring in beaten eggs to form threads.

Chicken and Galingale Soup [*Kai Tom Ka* Thailand]   Flavour chicken stock with lemon grass, sliced galingale, kaffir lime leaves, red chillies and nam pla. Garnish with julienne of chicken and sliced shiitake or oyster mushrooms. Finish with coconut milk, lemon or lime juice and chopped basil.

Chicken and Melon Soup [*Kang Kung* Thailand]   Flavour chicken stock with saké, dried shrimps, nuoc mam, dried mushrooms and grated root ginger. Garnish with melon balls cooked in the soup.

Chicken and Mushroom Soup [*Gai Gwoo Tong* China]   Flavour chicken stock with soy sauce, saké and grated ginger. Garnish with sliced chicken breast, ham, spring onions, sliced dried mushrooms, bamboo shoots and Chinese noodles. Serve with prawn crackers.

Chicken and Mushroom Soup [*Kang Hed Say Hom Pom* Thailand]   Flavour chicken stock with sautéed chopped onion, sliced mushrooms, ground coriander and cumin. Finish with slightly thickened coconut milk and chopped coriander leaves.

Chicken and Pasta Broth [*Stracciatelli alla Romana* Italy]   Whisk together beaten eggs, semolina, grated Parmesan cheese, salt, pepper and nutmeg and a little stock. Whisk the mixture into simmering chicken stock and cook.

Chicken and Pumpkin Soup [*Canh Ga Bi Doe* Thailand]   Flavour chicken stock with nuoc mam and garnish with cooked pumpkin balls and diced chicken.

Chicken and Sweetcorn Soup [*Tiansuan Gai Tong* China]   Flavour chicken stock with saké, soy sauce and white wine vinegar. Garnish with sliced button mushrooms, chopped coriander leaves, sliced chicken, julienne of spring onion and sliced baby sweetcorn.

Chicken Broth [GB]   Boil chicken stock with small dice of onion, carrot, celery and turnip, cook then garnish with diced cooked chicken and chopped parsley.

Chicken, Courgette and Sweetcorn Soup [*Sopa Xochitl* Mexico]   Sweat chopped onion in oil, moisten with chicken stock then add diced courgette, sweetcorn kernels and chopped green toasted chillies. Season with nutmeg, finish with milk and garnish with diced Monterey Jack cheese.

Chicken Liver Soup [*Minestra di Riso e Fegatini* Italy]   Cook long-grain rice and chopped and fried chicken livers in chicken and beef stock. Sprinkle with chopped parsley and serve with grated Parmesan cheese.

Chicken, Mushroom and Dill Dumpling Soup [Israel]   Sweat chopped onion and sliced mushrooms in olive oil, sprinkle with flour and moisten with chicken stock, then season with paprika and salt. Poach dill dumplings in the soup and finish with chopped dill.

    Dumplings: combine eggs, plain flour, chopped dill, paprika, cayenne and salt and mould into small balls.

Chicken, Prawn and Noodle Soup [*Mah Mee* China]   Lightly fry grated ginger and garlic in oil, add to chicken stock with bean sprouts and egg noodles and season with five-spice powder. Garnish with cooked chicken, peeled prawns, lardons of bacon and crab meat. Serve with coarsely grated cucumber and sliced spring onions.

Chicken Soup with Crabmeat Dumplings [**Bak Wan Kepiting** *China*] Golden
fry chopped spring onions, blanched bamboo shoots and crabmeat then season
with sareh powder. Combine with beaten eggs and form into garnish-size balls.
Poach the balls in chicken stock and garnish with chopped coriander leaves.

Chicken Soup with Farfel [*Israel*] Flavour chicken stock with chilli, coriander,
lemon and turmeric. Garnish with leaves of parsley and farfel and serve accompanied by lemon wedges.

Chicken Soup with Grated Potato [**Sopa de Patata Rallada** *Spain*] Cook
grated potato in chicken stock and serve sprinkled with chopped fresh herbs.

Chicken Soup with Kreplach [**Mark Kreplach** *Israel*] Garnish chicken stock
with kreplach, which are small triangular-shaped pieces of noodle paste filled
with a savoury mixture of veal, onion and breadcrumbs, poached in the soup.

Chicken Soup with Vegetables and Noodles [**Lapsha** *Russia*] Sweat brunoise
of carrot, parsnip and chopped onion in oil, moisten with chicken stock and
simmer. Add egg noodles and finish with chopped dill.

Corn Chowder [*USA*] Cook sweetcorn kernels with sweated chopped onion,
fresh red chillies and diced green pimento, celery, tomato flesh and potato;
season with salt, sugar and allspice and finish with cream.

Corn Soup [**Sopa de Elote** *Mexico*] Sweat chopped onion, fresh chillies and
green and red pimentos in oil, moisten with chicken stock and milk then add
the sweetcorn kernels and cook. Serve garnished with chopped coriander.

Courgette and Pumpkin Soup [**Potaje de Bubangos** *Spain*] Sweat diced carrot,
chopped onion and garlic in oil, moisten with stock then add diced courgettes,
pumpkin and potatoes and corn kernels, bayleaf, thyme and oil, and cook.

Dried Chestnut Soup [**Sopa de Castanhas Piladas** *Portugal*] Soak then cook
dried chestnuts in their soaking liquid then add rice and sliced onion sweated in
olive oil, and cook until tender.

Dry Soup, Minho Fashion [**Sopa Seca do Minho** *Portugal*] Line an earthenware dish with bread croûtons then add layers of cooked chickpeas, diced
cooked carrot, diamonds of french beans, tomato concassée and diced beef.
Moisten with chicken stock and bake in the oven for approx. 30 min.

Duck and Barley Soup [**Rassolnik** *Russia*] Cook pearl barley in duck stock with
chopped onion, diced potato, sliced gherkin and chopped dill. Serve accompanied by smetana.

Game Soup [*GB*] Sweat a brunoise of onion, carrot, celery, turnip and bacon,
moisten with game stock, thicken with arrowroot and finish with port wine.
Serve accompanied by diced croûtons.

Game Soup [**Sopa ou Lebre** *Portugal*] Cook pieces of hare in game stock with
vegetables, thyme and bayleaf. Liquidise the vegetables with the stock, thicken
lightly with cornflour, garnish with diced hare and finish with madeira.

Garlic and Coriander Soup [**Sopa a Alentejana** *Portugal*] Spread croûtons with
a garlic and fresh coriander paste, place into soup bowls, moisten with boiling
water, olive oil and seasoning; break an egg into each bowl, and allow to gently
simmer until poached.

Haricot Bean and Saffron Soup [**Arroz con Acelgas** *Spain*] Boil haricot beans
in chicken stock then add shredded Swiss chard, a few threads of saffron,
paprika, diced turnip and short-grain rice. Simmer until cooked then season to
taste and serve.

Leek and Caraway Soup [*GB*]   Sweat julienne of white of leek, moisten with chicken stock, add saffron and caraway seeds. Garnish with vermicelli and a julienne of cooked chicken breast.

Lentil Soup [***Sopa de Lentejas*** *Spain*]   Cook lentils in water with a bouquet garni for approx. 45 min. Sweat chopped onion, garlic and diced carrot in oil, stir in paprika then add to the lentils. Add diced potatoes, a little vinegar, and seasoning and allow to cook.

Lime Soup [***Sopa de Lima*** *Mexico*]   Flavour chicken stock with cloves, oregano and lime juice; garnish with julienne of chicken, crisp-fried strips of tortilla and sliced fresh green chillies. Lightly fry chopped onion, crushed garlic and brunoise of green pimento, add tomato concassée and cook and serve separately.

Mandura Beef Soup [***Soto Madura*** *Indonesia*]   Fry chopped onion and garlic in oil, add ginger and turmeric, moisten with beef stock, add chilli powder, simmer 2 min then add prawn stock flavoured with candlenuts. Garnish with bean sprouts, diced beef, picked parsley and fried shallots and serve with slices of lemon.

Meatball Soup [*Israel*]   Sweat diced carrot, moisten with chicken stock, add tomato purée and season with ground cumin, turmeric, cayenne and salt. Poach small meatballs in the soup together with diced potato and basmati rice and garnish with chopped parsley.

Meatballs: combine minced cooked beef, chickpea flour, chopped onion, parsley and seasoning.

Melon Soup [***Tung Kwah Chuk*** *China*]   Garnish chicken and pork stock with sliced dried mushrooms, diced bamboo shoots, shredded ham and grated ginger; pour onto melon pulp and allow to cook. Serve the soup in hollowed out melon halves.

Minestrone [*Italy*]   Crisp fry diced salt pork in olive oil, remove and retain. Add and sweat chopped onion and garlic and paysanne of carrots and celery, moisten with chicken stock then add diced potatoes and tomato flesh, shredded cabbage, a bouquet garni, the pork, cooked kidney beans and chickpeas. Allow to cook. Finish by adding elbow macaroni and peas and serve sprinkled with Parmesan cheese.

Mixed Vegetable Soup [***Gemüsesuppe*** *Germany*]   Sweat paysanne of carrot, turnip, leek, celery and shredded cabbage then moisten with vegetable stock; add florets of cauliflower and paysanne of potatoes and cook. Garnish with diced smoked ham and serve accompanied by frankfurter sausages and rye bread.

Mutton and Dill Soup [***Harcho*** *Hungary*]   Sweat chopped onion and celery with crushed garlic, add tomato purée and moisten with mutton stock. Rain in rice, add chopped pickled plums and allow to cook. Serve garnished with diced mutton and chopped dill.

Mutton Soup [***Chervah*** *Middle East*]   Lightly fry diced mutton in oil with chopped onion, add diced tomato flesh and mint, moisten with stock and cook. Garnish with rice or vermicelli.

Nettle Soup [***Zelonyeshchi*** *Russia*]   Cook potatoes and nettles in beef stock then liquidise. Garnish the soup with diced beef then ladle it into soup bowls in which one soft-boiled egg per portion has been placed; top with smetana.

Nettle Soup [*Zuppa di Ortiche* Italy]   Fry lardons of pancetta and chopped onion in olive oil. Add tomato concassée and shredded nettle leaves, moisten with chicken stock and simmer.

Onion and Almond Soup [*Cebollada con Almendras* Spain]   Heat olive oil in a pan, moisten with white wine and chicken stock, add a bouquet garni and sliced onion and simmer for 30 min. Blend blanched almonds with a little stock to a smooth paste, add to the soup and flavour with a little cumin and continue to cook for 10 min. Pour the soup into individual soup bowls, place toasted bread croûtons on top, sprinkle with Parmesan cheese and gratinate under a grill. Sprinkle the surface with toasted shredded almonds and serve.

Peas and Kleis [Israel]   Cook shelled peas in salted water and drain, moisten with boiling milk, add a knob of butter and chopped mint and cook. Drop table-spoons of kleis batter into the soup and poach.
     Kleis batter: whisk egg and milk into fine matzo meal and salt to make a soft mixture.

Pork Soup [*Samlor Chhrook* Thailand]   Fry chopped garlic and diced pork in groundnut oil. Add pork stock, nuoc mam, lemon juice, sugar and grated ginger. Garnish with chopped coriander leaves.

Pork and Chicken Soup [*Kaeng Chud Mu Kai* Thailand]   Garnish coriander-flavoured chicken and pork stock with cellophane noodles, sliced mushrooms, diced pork cooked in water with nam pla and palm sugar, chopped spring onions and coriander leaves.

Pork and Tannias Soup [*Tannia Soup* Caribbean]   Cut salt pork into 1.5-cm cubes and soak in cold water for 12 hr. Rinse the meat under cold water, place into a pan, cover with stock, add beef cut into 1.5-cm cubes and simmer until it is almost cooked. Sweat sliced onion and crushed cloves of garlic in oil, moisten with the cooking liquid and add the diced meats, then add diced tannias and a sprig of thyme and seasoning; cook for approx. 20 min and serve.

Prune, Apricot and Peach Soup [*Abgushte Miveh* Middle East]   Sweat sliced onion, add turmeric and cook until lightly browned. Moisten with lamb and beef stock, simmer and add chopped dried prunes, apricots and peaches; finish with demerara sugar and lime or lemon juice.

Pumpkin Soup [*Kürbissuppe* Germany]   Boil roughly chopped pumpkin in water with grated zest of lemon, cloves and cinnamon then liquidise. Finish with white wine vinegar, season, sweeten with sugar and serve.

Pumpkin and Basil Soup [*Kaeng Liang Fak Thong* Thailand]   Cook diced pumpkin in vegetable stock flavoured with lemon grass, galingale and basil. Garnish with basil leaves and diced creamed coconut.

Rice and Turnip Soup [*Minestra di Riso e Rape* Italy]   Sweat paysanne of tur-nip in butter. Separately fry sliced onion and lardons of bacon, moisten with beef stock then add rice and simmer, add the turnip and serve accompanied by grated Parmesan cheese.

Scotch Broth [GB]   Boil white beef or mutton stock with added diced onion, car-rot, celery and turnip; garnish with chopped parsley.

Seakale and Chickpea Soup [*Potaje de Acelgas* Spain]   Cook chickpeas in water with diced salt pork and sliced onion, add diced seakale, pumpkin, potato, tomato flesh and corn kernels and cook. Finish with olive oil, paprika and saffron.

Spicy Chicken Soup [***Soto Ayam*** *Indonesia*] Fry sliced onion in peanut oil, add crushed garlic, ginger, blanchan, ground turmeric, coriander, cumin, nutmeg, black pepper and fennel seeds. Moisten with chicken stock, cook and strain. Finish with lemon juice and garnish with cooked egg noodles, diced chicken, chopped hard-boiled egg, sliced and fried cloves of garlic, sliced spring onions, fried dried green chillies and fried onion flakes. Serve accompanied by fried fresh chillies, potato crisps and sambal bajak or sambal ulek.

Spinach Soup [***Shigumchiguk*** *Korea*] Marinate strips of beef in soy sauce with chopped spring onion, garlic, toasted sesame seeds, sesame oil and black pepper. Golden fry the meat in oil, moisten with water and the marinade and cook, then add shredded spinach and diced bean curd.

Spinach and Chickpea Soup [***Potaje de Espinacas y Garbanzos*** *Spain*] Cook chickpeas in water with an onion clouté and cloves of garlic. When cooked remove and discard the onion and garlic. Golden fry cloves of garlic and diced bread croûtons in olive oil, place into a blender with some of the cooking liquid from the chickpeas and blend to a smooth paste. Pour the mixture into the soup and simmer for 10 min. Cook leaves of prepared spinach in a little salted water, drain, cut into shreds then lightly sauté with lardons of serrano ham and add to the soup; season to taste and serve.

Spring Green Soup [***Caldo Verde*** *Portugal*] Sweat sliced onion in oil, moisten with chicken stock, add potatoes and cook. Liquidise and serve garnished with shredded and boiled spring greens and diced chorizo sausage.

Stone Soup [***Sopa de Pedra*** *Portugal*] Sweat paysanne of onion, carrot and turnip in oil, moisten with beef and ham stock, add paysanne of cabbage and potatoes and cook. Add cooked butter beans or chickpeas and garnish with sliced chorizo sausage.

Tomato and Egg Soup [***Sopa de Tomate com Ovo Pao*** *Portugal*] Golden fry sliced onion in oil then add diced tomato flesh, chopped garlic and parsley. Moisten with stock then add diced potato. Place bread croûtons into soup bowls, pour in the soup and poach an egg in each by gentle simmering.

Tripe Soup [***Menudo*** *Mexico*] Simmer strips of tripe studded with cloves, quartered onions, diced carrot, celery, tomato flesh and garlic in chicken stock flavoured with oregano and sage. Serve sprinkled with olive oil and chopped spring onions.

Vegetable and Fried Bean Curd Soup [***Noppei-Jiru*** *Japan*] Rinse 1-cm slices of fried bean curd in hot water. Simmer quarters of shiitake mushrooms, thinly sliced carrot, daikon, taro and chopped salsify in salted water for 2 min, drain then cover with first soup stock, add the bean curd and simmer for 15 min; lightly thicken with diluted arrowroot and season with monosodium glutamate and soy sauce. Arrange cooked noodles in soup bowls, pour in the soup, sprinkle the surface with finely chopped spring onions and parsley and serve.

Vegetable Soup [***Yachaeguk*** *Korea*] Marinade strips of beef in soy sauce with shredded spring onion, garlic, toasted sesame seeds, sesame oil and black pepper. Fry the meat in oil, moisten with stock and the marinade then add diced potato and courgette and paysanne of Chinese cabbage and cook.

Vegetable Soup with Chicken and Avocado Pear [***Caldo Tlalpeño*** *Mexico*] Simmer chicken stock with diamonds of french beans, roundels of carrot, fresh red chillies, tomato concassée and cooked chickpeas. Garnish with strips of fresh red chillies, avocado pear and chicken breast. Serve accompanied by quarters of lime.

Vegetable Soup with Dumplings [*Frischesuppe* Germany] Sweat a brunoise of carrot, turnip and celery, moisten with beef stock and add diamonds of French beans. Garnish with small dumplings, cooked in the soup.
   Dumplings: boil salted water with butter, stir in flour and cool, beat in eggs and egg yolks. Form into balls and poach in the soup.

Vegetable Soup with Matzo Balls [*Israel*] Sweat grated carrot, onion and courgettes, moisten with stock, add tomato flesh and bouquet garni and cook. Garnish with matzo balls cooked in the soup and finish with milk and chopped dill.
   Matzo balls: combine matzo meal, baking powder, salt, pepper and beaten eggs.

Vegetable Soup with Prawns [*Sajur* Indonesia] Blend onions, garlic, cumin, ginger, chillies, bayleaf and salt to a paste then fry in oil for 1 min. Add coconut milk, grated carrot, shredded cabbage, cauliflower florets, diced pimento and zest of lemon; allow to cook then garnish with cooked minced beef, prawns, crisply fried onion and grated coconut.

Vermicelli Soup [*Sopa de Fideo* Mexico] Golden fry vermicelli in oil, add chicken stock, flavour with tomato, garlic and chillies and simmer until it thickens. Serve accompanied by Parmesan cheese.

Watercress and Haricot Bean Soup [*Potaje de Berros* Spain] Cook haricot beans in water with diced salt pork and sliced onion then add chopped watercress, diced tomato flesh, potato and green pimento and corn kernels. Finish with crushed garlic, oil and saffron.

White Bean Soup [*USA*] Cook haricot beans in beef and chicken stock with sweated diced carrot, celery, leek, garlic and smoked bacon. Liquidise half the beans and return to the soup, serve garnished with diced bacon.

Yellow Split Pea Soup with Lemon [*Souvana* Greece] Cook yellow split peas and rice in chicken stock with potatoes and onion. Liquidise, finish with lemon juice and serve accompanied by black olives, olive oil and bread.

Yemenite Beef Soup [*Israel*] Sweat diced beef seasoned with ground cumin, turmeric, salt and pepper, moisten with beef stock then add diced tomato flesh and small new potatoes. Finish with chopped coriander leaves.

Yemenite Chicken Soup [*Israel*] Sweat diced chicken, seasoned with ground cumin, turmeric, salt and pepper, moisten with chicken stock then add diced tomato flesh and small new potatoes. Finish with chopped coriander leaves.

Chilled Soups

Chilled Almond and Grape Soup [*Sopa Blanca al Uvas* Spain] Pound whole almonds and gradually incorporate cloves of garlic, olive oil, wine vinegar and chicken stock. Garnish with white grapes.

Chilled Apple Soup [*Applesoppa* Scandinavia] Simmer sliced apples in water with sugar and lemon juice, thicken with diluted cornflour and chill before serving.

Chilled Avocado Soup [*USA*]   Liquidise avocado flesh with chicken stock and lemon juice, finish with cream and garnish with leaves of fresh chervil.

Chilled Beer Soup [*Bierkaltschale Germany*]   To German beer add brown breadcrumbs, lemon juice, ground cinnamon and warmed currants and simmer gently until it thickens.

Chilled Bortsch [*Israel*]   Add brunoise of cooked beetroot to boiling water and cook, then add lemon juice and salt, strain and chill.

Chilled Breadfruit Soup with Chives [*Caribbean*]   Sweat sliced white of leek and onion and crushed cloves of garlic in oil; moisten with stock, bring to the boil, add roughly cut breadfruit, a bouquet garni, chopped fresh red chillies and seasoning and simmer until cooked. When cooked liquidise, strain, reboil and season to taste. Garnish with chopped chives and finish with cream.

Chilled Cider and Herb Soup [*Okroshka Russia*]   Whisk cider or kvas into sieved yolks of hard-boiled egg, English mustard and sugar; chill. Stir in a fine paste of garlic and chives, garnish with diced white of hard-boiled egg, cooked veal, beef, ham, potato and chopped dill and serve with soured cream.

Chilled Cucumber Soup [*Oinaengguk Korea*]   Combine julienne of cucumber, chopped green and red pimento, shredded spring onions and strips of red chillies; moisten with water, cider vinegar, soy sauce and sesame oil and add sugar.

Chilled Horseradish and Kvas Soup [*Sup Kholodnyi iz Kvas Russia*]   Combine cooked sauerkraut, finely sliced raw onion, sliced cucumber, grated horseradish, chopped dill and mashed hard-boiled egg then moisten with cider or kvas and chill. Serve topped with a spoonful of smetana.

Chilled Orange Soup [*Caribbean*]   Simmer chicken stock with the peel only of oranges for approx. 10 min, add orange juice, cloves, cinnamon stick and seasoning and continue to cook for 5 min. Strain through a muslin into a clean receptacle and chill. Serve garnished with segments of orange.

Chilled Potato and Vegetable Soup [*Okroshka Russia*]   Combine cooked and grated potato, carrot and turnip, chopped raw onion, sliced cucumber, chopped hard-boiled egg and diluted mustard; add seasoning and chill. Serve topped with a spoonful of smetana and chopped dill.

Chilled Rosehip Soup [*Nyponsoppa Scandinavia*]   Cook soaked rosehips in the soaking liquid with grated zest of lemons; liquidise and thicken with arrowroot. Finish with lemon juice, garnish with shredded almonds and serve with cream on top.

Chilled Sorrel and Watercress Soup [*Shchav Israel*]   Cook watercress and sorrel in vegetable stock then liquidise. Finish with the grated zest and juice of lemon and sugar and serve chilled accompanied by soured cream.

Chilled Spinach and Fish Soup [*Botvinya Russia*]   Blend cooked spinach, grated horseradish and cider or kvas to a soup consistency, season and chill. Garnish with raw chopped onion and goujons of poached white fish. Serve topped with a spoonful of smetana.

Chilled Spinach, Sorrel and Cider Soup [*Botvinia Russia*]   Liquidise purée of cooked spinach with sweated shredded sorrel, sugar and English mustard. Add dry cider or kvas, boil and chill. Garnish with sliced pickled cucumber, chopped chives and dill, flaked cooked pike or perch and grated horseradish.

Chilled Tomato Soup [*USA*]   Sweat chopped onion and garlic in oil, add ground mace and flour, moisten with chicken stock, add crushed tomatoes and cook.

Add a reduction of vinegar and sugar then liquidise. Finish with soured cream and chopped chives.

Gazpacho [*Spain*]   Liquidise bread, previously soaked in white wine, cloves of garlic, wine vinegar, olive oil, tomato flesh, chopped green pimento, crushed cumin seeds and water. Serve accompanied by chopped parsley, onion, cucumber, red pimento and hard-boiled egg and fried bread croûtons, each in a separate dish.

Gazpacho with White Grapes [*Ajo Blanco con Uvas Spain*]   Liquidise bread, previously soaked in white wine, cloves of garlic, ground almonds, vinegar and water. Strain the soup and serve garnished with peeled seedless white grapes and diced bread croûtons.

Vichyssoise [*France*]   Sweat sliced leek and onion in butter, moisten with chicken stock, add diced potato and cook. Liquidise and finish with cream and garnish with chopped chives.

Yogurt and Raisin Soup [*Ash Mast Va Khir Middle East*]   Combine yogurt and cream and garnish with chopped hard-boiled egg, batons of cucumber, chopped dill and parsley and soaked raisins.

Clear Soups and Consommés

Beef and Bean Curd Soup [*Kogidubuguk Korea*]   Marinate garnish-size strips of beef in soy sauce with chopped spring onions, garlic, toasted sesame seeds and sesame oil. Golden fry the meat in oil, moisten with water and cook, then add cubes of bean curd. Serve garnished with julienne of spring onions.

Beef and Bean Paste Soup [*Twoenjang-Tchigae Korea*]   Marinate garnish-size strips of beef and kimichi in soy sauce with garlic. Sauté the beef and the kimichi, stir in twoenjang, moisten with water and simmer. Add diced bean curd, chopped fresh green chillies, diced courgette and diagonal sliced spring onions and cook.

Beef and Bean Sprout Soup [*Kong Namul Kuk Korea*]   Marinate strips of beef in soy sauce, sesame oil and garlic then golden fry in oil. Moisten with stock. Add soya bean sprouts and cook; finish with chopped spring onions.

Beef and Turnip Soup [*Komguk Korea*]   Cut a julienne of cooked brisket of beef and cooked turnip, add chopped spring onions, soy sauce, toasted sesame seeds and sesame oil. Add to simmering beef stock and serve with steamed rice.

Beef and Vegetable Soup [*Gogi Kuk Korea*]   Fry diced beef, spring onions and garlic in oil, add sliced mushrooms, moisten with stock, soy sauce and saké then add hot bean sauce and cook. Finish with a little sesame oil.

Beef Dumpling Soup [*Mandoo Korea*]   Flavour beef stock with soy sauce then add the dumplings and cook; garnish with strips of fried beaten egg and crumbled nori.

Dumplings: fry minced pork and beef in oil, moisten with stock and cook. Combine with blanched chopped bean sprouts and Chinese cabbage, mashed bean curd, chopped spring onion, garlic and toasted sesame seeds. Wrap and seal the mixture in wonton wrappers.

Beef Rib Soup [*Kalbitang Korea*]   Marinade pieces of rib of beef in soy sauce together with diagonal slices of spring onions, garlic, shredded ginger, sesame oil and black pepper. Golden fry the meat in oil, moisten with the marinade and water and cook. Serve garnished with strips of beaten fried egg and shredded spring onions.

Beef Soup [*Cocido* Mexico]   Boil beef stock with sliced carrot, courgette, potato, sweetcorn and onion. Pour the soup over arroz rojo in soup bowls, top with salsa roja and serve accompanied by segments of lime.

Beef Soup with Kasha [*Israel*]   Garnish beef stock with coarsely cut carrots, turnips, leeks and onion, diced beef and kasha.

Beef Soup with Meatballs [*Wanjaguk Korea*]   Combine minced beef, bean curd, garlic, soy sauce, toasted sesame seeds, sesame oil and chopped spring onions. Mould the mixture into balls, pass through beaten egg and cornflour then poach in beef stock. Serve garnished with chopped chives.

Beef Soup with Pork Meatballs [*Sopa de Albòndigas Mexico*]   Boil beef stock with chopped onion, diced carrot, green pimento and tomato flesh. Add beef and pork meatballs flavoured with fresh coriander and oregano and poach.

Bird's Nest Soup [*Yin Wor Tong China*]   Simmer soaked nests in chicken stock then transfer to a steamer dish, add legs of chicken and steam. Combine water chestnut flour and water and stir into the simmering stock to thicken; add cooked and diced egg white then garnish the nests with a brunoise of chicken leg, ham, mushrooms and spring onions.

Callaloo [*Caribbean*]   Fry lardons of bacon, chopped onion and garlic, and add shredded Chinese spinach or ordinary spinach. Moisten with chicken stock and coconut milk. Garnish with crabmeat and sliced okra and finish with Tabasco sauce.

Chicken Soup [*Soto Ayam Thailand*]   Fry chopped shallots and garlic in peanut oil, stir in blachan, coriander powder, turmeric powder and lemon juice. Moisten with chicken stock flavoured with lemon grass, ginger, galingale and curry leaves. Garnish with a julienne of chicken breast and serve sprinkled with crisp fried onions.

Chicken Soup with Meat Dumplings [*Manduguk Korea*]   Combine fried minced pork, beef, chopped garlic, soy sauce, toasted sesame seeds, sesame oil, grated ginger, chopped spring onions, chopped and squeezed kimichi, blanched and chopped bean sprouts, squeezed bean curd, salt and black pepper. Fill wonton wrappers with the mixture to make mandu then poach them in chicken stock. Serve garnished with chopped spring onions and accompanied by chojang vinegar.

Chicken Soup with Shredded Egg [*Paeksuk Korea*]   Flavour chicken stock with sliced ginger and garlic. Serve garnished with diced chicken, sliced spring onions and strips of fried beaten egg.

Chicken Soup with Stuffed Mushrooms and Water Melon [*Gaeng Jued Thailand*]   Blend minced pork, water chestnuts, garlic, spring onions, coriander leaves, soy sauce and saké to a paste. Fill soaked Chinese mushroom caps with this mixture then steam them. Garnish chicken stock with the mushrooms, balls of water melon and coriander leaves.

Clear Chicken Soup [*Toriniku No Tsumirejiru Japan*]   Combine a fine purée of raw chicken breast with flour, bean paste and sliced jelly mushroom; mould into small balls then poach for 2 min in first soup stock together with sliced mushrooms. Finish with light soy sauce, sliced spring onions and a little juice from grated ginger.

Clear Egg Drop Soup [*Kakitama-Jiru* Japan] Lightly thicken first soup stock with diluted cornflour, flavour with soy sauce then strain beaten eggs into the simmering soup to form threads. Place grated ginger and a few drops of ginger juice into soup bowls, pour in the soup and serve garnished with v-shaped pieces of lime peel.

Clear Egg Soup [*Consommé con Huevos* Spain] To chicken, veal and ham flavoured stock, add a lightly poached egg to each portion of soup. Serve on a base of bread croûtons in small marmites.

Clear Egg Soup [*Suimono* Japan] Lightly thicken dashi with diluted cornflour, garnish with chopped spring onions and finish by pouring beaten eggs into the simmering soup to form threads.

Clear Soup with Bean Curd and Seaweed [*Tofu To Wakame No Suimono* Japan] Poach 1-cm cubes of bean curd and coarsely chopped lobe-leaf sea-weed in first soup stock flavoured with light soy sauce.

Clear Soup with Okra and Ginger [*Okura To Hari Shoga No Suimono* Japan] Lightly flavour first soup stock with soy sauce and pour into soup bowls. Garnish with sliced blanched okra and slices of fresh ginger.

Cock-a-Leekie [GB] Sweat julienne of white of leek, moisten with chicken stock and add diced soaked prunes.

Consommé Crecy [France] Garnish chicken consommé with diamonds of carrot-flavoured royale, small balls of carrot and picked chervil.

Consommé Longchamps [France] Garnish beef consommé with shredded sorrel and vermicelli.

Consommé Madeleine [France] Garnish chicken consommé with shredded let-tuce, diced celery and quenelles. Serve with small profiteroles.

Consommé Madrilène [France] Consommé flavoured with tomato, pimento and celery; serve garnished with julienne of tomato, vermicelli and shredded sorrel.

Consommé Portugaise [France] Garnish beef consommé with rice and diced flesh of tomato.

Consommé with Eggs [*Zuppa alla Pavese* Italy] Place sliced fried bread croûtons in the bottom of individual soup bowls, then crack a small egg into each, sprinkle with grated Parmesan cheese, pour over boiling beef consommé and serve.

Croûtes-au-pot [France] Garnish beef stock with chicken winglets, diced car-rots, turnips, cabbage and celery. Serve with croûtes de flûtes.

Egg Soup [*Dahn Far Tong* China] To chicken stock add saké and a little sesame oil. Finish by pouring beaten eggs into the soup to form threads. Garnish with chopped spring onions.

Fresh Noodle Soup with Eggs and Chicken [*Tojikishimen* Japan] Poach goujons of breast of chicken in dashi flavoured with light and dark soy sauces, mirin and sugar; thicken with cornflour and whisk in beaten eggs to form threads. Arrange cooked noodles in soup bowls, top with chopped spinach, pour in the soup, and sprinkle the surfaces with finely chopped spring onions and seven-flavour spice.

Fresh Noodle Soup with Poached Egg [*Tsukimi Udon* Japan] Divide cooked noodles into china serving bowls, pour over dashi flavoured with light and dark soy sauces, mirin and sugar and place a slice of rolled cooked spinach on top of each. Place a poached egg in each bowl and garnish with small squares of crisp toasted dried seaweed.

Fresh Noodle and Pork Soup [*Buta Udon* *Japan*]   Poach strips of pork and julienne of leek in dashi flavoured with light and dark soy sauces, mirin and sugar. Remove from the stove and stir in light soy sauce, sugar and a pinch of monosodium glutamate. Add cooked noodles to the soup, serve in bowls and garnish with sprigs of spring onions and a little seven-flavour spice.

Garlic Soup [*Sopa de Ajo* *Spain*]   Heat olive oil in a pan, add cloves of garlic and cook until golden, stir in paprika and ground cumin, moisten with chicken stock, add a few strands of saffron and simmer for 5 min. Pour the boiling soup into individual soup bowls then crack a small egg in each, place sliced fried bread croûtons on top, allow the eggs to poach for a few moments and serve.

Miso Soup with Bean Curd and Seaweed [*Tofu To Wakame No Miso-Shiru* *Japan*]   Place coarsely chopped seaweed into hot first soup stock flavoured with bean paste and soy sauce. Place small cubes of bean curd into soup bowls, pour in the soup, sprinkle with chopped spring onions and serve.

Miso Soup with Mixed Vegetables [*Satsuma-Jiru* *Japan*]   Simmer 1-cm pieces of blanched breast of chicken or pork in second soup stock with the addition of sliced shiitake mushrooms and daikon, paysanne of carrot, sweet potato and salsify, and cook for 15 min. Finish with bean paste and serve sprinkled with chopped spring onions, accompanied by seven-flavour spice.

Mock Turtle Soup [*GB*]   Beef stock flavoured with calf's head, tomato and infusion of turtle herbs. Thicken with arrowroot and serve garnished with diced calves head and finished with dry sherry.

Petite Marmite [*France*]   Boil beef stock and add chicken winglets, diced beef, carrots, turnips, cabbage and celery and simmer. Pour into small marmite pots, top with slices of poached beef marrow and serve with croûtes de flûtes and grated Parmesan cheese.

Red Bean Paste Soup [*Akadashi* *Japan*]   To simmering dashi add finely sieved miso and diced tofu. Garnish with chopped spring onions.

Creams and Veloutés

Application

Cream soups and veloutés are both made in the same way, the only distinction being the kind of liaison used. Cream soups are finished with a liaison of cream and butter, whereas velouté soups are finished with a liaison of egg yolks and cream.

Chicken Soup with Rice Vermicelli [*Laksa Lemak* *Thailand*]   Sauté chopped shallots, garlic, dried red chillies and ginger in oil. Add prawn shells, coriander and turmeric, moisten with chicken stock, simmer then strain through a muslin. Finish with thick coconut milk and garnish with peeled prawns, diced chicken, rice vermicelli and fried sliced tofu.

Chocolate Soup [*Schokoladensuppe* *Germany*]   Thicken vanilla-flavoured hot milk with arrowroot, add grated chocolate, flavour with cinnamon and finish with a liaison of egg yolks and cream.

Cream of Almond Soup [*GB*]   Pour chicken stock flavoured with ham, mace, cloves and dill onto ground almonds and simmer. Garnish with flaked almonds and finish with almond essence and sherry and finish with whipped cream.

Cream of Asparagus and Mushroom Soup [*Zöldséges Csirkeraguleves Hungary*] Sweat chopped onion and diced carrot and celeriac, moisten with veal stock and cook. Add chicken velouté, finish with a liaison of soured cream, egg yolks and lemon juice and serve garnished with sliced mushrooms, asparagus and chopped parsley.

Cream of Avocado and Crab Soup [*Caribbean*] Sweat chopped onion in a little oil, moisten with chicken stock then add finely diced ham, chopped fresh red chillies and seasoning. Mix together flour and water to a paste, pour into the simmering soup to lightly thicken it and cook for 10 min. Add a purée of avocados and white crabmeat, season to taste and finish with cream.

Cream of Brussels Sprout Soup [*GB*] Stew chopped onion, brussels sprouts and ham in butter, moisten with white stock and simmer. Liquidise, add béchamel sauce, finish with cream and serve accompanied by bread sippets.

Cream of Caraway Soup [**Köménymagleves** *Hungary*] Flavour jus lié with caraway seeds then finish with a liaison of soured cream and egg yolks and garnish with thimble dumplings.

Thimble Dumplings [Csipetke]: Poach walnut-size pieces of noodle paste in simmering salted water or soup.

Cream of Cheese Soup [**Kasesuppe** *Germany*] To chicken velouté add grated Emmenthal cheese and finish with a liaison of cream. Garnish with toasted small onion rings and diced croûtons.

Cream of Cheese and Pork Soup [**Sajtleves** *Hungary*] Add grated Parmesan cheese to velouté made with stock from boiled smoked pork, finish with a liaison of soured cream and garnish with macaroni, diced pork and chopped chives.

Cream of Chervil Soup [**Korvelsuppe** *Scandinavia*] Finish a chervil-flavoured pork velouté with a liaison of cream and egg yolks. Serve garnished with brunoise of cooked carrot, blanched chervil and halves of soft boiled egg.

Cream of Chestnut Soup [**Crème de Marrons** *France*] Sweat shredded leek and onion then add chicken stock and shelled chestnuts and cook. Liquidise and finish with cream.

Cream of Chicken and Almond Soup [*Israel*] Combine chicken velouté with a purée of chicken, ground almonds and brunoise of mixed vegetables; finish with a liaison of cream.

Cream of Chicken and Rice Soup [**Gai Tom Kah** *Thailand*] Blend shallots, garlic, coriander root, lemon grass, peppercorns, curry paste and ginger to a paste. Add the paste to simmering thick and thin coconut milk then add sliced chicken, grated ginger, crushed fresh green chillies and kaffir lime leaves. Serve garnished with shredded coriander leaves and finish with lime juice and nam pla.

Cream of Chicken and Vegetable Soup [**Sayur Lodeh** *Indonesia*] Blend to a paste onion, garlic, fresh chillies, trasi or blachan, macadamia nuts and sugar. Stir-fry the mixture in oil, add sliced onion and diced cooked chicken, and moisten with stock and thin coconut milk. Add diced eggplant, cabbage, pimento and french beans. Garnish with prawns and finish with thick coconut milk.

Cream of Chicken Soup [**Jemangiri Skorba** *India*] Fry sliced onion in ghee, add turmeric, curry powder, tomato concassée and a liquidised paste of cloves of garlic and grated ginger. Moisten with chicken stock and simmer. Finish with a liaison of cream and lemon juice.

Cream of Courgette Soup [*Kousa* Middle East]   Mix together a purée of courgettes with stock and béchamel sauce, garnish with chopped parsley and finish
with yogurt.

Cream of Crab Soup [*USA*]   Combine a purée of crabmeat with béchamel sauce,
stock and dry sherry; season with mace, finish with Worcester sauce and garnish
with chopped hard-boiled egg.

Cream of Cucumber and Coconut Soup [*Caribbean*]   Sweat sliced white of leek
in oil, moisten with thick coconut milk and chicken stock, add grated cucumber
and seasoning and simmer for 20 min. Liquidise, strain, reboil and season to
taste. Serve garnished with chopped fennel leaves and chopped chives, finish
with sherry and serve.

Cream of Cucumber Soup [*GB*]   Stew chopped cucumber, onion and celery in
butter, moisten with stock and cook. Liquidise, add béchamel sauce and finish
with cream.

Cream of Egg and Lemon Soup Garnished with Meatballs [*Yuvarlakia
Avgolemono* Greece]   Combine minced meat, cooked rice and eggs and mould
into small balls. Poach the meatballs in chicken stock and finish with a liaison of
egg yolks and lemon juice.

Cream of Garlic Soup [*Sopa de Ajo* Mexico]   Golden fry crushed garlic and
diced croûtons in olive oil, moisten with chicken stock and finish with a liaison
of cream.

Cream of Haricot Bean Soup [*Palòc Soup* Hungary]   Fry crushed garlic,
chopped onion and lardons of bacon in oil. Sprinkle with paprika, add mutton
stock, caraway seeds, haricot beans, diced potatoes, diamonds of french beans,
diced mutton and chopped parsley. Cook and finish with cream.

Cream of Jerusalem Artichoke Soup [*GB*]   Stew sliced artichokes, onion and carrot in butter then moisten with chicken stock and cook. Liquidise, add milk and
a liaison of cream. Finish with pounded hazelnuts and serve accompanied by
slices of lemon and whipped cream.

Cream of Lamb and Tarragon Soup [*Tàrkonyos Bàràny-Vagy Borjúfejbecsinàlt
Leves* Hungary]   Finish a tarragon-flavoured lamb velouté with a liaison of
soured cream and egg yolks. Serve garnished with diced lamb and lamb's
tongue, chopped tarragon and butter dumplings.

Cream of Lemon Soup [*Citronsuppe* Scandinavia]   Flavour chicken velouté
with the grated zest of lemons and finish with a liaison of egg yolks, sugar and
lemon juice. Serve with croûtons, and yogurt or whipped cream.

Cream of Macaroni Soup [*Makarónileves* Hungary]   Finish a chicken velouté
with a liaison of soured cream, egg yolks and butter; serve garnished with
macaroni and a sprinkle of cheese.

Cream of Marrow and Ginger Soup [*GB*]   Sweat chopped onion and shredded
white of leek then add grated ginger, chopped vegetable marrow and chicken
stock. Liquidise and finish with cream.

Cream of Mussel Soup, or Billy-Bye [*GB*]   Cook mussels, chopped shallots and
parsley in dry white wine, fish stock and saffron. Thicken the strained liquid
with cornflour and finish with a liaison of egg yolks and cream; serve garnished
with small mussels.

Cream of Pea Soup [*Erbsensuppe mit Saurersahne* Germany]   Cook fresh
peas in stock and liquidise, finish with a liaison of egg yolks and soured cream,
and garnish with julienne of smoked tongue.

Cream of Peanut Soup [*Caribbean*]   Liquidise chopped onion cooked in ground-nut oil, ground roasted peanuts and dried red or green chillies, and add to chicken stock. Garnish with chopped chives and finish with a liaison of cream and angostura bitters.

Cream of Peanut Soup [***Ful Sudani*** *Middle East*]   Blend roasted peanuts to a fine paste with stock, moisten with milk and stock and simmer; finish with a liaison of cream and samneh.

Cream of Pigeon Soup [*USA*]   Sauté pigeons with parsnip, carrot, celery, leek, bayleaf and thyme, moisten with stock and poach. Liquidise the vegetables and replace in the stock with breadcrumbs and cream, and season with nutmeg. Garnish with sweated shredded spinach, diced pigeon and chopped parsley.

Cream of Potato and Saffron Soup [*GB*]   Sweat chopped onion and moisten with stock then add sliced potato and cook. Liquidise, stir in infused saffron and finish with a liaison of egg yolks and cream. Serve accompanied by slices of lemon and whipped cream.

Cream of Potato Soup [***Kartoffelsuppe*** *Germany*]   Sweat chopped carrot, celery and leek, moisten with chicken stock, add sliced potato and cook. Liquidise, season with salt, pepper and nutmeg and garnish with a julienne of boiled potatoes, diced and sautéed onion and chopped chives; finish with cream. Serve accompanied by diced croûtons.

Cream of Potato Soup with Cheese [***Potatissoppa med Ost*** *Scandinavia*]   Boil grated potato in stock until cooked. Add grated cheese and finish with cream and chopped parsley.

Cream of Pumpkin and Sweet Potato Soup [***Potaje de Leche*** *Spain*]   Boil diced pumpkin and sweet potato and corn kernels in stock. Cook short-grain rice in milk and add to the vegetables, and finish with cream.

Cream of Pumpkin Soup [*USA*]   Stew pumpkin in butter, season with ground mace, nutmeg and clove then liquidise. Moisten with milk and finish with a liaison of egg yolks.

Cream of Rabbit Soup [*GB*]   Combine rabbit velouté with a purée of rabbit, finish with a liaison of cream and serve accompanied by bread sippets.

Cream of Rice and Mushroom Soup [***Rizsleves*** *Hungary*]   Cook rice, sliced mushrooms and chopped parsley in stock then add to veal velouté. Finish with a liaison of soured cream and egg yolks.

Cream of Rice Soup [***Creme a Moda do Dao*** *Portugal*]   Sweat sliced carrot in oil, moisten with chicken stock then add short-grain rice, cook and liquidise. Serve garnished with diamonds of french beans and finish with a liaison of egg yolks and cream.

Cream of Sorrel Soup [***Potage à l'Oseille*** *France*]   Sweat sliced leek, sliced onion and shredded sorrel, then add chicken stock and roughly cut potatoes. Liquidise and garnish with shredded sorrel cooked in oil and finish with cream.

Cream of Spinach and Oyster Soup [*USA*]   Sweat chopped onion and garlic then add chicken velouté, rice and oyster juice, season with mace and cook. Liquidise then finish with cream and garnish with shredded stewed spinach and poached oysters.

Cream of Spinach Soup [***Spinatsuppe*** *Scandinavia*]   To chicken velouté add a purée of spinach and season with salt, pepper and nutmeg. Garnish with sliced hard-boiled egg and finish with cream.

Cream of Summer Vegetable Soup with Prawns [*Kesäkeitto Scandinavia*]
Cook carrots, cauliflower, french beans, radishes, peas and shredded spinach
in vegetable stock. Liquidise and garnish with peeled prawns and chopped dill
and finish with cream.

Cream of Sweetcorn and Prawn Soup [*Caribbean*]   Sweat chopped onion and
garlic, add chopped tomatoes and fish stock. Liquidise, and add new potatoes,
sweetcorn kernels and milk. Garnish with peeled prawns and finish with cream.

Cream of Veal and Vegetable Soup [*Borjùraguleves Hungary*]   Sweat chopped
onion, paysanne of carrot, parsnip and celeriac, moisten with stock then add paysanne of savoy cabbage, sliced mushrooms and sautéed minced veal. Add veal
velouté and finish with a liaison of soured cream, egg yolks and lemon juice.

Cream of Vegetable and Beer Soup [*Sopa de Cerveza y Queso Mexico*]   Sweat
sliced onion, diced carrot and celery, moisten with beer and chicken stock and
season with nutmeg, cumin and cloves. Finish with soured cream and sprinkle
with diced Monterey Jack cheese.

Cream of Vegetable and Citrus Fruit Soup [*Sopa de Pollo con Vegatales
Mexico*]   Sweat chopped onion and diced carrot and celery, moisten with
chicken stock and orange, lime and lemon juices. Finish with soured cream and
garnish with fried tortilla strips.

Cream of Walnut and Grape Soup [*Ash Sack Middle East*]   Sweat sliced onion
and leeks, moisten with chicken stock, add shredded spinach then thicken with
ground rice. Combine minced beef and beaten eggs, mould into small dumplings and cook in the soup, then finish it with beaten eggs, yogurt or cream,
and grape juice. Serve accompanied by chopped walnuts and peeled and
pipped grapes.

Mulligatawny Soup [*GB*]   Sauté roughly cut onion, carrot, turnip and apple in
oil, mix in curry powder, tomato purée and chutney. Moisten with white stock,
add bouquet garni, mace and clove and cook. Liquidise, garnish with boiled
rice and finish with cream.

Onion and Mint Soup [*Eshkaneh Middle East*]   Sweat sliced onion in samneh,
moisten with chicken stock then thicken with flour and cook. Finish with a liaison of egg yolks, sugar and lemon juice, season with cinnamon and garnish
with rubbed dried mint.

Rye Bread Soup [*Brotsuppe Germany*]   Sweat sliced onion, leek and celery,
moisten with beef stock, add diced fried rye bread croûtons and cook. Liquidise
then finish with a liaison of egg yolks and soured cream.

Soured Cream of Rice and Sorrel Soup [*Savanyú Rizsleves Hungary*]   Cook
rice and chopped parsley in stock, then add shredded sorrel and flavour with
tomato purée; finish with soured cream.

Soured Cream Soup [*Rovenskai Leves Hungary*]   Combine a little vegetable
stock, soured cream, egg yolks and lemon juice. Add caramelised sugar to more
vegetable stock, finish with the soured cream liaison and serve garnished with
rice.

Vermicelli Soup [*Sheriyeli Çorba Greece*]   Finish chicken stock with a liaison of
egg yolks and lemon juice and garnish with vermicelli.

Yogurt and Spinach Soup [*Labaneya Middle East*]   Sauté chopped onion in
samneh then add shredded spinach and stew; add long-grain rice, moisten with
stock and cook. Finish with yogurt and crushed garlic.

Fish Soups

Application

Methods of making this type of soup vary considerably. Most are moistened with dry white wine and fish stock, and the ratio of fish and shellfish to liquid should be higher when compared with vegetable-type soups.

Clam Chowder [*USA*]   Golden fry diced salt pork, add chopped onion, moisten with milk, add diced potato, dried thyme, chopped parsley and fish stock, whisk in beurre manié to thicken them and allow to simmer. Garnish with chopped clams and finish with soured cream.

Clam Soup [*Chogaetang Korea*]   Toss clams in sesame oil then add twoenjang and spring onions; moisten with stock, season with black pepper and simmer. Serve garnished with shredded spring onions.

Clam Soup [*Hamaguri No Sumashi-Jiru Japan*]   Soak clams in cold salted water then cook in first soup stock flavoured with saké and soy sauce and seasoned with salt. Serve in bowls and garnish with strips of raw spring onions and v-shaped pieces of lime peel.

Clear Fish Soup [*Shiromizakana No Suimono Japan*]   Cook small diagonally cut pieces of white fish in water and lemon juice, drain and place into soup bowls. Add cooked and coarsely chopped spinach, moisten with first soup stock flavoured with soy sauce and serve garnished with v-shaped pieces of lime peel.

Codfish Chowder [*USA*]   Sweat chopped onion, garlic, diced carrot, celery and green pimento, moisten with fish stock, add diced potato and cook. Add fish velouté and goujons of cod, allow to cook and finish with cream.

Cullen Skink [*GB*]   Thicken smoked haddock cooking liquid with mashed potato. Garnish with flaked smoked haddock and chopped parsley and finish with a liaison of cream and butter.

Fish Chowder [*USA*]   Fry lardons of salt pork and sliced onions, add flour to form a roux, moisten with fish stock and milk then add sliced potatoes and goujons of white fish. Garnish with chopped parsley and serve accompanied by broken cream cracker biscuits.

Fish Soup [*Caribbean*]   Sweat chopped onion and garlic, add tomato concassée, stir in paprika and moisten with fish stock, coconut milk and dry white wine; add sliced potatoes, sliced red or green chillies and allspice. Add goujons of white fish. Liquidise the vegetables and cooking liquor and strain back over the goujons. Finish with Pernod.

Fish Soup [*Bergens Fiskesuppe Scandinavia*]   Poach fillet of halibut in fish stock and white wine with sweated julienne of carrot, leek and parsnips. Finish by pouring beaten egg yolks into the soup to form threads. Garnish with the flaked fish and chopped fresh herbs. Serve accompanied by soured cream.

Fish Soup [*Maeuntang Korea*]   Marinate strips of beef in kochujang, soy sauce, sesame oil, garlic and black pepper. Fry the meat in oil, moisten with fish stock then add small red snapper steaks, sliced courgette, diced red and green pimento and sliced fresh chillies, and cook. Add diced bean curd and garnish with shredded spring onions.

Fish Soup [*Psarosoupa Greece*]   Simmer fish stock with strips of tomato flesh and olive oil. Rain in rice or tapioca, simmer and finish with lemon juice; garnish with chopped parsley.

Fish Soup [*Soupe de Poisson France*]   Sweat sliced onion, garlic, leek, carrot and celery. Moisten with fish stock, add tomato concassée and place in goujons of any kind of white fish. Liquidise the cooking liquor, and add saffron and vermicelli. Serve the soup with the goujons accompanied by fried bread croûtons rubbed with garlic, Parmesan cheese and Rouille.

   Rouille: soak pieces of diced french bread in a little of the soup and press to a paste. Blend to a purée with cloves of garlic, a pinch of saffron and yolk of egg, then whisk in olive oil to form the consistency of mayonnaise.

Fish Soup [*Zuppa di Pesce Lucana Italy*]   Fry goujons of any kind of white fish in oil with crushed garlic. Sprinkle with chopped parsley, chilli powder and whole dried chillies, cover with fish stock and cook. Line the bottom of a soup bowl with toasted bread croûtons rubbed with garlic, pour in the soup and serve.

Fish Soup Seville Style [*Caldo de Perro Gaditano Spain*]   Slice whiting into small 1-cm sections, sprinkle with coarse salt and retain for 1 hr in a refrigerator. Sweat chopped onion in garlic-flavoured olive oil, moisten with fish stock then add the whiting and simmer for approx. 15 min. Remove the skin and bones from the fish, place back into the soup, add orange and lime juice, season to taste and serve.

Fish Soup with Egg and Lemon [*Psarosouppa Avgolemoni Greece*]   Cook roughly chopped courgettes, carrot and celery and chopped parsley in fish stock then add flaked poached fish and liquidise. Add rice to the soup and cook; season with salt, pepper and cinnamon then finish with a liaison of eggs and lemon juice.

Fish Soup with Noodles [*Sopa de Pescado con Fideos Spain*]   To a fish velouté add and cook diced carrots and tomato flesh, garlic, roasted hazelnuts and saffron, then liquidise. Serve garnished with noodles and flaked monkfish and sprinkled with grated Gruyère cheese.

Herring Soup [*Sill Soppa Scandinavia*]   Cook herrings in water. Sweat diced carrot, celery, leek and parsnip in oil, moisten with the herring stock then add diced potato, thyme and bayleaf and cook. Garnish with pieces of boned herring and chopped dill and finish with cream.

Mussel Soup [*Zuppa di Cozze Italy*]   Sweat chopped onion, garlic and diced celery in olive oil. Add basil, oregano and diced tomato flesh; moisten with white wine and fish stock and cook. Add cleaned mussels and cook. Discard the top shells then transfer the mussels to a tureen and pour the soup over them.

Oyster and Bean Curd Soup [*Kaki Dofu Jiru Japan*]   To first soup stock add bean paste, 5-mm dice of bean curd, chopped parsley and oysters and simmer for 2 min. Pour into soup bowls, flavour with ginger juice and sprinkle with Japanese pepper.

Oyster Soup [*GB*]   Sauté chopped onion in butter, moisten with white wine, add roughly cut oysters and their liquid and gently stew. Add cream and heat through and finish with a liaison of egg yolks.

Prawn Soup [*Kung Tom Yam Thailand*]   Fry prawns in groundnut oil, moisten with fish stock and add lemon grass and sliced fresh green chillies. Strain the liquor, add nam pla and lemon juice and serve garnished with the peeled prawns, chopped coriander leaves and spring onions.

Prawn Soup with Lily Buds [*Kaeng Chüd Dok Mai Chin* *Thailand*] Fry chopped onion, peeled prawns and a paste of coriander leaves and garlic. Moisten with prawn stock, add cellophane noodles, halved lily buds, dried mushrooms, sliced spring onions, light soy sauce and sugar. Pour in beaten eggs to form threads and garnish with coriander leaves.

Salmon Chowder [*USA*] Sweat sliced onion and garlic, moisten with fish stock and chicken stock and add bayleaf, thyme, diced potato and tomato flesh. Add goujons of salmon, lemon juice and chopped dill and cook.

Shark's Fin Soup [*China*] Simmer dried shark's fin in water for 2 hr and remove. Garnish the liquid with julienne of smoked ham and chicken breast, spring onions and ginger. Finish with saké and dark and light soy sauces and retain au bain-marie for 2–3 hr. Garnish with the flaked shark's fin, lightly fried sliced abalone and chopped parsley.

Shrimp and Okra Gumbo [*USA*] Sweat chopped onion in butter, and add garlic, diced green pimento, okra and tomato flesh. Stir in red pepper flakes, bayleaf, allspice, thyme, Worcestershire sauce, shrimps and chicken velouté and simmer. Garnish with boiled rice and serve accompanied by hot pepper sauce.

Soured Fish Soup [*Tom Som Pla* *Thailand*] Blend to a paste shallots, ginger, garlic, coriander root, turmeric, peppercorns, salt and shrimp paste. Stir-fry the paste then add goujons of fish, moisten with fish stock and tamarind juice, add palm sugar and simmer. Add shredded cabbage and french beans and chopped spring onions. Garnish with shredded coriander leaves.

Soured Soup with Prawns [*Tom Yam Koong* *Thailand*] Flavour chicken stock with slices of tamarind, red chillies, kaffir lime leaves, ginger and lemon grass. Pour this simmering stock onto watercress leaves, sliced oyster mushrooms, chopped coriander leaves and nam pla. Finish with lemon juice and garnish with peeled prawns.

Whitebait Soup [*Minestra di Gianchetti* *Italy*] Cook peas, vermicelli and whitebait in fish stock and dry white wine, stir in beaten eggs and serve.

Purée Soups

Bortsch [*Israel*] Liquidise beef stock cooked and flavoured with young beetroots, beetroot tops, onion, garlic and bayleaf. Add sugar and vinegar, finish with a liaison of beaten egg yolks and garnish with diced beef.

Green Bortsch [*Zelyony Bortsch* *Russia*] Flavour veal velouté with a purée of ham. Sweat shredded sorrel then add boiled finely chopped spinach and soured cream and add to the velouté. Garnish with half a hard-boiled egg, chopped dill, parsley and coriander leaves. Serve accompanied by smetana.

Leek Soup [*GB*] Sweat chopped leeks, moisten with chicken stock, add potatoes and cook. Liquidise, add milk and serve accompanied by crumbled Caerphilly cheese.

Purée of Avocado Pear Soup [*Sopa de Aguacate* *Mexico*] Purée avocado flesh and cook in chicken stock. Serve accompanied by crisp fried tortilla squares.

Purée of Cabbage and Nettle Soup [*Zelonyeshchi* *Russia*] Cook cabbage, potatoes and young nettles in stock, liquidise and garnish with diced beef and a soft-boiled egg per portion. Serve accompanied by smetana.

Purée of Elderberry Soup with Dumplings [*Fliederbeersuppe* Germany] Cook elderberries in water, liquidise and garnish with diced dessert apple, stoned plums and small dumplings cooked in the soup.

Dumplings: boil milk with a pinch of salt and butter, stir in flour, cool then beat in eggs. Form into small balls, add and poach in the soup.

Purée of Parsnip and Apple Soup [*GB*] Sweat chopped onion, parsnips and unpeeled apples, moisten with chicken stock and add grated rind of lemons. Cook, liquidise and serve.

Purée of Pheasant Soup [*GB*] Moisten a purée of pheasant with brown pheasant stock flavoured with ham and mace, then thicken with breadcrumbs combined with sieved hard-boiled eggs.

Purée of Plum Soup with Dumplings [*Pflaumensuppe mit Keilchen* Germany] Poach plums in water with cinnamon stick, cloves, lemon juice and sugar. Liquidise then thicken with arrowroot and garnish with small dumplings.

Dumplings: combine eggs with flour and salt to form a firm dough.

Purée of Pumpkin Soup [*USA*] Sweat sliced onion, moisten with chicken stock, add pumpkin flesh and lemon juice and flavour with grated nutmeg or mace. Cook then liquidise.

Purée of Pumpkin Soup Creole Style [*Caribbean*] Cut salt pork into 1.5-cm cubes and soak in cold water for 12 hr. Rinse the meat under cold water, place into a pan, cover with stock and simmer until it is tender; remove the cooked meat and retain. Sweat sliced onion and crushed cloves of garlic in oil, moisten with the cooking liquid then add diced pumpkin flesh and seasoning. Cook for approx. 20 min then liquidise, strain, reboil and serve garnished with the cooked meat.

Sweet and Sour Cabbage Soup [*Israel*] Sweat sliced cabbage and onion, moisten with beef stock, and add brown sugar, lemon juice, caraway seeds, clove and tomato. Liquidise and garnish with diced beef.

Watercress Soup [*GB*] Sweat sliced white of leek, moisten with white stock and add roughly cut potatoes. When the potatoes are cooked, add watercress and liquidise. Garnish with blanched watercress leaves and top with a whirl of cream.

Chapter Four

Egg Dishes and Cheese Dishes

This chapter is divided into 13 main areas. Egg dishes are grouped according to methods of cookery and cheese dishes according to which cheese is featured as the main ingredient.

✧ Boiled Eggs ✧

✧ Moulded Eggs ✧

✧ Shallow- and Deep-Fried Eggs ✧

✧ Poached Eggs ✧

✧ Savoury Egg Custard ✧

✧ Savoury Omelettes ✧

✧ Chinese and Indonesian Omelettes ✧

✧ Japanese Omelettes ✧

✧ Middle Eastern Omelettes ✧

✧ Savoury Soufflés ✧

✧ Scrambled Eggs ✧

✧ Shirred Eggs ✧

✧ Cheese Dishes ✧

Boiled Eggs

Application

Cook the eggs in boiling water, allowing five min for soft-boiled and 10 min for hard-boiled eggs, then plunge them into cold water and remove the shell.

Curried Eggs [*Madras Anday India*]   Sauté chopped onion in ghee, add a sprinkling of ground coriander, cumin, turmeric, ginger and chilli powder then moisten with coconut milk and lemon juice. Place the 5-min boiled eggs cut into slices, quarters or halves on a bed of boiled rice, mask with the sauce and serve.

Eggs with Onion [*Israel*]   Golden fry chopped onion in olive oil, add chopped hard-boiled eggs, season and serve.

Eggs in Paprika Sauce [*Tojás Paprikamártában Hungary*]   Place the 5-min boiled and halved eggs on a bed of boiled rice, mask with paprika sauce then sprinkle with grated cheese.

Eggs with Peppers and Tomato [*Huevos a la Extemeña Spain*]   Place halved hard-boiled eggs in a serving dish, and top with fried pimentos and diced tomato flesh. Coat with onion sauce seasoned with paprika and bake.

Eggs with Soured Cream [*Sült Tojàs Hungary*]   Fill centres of hard-boiled eggs with the sieved egg yolks and chopped herbs. Mask with soured cream and bake.

Eggs with Soured Cream and Herbs [*Eier mit Kräutersahne Germany*]   Combine Quark and soured cream with chopped fresh herbs. Coat the 5-min boiled and shelled eggs with the sauce.

Eggs with Tripe [*GB*]   Thickly slice hard-boiled eggs, place in a serving dish and coat with diced cooked tripe in parsley sauce.

Eggs with Sweet and Sour Sauce [*Saure Eier mit Specksauce Germany*]   Sauté grated onion and lardons of bacon, moisten with vinegar, add sugar and boil to reduce by half; add jus lié then finish with a little cream. Place the 5-min boiled eggs on blinis and coat with the sauce.

Stuffed Eggs with Mushrooms and Cheese Sauce [*Oeufs Farcis Chimay France*]   Combine sieved hard-boiled yolks of egg with cooked chopped mushrooms and pipe into the centre of the whites. Coat with cheese sauce and gratinate.

Stuffed Eggs with Shrimps [*Huevos Rellenos de Gambas Spain*]   Combine sieved hard-boiled yolks of egg with chopped shrimps, lightly sautéed chopped onion and chicken velouté. Fill the egg whites with the mixture and bake. Serve sprinkled with chopped fresh herbs.

Moulded eggs [*Oeufs en Cocotte France*]

Application

Butter and season a ramekin or egg cocotte and break an egg into it. Cook au bain-marie covered with a lid in the oven and simmer until the white is firm and the yolk still soft.

Moulded Eggs with Chicken [*Oeufs en Cocotte à la Reine* France] Combine diced cooked chicken with sauce suprême and place a little in the bottom of each cocotte, break the eggs into the cocotte and cook. Serving by floating a little warmed cream on top.

Moulded Eggs with Ham, Sausage and Asparagus [*Huevos à la Flamenca* Spain] Pour tomato sauce into the bottom of each cocotte or ramekin, add eggs, arrange diced ham, strips of chorizo sausage, asparagus tips, peas and pimento on top and cook.

Moulded Eggs with Kidney [*Oeufs en Cocotte aux Rognons* France] Place diced sautéed lamb's kidney combined with a little jus lié in the bottom of each cocotte, add the eggs and cook.

Moulded Eggs with Tomato [*Oeufs en Cocotte Portugaise* France] Place cooked tomato concassée in the bottom of each cocotte, add the eggs and cook.

Moulded Eggs with Tripe [GB] Place diced tripe in parsley sauce in the bottom of each cocotte, add the eggs and cook. Serve by floating a little warmed cream on top.

Shallow-Fried and Deep-Fried Eggs

Egg Fritters [*India*] Pass slices of hard-boiled eggs through a mixture of equal quantities of pomegranate seeds and ground coriander, then coat in pakora batter and deep fry in peanut oil. Serve accompanied by mint chutney.

Fried Eggs French Style [*Oeufs Frits à la Française* France] Deep fry the eggs in an omelette pan in oil so that the egg white envelops the yolk, the outside of the egg becomes light golden and the yolk remains soft inside. Drain on a cloth, season with salt and serve.

Fried Egg Garnish [*Korea*] Shallow fry beaten eggs as for a flat omelette, then cut into thin ribbon strips.

Fried Eggs in Madeira Sauce [*Spejlaeg* Scandinavia] Place toasted bread croûtons into a porcelain ovenproof dish and arrange a slice of ham and a fried egg on top of each. Reduce Madeira and veal stock to a glaze, add knobs of butter to form a light sauce, mask the eggs with the sauce and serve.

Fried Eggs with Garlic and Paprika [*Huevos Fritos al Ajillo* Spain] Fry eggs in butter and transfer them to plates, then garnish with lightly sautéed strips of pimento. Golden fry slices of garlic in oil, cool, moisten with a little vinegar and paprika, pour over the eggs and serve accompanied by slices of fried bread.

Fried Eggs Yucatan Style [*Huevos Motulenos* Mexico] Spread fried tortillas with refried pinto beans, place a fried egg on each, mask with oregano-flavoured tomato concassée and serve sprinkled with chopped smoked ham, peas and cheese.

Fried Quail's Eggs [*Huevos de Codorniz a la Plancha* Spain] Deep fry the eggs in an omelette pan in olive oil so that the egg white envelops the yolk, the outside of the egg becomes light golden and the yolk remains soft inside. Drain on a cloth and serve on bread croûtons.

Fried Stuffed Eggs [Bundàs Töltött Tojàs Hungary] Fill the centres of hard-
boiled eggs with a mixture of the sieved egg yolks and duxelle of mushrooms.
Pass the eggs through flour and thick batter and deep fry. Serve sprinkled with
chopped chives.

Poached Eggs

Application

In a shallow pan add 1 part white vinegar and 10 parts water. Break the eggs into
the simmering water and cook so that the egg white envelops the yolk and when
cooked the white is firm but not hard. Drain on a cloth, trim and serve.

Eggs Poached in Sorrel Sauce [Buggyantott Tojás Sóskamártással Hungary]
Coat poached eggs with sorrel sauce finished with soured cream.
Poached Eggs in Cheese sauce [Buggyantott Tojás Fehér Mártásban Hungary]
Coat poached eggs with cheese sauce finished with soured cream.
Poached Eggs in Lemon Sauce [Buggyantott Tojás Citromos Mártással
Hungary] Coat poached eggs with lemon sauce made from velouté finished
with soured cream and lemon juice.
Poached Eggs in Yogurt [Yumurta Çilbir Greece] Serve poached eggs coated
with yogurt flavoured with garlic essence, vinegar and salt, sprinkled with
paprika pepper heated in butter.
Poached Eggs with Pinto Beans [Huevos Sonorenses Mexico] Spread fried
tortillas with refried pinto beans and place poached eggs on top. Mask with
chilli sauce garnished with chopped smoked ham, sprinkle with cheese then
gratinate.
Poached Eggs Yucatan Style [Huevos Yucatecos Mexico] Sauté chopped onion
then add diced tomato flesh, jalapeno pepper and cliantro and cook. Mask
poached eggs into the sauce and sprinkle with toasted and ground pumpkin
seeds.

Savoury Egg Custard

Application

Savoury custards consist of 6 eggs and 750 ml milk or stock in addition to an
appropriate herb, vegetable, fish, meat, poultry or game. The custard is poured
into oiled and seasoned ramekin dishes then baked au bain-marie in the oven at
160 °C for approx. 20 min until set.

Savoury Egg Custard Sephardi Fashion [Israel] Combine sautéed chopped
onion, sliced mushrooms, shrimps, chopped cooked spinach, chopped parsley,
chives and tarragon. Warm milk then pour onto beaten eggs and season. Pour
the mixture into ramekins quarter filled with the spinach mixture, and bake.

Savoury Egg Custard with Eggplant [*Kukuye Bademjan* Middle East]   Golden fry peeled and diced eggplant and chopped spring onions in samneh. Pour warm white stock onto beaten eggs then add to the eggplant mixture and season. Pour the mixture into ramekins and bake. Serve topped with warm cream.

Savoury Egg Custard with Goujonettes of Fish [*Kukuye Mohi* Middle East] Sauté chopped onion in samneh then add and golden fry goujonettes of white fish. Add chopped coriander leaves, turmeric and lemon juice. Pour warm white stock onto beaten eggs and season. Pour the mixture into ramekins garnished with the fish mixture and bake. Serve topped with warm cream.

Savoury Egg Custard with Mint [*Laban Bil Bayd* Middle East]   Mix together yogurt, cornflour and lightly beaten eggs. Pour the mixture into ramekins, break an egg into each, cover with a mixture of crushed garlic and chopped mint sautéed in samneh and bake.

Savoury Egg Custard with Mushrooms and Prawns [*Chawan Mushi* Japan] Warm white stock and shoyu sauce and pour onto beaten eggs and season. Pour the mixture into ramekins, garnish with sautéed sliced mushrooms, prawns and chopped fresh herbs then bake.

Savoury Egg Custard with Mushrooms, Prawns and Sesame Seeds [*Keran Chim* Korea]   Combine purée of garlic with sliced spring onions, sliced mushrooms and prawns, chicken stock, soy sauce, and beaten eggs. Pour the mixture into ramekins, sprinkle with toasted sesame seeds and bake.

Savoury Egg Custard with Tomato [*Ovos Portugueses* Portugal]   Place tomatoes with the insides hollowed out into ramekin dishes, break an egg into each tomato, top with a purée of tomato flesh and bake.

Savoury Omelettes

Oval-shaped omelette

Application

Heat an omelette pan, add a little butter and when it begins to foam add 3 well-beaten and seasoned eggs, shaking the pan and stirring with the back of a fork to evenly distribute the beaten eggs. When on setting point tilt the pan, and using the inside of the fork, roll over and fold into an oval shape. Turn out onto a plate and if necessary re-form with a very clean cloth.

Balinese Omelette [*Dadar Bali* Indonesia]   Sauté chopped onion then stir in Java curry powder and sambal ulek; add diced cooked chicken and diced tomato flesh and sprinkle with sweet soy sauce. Prepare the omelette and serve garnished with the chicken mixture and chopped coriander.

Carrot and Herb Omelette [*Omelette Crécy* France]   Add cooked sliced small carrots and chopped fresh herbs to the beaten eggs. Prepare the omelette and serve garnished with slices of cooked carrot on top.

Date, Shrimp and Ham Omelette [*Tortilla de Dátiles* Spain]   Combine shrimps, diced cured ham and chopped dates with the beaten eggs, then make the omelette and serve with a band of tomato sauce.

Eggplant Omelette [*Omelette Niçoise* France]   Add sautéed diced eggplant, grated Parmesan cheese and chopped parsley and chervil to the beaten eggs and make the omelette in the usual manner.

Sorrel Omelette [*Omelette à l'Oseille* France]   Add finely shredded sorrel stewed in butter, chopped chervil and garlic to the beaten eggs and make the omelette in the usual manner.

Tomato and Rice Omelette [*Omelette com Tomate a Portugusea* Portugal]   Serve a plain omelette on a base of tomato sauce, garnished with risotto.

Round Flat Omelette

Application

Beat 3 eggs with a little salt and pepper to blend the yolks. Heat an omelette pan, add a little butter and when it begins to foam, add omelette mixture with the stated garnish, shaking the pan and stirring with the back of a fork to evenly distribute the egg mixture. When on setting point and firm, turn over to set the other side then turn out onto a plate.

Artichoke Omelette [*Tortilla de Alcachofas* Spain]   Lightly fry sliced artichoke bottoms and lardons of bacon in olive oil, add to the egg mixture and make the flat omelette in the usual manner.

Chickpea Omelette [*Tortilla de Garbanzos* Spain]   Combine beaten eggs, sautéed chopped onion and garlic, cooked chickpeas and diced pimento and make a flat omelette.

Chive and Soured Cream Diamonds [*Tojáslepény* Hungary]   Combine beaten eggs, chives and soured cream and make a flat omelette, then cut it into diamond shapes and serve.

Cod Omelette [*Tortiulla de Bacalao* Spain]   Combine beaten eggs, cooked flaked salt cod, sautéed chopped onion and garlic and make a flat omelette.

Country Omelette [*Tortilla a la Payesa* Spain]   Combine fried diced potatoes, lardons of bacon, chopped onion and garlic, add to the beaten eggs with peas and diamonds of french beans then make the omelette.

Farmer's Omelette [*Käseomelette nach Bäuerinnenart* Germany]   Add sautéed chopped onion, diced potato, sliced mushrooms and lardons of bacon and grated Emmenthal cheese to the beaten eggs and make into a flat omelette.

Globe Artichoke Omelette [*Frittata di Carciofi* Italy]   Add sautéed chopped garlic, sliced globe artichoke cooked in olive oil and grated Parmesan cheese to the beaten eggs and proceed in the usual manner.

Lima Bean Omelette [*Tortilla de Habas* Spain]   Combine beaten eggs with sautéed chopped onion and garlic, cooked lima beans and diced cured ham and make a flat omelette in the usual manner.

Leek and Bacon Omelette [*Omelett mit Lauchringen* Germany]   Add sautéed shredded leek and fried lardons of bacon to the beaten eggs and make into an omelette.

Matzo Omelette [*Matzo Brei* Israel]   Soak a whole matzo biscuit in milk, drain then add to beaten eggs and make a flat omelette in the usual manner.

Potato and Soured Cream Soufflé Omelette [*Burgonyaomlett* Hungary]
Combine grated potato, flour, egg yolks and soured cream then fold in stiffly
beaten egg whites and make a flat omelette.

Sacro-Monte Omelette [*Tortilla al Sacro-Monte* Spain]   Fry sliced lamb's brain,
kidney and sweetbread with lardons of bacon and red pimentos in oil, add to
the beaten eggs and make a flat omelette in the usual manner.

Spanish Potato Omelette [*Tortilla Espagñola* Spain]   Fry diced potato and
chopped onion in olive oil, add to the beaten eggs and make into a flat
omelette.

Spanish Vegetable Omelette [*Tortilla a la Payesa* Spain]   Fry diced potato in
olive oil, reserve, then sauté chopped onion, garlic, green pimento and diced
tomato flesh in the same pan. Add the potato and vegetable garnish to the
beaten eggs and make into a flat omelette.

Spiced Omelette [*Tortilla en Salsa de Clavijo* Spain]   Soak breadcrumbs in
milk, squeeze out and add to beaten eggs; add chopped fresh herbs and make
a flat omelette. Mask the omelette with chicken velouté flavoured with ground
cloves and cinnamon and finished with cream.

Spinach and Pine nut Omelette [*Tortilla de Espinacas* Spain]   Add cooked
and shredded spinach and pine nuts to the beaten eggs and make a flat omelette in the usual manner.

Chinese and Indonesian Omelettes

Application

Heat a little vegetable oil in a wok or omelette pan, pour in beaten and seasoned
eggs and turn the mixture over several times until it is completely set. Turn out
onto a plate and sprinkle with soy sauce.

Bean Curd and Tomato Omelette [*Tahu Telur* Indonesia]   Garnish a prepared
omelette with cooked tomato concassée, diced bean curd, chopped spring
onions and tarragon, and sprinkle it with light soy sauce.

Crab Omelette [*Trung Chien Voicua* Indonesia]   Garnish an omelette with stir-
fried chopped onion in peanut oil, crabmeat and prawns; sprinkle with soy
sauce and chopped spring onions.

Ham and Bean Sprout Omelette [*Omelette Foo Yung* China]   Add diced ham,
blanched bean sprouts, chopped spring onions and a few drops of light soy
sauce to the beaten eggs. Prepare the omelette and garnish it with diamonds of
ham.

Spring Onion and Ginger Omelette [*Jang Chong Show Dan* China]   Stir-fry
grated ginger and chopped spring onions in sesame oil, pour in the beaten eggs
to which have been added sesame oil, light soy sauce and stock. Make the
omelette in the Chinese fashion, turn out and sprinkle with soy sauce and
chopped spring onions.

Japanese Omelettes

Application (2 portions)

Thoroughly beat 4 eggs and season with salt and pepper. Heat a tamago-yaki nabe or omelette pan, wipe with an oiled cloth then pour in one-third of the beaten egg, spreading it evenly. As it begins to set, roll up in the form of a swiss roll, place aside then cook a second and third omelette, rolling the previous one inside and rolling up. Cut into 5-cm slices and serve with the appropriate garnish.

Omelette with Chicken [*Torinuku Iri Omuretsu*]   Boil mirin, light soy sauce and water with finely sliced cooked chicken breast and reduce by two-thirds. Prepare an omelette, garnish with the chicken mixture and sprinkle with finely chopped spring onions.

Omelette with Mirin and Daikon [*Dshi-Maki Tamago*]   Mix together first soup stock, mirin and light soy sauce then combine with beaten eggs. Prepare the omelette and garnish with grated daikon, flavoured with soy sauce.

Omelette with Mushrooms [*Shiitake Iri Omuretsu*]   Stir-fry chopped spring onions and mushrooms in groundnut oil and moisten with light soy sauce. Mix together first soup stock, mirin and soy sauce and combine with beaten eggs. Prepare the omelette, folding in the mushroom mixture between the rolls, and garnish with cooked button mushrooms.

Omelette with Mushrooms and Prawns [*Fukusa Yaki*]   Mix together beaten eggs and mashed bean curd, julienne of mushrooms and prawns, and flavour with mirin, light soy sauce, sugar and monosodium glutamate. Prepare the omelette and garnish with grated daikon.

Omelette with Prawns [*Ebiiri-Tamago-Yaki*]   Blend prawns and first soup stock to a smooth paste. Mix together beaten eggs, saké, sugar, a little diluted arrowroot and the prawn mixture. Prepare the omelette, wrap in a cloth and allow to cool. Cut into slices and serve.

Omelette with Soup Stock [*Dashi-Maki Tamago*]   Mix together 4 parts beaten egg and 1 part first soup stock, and flavour with light soy sauce, mirin and monosodium glutamate. Prepare the omelette, wrap in a cloth, place a weight on top and allow to cool. Slice the omelette and serve garnished with grated daikon moistened with soy sauce.

Omelette with Spinach [*Horenso Tamago Maki*]   Place cooked and drained spinach in a cloth, sprinkle with soy sauce, season with monosodium glutamate then form into a small roll. Prepare the omelette, folding in the spinach roll between the rolls, and serve.

Middle Eastern Omelettes

Application

Thoroughly whisk eggs then add the main ingredients; transfer to a flan-type porcelain dish brushed with butter, cover with foil and bake for 20 min. Serve cut into wedge shaped portions.

Fish Omelette [***Kukuye Mohi***]   Sauté chopped onion in samneh, stir chopped coriander and flour then add cooked flaked fish. Add the beaten eggs and proceed as for the basic recipe.

Herb Omelette [***Kookoo Sabzi***]   Add chopped spring onions, mint, chive, chervil, watercress, basil, dill, shredded spinach, saffron, turmeric, salt and chilli powder to the beaten eggs. Proceed as for the basic recipe.

Herb and Walnut Omelette [***Kookoo Now Rooz***]   Add chopped spring onions, mint, parsley, chives, chervil, watercress, basil, dill, walnuts, dried fruit, shredded spinach, saffron, turmeric, salt and chilli powder to the beaten eggs. Proceed as for the basic recipe, mask with yogurt and garnish with cooked fennel quarters.

Leek Omelette [***Eggah bi Korrat***]   Golden sauté julienne of leek in oil, add sugar and lemon juice then cool. Combine with beaten eggs and proceed as for the basic recipe.

Onion Omelette [***Ajja***]   Add chopped onion and parsley to beaten eggs and proceed as for the basic recipe.

Potato Omelette [***Kukuye Sibzamini***]   Golden fry diced potato and grated onion in samneh then sprinkle with turmeric. Add to beaten eggs and proceed as for the basic recipe.

Pumpkin Omelette [***Kukuye Kadou Halvaii***]   Combine pumpkin purée, grated onion and turmeric with beaten eggs and proceed as for the basic recipe.

Spinach Omelette [***Ij-Jit Saban-Egh***]   Combine cooked and shredded spinach and garlic with beaten eggs and proceed as for the basic recipe.

Spiced Potato Omelette [***Eggah bi Lahma***]   Season beaten eggs with salt, pepper, allspice and cumin, then add mashed potato, lightly sautéed chopped onion and fresh herbs and cook the omelette in the usual manner.

Walnut and Chive Omelette [***Kuku Sabzy***]   Combine infused saffron, chopped walnuts and chives, currants, breadcrumbs and turmeric with beaten eggs and cook in the Middle Eastern style.

Savoury Soufflés

Application

Brush porcelain soufflé dishes with melted butter, two-thirds fill with a soufflé preparation and cook in the oven at 200 °C; serve immediately.

Savoury Soufflé Preparation   Whisk egg yolks into warm béchamel sauce and add the main flavouring ingredient and seasoning. Fold in stiffly beaten egg whites in two stages then pour the mixture into the soufflé dish and cook in the oven at 200 °C for 30 min; serve immediately.

Cheese Soufflé [*GB*]   Add grated Parmesan cheese to the basic recipe.

Chicken Soufflé [*GB*]   Add a purée of cooked chicken to the basic recipe.

Courgette Soufflé [*GB*]   Add a purée of cooked baby marrow to the basic recipe.

Crab Soufflé [*GB*]   Add a purée of cooked crab to the basic recipe, and season with salt, paprika and tabasco sauce.

Spinach Soufflé [*GB*]   Add spinach purée to the basic recipe and season with salt, pepper and grated nutmeg.

Scrambled Eggs

Application (2 portions)

Thoroughly beat 4 eggs with a fork then season with salt and pepper. Cook gently, stirring continuously until lightly set, then add a little butter and cream and serve immediately.

Scrambled Eggs Mexican Fashion [*Huevos a la Mexicana* Mexico]   Add chopped onion sautéed in bacon fat, chopped fresh green chillies and tomato concassée to beaten eggs.

Scrambled Eggs with Buckling Herring [*Rührei mit Bücklingen* Germany]   Serve scrambled eggs garnished with slices of buckling herring fillet heated in butter.

Scrambled Eggs with Chicken [*Kholee Coongee* India]   Add sautéed grated onion and ginger and diced cooked chicken to beaten eggs and season with ground cinnamon, turmeric and chilli powder. Finish the scrambled eggs with butter and cream.

Scrambled Eggs with Bacon and Chorizo [*Duelos y Quebrantos* Spain]   Add sautéed lardons of bacon and strips of chorizo sausage to beaten and seasoned eggs. Finish the scrambled eggs with knobs of butter.

Scrambled Eggs with Coriander [*Parsee Ekoori* India]   Add sautéed grated onion to beaten eggs then flavour with ground cinnamon, ginger and turmeric, and chopped coriander leaves. Finish the scrambled eggs with butter and cream.

Scrambled Eggs with Lobster [*Oeufs Brouillés aux Lames de Homard* France]   Garnish scrambled eggs with slices of lobster tossed in butter.

Scrambled Eggs with Mushrooms [*Rührei mit Champignons* Germany]   Garnish scrambled eggs with sautéed sliced mushrooms and lardons of bacon and sprinkle with chopped parsley.

Scrambled Eggs with Peppers [*Menemen* Greece]   Sauté diced green and red pimento and fresh chillies in oil then add whole cherry tomatoes, moisten with water and cook. Add beaten eggs to the mixture and cook. Serve sprinkled with chopped coriander.

Scrambled Eggs with Prawns [*Rührei mit Krabben* Germany]   Garnish scrambled eggs with prawns and serve sprinkled with chopped chives.

Scrambled Eggs with Shrimps and Spinach [*Revuelto de Langostino y Espinacas* Spain]   Add shrimps and cooked shredded spinach to the beaten and seasoned eggs, cook and serve garnished with diced bread croûtons.

Scrambled Eggs with Smoked Eel [*Räucheraal in Omelette* Germany]   Garnish scrambled eggs with slices of smoked eel and sliced cooked mushrooms tossed in butter.

Scrambled Eggs with Tomato [*Israel*]   Cook diced tomato flesh and its juice in oil with chilli powder. Add beaten and seasoned eggs to the mixture, cook and serve accompanied by pitta bread.

Scrambled Eggs with Tomato and Pimento [*Piparrada* Spain] Sauté chopped onion and garlic, diced cured ham and diced green and red pimento. Add beaten and seasoned eggs to the mixture, cook and serve garnished with bread croûtons.

Scrambled Eggs with Vegetables [*Piparrada* Spain] Lightly fry chopped onion, diced green pimento and tomato flesh in garlic-flavoured oil. Add beaten and seasoned eggs to the mixture, cook and serve on bread croûtons.

Scrambled Eggs with Vegetable Purée [*Ovos Mexidos a Estremenha* Portugal] Spread crisply fried bread croûtons with vegetable purée, top with scrambled egg mixture and garnish with fillets of anchovy and green olives.

Shirred Eggs

Application

Heat a little butter in a porcelain ovenproof dish and season with salt and pepper. Break the eggs into the dish and cook for 2 min either in the oven or on top of the stove until the whites are just set; garnish according to the recipe.

Shirred Eggs à la Flamenca [*Huevos a la Flamenca* Spain] Sweat chopped onion and garlic, add cooked broad beans, french beans, sliced carrot, quartered artichoke bottoms, diced tomato flesh and lardons of smoked ham, then moisten with tomato sauce. Garnish shirred eggs with the vegetable mixture.

Shirred Eggs Bercy [*Oeufs sur le Plat Bercy* France] Garnish shirred eggs with grilled chipolata sausages, grilled tomato and a ring of tomato sauce.

Shirred Eggs with Bacon [GB] Garnish shirred eggs with grilled rashers of bacon.

Shirred Eggs with Mushrooms [*Huevos con Picadilla de Champiñon* Spain] Sauté sliced mushrooms and garlic in oil then transfer the mixture to porcelain dishes, break the eggs into the dish and cook.

Shirred Eggs with Sorrel [*Sóskàs Tojàs Nyelvvel* Hungary] Combine shredded sorrel cooked in butter with soured cream then place the mixture into a porcelain dish; place the eggs onto the mixture and cook.

Shirred Eggs with Tomato and Sausage [*Huevos à La Madrileña* Spain] Garnish shirred eggs with sliced tomato sautéed in oil and sliced morcilla sausage, sprinkle with grated Parmesan cheese and gratinate.

Cheese Dishes

The following are examples of the wide range of dishes that can be made from cheese. They range from many well-known household dishes to fairly advanced ones from the international repertoire, and many are eminently suitable for vegetarian meals if one of the several kinds of vegetarian cheese is substituted for ordinary cheese. This section contains recipes where the main flavour is that of the cheese, and does not include any where cheese is a subsidiary ingredient, e.g. moussaka contains cheese but is mainly made from meat.

Beurrecks [*Turkey*]   Cut Gruyère cheese into small dice and mix with cold béchamel sauce. Roll out noodle pastry very thinly, cut into 8-cm squares and roll a cigar-shape piece of the cheese filling in each, sealing the ends well. Egg and breadcrumb and golden deep fry.

Bread and Butter and Cheese Pudding [*GB*]   Spread thin slices of crustless bread with butter, cut into quarters and arrange neatly overlapping in pie dishes. Warm milk and pour onto beaten eggs together with salt, pepper and a pinch of nutmeg and add grated Cheddar cheese. Pour the mixture over the bread and cook au bain-marie in the oven.

Buck Rarebit [*GB*]   Make a Welsh rarebit and serve with a well drained poached egg on top.

Calgore [*Italy*]   Roll out pizza dough and stamp out 8-cm rounds, lay half rounds of Bel Paese cheese and ham on each, and fold over to seal well. Allow to prove and bake in the oven.

Camembert Fritters [***Beignets au Camembert*** *France*]   Cut the rind off a Camembert and divide into eight pieces; dip into flour then into yeast batter and golden deep fry.

   Note: Brie can also be treated in this way, and these two cheeses can also be served warm and runny by keeping them in a hotplate.

Cheese Bakewell Tart [*GB*]   Line a flan ring with short pastry, cover the base with tomato concassée and fill with the following mixture: add yolks of egg, bread-crumbs, grated Cheddar cheese, salt and pepper to cream sauce and fold in stiffly beaten egg whites. Bake in the oven at 210 °C for approx. 40 min.

Cheese Blintzes [*Israel*]   Make small, thin pancakes and place an oblong of curd cheese mixed with milk, eggs and sugar in the centre; fold over, heat through and serve dredged with caster sugar.

   Note: fruit such as stoned cherries, segments of mandarins or slices of peach may be added to the cheese filling.

Cheese Fritters [*GB*]   Mix grated Cheddar cheese with white breadcrumbs and eggs to form a smooth paste. Divide into pieces, mould round, dip into frying batter and golden deep fry. Serve garnished with fried parsley.

Cheese Fritters [***Beignets Soufflés au Fromage*** *France*]   Bring water, butter and a pinch of salt to the boil; add flour, mix well over heat until it leaves the pan clean, then allow to cool. Add eggs one by one, mixing thoroughly. Add grated Parmesan and diced Gruyère cheese. Mould into pieces using two table-spoons and golden deep fry at 190 °C for approx. 5 min, moving them continu-ously in the hot oil. Serve sprinkled with grated Parmesan.

Cheese Kebabs [***Attereaux au Parmesan*** *France*]   Bring milk to the boil, rain in semolina and cook gently for 5 min, mixing well and adding a pinch of nut-meg, grated Parmesan cheese, yolks of egg, butter and seasoning. Spread on an oiled tray 0.5 cm thick, butter the surface and allow to cool. Cut out 2.5-cm rounds and thread on skewers, alternating with 2.5-cm round slices of Gruyère cheese. Coat with egg and breadcrumbs and deep fry.

Cheese Pancake Fritters [***Nalesnikis*** *Russia*]   Mix together pressed curd cheese and butter with beaten egg and seasoning; mould into 25 g squares, wrap each in a small pancake forming them square, dip into yeast batter and deep fry until crisp and golden.

Cheese Straws [*Paillettes au Parmesan* France] Roll out puff pastry, sprinkle with grated Parmesan cheese and a tiny pinch of cayenne and press in. Fold into three, roll out 3 mm thick and brush with eggwash. Sprinkle with grated Parmesan and roll it in to make it stick. Cut into 15-cm lengths 1 cm in width, twist into spirals and press onto a damp baking sheet, also making a few circles of the pastry. Allow to rest for 15 min then bake at 220 °C for approx. 8 min. Fill the circles with the straws to look like sheaves.

Cottage Cheese Quiche [*Quiche au Fromage* France] Line a .flan ring with short pastry and fill with a mixture of cottage cheese, double cream, sautéed chopped onion and eggs. Bake at 200 °C for approx. 25 min.

Croque Monsieur [*France*] Spread thin slices of bread with butter and sandwich with slices of Gruyère cheese and ham. Seal well, cut off the crusts and golden shallow fry in vegetable oil or clarified butter.

Fried Cheese [*Saganaki* Greece] Pass slices of Feta, Kefalotíri or Kasseri cheese through flour then golden shallow fry in olive oil. Serve with a sprinkling of lemon juice and chopped fresh herbs.

Fried Cheese Crescents [*Piroguis* Russia] Mix jus lié with breadcrumbs and butter and heat until it becomes quite stiff. Spread on a tray to cool then cut out crescents and sandwich two together with twarogue. Shallow fry in vegetable oil or clarified butter.

Note: to make twarogue, mix together cream cheese and butter with egg and seasoning.

Fried Cheese Puffs [*Tirakia Tiganita* Greece] Stiffly beat egg whites, fold in finely grated kefalotíri cheese and seasoning of milled pepper. Drop teaspoonsful of the mixture into hot olive oil and fry until golden.

Galette au Fromage [*France*] Mix together flour, grated Emmenthal, vegetable oil or butter and eggs to make a firm dough. Roll to a circle, brush with eggwash and bake in the oven at 220 °C.

Kreplach [*Israel*] Roll out noodle pastry very thinly and cut into 6-cm squares. Mix cottage cheese with egg and sugar, place some in the centre of each piece of pastry, fold over as triangles and seal well. Allow the kreplachs to dry then simmer in boiling water for approx.15 min, drain well and serve sprinkled with melted butter and sugar.

Macaroni Cheese [*GB*] Cook elbow macaroni in plenty of boiling salted water until tender; drain well and mix into cheese sauce. Pour into a buttered earthenware dish, sprinkle with a mixture of grated Gruyère and Parmesan cheese and vegetable oil or melted butter, and gratinate.

Mozzarella in Carozza [*Mozzarella Carozza* Italy] Sandwich a slice of Mozzarella between two buttered slices of bread, trim the crusts, dip into beaten eggs and golden shallow fry in vegetable oil or clarified butter.

Roulettes [*GB*] Mix together St Ivel cheese with white breadcrumbs and season- . ing. Mould into 45-g flat cakes, pass through flour then through beaten egg and shallow fry in vegetable oil or clarified butter until golden.

Savoury Cheese Cakes [*Israel*] Combine finely grated Cheddar cheese with beaten eggs and seasoning of salt and a little cayenne. Roll out puff pastry to 3 mm thick then cut into 5-cm rounds. Fill the centre of each with 1 teaspoonful of the cheese mixture, eggwash the edges then fold in two to form crescents. Place onto a dampened baking sheet, egg wash and bake at 220 °C for approx. 12 min.

Welsh Rarebit [*GB*] Mix grated Cheddar cheese into hot béchamel sauce and
when melted add yolks of egg, a few drops of Worcester sauce, English mustard, a small pinch of cayenne and reduced ale. Spread liberally on slices of
buttered toast, trim and colour under a salamander grill.

Chapter Five

Farinaceous Dishes, Pizzas, Dumplings, Bulgar or Cracked Wheat and Savoury Pancakes

This chapter is divided into ten categories according to product type:

✧ Pastas ✧

✧ Cannelloni ✧

✧ Ravioli ✧

✧ Lasagne and Fillings ✧

✧ Spaghetti ✧

✧ Noodle Dishes and Asian Noodles ✧

✧ Pizzas ✧

✧ Dumplings ✧

✧ Bulgar, or Cracked Wheat ✧

✧ Savoury Pancakes ✧

Pastas [*Italy*]

Allow 75 g dry or 90 g fresh pasta per average portion as a first course or as an accompaniment. Allow 100 g dry uncooked pasta per average portion as a main dish.

All pasta items are cooked in simmering salted water. Cooking time varies according to type: fresh pasta takes approx. 5 minutes to cook, and for the dried type, 5–10 minutes is considered sufficient, though the quick-cook types may need only 3 minutes. Pastas should be cooked slightly underdone to the stage known as 'al dente'.

Fresh Noodle Paste

To 500 g plain or durum flour or fine semolina and 2 teaspoons of salt add 5 beaten eggs, 25 ml olive oil and 75 ml water, and knead well until smooth and elastic.

Pasta Verde   Add 75 g finely sieved cooked spinach to the flour at the same time as the eggs.
Pasta Rossa   Add 150 g concentrated tomato purée to the flour at the same time as the eggs.
Wholemeal Pasta   Use 400 g wholemeal flour sieved with 100 g ordinary white flour and proceed as for fresh noodle paste.

Cannelloni

Cut the very thinly rolled fresh noodle paste into 8 cm × 8 cm squares. Plain boil and refresh, lay on a cloth and pipe the filling across each. Roll up, place into a buttered dish, add the sauce, sprinkle with grated cheese and oil or butter, and gratinate.

Cannelloni Piacentini   Filling: beat together chopped cooked spinach, chopped parsley and ricotta cheese then add Mascarpone, grated Parmesan, beaten egg and seasoning of salt, pepper and nutmeg.

Ravioli

Cut very thinly rolled fresh noodle paste into two 40 cm × 20 cm pieces. Mark into 3-cm squares and eggwash. On one piece pipe the filling into the centre of each square, cover with the other piece, seal and cut into squares or rounds. Cook, drain, place into a buttered dish, add the sauce, sprinkle with grated cheese, and oil or butter and gratinate.

Ravioli Calzoni di Ricotta alla Molisana   Filling: combine diced ham, Ricotta, Provolone, egg yolk and seasoning. Make into ravioli, cook in boiling salted water for approx. 5 min and drain. Golden deep fry the ravioli in olive oil, drain and serve.

Ravioli Coligniones   Filling: combine grated Pecorino cheese, chopped cooked spinach, saffron, egg yolks and seasoning. Sauce: lightly fry chopped onion and diced bacon, add minced veal, chopped parsley and basil and cook. Add diced tomato flesh and stock, simmer and reduce the liquid to a râgout consistency. Serve sprinkled with grated Pecorino cheese.

Further ravioli fillings are listed under Lasagne, below.

Lasagne

Cut the thinly rolled paste into 8 cm × 3 cm rectangular shapes, cook and refresh. Layer trellis-fashion in a buttered dish alternating with layers of the selected filling, sprinkle with grated cheese, oil or butter and gratinate.

Fillings for Lasagne and Ravioli

Beef, Pork, Rabbit or Veal   Sweat chopped onion and garlic in olive oil, add the selected minced meat, moisten with dry white wine and cook.

Fontina Cheese and Chive Filling   Combine grated Fontina cheese with chopped chives.

Cheese, Ham and Mushroom   Combine sliced button mushrooms, julienne of prosciutto crudo and grated Gruyère cheese with béchamel sauce.

Chicken and Ham   Sauté chopped onion, diced carrot and celery in olive oil. Add finely diced chicken breast, chopped prosciutto crudo and mushrooms then add basil and tomato concassée. Moisten with dry white wine, reduce then add jus lié and season with nutmeg.

Spinach and Ricotta Cheese   Mix together finely chopped cooked spinach, Ricotta cheese, salt, and nutmeg and diced Mozzarella.

Spaghetti

Application

Plunge the dried pasta into boiling salted water and fast simmer for nine min. Once cooked and drained, the pasta can be tossed in plain or garlic-flavoured olive oil or butter. As a general rule grated Parmesan cheese accompanies all pasta dishes except those that contain shellfish.

The following spaghetti dishes are given as foundation formulas that are suitable for most other plain pasta items.

Spaghetti with Baby Clams [*Spaghetti alla Vongole*]   Fry garlic in olive oil then stir in passata and simmer. Add the clams, seasoning and chopped parsley. Add to the cooked spaghetti and toss over to mix.

Spaghetti with Baby Marrow [*Spaghetti con Zucchine*]   Sauté finely chopped shallot, garlic, carrot and celery in olive oil. Add tomato concassée and tomato sauce and cook. Toss the spaghetti in this sauce and serve with a layer of roundels of crisp, deep fried baby marrow on top.

Spaghetti with Bacon, Egg and Cream [*Spaghetti alla Carbonara*]   Crisp fry lardons of bacon in garlic-flavoured olive oil, add the pasta and a liaison of egg yolks and cream to lightly cook and bind.

Spaghetti with Bacon and Onion [*Spaghetti con Guanciale e Cipolla*]   Crisp fry lardons of unsmoked bacon in garlic-flavoured olive oil, add sliced onion and sweat. Add the pasta and grated Pecorino cheese and sprinkle with chilli powder.

Spaghetti with Basil Sauce [*Spaghetti al Pesto*]   Liquidise garlic, basil leaves and pine nuts or walnuts, then whisk in olive oil and grated Parmesan or Pecorino cheese. Toss the cooked and drained spaghetti in this sauce.

Spaghetti Bolognaise [*Spaghetti con Salsa alla Bolognese*]   Fry lardons of prosciutto crudo, chopped onion, garlic, brunoise of carrot and celery and sliced, dried mushrooms in olive oil. Add minced or finely diced tail end of fillet of beef, dry red wine, tomato concassée, chopped parsley and marjoram; season with nutmeg and cook. Toss the pasta in this sauce and sprinkle with Parmesan cheese.

Spaghetti with Cheese and Pepper [*Spaghetti con Casio e Pepe*]   Serve the spaghetti seasoned with coarsely ground black peppercorns and melted grated Pecorino cheese.

Spaghetti with Chilli Sauce [*Spaghetti al Fuoco*]   Sauté garlic and fresh red chillies in olive oil and liquidise, then fry the mixture in garlic-flavoured olive oil. Toss the pasta in this sauce and serve.

Spaghetti with Garlic, Oil and Chilli Peppers [*Spaghetti con Aglio, Olio e Peperoncino*]   Toss the pasta in olive oil flavoured with garlic and dried red chillies.

Spaghetti with Ham and Mushrooms [*Spaghetti con Prosciutto e Funghi*]   Sauté sliced mushrooms in garlic-flavoured olive oil. Add lardons of prosciutto crudo and chopped basil. Add the fried mixture to the pasta and sprinkle with Parmesan cheese.

Spaghetti with Mussels and Garlic [*Spaghetti alla Tarantina*]   Sauté chopped garlic in olive oil and add chopped parsley. Toss the spaghetti in the flavoured oil together with cooked mussels.

Spaghetti with Peas [*Spaghetti con Piselli*]   Sauté chopped onion and lardons of bacon in olive oil. Add tomato purée, chicken stock and peas and cook. Toss the spaghetti in this mixture.

Spaghetti with Tomatoes [*Spaghetti con Pomodoro*]   Sauté chopped garlic and fresh red chillies in olive oil, add strips of tomato flesh and cook. Toss the spaghetti in this mixture.

Spaghetti with Tomatoes and Basil [*Spaghetti con Pomodoro e Basilico*]   Sauté chopped garlic and fresh red chillies in olive oil, add strips of tomato flesh and chopped basil and cook. Toss the spaghetti in this mixture.

Noodle Dishes and Asian Noodles

German Swabian Noodles [*Spätzle*]   Combine flour, beaten eggs, water and salt to form a light, firm dough. Force the mixture through a colander into boiling salted water, poach and drain.

Hungarian Noodle Paste   Combine flour, beaten eggs, water and salt to form a light, firm dough. Roll out the paste 5 mm thick, cut into desired shape then poach in boiling salted water.

Noodles with Cottage Cheese [*Túrós Metélt* Hungary]   Toss cooked noodles in bacon fat, moisten with soured cream and finish with crumbled cottage cheese and chopped dill. Serve topped with lardons of bacon.

Noodles with Eggs [*Tojásos Tészta* Hungary]   Toss cooked noodles in butter then moisten with beaten eggs and lightly cook to coat the noodles.

Noodles with Ham [*Sonkás Kocka* Hungary]   Toss very thin noodles in butter then combine with egg yolks and soured cream, grated cheese and diced ham.

Asian Noodles

Applications

Egg noodles – soak noodles in hot water for 10 min, drain then plunge into boiling water to which a little oil has been added and cook for 3 min. Drain, spread on a cloth to dry then golden deep fry in peanut oil and drain.

Rice Vermicelli Noodles [*Mi Fun* China]   Place into boiling water and cook for 2–3 min, drain and use as required. Alternatively fry in small batches in oil until they puff-up and are crisp and golden, then drain on kitchen paper.

Korean Noodles – cook noodles in simmering water for 2 min, refresh and drain.

Cellophane or Bean Starch Noodles [*Fun See* China]   Soak for 20 min in hot water, drain then cook in boiling water for 15 min. Alternatively, for crisp noodles fry in small batches in oil until they are crisp and golden, then drain on kitchen paper.

Buckwheat Noodles with Chilli Sauce [*Pibimnaengmyon* Korea]   Combine kochujang, chilli powder, rice vinegar, sesame oil, toasted sesame seeds, sugar and chopped spring onions. Cook noodles in simmering water for 2 min then drain. Serve warm noodles topped with the dressing, slices of boiled beef, sliced Korean radish and hard-boiled egg. Serve accompanied by beef stock.

Chilled Buckwheat Noodles [*Naengmyon* Korea]   Marinate strips of boiled beef in soy sauce, sesame oil, toasted sesame seeds, garlic and black pepper. Sprinkle sliced cucumber with salt, allow to stand for 30 min, rinse and drain then combine with cider vinegar, sugar and chilli powder. Combine beef stock with kimichi juice and vinegar. Cook noodles in simmering water for 2 min then drain. Serve the noodles moistened with the stock and topped with the beef, cucumber and hard-boiled egg, accompanied by mustard dressing.

Chilled Son Myon Noodles with Vegetables [*Pibimguksu* Korea]   Cook noodles in simmering water for 2 min then drain. Moisten the noodles with a dressing of kochujang, cider vinegar, sesame oil, toasted sesame seeds and garlic. Serve topped with julienne of carrot and ham, shredded Chinese cabbage and strips of fried beaten egg.

Crispy Egg Noodles with Chicken and Bamboo Shoots [*Kai See Jar Mein China*] Cook noodles in peanut oil until gold and crispy and form into nests and drain. Stir-fry strips of chicken, add sliced mushrooms and bamboo sprouts then season with salt and pepper. Dilute cornflour in a little water and soy sauce, pour onto the preparation and cook for 2 min. Serve sprinkled with chopped spring onions.

Crisp Fried Noodles [*Chow Min China*] Fry crushed garlic and grated ginger in peanut oil then add and stir-fry strips of fillet of pork and chicken breast, then add sliced abalone, Chinese cabbage, spring onions, bean sprouts and bamboo shoots. Moisten with thickened chicken stock. Serve on top of deep fried egg noodles.

Crisp Fried Vermicelli Noodles [*Mee Grob Thailand*] Golden stir-fry soaked and drained noodles and retain. Golden stir-fry chopped shallot and garlic in oil, and add goujons of chicken and pork. Add crisply fried yellow bean curd and bean sprouts then stir in beaten eggs to set. Stir in rice vinegar and nam pla, then add the noodles and finish with roasted chilli powder and chopped coriander.

Egg Noodles with Lobster and Vegetables [*Chow Mai China*] Stir-fry sliced onion and mushrooms in oil, and add bean sprouts, sliced water chestnuts, celery and cucumber, add sliced, cooked lobster. Moisten with a little soy sauce and stock, add noodles, season to taste and cook for 2 min.

Egg Noodles with Prawns [*Laksa Lemak Thailand*] Blend onion, garlic, almonds, turmeric, ginger and blachan to a paste. Cook the mixture in oil, moisten with coconut milk then add prawns. Serve the prawn mixture on a base of cooked laksa (noodles) and garnish with julienne of cucumber and shredded basil. Serve accompanied by red and green chillies.

Fried Crisp Noodles [*Mee Krob Thailand*] Deep fry broken vermicelli noodles. Fry chopped onion and garlic in oil then add strips of fillet of pork and chicken, finely sliced dried mushrooms and fresh chillies. Moisten with soy sauce, lime juice, rice vinegar and nam pla then reduce the sauce by half. Add prawns, pour in beaten eggs and stir until they begin to thicken. Add bean sprouts and the cooked noodles. Serve with segments of lime, sprinkled with chopped spring onions and coriander leaves.

Fried Egg Noodles [*E Min China*] Boil, drain and dry egg noodles. Fry the noodles in peanut and sesame oil until golden and serve with vegetables, poultry or meat dishes.

Fried Noodles [*Pad Thai Thailand*] Fry garlic in peanut oil then add shrimps, sugar, nam pla and tomato ketchup. Pour in beaten eggs and stir until the mixture begins to thicken. Add rice vermicelli and cook for a few minutes then stir in bean sprouts. Place the mixture onto a serving dish, surround with segments of lime, and sprinkle with raw bean sprouts, shrimp powder, peanuts, chilli flakes, chopped spring onions and coriander leaves.

Fried Noodles Indonesian Style [*Bahmi Goreng Indonesia*] Golden fry strips of pork in peanut oil, remove the meat and retain. Add chopped garlic, onion and grated ginger and cook for 2 min then add strips of celery, shredded cabbage, French beans and bean sprouts, cook for a further 2 min then add the pork and prawns, sprinkle with soy sauce and season to taste. Golden fry cooked noodles in oil and serve with the vegetables, pork and prawns arranged on top.

Rice Noodles Thai Style [*Guay Tiaw Pad Thai Thailand*] Blend fresh red chillies, shallots, nam pla, sugar, lime juice and tamarind liquid to a paste. Stir-fry the paste then add shrimps and noodles, moisten with soy sauce and water, toss in stir-fried strips of pork and bean sprouts and serve garnished with shredded fresh red chillies.

Rice Vermicelli Noodles with Prawns [*Choy Yuen Har Kau Chow Mi Fun China*] Stir-fry prawns in peanut oil, remove and retain. Add shredded Chinese cabbage and fry for 2 min, moisten with stock, saké and light soy sauce then add crushed garlic, grated ginger and seasoning and cook for a further 2 min. Toss in rice vermicelli then add the prawns and serve.

Japanese Noodle Dishes

Application

To cook dried and fresh noodles place them into boiling salted water, immediately add a small amount of cold water and bring back to the boil then repeat this process three times; when cooked, drain and serve. Thin ordinary, vari-coloured and buckwheat noodles are cooked in the same way, adding cold water during the cooking three times only. For fresh, thick noodles, place into a saucepan, cover with boiling water and let them stand for a few minutes to heat through. Separate the noodles, drain and serve.

Fresh Noodles [*Teuchi Udon,* or *Saba*] Sift 500 g plain flour, or 375 g buckwheat mixed with 125 g strong flour, into a bowl, make a bay in the centre and gradually add 175 ml warm water with 1 tsp salt added, mixing to a firm dough. Knead the dough until it is smooth and elastic, cover with a cloth and allow to rest for 1 hr. Knead the dough then roll out into a rectangle 3 mm thick and cut into 4-mm strips for udon noodles or 3-mm strips for saba. Place the noodles into boiling salted water, immediately add a small amount of cold water and bring back to the boil, then repeat this process three times; cook for 2 min, drain and serve.

Noodle Broth – Simmer together dashi, salt, dark and light soy sauces, sugar and mirin.

Tentsuyu Dipping Sauce – Simmer first soup stock flavoured with soy sauce and mirin for 1 min, cool and serve.

Buckwheat Noodles with Chicken [*Torinanban*] Slice poached chicken breasts then marinate in soy sauce and saké. Cook spinach, drain, refresh, squeeze into a cloth to form a roll and cut into slices. Place cooked noodles into china bowls, arrange the chicken, spinach slices and paysanne of spring onions on top. Moisten with noodle broth and serve accompanied by seven-flavour spice.

Chilled Buckwheat Noodles on Bamboo [*Zaru Soba*] Chill cooked noodles in iced water, drain well and divide into bowls or onto bamboo strainers, place a small amount of green horseradish paste on each and sprinkle with crumpled seaweed. Serve accompanied by finely chopped spring onions and tentsuyu dipping sauce.

Chilled Noodles with Eggs [*Hiyamugi*]   Chill cooked noodles in iced water, drain well then place into a large serving bowl. Arrange sliced cucumber, diamonds of tomato flesh and slices of hard boiled egg on top and serve accompanied by tentsuyu dipping sauce and chopped spring onions.

Chilled Noodles with Prawns [*Hiyashi Somen*]   Chill cooked noodles in iced water, drain well then place into a large serving bowl. Arrange prawns and blanched seeded slices of cucumber on top and serve accompanied by tentsuyu dipping sauce, chopped spring onions and 5-cm slices of daikon stuffed with hot chilli peppers.

Fried Noodles [*Wu-Dung*]   Stir-fry chopped spring onion, garlic, strips of fillet steak and sliced mushrooms. Add chopped tofu, peeled prawns, soy sauce, sugar and toasted sesame seeds. Stir in cooked noodles and serve.

Noodles in Dashi with Poached Egg [*Tsukimi Udon*]   Divide cooked noodles into china serving bowls; pour over dashi flavoured with mirin, dark and light soy sauces and sugar and place a slice of rolled cooked spinach on top of each. Poach eggs in simmering water, place an egg in each bowl and garnish with small squares of crisp toasted dried seaweed.

Noodles in the Pot [*Nabeyaki Udon*]   Serve portions of cooked udon noodles, arrange shrimps, kamaboko slices and trefoil on top moistened with dashi flavoured with mirin, dark and light soy sauce and sugar. Poach an egg in the centre bay of the noodles and serve.

Noodles with Bean Curd [*Kitsune Udon*]   Cook small triangles of bean curd in a small amount of second soup stock flavoured with soy sauce, mirin and sugar for 10 min, by which time the liquid should have almost evaporated. Divide the cooked noodles and the bean curd into china serving bowls, moisten with noodle broth and serve garnished with julienne of spring onion and seven-spice powder.

Noodles with Bean Paste [*Miso Udon*]   Combine red miso and a little hot chicken stock in a pan, add sliced mushrooms and chopped spring onions and cook for 2 min. Add cooked noodles and poached chicken thighs to the sauce and serve.

Noodles with Cucumber [*Somen To Kyuri No Suimono*]   Arrange cooked noodles in bowls and moisten with first soup stock flavoured with saké and soy sauce. Place seeded, sliced cucumber on top and serve.

Noodles with Eggs and Chicken [*Tojikishimen*]   Poach goujons of breast of chicken in dashi flavoured with mirin, dark and light soy sauces and sugar. Thicken with cornflour and whisk in beaten eggs to form threads. Serve noodles in bowls, topped with chopped spinach. Pour in the liquid and the pieces of chicken and sprinkle the surfaces with finely chopped spring onions and seven-spice powder.

Noodles with Poached Egg [*Tsukimi Udon*]   Divide cooked noodles into china serving bowls, pour over dashi flavoured with light and dark soy sauces, mirin and sugar and place a slice of rolled cooked spinach on top of each. Place a poached egg into each bowl and garnish with small squares of crisp toasted dried seaweed.

Noodles with Pork [*Buta Udon*]   Poach strips of pork and julienne of leek in dashi flavoured with light and dark soy sauces, mirin and sugar. Remove from the stove and stir in more light soy sauce, sugar and a pinch of monosodium glutamate. Add cooked noodles to the soup, serve in bowls and garnish with sprigs of spring onions and a little seven-spice powder.

Pizzas

Pizza Dough

Sift 800 g strong flour and 2 tsp salt into a bowl. Make a well in the centre, add 40 g yeast dissolved in 375 ml warm water and allow the mixture to ferment. Add 75 ml olive oil and make into a smooth dough. Allow to prove, then knock back and use.

Pizza Tomato Topping [*Passata*]

Sweat chopped onion and garlic in olive oil. Add tomato concassée, tomato purée, chopped oregano and basil, bayleaf, demerara sugar and seasoning. Simmer to a smooth consistency, which may also be obtained by liquidising the mixture.

Application

For a 20-cm one portion pizza, roll out a 250-g piece of the dough and place onto an oiled baking sheet. Spread with passata leaving 1-cm space around the edges, then top with the other pizza ingredients. Sprinkle with olive oil and bake at 230 °C for approx. 20 min. If using a traditional wood-burning oven cook for only 5–8 min.

Pizza with a Tomato (Passata) and Cheese Topping

Pizza ai Funghi   Spread bases with passata, and sprinkle with sliced mushrooms, chopped Mozzarella cheese, oregano and seasoning.

Pizza ai Quattro Formaggi   Spread bases with passata, sprinkle with chopped Mozzarella, Gorgonzola, grated Pecorino and Parmesan cheeses; then sprinkle with chopped oregano.

Pizza ai Sardine   Spread bases with passata, sprinkle with chopped Mozzarella cheese and onion, arrange sardines on top and sprinkle with chopped oregano.

Pizza al Tonno   Spread bases with passata, and sprinkle with chopped Mozzarella cheese, flaked tuna fish and chopped oregano.

Pizza alla Gorgonzola   Spread bases with passata, and sprinkle with chopped Mozzarella and Gorgonzola cheeses and chopped oregano.

Pizza Capricciosa   Spread bases with passata, and sprinkle with sliced mushrooms, diced ham, chopped Mozzarella cheese and oregano.

Pizza con Salami   Spread bases with passata, sprinkle with chopped Mozzarella cheese and layer with slices of salami.

Pizza Lazio   Spread bases with passata and chopped Mozzarella cheese and julienne of pimento and onion.

Pizza Margherita   Spread bases with passata, and sprinkle with chopped Mozzarella cheese, oregano and fresh basil leaves.

Pizza Marinara   Spread bases with passata, and sprinkle with mussels, shrimps, chopped Mozzarella cheese and oregano.

Pizza Napoletana   Spread bases with passata, and sprinkle with chopped Mozzarella cheese and chopped anchovy fillets.

Pizza Piccola Roma   Spread bases with passata, and sprinkle with chopped Mozzarella cheese, chopped ham, diced pineapple and oregano.

Pizza Quattro Stagione   Spread bases with passata then spread a quarter of each base with diced ham, a quarter with sliced button mushrooms, a quarter with sautéed quartered artichoke bottoms, a quarter with grated cheese, and sprinkle all over with oregano.

Pizza Romana   Spread bases with passata, and sprinkle with diced artichoke bottoms, chopped Mozzarella cheese and oregano.

Pizza Sardegniara   Spread bases with passata, arrange fillets of anchovy, stoned black olives and slivers of garlic on top, and sprinkle with basil.

Pizza Tropicale   Spread bases with passata, and sprinkle with chopped Mozzarella cheese, ham and pineapple, sliced banana and oregano.

Pizzas without a tomato and cheese topping

Pizza Andréa   Spread bases with stewed sliced onion, anchovy and sliced olives. Sprinkle with a few drops of olive oil and bake.

Pizza Calabrese   Spread bases with anchovy fillets, flaked tuna, capers and sliced olives. Sprinkle with a few drops of olive oil and bake.

Pizza Cinquemilli   Spread bases with raw whitebait, chopped garlic and oregano. Sprinkle with a few drops of olive oil and bake.

Pizza Fitascetta   Spread bases with sautéed sliced onion, sprinkle with sugar and bake.

Pizza Francesco   Spread bases with small slices of ham and tongue and cooked sliced mushrooms. Sprinkle with a few drops of olive oil and bake.

Pizza Gardiniera   Spread bases with blanched slices of carrot, eggplant, courgette and pimento. Sprinkle with a few drops of olive oil and bake.

Pizza Religioso   Spread bases with cooked sliced cep mushrooms, anchovy and flaked smoked mackerel. Sprinkle with a few drops of olive oil and bake.

Pizza Vesuvio   Spread bases with cooked sliced mushrooms, small pieces of salami and red pimento. Sprinkle with a few drops of olive oil and bake.

Dumplings

Bread Dumplings [*Semmelknödel* Germany]   Combine stale bread soaked in milk and squeezed out with sautéed chopped onion, beaten eggs, chopped parsley, salt, pepper and nutmeg. Poach small balls of the mixture in salted water.

Buckwheat and Garlic Dumplings [*Pampushki* Russia]   Make a yeast dough with buckwheat flour, yeast, water and salt. Poach small balls in salted water then fry in garlic-flavoured sunflower oil.

Butter Dumplings [*Vajguluska* Hungary]   Cream butter and eggs then fold in flour, salt and mixed herbs. Form almond shapes then poach in soup.

Cabbage Dumplings [*Kàposztàs Gombóc* Hungary]   Make a smooth dough with flour, butter, eggs and water then roll out 5 mm thick. Grate a raw white cabbage, sprinkle it with salt and rest for 30 min. Heat sugar in lard, add the squeezed out cabbage and sauté until lightly browned. Spread the mixture over the dough then roll up Swiss-roll fashion, sealing the edges with water. Cut into 5-mm thick slices then poach in salted water and serve sprinkled with grated cheese.

Caraway Dumplings [*Galushki Russia*] Combine flour, eggs, melted butter, milk, chopped cooked onion and caraway seeds; form into small balls and poach in salted water. Serve accompanied by crisp fried lardons of bacon.

Cheese Dumplings [*Sajtos Gombóc Hungary*] Beat together egg yolks, flour, melted butter, milk and grated cheese then fold in stiffly beaten egg whites. Poach teaspoonfuls of the mixture in simmering soup.

Cheese Dumplings [*Glumskeilchen Germany*] Combine cottage cheese, sugar, salt and beaten eggs then stir in flour and cornflour. Mix in dry mashed potato and currants. Poach wedge-shaped pieces in simmering salted water, drain and serve sprinkled with sugar and cinnamon.

Chicken and Bean Curd Dumplings [*Man-Doo Korea*] Lightly fry diced chicken, blanched bean sprouts, prawns and bean curd in sesame oil and season with chilli powder and soy sauce. Cut out 7-cm diameter circles of hot water paste, fill the centres with the mixture, fold in half and seal then steam them.

Cottage Cheese Dumplings [*Velos Burgonyagombóc Hungary*] Press cottage cheese through a sieve, add beaten egg yolks and melted butter then fold in stiffly beaten egg whites. Mould into walnut-sized dumplings using spoons and poach in simmering salted water. Roll the drained dumplings in golden fried breadcrumbs then sprinkle with soured cream.

Curd Cheese Dumplings [*Galushki Russia*] Combine curd cheese, butter, flour, salt and sugar then fold in stiffly beaten egg whites. Poach teaspoonfuls of the mixture in simmering salted water, remove, drain and serve coated with a sauce of soured cream and chopped mixed herbs.

Note: fruit such as stoned cherries, segments of mandarins or slices of peaches may be served to accompany them.

Fish Liver Dumplings [*Israel*] Poach a fish liver in salted water then blend it to a paste. Combine with fine matzo meal, chopped parsley, eggs and seasoning. Mould into small balls and poach in the stock of a fish stew.

Gnocchi with Cream Sauce [*Gnocchi Parisienne France*] Pipe 2-cm lengths of chou paste into simmering salted water and cook. Drain, toss in butter and combine with cream sauce. Sprinkle with butter and grated Parmesan cheese and gratinate.

Gnocchi with Potatoes [*Gnocchi Piémontaise France*] Combine dry purée of potatoes with egg yolks. Form into walnut-sized pieces and poach in simmering salted water. Sprinkle with butter and Parmesan cheese and gratinate

Gnocchi with Potatoes [*Gnocchi della Carnia Italy*] Combine dry purée of potatoes with flour, grated Parmesan cheese, egg, salt, pepper and nutmeg. Form into walnut-sized pieces and poach in simmering salted water. Sprinkle with butter, sugar, cinnamon and Parmesan cheese and gratinate.

Gnocchi with Semolina [*Gnocchi Romaine Italy*] Boil milk and rain in semolina, add butter and salt and cook, then add egg yolks. Cool in a dish 1 cm thick then cut into shapes. Place into a dish, sprinkle with oil and grated Gruyère, Emmenthal or Parmesan cheese and gratinate.

Gnocchi with Spinach and Ricotta Cheese [*Gnocchi di Ricotta Italy*] Combine Ricotta cheese, spinach purée, Parmesan cheese, eggs, salt, pepper, nutmeg and flour to make a soft mixture. Form croquette shapes and poach in simmering salted water. Place into a dish, sprinkle with oil and grated Gruyère, Emmenthal or Parmesan cheese and gratinate.

Kugel [*Israel*]   Combine breadcrumbs, flour, chicken fat, eggs and seasoning. Place the mixture into a greased and breadcrumbed mould, cover with foil and bake slowly for 4 hr. Serve accompanied by cholent.

Matzo Dumplings [*Matzo Cleis Israel*]   Pour boiling water over matzo meal then add ground almonds, chopped parsley, lightly sautéed chopped onion, ground ginger, nutmeg, salt, pepper and eggs to bind. Form into walnut-sized balls and poach in the soup.

Mushroom, Pork and Prawn Dumplings [*Wun Tun China*]   Combine finely minced pork, chopped dried Chinese mushrooms, prawns, chopped spring onions, cornflour diluted with a little soy sauce, brandy, oil and beaten egg and season to taste. Envelop teaspoons of the mixture in 2.5-cm squares of thinly rolled noodle paste, brush with eggwash and seal. Poach in simmering salted water for 5 min. Sprinkle with chopped spring onion and serve in clear chicken stock.

Nockerel [*Israel*]   Make a batter using eggs, water, flour, baking powder and salt. Drop teaspoonfuls into simmering salted water or soup. When the dumplings rise to the surface remove and serve.

Polenta – Basic Method [*Italy*]   Rain cornmeal into boiling salted water and cook whilst stirring for 10 min, then add egg yolks and grated Parmesan cheese. Cool in a greased dish 1 cm thick then cut into shapes. Place into a dish, sprinkle with oil and grated Parmesan cheese and gratinate. Polenta shapes may also be shallow fried.

Polenta with Fontina Cheese [*Polenta a Concia Italy*]   Stir diced Fontina cheese into made polenta and proceed as for the Basic Method.

Polenta with Mushrooms [*Polenta con Funghi Italy*]   Proceed as for the Basic Method, cut the polenta into shapes then place on a base of sautéed chopped onion and garlic and quartered mushrooms. Sprinkle with oil and grated Parmesan cheese and gratinate.

Polenta with Mushrooms and Ham [*Gnocchi di Polenta Italy*]   Proceed as for the Basic Method, substituting milk for water. Sweat chopped onion in olive oil, add sliced mushrooms and cook then add diced ham and tomato flesh and chopped rosemary, and moisten with red wine to make a sauce. Arrange the polenta on the sauce base then gratinate.

Pork Dumplings [*Char Shiu Bao China*]   Stir-fry cooked minced pork in peanut oil, sprinkle with soy sauce, add a little sugar and season with salt. Moisten with diluted cornflour and cook for 2 min, add oyster sauce to the mixture then cool. Sift flour and baking powder in to a bowl, add water to form a dough, knead well then roll into a sausage shape. Roll out the dough into 2.5-cm diameter pieces, envelop teaspoonfuls of the mixture in the middle of each, and pinch the edges together to form small round bun shapes with a twisted top. Steam for approx. 20 min and serve.

Potato Dumplings [*Buabaspitzle Germany*]   Combine boiled dry sieved potato, butter, flour and egg yolks and season with nutmeg. Mould into cigar-shaped pieces, poach in simmering salted water, drain and serve with sauerkraut.

Raw Potato Dumplings [*Rhoe Kartoffelklöbe Germany*]   Mash plain boiled potatoes and refrigerate. Combine the dry mashed potato with grated raw potato, flour, salt and marjoram. Shape the mixture around cubed fried bread croûtons to form large dumplings then poach them in simmering salted water. Drain and serve with roast meat, goose or duck.

Salami Dumplings [*Canderli Italy*]   Soak stale bread in milk then squeeze dry. Combine with chopped and fried smoked bacon, salami, parsley, flour and eggs. Poach walnut-sized pieces of the mixture in beef stock, drain then toss the dumplings in butter and serve accompanied by tomato sauce.

Semolina Dumplings [*Griebklöbe Germany*]   Rain semolina into boiling salted water and butter and cook, stirring all the time. Allow to cool then mould the mixture into balls and poach in simmering salted water. Serve the drained dumplings coated with sautéed chopped onion.

Semolina Dumplings [*Daragaluska Hungary*]   Cream lard and eggs then add semolina and chopped parsley. Form walnut shapes then poach in soup.

Spinach Dumplings [*Strangolapreti Italy*]   Soak stale bread in boiling water for 1 hr then drain and squeeze dry. Combine the bread with cooked chopped spinach, eggs, flour, salt, pepper and nutmeg. Poach spoonfuls of the mixture in salted water, drain then toss the dumplings in sage-flavoured butter and sprinkle with grated Parmesan cheese.

Steamed Pork Dumplings [*Har Gow China*]   Stir-fry minced pork in sesame oil then add chopped onions, mushrooms, bamboo shoots and grated ginger, and moisten with cornflour diluted with a little water, saké and soy sauce. Simmer for 2 min then add chopped prawns, transfer the mixture to a bowl and cool. Add Chinese wheat starch or flour to boiling water to form a dough, knead well then roll into a sausage shape. Roll out the dough into 2.5-cm diameter pieces, envelop teaspoonfuls of the mixture in the middle of each, pinch the edges together to form a semicircle. Steam for approx. 12 min and serve.

Steamed Pork and Chestnut Dumplings [*Shao Mai China*]   Combine minced pork, chopped water chestnuts, prawns, bamboo shoots, a little sugar, light soy sauce, grated ginger, saké and seasoning of salt. Break off pieces of noodle paste and roll out very thinly, cut into 2.5-cm diameter pieces, envelop teaspoonfuls of the mixture in the middle of each, and pinch the edges together to form small dumplings. Place a prawn on top of each and steam for approx. 15 min.

Steamed Pork and Prawn Dumplings [*Shiumai China*]   Combine chopped water chestnuts, bamboo shoots and spring onions, minced pork, prawns, light soy sauce, saké, sesame oil, egg whites and chopped dried Chinese mushroom caps. Envelop teaspoonfuls of the mixture in wonton wrappers to form purses. Place a whole prawn on top of each, and steam. Serve with a dipping sauce, e.g. Soy Sauce with Ginger.

Steamed Prawn and Chicken Wonton Dumplings [*Siu Mai Thailand*]   Combine minced chicken, chopped prawns, shiitake mushrooms and spring onions, sugar and soy sauce. Fill wonton wrappers with the mixture and steam them. Serve accompanied by sweet chilli sauce.

Steamed Savoury Pudding [*Serviettenklob Germany*]   Soak diced stale bread in a mixture of beaten egg yolks and milk for 3 hr. Combine the bread mixture with golden fried chopped onion, chopped parsley, salt, pepper and nutmeg, then fold in beaten egg whites. Mould the mixture into a ball, tie in a cloth and steam. Serve with braised or roast meats or with roasted or grilled poultry.

Wonton Savoury Dumplings [*Wonton China*]   Combine blanched, chopped bamboo shoots, raw prawns and spring onions, minced pork, soy sauce, sesame oil and chopped dried Chinese mushrooms. Envelop teaspoonfuls of the mixture in wonton wrappers to form triangle shapes. Deep fry in peanut oil and serve with sweet-and-sour type sauce.

Bulgar, or Cracked Wheat

Application

Place the cracked wheat in a pan, cover with stock or cold water, bring to the boil and simmer for 10 min, until the water has been absorbed. Cover with a cloth and allow to stand, or cover with boiling water and allow to stand for 30 min, then drain.

Cracked Wheat Pilaf [*Pourgouri Pilafi* Greece]   Sweat chopped onion in olive oil, add cracked wheat, cover with chicken stock and cook.

Cracked Wheat Pilaf [*Tabbouleh* Middle East]   Mix cooked cracked wheat with chopped mint and parsley, tomato concassée and lemon juice.

Cracked Wheat Pilau [*Burghal Pilaf* Middle East]   Sweat chopped onion in samneh, add cracked wheat, moisten with chicken stock and cook.

Savoury Pancakes

Pancake Batter   Sift 250 g flour and 2 g salt, make a bay and add 2 eggs beaten with 500 ml milk, whisk to a smooth batter and allow to rest for 30 min before using.

Bacon and Chive Pancakes [*Fleskepannekaker* Scandinavia]   Add chopped chives and lightly sautéed lardons of bacon to pancake mixture and make pancakes in the usual way.

Cabbage and Caraway Pancakes [*Káposztás Palacsinta* Hungary]   Lightly caramelise sugar and lard then add finely shredded cabbage and caraway seeds and lightly cook; add to a pancake batter and make the pancakes. Fill with chopped ham, roll up and serve the pancakes sprinkled with soured cream and grated cheese.

Dill and Cabbage Pancakes [*Farshirovanii Blinchiki* Russia]   Sweat chopped onion in oil then mix in boiled and drained shredded cabbage, chopped hard-boiled egg and dill. Spread pancakes with the mixture, roll up, sprinkle them with grated cheese and butter and gratinate.

Dill and Coriander Pancakes [*Sabzi Kuku* Israel]   Blend parsley, coriander, dill and spinach to a paste. Whisk eggs and matzo meal to a dropping consistency, then add the paste. Make pancakes with the mixture and serve with cream or cottage cheese.

Goose Liver Pancakes [*Libamájjal Töltött Palacsinta* Hungary]   Arrange alternate layers of pancakes and a mixture of mushroom duxelle and foie gras in a buttered shallow dish, finishing with pancakes. Sprinkle with soured cream and dot with butter and bake in the oven. Serve cut into portions.

Mandarin Pancakes for Peking Duck [*China*]   Beat 230 ml boiling water onto 500 g sifted plain flour and knead well to a smooth dough. Allow to rest then divide into 20 equal pieces and roll each to 8 cm in diameter. Brush five of them lightly with sesame oil and allow to rest. Place two rounds together and roll out into flat 17-cm diameter pieces. Cook on a non-greased heated griddle plate until cooked on both sides and a few golden bubbles appear. Remove from the griddle plate, gently peel each pancake apart into two and retain. Continue to brush, roll out and cook the other rounds of dough. Place the pancakes on a clean cloth and reheat in a steamer.

Potato and Mushroom Pancakes [*Israel*] Sweat chopped onion and chopped mushrooms in butter, and combine with dry mashed potato, egg yolk and seasoning. Spread the pancakes with this mixture, roll up, place in a dish, sprinkle with matzo meal or farfel, melted butter and the grated zest of lemon, and gratinate in a hot oven.

Shellfish, Mushroom and Cheese Pancakes [*Fyllda Pannkakor* *Scandinavia*] Combine sautéed sliced mushrooms and shredded white crabmeat with cream sauce. Spread pancakes with the mixture, roll up and place into a shallow earthenware dish. Sprinkle with grated Parmesan cheese and melted butter and gratinate.

Chapter Six

Savoury Rice Dishes

This chapter is divided into three main categories:

✧ Boiled Rice ✧

✧ Pilaff ✧

✧ Risotto ✧

Boiled Rice

Application – boiled rice dry or conservative method

Wash short-grain rice until the water runs clean. Place the rice in a pan, barely cover with cold water, season with salt and bring to the boil. Boil rapidly for 1 min, then cover with a lid and simmer until cooked. Remove from heat and allow to stand for 10 min before serving.

Boiled Glutinous Rice [*Nasi Kunyit* Indonesia]   Place pulot rice in a pan with water, salt, garlic, turmeric and duan pandan leaf. Bring to the boil and boil rapidly for 1 min, then cover with a lid and simmer until cooked. Serve garnished with crisply fried onion flakes.

Boiled Rice and Pine nuts [*Chatchuk* Korea]   Blend pine nuts and water to a paste. Wash rice until the water runs clean then soak for 3 hr and drain. Simmer the pine nut mixture, sesame oil and the rice in an equal quantity of water for 45 min. Season and garnish with whole pine nuts.

Boiled Rice in Stock [*Gohan* Japan]   Place short-grain rice in a pan, add second soup stock, cover and cook for 12 min until most of the liquid has been absorbed. Remove from the stove and allow to stand for 15 min and serve.

Boiled Rice Japanese Style [*Japan*]   Place 1 part short-grain rice in a pan, add 2 parts second soup stock, cover and cook until most of the liquid has been absorbed. Wrap the pan in a cloth for 15 min and serve.

Boiled Rice Mexican Style [*Arroz à la Mexicana* Mexico]   Golden fry long-grain rice in garlic-flavoured olive oil, then add chicken stock and chilli sauce. Cover and cook.

Boiled Rice with Abalone [*Chonbokchuk* Korea]   Wash rice until the water runs clean then soak for 3 hr and drain. Sauté diced abalone in oil then add the rice, moisten with half the quantity of water and simmer for 30 min, then add a similar quantity of water and simmer for a further 30 min. Serve accompanied by chojang vinegar soy sauce.

Boiled Rice with Barley [*Poribap* Korea]   Soak 2 parts washed rice and 1 part pearl barley separately in cold water for 3 hr, drain then combine and cook in 3 parts water under cover for 30 min.

Boiled Rice with Beef [*Gyudon* Japan]   Simmer strips of beef, blanched noodles cut into 1-cm lengths, sliced spring onion and 1-cm pieces of bean curd in second soup stock flavoured with soy sauce, mirin and monosodium glutamate for 3 min. Place boiled rice in bowls, top with the beef mixture and serve.

Boiled Rice with Beef and Eggs [*Gyutama Donburi* Japan]   Place boiled rice in bowls. Simmer together water flavoured with soy sauce, mirin and bonito flakes for 1 min then strain. Place thin slices of fish sausage, strips of beef and sliced mushrooms into the liquid and cook for 3 min. Pour portions of beaten eggs into a shallow pan and cook au bain-marie until it begins to set. Place boiled rice in bowls, add the fish and mushroom mixture then top with the cooked egg.

Boiled Rice with Chestnuts [*Kuri Cohan* Japan]   Proceed as for boiled rice dry method, with the addition of cooked, quartered chestnuts. When cooked sprinkle with saké.

Boiled Rice with Chestnuts [*Pambap Korea*] Proceed as for boiled rice dry method and add cooked chestnuts.

Boiled Rice with Chicken [*Nasi Goreng Indonesia*] Liquidise onion, garlic, sambal ulek and groundnut oil to form a paste. Fry the mixture in groundnut oil until golden red. Add diced chicken and boiled rice and stir-fry until the rice begins to colour. Add peeled prawns and sprinkle with Indonesian soy sauce.

Boiled Rice with Chicken and Bamboo Shoots [*Takenoko Goban Japan*] Add diced cooked chicken and strips of bamboo shoots to plain boiled rice.

Boiled Rice with Chicken and Eggs [*Oyako Donburi Japan*] Simmer small slices of cooked chicken, sliced mushrooms and strips of spring onions in second soup stock flavoured with soy sauce and mirin for 2 min. Pour portions of beaten eggs into a shallow pan and cook au bain-marie until they begin to set, then place each portion in a separate bowl. Add boiled rice and the chicken mixture and serve.

Boiled Rice with Chicken and Mangetouts [*Soboro Goban Japan*] Pour portions of beaten eggs flavoured with sugar and mirin into a shallow pan and cook au bain-marie until it begins to form threads, then transfer into bowls. Mix together grated ginger, ginger juice, soy sauce, mirin and cooked minced chicken. Cook over moderate heat until the liquid has completely reduced. Cook blanched mangetouts in soup stock until the liquid has evaporated. Serve boiled rice flavoured with soy sauce in bowls, top with the egg and the chicken mixtures and decorate with mangetouts.

Boiled Rice with Crabmeat and Prawns [*Moo Yong Thailand*] Three-quarters cook basmati rice using the dry method and drain. Lightly fry chopped shallots, garlic and fresh green chillies in groundnut oil. Add peeled prawns, crabmeat, the rice, water and saffron and continue cooking. Fill quarters of scooped out pineapple with the rice mixture. Garnish with diced pineapple, sprinkle with crisp fried onions and bake in the oven.

Boiled Rice with Ginger [*Nasi Kebuli Indonesia*] Stir soaked and rinsed rice into heated groundnut oil. Moisten with chicken stock, ground ginger and coriander and proceed as for boiled rice dry method, then add sautéed onions and garlic and sprinkle with nutmeg.

Boiled Rice with Lemon and Saffron [*Kesar Pilau India*] Fry crushed cardamom pods, cloves and cinnamon stick in ghee. Add long-grain rice, water, lemon juice, sugar and salt. Cover with a lid and cook for 10 min then add infused saffron, but do not stir the rice.

Boiled Rice with Lentils and Macaroni [*Koushari Middle East*] Proceed as for boiled rice dry method. Fry sliced onion and garlic in olive oil, stir in tomato purée then fork it into cooked rice together with cooked brown lentils and cooked short-cut macaroni.

Boiled Rice with Mushrooms [*Song i Pahb Japan*] Lightly fry chopped spring onions, sliced mushrooms and diced cooked chicken in sesame oil. Add soy sauce, toasted sesame seeds and previously soaked long-grain rice. Add cold water and seasoning. Boil rapidly for 1 min, cover with a lid and cook for 10 min. Allow the covered rice to stand for 10 min then serve.

Boiled Rice with Mushrooms and Beef [*Posotbap Korea*] Marinate strips of beef and mushrooms in soy sauce, sesame oil, toasted sesame seeds, chopped spring onions and black pepper. Sauté the meat and mushroom mixture in oil, add the soaked rice, moisten with stock or water and cook under cover for 30 min.

Boiled Rice with Oysters [*Kaki-Zousi* Japan]   Wash boiled rice in cold water and drain. Place the rice into a pan, barely cover with first soup stock flavoured with soy sauce, simmer for 3 min then add oysters. Cook for 1 min and serve.

Boiled Rice with Peas [*Endo Gohan* Japan]   Mix together 10 parts short-grain rice and 1 part glutinous rice and proceed as for plain boiled rice. When cooked fork in cooked peas and serve sprinkled with saké.

Boiled Rice with Pineapple [*Kao Pad Supparot* Thailand]   Sauté strips of pork and sliced onion in oil, stir in shrimp paste, soy sauce and cooked rice then add prawns. Fill small, warmed and hollowed pineapples with the rice mixture, and sprinkle with chopped fresh red chillies and coriander.

Boiled Rice with Prawns and French Beans [*Tendon* Japan]   Pass unpeeled prawns and small bundles of blanched French beans through tempura batter and fry until lightly golden. Place boiled rice into bowls, top with the prawns and the beans and serve accompanied by a dipping sauce made with second soup stock flavoured with soy sauce and mirin.

Boiled Rice with Prawns, Chicken and Mushrooms [*Kamameshi* Japan]   Place washed and drained short-grain rice into a casserole dish, moisten with first soup stock flavoured with soy sauce and saké and season. Add strips of breast of chicken, prawns previously marinated in soy sauce and sliced mushrooms. Cover with a lid and cook for 15 min. Allow to stand for 10 min then serve in bowls and garnish with spring onions.

Boiled Rice with Seaweed [*Sushi* Japan]   Proceed as for boiled rice dry method, with the addition of cubes of dried seaweed. When cooked remove the seaweed, fluff the grains then incorporate rice vinegar and caster sugar.

Boiled Rice with Spices [*Parsi Pilau* India]   Lightly fry crushed cardamom pods, cinnamon stick, cloves and black peppercorns in ghee. Add long-grain rice and stir in the fat. Add water, salt, saffron and grated rind of oranges. Proceed as for boiled rice dry method. When cooked add sultanas, blanched almonds and pistachio nuts.

Boiled Rice with Spices [*Kahu Buth* India]   Sweat chopped onion and lemon grass, crushed cardamom pods, peppercorns, garlic and curry leaves in ghee then add basmati rice, turmeric and a cinnamon stick. Proceed as for boiled rice dry method, substituting coconut milk for water.

Boiled Rice with Spring Onions [*Ching Choong Chow Fan* China]   Fry boiled rice in sesame oil until it begins to colour. Sprinkle in light soy sauce and chopped spring onions. (Any number of other ingredients or combination of ingredients may be added to this basic recipe).

Boiled Rice with Vegetables [*Chai Chow Fan* China]   Sauté chopped garlic, grated ginger, chopped spring onions, diced celery and soaked and sliced dried mushrooms in sesame oil. Stir in sliced bamboo shoots and boiled rice. Add light soy sauce and the mushroom soaking liquid and mix in.

Boiled Rice with Vegetables and Prawns [*Maze Gohn* Japan]   Proceed as for boiled rice dry method with the addition of diced carrot and celery, sliced dried mushrooms, soy sauce and saké. When cooked, fork in cooked peas and peeled prawns.

Boiled Spiced Rice [*Nasi Lemak* Thailand]   Sweat chopped onion in ghee, and add crushed cardamom pods, garlic and cinnamon. Add long-grain rice, moisten with boiling chicken stock and add seasoning. Proceed as for boiled rice dry method.

Boiled Spiced Rice with Coconut Milk [*Nasi Uduk* *Indonesia*]   Boil water and add coconut milk, chopped onion and garlic, ground cumin and coriander, trasi and lemon grass. Add rice and proceed as for boiled rice dry method.

Caribbean-style Boiled Rice   Rain rice into boiling salted water and boil for 15 min without the lid. Drain, rinse under cold water and return to the saucepan. Cover with the lid and continue to cook on a very low heat and lightly stir occasionally with a fork to fluff the grains of rice.

Fried Rice with Pork and Chicken [*Nasi Goreng* *Indonesia*]   Stir-fry chopped onion, garlic and shredded fresh red chillies in peanut oil. Add strips of pork and chicken then add cooked rice and cook for 3 min. Pour in beaten eggs and stir until cooked, season to taste then add prawns and serve sprinkled with shredded egg and garnished with sliced cucumber.

Middle Eastern-style Boiled Rice   Add washed rice to boiling salted water, boil for 5 min then drain. Heat oil with water, pour half into a pan, swirl to coat the sides and bottom and add the rice to form a mound. Make a hole in the centre and pour in the remainder of the oil and water. Cover with a cloth and lid and cook for 35 min on a low heat. Lightly stir with a fork to fluff the grains of rice.

Most Precious Rice [*Bark Bow Fan* *China*]   Stir-fry strips of pork and sliced mushrooms in oil, moisten with a little soy sauce, and add cooked rice, prawns, cooked peas and sliced French beans. Pour in beaten eggs and stir until cooked, season to taste and serve sprinkled with chopped spring onions.

Rice Balls [*Onigiri* *Japan*]   Mould 5-cm balls of boiled rice, stuffing some with a pickled plum, some with salt-cured salmon or gravlax and others with bonito flakes flavoured with soy sauce. Press squares of seaweed on the top and bottom of each and arrange on a sushioke and serve at room temperature.

Rice Calypso [*Caribbean*]   Proceed as for Caribbean-style rice. When cooked combine with sweated chopped onion and julienne of red pepper and ham. Serve sprinkled with grated Cheddar cheese.

Rice Creole [*Caribbean*]   Proceed as for Caribbean-style rice. When cooked combine with sliced mushrooms, ham and tomato concassée. Serve sprinkled with cheese.

Rice with Honey [*Muhammar* *Middle East*]   Proceed as for boiled rice Middle Eastern style and cook for 8 min. Drain and fork in honey. Heat samneh in a pan and add the cooked rice, sprinkle with rose-water and add infused saffron and cardamom pods liquid. Make three indentations in the rice, cover with greased greaseproof paper and a lid and cook in the oven.

Rice with Lamb and Cherries [*Miveh Dami* *Middle East*]   Proceed as for boiled rice Middle Eastern style with the addition of chopped onion and diced lamb lightly fried in samneh. Season with ground cinnamon and salt and add stoned sour cherries, chopped walnuts and currants during the last minutes of cooking.

Rice with Mushrooms [*Song i Pabb* *Japan*]   Lightly fry chopped spring onions, sliced mushrooms and diced cooked chicken in sesame oil. Add soy sauce, toasted sesame seeds and previously soaked long-grain rice. Add cold water and seasoning. Boil rapidly for 1 min, cover with a lid and cook for 10 min. Stand for 10 min covered with the lid.

Rice with Pigeon Peas [*Caribbean*]   Proceed as for Caribbean-style rice, then mix in peas, tomato concassée and lime juice.

Rice with Red Kidney Beans [*Caribbean*]   Add 2 parts washed and drained long-grain rice to 1 part cooked red kidney beans and proceed as for Caribbean-style rice.

Steamed Pink Rice with Red Beans [*Sekiban* Japan]   Cook red azuki beans in water, drain and reserve. To the cooking liquid add more water then soak previously washed short-grain rice in it for 8 hr. Drain the rice thoroughly, reserving the liquid, then combine the rice and the beans and steam for 40 min. When cooked cover with all the reserved liquid. Serve in bowls, sprinkled with toasted sesame seeds.

Steamed Rice Thai Method   Wash 1 part long-grain rice until the water runs clean. Place the rice in a pan with 3 parts cold water and cook until all the water has been absorbed. Transfer to a steamer tray and steam.

Steamed Rice with Crab, Prawns and Pork [*Khao Phat* Thailand]   Stir-fry chopped onion in oil then add diced pork and cook, then add prawns, crab-meat and beaten eggs. Add steamed rice, mix in nam pla, chilli sauce and tomato purée and serve sprinkled with chopped coriander.

Stir-Fried Rice [*Khao Phat Prik* Thailand]   Stir-fry sliced fresh red and green chillies in peanut oil, stir in red curry paste and cook. Add diced pork and prawns and fry, then add steamed rice. Add beaten eggs and allow to set, sprinkle with nam pla and serve sprinkled with chopped spring onions and coriander leaves.

Sushi Vinegared Rice [*Zushi* Japan]   Place washed short-grain rice in a pan, add water and kelp, cover, bring to the boil then remove the kelp. Replace the lid and boil for 5 min then simmer for 15 min. Remove from the stove, allow to stand for 15 min then fork in rice vinegar, sugar and salt.

Sushi Vinegared Rice Squares with Crab [*Kani-Zushi* Japan]   Proceed as for Sushi Vinegared Rice and mix in crabmeat. Make plain Japanese omelettes. Arrange layers of squares of rice with crabmeat, cooked peas and slices of omelette in an oiled square tin or an oshiwaku. Allow to set under pressure. De-mould and serve cut into small squares, garnished with pickled ginger.

Sushi Vinegared Rice with Bean Curd [*Inari-Zushi* Japan]   Proceed as for Sushi Vinegared Rice. Rinse bean curd in hot water, dry then cut in half to make little bags. Cook the curd bags in second soup stock flavoured with mirin and sugar, reducing the liquid by half, then add light soy sauce and cook until all the liquid has evaporated. Drain the curd pieces, stuff each with rice and serve garnished with red ginger and cucumber pickle.

Sushi Vinegared Rice with Vegetables [*Chirashi-Zushi* Japan]   Prepare plain Japanese omelettes. Cook mangetouts and lotus root in second soup stock flavoured with sugar and seasoned with salt for 1 min, then drain, keeping the liquid. Flavour the liquid with soy sauce then add sliced mushrooms and blanched strips of gourd and cook for 5 min. Remove the gourd then reduce the liquid to a glaze. Place the sushi rice into bowls, add prawns, the vegetables and slices of omelette, sprinkle with toasted and crushed seaweed and serve.

Pilaff Rice

Application

Using a ratio of 1 part long-grain rice and 2 parts chicken or vegetable stock, sweat chopped onion in oil, stir in the rice then moisten with boiling stock and add a bayleaf, a clove of garlic and seasoning. Cover with a lid and cook in the oven at 200 °C for 16 min.

Pilaff with Orange [*Zarda Palau* Turkey] Boil basmati rice in salted water for 10 min and drain. Golden fry chopped onion and slivered almonds in ghee and combine with julienne of orange peel cooked in a syrup. Add the rice, moisten with saffron-flavoured stock and cook in the oven at 150 °C for 40 min.

Pilaff with Pimento and Coriander [*Arroz Verde* Mexico] Using long-grain rice proceed as for pilaff, adding chopped fresh green chillies, green pimento and coriander leaves.

Pilaff with Saffron [*Riz Pilaff Safrané* France] Proceed as for pilaff with the addition of saffron infused in the chicken stock.

Pilaff with Saffron and Tomato [*Riz Pilaff à la Turque* France] Proceed as for pilaff with the addition of saffron infused in the chicken stock and tomato concassée.

Pilaff with Spices [*Yakhni Pilau* India] Proceed as for pilaff with the addition of grated ginger, saffron, garam masala, ground cardamom, rose-water and sultanas. Garnish with diced chicken, toasted flaked almonds, cooked peas and hard-boiled eggs.

Pilaff with Spinach [*Spanahorixo* Greece] Proceed as for pilaff, adding coarsely cut spinach to the sweated onion.

Pilaff with Tomato [*Arroz Rojo* Mexico] Using long-grain rice, proceed as for pilaff, with the addition of diced tomato flesh and tomato purée.

Risotto

Application

Using a ratio of 1 part rice and 3 parts chicken or vegetable stock, sweat chopped onion in oil, stir in the rice then moisten with ladlefuls of boiling stock in stages throughout the cooking process.

Risotto with Chicken Livers [*Pilaff Bokhari* Israel] Proceed as for risotto and garnish with sweated julienne of carrot with turmeric, diced fried chicken livers and tomato concassée.

Risotto with Cream Cheese and Pimento [*Arroz Poblano* Mexico] Proceed as for risotto with the addition of dried green chillies, garlic and chopped coriander leaves. Layer a dish with the cooked risotto, julienne of green and red pimento, soured cream and grated Cheddar cheese. Sprinkle the surface with grated cheese and gratinate.

Risotto with Fennel [*Risotto al Finocchi* Italy]   Proceed as for risotto with the addition of lardons of unsmoked bacon or pancetta and sliced fennel.

Risotto with Ham, Tongue and Mushrooms [*Risotto Milanaise* France] Proceed as for risotto, and garnish with julienne of ham, ox tongue and mushrooms. Serve with tomato sauce and grated Parmesan cheese.

Risotto with Lentils and Pine nuts [*Mejedrah* Turkey]   Proceed as for risotto with the addition of cooked whole brown lentils and fried pine nuts.

Risotto with Mushrooms [*Riz an Djon-Djon* Caribbean]   Proceed as for risotto with the addition of sliced dried mushrooms and diced salt pork, green pimento and ham. Garnish with prawns, chopped chives and parsley.

Risotto with Pistachio Nuts [*Dugun Pilav* Turkey]   Proceed as for risotto using beef stock and pistachio nuts added to the rice.

Risotto with Prawns [*Arroz con Camarones* Caribbean]   Proceed as for risotto with the addition of tomato concassée, crushed dried chillies, chopped coriander and paprika. Garnish with prawns.

Risotto with Saffron [*Risotto alla Milanese* Italy]   Proceed as for risotto, infusing saffron in chicken stock. When cooked add butter and grated Parmesan cheese.

Risotto with Saffron and Almonds [*Timman Zaffaran* Middle East]   Proceed as for risotto with the addition of saffron infused in rose-water. Garnish with fried diced lamb, slivered almonds and sultanas.

Risotto with Spinach [*Spanakorizo* Greece]   Proceed as for risotto with the addition of lemon juice and chopped dill and shredded spinach previously sweated in oil.

Risotto with Tomato [*Pillaff me Domates Glace* Greece]   Proceed as for risotto and serve moulded and masked with cooked tomato concassée made using plum tomatoes.

Chapter Seven

Single Hors-d'oeuvres and Salads

This chapter is divided into six main categories:

✧ Chopped Items ✧

✧ Pâtés and Terrines ✧

✧ Potted Items ✧

✧ Mousses ✧

✧ Warm Salads ✧

✧ Composite Salads ✧

Chopped Items

Chopped Chicken Liver and Salami [*Peverada Veneziana* Italy] Sauté chopped chicken livers and salami, fillets of anchovy and garlic with grated zest of lemon. Moisten with white wine and lemon juice and cook until reduced to a smooth consistency. Serve with grilled chicken.

Chopped Herring [*Gebackte Herring* Israel] Remove the heads and entrails of salt herrings, place the fish under running cold water for 1 hr and retain in cold water for 12 hr. Finely chop the flesh together with hard-boiled eggs, tart dessert apples and grated onion. Combine with fine matzo meal, vinegar, caster sugar and seasoning. Chill before using.

Chopped Liver [*Gebackte Leber* Israel] Sauté sliced onion in chicken fat then add chicken, calf's or ox liver and cook. Finely chop or pass through a fine mincer and add sieved hard-boiled egg. Serve chilled, sprinkled with sieved egg and chopped parsley accompanied by finger toast, challah or matzo.

Pâtés and Terrines

Country Pâté [*Terrine de Campagne* France] Blend to a coarse texture pig's liver, belly of pork, pork flesh and pork fat, adding mixed spice, brandy, white wine, garlic, bayleaf, thyme and seasoning; refrigerate for 12 hr. Mix in beaten eggs, melted butter and double cream and fill into a terrine previously lined with thin rashers of streaky bacon. Turn the ends over the top, cover with the lid and cook au bain-marie in the oven at 160 °C for 2.5 hr. Place under weight until cool then cover with a film of melted lard.

Fish Pâté in Brioche Pastry [*Pâté de Poisson en Croûte* France] Mix puréed sole with warm frangipane panada and egg whites and chill for 30 min. Add cream, chopped tarragon and dill and seasoning. Cut out two fish-shaped pieces of brioche pastry and cover one with the pâté, lay strips of fillet of salmon on top then cover with more pâté. Encase with the pastry, decorate and eggwash then bake at 200 °C for 40–45 min.

Game Pâté [*Terrine de Gibier* France] Cut the flesh of a hare into 1-cm pieces and marinate for 12 hr in brandy and mixed spice. Finely mince venison meat, lean pork and chicken livers, and mix in beaten eggs and the hare and its marinade. Line a terrine with thin slices of salt pork fat, half fill with the mixture, arrange strips of the pork fat along the length of the terrine and fill with the rest of the mixture. Turn in the overlapping slices of pork fat, cover with a lid and cook au bain-marie in the oven at 160 °C for 2.5 hr. Place under weight until cool then cover with a film of melted lard.

Game Terrine or Aylesbury Game Pie [GB] Marinate diced breast of chicken, pheasant, hare and veal flesh in brandy with thyme, bayleaf and sliced onion. Make a forcemeat with chicken legs and veal trimmings, the hare and pheasant livers and pork fat. Line a shallow earthenware dish with rashers of bacon, cover with alternate layers of forcemeat and the meats, finishing with forcemeat. Cover over with bacon, and place a sprig of thyme and bayleaf from the marinade on top. Cover with a lid and bake au bain-marie in the oven at 125 °C for 1·5 hr. When cooked, place under weight until cold.

Pâté Maison [*France*]   Sauté diced bacon and chopped onion then add chicken livers, diced lean pork, garlic, thyme, bayleaf and mixed spice. Finely mince then pass through a fine sieve, and add brandy, double cream and seasoning. Line terrines with thinly sliced bacon, place in the mixture and fold over the end of the bacon. Cover with a lid and cook au bain-marie in the oven at 125 °C for 2 hr. When cooked, place under a weight until cold.

Potted Items

Potted Avocado [*GB*]   Blend the flesh of avocado pears with garlic, onion, lime juice, tomato flesh, chilli powder, a pinch of fresh herbs and a few drops of Tabasco. Serve chilled, garnished with segments of lime.

Potted Beef [*GB*]   Layer small cubes of rump of beef in a terrine and season with ground cloves, salt, pepper and anchovy essence. Moisten with stock, cover with a lid and bake. When well cooked place under weight until cold then cover with clarified butter.

Potted Bloater [*GB*]   Poach bloaters in water then remove the flesh. Purée the flesh with lemon juice and butter to form a paste then season as necessary. Portion into ramekin dishes, cover with clarified butter and refrigerate.

Potted Char [*GB*]   Sauté fillets of char in hot butter. Arrange layers in a ravier, brushing each with melted butter, then cover with clarified butter and refrigerate.

Potted Duck [*GB*]   Cut breast of duck and belly of pork into small pieces, place in layers in a terrine and add sage leaves, sprig of thyme, mace, salt and pepper, and moisten with claret. Bake in the oven. When cooked place under weight until cold then cover with clarified butter.

Potted Goose [*Confit d'Oie France*]   Cut the flesh of a goose into small pieces and rub well with a mixture of coarse salt and a pinch each of saltpetre, powdered bayleaf, clove and thyme. Refrigerate for 24 hr. Gently sauté the goose in goose fat for 1.5 hr. Portion the flesh into ramekin dishes, cover with the cooking fat and refrigerate.

Potted Grouse [*GB*]   Rub cayenne and black pepper into breasts of grouse and place in a terrine on top of the giblets, necks and livers. Moisten with stock, cover with a lid and bake until well cooked. Mash the grouse meat and cooking liquid with butter and a little port; portion into ramekin dishes, cover with clarified butter and refrigerate.

Potted Hare [*GB*]   Cut the flesh of a hare into 5-cm pieces and soak in cold water and vinegar. Sauté the hare with chopped onion, bayleaf and garlic, cover with stock and cook for 2 hr. Finely mince the hare, and mix in melted butter, zest of lemon, nutmeg and dry sherry. Portion into ramekin dishes, cover with a layer of clarified butter and refrigerate. Serve accompanied with hot toast.

Potted Hough [*GB*]   Cut shin of beef into 5-cm pieces, cover with stock and cook. Chop or mince the meat, mix with the cooking liquor and season. Pour into a mould and refrigerate. De-mould and serve cut into slices.

Potted Oysters [*GB*]   Blend cooked oysters, anchovy fillets, lemon juice and butter. Portion into ramekin dishes, cover with clarified butter and refrigerate.

Potted Pigeon [*GB*]   Layer a terrine with alternate layers of slices of pigeon breasts and minced pork and pork fat seasoned with garlic, thyme, juniper berries and brandy; cover with a lid and bake. Cover with clarified butter and refrigerate.

Potted Pigeon and Walnuts [*GB*]   Combine the flesh from pot roasted pigeons with half its weight in shelled walnuts and pass through a fine mincer. Add butter and brandy. Fill into ramekin dishes, cover with clarified butter and refrigerate.

Potted Pork [***Sobrasada*** *Spain*]   Blend chorizo sausages, pork dripping, paprika, chopped marjoram and dry sherry to form a fine purée. Portion into ramekin dishes, cover with pork dripping and refrigerate.

Potted Salmon [*GB*]   Place fillets of salmon in a buttered dish, season and flavour with nutmeg, mace and cloves, and sprinkle with chopped shallots and anchovy fillets. Moisten with a little cream, add bayleaves, cover with kitchen foil and bake. Purée the fish, add butter and portion into ramekin dishes, cover with clarified butter and refrigerate.

Potted Shrimps [*GB*]   Warm peeled shrimps in frothing melted butter with salt, pepper and ground mace, portion into ramekins and refrigerate.

Potted Smoked Cod Roe [*GB*]   Blend smoked cod roe, sautéed shallots, vinegar and English mustard to a smooth paste. Portion into ramekin dishes, cover with clarified butter and refrigerate.

Potted Smoked Salmon [*Israel*]   Blend cream cheese, cream, garlic, zest of lemon and smoked salmon to a purée, and flavour with chopped chives, parsley and seasoning. Portion into ramekins and refrigerate.

Potted Smoked Salmon [*GB*]   Blend finely minced smoked salmon trimmings with butter, mixed herbs and Tabasco. Portion in ramekins and chill. Garnish with segments of lemon.

Potted Smoked Trout [*GB*]   Blend béchamel sauce, flaked smoked trout and sweated chopped onion to a purée, adding a little lemon juice and dry white wine. Fold in cream, portion into ramekins and refrigerate.

Potted Veal [***Papreikaspástéton*** *Hungary*]   Sauté chopped onion, add paprika and diced stewing veal, fry to colour then add tomato purée and a little veal stock. Simmer until tender then finely mince. Reheat the veal, add yolks of egg and cook to bind. Mix in butter, season, fill into ramekins and refrigerate.

Mousses

Carolina Shrimp Mousse [*USA*]   Combine a purée of shelled prawns, chopped celery and green and red pimentos, tomato purée, fish velouté or mayonnaise and a little soaked and melted leaf gelatine. When at setting point fold in stiffly beaten egg whites and pour into a mould. Refrigerate then turn out onto a dish coated with tomato-flavoured jelly and decorate with shrimps.

Chicken Liver Mousse [*GB*]   Soak chicken livers in milk for 8 hr. Sauté the livers in butter with thyme and bayleaf and blend to a fine purée. Allow to cool then mix in melted butter and double cream. Serve by the spoonful accompanied by hot toast.

Chicken Mousse [*Mousse de Volaille* France] Mince cooked chicken breast, add chicken velouté and aspic jelly, bring to the boil and season. Stir on ice until setting then add whipped double cream. Pour into dishes, decorate with diamonds of white of egg and truffle and cover with a layer of aspic jelly.

Crab Mousse [USA] Process crabmeat with egg yolks, lemon juice, brandy, mayonnaise and fish aspic jelly and flavour with a little curry powder. Fold in stiffly whisked whites of egg and pour into moulds. Serve with avocado and tomato sauce made by combining avocado flesh, garlic, lemon juice, soured cream and tomato ketchup.

Warm Salads

Asparagus with Mustard Dressing [*Asuparagasu Karashi-Ae* Japan] Moisten cooked sprue asparagus with warm mustard and egg dressing.

Bean and Potato Salad [USA] Sauté chopped onion, moisten with red wine vinegar and reduce. Toss in sliced cooked potato and diamonds of cooked French beans then add lardons of bacon.

Bean and Sesame Salad [*Sandomame Goma-Miso Ae* Japan] Blend toasted, ground sesame seeds with red miso, sugar and mirin then mix into cooked French beans.

Beetroot and Horseradish Salad [Russia] Boil wine vinegar with bayleaf, peppercorns and sugar then strain over sliced beetroot; sprinkle with grated horseradish and marinate. Mix the beetroot with oil and cream and heat through.

Bellflower Salad [*Torajisaengchae* Korea] Tear rootlets of soaked toraji, lightly fry them in sesame oil until tender then add cider vinegar, chilli powder, sugar, garlic and toasted sesame seeds.

Cabbage and Bacon Salad [*Weisskrautsalat* Germany] Blanch shredded white cabbage then drain and sprinkle with vinaigrette sauce. Crisp fry lardons of bacon and sprinkle over the cabbage together with chopped fresh herbs.

Celeriac Salad [*Selleriesalat* Germany] Cook batons of celeriac in beef stock with chopped onion, olive oil, wine vinegar, lemon juice and sugar, allowing the cooking liquid to reduce by half. Sprinkle with chopped walnuts.

Cucumber Salad [*Kūri no Sumomi* Japan] Sprinkle sliced cucumber with salt, then drain off the liquid. Simmer dashi flavoured with rice vinegar, dark soy sauce and sugar and pour over the cucumber, allow to macerate then squeeze out and retain the liquid. Moisten again with a little of the liquid and serve.

Dandelion Salad [*Löwenzahnsalat* Germany] Toss dandelion leaves in a dressing of warmed sesame oil, wine vinegar and sugar. Add diced boiled potato and crisp lardons of bacon.

Eggplant Salad [*Melintzanosaláta* Greece] Dice eggplant, bake then allow to cool. Combine the diced eggplant with diced tomato flesh, chopped onion and parsley then dress with olive oil and lemon juice.

Five Salad [*Goshiki Namasu* Japan] Combine blanched julienne of persimmons, daikon, carrots, French beans and grilled shiitake mushrooms with white miso dressing.

Goat Cheese Salad [*USA*]   Sprinkle cubes of goat's cheese with olive oil and retain for 12 hr. Sauté the cheese in oil then sprinkle it over shredded spinach leaves and top with crisp fried lardons of bacon. Serve accompanied by tarragon dressing.

Grapes in Mustard Dressing [*Masukatto Karashi-Ae Japan*]   Combine seedless muscat grapes with warm mustard dressing.

Mustard Dressing: mix dry English mustard to a paste with water, then stir in dashi, miso and light soy sauce and heat without boiling.

Mushroom and Vegetable Salad [*Salpicon de Hongos Mexico*]   Sauté the following in garlic-flavoured oil: chopped onion and fresh red chillies, brunoise of carrot, celery and green pimento, and sliced mushrooms. Sprinkle with lemon juice and chopped coriander and stew for 5 min.

Spinach and Bacon Salad [*GB*]   Crisp fry lardons of bacon and sliced mushrooms in hazelnut oil then add a few drops of cider vinegar, some chopped mixed herbs and fried diced bread croûtons. Pour the preparation over finely shredded spinach.

Spinach Salad [*Lalab Bayam Indonesia*]   Moisten coarsely shredded, blanched spinach with a hot dressing of sambal ulek, crushed garlic, lemon juice and seasoning.

Warm Potato Salad [*Kartoffelsalat Germany*]   Marinate sliced steamed jacket potatoes in a hot dressing of beef stock, olive oil, wine vinegar, mixed herbs, onion juice, Dijon mustard, sugar and seasoning.

Warm Potato Salad [*Varm Kartoffel Salat Scandinavia*]   Combine freshly cooked and sliced potato, chopped onion and warm diced ham with French dressing flavoured with a little sugar.

Wilted Green Salad [*USA*]   Whisk together eggs, water and red wine vinegar, pour into a hot pan brushed with bacon fat and stir until the sauce thickens. Pour over lettuce leaves and sprinkle with lemon juice.

Composite Salads

American Salad [*USA*]   Toss together leaves of crisp lettuce, sprigs of watercress, julienne of ham and Emmenthal cheese, quartered tomatoes and hard-boiled eggs, stoned black olives and chopped anchovy fillets with a dressing of sunflower oil, cider vinegar, Dijon mustard and seasoning.

Artichoke, Eggplant, Pimento and Tomato Salad [*Ensalada de Escalibada Spain*]   Combine baked strips of eggplant and red and green pimento, cooked and sliced artichoke bottoms, strips of tomato flesh, capers and sliced onion, moisten with lemon juice and olive oil and serve chilled.

Asparagus Salad [*Trigueros en Vinagrillo Spain*]   Marinate cooked sprue asparagus with red wine vinegar, olive oil, chopped garlic, paprika and seasoning.

Asparagus with Mustard and Egg Dressing [*Asuparagasu Karashi-Ae Japan*]   Moisten cooked sections of sprue asparagus with warm mustard and egg dressing.

Mustard and Egg Dressing: mix dry English mustard with a little water, whisk in a raw egg yolk and dark soy sauce.

Avocado and Beef Salad [*Salpicon de Res Poblano* *Mexico*]   Combine diced cooked beef, potato, Féta cheese, chopped fresh green chillies, onion and avocado balls with French dressing.

Bamboo Shoots and Pork Salad [*Yam No Mai Gup Moo* *Thailand*]   Blend shallots and garlic to a paste, wrap in foil and grill for 1 min. Combine the paste with bamboo shoots, nam pla, lime juice, sugar, chopped spring onions and slices of cooked pork. Serve on a bed of lettuce, sprinkled with dried chilli flakes and leaves of mint.

Banana Salad [*Caribbean*]   Combine slices of boiled unripe green bananas with strips of tomato flesh, julienne of cucumber, carrot and celery, and sliced avocado with mustard dressing.

Banana and Nut Salad [*Banan och Nöt Sallad* *Scandinavia*]   Combine sliced banana, lemon juice, chopped nuts and mayonnaise.

Bean Salad [*Foul Madumnas* *Middle East*]   Combine cooked haricot beans, chopped garlic, olive oil, lemon juice and sieved hard-boiled egg.

Beef and Coriander Salad [*Yam Neua* *Thailand*]   Blend garlic and fresh green chillies to a paste then add nam pla, lime juice and sugar. Dress strips of cooked beef on a bed of lettuce, sprinkle with chopped coriander and lemon grass and mask with the dressing.

Beetroot Salad [*Rote-Bete-Salat* *Germany*]   Combine diced beetroot and grated horseradish then toss with olive oil, wine vinegar, sugar, cumin and crushed mustard seeds. Allow to marinate then serve topped with sliced onion rings.

Beetroot, Nut, Olive and Egg Salad [*Rödbeta, Nöt, Oliv och Agg Sallad* *Scandinavia*]   Combine beetroot, chopped nuts and olives; sprinkle with a French dressing and serve sprinkled with chopped whites and yolks of hard-boiled eggs.

Beetroot, Walnut and Yogurt Salad [*Svyokla* *Russia*]   Grate beetroot and allow to drain in a colander then combine with yogurt, chopped walnuts and seasoning.

Cabbage Salad [*Salat Kruv-Shoshana* *Israel*]   Toss together shredded white and red cabbages, grapefruit segments, julienne of celeriac, apple and pimento and chopped walnuts. Combine with cream mixed with mayonnaise.

Cabbage Salad [*Lahanosaláta* *Greece*]   Toss together shredded cabbage and sliced onion with red wine, tarragon vinegar, sugar and seasoning.

Cabbage, Coconut Milk and Prawn Salad [*Yam Galumblee* *Thailand*]   Combine blanched shredded cabbage, diced cooked pork, fried chopped onion and garlic, crushed roasted peanuts, prawns, nam pla, lime juice and thick coconut milk.

Cabbage Salad with Coconut [*Lalab Kubis* *Indonesia*]   Brush between layers of blanched cabbage leaves with a dressing of lemon juice, soy sauce, sugar, sambal ulek, garlic and oil. Place them under weight then cut into fingers and serve sprinkled with desiccated coconut.

Cabbage and Cumin Salad [*Krautsalat* *Germany*]   Season shredded white cabbage with salt and pound to break down the fibres. Season with cumin, add white wine vinegar and serve sprinkled with sautéed lardons of bacon.

Cabbage and Celery Salad [*Salat s Kapustoi* *Russia*]   Sprinkle shredded cabbage with salt to reduce crispness then squeeze out excess moisture. Combine the cabbage with sliced celery, and sprinkle with a dressing of oil, lemon juice, a little sugar and seasoning.

Caesar Salad [*USA*]   Toss together lettuce leaves with olive oil and seasoning; break a 1-min boiled egg on top and moisten with lemon juice and Worcester sauce. Sprinkle with grated Parmesan cheese and fried diced bread croûtons cooked in garlic-flavoured olive oil, and mix gently.

Carrot and Apple Salad [*Gulróta-Eplisalat Scandinavia*]   Combine grated carrot and apple, raisins, cream and lemon juice, flavour with sugar and season to taste.

Carrot and Turnip Escabèche [*USA*]   Heat olive oil, white wine vinegar, garlic and seasoning then allow to cool. Pour the dressing over sliced cooked carrot and turnip then sprinkle with vodka and chopped parsley.

Cauliflower Salad [*Lalab Bunga Kol Indonesia*]   Moisten cooked cauliflower florets with a dressing of lemon juice, soy sauce and sambal ulek.

Cauliflower and Anchovy Salad [*Insalata di Rinforzo Italy*]   Combine blanched cauliflower florets with chopped fresh mixed herbs and anchovy fillets, stoned black olives, capers, quarters of hard-boiled egg and lemon dressing.

Cauliflower and Avocado Salad [*Ensalada de Coliflor Mexico*]   Moisten florets of cooked cauliflower with chilli mayonnaise dressing and serve topped with avocado dip and sprinkled with slivered almonds.

Chicken and Vegetable Salad [*Toriniku No Oroshi-Ae Japan*]   Sprinkle chicken fillets with saké, grill then cut into strips. Combine with strips of grilled mushroom, julienne of celery, grated daikon squeezed out to remove excess moisture, and blanched small florets of parsley. Dress in bowls moistened with a dressing made of light soy sauce and mirin, seasoned with monosodium glutamate.

Chickpea Salad [*Garbanzos Aliñados Spain*]   Combine cooked chickpeas with chopped onion, garlic, capers and parsley and moisten with red wine vinaigrette and seasoning.

Christmas Salad [*Jólasalat Scandinavia*]   Place shredded cabbage under weight to remove excess moisture. Combine cabbage with redcurrant jelly, rhubarb preserve and lemon juice.

Cod Fish Salad [*Empedrat Tarragoni Spain*]   Combine cooked and flaked dried salt cod with julienne of tomato flesh, cooked haricot beans, onion rings, quarters of hard-boiled egg, black olives, chopped parsley, red wine vinaigrette and seasoning.

Cole Slaw Salad [*Salat s Kapustoi Russia*]   Sprinkle shredded red cabbage with salt to reduce crispness then squeeze out excess moisture. Sprinkle with a dressing of oil, lemon juice, a little sugar and seasoning.

Cole Slaw Salad [*USA*]   Combine shredded white cabbage, chopped onion and green pimento and grated carrot with chilli mayonnaise and serve sprinkled with crisp fried lardons of bacon.

Corn Salad [*USA*]   Combine diced green pimento, celery, spring onions and tomato flesh and sweetcorn kernels then moisten with soured cream dressing.

Cracked Wheat Salad [*Tabbouleh Middle East*]   Combine soaked cracked wheat with chopped spring onions and mint, strips of tomato flesh, olive oil, lemon juice and seasoning.

Cucumber Salad [*Küri No Sumomi Japan*]   Sprinkle sliced peeled cucumber with salt then drain off the liquid. Simmer dashi flavoured with rice vinegar, dark soy sauce and sugar and pour over the cucumber, allow to macerate then squeeze out and discard the liquid. Moisten again with a little more fresh liquid and serve.

Cucumber Salad [*Oinamul Korea*]   Sprinkle salted and drained sliced cucumber with a dressing made with cider vinegar, sugar and chilli powder and mix together.

Cucumber Salad [*Pressgurka Israel*]   Combine salted and drained sliced cucumber with wine vinegar, sugar, caraway seeds and chopped dill.

Cucumber and Dill Salad [*Ogursty Russia*]   Combine sliced, salted and drained cucumber with soured cream, chopped dill and seasoning.

Cucumber and Yogurt Salad [*GB*]   Combine salted and drained sliced cucumber with a dressing of yogurt, cream, lemon juice, chopped mint and crushed garlic.

Cucumber and Yogurt Salad [*Khira Raita India*]   Combine salted and drained sliced cucumber with yogurt flavoured with garlic, grated ginger and lemon juice.

Cucumber in Yogurt Salad [*Angúri me Yaoúrti Greece*]   Combine yogurt, garlic, olive oil, seasoning and finely diced cucumber.

Cucumber, Yogurt and Dill Salad [*Tarator Israel*]   Combine diced cucumber with a dressing made with yogurt, garlic, olive oil, lemon juice and chopped dill.

Cucumber, Tomato and Féta Cheese Salad [*Salata Therini Greece*]   Combine salted and drained sliced cucumber with strips of tomato flesh, onion rings, julienne of green pimento, cubes of Féta cheese, stoned black olives and chopped parsley and marjoram with lemon dressing.

Eggplant 'Caviar' [*Baklazannaya Russia*]   Sauté chopped onion and garlic in oil, and add sliced tomato flesh and peeled and diced eggplant. Moisten with a little stock and allow to cook for approx. 10 min. Cool and serve accompanied by caviar and toasted bread fingers.

Eggplant Salad [*Kajinamul Korea*]   Moisten steamed and sliced peeled eggplant with a dressing of soy sauce, cider vinegar, sesame oil, chopped spring onion, garlic and toasted sesame seeds.

Endive with Blue Cheese Salad [*Endivias con Queso Cabrales Spain*]   Mix blue cheese with mayonnaise, spread onto endive leaves and sprinkle with chopped fresh herbs.

Fennel and Orange Salad [*Salade de Fenouil aux Oranges France*]   Combine julienne of raw fennel with orange segments and chopped walnuts mixed with lemon juice and walnut oil.

Fish Salad [*Salatit Samak Middle East*]   Combine poached and flaked white fish, boiled rice, sweated chopped onion, chopped anchovy fillets, stoned olives, soaked sultanas, diced tomato flesh and lemon juice.

French Bean and Coriander Salad [*Lalab Buncis Indonesia*]   Cook small whole or cut French beans in salted water with grated zest and juice of lemon; drain and cool. Moisten with a dressing of lemon juice, soy sauce, sugar, sambal ulek, garlic and oil. Garnish with diced tomato flesh and chopped coriander leaves.

French Bean and Sesame Salad [*Sandomame Goma-Miso Ae Japan*]   Blend toasted and ground sesame seeds with red miso, sugar and mirin then mix into cooked French beans.

Fruit and Herb Salad [*Yaam Polamai Thailand*]   Mix together halves of grapes, sliced lychees and water chestnuts, prawns, diced cooked chicken, lime juice, sugar, salt, crisply fried chopped garlic and shallots, crushed roasted peanuts, chopped coriander leaves and fresh red chillies.

Fruit and Prawn Salad [*Yaam Polamai* Thailand]   Combine segments of orange, diced apple, halves of grapes, sliced lychees and water chestnuts, prawns, crisp fried chopped garlic and shallots, crushed roasted peanuts and lime juice. Serve sprinkled with chopped coriander and fresh red chillies.

Fruit and Vegetable Salad [*Caribbean*]   Moisten diced pineapple, diced firm mangos, segments of orange, sliced bananas and diced cucumber with a dressing of crushed cloves of garlic, juice from the fruits, olive oil and chopped chives and seasoning. Serve on a bed of watercress and crisp lettuce leaves.

Grapefruit Salad [*USA*]   Sprinkle grapefruit segments with julienne of orange peel and red onion rings then moisten with orange dressing.

Ham, Cucumber and Potato Salad [*Skinke, Agurk og Kartoffel Salat* Scandinavia]   Combine diced ham, diced cooked potato, pickled cucumber, sliced cucumber and mayonnaise.

Herring Salad [*Sildesalat* Scandinavia]   Flavour béchamel sauce with vinegar from pickled beetroot, flavour with sugar, English mustard and curry powder then add grated onion and olive oil. Combine with soaked fillets of salted herrings cut on the slant, with diced cooked potato, beetroot and cooked meat, grated apple and sliced gherkin.

Herring, Beetroot and Apple Salad [*Sillsallad* Scandinavia]   Combine soaked fillets of salted herrings cut on the slant with diced apple, cooked potato, beetroot and cream. Flavour with sugar and season to taste.

Herring, Potato and Dill Pickle Salad [*Sillsallad* Scandinavia]   Combine soaked fillets of salted herring cut on the slant with diced cooked potato, beetroot, dill pickled gherkin, chopped onion and diced cooked veal. Moisten with French dressing and serve garnished with chopped hard-boiled egg and chopped dill.

Horseradish and Macaroni Salad [*Piparrótasalat meo Makkaronur* Scandinavia]   Combine cooked macaroni, grated horseradish and cream, flavour with sugar and season to taste.

Kohlrabi Salad [*Salat Kohlrabbi* Scandinavia]   Combine julienne of kohlrabi and stoned black olives with lemon dressing.

Lamb's Lettuce and Orange Salad [*Feldsalat mit Orangen* Germany]   Serve segments of oranges on lamb's lettuce, masked with lemon dressing.

Mango Salad [*Caribbean*]   Moisten diced firm mangos with a dressing of crushed cloves, garlic, lime juice, olive oil, chopped chives, a little sugar and seasoning.

Mango Salad [*Yam Ma Muang* Thailand]   Sauté sliced spring onions, garlic and strips of pork in oil, sprinkle with prawn powder, nam pla and roasted nibbed peanuts then combine with julienne of mangos and chopped fresh red chillies.

Mung Bean Salad [*Sukchunamul* Korea]   Moisten blanched mung beans with a dressing of soy sauce, sesame oil, garlic, red pepper threads and toasted sesame seeds.

Mushroom and Yogurt Salad [*Borani Garch* Middle East]   Combine sautéed sliced mushrooms and chopped onion with yogurt and dried mint.

Mushroom Salad [*Insalata di Funghi* Italy]   Moisten sliced raw mushrooms with lemon juice and olive oil then sprinkle with chopped hard-boiled egg yolk, parsley, anchovy fillets and garlic.

Mushroom Salad [*Sienisalaatti* Scandinavia]   Cook quarters of mushrooms in water with grated zest and juice of lemon, drain and cool then combine with chopped chives and cream and season to taste.

Mushroom, Sweetcorn and Pimento Salad [*Lalab Cendawan* Indonesia] Cook quarters of mushrooms in water with grated zest and juice of lemon, drain and cool then combine with cooked sweetcorn kernels and blanched strips of red pimento. Moisten with a dressing of lemon juice, soy sauce, sugar, sambal ulek, chopped shallots, garlic and oil.

Onion Salad [*Tamanegi No Sunomono* Japan] Soak thinly sliced onion in iced water for 30 min then drain. Flavour with a dressing made with rice vinegar, soy sauce and bonito flakes and serve.

Onion and Coriander Salad [*Piaz Ka Dhania Pattar Salat* India] Moisten sliced spring onions with lemon juice and sprinkle with chopped coriander leaves.

Onion Salad Parsi Style [*Kachumbar* India] Sprinkle chopped onion with salt, leave for 1 hr then drain off the liquid and rinse the onion in cold water. Combine the onion with tamarind liquid, palm sugar, tomato concassée, grated ginger, garam masala, sliced green chillies and chopped coriander leaves.

Onion, Tomato and Ginger Salad [*Kachumbar* India] Sprinkle sliced spring onions with salt, leave for 1 hr then drain off the liquid and rinse in cold water. Combine the onions with tamarind liquid, palm sugar, strips of tomato flesh, grated ginger, sliced fresh green chillies and chopped coriander leaves.

Orange Salad [*Bourekakia Salata* Greece] Season segments of orange with ground cinnamon and garnish with stoned black olives and sliced radishes; serve sprinkled with blanched grated zest of orange.

Orange Salad [*Insalata di Arance* Italy] Sprinkle segments of blood oranges with chopped shallots, grated blanched zest of oranges and olive oil.

Orange and Banana Salad [*Caribbean*] Combine segments of orange, sliced banana, strips of red pimento, olive oil, lemon juice and grated coconut.

Orange and Carrot Salad [*Israel*] Marinate grated carrot in orange and lemon juices and honey then combine with segments of orange, raisins and chopped mint.

Orange and Prawn Salad [*Pla Gung Sod Gup Som Keo Wan* Thailand] Combine orange segments, prawns, dried red chilli flakes, chopped mint and garlic, nam pla and lime juice.

Orange Salad with Pecan Dressing [*Ensalada de Naranja con Salsa de Nuez* Mexico] Combine orange segments and lettuce with a dressing of mayonnaise, soured cream, lime juice, sugar, ground pecan nuts and cinnamon.

Paw-Paw Salad [*Ensalada Paw Paw* Thailand] Marinate diced paw-paw and pineapple and sliced passion fruit in pineapple juice and rum.

Pimento and Tomato Salad [*Ensalada de Pimiento y Tomate* Spain] Moisten strips of pimento, sliced tomato and onion rings with French dressing, chopped anchovy and mixed herbs and marinate.

Pineapple Salad [*Lalab Nenas Muda* Indonesia] Sprinkle cubes of pineapple with salt and leave to drain in a colander. Combine the pineapple with strips of red pimento then moisten with a dressing of lemon juice, sambal ulek and sugar.

Pineapple and Pimento Salad [*Lalab Nenas Muda* Indonesia] Sprinkle diced unripe pineapple with salt and retain for 30 min then drain. Combine the pineapple with diced red pimento and chopped chives then moisten with a dressing made of 1 part Indonesian sweet soy sauce, 1 part lemon juice, sambal ulek and brown sugar.

Pinto Bean Salad [*Ensalada de Frijoles* Mexico]   Combine cooked pinto beans, diced celery and chopped onion, garlic and parsley. Season with ground cumin then toss together with mayonnaise made with lime juice and olive oil.

Potato Salad [*Kartoffelsalat* Germany]   Moisten coarsely grated steamed potatoes with hot beef stock then add chopped onion, mixed herbs, wine vinegar and olive oil and marinate.

Potato and Dill Salad [*Kartofelnyi Salat* Russia]   Moisten cooked diced potato with vinegar and oil, and add chopped onion, dill and seasoning.

Potato and Orange Salad [*Ensalada Valenciana* Spain]   Moisten cooked diced potato with red wine vinegar and olive oil, and add chopped onion, orange segments, strips of pimento and seasoning.

Radish Salad [*Muusaengchae* Korea]   Grate radishes, add salt and leave for 15 min. Drain and squeeze out the liquid. Add a dressing made of cider vinegar, sesame oil, ginger, sugar and chilli powder.

Radishes in Soured Cream [*Ritachlich mit Smeteneh* Israel]   Combine sliced radishes with soured cream mixed with wine vinegar and sugar.

Radishes and Dill in Soured Cream [*Rediska so Smetanoi* Russia]   Combine sliced radishes with sieved hard-boiled egg, chopped dill and soured cream.

Red Cabbage Salad [*Rotkrautsalat* Germany]   Combine shredded red cabbage, sliced dessert apples and onion, caraway seeds and sugar, then moisten with French dressing.

Rice Salad [*Ensalada de Arroz* Spain]   Combine cooked rice Spanish style with quarters of cooked mushrooms and moisten with French dressing with chopped anchovy and herbs.

Romaine Salad [*Ensalada de Romanita* Mexico]   Combine mashed anchovy fillets with grated Parmesan cheese, lime juice and Worcester sauce then toss together with leaves of cos lettuce and diced bread croûtons.

Seaweed Salad [*Miyoknamul* Korea]   Wash sliced seaweed, drain then moisten with a dressing of soy sauce, cider vinegar, sesame oil and toasted sesame seeds.

Soy Bean Sprout Salad [*Kongnamulmuchim* Korea]   Moisten blanched bean sprouts with a dressing of soy sauce, rice vinegar, sesame oil, toasted sesame seeds and sugar.

Spinach Salad [*Shigumchinamul* Korea]   Moisten blanched and coarsely shredded spinach with a dressing of soy sauce, toasted sesame seeds, sesame oil, garlic and sugar.

Spinach and Spiced Yogurt Salad [*Palak Raita* India]   Fry mustard seed in ghee, and when the seeds pop add cumin seeds, ground cumin, fenugreek seeds and chilli powder. Combine with yogurt and mix into cooked chopped spinach.

Spinach with Sesame Dressing [*Horenso no Goma-Ae* Japan]   Combine blanched and coarsely shredded spinach with sesame dressing.

Sweet and Sour Eggs [Israel]   Marinate sliced hard-boiled eggs in olive oil and cider vinegar with chopped onion, salt, black pepper and sugar. Serve accompanied by sweet beetroot preserve.

Tomato and Anchovy Salad [*Salade de Tomate et Anchois* France]   Sprinkle sliced tomatoes with chopped anchovies and their oil and chopped fresh mixed herbs.

Tomato and Dill Salad [*Tomaty* Russia] Sprinkle sliced tomato with chopped dill and seasoning.

Tomato and Mint Salad [*Tamatar Salat* India] Sprinkle sliced tomatoes with lemon juice, chopped mint leaves, sugar, chilli powder and chopped spring onions.

Tomato and Onion Salad [*Kachoombar* India] Combine strips of tomato flesh with chopped spring onions, fresh green chillies, coriander and mint leaves, lemon juice and sugar.

Vegetable and Lime Salad [*Ensalada Mixta* Mexico] Combine diced cooked carrot, beetroot and potato, diamonds of French beans, peas, strips of tomato flesh and sliced cucumber, then moisten with lime dressing and sprinkle with chopped coriander leaves.

Water Chestnut and Prawn Salad [*Yam Krachup* Thailand] Sauté sliced onion in oil, cool then mix with strips of water chestnuts, nam pla, sugar, lemon juice, prawns, diced cooked pork, crabmeat and chopped coriander leaves and fresh red chillies.

Watercress Salad [*Minarinamul* Korea] Moisten blanched and chopped watercress with a dressing of soy sauce, toasted sesame seeds, sesame oil, garlic and sugar.

Chapter Eight

Fish Dishes

In this chapter fish dishes are assigned to nine main areas according to method of cookery:

✧ Baked Fish ✧

✧ Deep-fried Fish ✧

✧ Deep-poached and Boiled Fish ✧

✧ Grilled Fish ✧

✧ Marinated and Pickled Fish ✧

✧ Shallow-fried Fish ✧

✧ Shallow-poached Fish ✧

✧ Steamed Fish ✧

✧ Stewed Fish ✧

Allow the following amounts of prepared raw fish per portion:

85–100 g – fillets, suprêmes and goujons
150–200 g – cuts of fish on the bone, e.g. tronçons, steaks (darnes)
200–250 g – whole small fish, e.g. herring, mackerel, mullet, trout

Cuts of fish suggested in this section are intended as a guide and may be substituted by others.

Baked Fish

Application

Cook whole or portions of fish moistened with a marinade, oil, sauce, wine or oil by dry heat in the oven at 180–200 °C until coloured golden brown.

Fish can also be baked in parcels – cut kitchen foil into a heart shape, brush with oil, enrobe the fish with any garnish, and fold and pleat the foil to seal. Bake in the oven at 175 °C for approx. 20 min according to size.

Baked Carp in Cider [*Pechionyi Karp v Pive Russia*]   Place a carp into a shallow dish, sprinkle with sweated diced carrot and onion, moisten with a little cider and bake. Reduce the liquor by two-thirds and finish with cream. Mask the fish with the sauce and serve.

Baked Fillet of Bream and Cod [*Caldeirada Estilo Nazaré Portugal*]   Fry chopped onion in oil then add diced tomato flesh, red pimento and garlic, moisten with white wine and add a bayleaf and some saffron. Place fillets of cod and bream, allowing one of each per portion, in a shallow dish, moisten with the sauce and bake.

Baked Fillet of Cod with Fresh Herbs [*USA*]   Place cooked fillets of cod on a base of sautéed chopped onion, sprinkle with chopped mixed herbs and paprika, coat with cream then bake.

Baked Fillet of Cod with Sauerkraut [*Fisch mit Sauerkraut Germany*]   Place sauerkraut into a shallow dish, arrange fillets of cod on top and moisten with milk; sprinkle with butter and bake.

Baked Fillet of Cod with Vegetables [*Samak Yakhin Middle East*]   Marinate fillets of cod in lemon juice, cumin seeds, salt and pepper. Sauté chopped onion and garlic in olive oil, add chopped parsley and celery leaves, diced tomato flesh and a bayleaf and cook. Coat over the marinated fish and bake in the usual way.

Baked Fillet of Flounder with Almonds [*Filletes de Lenguado con Almendra Spain*]   Blend sautéed chopped onion and garlic, golden fried bread slices, blanched almonds, chopped parsley, white wine and fish stock to a coarse mixture. Boil the mixture for 5 min then blend and reserve. Cut potatoes into 5-mm thick slices and shallow fry in oil until cooked but only lightly browned, drain and transfer to a shallow dish. Shallow fry flounder fillets in oil then place them on top of the potatoes. Mask the fish with the almond-flavoured mixture and bake.

Baked Fillet of Haddock [*USA*]   Pass fillets of haddock through flour, milk and breadcrumbs mixed with chopped fresh herbs, then shallow fry. Place in a dish, sprinkle with red wine vinegar and bake.

Baked Fillet of Hake with Anchovies and Rosemary [*Nasella alla Palermitana Italy*]   Place fillets in a shallow dish on sprigs of rosemary dipped in oil. Lightly sauté anchovy fillets in oil, mash them and mask over the fish. Sprinkle with bread-crumbs, chopped parsley, grated zest and juice of lemon and butter, and bake.

Baked Fillet of Hake with Asparagus [*Merluza a la Vasca Spain*]   Place fillets of hake in a buttered shallow dish, moisten with white wine fish sauce diluted with fish stock and add sweated chopped onion and garlic. Bake in the oven and serve garnished with asparagus tips and chopped hard-boiled egg.

Baked Fillet of Hake with Potatoes and Cider [*Merluza a la Sidra Spain*]   Golden fry sliced potato and garlic in olive oil, drain off the oil then place in a dish; place fillets of hake on top, season with paprika and moisten with cider and fish stock. Bake until cooked and golden brown.

Baked Fillet of Mackerel in Cider with Gooseberry Sauce [*GB*]   Butter and season a dish with salt and add peppercorns. Place rolled fillets of mackerel secured with cocktail sticks with a bayleaf attached in a baking dish. Moisten with dry cider, brush with butter, cover with foil and bake. Serve accompanied by gooseberry sauce.

Baked Fillet of Plaice with Spinach [*Rauosprettur meo Spinati Scandinavia*]   Place cooked, chopped and seasoned spinach into a shallow buttered and seasoned dish, arrange fillets of plaice on top, coat with cheese sauce, sprinkle with breadcrumbs, grated zest of lemon and melted butter and bake until golden.

Baked Fillet of Salmon-trout in Ham [*Truite-saumonée au Jambon France*]   Wrap fillets of salmon-trout in sliced ham, place in a shallow buttered dish, moisten with fish stock and bake until almost cooked. Drain off the liquid, add cream and pour back over the fish. Bake until fully cooked. Serve sprinkled with chopped chives.

Baked Fillet of Swordfish with Tomato and Olives [*Agghiotta di Pesce Spada Italy*]   Shallow fry fillets of swordfish in olive oil then transfer to a shallow dish. Sauté chopped garlic and celery in oil, add diced tomato flesh and soaked raisins, pine nuts, stoned green olives and a bayleaf and cook. Coat the fish with the tomato mixture, cover and bake.

Baked Fish Terrine [*Fiskfärs Scandinavia*]   Combine finely minced raw white fish, anchovy fillets, beaten eggs and seasoning. Mix in flour to bind then add cream to form a light mixture. Fill buttered terrines with the mixture, sprinkle with breadcrumbs and bake au bain-marie for approx. 1 hr. Serve garnished with lemon wedges, prawns and dill.

Baked Goujons of Cod in Cider [*GB*]   Butter a shallow dish and fill with alternate layers of sliced potato, goujons of cod and tomato concassée. Sprinkle the top layer of sliced potato with grated cheese and butter, moisten the dish with cider and fish stock and bake.

Baked Goujons of Cod with Vegetables [*Dum Muchli India*]   Marinate goujons of cod in a liquidised mixture of yogurt, ground coriander, cinnamon, cardamoms, cloves, chickpea flour, aniseed, chopped shallots and saffron. Shallow fry the goujons in ghee, transfer to a dish and cover with a layer of sliced baby marrow and julienne of carrot. Moisten with the marinade paste and bake in the oven.

Baked Herring in Cream [*Forshmak* Russia] Combine finely minced fillets of herring with lightly sautéed chopped onion, milk-soaked and squeezed breadcrumbs, grated apple, cream and seasoning. Place mixture into a shallow dish, sprinkle with breadcrumbs, grated nutmeg, zest of lemon and butter and bake for approx. 30 min.

Baked Lobster [*Istakoz Firinda* Greece] Lightly fry chopped onion and garlic in olive oil, stir in paprika, chopped parsley and dill then moisten with soured cream and add diced lobster flesh. Fill the half lobster shells with the mixture and bake.

Baked Lumpenfish and Dill Moulds [*Kaviarlada* Scandinavia] Boil cream, pour onto white breadcrumbs and cool. Add lumpenfish roe, dill and lightly beaten eggs. Pour into buttered and seasoned ramekins and bake au bain-marie.

Baked Mackerel and Prawn Parcels [*Saba No Ginshiyaki* Japan] Marinate fillets of mackerel and prawns in red wine, mirin and soy sauce. Enrobe each piece of fish with duxelle of shiitake mushrooms moistened with soy sauce and flavoured with sugar. Seal in foil wrappers and bake.

Baked Mussels [*Gratin de Moules* France] Sweat chopped shallot, add cleaned mussels and dry white wine, cover with a lid and boil for 5 min, then reduce the liquor. Open and spread the mussels with a mixture of chopped shallots, crushed garlic, chopped parsley and butter, place in a serving dish then surround with the liquor, sprinkle with curry powder and breadcrumbs and gratinate.

Baked Pike with Soured Cabbage [*Fogas Varza Calita* Hungary] Lightly fry bayleaf in oil, add tomato purée, moisten with white wine then add finely shredded cabbage, crushed peppercorns, juniper berries and rubbed thyme. Place into an earthenware dish and braise in an oven for approx. 45 min. Place fillet of pike on top of the cabbage, brush with oil and bake for 1 hr until lightly golden.

Baked Red Mullet Parcels [*Samak Maschwi* Middle East] Shallow fry red mullet in olive oil, seal in foil wrappers and bake. Serve accompanied with a lemon dressing.

Baked Salt Codfish with Tomato and Pimento [*Bacalhau Dourado* Portugal] Sweat chopped onion in olive oil, add diced red pimento and tomato flesh, chopped parsley and garlic then moisten with white wine. Shallow fry the previously soaked fish in olive oil, flake it then place into a shallow dish. Mask with the sauce, sprinkle with sieved hard-boiled egg and bake.

Baked Sardines [*Psari Riyànato* Greece] Place sardines in a shallow dish, moisten with lemon juice and olive oil, add chopped oregano and salt then bake.

Baked Skate with Sauerkraut [*Rochen mit Sauerkraut* Germany] Poach skate portions in milk flavoured with cloves, bayleaf and peppercorns. Drain the fish, pass through butter and flour, wrap in foil and bake. Serve with sauerkraut.

Baked Snapper Parcels [*Ikann Bandeng* Indonesia] Marinate suprêmes of snapper with sambal bajak, turmeric and soy sauce. Wrap the fish in foil wrappers with some of the marinade and bake.

Baked Spiced Mackerel Parcels [*Mulu 'Minah'* India] Marinate fillets of mackerel in lemon juice, turmeric, bayleaf and thyme. Blend chopped shallots, garlic, curry powder, chilli powder and water to a paste. Enrobe the fish with the paste, seal in foil wrappers with some of the marinade and bake.

Baked Stuffed Bream [*Farshirovanyi Lieshch* Russia] Stuff a whole bream with cooked buckwheat combined with golden fried chopped onion, chopped hard-boiled eggs and raw egg to bind. Place it in a shallow dish, moisten with crème fraîche and bake.

Baked Stuffed Mackerel Parcels [*Hel-Fisk i Kapprock* Scandinavia] Mix together butter, chopped chives, parsley, onion and lemon juice to make the stuffing. Remove the backbone from the mackerel, open up and fill the cavity with the stuffing. Wrap the fish in foil wrappers and bake.

Baked Stuffed Monkfish [*Mahi Now Rooz* Middle East] Sauté chopped onion in samneh, add sugar and allow to melt, then add blanched shredded spinach, sultanas, chopped dates, diced tomato flesh, quarters of dried lime and barberries to form a stuffing. Use it to stuff a monkfish, cover with a mixture of yogurt, tomato ketchup, garlic, turmeric, cinnamon and chopped walnuts, then bake. Serve with a sprinkling of chopped mint and wedges of lime.

Baked Stuffed Pike [*Brocheton à la Quincy* France] Combine breadcrumbs, chopped fresh herbs and beaten eggs. Stuff a small boned pike with the mixture and place in a shallow dish on a base of sautéed sliced onion. Moisten with white wine and bake. Liquidise the onion and the cooking liquor to form a sauce, enrich with butter and mask over the fish.

Baked Stuffed Rainbow Trout [*Pesxado Relleno* Mexico] Sweat chopped onion in oil, add diced tomato flesh and potato and cook, then add capers, lime juice and chopped almonds. Stuff a boned trout with this mixture and bake.

Baked Stuffed Sardines [*Sarde Ripiene* Italy] Remove the backbones and stuff sardines with a mixture of breadcrumbs, parsley, capers, garlic and Parmesan cheese. Place into an oiled dish, sprinkle with breadcrumbs and Parmesan cheese and bake.

Baked Stuffed Squid [*Calamari Ripieni al Forno* Italy] Combine chopped boiled squid tentacles with chopped anchovies, garlic, mixed fresh herbs, eggs, zest and juice of lemon, breadcrumbs and seasoning. Stuff the squid with this mixture, sew up and bake. Garnish with leaves of fennel.

Baked Stuffed Trout [GB] Stuff a boned trout with veal forcemeat, place in a buttered dish, moisten with white wine and fish stock and bake. Serve coated with white wine fish sauce containing chopped capers and seasoned with nutmeg, anchovy essence and lemon juice.

Baked Suprême of Halibut [*Fischragout* Germany] Season the base of a shallow dish, sprinkle with salt and pepper, and add chopped shallots and parsley and sliced mushrooms. Place suprêmes of halibut on top, moisten with white wine and fish stock, sprinkle with breadcrumbs, grated zest of lemon and oil and bake.

Baked Suprême of Halibut with Tahina and Walnuts [*Samak Bil Rashi* Middle East] Marinate halibut suprêmes with lemon juice then golden shallow fry in olive oil. Place the fish in a shallow dish, spread with a paste made of sautéed chopped onion, chopped walnuts, tahina, lemon juice and water then bake gently.

Baked Suprême of Salmon with Cream and Cucumber [GB] Place salmon suprêmes in a buttered dish, cover with sliced cucumber, moisten with lemon juice and cream and bake.

Baked Suprême of Swordfish with Tomato and Herbs [*Sarde à Beccafico* Mexico] Shallow fry suprêmes of swordfish and place in a dish. Sweat shallots,

garlic, brunoise of celery and white of leek, tomato concassée, bayleaf, pine
nuts, capers and stoned green olives; pour over the fish and bake. Garnish with
seeded white grapes and chopped fresh herbs.

Baked Trout [*Israel*] Place trout in a shallow dish, sprinkle with salt, pepper,
lemon juice and sliced onion and coat with soured cream. Bake until golden
and serve.

Coulibiac of Salmon [*Kulebiaka Russia*] Lightly fry suprêmes of salmon then
add cooked and chopped vésiga. Roll out puff pastry to the required size, spread
with cooked rice, then with alternate layers of sautéed chopped mushrooms,
chopped hard-boiled eggs, and the fish and vésiga. Encase in the pastry and
bake. When cooked pour melted butter into a hole in the top.

Crab Turnovers [*USA*] Sweat chopped onion, garlic, green pimento and celery.
Add tomato sauce and crabmeat and finish with cream. Fill 10-cm diameter
pieces of sweetened short pastry with the mixture, fold over to seal, brush with
cream and bake.

Red Mullet in Parcels [*Pepesan Ikan Indonesia*] Marinate red mullet in lemon
juice with bayleaf, thyme and seasoning. Shallow fry the fish and retain. Blend
roasted candel nuts, ginger, shallot, sambal ulek, water, tomato concassée and
red pimento to a paste. Enrobe the fish with the paste, seal in foil wrappers
with the marinade and bake.

Snails Burgundy Style [*Escargots à la Bourguignonne France*] Combine butter, chopped shallots, garlic, parsley, chervil, lemon juice and Pernod. Half fill
snail shells with the mixture, place in a cooked snail and seal with more butter.
Heat in the oven and serve with French bread.

Sole and Oyster Custard [*GB*] Butter a dish and sprinkle with breadcrumbs and
chopped mixed herbs, place in fillets of sole and oysters and cover with savoury
egg custard. Sprinkle with breadcrumbs and chopped mixed herbs and bake.

Soused Herring [*Israel*] Layer herring fillets with onion rings, roll up tail to head
and pack in a dish. Add onion rings, vinegar, peppercorns, bayleaf, mace, sugar,
salt and corn syrup. Bake until the liquor has reduced by half. Serve chilled.

Deep-fried Fish

Application

Deep frying involves cooking small cuts of fish in oil or fat at high temperature
with the fish totally immersed in the fat. To prevent fat penetrating the fish during
cooking, all deep-fried fish must have some form of outer coating.

Assortment of Fried Fish [*Fritura de Pescado Spain*] Pass goujons of red mullet, halibut and squid through flour then deep fry in olive oil and serve garnished with segments of lemon.

Fried Clams [*Ameijoas Fritas Portugal*] Pass shelled clams through massa
vinhe batter then fry in olive oil and serve accompanied by tomato sauce.

Fried Codfish with Garlic Sauce [*Bakaliáros Tiganitós Skorthaliá Greece*] Cut
soaked codfish into goujons, pass through flour and batter (Kourkoúti-
Salangoúta) then golden fry in olive oil. Mask the fish with garlic sauce and serve.

Fried Fillets of Herring Norfolk Style [GB]   Coat the fillets of herring with semolina, deep fry and serve with segments of lemon.

Fried Fillet of Plaice with Sweet and Sour Sauce [*Pla Priou Wan Khing Thailand*]   Marinate fillets of plaice in lemon juice. Pass through oil and corn-flour and deep fry. Serve with the following sauce: blend fresh red chillies and water to a paste then fry in oil for 2 min; add a julienne of spring onions and moisten with a reduction of wine vinegar, grated ginger and soft brown sugar, then finish with nam pla and sesame oil. Garnish with cucumber fans.

Fried Fish Balls [*Fiskbullar* Scandinavia]   Boil fillet of halibut, salt cod and pota-toes together. Drain and mash, add knobs of butter, beaten eggs, lemon juice, juice from chopped and squeezed onion, a little flour and seasoning. Spoon-mould the mixture, drop into hot fat and fry in oil until golden. Serve garnished with wedges of lemon and sprigs of dill.

Fried Fish with Sweet and Sour Sauce [*Gwoo Lo Yue Lau* China]   Rub goujons of white fish with five-spice powder and salt, then pass through eggwash and cornflour and fry in groundnut oil. Serve coated with the following sauce: boil soy sauce, Chinese tomato sauce, saké and wine vinegar then add crushed gar-lic, grated ginger, carrot and onion and simmer for 2 min, then thicken with arrowroot. Garnish the goujons with sliced cucumber, melon or cooked pump-kin pieces.

Fried Lobster with Pineapple [*Tong Cho Loong Har* China]   Marinade pieces of lobster tail in soy sauce with a little sugar and salt for 20 min. Dip the pieces of lobster in beaten egg and deep fry until lightly golden. Serve the lobster pieces immersed in pineapple sauce, accompanied by boiled rice and prawn crackers.
    Pineapple sauce: simmer together peanut oil, vinegar, a little sugar and pine-apple pieces, and thicken with diluted cornflour to form a light sauce.

Fried Oysters [*Kaki No Koganeyaki* Japan]   Blanch spinach, drain, roll in a cloth and cut into 1-cm thick slices. Marinate oysters in saké for 5 min, drain then pass through flour then beaten egg and deep fry until lightly golden. Serve garnished with the spinach slices.

Fried Plaice [*Karei No Karaage* Japan]   Score small plaice diamond fashion, pass through flour and deep fry in oil. Finely grate peeled daikon, add dried red chilli pepper, mix together then squeeze out excess moisture. Garnish the fish with the grated daikon and strips of spring onion, accompanied by the dipping sauce.
    Dipping sauce: flavour moisture extracted from the daikon with soy sauce and second soup stock.

Fried Prawns [*Saeutwigim* Korea]   Pass shelled prawns through a light batter of flour, egg, water and toasted sesame seeds and deep fry in oil. Serve accom-panied by chojang vinegar.

Fried Salt Codfish with Garlic Sauce [*Bakaliaros Skorthalia* Greece]   Pass portions of soaked salt cod through batter and deep fry. Serve accompanied by garlic sauce and radishes.

Fried Sardines [*Sardinhas Fritas* Portugal]   Split, remove backbones and heads then pass through flour, eggwash and breadcrumbs combined with crushed gar-lic. Deep fry in olive oil.

Fried Scallops [GB]   Marinate scallops in olive oil, lemon juice and chopped parsley. Pass through flour, eggwash and a mixture of breadcrumbs, chopped onion, grated cheese and minced ham. Deep fry, sprinkle with lemon juice and serve with segments of lemon and deep-fried parsley.

Fried Shrimp [*USA*]   Pass shrimps through garlic-flavoured mayonnaise thinned with milk then through breadcrumbs mixed with chopped fresh herbs. Deep fry in the usual manner.

Fried Smelts in Pickle [*Inlagd Stekt Strömming* *Scandinavia*]   Pass filleted smelts through flour, eggwash and breadcrumbs and deep fry them in butter. Drain well and marinate in brine of vinegar, sugar, chopped parsley and dill and seasoning for approx. 2 hr. Serve with some of the marinade garnished with fresh dill.

Fried Squid [*Calamares Fritos* *Spain*]   Cut a squid into rings and the tentacles into lengths, pass through flour and beaten egg then deep fry in mixed olive oil and sunflower oil. Serve with segments of lemon.

Fried Stuffed Fillet of Plaice [*Riga Tel'noe* *Russia*]   Marinate fillets of plaice in oil, lemon juice, chopped dill and parsley for 1 hr. Spread fillets with duxelle of mushrooms then roll them up and secure with a cocktail stick. Pass through seasoned flour, eggwash and breadcrumbs, deep fry in oil and serve garnished with picked parsley.

Golden Fried Baby Squid [*Kalamarakia* *Greece*]   Pass whole baby squid through seasoned flour and deep fry in olive oil. Sprinkle with lemon juice and serve with segments of lemon and deep-fried parsley.

Goujons of Whiting in Sesame Seeds [*Tomi Gun* *Korea*]   Rub goujons of whiting with salt then pass through a cornflour and egg batter. Deep fry and serve sprinkled with toasted sesame seeds.

Noodle-coated Prawns [*Ebi No Shibaage* *Japan*]   Sprinkle prawn tails with salt and saké and pass through cornflour diluted with a little saké, then through eggwash and broken fine noodles. Deep fry in hot oil and serve.

Prawn Butterflies [*Woo Dip Har* *China*]   Prepare prawns butterfly-fashion and marinate in saké, light soy sauce, crushed garlic, grated ginger and salt. Pass the prawns through cornflour, eggwash and breadcrumbs then deep fry in peanut oil. Serve with segments of lemon and accompany with chilli sauce.

Prawn and Potato Balls [*Caribbean*]   Combine dry mashed potato, butter, egg yolks, grated Cheddar cheese, chopped parsley, sweated chopped onion, prawns and seasoning. Form into small balls, pass through flour, eggwash and breadcrumbs then deep fry. Serve with segments of lemon.

Prawns in Beer Batter [*Gambas con Gabardina* *Spain*]   Make a batter of plain flour, light ale, salt and a few strands of infused saffron. Pass peeled king prawns through this batter and deep fry. Serve with segments of lemon.

Seafood and Vegetables in Batter [*Tempura* *Japan*]   Golden deep fry the following in tempura batter: goujons of sole, large peeled prawns, scallops, sliced squid, slices of eggplant, button mushrooms, squares of green pimento and squares of dried lava seaweed, keeping them slightly soft. Serve accompanied by tempura dip.

Spring Rolls with Scallop [*Dai Tze Guen* *China*]   Combine sliced scallops, chopped dried mushrooms, water chestnuts, spring onions, grated ginger, light soy sauce, sesame oil and seasoning. Enrobe portions of this filling in spring roll wrappers then deep fry in peanut oil.

Deep-poached Fish

Application

Deep poaching fish (which may also be termed boiling fish) means cooking fish completely submerged in a cooking liquid at just below boiling point.

Court-bouillon for poaching fish

Simmer all of the following ingredients in salted water for 20 min then strain: vinegar, sliced carrot and onion, thyme, bayleaf, parsley stalks and peppercorns.

Blue Eel [*Blau Aal* Germany]   Season an unskinned eel with salt then marinate in hot tarragon vinegar. Cut into sections and poach in court-bouillon. Serve accompanied by melted butter.

Boiled Carp [*Carpion Me'vushal* Israel]   Rub a carp with salt and retain for 30 min, then cut into portions. Poach the fish in water with salt, pepper, sugar, shredded almonds and raisins. Serve with some of the reduced cooking liquid.

Boiled Halibut Steaks with Saffron Rice [*Plov* Russia]   Poach steaks in water with onion, carrot, parsnip, peppercorns, bayleaf and salt for approx. 10 min. Transfer the fish to a buttered earthenware dish, sprinkle with chopped onion, chopped dill, crushed fennel seeds and a little saffron or turmeric, moisten with cream and steam. Make a risotto with the vegetables and liquor in which the fish was cooked, with the addition of a little saffron. Serve the fish accompanied by the rice, sprinkled with grated zest of lemon on top.

Boiled Herring with Dill and Horseradish Dressing [*Selyodka Kortoshkoi* Russia]   Poach the fish in water and serve with some of the cooking liquid, garnished with boiled potatoes and accompanied by horseradish sauce combined with chopped dill.

Clams in White Wine [*Ameijoas a Nazaré* Portugal]   Cook clams in white wine and fish stock with chopped shallots and parsley. Liquidise the liquid with the shallots and serve the clams in their shells, moistened with the liquor and sprinkled with lemon juice.

Fried Stuffed Fillet of Plaice [*Riga Tel'noe* Russia]   Marinate fillets of plaice in oil, lemon juice, chopped dill and parsley for 1 hr. Spread fillets with duxelle of mushrooms then roll them up and secure with a cocktail stick. Pass through seasoned flour, eggwash and breadcrumbs

Gefillte Fish [Israel]   Combine 2 parts minced hake with 1 part each of minced haddock and cod, and add grated onion, beaten eggs, ground almonds, medium matzo meal, parsley, eggs to bind and seasoning. Mould the mixture into balls and place in gently simmering fish stock with sliced carrot, onion, sugar, and salt for 1.5 hr. Reduce the liquor by half. Allow to get cold and serve with the jellied liquor, accompanied by chollah or matzo.

Jellied Salmon [*Lax i Gelé* Scandinavia]   Poach goujons of salmon in water with allspice, bayleaf, sliced carrot and onion and seasoning. Drain then strain the cooking liquid, and add soaked leaf gelatin. Place the goujons into moulds, fill with the liquid and allow to set in a refrigerator. When set, turn out onto a serving dish and garnish with sprigs of fresh herbs.

Kedgeree [*GB*]   Poach smoked haddock in water, drain, skin and flake then combine loosely with risotto made with fish stock, diced hard-boiled egg and diced tomato flesh. Serve the mixture in a dish, sprinkled with chopped parsley and accompanied by curry sauce.

Mussels in Sherry [*Mejillones a la Marinera* Spain]   Sauté chopped onion and garlic in oil, add mussels and chopped parsley, moisten with sherry and cook until the shells open. Serve in the half shells with the reduced cooking liquor.

Mussels with Lemon [*'Mpepata di Cozze* Italy]   Cook mussels with garlic, white wine, fish stock, segments of lemon, crushed peppercorns and chopped parsley. Serve in the half shells with the reduced cooking liquor.

Poached Bass with Ginger Sauce [*Gung Pin Loo Yu* China]   Poach bass steaks in salted water with lemon juice. Serve the drained fish coated with ginger sauce and garnished with chopped spring onions.

Ginger sauce: combine sesame oil, soy sauce and grated ginger.

Poached Cuttlefish with Ink [*Chocos com Tinta* Portugal]   Golden fry chopped garlic in olive oil then add breadcrumbs and sauté. Add prepared cuttlefish, moisten with a little water, season with paprika then poach. Serve accompanied by boiled potatoes.

Poached Darne of Carp [*Israel*]   Simmer darnes of carp in fish stock made from the trimmings and blood from the carp. When cooked, reduce the cooking liquor by half, strain over the fish and refrigerate. Serve accompanied by sweet beetroot relish.

Poached Darne of Salmon with Dill Sauce [*USA*]   Poach a darne of salmon in white wine and fish stock; serve accompanied by dill sauce.

Poached Eel in Dill Sauce [*Aal in Grüner Sobe* Germany]   Cut prepared eels into sections, rub with salt then marinate in hot wine vinegar. Poach the eel in court-bouillon made with the wine vinegar and serve accompanied by white wine fish sauce containing chopped dill.

Poached Herring [*GB*]   Poach a herring in salted water and serve garnished with plain boiled potatoes accompanied by mustard sauce or horseradish sauce.

Poached Octopus with Rice [*Polvo com Arroz* Portugal]   Sauté chopped onion in olive oil, and add chopped parsley and octopus pieces. Moisten with white wine vinegar and water to cover, flavour with chilli powder then poach. Season with salt and serve with risotto made with the liquor in which the octopus has been cooked.

Poached Red Mullet with Fennel [*GB*]   Sprinkle a dish with chopped fennel, parsley and shallots, place in a red mullet, moisten with white wine, fish stock and lemon juice and poach.

Poached Skate with Sorrel and Lovage Sauce [*GB*]   Poach skate wings in water, vinegar, sliced onion, peppercorns, parsley stalks and salt. Serve coated with white wine fish sauce finished with sweated shredded sorrel, chopped lovage and lemon juice.

Poached Suprême of Turbot with Cauliflower [*Fisch mit Blumenkokl* Germany]   Marinate turbot suprêmes in lemon juice then poach in a court-bouillon. Serve the fish coated with white wine fish sauce and garnished with florets of cauliflower.

Skate with Capers and Black Butter [*Raie au Beurre Noir* France] Poach portions of skate wings in court-bouillon for approx. 10 min. Transfer drained fish to an earthenware dish, sprinkle with capers and retain. Place knobs of butter into a frying pan and cook until brown, add vinegar and chopped parsley and pour over the fish.

Grilled Fish

Application

Prepared fish are passed through seasoned flour, placed on an oiled grid, brushed with melted butter or oil to prevent sticking and cooked under or over direct heat. Some items are marinated before cooking, in which case the fish is brushed with the marinading liquid during cooking.

Barbecued Trout [*Eaengsongui* Korea] Marinate trout in soy sauce, sesame oil, garlic, ginger, toasted sesame seeds, chilli powder and sugar. Grill on a barbecue and serve accompanied by chojang vinegar.

Glazed Fillet of Mackerel [*Sawara No Teriyaki* Japan] Marinate mackerel fillets in mirin, saké and soy sauce for 30 min. Boil and reduce the marinade by a quarter. Skewer the fillets, brush with oil and the marinade then grill and serve.

Grilled Cod Kebabs [*Samak Kebab* Middle East] Marinate cubes of cod in lemon and onion juice, cumin, bayleaves and seasoning. Skewer alternate pieces of fish and quarters of tomato then grill them. Serve on a bed of watercress with wedges of lemon, accompanied by eggplant purée.

Grilled Cod Steaks [GB] Grill cod steaks on one side, turn them over and coat with cheese paste consisting of grated cheese combined with a little thick béchamel sauce; continue to grill until golden. Garnish with segments of lemon and tomato.

Grilled Crabmeat and Pork Rolls [*Tod Nam Pla* Thailand] Combine crabmeat, minced pork, crushed garlic, chopped coriander leaves, chopped shallots, ground toasted peanuts, red spice paste, nam pla, thick coconut milk and seasoning. Divide into small rolls, steam for 20 min then grill until golden. Serve with segments of lime.

Grilled Fillet of Carp [*Saramura* Hungary] Season fillets with chopped fresh herbs, oil and salt for 30 min. Grill until golden. Reduce fish stock, salt and chopped chillies to a coating consistency then add butter to make a light sauce. Serve fillets on a bed of polenta coated with the sauce.

Grilled Fillet of Mackerel [*Saba No Shioyaki* Japan] Sprinkle mackerel fillets with sea salt and allow to stand for 30 min. Rinse the fish and repeat the salting process. Grill until golden. Sprinkle with grated daikon and lightly mask with warm soy sauce.

Grilled Fillet of Whiting with Ginger [*Gun Saengsun* Korea] Combine light soy sauce, sesame oil, grated root ginger, crushed garlic and seasoning. Pass fish through this mixture and grill until golden. Garnish with segments of lime and red chilli flowers.

Grilled Goujonettes of Fish and Beef [*Saengonsanjok* Korea]   Marinate goujonettes of cod, sole and beef steak with soy sauce, sesame oil, toasted sesame
seeds, garlic, ginger and chopped spring onions. Skewer alternate pieces of
both kinds of fish and meat then grill them in the usual manner.

Grilled Marinated Fillet of Red Mullet [*Triglie in Graticola* Italy]   Marinate fillet of red mullet in olive oil with garlic and chopped parsley. Grill until golden,
then serve decorated with bayleaves and with segments of lemon.

Grilled Marinated Scallops [*Paejusanjok* Korea]   Skewer scallops and pieces of
red pimento and marinate with soy sauce, sesame oil, toasted sesame seeds,
rice vinegar, garlic and ginger. Grill the skewers in the normal manner.

Grilled Marinated Turbot Steak [*Ikan Panggang* Indonesia]   Marinate turbot
steaks in sambal bajak with kencur powder and thick coconut milk then grill
them. Simmer the marinade with additional coconut milk, lemon grass and
chopped basil and serve the fish coated with the sauce.

Grilled Scallops [*Tairagai No Sansho Yaki* Japan]   Gently heat soy sauce,
mirin and saké in a pan to blend, then cool. Marinate sliced scallops in the mixture for 5 min, remove and thread onto skewers. Grill until golden, basting with
the marinade and serve sprinkled with Japanese pepper.

Grilled Skewered Prawns [*Saté Udang* Indonesia]   Marinate prawns in lemon
juice, coconut milk, sambal ulek, dark soy sauce and salt. Skewer the prawns
and grill them. Simmer the marinade and finish with coconut to form a sauce to
accompany the prawns.

Grilled Skewered Prawns and Scallops with Mango Sauce [*USA*]   Marinate scallops and prawns in a liquidised blend of mango flesh, olive oil and lime juice.
Skewer cooked snow peas between the prawns and scallops, and grill. Serve
accompanied by the mango marinade made into a sauce.

Grilled Skewered Scallops [*GB*]   Pass coral pieces of scallops through eggwash
and breadcrumbs mixed with chopped fresh mixed herbs, and skewer them
between white pieces of scallop wrapped in bacon, and mushrooms. Sprinkle
with lemon juice, season and grill.

Grilled Skewered Swordfish [*Kilich Shish* Greece]   Marinate cubes of swordfish in olive oil, lemon juice, chopped onion, bayleaf, salt, paprika and pepper.
Skewer the fish and grill.

Grilled Sour and Spiced Trout [*Ikan Panggang* Indonesia]   Blend soaked dried
red chillies, galingale, garlic, ginger, lemon grass, lime juice, red pimento, shallots and coconut milk to a paste then marinade prepared trout in the mixture.
Grill the fish and serve with wedges of lemon.

Grilled Suprême of Cod with Garlic [*Bacalao al Mojo de Ajo* Mexico]   Brush
suprêmes of cod with garlic-flavoured olive oil then grill until golden brown.

Grilled Suprême of Halibut with Orange Sauce [*Pescado en Salsa de Naranja*
Mexico]   Marinate halibut suprêmes in lime juice and olive oil. Grill and serve
garnished with segments of orange and accompanied by orange sauce.

Grilled Suprême of Salmon [*Saké No Isobeyaki* Japan]   Marinate salmon
suprêmes in mirin, soy sauce and seasoning. Boil and reduce the marinade by
half. Pass the fish through the reduced marinade, brush with vegetable oil then
grill. Serve coated with a sprinkling of toasted crushed seaweed and accompanied by pickled ginger.

Grilled Suprême of Tuna Fish [*Costoletta di Tonno* Italy]   Marinate a suprême of tuna in dry white wine with rosemary, garlic and seasoning. Grill, sprinkle with breadcrumbs and chopped parsley and continue to grill. Serve sprinkled with a dressing of olive oil and lemon juice.

Grilled Suprême of Turbot with Sesame and Ginger [*Gun Saengsun* Korea]   Marinate turbot suprêmes in soy sauce, roasted sesame seeds, grated ginger, sugar, garlic and sesame oil then grill them.

Grilled Tuna Fish Steaks [*Costolette di Tonno* Italy]   Marinate tuna steaks in crushed garlic, chopped rosemary, dry white wine and seasoning. Grill the fish, transfer to an earthenware dish, sprinkle with breadcrumbs, chopped fresh herbs, the juice and zest of lemons and olive oil, and gratinate. Serve with wedges of lemon.

Monkfish Kebabs [*Pinchitos de Rape* Spain]   Marinade skewered pieces of monkfish and green and red pimentos in oil, garlic, lemon juice and cumin. Grill and serve with wedges of lemon.

Spatchcocked Eel [GB]   Sauté chopped shallots in butter, add rubbed thyme, chopped parsley and hard-boiled yolks of egg and seasoning. Pass skinned eel pieces through the mixture and then through breadcrumbs and grill until crisp and serve.

Marinated and Pickled Fish

Application

To marinate, place the prepared fish in an earthenware or porcelain dish, add the marinating mixture, cover with clingfilm and place in a refrigerator for the prescribed time of 2 hours, or longer if stated.

Gravlax [*Scandinavia*]   Combine coarse salt, caster sugar and crushed black peppercorns. Spread a prepared fillet of salmon with dill, sprinkle with whisky and the seasoning, and lay a second fillet on top. Cover and allow to marinate for 2–3 days, turning occasionally.

Herrings in Cream [*Bondesild* Scandinavia]   Cut milk-soaked fillets of herring into pieces on the slant, add grated onion and grated apple, and combine with whipped cream mixed with white wine vinegar, sugar and black pepper. Cover and allow to marinate for 4 hours.

Pickled Fish [*Boquerones en Vinagre* Spain]   Split sardines, sprats or anchovies butterfly-fashion, removing the back bone, then marinate for 2 days in sherry vinegar, water, olive oil, sliced garlic, chopped parsley and seasoning.

Pickled Fish [*Caveached Fish* Caribbean]   Boil cider vinegar, olive oil, julienne of green pimento, julienne of carrot, sliced onion, bayleaf, grated ginger, mace, chilli powder, peppercorns and salt. Shallow fry fillets of white fish and moisten with this marinade. Serve hot or chilled with the marinade.

Pickled Herring [*Rollmops* or *Bismarcks* Israel]   Place fillets of herrings under running cold water for 1 hr then retain in cold water for 12 hr. Layer the fillets with onion rings, roll up tail to head, skewer and place in a dish with sliced lemon, bayleaves and pickling spice. Moisten with boiled acetic acid, water and brown sugar and leave to cool and marinate for 4 days.

Prawn Sushi [*Ebi No Kimi-Zushi Japan*]   Skewer large raw shelled prawns on toothpicks to straighten them and blanch for 2 min. Open the prawns from the underside and slightly flatten them, then marinate in rice vinegar, sugar and salt for 1 hr. Lightly scramble beaten eggs flavoured with rice vinegar, then process in a blender for 3 seconds until very light in texture. Form the egg mixture into small oval patties, arrange the prawns on top and serve.

Sliced Raw Fish [*Sashimi Japan*]   Suitable fresh fish and methods of preparation are as follows:

bream, flounder, halibut, mackerel, red snapper and sole – cut fillets into 1 cm × 2.5 cm slices on the slant;

tuna – cut fillets into straight 5-mm slices;

squid – cut open into two pieces, cut in half making four pieces then cut into very thin slices on the slant.

Arrange the fish on serving dishes garnished with daikon, carrot, cucumber, julienne of spring onion and celery. Serve accompanied by any of the following dipping sauces: soy sauce; horseradish flavoured with soy sauce; soy sauce mixed with grated root ginger; soy mixed with mustard; soy sauce mixed with saké and dried bonito flakes, simmered for 1 min and strained.

Soused Red Snapper [*Escovitch Caribbean*]   Boil white wine vinegar, olive oil, julienne of green pimento and carrot, sliced onion, chopped chives, peppercorns and salt. Shallow fry fillets of snapper and moisten with the marinade and lime juice. Serve hot or cold with the marinade.

Shallow-fried Fish

Application

To shallow fry fish, cook in a small amount of oil or clarified butter in a balti pan or frying pan; also known as cooking à la poêle.

Balti Prawns [*India*]   Stir-fry white cumin seeds, coriander seeds, fennel seeds, lovage seeds, chopped garlic and onion. When golden, add diced red pimento, chopped fresh green chillies, chopped coriander, a little tomato purée, balti spice mixture and a little water to form a paste. Add prepared prawns, allow to simmer for 2 min and serve.

Glazed Smelt with Ginger [*Wakasagi No Ageni Japan*]   Pass smelts through cornflour then golden shallow fry in oil. Simmer saké, sugar and soy sauce in a shallow pan, add the fish and cook for 2 min to allow them to glaze. Serve garnished with grated ginger.

Glazed Suprême of Salmon [*Saké No Teriyaki Japan*]   Golden shallow fry suprêmes for 4 min, moisten with a little soy sauce and mirin then cook and reduce the liquor, basting frequently until the fish is glazed. Serve garnished with pickled ginger.

Prawn and Sesame Toasts [*Zah Xia Bao China*]   Blend peeled prawns and grated ginger to a paste then add a chilled mixture of cornflour diluted with saké, beaten egg white and salt. Spread the mixture onto slices of bread, dip in sesame seeds and fry in oil. Cut into shapes, garnish with spring onion flowers and accompany with chilli sauce.

Sautéed Eel [*Héli Tiganitó Greece*]   Cover sections of eel with boiling water and allow to stand for 10 min. Drain, season and pass through beaten egg and flour, then sauté in olive oil. Serve with lemon wedges.

Sautéed Eel in Cream Sauce [*Ugor Russia*]   Sauté sections of eel in oil, moisten with fish velouté and lemon juice and thicken with a liaison of egg yolks and smetana.

Sautéed Frogs' Legs [*Ancas de Rana Spain*]   Marinate frogs' legs in sherry, lemon juice, thyme, garlic and oil. Pass through flour, eggwash and bread-crumbs mixed with chopped parsley, then golden fry in olive oil and serve with segments of lemon.

Sautéed Squid in Chilli and Garlic Sauce [*Sotong Dan Chilli Dan Bawang Putih Thailand*]   Blend soaked dried red chillies, sambal ulek and lime juice to a paste. Sauté squid pieces in peanut oil with garlic, remove and retain. Sauté sliced onion in the oil, add the paste and cook for 2 min, then add the squid and mix in.

Shallow-fried Cod Steaks with Peanut Sauce [*Ikan Kacang Indonesia*]   Marinate cod steaks with lemon juice then shallow fry and serve coated with peanut sauce and sprinkled with chopped coriander.

Shallow-fried Curried Fish Cakes [*Muchli Kofta India*]   Flake poached white fish and combine with chopped shallots and fresh green chillies, dry mashed potato, beaten egg, chopped coriander leaves and seasoning. Form into fish cakes and shallow fry, then simmer the cakes in spiced sauce and serve sprinkled with chopped coriander leaves.

Sauce: sweat chopped garlic, cardamoms and crushed cinnamon and cook for 1 min, then add garam masala, ground coriander, turmeric, cumin and a bay-leaf. Moisten with lemon juice and fish stock and add desiccated coconut.

Shallow-fried Fillet of Coley in Curry Sauce [*Malu Kari India*]   Combine black pepper, salt and turmeric and rub into coley fillets, then shallow fry in ground-nut oil. For the sauce stir-fry chopped shallot, crushed garlic, fenugreek seeds, grated ginger and curry powder; moisten with mirin, tamarind juice and thi coconut milk. Place the fish in the sauce and serve.

Shallow-fried Fillet of Mackerel with Piccalilli Sauce [*GB*]   Shallow fry mac fillets and serve on white wine fish sauce containing piccalilli.

Shallow-fried Fillet of Red Mullet in Coconut Sauce [*Ikan Bumbu Indonesia*]   Marinate fillets in lemon juice and seasoning then shall groundnut oil. For the sauce, stir-fry chopped shallot, garlic, grated gir ulek and soft brown sugar, moisten with soy sauce and thin and t milks. Mask the fish with this sauce.

Shallow-fried Fillet of Red Mullet in Vinaigrette Sauce [*GB*]   S with the minimum colour, then marinate for 1 hr in vinaigrette diced tomato flesh and chopped basil. Serve the fish coated and garnish with segments of lime and basil leaves.

Shallow-fried Fillet of Sole with Mushrooms and Pr *Bretonne France*]   Shallow fry sole fillets in oil and sliced mushrooms and prawns. Serve coated with lem and chopped parsley.

Shallow-fried Fillet of Sole with Pine Nuts [*Lenguado Con Piñones* Mexico]
Shallow fry sole fillets in oil and butter. Serve coated with veal velouté flavoured
with zest and juice of lemon sprinkled with pine nuts.

Shallow-fried Fish Fans [*Boquerones Fritos* Spain]   Pass prepared small fish
such as anchovies, sardines, sprats or whitebait through seasoned flour, press
their tails together to form fan shapes then shallow fry in olive oil. Serve with
segments of lemon.

Shallow-fried Gefillte Fish [*Israel*]   Combine 2 parts minced hake with 1 part
each of minced haddock and cod, and add grated onion, beaten eggs, ground
almonds, medium matzo meal, parsley, eggs to bind and seasoning. Mould the
mixture into fish cakes, pass through fine matzo meal then fry in oil and serve
accompanied by green olives, pickled cucumber and chollah or matzo.

Shallow-fried Goujons of Plaice with Onion Rings [*Steiktur Fisk meo Lauk*
Scandinavia]   Pass goujons of plaice through seasoned flour then shallow fry
in oil and serve garnished with sliced sautéed onion rings, segments of lemon
and boiled potatoes.

Shallow-fried Goujons of Sole with Artichokes [*Goujons de Sole Murat* France]
Pass goujons of sole through seasoned flour then shallow fry in oil. When
golden toss in batons of cooked fonds of artichoke, shallow-fried batons
of potato and chopped parsley, and sprinkle with lemon juice and chopped
parsley. Place knobs of butter into a hot frying pan and cook until nut-brown
in colour, mask the fish with the butter and serve.

Shallow-fried Halibut Steak Balinese Style [*Ikan Bali* Indonesia]   Golden fry
chopped onion, garlic and ginger in peanut oil, add sambal ulek, grated zest
and juice of lemon, sugar and dark soy sauce and simmer for 2 min. Shallow fry
the halibut steak in peanut oil and serve coated with the sauce.

·llow-fried Herring in Oatmeal [GB]   Remove the backbone from the herring,
        ʼhrough fine oatmeal and shallow fry. Garnish with oatcakes and segments

Lobster with Rice Noodles [*Loong Har Chow Mai* China]
        ·d lobster in oil with sliced onion, mushrooms, water chestnuts,
        ·r and bean sprouts. Add soaked rice noodles, moisten with soy
        . add a little sugar and season with salt. Cook for 2 min and

s in Garlic [*Gambas al Ajillo* Spain]   Lightly fry chopped
        ·live oil, add peeled king prawns and toss over. Serve with

·an Garlic with Chillies [*Gambas Pil-Pil* Spain]   Lightly
        drained red chillies and salt in olive oil, add peeled king
        ·erve with segments of lemon.

·ut [*Nijimasu No Karaage* Japan]   Season trout with
        for 30 min. Grate cucumber, sprinkle with salt and
        ·flavour with rice vinegar, ginger juice and sugar and
        dry the trout, pass through cornflour and shallow fry
        ·nished with fresh green chillies, pickled red ginger
        · mixture.

·ed with Spices [*Samak Mahshi* Middle East*]
        ·nd turmeric. Sauté chopped onion and garlic in

samneh then stir in the baharat and turmeric. Stuff the fish with the mixture and shallow fry. Serve with wedges of lime and coriander.

Shallow-fried Red Mullet with Salted Black Beans [*Saengsonjon Korea*] Shallow fry red mullet in sesame oil. Drain the oil from the pan, add soy sauce, kochujang, sesame oil, Chinese salted black beans and sugar, and cook to form a sauce. Mask the fish with this sauce, and serve sprinkled with chopped coriander.

Shallow-fried Salt Codfish [*Bacalhau à Lisbonense Portugal*] Sauté chopped onion with flaked, poached salt cod in olive oil and place in a dish. Mix deep-fried but uncoloured and soft straw potatoes with beaten eggs and chopped parsley and cook until it becomes creamy in texture. Pour this mixture over the fish and serve.

Shallow-fried Salt Codfish and Ackee [*Caribbean*] Soak the salt cod in water for 12 hr, drain then poach in water until tender. Remove the skin and bones and flake. Sauté lardons of salt pork, chopped onion and garlic in oil, and add diced tomato flesh, thyme, chopped fresh red chillies, the fish and ackee. Serve accompanied by boiled green bananas, plantain or breadfruit.

Shallow-fried Salt Codfish Balls [*USA*] Combine flaked poached codfish, mashed potatoes, egg, butter and cream. Form into small ball shapes, flatten slightly and golden fry.

Shallow-fried Salt Codfish with Tomatoes and Lime [*Caribbean*] Soak the salt cod in water for 12 hr, remove the skin and cut into suprêmes, then shallow fry in olive oil, remove and keep hot. Lightly fry chopped shallots, crushed garlic and chopped red chillies in the same pan, add lime juice and chopped parsley, mask over the fish and serve.

Shallow-fried Sardines with Tomato [*Sardinhas Pamplinas Portugal*] Split and remove the backbones and heads of sardines, then marinate in lemon juice. Pass the fish through flour, eggwash and breadcrumbs then fry in olive oil. Serve with a band of cooked tomato concassée seasoned with nutmeg and garnish with slices of warm hard-boiled egg.

Shallow-fried Scallops and Mussels with Snow Peas [*Hu Lan Du Chow Tsi Tsei China*] Sauté cooked scallops and cooked mussels in groundnut oil, remove and add grated ginger, julienne of leek and snow peas. Add soy sauce and fish stock, thicken with cornflour, then add the fish and serve sprinkled with chopped spring onions.

Shallow-fried Scallops in Tarragon Sauce [*USA*] Sauté scallops in garlic butter and retain. Swill the pan with white wine and lemon juice, add fish velouté then strain the sauce. Add chopped tarragon and the scallops to the sauce and serve.

Shallow-fried Sole with Ginger Sauce [*Pla Brio Wan Thailand*] Shallow fry a sole in peanut oil, remove and sauté chopped garlic in the oil, moisten with soy sauce and add palm sugar, nam pla and tamarind liquid. Return the fish to this sauce to coat it then sprinkle with grated ginger. Serve sprinkled with fried onion flakes and chopped coriander.

Shallow-fried Suprême of Halibut with Sesame Seeds [*Tuigim Saengsun Korea*] Marinate halibut suprêmes in a mixture of soy sauce, sesame seeds, chopped spring onions and sesame oil, then shallow fry in oil. Serve sprinkled with fried sesame seeds.

Shallow-fried Suprême of Salted Cod Florentine Style [*Baccalà alla Firenziana Italy*]   Soak salt cod in water for 12 hr, remove the skin and cut into suprêmes, then shallow fry in olive oil. Remove and keep hot. Lightly fry chopped shallots, crushed garlic, crumpled bayleaf, thyme and tomato concassée in the same pan. Mask over the fish and serve sprinkled with chopped basil.

Shallow-fried Suprême of Tuna with Saffron [*Atum à Algarvia Portugal*]   Marinate suprêmes in lemon juice and chopped parsley then shallow fry in olive oil. Serve masked with chopped onion cooked in butter and moistened with white wine vinegar with a pinch of saffron added.

Shallow-fried Suprême of Turbot in Lemon Sauce [*Psari me Selino Avgolemono Greece*]   Shallow fry suprêmes in olive oil and remove. Add dry white wine, fish stock and chopped dill to the pan and cook. Reduce by half, and add a liaison of eggs, zest and juice of lemons and cream. Mask the fish with the sauce and garnish with a sprig of dill.

Shallow-fried Trout in Cream [*Truite à la Crème France*]   Shallow fry trout in oil, pour off the fat and flambé with brandy, then add cream. Mask the fish with the resultant sauce and serve sprinkled with fried chopped almonds.

Shallow-fried Trout with Cured Ham [*Trucha à la Navarra Spain*]   Sprinkle trout inside and out with salt and lemon juice. Place a slice of jambón serrano in the cavity and a slice around each fish. Shallow fry the trout in oil and serve garnished with strips of pimento and wedges of lemon.

Shallow-fried Trout with Turmeric [*Pla Too Tord Thailand*]   Pass through flour and turmeric then shallow fry.

Shallow-fried Whiting Szechwan Style [*Sichuan Yaujar Yue China*]   Marinate whiting in saké, groundnut oil and seasoning. Shallow fry the fish in groundnut oil. Remove and keep hot. Add and lightly fry grated ginger and crushed garlic, then moisten with dark soy sauce, fish stock and bean sauce, simmer and thicken with cornflour. Place the fish in the sauce and serve sprinkled with chopped spring onions.

Snails in Tomato and Herb Sauce [*Caracoles en Salsa Spain*]   Sauté chopped onion and garlic in oil then add diced tomato flesh, bayleaf and thyme and cook. Add prepared snails to the mixture, finish with chopped fresh herbs then transfer to a shallow dish. Sprinkle with breadcrumbs, grated zest and juice of lemon and oil, and gratinate.

Snails with Ham and Chorizo [*Caracoles à la Burgalesa Spain*]   Sauté chopped garlic, lardons of bacon and diced chorizo in olive oil; add breadcrumbs and chopped fresh green chilli then moisten with white wine and cook. Add prepared snails, season and serve sprinkled with chopped fresh herbs.

Stir-fried Octopus [*Nakchibokkum Korea*]   Stir-fry crushed garlic and diagonal slices of carrot in sesame oil, add octopus rings then add kochujang, chilli powder and spring onions and moisten with soy sauce. Serve sprinkled with toasted sesame seeds.

Stir-fried Spiced Prawns [*Nachbous Middle East*]   Blend baharat, turmeric, cumin, curry powder, chilli powder and water to a paste. Stir-fry chopped garlic in samneh then add the spice paste and chopped onion. Add and cook prawns and finish with chopped coriander leaves.

Shallow-poached Fish

Application

Small whole fish and cuts of large fish are barely covered with appropriate liquid and greaseproof paper and cooked in the oven at 175 °C. The liquid should not be allowed to boil.

Poached Darne of Carp in Brandy and Fruit Sauce [*Schwarzfisch Germany*]
Shallow poach thin darnes of carp in fish stock. For the sauce, caramelise sugar and butter and add chopped almonds, walnuts, sultanas and fresh figs. Flambé with brandy then add the cooking liquid from the fish, boil and reduce. Thicken with white breadcrumbs and finish with lemon and orange juices. Serve the fish coated with the sauce.

Poached Darne of Cod in Green Curry Sauce [*Kaeng Khieu Wan Pla Thailand*] Simmer green curry paste with coconut milk, add darnes of cod and poach. Finish by sprinkling with chopped fresh green chillies and basil.

Poached Darne of Cod with Coconut Milk [*Gulia Ikan Indonesia*] Rub thin darnes with salt and marinate in lime juice. Blend soaked dried red chillies and the soaking liquid, lemon grass, galingale, pimento, shallots, ginger, garlic, turmeric and paprika to a paste. Fry the paste in oil, moisten with thin coconut milk, simmer for 15 min then pass through a strainer. Add lemon grass, zest of lemon, curry leaves, mint and lime juice to the sauce and poach the fish in it; finally finish it with coconut cream and serve masked over the fish.

Poached Eels in Tomato and Basil Sauce [*Anguilla alla Comacchiese Italy*]
Shallow fry sections of eel in olive oil and retain. Add and fry chopped shallots, crushed garlic, tomato concassée, tomato purée and chopped basil, and moisten with dry white wine and fish stock. Replace the eels, simmer for a few minutes and serve in the sauce, accompanied by polenta.

Poached Eels with Sorrel [*Anguille au Vert France*] Blanch sections of eel in salted water then stew the eel in oil with chopped shallot, parsley, chervil, mint, shredded sorrel and fresh sage, then moisten with fish stock and cook. Finish with zest and juice of lemon.

Poached Fillet of Herring in Saké [*Nishin No Nitsuke Japan*] Poach blanched fillets of herring in saké, mirin, dark soy sauce, flaked kombu, bean curd and grated ginger. Discard the kombu and serve the fillets sprinkled with grated ginger.

Poached Fillet of Mackerel in Coconut Milk [*Gulai Ikan Indonesia*] Simmer thin coconut milk with chopped onion, garlic, grated ginger, turmeric, trasi, sambal ulek, lemon grass and salt. Add fillets of mackerel, chopped basil and tamarind liquid and poach. Finish with thick coconut milk, and serve the fish in the sauce accompanied by boiled rice.

Poached Fillet of Mackerel with Daikon [*Saba Oroshi-ni Japan*] Lightly shallow fry mackerel fillets then poach in saké flavoured with grated ginger and remove the fish. Combine dashi, mirin, salt and light soy sauce, pour it into the simmering liquid and cook until it has reduced by half. Replace the fillets, sprinkle with shredded daikon and chopped spring onions, simmer for 2 min and serve accompanied by seven-spice powder.

Poached Fillet of Perch [*Zander Balaton* Hungary]   Sprinkle fillets with salt and lemon juice and allow to marinate for 30 min. Place duxelle of mushrooms into a shallow dish, lay the fillets on top, cover with white wine and fish stock and poach. Remove fillets and retain. Reduce the strained cooking liquor, add soured cream and season. Garnish fish with sliced boiled potatoes, coat with the sauce and serve.

Poached Fillets of Sole in White Wine Sauce with Mushrooms, Tarragon and Tomato [*Filets de Sole Palace* France]   Poach fillets in white wine and fish stock with strips of mushroom, tomato concassée and chopped tarragon. Remove fillets and retain, sprinkled with the garnish. Reduce strained cooking liquor, add fish velouté and cooked egg yolks then strain through a muslin. Finish sauce with cream, knobs of unsalted butter and a little brandy. Coat the fish with the sauce and glaze under the salamander.

Poached Fillets of Sole with Chilled Grapes [*Fillet de Sole Véronique* France]   Poach fillets of sole in white wine and fish stock. Remove fillets and retain. Place strained cooking liquor into a pan, add fish velouté and cream, reduce to a light coating consistency, add cooked egg yolks (sabayon) then strain through a fine strainer. Finish the sauce with knobs of unsalted butter and season to taste. Coat fish with the sauce, garnish with peeled grapes and glaze under the salamander.

Poached Sole in Saké with Chillies [*Karei No Nitsuke* Japan]   Score sole to form a diamond pattern, then poach in second soup stock flavoured with saké, mirin and soy sauce. Serve garnished with de-seeded green chilli peppers blanched in soy sauce.

Poached Suprême of Turbot with Pickled Walnuts and Watercress [GB]   Shallow poach turbot suprêmes in fish stock with chopped pickled walnuts and watercress. Reduce the cooking liquid by half and add to white wine fish sauce. Serve the suprêmes coated with the sauce.

Poached Suprême of Turbot with Rice [*Sayyadiyya* Middle East]   Soak fish in salted iced water for 1 hr. Cook chopped onion in olive oil until soft and dark brown, moisten with water and cook, then coarsely liquidise. Flavour with salt and cumin, add suprêmes of turbot and cook. Reduce the cooking liquor with lemon juice to a coating consistency. Serve the fish on a bed of rice cooked in fish stock and coat with the sauce.

Poached Tail-end of Hake with Hazelnuts [*Cola de Merluza a la Marichu* Mexico]   Poach tail pieces of hake in white wine and fish stock with sliced carrot and onion. Reduce the liquor with the vegetables by half, add roasted and crushed hazelnuts, garlic, fried breadcrumbs and chopped parsley, then liquidise to form a sauce and finish with a liaison of egg yolks and cream. Serve the fish coated with the sauce.

Shirred Scallops [GB]   Poach scallops in sherry and fish stock then drain and toss in melted butter. Reduce the cooking liquid to a glaze, and add knobs of butter, cream and chopped parsley to form a sauce; add to the scallops and serve.

Soused Anchovies [*Hamsi Bugulamsi* Greece]   Poach fresh anchovies in water with olive oil, chopped dill and parsley and lemon juice. Serve with the cooking liquor.

Steamed Fish

Application

Fish prepared for shallow or deep poaching may also be steamed. There are various types of equipment available for steaming. When using a pressure steamer it is advisable to cover the dish with a lid. When using a Chinese bamboo steamer the fish is usually previously marinated, placed onto an oiled heatproof plate or in kitchen foil and then steamed.

Eel Pudding or Pulborough Eels [*GB*]   Line a pudding basin with suet pastry and fill with a mixture of blanched sections of boned eel, chopped onion, mixed fresh herbs, quarters of hard-boiled egg and diced pickled pork. Moisten with fish stock, cover with suet pastry then steam.

Steamed Fillet of Red Snapper [*Pla Nerng Leung* Thailand]   Blend dried red chillies, garlic, onion, coriander, turmeric, nam pla, thick coconut milk and beaten eggs to a paste. Pass fillets of snapper through the spiced mixture; dust with rice flour then steam.

Steamed Suprême of Cod with Turmeric and Coriander [*Pla Nerng Leung* Thailand]   Blend dried red chillies, onion, garlic, ground coriander, turmeric, thin coconut milk and beaten eggs to a paste. Pass suprêmes through this mixture then through cornflour and place to steam. Serve with boiled rice and a liquid made of 1 part light soy sauce, 1 part nam pla and 1 part boiling water.

Steamed Suprême of Halibut with Lemon Grass [*Tom Som Pla* Thailand]   Sprinkle a shallow dish with grated ginger, chopped galingale, lemon grass, shallots and coriander. Add suprêmes of halibut, moisten with nam pla and fish stock then place to steam. Serve sprinkled with chopped fresh red chillies and coriander.

Steamed Suprême of Salmon with Bean Curd [*Sake No Kenchin-Mushi* Japan]   Sprinkle suprêmes with salt and mirin and set aside for 30 min. Combine mashed bean curd, strips of jelly mushrooms, prawns and peas with beaten egg and flavour with mirin and soy sauce. Rinse the suprêmes in cold water, dry them and place each in the centre of a piece of muslin; spread with the bean curd mixture, form into small parcels then steam for 30 min. Serve the unwrapped suprêmes coated with first soup stock which has been flavoured with light soy sauce and thickened with diluted cornflour; garnish with julienne of root ginger.

Stewed Fish

Application

Stewed fish is prepared using a mixture of fish or shellfish, vegetables, spices and herbs, moistened with fish stock and wine and simmered under a lid on top of the stove or in the oven.

Bouillabaisse [*France*]   Sweat julienne of white of leek, sliced onion, chopped garlic, bayleaf, thyme and fennel seeds in oil. Add 5-cm pieces of brill, conger eel, mackerel, John Dory, red mullet, whiting and squid, mussels, scampi and tomato concassée. Moisten with dry white wine, flavour with saffron then allow to stew until cooked. Serve with French bread.

Casserole of Goujons of Fish [*Casserola Italy*]   Sauté chopped onion, garlic and diced green and red pimento in oil then add diced tomato flesh; moisten with white wine and fish stock and cook. Add sautéed goujons of white fish and squid to the mixture and stew until cooked. Serve in a casserole on a base of toasted bread.

Casserole of Salt Codfish [*Bakaliáros Yahnistós Greece*]   Cut soaked codfish into portions, sauté in olive oil, add diced tomato flesh, tomato sauce, chopped parsley and seasoning then place in a casserole, cover with a lid and allow to stew gently.

Crab in Curry Sauce [*Poo Paad Gari Thailand*]   Chop a boiled crab into pieces and deep fry in oil, remove and drain. Sauté sliced fresh red chillies and garlic, stir in red curry paste then moisten with thick coconut milk, add chopped spring onion then add in the crab pieces and stew; serve sprinkled with chopped coriander leaves.

Curried Fish [*Ikan Moolie Thailand*]   Blend dry fried sliced onion, macadamia nuts, ginger, lemon grass and turmeric to a paste. Grind roasted desiccated coconut. Golden stir-fry sliced onion and garlic in coconut oil, add the paste, moisten with coconut milk, add the ground coconut, shredded fresh red chillies and goujons of fish. Stew in the sauce for a few minutes then finish with thick coconut milk.

Curried Squid [*Gulai Cumi-Cumi Indonesia*]   Simmer the following preparation until it begins to thicken: coconut milk, chopped onion, garlic, grated ginger, salt, chilli powder, trasi, grated kemiri nuts and lemon grass. Add pieces of squid and simmer then add tamarind liquid, palm sugar and seasoning and stew until tender.

Curried Suprême of Halibut [*Israel*]   Sauté sliced onion and garlic in oil, add suprêmes of halibut and stiffen quickly without colouring. Add fresh coriander, ground cumin, turmeric, dried red chillies and tomato purée then moisten with fish stock, a little herb vinegar and seasoning. Strain the liquor over the fish, allow to stew gently and serve with boiled rice.

Fillets of Herring in Saké [*Nishin No Nitsuke Japan*]   Blanch fillets of herring, cut into two on the slant then stew them in saké, mirin, dashi and dark soy sauce, and kelp. Discard the kelp, add cubes of tofu and cook for 1 min. Serve sprinkled with grated ginger.

Fillet of Red Mullet in Tomato [*Triglie alla Livornese Italy*]   Cook diced tomato flesh in garlic-flavoured butter. Shallow fry fillets of red mullet in olive oil then transfer to the tomato mixture and allow to stew. Serve sprinkled with chopped parsley.

Fish Ratatouille [*Chiveci Hungary*]   Sauté chopped onion, diced carrot, celery and parsnip in oil. Add diced tomato flesh, stir in tomato purée, moisten with fish stock and simmer for 10 min. Add 5-cm pieces of carp, brill, halibut and grey mullet, peas and diamonds of French beans, and allow to stew until most of the liquid has evaporated and the fish is cooked. Serve accompanied by polenta.

Fish Stew Italian Style [***Brodetto all' Anconetana*** *Italy*] Sweat sliced onion, garlic, bayleaf and diced red pimento then add tomato concassée. Add pieces of red or grey mullet, bass, sole and halibut, then add shrimps, clams or mussels, moisten with dry white wine and allow to stew. Serve on slices of toast.

Goujons of Cod in Broth [***Tara No Age-ni*** *Japan*] Deep fry blanched goujons of cod then stew them in dashi, mirin, sugar, dark soy sauce and saké. Serve sprinkled with grated ginger and chopped green onion.

Goujons of Sole with Bean Curd and Mushrooms [***Hirame No Ageni*** *Japan*] Deep fry floured goujons of fillet of sole, mushrooms and cubes of bean curd then stew them in first soup stock flavoured with mirin, soy sauce and sugar. Serve in bowls with the sauce.

Herrings Stewed in Milk with Dill [***Selyodka Tushennaya v Moloke*** *Russia*] Place salted herrings in a shallow-sided pan, moisten with milk, and add sliced onion and chopped dill, bayleaf and marjoram. Cover with a lid and stew for approx. 40 min. Blend the liquid, onion and dill to form a light sauce. Serve the fish masked with the sauce, garnished with sprigs of dill.

Jellied Eels [*GB*] Pack skinned sections of eel into a pan, just cover with 2 parts water to 1 part vinegar and add sliced onion, bayleaves, peppercorns, salt and parsley stalks. Stew for 2 hr. Allow to get cold and serve the eel in its own jelly.

Lobster in Beer [***Hummer in Weissbier*** *Germany*] Sweat chopped shallots in oil, moisten with light beer, season, add caraway seeds and thicken with arrow-root, cook and strain. Reheat flesh of cooked lobster in butter, flambé with brandy then add the beer sauce.

Lobster with Ginger [***Ching Yu Chowl Loon Joo*** *China*] Lightly sauté sections of raw lobster in corn oil, add julienne of root ginger and spring onions and stew until cooked. Flambé with brandy, and moisten with Shaohsing wine, soy sauce, oyster sauce and fish stock. Stew for 10 min then remove the lobster. Thicken the sauce with the lobster butter and season. Coat the lobster with the sauce and serve decorated with the tail.

Lobster with Pimento and Ginger [***Ching Yu Chowl Loon Joo*** *China*] Heat cooked sliced lobster flesh in groundnut oil. Stir-fry diced red and green pimento, crushed garlic and grated ginger. Moisten with yellow bean sauce, fish stock and saké, then add beaten eggs to this simmering sauce to form threads and thicken with cornflour. Add the lobster and serve with boiled rice.

Octopus in Tomato and Basil Sauce [***Polpi in Umido*** *Italy*] Lightly fry pieces of octopus in olive oil, add dry white wine, reduce by half then add tomato concassée and stew. Serve coated with the sauce and sprinkled with chopped basil combined with chopped garlic.

Paella [*Spain*] Simmer the following in seasoned chicken stock flavoured and coloured with saffron until cooked, using a paellera: mussels, prawns, lobster, cubes of monkfish and small squid, the tentacles cut into lengths and the bag cut into rings. Shallow fry chicken pieces in olive oil with crushed garlic and strips of red and green pimentos. Stir in short-grain rice and strips of tomato flesh, ladle in boiling chicken stock and cook. Fork in the mussels, squid, prawns and lobster. Serve with wedges of lemon.

Prawn and Cucumber Curry [***Gulia Labu*** *Thailand*] Combine chopped shallots, garlic, ground coriander, fennel, cumin, white pepper, turmeric, crumbled dried red chillies and water. Simmer the mixture, add sliced cucumber then prawns and sugar and finish with thick coconut milk. Golden stir-fry chopped shallot and garlic, add fennel seeds and add to the prawn curry, cover for a while then serve with rice.

Prawns in Coconut Cream [*Sambal Goreng Udang* Indonesia]   Sauté chopped onion, garlic, fresh red chillies and curry leaves in peanut oil. Add sambal ulek and laos powder then add prawns; moisten with fish stock, add grated creamed coconut, salt and sugar and allow to stew. Serve accompanied by boiled rice.

Prawns in Coconut Cream [*Udang Masak Lemak* Thailand]   Sauté chopped onion, dried red chillies and strips of green pimento in ghee, stir in curry powder, add prawns then moisten with coconut cream and allow to stew.

Prawns in Piquant Sauce [*Sambal Goreng Udang Asam* Indonesia]   Sauté chopped onion, garlic and grated ginger in peanut oil. Add sambal ulek, laos powder, grated zest of lemon and tamarind liquid then simmer until the sauce thickens. Season with salt and sugar then add chopped prawns, reheat and serve.

Seafood Chongol [*Haemuljongol* Korea]   Stew sections of squid, goujons of white fish, Pacific prawns, clams, shredded watercress or spinach, diced bean curd, strips of spring onion and fresh chillies and grated ginger in fish stock until all is cooked and the liquid is slightly thickened.

Seafood with Rice and Dried Red Peppers [*Arroz en Caldero à la Murciana* Mexico]   Blend together garlic, beaten egg, lemon juice, olive oil and seasoning, strain and pour into a sauceboat. Season goujons of hake or halibut with salt and allow to stand for 1 hr, then rinse and dry. Golden fry dried sweet red pepper and garlic then blend together with parsley, a few strands of saffron, paprika, salt and prawn-flavoured fish stock. Lightly sauté rings of squid, prawns and the goujons in oil, remove and retain. Add diced tomato flesh to the pan then stir in short-grain rice, moisten with the blended saffron mixture and simmer, then transfer to a shallow dish and bake. Layer the fish on top of the rice and finish cooking. When cooked serve accompanied by the egg and lemon sauce.

Shrimps in Sweet and Sour Sauce [*Paad Priew Wan Goong* Thailand]   Marinate peeled shrimps in lime juice and saké. Sauté chopped shallot, garlic and pimento, and add the shrimps, diced tomato flesh, batons of cucumber, palm sugar and shrimp paste. Moisten with the marinade, soy sauce, fish and chicken stock, add pineapple pieces then thicken the liquor with cornflour and serve sprinkled with chopped coriander.

Spicy Fish Stew [*Saengsun Chigae* Korea]   Marinate thin slices of fillet of beef, sliced courgettes and shiitake mushrooms in soy sauce, sesame oil, garlic and hot fermented bean paste. Stir-fry the beef and the vegetables in oil, moisten with fish stock and simmer. Add sliced spring onions and diced green pimento, then add darnes of cod, clams and squares of bean curd and allow to stew. Sprinkle with chopped celery leaves and serve a darne of cod with a slice of beef and a good ladleful of the other ingredients per portion.

Squid in Black Bean Sauce [*Sotong Masak Kicap* Thailand]   Stir-fry chopped onion in oil then add the squid, black bean sauce and soy sauce and allow to stew. Serve sprinkled with chopped coriander leaves.

Squid Stewed in Red Wine [*Kalamarakia Krassata* Greece]   Lightly fry chopped shallots and garlic and diced green pimento in olive oil, then add strips of squid and continue to fry until any liquid has been reduced. Moisten with red wine and fish stock, add bayleaf, thyme and tomato concassée then stew. Serve on a base of boiled rice, sprinkled with chopped fresh basil.

Stewed Eel [*Héli Yahnistó Greece*]   Stew sections of eel in fish velouté sauce with the addition of sweated chopped onion and garlic, bayleaf, sage, parsley and lemon juice.

Stewed Eel in Tomato [*Anguilla alla Comacchiese Italy*]   Sauté chopped onion and garlic in olive oil, add diced tomato flesh, tomato purée and chopped basil. Place the tomato mixture on a layer of sections of eel in a shallow dish. Moisten with white wine and fish stock and simmer until tender. Serve with polenta.

Stewed Marinated Hake Steaks [*Ryba v Marinade Russia*]   Marinate hake steaks for 1 hr in lemon juice, oil, chopped dill and seasoning. Sweat chopped onion, chopped cloves of garlic and finely grated carrot in oil, add diced tomato flesh, marjoram and chopped parsley and cook for 5 min. Place in the fish portions, moisten with fish stock and a little sugar dissolved in red wine, cover with a lid and simmer for approx. 1.5 hr. Serve garnished with sprigs of fresh herbs.

Stewed Octopus in Red Wine [*Octopus Stifado Greece*]   Sauté sliced onions with pieces of octopus in corn oil, then add cinnamon, bayleaf, peppercorns, garlic and blanched button onions. Moisten with red wine and vinegar and stew until nearly all the liquid has been absorbed.

Stewed Shark Suprêmes, Creole Style [*Caribbean*]   Marinate suprêmes of shark for 2 hr in lime juice, rum, water, crushed cloves of garlic, chopped chives, chopped fresh red chillies and seasoning. Shallow fry the fish portions in oil, remove and retain. Add chopped onion and allow to cook, then add diced tomato flesh and the marinade and gently cook. Place in the fish and simmer for 15 min.

Stewed Snapper in Curry Sauce [*Muchli ka Salin India*]   Sweat chopped shallots and garlic in ghee, add ground coriander and cumin, chilli powder and black pepper. Stir in tomato purée and moisten with fish stock. Add goujons of snapper then stew. Serve sprinkled with chopped coriander leaves.

Stewed Squid in Ink [*Calamares en su Tinta Spain*]   Sauté chopped onion and garlic in oil, add diced tomato flesh and tomato juice and cook. Arrange the squid stuffed with the chopped tentacles on top of the mixture, moisten with fish stock and white wine and cook. Liquidise the ink of the squid with breadcrumbs and chopped parsley, add it to the cooking liquid to thicken and serve.

Stewed Suprême of Halibut with Cabbage and Caraway [*Fische mit Kümmelkraut Germany*]   Sweat shredded cabbage in oil then add paysanne of potatoes and moisten with fish stock and water, add caraway seeds and stew until nearly cooked. Place suprêmes of halibut on top of the vegetables and continue cooking.

Stewed Suprême of Halibut with Fish Liver Dumplings [*Israel*]   Sweat sliced onion in oil, add suprêmes of halibut, sprinkle with salt and lemon juice and allow to stiffen over heat. Moisten with fish stock and simmer, adding fish liver dumplings. Thicken the strained cooking liquor with cornflour and finish with a liaison of egg yolks. Mask the fish and dumplings with the sauce and serve.

Stewed Tuna Steaks Caribbean Style [*Caribbean*]   Marinate tuna steaks for 4 hr in lime juice, chopped fresh red chillies and seasoning. Golden shallow fry the fish portions in oil, add chopped onion and diced tomato flesh then moisten with fish stock and add cloves, bayleaf, thyme, parsley and seasoning. Stew for 20 min and serve with rice creole style or mixed vegetables.

Chapter Nine

Meat Dishes

This chapter is divided into 14 main categories according to methods of cookery:

✧ Baked Meats, Game and Offal ✧

✧ Pies ✧

✧ Boiled Meats, Game and Offal ✧

✧ Braised Meats, Game and Offal ✧

✧ Deep-fried Meats, Game and Offal ✧

✧ Food Cooked at Table ✧

✧ Grilled Meats ✧

✧ Roast Meats and Game ✧

✧ Pot Roasted Meat and Game ✧

✧ Shallow-fried or Sautéed Meat and Offal ✧

✧ Shallow-fried Breaded Meats ✧

✧ Steamed Meats ✧

✧ Stewed Meats, Game and Offal ✧

✧ Stir-fried Meats ✧

Allow the following amounts of prepared raw meat per average portion:

100 g – prepared cutlets and escalopes
150–200 g – prepared steaks and chops
1.5 kg meat cut into 2.5-cm cubes for stewing for 10 portions
150–200 g – joints of meat on the bone
120–150 g – joints of meat off the bone

Baked Meats, Game and Offal

Application

Dry heat is applied in an oven, moisture coming from the item being cooked. Meats usually form part of dishes such as pies, filo pastry parcels, pasties and hot pots which are baked in an oven at 150–200 °C.

Baked Lamb [*Kleftiko* Greece]   Rub cubes of lamb with lemon juice and season with salt and oregano. Place into earthenware dishes, moisten with a little dry white wine, cover with a lid and bake very slowly.

Baked Lamb with Onions [*Tavas* Greece]   Place equal quantities of lamb and diced tomato flesh with sliced onion in an earthenware dish, flavour with artisha (optional) and season with salt, moisten with a little water, cover with a lid and bake very slowly.

Baked Leg of Lamb with Potatoes [*Arní tou Foúrnou* Greece]   Cut slits to the bone into the leg and insert cloves of garlic and rosemary sprigs. Place the leg into a casserole, sprinkle with olive oil, rosemary and salt, arrange quarters of potato around the meat, and sprinkle them with tomato purée diluted with water and then with olive oil. Moisten with a little stock and bake.

Baked Meat Pie [*Kjötbuoingur* Scandinavia]   Combine minced beef, lightly sautéed chopped onion, egg yolks and stiffly beaten egg whites, flavour with a little sugar and season with salt and pepper. Moisten with veal velouté and place into a shallow earthenware dish, sprinkle with breadcrumbs combined with grated zest of lemon, chopped parsley and melted butter and bake.

Baked Minced Beef with Pine Nuts [*Siniyeh* Israel]   Blend minced beef or lamb, parsley, onion, garlic and seasoning of salt, pepper and cinnamon to a fine purée. Spread the mixture in an oiled dish, sprinkle with golden fried pine nuts then bake. When golden and almost cooked moisten with tahina.

Baked Topside of Beef Colorado Style [USA]   Combine liquidised tomatoes, brown sugar, paprika, mustard, lemon juice, ketchup, cider vinegar and Worcester sauce. Rub the joint with garlic, place in an oven dish on a bed of sliced carrot, onion, bayleaf and thyme and pour the mixture over. Brush the joint with oil and bake.

Baked Turkey Pieces Mexican Style [*Mole Poblano de Guajolote* Mexico]   Pan fry dried chillies mulatos, dried chillies anchos and dried chillies pasillas, sesame seeds and coriander seeds, and retain. Lightly fry chopped onion and garlic in oil, add diced tomato flesh and grated Mexican chocolate or unsweetened cocoa. Add lightly fried raisins and browned unpeeled almonds. Add fried and crumbled tortilla bread and cubes of white bread to the mixture. Add the chillies and seeds to the mixture, moisten with stock and simmer for 30 min, season with salt and sugar then blend the mixture to a smooth sauce. Sauté legs, thighs and breasts of turkey in oil then transfer to a shallow dish, pour the sauce over the turkey and bake for approx. 2 hr. When cooked carve the turkey into portions, mask with the sauce, sprinkle with sesame seeds and serve.

Baked Venison Steaks [*Dyresteg* *Scandinavia*] Lightly brown seasoned steaks in oil then place in an earthenware dish and bake. Serve accompanied by veal velouté with the addition of sautéed chopped onion.

Beef and Macaroni Bake [*Pastitso* *Greece*] Sauté minced beef, chopped onion and garlic in olive oil then add tomato purée. Moisten with red wine and brown beef stock and cook, then finish with a liaison of cream. Toss cooked macaroni in oil with grated Kefalotíri cheese and beaten eggs and season with nutmeg. Place alternate layers of the macaroni and the meat in dishes, coat with cream sauce, sprinkle with grated Kefalotíri cheese and olive oil and gratinate in the oven.

Beef and Onions in Red Wine [*Stiffàto* *Greece*] Combine cubes of beef, blanched button onions, garlic, bayleaves, peppercorns, cinnamon stick and diced tomato flesh. Place into shallow dishes, moisten with red wine, vinegar, stock and olive oil, cover with a lid and bake slowly until the liquid has been almost completely absorbed.

Ham Loaf [*USA*] Combine equal amounts of minced smoked bacon and pork with breadcrumbs, Dijon mustard, sugar and sufficient beaten egg and milk to bind. Form a loaf shape, sprinkle with breadcrumbs and bake.

Hungarian Hot Pot [*Aratógulàs* *Hungary*] Arrange alternate layers of lardons of bacon, sautéed sliced onion and paprika, sliced spare rib of pork, sliced tomato and green pimento in a shallow dish then top with a layer of sliced potato. Moisten with stock, cover with a lid and bake.

Lancashire Hot Pot [*GB*] Combine sautéed cubes of lamb and lamb kidneys, sliced onion, shredded white cabbage, chopped parsley and seasoning. Arrange layers of the vegetables and meats in shallow dishes and top with slices of potato. Moisten with stock, sprinkle with melted butter and bake.

Meat Loaf [*USA*] Combine equal amounts of minced beef and veal and a quarter the amount of minced pork, chopped shallots and basil, breadcrumbs, chilli sauce, soy sauce and sufficient beaten egg and milk to bind. Form a loaf shape, cover with rashers of bacon and bake.

Moussaka [*Moussaká* *Greece*] Fry or grill sliced eggplant in olive oil. Fry minced beef in oil with chopped onion and garlic, and add tomato purée and tomato concassée. Moisten with white wine, add herbs, sugar and cinnamon and cook. Place alternate layers of eggplant and meat in shallow dishes, finishing with a layer of eggplant. Mask with cheese sauce made with Kefalotíri cheese, and gratinate.

Pomey's Head [*USA*] Combine equal amounts of minced beef and veal and half the amount of pork sausage meat, chopped shallots, Dijon mustard, rubbed thyme and sage and sufficient beaten egg and stock to bind. Form into a round dome shape and press a 2.5-cm hole in the centre. Sprinkle with flour and butter and bake.

Tattie Pot [*GB*] Arrange layers of cubed beef and lamb and sliced potatoes, onion and black pudding in shallow dishes; top with sliced potatoes and moisten with stock. Sprinkle the surface with oil and bake. Serve accompanied by pickled red cabbage.

Toad in the Hole [*GB*]   Heat dripping in shallow dishes then place in cooked beef or pork sausages. Pour in Yorkshire pudding batter and bake. Serve with HP Sauce.

Pies

Beef and Polenta Pie [*Tamal Mexico*]   Sauté minced beef and chopped onion until brown, add diced tomato flesh, flavour with chilli powder and cayenne then moisten with stock and cook. Place the mixture into shallow dishes, cover with a layer of polenta mixture then bake until golden.

Beef, Leek and Potato Pie [*GB*]   Sauté 2-cm cubes of beef, moisten with stock, add chopped parsley, thicken with arrowroot and cook. Place the cooled mixture into pie dishes, add a layer of sliced leek and diced potato, cover with suet pastry then bake.

Beef, Onion and Mushroom Pie or London Double Crust Pie [*GB*]   Sauté minced beef, chopped onion and sliced mushrooms in dripping, add a little curry powder then moisten with stock and red wine; season and cook. Line pie dishes with short pastry, fill with the cooked meat, cover with pastry and bake.

Cornish Pasties [*GB*]   Combine finely diced raw beef, swede and potato with chopped parsley and seasoning. Roll out short pastry and cut 10-cm diameter pieces, place a pile of the filling in the centre, fold in half, seal, crimp the edge then bake.

Egg and Bacon Pie [*GB*]   Line a pie dish with puff pastry, sprinkle with fried lardons of bacon then break eggs over them and sprinkle the top with more lardons, cover with puff pastry and bake.

Hare and Grouse Pie [*GB*]   Combine cubes of grouse, hare and lamb's kidney, sliced mushrooms, lardons of bacon, veal forcemeat balls and chopped onion, basil, marjoram and parsley. Place into pie dishes. Moisten with port and brown game stock, cover with short pastry and bake.

Lamb, Féta and Mitzithra Cheese Pie [*Kreatopita Greece*]   Fry cubed lamb and chopped onion until coloured, moisten with stock then reduce the liquid by half. Add grated Mitzithra cheese and Féta cheese, chopped dill and parsley. Line flat dishes with short pastry, fill with the lamb then cover with short pastry and bake.

Lamb and Sage Cobbler [*GB*]   Fry cubes of lamb and sliced onion until coloured, add drained soaked dried peas and chopped parsley, basil and marjoram. Moisten with lamb stock and cook. Place the mixture into suitable pie dishes, cover with squares of sage-flavoured scone pastry then bake.

Loin of Veal Baked in Pastry [*Longe de Veau Farcie en Croûte France*]   Pot roast a boned loin of veal; when cooked allow to cool. Cover the joint with sage and lemon stuffing then envelop in puff pastry and bake. Serve accompanied by lime sauce.

Mutton Patties [*GB*]   Line patty tins with short pastry. Combine cooked minced lamb with cooked chopped onion, chopped parsley and walnuts, grated zest of orange, mace, cinnamon, nutmeg and jus lié. Fill into patty tins, cover with pastry and bake.

Pork Cobbler [*GB*]   Combine cubes of pork, diced onion, carrot, turnip and leek, chopped parsley, basil and marjoram and suitable stock. Place the mixture into dishes, cover with foil and bake until half cooked. Remove the foil and arrange squares of savoury scone pastry on top, then bake again until cooked.

Pork Pie [***Empanada de Lomo** Spain*]   Marinate cubes of pork in white wine with thyme, marjoram, paprika and ground pepper. Sauté the meat with chopped onion and green pimento, moisten with the marinade liquid then add diced potato and cook. Line pie dishes with short pastry, fill with the pork mixture then cover with pastry lids, decorate and bake.

Rabbit Pie [*GB*]   Combine rabbit joints, lardons of bacon, veal forcemeat balls and chopped onion, basil, parsley and marjoram, and season with salt, pepper and mace. Place the mixture into pie dishes, moisten with game stock, cover with puff pastry, decorate and bake.

Raised Beef and Egg Pie [*GB*]   Line raised pie moulds with hot water pastry. Combine minced beef, shredded suet and seasoning. Fill the moulds with the mixture and place hard-boiled eggs in the centre of the meat. Cover with a puff pastry lid, decorate and bake. When cooked fill the pie with beef jelly.

Raised Mutton Pie or Cumberland Pie [*GB*]   Line raised pie moulds with hot water pastry. Combine minced mutton, currants, raisins, candied peel and soft brown sugar and flavour with mixed spice and a sprinkling of rum. Fill the moulds with the mixture, cover with puff pastry lids, decorate and bake.

Raised Veal and Ham Pie [*GB*]   Line raised pie moulds with hot water pastry. Layer with diced shoulder of veal, diced gammon, chopped walnuts, mushrooms, grated zest of lemon, parsley and seasoning. Place hard-boiled eggs amongst the meat, cover with puff pastry lids, decorate and bake. When cooked fill the pie with veal jelly.

Steak and Kidney Pie [*GB*]   Combine cubes of beef and ox kidney, chopped onion and parsley, brown beef stock, Worcester sauce and seasoning. Place the mixture into pie dishes, cover with puff pastry, decorate and bake.

Veal and Plum Pie [*GB*]   Combine diced veal, stoned plums, dates, chopped parsley, basil and marjoram and season with salt, pepper, cinnamon and sugar. Place the mixture into pie dishes, moisten with white wine and stock, cover with short pastry and bake.

Veal and Pork Pot Pie [*GB*]   Combine cooked diced veal, strips of boiled pickled pork, sliced onion, chopped parsley, veal stock and seasoning. Place into pie dishes with alternate layers of sliced parboiled potatoes. Cover with short pastry and bake.

Venison Pie [*GB*]   Arrange layers of fried venison steaks and lamb kidney fat in pie dishes. Season with salt, pepper, nutmeg and chopped fresh herbs and moisten with port, lemon juice and game stock. Cover with puff pastry, decorate and bake.

Boiled Meats, Game and Offal

Application

Boiling is generally carried out by gentle simmering of joints, cuts and other meat items in stock or water with the addition of vegetables and herbs.

Boiled Beef, Chicken and Calf's Liver [*Shin Sullro* Korea]   Combine minced beef, chopped onion, garlic and beaten egg and mould into small oval shapes. Poach them together with goujons of chicken, strips of beef and of liver, diced onion, carrot, celery and pine nuts in chicken stock until they are all cooked.

Boiled Beef, Chicken and Pork with Vegetables [*Cozido à Portuguesa* Portugal]   Boil diced beef, pork and chicken in water, staging the cooking times together with turned carrots, turnips, potatoes and quartered cabbage. Serve the meats with the vegetables in an earthenware tureen, moistened with the cooking liquor and accompanied by boiled rice and garnished with sliced chorizo sausage.

Boiled Beef French Style [*Boeuf Bouilli à la Française* France]   Cook fresh brisket of beef in water with peppercorns, thyme, bayleaf and cloves. Simmer then add turned carrots and turnips, button onions, leeks, celery and cabbage. Serve the sliced meat with the vegetables, accompanied by coarse salt, gherkins and French mustard.

Boiled Beef, Pork and Lamb with Vegetables [*Burgoo* USA]   Boil a shin of beef, hand of pork, breast of lamb and a chicken with button onions, sliced carrot and okra, diced potato, lima beans and fresh red chillies. When cooked add tomato concassée, season with Worcester and Tabasco sauces and cayenne pepper. Reduce the cooking liquor to a thickish consistency, then add carved portions of the meats.

Boiled Beef Russian Style [*Varyonaya Govyadina s Khrenom* Russia]   Cook a joint of brisket of beef in water with fresh red chillies, peppercorns, bayleaf and thyme. Add turned carrots and turnips, button onions and small potatoes. Combine grated horseradish and soured cream with some of the cooking liquor to form a sauce. Serve the sliced meat and vegetables accompanied by the sauce.

Boiled Beef with Chillies and Carrots [*Changjorim* Korea]   Cook a joint of beef in water with soy sauce, fresh chillies and turned carrots.

Boiled Beef with Farfel and Prunes [*Prune Tsimmes* Israel]   Poach a seared joint of brisket of beef in water with sliced onion and flavourings of ground cinnamon, nutmeg and salt, and simmer. Add farfel and cook, then add stoned prunes, honey and grated zest and juice of lemon. When cooked, cover the sliced meat, farfel and prunes with some of the cooking liquor and bake. Serve accompanied by boiled rice, barley or kasha.

Boiled Beef with Honey [*Israel*]   Cook a joint of brisket of beef in water with root vegetables, bayleaf and thyme. Soak slices of rye bread in water, mash and add honey and lemon juice, add to some of the cooking liquid, boil and strain. Serve the sliced meat and vegetables coated with the liquid.

Boiled Beef with Horseradish Sauce [*Papparrotskött* Scandinavia]   Cook a joint of brisket of beef in water with root vegetables, bayleaf and thyme. Serve the sliced meat and vegetables coated with the cooking liquid, accompanied by horseradish sauce.

Boiled Beef with Red Chillies [*Gangas* Indonesia]   Boil a joint of brisket of beef in water with root vegetables, remove the meat and cut into cubes while reducing the strained stock by half. Blend ground cumin, coriander and ginger, garlic, trasi and oil to a paste. Add the paste to the cooking liquor, replace the meat, add chillies cut into rings and simmer until most of the liquor has reduced, then finish with lime juice.

Boiled Beef with Red Kidney Beans [*Caribbean*]   Boil cubes of salted silverside with turned carrots, button onions, thyme, bayleaf, cloves, marjoram and mace. Combine the meat with cooked red kidney beans, coconut milk and diced fresh red chillies and moisten with liquid from the meat. Thicken with arrowroot and serve with the carrots and onions accompanied by boiled rice.

Boiled Beef with Rice Vermicelli [*Yukkae Jang Kuk Korea*]   Cook a brisket of beef in water with root vegetables until very well done. When cooked, break the meat into shreds, cover it with stock, and add sliced spring onions, sugar, seasoning and the soaked rice vermicelli. Bring to the boil, add a paste made of sesame oil and chilli powder then pour in beaten eggs to form threads. Serve accompanied by boiled rice.

Boiled Beef with Spiced French Beans [*Sajoer Asem Indonesia*]   Boil a joint of brisket of beef in water with duan leaf, lemon grass, mace and peppercorns. Cut the meat into cubes, add to the stock with sliced onion, sambal ulek, laos powder, sugar, French beans, strips of red and green pimento and leek. Cook until tender then finish by flavouring with lemon juice.

Boiled Beef and Pork with Vegetables [*Kokt Middags Mal Albert Scandinavia*]   Fry a joint of brisket in oil until brown on all sides, barely cover with water, season and cook. When three-quarters cooked add turned carrots, turnips and potatoes. In a separate pan boil a joint of salt pork in water, and when almost cooked add quarters of cabbage. Serve the carved meats garnished with the vegetables and moistened with some of the cooking liquor.

Boiled Brisket of Beef [*Pyonyuk Korea*]   Boil a joint of brisket in water with root vegetables and herbs. Press the cooked meat under weight until cold. Serve cut in slices garnished with the vegetables, cucumber and hard-boiled eggs, masked with a dressing made of cider vinegar, sesame oil, garlic, chopped spring onions and toasted sesame seeds.

Boiled Hand of Pork with Beer [*Schweinshaxe Germany*]   Boil a joint of pork in salted water with carrot, celery, leek, onion, bayleaf and peppercorns. Place the joint into a shallow dish, moisten with some of the stock and beer and glaze it in the oven. Serve accompanied by knödel dumplings or sauerkraut.

Boiled Knuckle of Pork [*Eisbein Germany*]   Boil fresh or salted knuckles of pork in water with carrot, celery, leek, onion, bayleaf, cloves and peppercorns. Remove the bones from the knuckles and serve accompanied by purée of peas.

Boiled Leg of Lamb with Dill Sauce [*Kokt Lamm i Dill Sas Scandinavia*]   Boil a leg of lamb in water with root vegetables, dill and seasoning. Serve the carved meat coated with the cooking liquid, accompanied by dill sauce.

Boiled Leg of Lamb with Parsley Dumplings [*GB*]   Boil a leg of lamb in water with turned carrots, sliced onion, a bouquet garni and seasoning. When nearly cooked add suet dumplings made with the addition of chopped parsley and cook in the simmering liquid. Serve carved meat, coated with lightly thickened cooking liquid, carrots and the dumplings.

Boiled Leg of Pork with Broad Beans [*GB*]   Boil a salted leg of pork in water with turned carrots, turnips, sliced onion and a bouquet garni. When almost cooked add broad beans and cook until tender. Coat carved slices of the meat moistened with cooking liquid with the vegetables and serve accompanied by parsley sauce.

Boiled Loin of Pork with Eggplant [*Caribbean*]   Seal a boned and rolled loin of pork in groundnut oil, moisten with brown stock and jus lié, add thyme, sage, allspice and crushed green chillies, simmer then add diced eggplant. Serve accompanied by boiled rice.

Boiled Loin of Pork with Mustard Sauce [*Yudebuta Japan*]   Simmer a boned, rolled and tied loin of pork in white stock with sliced onion, ginger and mirin. Serve slices of the joint accompanied by mustard sauce.

Mustard Sauce: mix Japanese or English mustard to a paste with boiling water, add soy sauce and season with monosodium glutamate.

Boiled Ox Tongue in Mushroom Sauce [*Marhanyelv Gombamàrt Pssal Hungary*]   Boil an ox tongue in salted water with celery and parsley. Serve the sliced tongue coated with mushroom sauce finished with red wine.

Boiled Ox Tongue with Sweet and Sour Sauce [*Israel*]   Simmer a picked ox tongue in water. Serve the sliced tongue coated with sweet and sour sauce.

Boiled Pig's Tail with Rice and Cabbage [*Caribbean*]   Boil unsmoked cubes of pork and sliced pig's tail in water, then add the following and continue cooking: whole onion, cloves of garlic, sliced red pimento, red chillies, thyme, fennel seeds, allspice, lime juice and seasoning. Simmer and when almost cooked add long-grain rice, then add a layer of sliced cabbage. When cooked combine the ingredients and serve with knobs of butter on top.

Boiled Salt Pork with Pease Pudding [*GB*]   Boil the salted joint of pork in water with turned carrots, turnips and parsnips, batons of celery, small onions, quarters of cabbage and herbs. Serve carved into slices with the vegetables and pease pudding.

Boiled Short Rib of Beef [*Kalbi-Tchim Korea*]   Marinate lengths of ribs of beef in soy sauce, cider vinegar, rice wine, sesame oil, garlic, ginger, toasted sesame seeds and sugar. Fry the ribs in oil, add diced carrot and onion, moisten with the marinade and stock and cook. Glaze the ribs by reducing the liquid to a syrup and serve sprinkled with pine nuts, toasted sesame seeds and strips of fried egg.

Boiled Shoulder of Mutton with Cabbage and Caraway [*Ürühús Édes Kàposztàval Hungary*]   Boil a boned and rolled shoulder of mutton or lamb in salted water with caraway seeds, green pimento, quarters of cabbage and turned potatoes. Serve the sliced meat with the cabbage and boiled potatoes, moistened with the liquor and accompanied by paprika-flavoured mutton velouté made from the cooking liquor and finished with soured cream.

Boiled Silverside and Dumplings [*GB*]   Boil the salted silverside in water with turned carrots, small onions and herbs. Mould suet pastry into small dumplings and cook in the simmering liquid. Serve slices of the meat with the carrots, onions, dumplings and the cooking liquid.

Boiled Silverside with Pease Pudding [*GB*]   Boil the salted silverside in water with turned carrots, small onions and herbs. Serve the sliced meat with the vegetables accompanied by pease pudding.

Boiled Smoked Hock with Red Beans [*Caribbean*]   Boil hocks of bacon then add half-cooked red kidney beans, sliced onion with a flavouring of brown sugar, ground cloves, grated nutmeg, garlic, thyme and bayleaf and simmer until cooked. Serve sprinkled with chopped chives and accompanied by boiled rice or cooked yams.

Boiled Soured Pork [*Schweinesauer Germany*]   Boil a leg of pork in salted water with wine vinegar, diced carrot, celery, onion, leek, bayleaf and thyme. Thicken the liquor with arrowroot and sweeten with sugar. Serve carved slices of pork on a bed of sauerkraut, coated with the cooking liquor.

Boiled Spiced Beef [*Changjorim Korea*]   Boil a piece of beef in water flavoured with soy sauce and sesame oil with fresh red and green chillies and quarters of green pimentos. When cooked, cut strips from the joint and set with the chillies and pimento in some of the cooking liquid, reduced so that it sets to a jelly. Carve the rest of the beef into slices and serve with boiled rice and kimichi and some of the jellied garnish.

Boiled Tripe Oporto Style [***Tripas à Modo do Porto** Portugal*]   Boil squares of veal tripe, pieces of chicken and bacon, slices of chorizo sausage, presunto, calf's or pig's trotter, turned carrots, button onions, a bouquet garni and cumin seeds in salted water. Combine the meat pieces with cooked butter beans and a little of the liquid. Serve garnished with the carrots and onions accompanied by braised rice.

Calf's Cheek with Vinaigrette Sauce [***Tête de Veau Vinaigrette** France*]   Soak a boned calf's cheek and tongue for 12 hr and the brain for 2 hr. Blanch the cheek and the tongue; discard the ears, nostrils and eye apertures then cut cheek and tongue into 5-cm squares. Cook the cheek and tongue in a blanc and the brain in a court-bouillon. Serve garnished with picked parsley, accompanied by vinaigrette sauce.

Pepperpot [*Caribbean*]   Cut stewing beef and salt beef into 2.5-cm cubes, a boiling fowl into 10 pieces, oxtail into sections and pigs' trotters into sections. Wash the meats under cold water, place into a pan, cover with cold water and blanch; drain and rinse under cold water. Place into a clean pan, cover with cold water, bring to the boil and simmer for approx. 1 hr. Add cassareep, cook for 30 min then add chopped fresh red chillies, cloves, bayleaves, lemon juice, vinegar, brown sugar, stick cinnamon, salt and pepper. When all is cooked serve with plain boiled rice.

Poached Beef with Ginger [***Gyuniku No Tsudani** Japan*]   Simmer water flavoured with thinly sliced fresh root ginger, soy sauce, mirin, saké, sugar and monosodium glutamate for 4 min. Add strips of fillet of beef and simmer for 15 min until tender and most of the liquid has reduced to a glaze. Serve slightly chilled.

Poached Veal Meatballs in Egg and Lemon Sauce [***Youvarlákia** Greece*]   Combine minced veal, chopped onion boiled in water with butter, uncooked rice, chopped parsley and beaten eggs. Form the mixture into walnut-sized balls. Poach the meat balls in chicken stock for at least 30 min and serve them coated with egg and lemon sauce.

Tripe and Onion [*GB*]   Cook squares of tripe in water with sliced onion and seasoning. Drain the tripe and onions, add parsley sauce, mix in and serve.

Braised Meats, Game and Offal

Application

Brown braising is the cooking of small joints and cuts of meat which are first passed through seasoned flour then shallow fried with a mirepoix of vegetables and herbs. Two-thirds cover with brown stock or jus lié, cover with a lid and cook in an oven at 180 °C.

White braising is the cooking of small joints and cuts of meat with vegetables and herbs. Two-thirds cover with white stock, cover with a lid and cook in an oven at 180 °C.

Braised Beef Olives with Gherkins [*Rindsrouladen* Germany] Spread thin beef steaks with mustard then place a pickled gherkin wrapped in bacon in each; roll up and tie. Brown the floured olives in oil then braise in jus lié.

Braised Beef Olives with Mushrooms [*Töltött Felsàl* Hungary] Spread thin beef steaks with mustard then place mushroom duxelle combined with milk-soaked bread in each; then roll up and tie. Brown the floured olives in oil, moisten with stock then braise. Strain and thicken the cooking liquid and enrich with soured cream.

Braised Beef Olives with Veal Forcemeat [GB] Encase veal forcemeat in flattened steaks then flour and fry them in oil with sliced onion. Moisten with stock then braise and serve in the usual manner.

Braised Beef Olives with Vegetables [*Töltött Felsàl Zöldséggel* Hungary] Combine duxelle of mushrooms with cooked rice, strips of ham, fresh mixed herbs and eggs then enclose portions of the mixture in thinly flattened steaks. Roll up and tie then brown the olives in oil with sliced onion, carrot and celery. Moisten with stock then braise. Finish the sauce with soured cream and serve garnished with a selection of boiled vegetables.

Braised Beef, Bacon and Veal Olives [*Erdélyi Hústekercs* Hungary] Flavour minced bacon and calf's liver with marjoram, then encase portions in flattened steaks with strips of veal. Brown the floured steaks in oil, sprinkle with paprika, moisten with stock then braise. Finish by adding soured cream to the cooking liquor.

Braised Beef with Lotus Roots and Ginger [*Lien Tzu Ngow Yuk* China] Fry thin slices of steak in garlic-flavoured oil, add grated ginger, grated zest of orange, oyster sauce, soy sauce, stock and lotus roots then braise.

Braised Calf's Liver Cholent Style [Israel] Fry slices of calf's liver in chicken fat, add sliced carrot and onion, season with salt and paprika, moisten with stock and braise.

Braised Calf's Liver with Soured Cream [*Lever med Sur Gradde* Scandinavia] Soak larded whole liver in water for 30 min, drain and dry. Fry the seasoned liver in oil until golden on all sides, moisten with milk and braise for approx. 1 hr, then add soured cream. When cooked lightly thicken the cooking liquid with diluted arrowroot and serve carved slices coated with the sauce.

Braised Calf's Sweetbreads [*Ris de Veau à la Soubise* France] Blanch then braise veal sweetbreads on a bed of sliced onion with white wine. Reduce the cooking liquor then add cream to make the sauce. Arrange the sweetbreads on a base of the puréed onion, sprinkle with sautéed sliced mushrooms and diced ham and coat with the sauce. Sprinkle with grated cheese and butter and gratinate.

Braised Fillets of Veal with Vegetables and Soured Cream [*Pàrlot Borjúhús Szt. Julien Módon* Hungary] Brown floured fillets of veal in oil then braise with lardons of bacon, sliced mushrooms, julienne of carrots and celery and white wine. Serve the fillets covered with the garnish and coated with the reduced cooking liquid finished with soured cream.

Braised Knuckles of Pork with Sauerkraut [*Schweinshaxen mit Kraut Germany*] Fry chopped onion and diced dessert apples in oil, add the sauerkraut and bayleaf and moisten with white wine, pork or chicken stock. Press knuckles of pork into the sauerkraut and braise until tender.

Braised Leg of Lamb Castilian Style [*Cordero Asado, Estilo Castellano Spain*] Rub a leg of lamb with garlic, season with salt, pepper and paprika and brown in the oven. Simmer stock, vinegar, cloves of garlic, sliced onion, bayleaf, sprigs of parsley, rosemary, oregano, ground cumin and lemon juice for 15 min. Moisten the joint with the mixture, cover with a lid and braise.

Braised Loin of Pork with Soured Cream [*Schweinefilet Germany*] Brown a loin of pork in oil with a mirepoix of vegetables and herbs; moisten with jus lié then braise. Reduce the strained liquor and add dry red wine and soured cream. Serve slices of the pork with braised red cabbage.

Braised Oxtail with Haricot Beans [*GB*] Brown sections of oxtail in oil with a mirepoix of vegetables, lardons of bacon and herbs. Stir in tomato purée and moisten with stock; add squashed tomatoes then braise. Strain and thicken the braising liquid, add cooked haricot beans and serve.

Braised Paprika Steaks with Soured Cream [*Alföldi Felàl Hungary*] Brown floured larded beef steaks in oil, sprinkle with paprika, add sautéed sliced onion, thyme and bayleaf then moisten with stock and braise. Finish the sauce with soured cream and serve garnished with braised green pimentos.

Braised Soured Beef [*USA*] Marinate a joint of beef for 3 days in vinegar, lemon juice, water, garlic, celery, carrot, parsley, bayleaf, thyme, cloves and Worcester sauce. Brown the joint in oil with cubes of salt pork, moisten with stock and the marinade then braise until tender.

Braised Steaks California [*Manzo alla Californiana Italy*] Brown beef steaks in hot oil, moisten with red wine vinegar, brown stock and yogurt then braise. Serve coated with the cooking liquor, topped with a swirl of cream and sprinkled with chopped dill.

Braised Steaks Hungarian Style [*Esterhazy Rosteloys Hungary*] Brown beef steaks coated with flour mixed with paprika in hot oil. Moisten with brown stock and wine vinegar, flavour with caraway seeds, thyme, bayleaf and zest of lemon and braise. Finish the thickened cooking liquor with soured cream and serve garnished with turned carrots.

Braised Steaks in Beer [*Ochsenfleisch in Bier Germany*] Brown floured beef steaks in hot oil and moisten with brown stock, beer, vinegar and corn syrup. Add lardons of bacon, sliced onion, diced carrot and herbs then braise in the usual manner.

Braised Stuffed Shoulder of Veal Hanover Style [*Kalbsschulter auf Hannoverische Art Germany*] Stuff a boned shoulder of veal with sausage meat or parsley, thyme and lemon stuffing, cover with bacon rashers and tie. Braise in veal stock and a little vinegar with turned carrots and turnips, button onions, batons of celery and herbs. Serve carved in slices coated with the reduced cooking liquid finished with cream, chopped anchovy fillets and chopped fresh herbs, accompanied by the vegetables.

Braised Topside of Beef with Savoy Cabbage [*Kelkàposztàs Marhasült Hungary*] Brown a larded joint of beef in hot oil then moisten with stock and jus lié. Add grated carrot, celeriac, onion and parsnip and shredded savoy cabbage, then braise. Finish by adding soured cream to the reduced cooking liquid. Serve the drained cabbage and vegetables at the side.

Braised Venison in Red Wine [*Guiso de Venado o Buey* Spain] Marinade venison steaks in oil with garlic, red wine, bayleaf, thyme, carrot, onion and celery. Brown the floured steaks in hot oil with lardons of bacon and the marinade vegetables. Moisten with the marinade liquid and brown stock then braise in the usual manner.

Braised Venison Steaks [*USA*] Brown floured venison steaks in oil then add chopped onion, garlic and squashed tomatoes. Moisten with red wine, add diced carrot and celery and Worcester sauce, then braise.

Meat Loaf [*Israel*] Combine minced beef with matzo meal, eggs, chopped onion and English mustard. Mould the mixture to a loaf shape in a dish, add lightly fried onions, moisten with brown stock and braise.

Deep-fried Meats and Offal

Application

Items need to be coated with either batter, beaten eggs or breadcrumbs to prevent fat from penetrating the meat during cooking. Meats are deep fried in hot fat at a temperature of 170–180 °C until golden and crisp.

Breaded Pork Escalopes [*Tonkatsu* Japan] Pass escalopes through flour, egg-wash and breadcrumbs and deep fry until golden. Serve garnished with lettuce and lemon wedges, accompanied by Worcester sauce.

Breaded Veal Escalopes [*Schnitzel* Germany] Coat veal escalopes with flour, eggwash and breadcrumbs, deep fry and serve with lemon wedges.

Calf's Liver Fritters [*Kanjon* Korea] Cut thin slices of liver into squares then pass through flour and beaten egg and deep fry in sesame oil. Serve accompanied by chojang vinegar dipping sauce.

Fried Beef Kebabs [*Gyuniku No Kushiyaki* Japan] Thread cubes of beef onto bamboo skewers with pieces of onion and marinate in soy sauce, mirin, sugar and seasoning. Pass through flour, eggwash and breadcrumbs then deep fry. Serve accompanied by boiled rice.

Fried Calves' Feet [*Gebackene Kalbsfüsse in Teig* Germany] Marinate squares of cooked calves' feet in dry white wine with peppercorns, parsley stalks, carrot, leek and seasoning. Coat with a batter made with beer and deep fry. Serve with sprigs of parsley and wedges of lemon.

Fritto Misto [*Italy*] Deep fry goujons of chicken, sliced eggplant and courgettes, mushrooms and pieces of sweetbread in yeast batter. Serve with segments of lemon.

Fried Pork Balls [*Padd Loog Chin* Thailand] Blend garlic, coriander root, lime juice and sugar to a paste. Combine the paste with minced pork and chopped dried Chinese mushrooms, shallots, water chestnuts and bamboo shoots, beaten eggs and flour. Form the mixture into small balls then deep fry in oil.

Noisettes of Lamb in Spiced Batter [*Kamargah* India] Cook noisettes of lamb in stock with cardamom pods, cloves, a cinnamon stick and black peppercorns. Drain well then pass through pakora batter and deep fry.

Steak Fritters [*Kanjon Korea*]   Pass thin slices of steak through flour and beaten egg then fry in sesame oil. Serve cut into squares accompanied by chojang vinegar dipping sauce.

Sweet and Sour Pork [*Gu Lo Yuk China*]   Pass cubes of pork through cornflour and beaten egg then fry in oil. Serve coated with sweet and sour sauce.

Sweet and sour sauce: sauté diced green and red pimento in oil, moisten with a mixture of cornflour diluted with soy sauce, saké, and vinegar flavoured with a little sugar, grated ginger and Chinese tomato sauce, and simmer for 2 min to form a light sauce.

Food Cooked at Table

Application

The raw food, garnishes and dipping sauces are prepared and presented to the diners who using sets of chop-sticks select pieces of food from the display and dip it into a donabe or sukiyaki-nabe containing simmering stock made with water flavoured with dried seaweed which is set on an on-the-table heater. The food is swished back and forth in simmering liquid until cooked then dipped into one of the accompanying sauces or dips.

One-pot Dishes [Nabemono, Japan]

One-pot Bean Curd [*Yudofu*]   Assemble slices of bean curd, grated ginger, finely sliced spring onion, julienne of toasted lava seaweed and bonito flakes in individual serving dishes. Pour water into a donabe and bring to boiling point, adding a section of dried seaweed, leaving for a few moments to extract its flavour and removing before boiling point is reached. Bean curd is cooked in the simmering liquid as required.

Accompanying dipping sauce: place dried seaweed in a pan, cover with cold water and bring to boiling point, and remove and discard the seaweed. Add bonito flakes and simmer for 2 min, flavour with soy sauce and mirin, strain and pour into bowls.

One-pot Chicken, Seafood and Vegetables [*Yosenabe*]   Assemble and serve in bowls peeled prawns, oysters, goujons of fillet of sole, strips of chicken fillet, grooved, sliced and blanched carrot, sliced bamboo shoots, julienne of spring onion, sliced bean curd, 7-cm pieces of bean gelatine noodles, mushroom caps, sliced Chinese cabbage and finely grated daikon, squeezed of excess moisture. Simmer second soup stock flavoured with saké, mirin, soy sauce and seasoning in donabe and set on a table heater. Food selected is cooked in the simmering liquid as required.

Accompanying dipping sauce: combine equal quantities of soy sauce and rice vinegar for the dipping sauce and pour into bowls.

One-pot Chicken with Vegetables [*Tori No Mizutaki*]   Cut a chicken as for sauté, removing all the bones, and poach in salted water. Prepare bowlfuls of shredded Chinese cabbage, button mushrooms, soaked and drained bean gelatine noodles, slices of bean curd, blanched chrysanthemum or spinach leaves, sections of spring onions, grated daikon squeezed of excess moisture, shredded dried red chillies and grated root ginger. Place a donabe pot containing the cooking liquor from the chicken on a table heater. Assemble bowls of prepared vegetables and cooked chicken to be cooked in the simmering liquid as required.

Accompanying dipping sauce: combine rice and citrus vinegars and soy sauce and pour into bowls.

One-pot Oysters with Bean Paste [*Kaki No Dotenabe*] Layer the bottom and sides of a donabe with a paste of red and white miso, pour in second soup stock flavoured with seven-spice powder and mirin and set on a table heater. Assemble and serve in bowls prepared oysters, small squares of grilled bean curd, diagonally sliced spring onion, chrysanthemum leaves or blanched spinach and mushroom caps.

Accompanying dipping sauce: moisten finely ground, toasted white sesame seeds with second soup stock flavoured with rice vinegar and light soy sauce and pour into bowls.

One-pot Red Snapper with Vegetables [*Ishikari-Nabe*] Assemble and serve in bowls goujons of red snapper, blanched Chinese cabbage leaves cut into strips, grooved, sliced and blanched carrot, boiled 5-mm slices of potato flavoured with devil's-tongue-root cake, mushroom caps, soaked and drained bean gelatine noodles, sliced bean curd, grated daikon squeezed of excess moisture and grated dried chillies, flavoured with second soup stock, citrus vinegar, soy sauce and monosodium glutamate. Pour water into a donabe and bring to boiling point, place in a section of dried seaweed, leave for a few moments to extract its flavour and remove before boiling point is reached. Food selected is cooked in the simmering liquid as required.

Accompanying dipping sauce: combine citrus vinegar, soy sauce and second soup stock flavoured with monosodium glutamate; pour into small bowls.

One-pot Simmered Beef with Vegetables [*Shabu Shabu*] Assemble in bowls strips of fillet of beef, sliced bean curd, blanched devil's-tongued noodles, mushroom caps, sliced trefoil or trimmed spinach and sliced Chinese cabbage, chopped spring onion and grated daikon, moistened with second soup stock flavoured with soy sauce and citrus vinegar. Place prepared seaweed on the bottom of a sukiyaki or donabe set on a table heater. Pour in water and bring to boiling point, removing the seaweed before boiling point is reached. Food selected is cooked in the simmering liquid as required.

Accompanying dipping sauce: moisten finely ground toasted sesame seeds with second soup stock flavoured with rice vinegar and light soy sauce; pour into small bowls.

Sin Sul Lo [Korea]

To serve food in true Korean fashion is to cook it at table, as best highlighted in their national dish Sin Sul Lo. The food is served in a charcoal-heated shin seol ro, or firepot as it is sometimes called. This table-sized pot has a central chimney for holding hot charcoal which is surrounded by a moat filled with simmering stock in which food is cooked to completion. Food is served with rice and an accompanying dipping sauce into which guests place the food they have selected with chopsticks.

Sin Sul Lo [*Korea*]   Make two omelettes, one with egg yolks and the second with egg whites only; roll them up and cut into strips. Pass small thin strips of calf's liver through seasoned flour and beaten egg yolks and lightly sauté in hot oil. Pass goujons of white fish through seasoned flour and beaten egg whites and quickly sauté in oil. Arrange strips of beef in the very hot moat of the firepot then add chopped onion, the liver, fish, strips of omelettes, strips of spring onion and carrot and a sprinkling of chopped walnuts and pine nuts. Moisten with beef stock, place the cover on the pot and place on the table accompanied by bowls of boiled rice. Guests help themselves to the cooked food then dip it into sesame seed sauce before eating.

Sesame seed sauce: blend golden dry-fried sesame seeds with sugar and moisten with soy sauce and vinegar. The cooking liquid is subsequently served as a soup.

Grilled Meats

Application

Cooking by direct heat items of meat that are not thicker than 7–8 cm. Some items are marinated before cooking and the marinade liquid is then used to brush them during cooking. Barbecueing is the outdoor version of grilling.

Barbecued Spare Ribs [*Siu Pai Gwut China*]   Season spare ribs of pork with salt and chopped garlic then marinade in hoisin sauce. Grill on a barbecue and serve with wedges of lemon.

Barbecued Spare Ribs [*Twaejigalbigui Korea*]   Marinate blanched spare ribs in soy sauce, sesame oil, sugar, garlic, ginger and toasted sesame seeds. Grill on a barbecue and serve with wedges of lemon.

Beef and Mushroom Kebabs [*Songisanjok Korea*]   Skewer alternate slices of steak and cooked mushrooms then marinate in soy sauce, rice vinegar, sesame oil, toasted sesame seeds, garlic and sugar. Grill and serve.

Beef Kebabs [*Pasanjok Korea*]   Skewer alternate slices of steak and spring onions then marinate in soy sauce, rice vinegar, sesame oil, toasted sesame seeds, garlic and sugar. Grill and serve.

Beef Satés [*Satay Daging Thailand*]   Marinate cubes of beef in lemon juice, ground turmeric, curry powder, cumin, sambal ulek, brown sugar, thick coconut milk and salt. Skewer the beef then grill and serve accompanied with sweet soy sauce or peanut sauce.

Broiled Lamb Chops with Dill [*Lamm Kotletter med Dill Scandinavia*]   Combine butter, chopped dill and onion. Brush chops with the butter mixture and grill them. Serve garnished with sprigs of dill.

Grilled Butterfly Lamb [*USA*]   Open up a leg of lamb while boning it out completely. Marinate for 12 hr in yogurt, garlic and mint then grill on a barbecue and serve carved into slices.

Grilled Lamb Cutlets with Garlic Mayonnaise [*Chuletas de Cordero con Ajioli Spain*]   Marinate lamb cutlets in olive oil and oregano. Grill the cutlets and serve accompanied by garlic-flavoured mayonnaise.

Grilled Marinated Fillet of Beef-[*Tereyaki Japan*]   Marinate strips of fillet of beef in diluted soy sauce, grated ginger, soft brown sugar, garlic and seasoning. Grill and serve.

Grilled Marinated Steak Korean Style [*Pulgogi Korea*]   Marinate steaks in soy sauce, garlic, ginger, sesame oil, toasted sesame seeds, sugar, sliced spring onion and black pepper. Grill and serve accompanied by boiled rice.

Grilled Marinated Steak Mexican Style [*Carne Asada Mexico*]   Marinate steaks in lime juice, corn oil and chilli powder. Grill and serve with segments of lime.

Grilled Marinated Steak with Fried Egg [*Bélszín Tükörtojàssal Hungary*]   Marinate beef steaks in oil with coarsely crushed black peppercorns and parsley, then grill and serve with a fried egg on top.

Grilled Meat Balls [*Koftah Greece*]   Combine minced beef or lamb, chopped garlic, fenugreek, coriander leaves and dried mint and beaten eggs then season with baharat and salt. Form into balls then grill and serve with rice and a relish.

Grilled Steak Flambéd with Rum [*Caribbean*]   Marinate beef steaks in olive oil, red wine vinegar, crushed garlic and seasoning. Grill then transfer to a serving dish, and flambé with rum. Slice the steaks, re-form them and serve sprinkled with chopped fresh herbs.

Grilled Sweetbreads [*GB*]   Wrap calf's sweetbreads in bacon rashers, skewer and grill them. Serve coated with breadcrumbs golden fried in butter, accompanied by bread sauce.

Lamb Kebabs [*Arni Souvláki Greece*]   Marinate cubes of lamb in olive oil, dry white wine, lemon juice, oregano, crushed garlic and bayleaves. Skewer the lamb between bayleaves and grill. Serve the kebabs on their skewers on a bed of rice with lemon wedges and picked parsley.

Lamb Kebabs with Yogurt Sauce [*Yogurtlu Kebabs Greece*]   Marinate cubes of lamb in olive oil, lemon juice, crushed garlic and seasoning. Skewer the lamb and grill the kebabs. Serve the kebabs on their skewers on a base of toasted strips of pitta bread, topped with strips of tomato flesh sautéed in oil. Mask with plain yogurt seasoned with cayenne pepper and salt.

Lamb, Pork and Veal Kebabs with Polenta [*Polenta con Scappate Italy*]   Marinate cubes of lamb, lamb's liver, pork, pig's liver, veal and calf's liver in olive oil and lemon juice. Skewer the meats between sage leaves, grill the kebabs and serve on fried lengths of polenta.

Lamb Sweetbread, Liver and Heart Kebabs [*Koloretsi Tis Souvlas Greece*]   Blanch lamb sweetbreads. Soak lambs' livers, lambs' kidneys and lambs' hearts in cold water and lemon juice, then cut into 2.5-cm squares. Marinate in olive oil, lemon juice, oregano, grated onion and bayleaves. Skewer the offals between bayleaves and grill the kebabs. Serve garnished with lemon wedges.

Lamb Tikka Kebab [*Tikka Kebab India*]   Blend lemon juice, onion, garlic, vinegar, yogurt, garam masala, paprika, root ginger and seasoning to a paste. Marinate cubes of lamb in the mixture then skewer them between pieces of onion and bayleaves and grill the kebabs. Serve the kebabs on their skewers on a base of rice with lemon wedges.

Mixed Grill [*Fatànyéros Hungary*]   Marinate beef steaks and pork chops with sliced onion, parsley, black pepper and oil. Grill the meats and serve garnished with game chips, braised cabbage, pickled gherkins, beetroot, green·pimento and boiled rice.

Mixed Grill Japanese Style [*Teppan-Yaki Japan*]   Cook sirloin steaks, scallops, prawns, pieces of green pimento, mushroom caps and mangetout on tepan-yaki grilling plates. Serve accompanied by dipping sauce.
   Dipping Sauce: combine soy sauce, mirin, saké, ginger juice and sesame oil.

Mutton or Lamb Kebabs Armenian Style [*Shashlik Kebab Russia*]   Marinade cubes of lamb in olive oil, ground cumin, cassia bark, red wine, lemon juice, tomato purée and garlic. Skewer the meat between pieces of red and green pimento, onion, fresh green chillies and cloves of garlic and grill them.

Mutton or Lamb Kebabs Indian Style [*Bottee Kebab India*]   Blend toasted desic-cated coconut, yogurt, onion, garlic, root ginger, nutmeg, cinnamon, cloves, car-damoms, black pepper and poppy seeds to a paste. Marinate skewered cubes of lamb or mutton in the mixture then grill them. Serve the kebabs on their skewers on a base of rice, accompanied by chapatis and onion sambals.

Noisettes of Lamb with Redcurrant Sauce [*GB*]   Wrap noisettes in bacon, set on slices of onion and grill. Serve coated with redcurrant sauce or with redcur-rant jelly.

Shashliks with Pomegranate [*Shashlyk s Granatovym Sokom Russia*]   Marinate cubes of lamb in red wine vinegar with onion, bayleaf and seasoning. Skewer the lamb between bayleaves and onion pieces and grill. Serve the shashliks on their skewers on a bed of rice with lemon wedges and accom-panied by pomegranate sauce.

Veal Saté [*Saté Lembu Indonesia*]   Blend ground almonds, ginger, coriander and turmeric then add coconut milk to form a paste. Marinate skewered cubes of veal in the mixture then grill them and serve accompanied by saté sauce.

Roast Meats and Game

Application

Joints and other meat items are cooked by radiated heat in the oven at 200 °C using fat as a basting agent.

Meat Loaf American Style [*USA*]   Combine 2 parts minced beef with 1 part minced pork or veal, sweated chopped onion, breadcrumbs, chopped parsley, beaten eggs, Worcester sauce and seasoning. Mould to a loaf shape in a roasting tray, cover with rashers of bacon and roast. Serve accompanied by jus lié.

Roast Kid [*Cabrito Assado Portugal*]   Mix paprika, garlic, salt, pepper and vinegar to a paste and smear it over a young kid. Roast it with sliced onion, bayleaves and pork fat. Swill the pan with white wine to make the gravy.

Roast Leg of Lamb Roman Style [*Abbacchio alla Romana Italy*]   Roast small cuts of leg of lamb on the bone then add lambs' kidneys and continue to cook. Liquidise red wine vinegar, rosemary, anchovy fillets, crushed garlic and seasoning. Pour the mixture over the meats and finish cooking. Serve with watercress, accompanied by the cooking liquor made into a sauce.

Roast Leg of Lamb with Buttermilk and Rosemary [*USA*]   Make incisions in the leg of lamb and insert a quarter clove of garlic in each. Combine crushed garlic, rosemary, Dijon mustard, buttermilk, oil and seasoning, spread over the leg and leave for 8 hr. Roast the meat then swill the pan with stock and the marinade to form the gravy.

Roast Leg of Lamb with Rosemary Sauce [*GB*] Rub rosemary and seasoning into the flesh of the boned leg of lamb, tie up and roast. Serve with lightly thickened roast gravy flavoured with chopped rosemary and finished with brandy and cream.

Roast Leg of Lamb with Savoury Potatoes [*Arni Psito Greece*] Half roast a leg of lamb. Combine sliced potatoes, sliced onion, tomato concassée, chopped parsley and seasoning, place in the roasting tray with the meat and moisten with white stock and lemon juice. Brush the surface of the potato with oil and continue to roast. Serve slices of the joint with the potatoes and sprinkled with chopped fresh herbs.

Roast Leg of Lamb with Tarragon and Orange [*Bàrànycomb Frascati Módra Hungary*] Score a leg of lamb, rub with salt and fill with strips of bacon, lamb's liver and ham. Roast the joint with chopped tarragon, sliced mushrooms, grated zest and juice of orange and white wine. Swill the pan with stock and finish with a liaison of egg yolks and cream to make a sauce.

Roast Leg of Lamb with Vegetables [*Fejér Megyei Sült Bàrány Hungary*] Roast a leg of lamb with the following blanched vegetables: florets of cauliflower, Brussels sprouts, batons of carrots, crescents of celeriac and mushrooms. When half cooked, stir in tomato juice. Swill the pan with stock and make into a sauce with soured cream. Serve slices of lamb with a portion of each of the vegetables, coated with the sauce.

Roast Loin of Pork with Apples [*USA*] Score a loin, rub with a mixture of salt, pepper and flour then roast for 30 min. Moisten with a mixture of boiled vinegar and sugar and when almost cooked add quartered apples sprinkled with sugar. Swill the pan with stock and cream to make the accompanying sauce.

Roast Loin of Pork with Apricots [*GB*] Make incisions in a skinned loin, fill them with cooked stoned apricots, replace the scored skin and roast.

Roast Loin of Pork with Caraway Seeds [*Köményes Sertéscomb Hungary*] Rub a skinned loin with crushed caraway seeds combined with salt, refrigerate for 1 hr then roast.

Roast Loin of Pork with Herbs [*Asado de Puerco Mexico*] Marinate a loin of pork in lime juice, chilli powder, orange juice, garlic, oregano and cumin. Roast the joint then swill the pan with white wine, add the marinade and stock then finish with soured cream.

Roast Loin of Pork with Pimentos and Eggplant [*Lomo de Cerdo con Escalibada Spain*] Rub a loin of pork with crushed garlic, thyme and seasoning and roast for 30 min. Add whole skinned red and green pimentos and peeled eggplant and continue to cook. Serve slices of pork garnished with strips of pimento and eggplant accompanied by salsa picante.

Picante sauce: simmer sliced onion in white wine and tarragon vinegar. When the liquid has almost reduced add chopped pickled cucumber, parsley and capers then add tomato sauce, simmer and season to taste.

Roast Loin of Pork with Prunes [*GB*] Make incisions in a loin of pork, fill with cooked stoned prunes, replace the scored skin and roast. When almost cooked moisten and baste frequently with prune juice mixed with lemon juice.

Roast Loin of Veal with Tarragon [*Tàrkonyos Borjúsült Hungary*]   Cut incisions into a loin of veal and fill with slices of anchovy-flavoured butter, then sprinkle with chopped tarragon. Roast the joint with clarified butter, soured cream and white wine, basting frequently.

Roast Marinated Rabbit [*Arnbab Chermpoula Middle East*]   Rub a whole rabbit with vinegar and leave for 2 hr. Blend onion, garlic, coriander leaves, fresh red chillies, paprika, saffron and seasoning to a paste. Smear the rabbit with the spice paste then truss and roast. Serve with rice or couscous.

Roast Ox Tongue in Wine Sauce [*Marbanyelv Vadasan Hungary*]   Boil an ox tongue in water with carrot, celeriac, onion, mushrooms and potato. Liquidise the vegetables with a little stock then roast the skinned tongue with the vegetable purée, basting occasionally. Add soured cream and stock to make a sauce. Serve the sliced tongue masked with the sauce.

Roast Saddle of Hare [*Marinerad Stekt Hare Scandinavia*]   Marinate a larded saddle of hare in red wine, olive oil, roughly cut carrot, onion and celery, crushed garlic, allspice, crushed juniper berries and crushed peppercorns, thyme and bayleaves. Roast the saddle and swill with the marinade and brown stock to make the gravy.

Roast Saddle of Hare with Cream Sauce [*Stekt Hare Scandinavia*]   Marinate a larded saddle of hare in red wine, olive oil, roughly cut carrot, onion and celery, crushed garlic, allspice, crushed juniper berries and crushed peppercorns, thyme and bayleaves. Roast the saddle, swill with the marinade and brown stock and finish with a liaison of cream and redcurrant jelly.

Roast Sirloin of Beef with Yorkshire Pudding [*GB*]   Roast a Sirloin of beef, remove and retain. Drain off surplus fat from the roasting tray, add brown stock and simmer for a few min then strain. Arrange carved slices on a flat dish, coat with a little gravy and garnish with Yorkshire pudding and watercress, accompanied by horseradish sauce.

Yorkshire pudding: heat beef dripping in individual moulds or two 15-cm frying pans, pour in the Yorkshire pudding batter and bake in the oven at 200 °C for approx. 45 min until crisp and golden.

Roast Stuffed Breast of Veal [*Telyachya Grud Russia*]   Stuff a breast of veal with cooked buckwheat mixed with sliced cooked mushrooms, butter and soured cream. Roast and serve with watercress and accompanied by roast gravy.

Pot Roasted Meat and Game

Application

Place joints of meat, poultry or game on a bed of root vegetables and herbs, brush with oil or butter, cover with a lid and cook in an oven at 175–180 °C. During the latter stages of cooking remove the lid to allow the surface of the items to lightly colour.

Pot Roasted Leg of Lamb Kashmiri Style [*Rann India*]   Cut incisions into a leg of lamb. Combine grated ginger, crushed garlic, salt, ground cumin, turmeric, black pepper, cardamom, cloves, chilli powder and lemon juice and rub it into the incisions. Blend yogurt, almonds, pistachios, infused saffron and water to a paste. Coat the leg with the paste, cover with clingfilm and marinate for 12 hr. Pot roast the joint then serve accompanied by rice pilaff.

Pot Roasted Rabbit with Vegetables [*Krolik Russia*]   Marinate portions of rabbit in wine vinegar, water, bayleaf, thyme and seasoning. Pot roast with turned carrots and turnips and button onions. Swill the pan with stock and soured cream and serve the rabbit coated with the sauce, garnished with the vegetables.

Pot Roasted Saddle of Hare [*Haresteg Scandinavia*]   Marinate a larded saddle in red wine with bayleaf and thyme. Pot roast with sliced vegetables. Moisten with the marinating liquid and cream to make the sauce. Serve coated with the sauce, accompanied by sweetened loganberries or loganberry jelly.

Pot Roasted Saddle of Venison [*Selle de Venaison Tourangelle France*] Marinate a larded saddle in red wine with bayleaf and thyme. Pot roast it with sliced vegetables then glaze. Flambé with brandy and moisten with the marinating liquid and cream to make the sauce. Serve coated with the sauce, garnished with prunes filled with foie gras purée, and braised chestnuts.

Pot Roasted Shoulder of Lamb with Lemon [*Psito Katsarolas Lemonato Greece*]   Rub lemon juice, oregano and seasoning into the flesh of a boned shoulder, tie up and pot roast. Serve with watercress, accompanied by lemon-flavoured, lightly thickened gravy.

Pot Roasted Shoulder of Pork [*Schweinbraten Germany*]   Rub a shoulder of pork with salt, pepper and French mustard then seal it in hot fat. Pot roast the joint on a bed of sliced carrot and onion, thyme, bayleaf, parsley, clove and tomato. When cooked swill the pan with red wine and stock, thicken with arrowroot then strain. Coat the carved slices of pork with the gravy and garnish with potato dumplings.

Pot Roasted Sirloin of Beef Greek Style [*Moskhari Psito Greece*]   Rub lemon juice, oregano and seasoning into a sirloin then pot roast. Serve with watercress, accompanied by lemon-flavoured, lightly thickened gravy.

Pot Roasted Sirloin of Beef Yankee Style [*USA*]   Place a sirloin of beef on a bed of sliced onion, surround with batons of carrot and parsnips, moisten with stock then add turned potatoes and pot roast. Carve and serve with the vegetables and the thickened cooking liquor.

Pot Roasted Sirloin of Beef in Garlic Sauce [*Solomillo All-i-Pebre Spain*] Brown the joint in oil then place on a bed of sliced onion, moisten with a little vinegar and pot roast. Blend together garlic, parsley and stock then pour the mixture over the beef and continue to cook. Carve and serve with the onions and the cooking liquor.

Shallow-fried or Sautéed Meat and Offal

Application

All forms of meat including offals, provided they are not cut too thick, lend themselves to shallow frying, which is cooking done in a small amount of frying medium in a frying pan or sauté pan over heat. This process is also called sautéing, which really means tossing food over and over whilst shallow frying it; in France it is often referred to as 'à la poêle', not to be confused with poêléing which is akin to braising.

Shallow frying is a very popular way of cooking because it is quick and easy to do and is less fatty than deep frying. It is possible to shallow fry without any fat by using a non-stick frying pan. Some foods may need to be coated before frying by coating with flour or egg and breadcrumbs, though most cuts of meat can be cooked directly, being placed into hot frying medium so as to seal the surface thus preventing loss of natural juices. Any juices that do escape can be used to flavour any accompanying sauce by deglazing the pan with an appropriate liquid.

Shallow frying should not be confused with stir-frying, which is done by a completely different technique using different equipment.

Beef and Soya Bean Curd Medallions [*Wanjajon Korea*]   Combine minced beef, squeezed and crumbled bean curd, soy sauce, sesame oil, toasted sesame seeds and chopped onion. Form into small medallions, pass through flour and beaten egg then shallow fry. Serve accompanied by chojang dipping sauce.

Beef and Vegetable Sukiyaki [*Sukiyaki Japan*]   Fry strips of fillet of beef in oil, moisten with second soup stock, soy sauce and mirin, add sugar and monosodium glutamate, cooked shirataki noodles, pieces of grilled bean curd and chrysanthemum leaves or shredded spinach and cook quickly. Serve in bowls accompanied by a bowl of beaten egg for dipping the meat, vegetables and noodles in.

Beef Rissoles [*Keftethes Greece*]   Combine finely minced beef, chopped onion, breadcrumbs, chopped parsley, mint and oregano, crushed garlic, beaten eggs, olive oil, vinegar, water and seasoning. Shape into small balls and shallow fry in olive oil.

Beef Rissoles Florentine Style [*Polpette alla Fiorentina Italy*]   Combine cooked minced beef, garlic, dry mashed potatoes, chopped parsley, grated Parmesan cheese, bread soaked in milk and squeezed dry, beaten egg to bind and seasoning. Shape the mixture into flat rounds and shallow fry in olive oil.

Beef Steak in Cream Sauce [*Bifé à Marrare Portugal*]   Rub beef steaks with garlic and shallow fry in butter. Swill the pan with cream then replace the steaks. Serve accompanied by batatas fritas.

Beef Steak Stroganoff [*Bef Stroganoff Russia*]   Fry sirloin steaks in oil and retain. Lightly fry chopped onion and sliced button mushrooms in the same pan, moisten with soured cream and finish the sauce with mustard. Serve the steaks coated with the sauce and garnished with deep-fried matchstick potatoes.

Beef Steak with Paprika Sauce [*Bélszín Magyarosan Hungary*]   Fry beef steaks in oil and retain. Sauté chopped onion then stir in paprika and diced tomato flesh; moisten with wine vinegar and finish with soured cream. Serve the steaks coated with the sauce, accompanied by boiled noodles.

Beef Stroganoff [*Stroganoff Russia*]   Quickly fry floured strips of fillet of beef in oil, remove and add chopped onion to the pan and allow to sweat. Add diluted English mustard, moisten with stock and finish with smetana. Replace the beef, toss to mix in and serve.

Beef with Oyster Sauce [*Ho Yow Ngow Yuk China*] Pass thin slices of steak through a mixture of cornflour, ground ginger, soy sauce, saké and seasoning. Shallow fry in garlic-flavoured oil. Remove and retain the meat, add oyster sauce and a little water, simmer for 1 min then replace the meat and serve immediately.

Calf's Liver with Tomatoes [*Fegato al Pomodoro Italy*] Marinate slices of calf's liver in lemon juice. Sauté sliced onion and garlic in butter then add diced tomato flesh, sage and basil and simmer. Shallow fry the liver in olive oil and serve coated with the sauce.

Calves' Kidneys in Port [*Rim Salteado com Porto Portugal*] Sauté quartered kidneys in olive oil then retain. Sweat chopped shallots, moisten with port and jus lié then add chopped mushrooms. Serve the kidneys on fried bread croûtons and coat with the sauce.

Corned Beef Hash [*USA*] Combine equal quantities of chopped corned beef and diced boiled potatoes. Fry the mixture in an omelette pan until golden and crisp on both sides.

Escalope of Pork with Marjoram [*Lomo de Cerdo con Limón y Mejorana Spain*] Marinate escalopes of pork in oil, lemon juice, garlic and marjoram. Fry the escalopes in oil and serve on fried bread croûtons.

Escalope of Veal Milanese [*Costolette alla Milanese Italy*] Pass the escalopes through flour, eggwash and breadcrumbs and shallow fry in butter. Garnish with segments of lemon and sprigs of parsley.

Escalope of Veal with Cream Sauce [*Kalv Ruller Scandinavia*] Spread veal escalopes with butter combined with chopped parsley and grated zest of lemon. Roll into parcels, pass through flour, eggwash and breadcrumbs and shallow fry in butter. Serve garnished with segments of lemon and sprigs of parsley.

Escalope of Veal with Ham, Cheese and Tomato [*Costoletta alla Bolognese Italy*] Sauté chopped onion and garlic in olive oil then add diced tomato flesh and chopped basil and cook. Pass veal escalopes through flour, eggwash and breadcrumbs and shallow fry in butter. Serve with a slice of prosciutto and Gruyère on each and gratinate, then mask with the tomato sauce.

Escalope of Veal with Marsala [*Scaloppine alla Marsala Italy*] Marinate small veal escalopes with lemon juice then season and sauté in butter. Add lemon juice and Marsala to the pan and simmer for 2 min. Serve the veal coated with the slightly reduced sauce.

Escalope of Veal with Proscuitto [*Saltimbocca Italy*] Marinate small veal escalopes with lemon juice then sprinkle with sage and seasoning. Attach a slice of proscuitto to each escalope with a cocktail stick then shallow fry in sage-flavoured butter. Swill the pan with white wine and serve the escalopes coated with the cooking liquor.

Fried Gammon Rasher with Redeye Gravy [*USA*] Sauté gammon steaks in oil then swill the pan with black coffee and fresh cream. Serve the gammon coated with the sauce.

Fried Liver in Wine Sauce [*Lebergeschnetzeltes Germany*] Sauté slices of liver in oil and retain. Fry lardons of bacon and chopped onion in the same pan, swill with red wine, moisten with jus lié then add thyme and rosemary. Serve the liver coated with the sauce accompanied by knödel dumplings.

Fried Liver with Apple and Onion [*Leber Berliner Art Germany*] Sauté slices of liver in oil and serve garnished with shallow-fried apple and onion rings and grilled tomatoes.

Fried Liver with Cream [*Zharenaia Pechen Russia*] Sauté slices of liver in oil and retain. Add and sweat chopped onion, moisten with smetana and season. Serve the liver coated with the cream sauce.

Ginger Glazed Escalopes of Pork [*Butaniku No Shogazukeyaki Japan*] Marinate slices of boned loin of pork in fresh ginger juice, mirin, soy sauce and seasoning. Fry the pork in a pan brushed with oil and remove. Swill the pan with the marinade then replace the pork and reduce the liquid to a glaze. Serve accompanied by boiled rice and salad.

Glazed Escalopes of Pork [*Butaniku No Teriyaki Japan*] Marinate slices of boned loin of pork in fresh ginger juice, mirin, soy sauce and seasoning. Fry the pork in a pan brushed with oil and remove. Swill the pan with the marinade then replace the pork and reduce the liquid to a glaze. Serve accompanied by sliced pickled cucumber, pickled ginger and wedges of tomato.

Goujons of Beef with Marjoram [*Majorannàs Vetrece Hungary*] Marinate goujons of beef in oil with marjoram then shallow fry in oil with chopped onion. Add soured cream and mix with the goujons; serve accompanied by boiled rice.

Goujons of Pork in White Wine Sauce [*Rojoes à Moda de Tràs-os-Montes Portugal*] Marinate goujons of pork in white wine with garlic, thyme, bayleaf, cloves and paprika. Crisp fry the goujons in oil, remove and retain. Swill the pan with the marinade and reduce to a sauce consistency. Serve the goujons on the sauce accompanied by sautéed potatoes and sautéed boiled chestnuts.

Goujons of Pork with Cockles [*Porco à Alentejana Portugal*] Marinate goujons of pork in white wine with garlic, thyme, bayleaf, cloves and paprika. Golden fry the goujons in oil, moisten with the strained marinade and reduce it to a sauce consistency. Serve the goujons coated with the sauce and garnished with cockles cooked with tomato concassée.

Goujons of Pork with Cumin [*Rojoes à Mode de Viana do Castelo Portugal*] Marinate goujons of pork in white wine and white wine vinegar with garlic, thyme, bayleaf, cumin seeds and paprika. Sauté lardons of bacon and the goujons in oil then moisten with the marinade liquid and cook it to a coating consistency.

Jambalaya Louisiana Style [*USA*] Sauté a spicy smoked Spanish sausage in oil, add garlic, diced green pimento, tomato flesh, sugar, rubbed thyme, chilli powder and cayenne and simmer for 15 min. Slice the sausage and return to the pan, add long-grain rice, diced smoked ham and chicken stock and simmer until the rice is cooked, then add prawns and chopped parsley.

Korean Shinsollo [*Shinsollo Korea*] Cut sirloin steaks, suprêmes of chicken, calves' livers and fillet of halibut into strips. Pass them through flour and beaten eggs then shallow fry and reserve. Combine minced beef, chopped spring onions, garlic, ginger and soy sauce; form into small balls and shallow fry. Place chopped bean sprouts in shinsollo pots then add alternate layers of the meats, fish and meatballs. Top with a garnish of strips of fried egg white and yolk, sliced mushrooms, carrots, spring onions, gingko and pine nuts, and moisten with boiling chicken stock.

Lamb and Lentil Rissoles [*Shami Kebab Thailand*] Cook minced lamb with lentils and chopped onion. When cooked allow to cool. Add ground cinnamon, cardamom, cloves, chopped mint and beaten eggs, mould into round flat cakes and shallow fry.

Lamb Cutlet Portugese Style [*Costeletas de Cordeiro em Béchamel* Portugal]
Seal lamb cutlets in oil, coat them in stiff béchamel sauce then pass through
beaten eggs and breadcrumbs. Shallow fry in olive oil.

Lamb Steak with Rosemary [*Prizóles Arnioú* Greece]   Marinate lamb steaks in
olive oil, red wine, rosemary and garlic. Fry the steaks in oil to the desired
degree and serve.

Marinated Calf's Liver [*Iscas à Portuguesa* Portugal]   Marinate slices of liver
in white wine with garlic, bayleaf, chopped parsley and olive oil. Shallow fry the
liver in butter with lardons of bacon and sliced boiled potatoes. Moisten with
the marinade and white wine vinegar to form a thin sauce.

Medallions of Fillet of Beef with White Wine [*Párlot Mignonfilé* Hungary]
Combine grated onion and chopped parsley and spread it over medallions of
beef, place rashers of bacon on top and secure with toothpicks. Fry the medallions in lard, moisten with white wine and cook.

Minced Lamb Balls [*Köfte* Greece]   Combine minced lamb, grated onion,
chopped mint, crushed garlic, soaked and squeezed bread, seasoning and beaten
eggs. Mould the mixture into walnut-sized balls, roll in flour and fry in oil.

Minute Steaks with Tabasco [*Bulkoki* Korea]   Marinate thin beef steaks with
chopped shallots, garlic and spring onions, sugar, soy sauce, sesame oil and
Tabasco. Fry the steaks in peanut oil and serve accompanied by a dip.

Peppered Sirloin Steaks [*Entrecôtes au Poivre* France]   Sprinkle steaks with
salt and crushed peppercorns, lightly pressing them in. Sprinkle with oil and
marinate for approx. 1 hr. Fry the steaks quickly in butter, remove and retain.
Drain off surplus fat from the pan, add brown stock, simmer and reduce by
half, then whisk in knobs of unsalted butter to form a light sauce. Coat the
steaks with the sauce and serve sprinkled with chopped parsley.

Pork Chops in Beer Sauce [GB]   Season loin chops with salt, pepper and nutmeg and shallow fry in oil, then moisten with ale. Thicken the liquor with a
liaison of egg yolks and cream and add chopped capers and basil. Serve the
chops with the sauce, garnished with fried apple rings that have been sprinkled
with brown sugar and cinnamon, and glaze.

Pork Chops in Port and Rosemary Sauce [*Costeletas de Porco* Portugal]   Sauté
pork chops in oil with rosemary and retain. Sauté chopped onion, garlic and
diced tomato flesh then moisten with port. Serve the chops coated with this
sauce.

Pork Noisettes with Prunes [*Noisettes de Porc aux Pruneaux* France]   Fry
the noisettes in butter then retain. Flambé the pan with brandy and add cream
to make the sauce. Garnish the noisettes with stoned cooked prunes and mask
with the sauce.

Pozharshie Cutlets [*Pozharskie Kotlety* Russia]   Combine finely minced veal
with white breadcrumbs soaked in milk and squeezed out, cream, beaten eggs,
chopped dill, salt, pepper and nutmeg. Mould cutlet shapes and pass through
breadcrumbs. Shallow fry and serve garnished with sprigs of dill, accompanied
by mushroom sauce.

Red Flannel Hash [USA]   Combine equal quantities of diced corned beef, boiled
potatoes, cooked beetroot, chopped onion and parsley, lardons of bacon, cream
and seasoning. Fry the mixture in omelette pans until golden and crisp on both
sides.

Sautéed Beef with Five-spice Powder [*Ng Heung Ngau Yook Szee China*]
Combine five-spice powder, crushed garlic, grated ginger, cornflour and soy sauce. Marinate thinly sliced beef in the mixture for 2 min then shallow fry in sesame oil. Remove and retain the meat, add the marinade, simmer for 2 min to form a thin sauce then replace the meat and serve immediately with boiled rice or noodles.

Sautéed Belly of Pork with Apples [*Aebleflaesk Scandinavia*]
Shallow crisp fry slices of slightly salted belly of pork, remove from the pan and retain. Shallow fry apple rings in the pork fat, sprinkle with sugar and allow to caramelise. Serve the fried pork garnished with the apple rings.

Sautéed Calf's Liver, Heart and Kidney in Spiced Sauce [*Kirshub Middle East*]
Blend turmeric, ground coriander, cumin, baharat and water to a paste. Sauté chopped onion, garlic and ginger in oil then add diced calf's liver, heart and kidney. Cook and add the spice mixture, diced tomato flesh and chopped coriander.

Sautéed Escalopes of Pork with Red Wine and Coriander [*Afelia Greece*]
Marinate pork escalopes in red wine, crushed coriander seed, black peppercorns, cinnamon stick and salt. Crisp fry the escalopes in corn oil then add the marinade and simmer to reduce the liquid to a coating consistency. Serve the escalopes coated with the sauce and sprinkled with chopped mint.

Sautéed Escalopes of Pork with Sesame Seeds [*Buta No Gomayaki Japan*]
Marinate small escalopes of pork in soy sauce and ginger juice. Blend toasted white sesame seeds with soy sauce, saké and cornflour, add sugar and cook to a smooth paste. Sauté the escalopes in oil, spread them with the sesame paste and serve.

Sautéed Fillet of Lamb with Peas [*Arnaki me Araka Greece*]
Sauté slices of fillet of lamb in corn oil, add chopped spring onion, moisten with lemon juice and brown stock then add peas and chopped dill.

Sautéed Grenadins of Veal with Wild Mushrooms [*Fricando con Setas Spain*]
Sauté grenadins of veal in olive oil and retain. Add chopped Spanish onions, crushed garlic and diced carrot to the pan then add tomato concassée. Moisten with white wine and brown stock and add thyme, bayleaf and oregano. Add sautéed wild mushrooms and toasted nibbed almonds and replace the grenadins. Serve coated with the thickened sauce, sprinkled with chopped fresh herbs.

Sautéed Lambs' Kidneys with Sherry [*Riñones al Jerez Spain*]
Soak halves of lambs' kidneys in vinegar water. Fry chopped onion and crushed garlic in olive oil, add and sauté the kidneys then stir in paprika, breadcrumbs and marjoram. Moisten with dry sherry and stock. Serve sprinkled with chopped fresh herbs.

Sautéed Meat Balls [*Tod Man Nuer Thailand*]
Combine finely minced beef, minced pork, nutmeg, chopped coriander leaves, garlic, spring onions, nam pla, beaten eggs and seasoning. Divide into small balls then sauté in oil and serve accompanied by a salad.

Sautéed Pork Chops in Watercress Sauce [*Caribbean*]
Fry pork chops in oil and retain. Lightly fry chopped garlic, add ground cloves and moisten with lemon juice, white wine and stock. Reduce by half, and add rum, blanched chopped watercress and cream to make a sauce. Serve the chops coated with the sauce, garnished with blanched leaves of watercress and accompanied by boiled potatoes flavoured with fennel.

Sautéed Sirloin Steak in Red Wine Sauce [*Entrecôte Bordelaise France*] Sauté sirloin steaks in oil and retain. Swill the pan with red wine, reduce by half then add jus lié and seasoning. Serve the steaks with a slice of poached beef marrow on top, coated with the sauce.

Sautéed Steak in Soured Sauce [*Neua Brio Wan Thailand*] Golden fry chopped garlic in oil, add beef steaks and sauté then retain. Add chopped onion, batons of cucumber, diced tomato flesh and chillies. Moisten with soy sauce and white wine vinegar, add sugar then thicken with cornflour and garnish with chopped spring onions and coriander leaves. Return the steaks to reheat in the sauce.

Sirloin Steak Pizzaiola [*Costata alla Pizzaiola Italy*] Sauté crushed garlic in olive oil, moisten with passata then add chopped parsley and basil. Sauté sirloin steaks in garlic-flavoured olive oil and transfer to the sauce for 2 min. Serve coated with the sauce, sprinkled with chopped fresh basil.

Tournedos Rossini [*France*] Fry seasoned tournedos quickly in butter, remove and retain. Drain off surplus fat from the pan, add Madeira and reduce by half, then add jus lié to form a light sauce. Place steaks on round croûtons, garnish each with a slice of foie gras, coat with the sauce and serve with slices of truffle on top.

Tripe with Chickpeas [*Callos con Gabanzos en Salsa Picante Spain*] Sauté chopped onion in oil then add diced cooked tripe and salami. Add sherry, diced tomato flesh, bayleaf, thyme and chopped fresh green chillies and simmer to reduce the liquid. Stir in cooked chickpeas, chopped parsley and seasoning.

Veal and Potato Galettes [*Kjötkökur meao Kartöflum Scandinavia*] Combine finely minced veal with breadcrumbs soaked in milk and squeezed out, mashed potato, beaten eggs, chopped parsley, salt, pepper and nutmeg. Mould the mixture into round shapes and pass through breadcrumbs. Shallow fry and serve garnished with sprigs of parsley.

Veal Cutlets with Cured Ham and Pimento [*Ternera à la Extremeña Spain*] Season veal cutlets with salt, sprinkle with thyme and sauté in oil, add chopped onion and garlic, strips of green pimento and thinly sliced chorizo sausage. Moisten with sherry, chicken stock and tomato sauce and simmer until cooked.

Veal Cutlets with Ham, Mushrooms and Pimento [*Chuleta de Ternera Hortelana Spain*] Season veal cutlets with salt, sprinkle with thyme and sauté them in oil. Add chopped onion, garlic, sliced green pimento, mushrooms and jambón serrano. Moisten with white wine and chicken stock and reduce the liquid by half. Serve the cutlets coated with the sauce and garnished with the vegetables.

Veal Cutlets with Paprika [*Chuleta de Ternera al Ajo Cabañil Spain*] Sauté veal cutlets in oil, add chopped garlic, sprinkle with paprika, moisten with vinegar and stock and simmer.

Veal Cutlets with Sage and Rosemary [*Rustin Neggà Italy*] Sauté veal cutlets and lardons of bacon in butter and add chopped fresh sage and rosemary. Moisten with white wine and reduce the liquid completely, then add veal stock and simmer. Serve with risotto.

Veal Cutlets with Soured Cream and Paprika [*Paprikaschnitzel Germany*] Season veal cutlets with salt and paprika then sauté them in oil. Add strips of green pimento, sliced onion and diced tomato flesh. Moisten with jus lié and finish with soured cream.

Shallow-fried Breaded Meats

Breaded Beef Steak [*Filete Empanado* Spain]   Blend crushed garlic and chopped parsley to a paste then spread over flattened steaks, pass through flour, eggwash and breadcrumbs and shallow fry in oil and butter.

Breaded Pork Steaks [*Filetes de Cerdo 'Cantamañanas'* Spain]   Place a slice of Fontina cheese and strips of pimento between slices of flattened pork. Pass through flour, eggwash and breadcrumbs and shallow fry in oil.

Lamb Cutlets Reform [*GB*]   Pass flattened lamb cutlets through flour, eggwash and breadcrumbs and shallow fry in oil. Toss julienne of ham and tongue in butter, add julienne of gherkins, whites of hard-boiled egg, beetroot and truffle. Serve the cutlets garnished at the side with the mixture, accompanied by Reform Club sauce.

Veal and Apple Rissoles [*Subrics* Italy]   Combine minced veal, chopped apple, eggs and seasoning. Shape the mixture into round flat cakes, pass through flour, eggwash and breadcrumbs then shallow fry in oil.

Veal and Pork Balls [*Karbonader* Scandinavia]   Combine finely minced veal and pork, beaten eggs, breadcrumbs, chopped parsley and seasoning. Mould into oval balls, pass through flour, eggwash and breadcrumbs and shallow fry in oil. Serve accompanied by cream sauce.

Veal Cutlets in Cider [*Côte de Veau Vallée d'Auge* France]   Pass veal cutlets through flour, eggwash and breadcrumbs and shallow fry in oil and retain. Add chopped shallots and sliced mushrooms to the pan, add cider and reduce, then moisten with cream and flavour with meat glaze. Serve the cutlets garnished with button onions on a bed of the sauce.

Veal Cutlets with Fontina Cheese [*Costolette alla Valdostana* Italy]   Cut pockets in veal cutlets and fill them with slices of Fontina cheese, then pass through flour, eggwash and breadcrumbs and shallow fry in oil.

Veal Cutlets with Lemon [*GB*]   Pass veal cutlets through flour, eggwash and breadcrumbs mixed with grated zest of lemon and chopped basil, marjoram and parsley. Shallow fry and serve on a base of lemon sauce, with slices of lemon on top.

Veal Escalope Holstein [*Holsteiner Schnitzel* Germany]   Sprinkle veal escalopes with lemon juice then pass through flour, eggwash and breadcrumbs and shallow fry in butter. Garnish with fried eggs, anchovy fillets and chopped parsley.

Veal Escalope Rolls [*Paraghemistá Thamalísia Roulá* Greece]   Combine sweated chopped onion, minced ham, garlic, chopped parsley, thyme and seasoning. Spread the mixture over veal escalopes and roll and tie them Swiss-roll fashion. Sprinkle with lemon juice, pass through flour, eggwash and breadcrumbs then sauté in olive oil. Add white wine and veal stock and simmer to reduce by half, then add tomato sauce. Serve the veal coated with the sauce and sprinkled with chopped coriander.

Veal Escalope Vienna Style [*Wiener Schnitzel* Germany]   Sprinkle veal escalopes with lemon juice then pass through flour, eggwash and breadcrumbs and shallow fry in butter. Decorate with sieved hard-boiled egg, slices of lemon, anchovy fillets and chopped parsley.

Steamed Meats

Application

Cook in a pressure steamer according to the manufacturer's guide for cooking times.

Steak, Kidney and Mushroom Pudding [*GB*]   Combine cubes of beef and ox kidney, quartered mushrooms, chopped onion, parsley, Worcester sauce, brown stock and seasoning. Line pudding basins with suet pastry, fill with the mixture, top with pastry lids and seal. Cover with greaseproof paper and a cloth and steam.

Steamed Bacon and Potato Roll, or Bacon Badger [*GB*]   Roll out suet pastry into a 25-cm square, layer with rashers of bacon, sprinkle with chopped onion, parsley and sage and cover with grated potato. Roll up Swiss-roll fashion then place in a pudding sleeve or wrap in a cloth, tie and steam.

Steamed Bacon Roll, or Quorn Bacon Roll [*GB*]   Roll out suet pastry into a 25-cm square, layer with rashers of bacon and sprinkle with chopped onion, parsley and basil. Roll up Swiss-roll fashion, place in a pudding sleeve or wrap in a cloth, tie and steam. Serve with boiled potatoes, carrots and turnips.

Steamed Beef and Pork Balls [*Ngau Yook Ju Yook Yin China*]   Soak short-grain rice for 2 hr in cold water then drain on a cloth. Combine equal quantities of finely minced beef and pork, chopped mushrooms, onions, garlic, water chestnuts, grated ginger, beaten eggs and seasoning. Form the mixture into 2.5-cm balls then pass them through the rice. Steam for approx. 25 min and serve.

Steamed Beef and Vegetables [*Mantali Middle East*]   Add finely minced beef to simmering jus lié then stir in beaten eggs. Stir in cream then pour the mixture into ring moulds and steam. De-mould and serve with boiled mixed vegetables and boiled rice.

Steamed Ham and Pork Roll [*GB*]   Combine finely minced ham and pork with breadcrumbs, chopped parsley and marjoram, beaten eggs, salt, cayenne and mace. Mould into a roll then place in a pudding sleeve or cloth and steam. Serve cold cut into slices.

Steamed Minced Beef Pudding or Farmhouse Pudding [*GB*]   Sauté minced beef and chopped onion in oil, add grated carrot, moisten with stock and cook. Thicken with arrowroot and add chopped parsley. Line pudding basins with suet pastry, and fill with alternate layers of the cold mixture and suet pastry, finishing with a top layer of pastry. Cover with greaseproof paper and a cloth and steam.

Steamed Pork and Chestnut Pudding, or Oxford Pudding [*GB*]   Combine diced pork and pig's liver, lardons of bacon, chopped onion, basil and parsley, cooked chestnuts, cooked haricot beans, Worcester sauce, brown stock and seasoning. Line pudding basins with suet pastry, fill with the mixture, top with pastry lids and seal. Cover with greaseproof paper and a cloth and steam.

Steamed Pork and Leek Pudding [*GB*]   Line pudding basins with suet pastry. Fill with alternate layers of diced pork and sliced leek, sprinkle with rubbed sage and moisten with brown stock or ale. Top with pastry lids and seal. Cover with greaseproof paper and a cloth and steam.

Steamed Pork and Prawn Balls [*Sija Mie Roewan China*] Work finely minced pork until it becomes sticky in texture, then combine with chopped prawns, saké, light soy sauce, shrimp sauce, salt, chopped spring onions and beaten eggs combined with cornflour. Form the mixture into balls then steam them for 25 min. Boil chicken stock, sesame oil, saké, dark and light soy sauces, oyster sauce, grated ginger and tomato concassée, then thicken with cornflour. Serve the pork and prawn balls coated with the sauce and garnish with prawns.

Steamed Rabbit and Mushroom Pudding [*GB*] Line pudding basins with suet pastry, and fill with layers of boneless rabbit pieces, chopped onion, sliced mushrooms and lardons of bacon. Season, sprinkle with rubbed sage and moisten with stock, then top with pastry lids and seal. Cover with greaseproof paper and a cloth and steam.

Stewed Meats, Game and Offal

Application

Stewing is a moist method of cooking small pieces and cuts of meat and game. Stews may be gently simmered on top of the stove or in the oven at 200 °C.

Bacon and Potato Stew or Alnwick Stew [*GB*] Arrange alternate layers of cubes of forehock of bacon, sliced onion and sliced potato in a shallow dish. Season with salt, pepper and mustard. Top with overlapping slices of potato, moisten with stock, cover with a lid and simmer.

Beef and Vegetable Stew [*Chongol Korea*] Fry strips of beef in oil then add diamonds of celery and carrot, julienne of bamboo shoots and sliced onion. Moisten with stock, rice wine and soy sauce, add sugar and simmer for 5 min. Add sliced dried mushrooms, julienne of spring onion and large paysanne of Chinese cabbage. Finish with sliced bean curd and konnyaku and cook for 2 min.

Beef Curry [*Gaeng Gari Nuea Thailand*] Blend dried red chillies, peppercorns, zest of lime, lemon grass, cumin and coriander seeds to a paste. Stir-fry the paste in oil, moisten with coconut milk then add the cubes of beef and stew. Add nam pla and serve with basil leaves and sliced fresh red chillies.

Beef Stew Creole Style [*Caribbean*] Liquidise lime juice, cloves of garlic, ground cinnamon, ground cloves, grated root ginger, grated nutmeg, chopped fresh red chillies, bayleaves, anatto liquid and seasoning to a smooth paste. Marinate cubes of beef in the mixture for 72 hr. Sauté the beef in melted butter, moisten with the marinade and stock to barely cover and simmer until cooked. Serve accompanied by creamed yams.

Beef Stew in Tequila [*Cocido de Carne de Res con Tequila Mexico*] Fry floured cubes of beef with chopped onion and garlic and lardons of bacon. Moisten with stock, tomato juice and tequila, add diced carrot, celery, and tomato flesh and stew. Add cooked garbanzo beans and serve.

Beef Stew Spanish Style [*Estofado à la Catalana Spain*] Fry floured cubes of beef with chopped onion and garlic, moisten with white wine and stock, add a bouquet garni with oregano, add fried lardons of bacon and stew until tender. Add a little grated bitter chocolate and some small potatoes and continue cooking. Serve garnished with sautéed chorizo sausage.

Beef Stew with Christophene [*Caribbean*]   Caramelise brown sugar with a little oil, incorporate cubes of beef then add flour to make a roux. Stir in tomato purée, moisten with beef stock then add chopped onion, diced carrot, chopped cloves of garlic, diced tomato flesh, chopped fresh red chillies, thyme, cloves and seasoning. Simmer for approx. 1 hr then add peeled, cored and sliced christophene and continue to cook. Serve with cooked red kidney beans accompanied by a salad.

Beef Stew with Plantains [*Cocido de Carne de Res con Plàtano* Mexico] Moisten cubes of beef with stock, add diced onion, celery, carrot and tomato flesh, thyme, oregano and garlic then stew. Reduce the liquor by one-third then add fried sliced plantains seasoned with chilli powder, and diced green pimento.

Butter Bean and Chorizo Stew [*Feijoada à Portuguesa* Portugal]   Cook butter beans in water with a studded onion and lardons of bacon. If necessary drain off some of the liquid and add sautéed sliced onion, diced tomato flesh, chopped garlic and cloves and stew. Add cubes of chorizo sausage and serve accompanied by rice pilaff.

Calf's Liver with Onion and Paprika [*Pirított Borjúmàj* Hungary]   Sauté chopped onion then stir in salt and paprika and moisten with stock. Add strips of liver and simmer then season and serve.

Chilli con Carne [*Carne con Chile Colorado* Mexico]   Blend together chopped toasted chillies and cumin seeds, garlic, oregano, paprika, sugar and salt. Fry cubes of shoulder of pork in oil until brown, moisten with stock, add the blended mixture and thicken with arrowroot. Serve accompanied with boiled pinto beans and plain boiled rice.

Chillied Green Pork [*USA*]   Sauté cubes of pork with chopped onion and garlic and diced skinned green pimento. Sprinkle with flour, moisten with stock, add diced green chillies and stew.

Couscous [*Middle East*]   Place fried cubes of shin of beef and scrag end of lamb in a pan and top with sliced browned onion and bone marrow, cover with water and simmer. Add saffron, cinnamon stick, tomato concassée, turned carrots, chickpeas tied in muslin and seasoning. Simmer and add a whole chicken, dried red chillies, sliced cabbage, sliced baby marrows, raisins and chopped coriander leaves. Cook the couscous and serve it sprinkled with melted samneh and the portioned meats and slices of bone marrow on top, accompanied by the chickpeas and some of the cooking liquid.

Curried Beef [*Masaman* Thailand]   Blend dry-fried dried red chillies, lemon grass, chopped coriander leaves, cumin seeds, cardamoms, cloves, chopped onion, garlic, olive oil, lemon juice and coconut milk to a paste. Boil the paste then stir in cubes of beef, moisten with coconut milk, add demerara sugar, kaffir lime leaves and seasoning then simmer. Serve accompanied by boiled rice.

Curried Mutton [*Mutton Kari* India]   Fry chopped onion, crushed garlic and grated ginger in ghee. Sprinkle with curry powder and add lemon juice. Stir in cubes of mutton and add tomato concassée, chopped fresh green chillies, chopped mint and stock. Finish with garam masala and chopped coriander leaves. Serve accompanied by boiled rice.

Fricassée of Lamb [*Arni Fricassée* Greece]   Seal cubes of lamb in oil, sprinkle with flour, moisten with white wine and stock then add chopped spring onions, sliced Belgian endives, young broad beans, shredded cos lettuce, bayleaf, thyme and dill. Cook until it is tender then finish with a liaison of cream, egg yolks and lemon juice.

Fricassée of Lamb Italian Style [*Agnello Stracotto a Ova* Italy]   Fry cubes of lamb and chopped onion in oil, moisten with white wine, completely reduce the liquid then moisten with stock and simmer. Finish with a liaison of egg yolks, cream, grated Parmesan cheese, lemon juice, chopped garlic and parsley.

Game Stew [*GB*]   Marinate cubes of venison, grouse and hare with sliced onion, carrot and celery, thyme, marjoram, basil, salt, pepper, nutmeg and red wine. Fry the floured pieces in oil, moisten with the marinade and game stock, then stew. Garnish with batons of cooked carrot and celery and serve accompanied by rowan jelly.

Goat Stew [*Chanfana da Bairrada* Portugal]   Combine cubes of goat meat, lardons of bacon, chopped onion, garlic and parsley, salt, pepper, paprika, nutmeg, Bairrada red wine and olive oil and stew. Serve accompanied by boiled potatoes.

Goulash of Beef [*Porkolt* Hungary]   Fry cubes of beef and chopped onion in oil, sprinkle with paprika, moisten with wine vinegar and stock then add caraway seeds and marjoram and allow to stew. Serve accompanied by sauerkraut and sauceboats of yogurt or soured cream.

Haricot of Mutton [*GB*]   Fry cubes of floured lamb in oil, moisten with stock then add soaked haricot beans, sliced onion, diced turnip and seasoning. Allow to cook until tender then add a few drops of Worcester sauce.

Irish Stew [*GB*]   Blanch pieces of scrag end and breast of lamb; cover with water, simmer and add shredded celery, onion and leek, sliced potatoes and seasoning. Allow to stew slowly. Liquidise the vegetables and liquid, pour back over the meat and garnish with cooked button onions, boiled turned potatoes and chopped parsley.

Jambalaya [*USA*]   Fry Spanish chorizo sausage or smoked spiced sausage in oil and retain. Sauté chopped onion and garlic and chopped green and red pimento in butter then add diced tomato flesh, chopped fresh and dried thyme, sugar and chilli powder. Add long-grain rice, the sliced sausage, chopped smoked ham and chicken stock and simmer until cooked. Stir in shelled shrimps and finish with chopped parsley.

Jugged Hare [*GB*]   Marinate joints of hare in cider with sliced onions, thyme, marjoram, basil, salt, pepper and nutmeg. Fry the floured joints in oil, moisten with the marinade and stock and stew. When cooked add redcurrant jelly and the diced liver then blend in the blood to thicken. Finish with port or claret and garnish with veal forcemeat balls.

Lamb and Rice Stew [*Kovyrama Palov* Russia]   Fry cubes of lamb and sliced onion in oil; stir in paprika, moisten with stock, add salt, pepper, cumin and grated carrot, then stew. When almost cooked arrange in layers with cooked long-grain rice and finish cooking in the oven covered with a lid. Serve sprinkled with chopped spring onions.

Lamb and Yogurt Stew with Pilau [*Mansaff* Middle East]   Stew cubes of lamb in stock with sliced onion. Finish with a liaison of yogurt and beaten eggs and serve on a bed of rice mixed with fried pine nuts.

Lamb Biriani [*Moglai Biriani India*]   Fry sliced onion, crushed garlic and grated ginger in ghee, sprinkle with curry powder, add lemon juice and season. Stir in cubes of lamb, add garam masala, ground cardamom, dried red chillies, chopped mint and tomato concassée, then stew. Layer a dish with rice pilau and the meat and sauce, finishing with rice, then bake in the oven. Serve garnished with pistachio nuts and edible silver leaf.

Lamb Casserole with Apricots [*Kaysi Yahnisi Greece*]   Fry cubes of lamb and sliced onion in oil, stir in ground cinnamon, moisten with stock and lemon juice then stew in a casserole, adding soaked dried apricots and sugar. Serve sprinkled with toasted pine nuts accompanied by plain boiled rice.

Lamb Casserole with Cannellini Beans [*Etli Kuru Fasulye Greece*]   Fry cubes of lamb, chopped onion and crushed garlic in olive oil, moisten with brown stock, add tomato concassée, tomato purée, oregano and cannellini beans, then stew in a casserole until all is tender.

Lamb Casserole with Fresh Peas [*Arnaki me Arake Greece*]   Fry cubes of lamb and sliced onion in sunflower oil, moisten with brown stock and lemon juice and place to stew. Add peas, chopped spring onions and chopped dill and finish cooking.

Lamb Casserole with Fruit [*Koresh* or *Korak Middle East*]   Sauté chopped onion in oil then add turmeric, cinnamon, cloves and pepper. Mix in cubes of lamb and dried apricots and prunes, sour cherries and dried limes, then place in a casserole, moisten with stock and stew until tender.

Lamb Stew with Cumin [*Kammouniat El-Lahm Middle East*]   Fry cubes of lamb in oil, add a paste of garlic and cumin, moisten with stock then stew.

Lamb Stew with Red Peppers [*Cordero al Chilindrón Spain*]   Fry cubes of lamb in garlic-flavoured oil, add chopped onion and stir in paprika and chilli pepper. Moisten with red wine and stock, add a bouquet garni and seasoning then simmer for 30 min. Blend fried cloves of garlic, red pimento, a little vinegar and stock to form a thick paste. Add this mixture to the stew and simmer until tender.

Lamb Stew with Saffron and Almonds [*Badami Gosht India*]   Marinate cubes of lamb in saffron-flavoured yogurt. Fry a cinnamon stick, cardamom pods and cloves in ghee then add sliced onion and garlic, grated ginger and ground cumin. Add the meat then moisten with the marinade and stock. Add nibbed almonds and simmer until cooked. Serve sprinkled with chopped mint, accompanied by boiled rice.

Meatballs in Brandy Sauce [*Albóndigas 'Saint Climent' Spain*]   Combine minced lamb, chopped garlic and parsley, breadcrumbs and beaten eggs and mould into marble-sized balls. Golden fry the meatballs in oil, add chopped onion, flambé with brandy, moisten with jus lié and simmer until cooked.

Meatballs in Tomato Sauce [*Albóndigas en Salsa Spain*]   Combine minced pork, breadcrumbs, chopped garlic and parsley and beaten eggs. Mould into marble-sized balls and simmer in tomato sauce mixed with sherry until cooked.

Medallions of Pork with Ginger [*Buta No Sakeni-Nabe Japan*]   Marinate seasoned medallions in ginger juice. Grate daikon and extract the juice. Simmer saké, soy sauce and the daikon juice, add sliced ginger, blanched and sliced devil's-tongue-root cake and sliced mushrooms; add the escalopes and simmer until cooked. Add chrysanthemum leaves or spinach and julienne of spring onion and cook for 3 min. Serve accompanied by grated ginger and daikon, moistened with soy sauce, in separate bowls.

Minced Lamb with Saffron Rice [*Kuzulu Pilav* Greece] Season minced lamb with cinnamon and allspice and sauté in oil. Moisten with stock, add grated zest of lemons, pine nuts and chopped walnuts then stew. Serve accompanied by saffron rice.

Mutton Curry [*Gulai Kambing* Thailand] Blend tamarind liquid, onion, garlic, ginger, coriander, cinnamon, fennel, nutmeg, black pepper, cloves, cardamom, candlenuts, dried chillies and roasted desiccated coconut to a paste, then fry the mixture in oil for a few minutes. Add cubed meat, diced tomato flesh and lemon grass, moisten with coconut milk and stew until tender.

Osso Bucco [*Ossi Bucchi* Italy] Fry sections of knuckle of veal on the bone in olive oil, stir in tomato purée and moisten with white veal stock then add tomato concassée and brunoise of carrot, turnip, celery and leek and a bouquet garni; allow to stew gently. Lightly thicken the cooking liquor with arrowroot and finish with zest of lemon, crushed garlic and chopped parsley. Serve accompanied by polenta or braised rice.

Pork and Bean Curd Stew [*Tubu-Tchigae* Korea] Sauté goujons of pork in sesame oil, and stir in kochujang, garlic, ginger, soy sauce and sesame oil. Moisten with stock and cook, then add diamonds of celery and green pimento, sliced courgette and sliced fresh green chillies. Add cubes of bean curd and garnish with shredded spring onion.

Pork and Beetroot Stew [*Vereshchaka* Russia] Fry cubes of pork in oil with lardons of bacon and chopped onion. Moisten with beetroot rassol and stock. Add sugar, black peppercorns, allspice berries, pearl barley and seasoning then stew. Serve sprinkled with chopped fresh herbs, accompanied by a sauceboat of smetana.

Pork and Chicken Stew [*Pozole* Mexico] Sauté cubes of pork and chicken pieces in oil with chopped onion and garlic. Moisten with stock, add sweetcorn kernels and chilli powder then stew. Serve accompanied by dishes of salsa roja, chopped onion, coriander leaves, lettuce and lime segments.

Pork and Tuna Stew [*Caribbean*] Boil smoked cubes of pork in water then add the following and continue cooking: small tannias cut in halves, sliced green bananas, sliced yam, whole okra, chopped onion, chopped cloves of garlic, sliced dasheen, lime juice, chopped fresh red chillies, cloves, thyme and seasoning. Cover with a lid and stew for approx. 1 hr. Place goujons of tuna fish on top and continue to cook. Serve sprinkled with chopped parsley.

Pork Gulyàs [*Kisalföldi Sertésgulyàs* Hungary] Sauté cubes of pork and chopped onion and garlic, add paprika and barely moisten with stock then simmer. Add diced tomato flesh and green pimentos, lengths of French beans and peas. Sprinkle rice on top, add more stock, cover and stew until the rice is cooked.

Pork in Orange Juice with Cumin [*Puerco al Comino* Mexico] Marinate cubes of pork in orange and lime juices with cumin seeds, oregano and lardons of bacon. Fry the meat and lardons in oil, moisten with stock and the marinade then stew. Finish with soured cream.

Pork in Red Wine with Coriander [*Afelia* Greece] Marinate cubes of pork in red wine with coriander seeds and a cinnamon stick. Fry the meat in oil, moisten with the marinade and stew until the meat is tender and the liquid is completely reduced.

Pork Medallions [*Lombo de Porco Frito Portugal*]   Marinate medallions of pork in wine vinegar, white wine, olive oil, garlic, bayleaf and chopped parsley. Sauté the meat in olive oil then add the marinade and reduce it to a coating consistency.

Pork Stew [*Hirino me Prassoselino Greece*]   Fry cubes of pork in sunflower oil with sliced onion. Add tomato purée, moisten with brown stock then stew. Add batons of blanched celery and sections of leek and continue to stew.

Pork Stew with Cabbage and Apples [*Bigos Russia*]   Fry cubes of pork in oil with chopped onion and crushed black peppercorns and garlic. Add shredded cabbage and sliced apples and moisten with stock. Add cucumber rassol and allow to stew. Serve accompanied by plain boiled potatoes.

Pork Stew with Eggplant [*Caribbean*]   Golden fry whole fillet of pork in oil, remove and retain. Add butter to the pan, sprinkle with chopped onion and allspice, replace the pork, moisten with stock, cover with a lid and cook in the oven. Cut peeled eggplant into half moon shapes, add to the meat and continue to stew. Serve accompanied by boiled sweet potato.

Pork with Sauerkraut [*USA*]   Fry cubes of pork in oil with chopped onion and garlic, then stir in caraway seeds, diced tomato flesh, juniper berries and sugar. Moisten with stock and stew. Add sauerkraut to the pork and finish by cooking in the oven.

Rabbit in Peanut Sauce [*Caribbean*]   Fry portions of rabbit in corn oil with chopped onion and garlic. Moisten with stock, and add a bouquet garni containing marjoram, grated nutmeg, chopped fresh red chillies and chopped parsley. Allow to stew then add ground roasted peanuts.

Rabbit Paella [*Arroz a la Catalana Spain*]   Roast portions of rabbit and spare ribs of pork for 20 min. Sauté chopped onion, garlic, diced cured ham and sliced chorizo sausage. Add diced tomato flesh then stir in short-grain rice. Moisten with chicken stock and simmer, then add mangetouts and transfer to a shallow dish. Place the rabbit pieces and spare ribs on top, decorate with strips of red pimento and bake until the liquid has been absorbed and all ingredients are cooked.

Rabbit Stew with Fruit, or **Elizabethan Rabbit** [*GB*]   Fry portions of floured rabbit in oil, and add chopped onion, crushed garlic, sliced Jerusalem artichokes and mushrooms and diced carrot. Moisten with red wine and stock, add a bouquet garni, diced apple, halves of grapes, raisins and grated zests of orange and lemon, and stew until the rabbit is tender.

Rabbit Stew with Wine and Port [*Coelho em Vinho Portugal*]   Place fried bread croûtons in a shallow dish, and add rabbit pieces and chopped onion and garlic. Moisten with white wine and port and stew until the rabbit is tender.

Rabbit with Mango [*Kelinchi Berkuah Mango Indonesia*]   Fry portions of rabbit in garlic-flavoured oil; moisten with mango purée, stock, sambal ulek, soy sauce and sugar and cook. Serve sprinkled with chopped coriander.

Savoury Meat Balls [*Albóndigas Israel*]   Combine minced lamb, soaked and squeezed bread, garlic, salt, pepper, cinnamon and beaten eggs. Mould into balls and cook them in light lamb velouté sauce flavoured with the grated zest and juice of lemon and chopped parsley.

Soured Tokàny [*Savanyú Tokàny Hungary*]   Sauté goujons of pork and chopped onion; moisten with sufficient stock, cover with a lid and allow to simmer. Add strips of pig's kidney and liver and continue to cook until tender. Finish the sauce with lemon juice and soured cream.

Tripe Stew [*Skembe Yahni* *Greece*]   Marinate squares of tripe in lemon juice with bayleaf, thyme and seasoning. Shallow fry the tripe in olive oil with chopped onion and crushed garlic. Add tomato purée then moisten with dry white wine and veal stock. Add chopped parsley then stew. Serve accompanied by rice pilaff.

Veal and Apricot Stew [*Mishmisheya* *Middle East*]   Blend together allspice, cinnamon, coriander and cumin. Sauté chopped onion, garlic and ginger in oil then add the spice mixture and cubes of veal, moisten with a little stock and stew. Finish by mixing in a purée of fresh apricots or peaches and serve with couscous.

Veal and Fennel Casserole [*Agnello coi Finocchietti* *Italy*]   Fry cubes of veal in olive oil with chopped onion and garlic, then add diced tomato flesh. Moisten with a little stock and allow to stew. When almost cooked, add blanched quarters of fennel and cook in a casserole in the oven until tender.

Veal Forcemeat [*GB*]   Combine finely minced veal with panada then pass through a sieve. Add beaten eggs, finish by gradually adding double cream and season to taste.

Panada: mix together flour and egg yolks, then add melted butter and mix in hot milk. Bring to the boil and cook while stirring for 5 min. Use when cool.

Veal Pörkölt [*Borjùpaprikàs* *Hungary*]   Sauté cubes of veal with chopped onion, add paprika, moisten with stock then add diced tomato flesh, caraway seeds and green pimento and place to stew. Serve with galushka dumplings.

Veal Stew with Cherries [*Khoreshe Albaloo* *Middle East*]   Sauté cubes of veal with chopped onion then stir in turmeric and cinnamon. Moisten with stock and stew. Finish by adding pitted sour morello cherries, lemon juice and brown sugar.

Stir-fried Meats

Application

Heat a minimum amount of oil in a wok or frying pan then add seasoned meat which has previously been cut into small pieces and fry very quickly, tossing continuously until evenly coloured and cooked.

Stir-fried Beef in Black Bean Sauce [*See Jup Ngau Yook* *China*]   Combine purée of black beans, soy sauce, a little water and sugar. Stir-fry goujons of beef in garlic-flavoured oil, remove and retain. Add the black bean mixture to the pan then add diluted cornflour to form a light sauce and simmer for 2 min. Replace the meat, simmer for 1 min and serve with boiled rice.

Stir-fried Beef in Green Curry [*Khiaw Waan Nuea* *Thailand*]   Stir-fry green curry paste in oil then add thin slices of beef. Moisten with thick coconut milk, sugar, nam pla and soy sauce. Finish with chopped basil, coriander and fresh green chillies.

Stir-fried Beef, or **Beef Bowl** [*Gyudon* *Japan*]   Stir-fry sliced onion and 2-cm lengths of thin slices of beef in oil, and moisten with water, dark soy sauce and mirin then ginger juice. Serve in donburi bowls on a base of rice.

Stir-fried Beef with Asparagus [*Seen Lo Shun Chow Ngau Yook China*]
Marinate goujons of beef in soy sauce, crushed garlic and seasoning for 10 min.
Stir-fry goujons in peanut oil, remove and retain. Add strips of asparagus stalks
and sliced onion, cook for a few moments then moisten with stock and add
bean sauce. Add asparagus tips and simmer. Thicken the liquid with diluted
cornflour to form a light sauce, replace the meat and serve with boiled rice.

Stir-fried Beef with Ginger [*Xin Jiang Chao Niu Rou China*] Marinate goujons of beef in soy sauce, saké, sesame oil, sugar, cornflour and seasoning for
5 min. Stir-fry goujons in sesame oil, remove and retain. Add grated ginger and
chopped garlic, then moisten with stock, oyster sauce and the marinade and
simmer for 2 min. Replace the meat and serve garnished with chopped spring
onions.

Stir-fried Beef with Mushrooms [*Doong Gwoo Chow Ngau Yook China*]
Marinate goujons of beef in soy sauce, five-spice powder, grated ginger and
crushed garlic for 10 min. Stir-fry goujons in sesame oil with sliced onion and
Chinese mushrooms, remove and retain. Moisten with stock and the marinade
then thicken with diluted cornflour to form a light sauce, replace the meat,
onions and mushrooms and serve sprinkled with chopped spring onions.

Stir-fried Beef with Peanuts [*Dendeng Belado Dan Katjang Indonesia*]
Marinate strips of beef in lime juice then stir-fry in oil and retain. Blend to a
paste onion, garlic, sambal ulek and peanut butter, then add the mixture to the
pan and stir in coconut milk and peanuts. Cook the sauce then add the meat
and serve garnished with sliced cucumber and chillies.

Stir-fried Beef with Snow Peas [*Ho Lan Dau Chow Ngau Yook China*] Stir-fry
goujons of beef in garlic-flavoured oil, remove and retain. Add sliced mushrooms and chopped spring onions, fry for 2 min then moisten with stock and
saké, add a little sugar, simmer then thicken with diluted cornflour to form a
light sauce, add blanched snow peas and cook for 4 min. Replace the meat and
serve with boiled rice or noodles.

Stir-fried Sweet and Sour Pork [*Kun Shao Pai Gu China*] Marinade 2.5-cm
pieces of spare rib in light soy sauce, saké and seasoning for 45 min. Drain, dry
then pass through cornflour, beaten egg and again through cornflour and deep
fry in peanut oil until cooked and golden. Stir-fry sliced onion and garlic for
2 min then add peas, moisten with stock and the marinade then thicken with
diluted cornflour to form a light sauce. Add a little tomato purée and simmer.
Add lychees and the pork to the sauce, cook for 1 min and serve.

Chapter Ten

Poultry and Game Birds

This chapter is divided into 12 main categories according to methods of cookery:

✧ Baked Poultry ✧

✧ Braised Poultry ✧

✧ Deep-fried Poultry ✧

✧ Grilled Poultry ✧

✧ Poached or Boiled Poultry ✧

✧ Roasted Poultry ✧

✧ Pot Roasted or Poêléd Poultry ✧

✧ Sautéed Poultry ✧

✧ Shallow-fried Poultry ✧

✧ Steamed Poultry ✧

✧ Stewed Poultry ✧

✧ Stir-fried Poultry ✧

Allow the following amounts of prepared raw poultry per average portion:

100–150 g – suprêmes and chicken jointed for sauté

a 1.5-kg prepared and trussed chicken and a 2.5-kg duck yield four average portions

100–150 g – turkey on the bone, raw weight.

Baked Poultry and Game Birds

Application

Baking involves cooking by dry heat in an oven at 200 °C.

Baked Chicken with Potato [*Burgonyàs Csirke* *Hungary*] Cover the bottom of a shallow dish with diced potato and chopped parsley then cover with chicken pieces and moisten with soured cream, stock and lemon juice. Top with a layer of sliced mushrooms and potatoes and grated cheese, then bake.

Baked Chicken with Sesame Seeds [*Simsim Daj* *Middle East*] Marinate goujons of chicken in oil, tahini paste, paprika, puréed garlic and salt. Sprinkle roasted sesame seeds into a shallow dish, place the goujons on top, moisten with the marinade, sprinkle with sesame seeds then bake.

Chicken and Mushroom Filo Parcels [*Kotopoulo* *Greece*] Enrobe suprêmes of chicken in duxelle of mushrooms, encase in filo pastry to form parcels, brush with oil then bake.

Chicken Patties [*Empadas de Calinha* *Portugal*] Sauté diced chicken and bacon in oil, add chopped onion and parsley and season with nutmeg, moisten with wine vinegar and white wine and simmer to reduce the liquid by half. Fill patty tins lined with puff pastry with the mixture, cover with pastry lids and bake.

Chicken Pie [*Empadas de Calinha* *Portugal*] Sauté diced chicken and bacon in oil, add chopped onion and parsley and season with nutmeg, moisten with wine vinegar and white wine then simmer reducing the liquid by half. Fill patty tins lined with puff pastry with the mixture, cover with pastry lids and bake.

Chicken, Bacon and Leek Pie [*GB*] Combine slices of poached chicken with fried lardons of bacon, julienne of sweated leek, chopped herbs and chicken velouté. Place into pie dishes, cover with puff pastry then bake.

Chicken Pot Pie [*USA*] Combine sliced poached chicken, diced vegetables cooked with the chicken, boiled diced potato and chicken velouté; season with ground mace and nutmeg and finish with cream. Place into pie dishes, cover with short pastry then bake.

Chicken and Rice Pie [*Kurnik* *Russia*] Combine beaten eggs with diced cooked chicken, cooked rice, chopped dill, chopped and sweated onion and seasoning. Line pie dishes with short pastry, place in the filling, cover with pastry then bake.

Chicken and Veal Forcemeat Pie, or Queen's Pie [*GB*] Sauté joints of chicken with lardons of bacon then transfer to pie dishes and season with salt, pepper and mace. Moisten with stock, add balls of veal forcemeat, cover with puff pastry then bake.

Chicken Pie with Filo Pastry [*Kotopitta* Greece]   Combine sliced cooked chicken, grated Kefalotíri cheese and velouté then season with salt, pepper and nutmeg. Line shallow dishes with filo pastry brushed between with oil, and fill with the chicken mixture. Cover with layers of filo pastry, brush with oil then bake.

Pigeon and Mutton Pie, or **Squab Pie** [*GB*]   Combine pigeon breasts, diced cooked mutton, chopped onion, apple and parsley, seasoning and mutton stock. Place into pie dishes, cover with short pastry then bake.

Vermont Chicken Pie [*USA*]   Add sliced chicken to chicken velouté then fill into pie dishes. Cover with 5-cm circles of rough puff pastry then bake.

Braised Poultry

Application

In braising, whole or jointed poultry is seared, placed on a bed of root vegetables, two-thirds covered with liquid, covered with a tight fitting lid and cooked in an oven at 180 °C.

Braised Chicken Stuffed with Rice and Pine Nuts [*Tavuk Dolmasi* Greece]   Sauté chopped onion and chicken livers in oil, add pine nuts and currants then combine with boiled long-grain rice and season with ground cinnamon, all-spice, salt and pepper. Stuff a chicken with the rice mixture then braise in chicken stock with potatoes, marjoram, lemon juice and oil.

Braised Duck and Cabbage [*Ente in Wirsing* Germany]   Sear the breast part only of ducks and braise with lardons of bacon and quartered savoy cabbage in duck stock. Thicken the braising liquid to a coating consistency.

Braised Duck with Sauerkraut and Dumplings [*Kacsa Savanyú Kàposztàval Hungary*]   Place sauerkraut, sautéed duck pieces and strips of duck liver in a pan, moisten with white wine and soured cream then braise. Serve with semolina dumplings.

Dumplings: cream lard and eggs then add semolina and chopped parsley. Form walnut shapes then poach.

Braised Duck with Vegetables [*Gaeng Phed Ped* Thailand]   Marinate ducks in soy sauce. Sear the ducks, then braise with sautéed chopped onion and garlic in duck stock. Add mushrooms and cubes of squash and pickled lime. Lightly thicken the braising liquid to a coating consistency.

Braised Goose with Apples [*Israel*]   Season a jointed goose with paprika and salt and fry in hot goose fat. Braise with fried chopped onion, quarters of apples and brown stock. Reduce the liquor to a glaze and serve portions coated with the liquor with the pieces of apple.

Braised Partridge with Grapes and Oranges [*Perdiz à Ribatejana* Portugal]   Seal partridges in oil, moisten with orange juice and jus lié then braise. Serve garnished with segments of orange and deseeded and peeled grapes.

Braised Partridge with Mushrooms [*Stekta Rapphöns med Champinjoner* Scandinavia]   Seal partridges in oil, moisten with Madeira and stock, add browned button onions and quartered button mushrooms then braise. Thicken the liquor with arrowroot and finish with cream.

Braised Partridge with Raisins [*Geschmorte Rebbühner* Germany]   Seal partridges in oil, moisten with red wine and stock, add fried lardons of bacon, juniper berries and mushroom trimmings, then braise. Thicken the liquor with arrowroot, finish with soured cream and add raisins macerated in brandy.

Braised Partridge with Savoy Cabbage [*Perdices con Col* Spain]   Marinate partridges in red wine, garlic, onion, parsley, bayleaves, thyme and cinnamon. Seal the birds in hot oil then moisten with the marinade, add tomato concassée and braise. Toss blanched shredded savoy cabbage in oil, add to the partridges and continue cooking.

Braised Pheasant with Sauerkraut [*Fasan auf Weinkraut* Germany]   Sauté chopped onion then add sauerkraut and juniper berries. Place pheasants on top of the sauerkraut, moisten with white wine and braise.

Braised Pigeon [*Tejfölös Galamb* Hungary]   Seal birds in hot oil, moisten with white wine and lemon juice and braise. Finish by adding soured cream to the liquor and thicken to form a sauce.

Braised Pigeon with Mushrooms [*Galambbecinàlt* Hungary]   Seal pigeons in hot oil, moisten with stock, add sliced mushrooms and braise. Add jus lié to the reduced cooking liquid and finish with soured cream.

Braised Pigeon with Olives [*Pigeon aux Olives* France]   Seal pigeons in hot oil and add chopped onion, lardons of belly of pork, diced carrot, garlic, thyme and bayleaf. Moisten with dry white wine, chicken stock and Madeira then braise. Add cooked button onions and stoned green olives. Reduce the liquor by half and thicken with cornflour.

Braised Quail with Grapes [*Codornices Braseadad con Uvas* Spain]   Half roast quail with sliced Spanish onions, quartered mushrooms, diced carrots, bayleaves and thyme. Liquidise peppercorns, nutmeg, grapes, garlic, dry white wine and Spanish brandy and strain. Add the quails and the mushrooms and braise, then garnish with peeled grapes, thicken the liquor with arrowroot and serve.

Braised Quail with Pimento [USA]   Sprinkle quails with salt and lemon juice then seal in hot fat. Place on a bed of chopped spring onions, diced green, red and yellow pimento, garlic and rosemary. Moisten with red wine, jus lié and stock, then braise.

Braised Stuffed Pigeon [*Gefüllte Tauben* Germany]   Combine minced beef and pigeon's liver, breadcrumbs, basil, eggs and cream then stuff pigeons with the mixture. Seal in hot oil, moisten with stock and red wine then braise. Thicken the liquor with arrowroot and finish with cream to form a sauce.

Chicken Casserole in Lemon Sauce [*Csirke Citromos Màrtàsban* Hungary]   Braise chicken pieces in a casserole with lardons of bacon and chopped parsley, stock and lemon juice. Reduce the liquor and add to a velouté, flavour with nutmeg and finish with a liaison of soured cream and lemon juice. Serve the chicken pieces in the sauce.

Chicken Casserole in Sherry Sauce with Almonds [*Pollo en Pepitoria* Spain]   Sauté chicken pieces in olive oil, add chopped onion, chopped garlic, julienne of jambón serrano and chopped parsley, and gently cook until the onion is tender. Moisten with sherry and chicken stock, add a few strands of saffron and season with salt, pepper and nutmeg. When cooked transfer the chicken and ham to a casserole. Blend blanched almonds with the cooking liquor to a smooth sauce, pour over the chicken pieces and bake. Serve sprinkled with chopped hard-boiled eggs.

Chicken Casserole Portuguese Style [*Frango na Púcara* Portugal] Braise a trussed chicken in a casserole with button onions, diced tomato flesh, lardons of smoked ham, garlic, sultanas and chopped fresh herbs, moistened with brandy, Madeira and white wine.

Chicken Casserole with Figs [*Pollo con Higos* Spain] Boil water, vinegar, sugar, lemon slices and cinnamon stick for 10 min then add figs and simmer for 10 min. Remove and discard lemon and cinnamon and retain for 4 hr. Place the drained figs in medium-sweet white wine with zest of lemon. Lightly sauté chicken pieces in olive oil, add lardons of bacon then moisten with the wine from the figs and chicken stock and boil to reduce the liquor to a light syrupy sauce. Transfer to a casserole and stew uncovered; when almost cooked, add the figs.

Chicken Casserole with Mushrooms and Cheese [*Pollo alla Parmigiana* Italy] Sauté chicken pieces with garlic, sliced mushrooms, diced green pimento, diced tomato and oregano. Moisten with white wine and stock then braise in an earthenware casserole. Sprinkle with grated Parmesan cheese and serve.

Chicken Casserole with Mushrooms and Ginger [*Tom Kem Gai* Thailand] Blend shallots, garlic, ginger and coriander leaves to a paste then stir-fry the mixture for 2 min in oil and discard, retaining only the oil. Add sugar and cook until syrupy then moisten with soy sauce and stock. Braise chicken pieces in a casserole in the sauce and serve garnished with coriander leaves and hard-boiled eggs.

Chicken Casserole with Rice [*Arroz de Frango à Portuguesa* Portugal] Sauté chicken pieces in oil with sliced onion and place in a casserole; add sliced chorizo sausage and lardons of smoked bacon, moisten with white wine and stock, cover with a lid and cook.

Chicken Casserole with Vegetables [GB] Braise chicken pieces in a casserole with batons of carrot, celery and swede, chopped onion, tomato concassée and peas, using chicken stock. Finish with chopped fresh herbs.

Duck Casserole with Apples [*Farshirovannaia Utka* Russia] Stuff a duck with diced apple, roast until half done then cook in a casserole with a little jus lié.

Duck Casserole with Cabbage and Potatoes [*Badbak Buffado* India] Fry chopped onion with cloves, cardamom pods, cinnamon stick, grated ginger and ground turmeric, pepper and coriander. Add duck cut into portions, fry and add sliced fresh green chillies. Place in a casserole, moisten with white stock and a little vinegar, add wedges of cabbage and small potatoes then cook until tender.

Duck Casserole with Olives [*Pato a la Sevillana* Spain] Place sliced onion and cloves of garlic in the duck cavity then half roast, transfer to a casserole, moisten with white wine, dry sherry and chicken stock, add coarsely chopped olives, thyme, bayleaf, diced carrot and seasoning and cook until tender.

Duck Casserole with Pistachio Nuts [*Vaatboo Pista* India] Sweat chopped onion and add coriander and cumin seeds, ground mace, chilli powder and black pepper. Add and combine dry mashed potato then add chopped hard-boiled eggs, pistachio nuts and fresh green chillies. Stuff a duck with the mixture, half roast in ghee then cook in a casserole with a little stock.

Partridge Casserole [GB] Place a shallot inside partridges, place into a casserole with lardons of bacon, diced carrot and onion, thyme and bayleaf. Moisten with game stock and jus lié and cook. When half cooked add blanched quarters of cabbage and continue to cook until all is tender.

Pheasant Casserole [*GB*]   Sauté pheasant pieces in oil with sliced mushrooms, diced carrot, onion and tomato flesh. Place into a casserole, moisten with red wine and jus lié and cook until tender.

Pheasant with Madeira and Truffles [***Faisan Souvaroff*** *France*]   Half roast pheasants then transfer to an earthenware cocotte, moisten with game stock and Madeira and add diced truffle and foie gras. Place the lid on the cocotte, seal with a stiff paste made from a mixture of flour and water and bake for approx. 30 min. Serve without breaking the pastry seal.

Deep-fried Poultry

Application

Items need to be coated with either flour, batter, beaten eggs or breadcrumbs to prevent fat from penetrating the poultry during cooking. Poultry items are deep fried in hot fat at a temperature of 170–180 °C until golden and crisp.

Chicken Suprêmes Kiev [***Kotlety Po-Kievski*** *Russia*]   Stuff suprêmes with a mixture of butter, chopped parsley and a little lemon juice. Pass the chicken through seasoned flour, eggwash and breadcrumbs and deep fry until golden. Drain, season with salt and serve accompanied by buckwheat kasha.
    Buckwheat kasha: boil buckwheat in salted water, when cooked add a little butter.

Flautas [*Mexico*]   Fill tortillas with strips of cooked chicken, secure with cocktail sticks and deep fry in oil. Sprinkle with lemon juice and grated cheese and serve accompanied by soured cream or guacamole.

Fried Chicken [***Toriniku No Tatsuta-Age*** *Japan*]   Marinate skinned chicken pieces in soy sauce and saké for 30 min. Pass through cornflour and deep fry until golden. Serve garnished with strips of spring onion.

Fried Chicken Goujons Japanese Style [***Tatsuta Age*** *Japan*]   Marinate chicken goujons in soy sauce, mirin and sugar. Coat with cornflour then deep fry.

Fried Chicken Goujons with Yellow Bean Sauce [***Kai Tod Taucheo*** *Thailand*]   Pass chicken goujons through a batter of lightly beaten egg whites mixed with cornflour and water chestnut flour and deep fry. Fry yellow bean paste in oil, add sugar, saké and sesame oil, then add the goujons and serve with boiled rice.

Fried Chicken Meat Balls [***Koftit Ferakh*** *Middle East*]   Combine finely minced chicken, garlic, onion, cumin, fresh green chillies and coriander. Form into small balls then deep fry.

Fried Chicken Winglets Buffalo Style [*USA*]   Deep fry boned chicken winglets until crisp then stir them into a hot spicy sauce. Serve accompanied by sticks of celery and blue cheese dressing.

Fried Duck Chinese Style [***Shanghai Yu Yian Ya*** *China*]   Marinate duck portions in saké, light and dark soy sauces, sugar, grated ginger, garlic and five-spice powder. Steam the duck pieces then deep fry them and add to the strained and boiled marinade flavoured with lime juice and serve.

Fried Marinated Chicken [***Toriniku Tatsuta-age*** *Japan*]   Marinate cubes of chicken in saké, light soy sauce, ginger juice and chopped onion. Pass through flour then deep fry them.

Fried Quails [*Codornices con Ajo* Spain]   Split the birds as for spatchcock then marinate in sherry and garlic. Deep fry in olive oil and serve on bread croûtons, with sprigs of watercress.

Fried Sesame Chicken [*Toriniku No Goma-Goromo-Age* Japan]   Marinate skinned chicken pieces in soy sauce, mirin and ginger juice. Pass through the batter and deep fry until golden; serve garnished with fried fresh green chillies.

  Batter: Blend together beaten eggs, saké, water, black sesame seeds and flour to form a light batter, then flavour with monosodium glutamate.

Fried Skewered Chicken [*Toriniku No Kushiage* Japan]   Thread skinned pieces of floured breast of chicken and strips of spring onion on bamboo skewers. Coat with tempura batter and deep fry until lightly browned. Serve accompanied by a dipping sauce.

  Tempura batter: combine beaten eggs and water and whisk into flour then strain.

Grilled Poultry

Application

Flattened whole and small pieces of poultry are seasoned, brushed with oil then grilled over or under direct heat. When items are marinated before grilling, the marinade is usually used to brush over the food during cooking.

Barbecued Chicken [*Gai Yaang* Thailand]   Blend garlic, peppercorns and coriander root to a paste, spread over the chicken which has been previously prepared for grilling, and allow to marinate. Grill the chicken and serve with a dipping sauce.

Barbecued Chicken [*Taksanjok* Korea]   Thread alternate pieces of chicken and spring onion on bamboo skewers then marinate in soy sauce, sesame oil, toasted sesame seeds, garlic, ginger and sugar for 1 hr, then grill.

Chicken Saté [*Saté Ajam Dengan Bumbu Katjang* Indonesia]   Grill skewered cubes of seasoned chicken previously marinated in coconut cream. Serve accompanied by saté sauce.

Chicken Tikka [*Murgh Tikka* India]   Marinate chicken pieces in sesame oil, plain yogurt, lemon juice, ground coriander, turmeric, chillies, ginger, chopped onion, crushed garlic and salt. Grill and garnish with segments of lemon.

Chicken Tikka 2 [*Murgh Tikka* India]   Marinate chicken pieces in oil with chopped onion, tomato purée, ground black pepper, cumin, ginger, mango powder and red colouring. Grill and garnish with segments of lemon.

Grilled Chicken and Chicken Livers [*Yakitori* Japan]   Thread alternate pieces of chicken, chicken liver, cubes of onions or leeks and green and red pimento on bamboo skewers. Dip into yakitori sauce then grill.

  Yakitori sauce: boil dark soy sauce, saké, mirin and sugar for 2 min.

Grilled Chicken Brochettes with Spices [*Saté Ayam* Indonesia]   Blend crushed dried red chillies, chopped onion, grated ginger, lemon juice, light and dark soy sauces, sugar and sesame oil to a paste. Marinate skewered pieces of chicken in the paste then grill them. Serve garnished with segments of lemon and accompanied by a sauce of the boiled marinade finished with coconut cream.

Grilled Chicken Hearts [*Israel*] Grill skewered hearts of chicken, sprinkle with Tabasco sauce and serve in pitta bread with tomato and cucumber salad.

Grilled Chicken Kebabs [***Pinchos de Pollo con Salsa Picada*** *Spain*] Marinate skewered boned chicken pieces in olive oil, garlic, lemon juice and marjoram, then grill them. Liquidise the marinade to a sauce consistency and add a brunoise of cucumber and tomato flesh with sherry and parsley. Serve the kebabs accompanied by the sauce.

Grilled Chicken Ohio Style [*USA*] Marinate chicken pieces in mustard powder combined with melted butter, maple syrup, chilli sauce, tomato ketchup, cider vinegar, salt, celery salt and cayenne. Grill the chicken and serve accompanied by the heated marinade.

Grilled Chicken Tandoori [***Tandoori Murgh*** *India*] Blend chopped onion, garlic and ginger, lemon juice, yogurt, garam masala, mace, nutmeg, cinnamon, cloves, coriander, cumin, tumeric, groundnut oil, red food colour and seasoning to a paste. Spread chicken pieces in the paste then grill them and serve garnished with segments of lemon.

Grilled Chicken Texas Style [*USA*] Blend garlic, chilli powder, cayenne and lemon juice to a paste. Marinate chicken pieces in the paste then grill them.

Grilled Chicken Yuan Style [***Tori no Yuan-yaki*** *Japan*] Grill skewered boned chicken, previously marinated in saké, mirin, soy sauce and yuzu rind. Grill, cut the chicken into slices and serve garnished with marinated and grilled pieces of leek.

Grilled Chicken with Garlic [***Kai Yang*** *Thailand*] Marinate chicken pieces in oil with garlic, salt, crushed peppercorns and coriander leaves. Grill and serve sprinkled with lemon juice.

Grilled Chicken with Garlic and Chillies [*USA*] Blend garlic, green chillies, lemon juice and chopped coriander leaves to a paste. Marinate skewered chicken pieces in the paste then grill them.

Grilled Chicken with Green Peppers [***Wakadori No Nanbanyaki*** *Japan*] Skewer chicken pieces, previously marinated in soy sauce, mirin and saké. Blend spring onions and dried red chillies to a smooth paste, and add the remaining marinade and beaten egg to form a light sauce consistency. Grill the chicken, basting frequently with the sauce mixture, and serve garnished with grilled fresh green peppers.

Grilled Devilled Chicken [*GB*] Coat skinned chicken pieces with a blend of butter, mustard, fruit chutney and Worcester sauce. Grill and serve accompanied by jus lié finished with some of the mustard and chutney mixture and chopped fresh herbs.

Grilled Marinated Chicken [***Masala Murghi*** *India*] Marinate chicken pieces in garam masala, garlic, ginger, paprika, rice flour, water, lemon juice and seasoning. Grill and garnish with segments of lemon.

Grilled Spiced Chicken with Coriander [***Pollo an Adobo a la Plancha*** *Mexico*] Marinate chicken pieces in olive oil with garlic, paprika, marjoram, cumin, coriander and lemon juice. Grill and serve garnished with segments of lemon.

Poached or Boiled Poultry

Application

Simmer chicken pieces or trussed chicken in stock or in water with root vegetables and herbs until cooked.

Boiled Salted Goose [*Språngd Gås* Scandinavia] Rub a combination of coarse salt, sugar and saltpetre into the goose inside and outside. Retain in a refrigerator under lid for 72 hr. Rinse the bird in warm water then boil in water with small carrots, onions, celery and herbs. Serve accompanied by horseradish sauce.

Brunswick Stew [*USA*] Poach chicken pieces in chicken stock with diced potatoes, tomato flesh, corn kernels and lima beans then sprinkle with chopped parsley.

Poached Chicken and Eggs [*Oyako Donburi* Japan] Poach chicken pieces in stock flavoured with light and dark soy sauces and chopped onion. Pour beaten eggs into the liquid to form threads and serve the chicken and egg on boiled rice with some of the liquor.

Poached Chicken and Mushrooms [*Tak Pok-Kum* Korea] Poach chicken pieces in chicken stock with light soy sauce, chopped spring onions, garlic, sliced mushrooms and sugar. Reduce the liquid by half, add a little sesame oil and serve sprinkled with chopped fresh green chillies.

Poached Chicken Burgundy Style [*Poulet Poché à la Bourguignonne* France] Poach a trussed chicken in equal quantities of white Burgundy wine and water with diced turnips. Make a velouté from the liquor and finish with cream. Coat portions of the chicken with the sauce and garnish with the turnips.

Poached Chicken Stuffed with Rice [*Poularde Stanley* France] Poach chicken stuffed with pilaff of rice combined with slices of truffle. Serve portions coated with curry-flavoured chicken velouté finished with cream.

Poached Chicken in Coconut Milk [*Gulai Ayam* Thailand] Poach a trussed chicken in coconut milk seasoned with chilli powder, ground cumin, turmeric and cinnamon, fenugreek seeds, sliced onion, crushed garlic, fennel, grated ginger and zest of lemon. Coat the chicken portions with the reduced liquor and serve with boiled rice.

Poached Chicken with Capers and Mushrooms [*Magyaros Csirkebecsinált* Hungary] Poach a trussed chicken in water with carrot, onion, celery, bayleaf and thyme. Make a velouté from the liquor, finish with a liaison of egg yolks and garnish with capers, chives, chopped mushrooms and grated cheese. Add cubes of the chicken to the sauce, transfer to a shallow dish, sprinkle with cheese and gratinate.

Poached Chicken with Carrots and Potatoes [*Tak Tori Tang* Korea] Simmer chicken pieces in water with soy sauce, sugar and hot fermented bean paste then add diced potato and carrot. Garnish with diced cooked red and green pimento and sprinkle with toasted sesame seeds.

Poached Chicken with Chinese Vermicelli [*Soto Ajam* Indonesia] Poach a trussed chicken in water with carrot, onion, celery, bayleaf and thyme. Blend turmeric, ginger, garlic and onion to a paste then fry the mixture in oil, add to the reduced chicken cooking liquid then add vermicelli and cook. Serve the sliced chicken on the vermicelli and sprinkle with chopped spring onions.

Poached Chicken with Egg and Lemon Sauce [*Israel*]   Poach a trussed chicken in water with carrot, studded onion, celery, turnip, bayleaf, thyme and seasoning. Reduce the liquor by half, thicken with arrowroot and finish with grated zest and juice of lemon and a liaison of egg yolks. Serve poured over the carved chicken.

Poached Chicken with Spiced Sauce [*Sie Hiung Tse China*]   Pour boiling water inside and over the chicken and dry on a wire grid. Boil and reduce by two-thirds water, light and dark soy sauces, grated nutmeg, cinnamon sticks, crushed peppercorns, cloves, five-spice powder, fennel seed, brown sugar, sliced ginger, leek and garlic. Poach a trussed chicken in this liquid. Carve the chicken, brush portions with sesame oil, mask with the strained liquid and serve sprinkled with chopped coriander leaves.

Poached Chicken with Truffle and Mushrooms [*Poularde Stanley France*]   Poach a chicken stuffed with pilaff of rice combined with strips of truffle and mushrooms. Coat portions of the chicken with curry-flavoured chicken velouté.

Poached Chicken with Vegetables [*Toriniku No Jubuni Japan*]   Marinate sliced raw chicken breast in soy sauce, saké and ginger juice. Place the lightly floured chicken in simmering second soup stock flavoured with mirin and soy sauce then add grooved and sliced carrot and cooked gingko nuts. Serve in bowls with mushroom caps and sliced spring onions previously cooked and glazed in second soup stock with the addition of a little sugar.

Poached Chicken with Yogurt and Almonds [*Shahjahani Murghi India*]   Poach a trussed chicken. Blend grated ginger, garlic, almonds, ground cumin, groundnut oil and water to a paste. Fry cardamoms, crushed cinnamon stick, bayleaves, cloves and chopped onion, add the paste, raisins and cubes of the poached chicken, then moisten with yogurt and cream, cook and finish with garam masala and toasted flaked almonds.

Poached Duck with Cabbage and Mushrooms [*Wuxiang Ya China*]   Poach a duck in duck stock with sliced ginger, chopped shallots, light and dark soy sauces, saké, sugar, five-spice powder and salt. Remove and retain. Reduce the liquor by half, then thicken with arrowroot, add quartered Chinese mushrooms, diced carrot and shredded Chinese cabbage and cook. Serve the duck cut into portions in the sauce together with the vegetables.

Poached Duck with Chilli Oil [*Hong Shu Ya China*]   Poach ducks in duck stock with chopped onion, diced fennel, carrot, celery, grated ginger, light and dark soy sauces, saké, five-spice powder, sugar, chilli oil and salt. Remove and retain. Reduce the liquor by half, add red colour and thicken with arrowroot. Coat the duck with the sauce and serve garnished with pickled cucumbers.

Poached Duck with Onion Sauce [*GB*]   Poach ducks in duck stock with basil, marjoram, celery and a studded onion. Add a reduction of the cooking liquid to a prepared onion sauce and finish it with cream. Serve the skinned duck portions coated with the sauce.

Poached Duck with Orange [*Pato com Arroz e Laranja Portugal*]   Poach ducks in duck stock with a piece each of smoked ham and bacon, lemon juice and cloves. Brush the duck with butter and crisp the skin under the grill. Serve on a bed of braised rice made with duck stock with slices of the smoked ham and bacon and of chorizo sausage. Garnish with segments of orange.

Poached Duck with Rice [*Pato com Arroz* Portugal] Poach ducks with lardons of bacon and pig's ears or trotters in duck stock. Serve garnished with sliced chorizo sausage accompanied by rice braised in the duck stock.

Poached Pigeons and Bacon [GB] Poach the pigeon and bacon pieces in water with turned carrots, batons of celery, button onions and a bouquet garni. Serve with the vegetables and cooked leaf spinach.

Poached Turkey with Celery Sauce [GB] Stuff a turkey with veal forcemeat and poach in water with a garnish of carrot, celery, onion and a bouquet garni. Serve with the vegetables, moistened with the liquor and accompanied by celery sauce.

Roasted Poultry

Application

A trussed whole bird is cooked in an oven at 200 °C using fat, marinade or wine for basting. It may also be spit-roasted.

Peking Duck [*Peh-ching K'ao Ya* China] Plunge a duck into boiling water then hang to dry for 12 hours. Three hours before roasting, brush with a cooked solution of honey, water and salt. Roast the duck until well cooked and the skin crisp. Serve the crisp skin and flesh cut into small pieces accompanied by mandarin pancakes, plum sauce, strips of spring onions and strips of cucumber.

Roast Chicken Algerian Style [*Djej Mechoui* Middle East] Marinade a chicken in olive oil, lemon juice, turmeric, cumin, coriander, baharat and dried mint for 12 hr, then roast in the usual manner.

Roast Chicken Cantonese Style [*Cha Tsa* China] Pour boiling water inside and over a chicken and dry it for 12 hr. Heat salt carefully until golden, mix with five-spice powder and use it to season the chicken. Thicken boiled Chinese rice vinegar and honey with arrowroot, cool it and brush over the surface of the chicken. Hang for a further four hours then roast in the usual manner.

Roast Chicken Stuffed with Cheese [*Pollo Ripieno al Forno* Italy] Sauté chopped heart and liver of a chicken, and combine with fried breadcrumbs, beaten eggs, milk, cream, grated Pecorino cheese and seasoning. Enrobe a hard-boiled egg with this stuffing, place inside the bird and roast in the usual manner.

Roast Chicken Stuffed with Couscous [*Djej M'Ahmar* Middle East] Combine couscous, pine nuts, sultanas and saffron with a little milk. Stuff a chicken with it then marinate in oil, turmeric, cumin, coriander, baharat and dried mint for several hours. Roast the chicken then glaze it with honey. Serve accompanied by chicken gravy flavoured with saffron, paprika, cumin and tomato purée.

Roast Chicken Stuffed with Ham [*Pollo alla Spiedo* Italy] Stuff a chicken with chopped ham mixed with garlic, sage, rosemary and breadcrumbs. Brush the bird with olive oil, sprinkle with sage and rosemary and leave for one hour. Bard with thin slices of smoked ham then roast on a spit.

Roast Chicken Stuffed with Oranges [Israel] Season a chicken inside and out with a mixture of salt, crushed garlic, paprika, ground coriander and chilli powder. Stuff with orange segments then roast, adding orange and lemon juices. Serve garnished with segments of orange.

Roast Chicken Stuffed with Rice [*Amich* Russia]   Combine boiled rice with soaked and chopped apricots, soaked raisins, blanched almonds, chopped hazelnuts and chopped basil. Season with ground cloves and cinnamon then stuff the chickens with the mixture and roast.

Roast Chicken Stuffed with Rice and Pine Nuts [*Ornitha Kokkinisti* Greece]   Rub a chicken with lemon, fill with braised rice and pine nut stuffing then roast in the usual manner. Swill the roasting tray with chicken stock, add tomato purée and crushed garlic then strain and serve as the gravy.

Roast Chicken with Honey and Cumin [*Pollo al ast Glaseado* Mexico]   Mix together olive oil, vinegar, ground cumin, crushed garlic, honey and salt. Marinate a chicken in the mixture for approx. 2 hr then roast in the usual manner, basting with the marinade as it cooks.

Roast Chicken with Liver and Marjoram Stuffing [*Egri Töltött Kappan* Hungary]   Stuff a bird under the breast skin with liver and marjoram stuffing then at the neck end with a mixture of chopped mushrooms and parsley. Roast the bird adding a little red wine. Swill the pan with stock and add soured cream to make an accompanying gravy.

Roast Chicken with Oranges [USA]   Season a chicken inside and out with garlic salt, stuff with orange stuffing then roast. Serve accompanied by orange-flavoured jus lié, sprinkled with julienne of orange peel.

Roast Chicken with Orange Sauce [*Pollo Asado con Salsa de Naranja* Spain]   Season a chicken inside and out with salt and roast. Pour off the fat and swill with chicken stock and jus lié, strain and reserve. Boil sugar until it begins to caramelise then add a little vinegar and orange juice, pour in the jus lié, simmer for a few minutes then strain through a fine strainer. Serve chicken portions coated with the sauce, accompanied by orange salad.

Roast Chicken with Vegetables [USA]   Sweat chopped onion with diced carrot, courgette and potato, and add soy sauce and chopped parsley. Rub a chicken inside and out with crushed garlic, stuff with the vegetable mixture and roast in the usual manner. Swill the pan with bourbon whiskey and jus lié and finish with a little cream.

Roast Duck [*Faisinjan Koresh* Middle East]   Sauté chopped onion and garlic in duck fat, stir in ground cumin, turmeric and cinnamon and blend to a paste with a little stock. Simmer the mixture then add ground almonds and more stock to form a sauce; add brown sugar and lemon and pomegranate juices. Coat portions of roast duck with this sauce, and sprinkle with pomegranate seeds and chopped coriander.

Roast Duck and Kasha [*Utka Zharenaya* Russia]   Stuff ducks with shallow-fried and diced duck giblets combined with buckwheat that has been boiled in salted water. Roast in the usual way.

Roast Duck with Honey, Lemon and Mint [GB]   Combine honey, butter and zest of lemon, rub over the surface and the inside of a duck and roast until almost cooked, then moisten with duck stock. Thicken the cooking liquor, and add honey, lemon juice and chopped mint. Mask portions of duck with this sauce and garnish with segments of lemon and sprigs of mint.

Roast Duck with Port Wine Sauce [GB]   Roast a duck and when almost cooked, sprinkle the duck with lemon juice and continue to cook until done. Swill the pan with port wine and brown stock then add jus lié; strain, and finish with orange marmalade and mushroom ketchup.

Roast Goose Stuffed with Apples [*Gus s Yablokami* Russia] Stuff a goose with quarters of peeled apples and fresh thyme then roast. Serve garnished with sprigs of mint.

Roast Goose with Apples and Prunes [*Stekt Gas* Scandinavia] Stuff a goose with poached and pitted prunes and lightly sautéed sliced apple then roast. Swill the pan with liquor from the prunes and red wine and reduce by half; add jus lié and finish with pieces of butter.

Roast Goose with Fruit and Nut Stuffing [USA] Stuff a goose with poached soft fruits and nut stuffing; rub over with a lemon then roast. Swill the pan with the liquor from the poached fruits and brandy and reduce by half; add jus lié and finish with pieces of butter.

Roast Goose with Pears [*Oca Amb Peres* Spain] Sauté chopped onion and garlic, pine nuts and raisins in oil; add chopped parsley and cinnamon, diced tomato flesh and milk and cook to a sauce consistency; finish with aniseed and brandy. Cook peeled, cored and halved pears in this sauce. Roast the goose, glazing it with the sauce during the last stages of cooking. Serve the carved bird garnished with the pears.

Roast Pheasant with Grapes [*Vivdruva-fylld Stekt Fasan* Scandinavia] Stuff barded pheasant with pitted grapes and roast. Serve garnished with chilled pitted green, black and white grapes, accompanied by roast gravy.

Roast Pheasant with Wild Rice Stuffing [USA] Stuff a pheasant with pilaff of wild rice combined with sautéed sliced mushrooms and chopped rosemary, then roast in the usual manner. Serve with jus lié finished with cream.

Roast Spiced and Stuffed Chicken [*Murgh Masalewala* India] Blend ground cardamoms, cloves, mace, nutmeg and saffron with yogurt to a paste then rub it over the inside of a chicken. Fry chopped onion and garlic in ghee, add seeded cardamoms, cloves, ground black pepper, chillies, turmeric, coriander and cinnamon and a little vinegar. Liquidise then pour over the surface of the chicken and refrigerate for 12 hr. Stuff the chicken with walnut, ginger, sultana and onion stuffing then roast.

Roast Stuffed Goose [*Töltött Liba* Hungary] Combine chopped mushrooms, chives, goose liver and chopped hard-boiled egg, marjoram, white wine, beaten eggs and soured cream. Stuff a goose with this mixture and roast.

Roast Stuffed Goose Neck [*Tötlött Libanyak* Hungary] Combine minced goose liver, heart, boiled potatoes, sautéed chopped onion, parsley, marjoram and beaten egg yolks. Stuff the neck skins with this mixture and roast. Serve with braised red cabbage.

Roast Stuffed Neck of Chicken [*Derma* Israel] Combine ground almonds, matzo meal, chopped parsley, egg and seasoning of salt, pepper and allspice. Fill the necks with the stuffing then roast.

Roast Stuffed Pigeons, or **Pigeons in Pimlico** [GB] Sauté blanched pigeon livers then blend to a coarse mixture with ham, mushrooms, parsley, marjoram, sage and mace, bound together with egg yolks. Stuff the birds with it, cover with a bard then roast them. Serve garnished with puff pastry tartlets filled with some of the cooked stuffing mixture.

Tandoori Chicken [*Tandoori Murch* India] Blend saffron-flavoured water, lemon juice, crushed garlic, grated ginger, chilli powder, paprika, garam masala and salt to a fine paste. Marinate skinned chicken pieces in the mixture for 2 hr. Brush with ghee and roast.

Pot Roasted or Poêléd Poultry

Application

Pot roasting means moist cooking with butter or oil on a layer of root vegetables and herbs in a deep sided pan, covered with a lid, at 180 °C. When cooked, swill with jus lié or stock and lightly thicken with arrowroot.

Pot Roast Chicken Georgian Style [*Israel*] Rub chickens inside and out with lemon juice and salt. Stuff with sautéed minced beef seasoned with cinnamon, nutmeg, cloves, sugar, salt, grated zest and juice of lemon and almonds, then pot roast. Swill the pan with stock, lemon and grape juice. Garnish with warm, depipped and peeled grapes.

Pot Roast Chicken Greek Style [***Kotopoulo Yemisto*** *Greece*] Stuff chickens with almond, sultana, liver and rice stuffing then pot roast with the addition of cinnamon sticks.

Pot Roast Chicken Hamburg Style [***Stubenküken*** *Germany*] Pot roast chickens stuffed with chicken liver, mushroom and basil stuffing.

Pot Roast Chicken with Foie Gras [***Poularde Poêlé Derby*** *France*] Pot roast chicken stuffed with pilaff of rice. Serve in an earthenware dish surrounded with jus lié and garnished with croûtons with a slice of truffle on each.

Pot Roasted Chicken with Mushrooms [***Poulet en Cocotte Grand'Mère*** *France*] Pot roast chickens and serve in an earthenware casserole garnished with sautéed button mushrooms and fried diced bread croûtons.

Pot Roasted Pigeon with Onions, Olives, Potatoes and Truffle [***Pigeon Poêlé Nana*** *France*] Pot roast pigeons and moisten with white wine and jus lié. Serve garnished with glazed button onions, stoned olives, noisette potatoes and diced truffle.

Pot Roast Chicken with Pork and Orange Stuffing [*Caribbean*] Pot roast chickens stuffed with pork and orange stuffing. Swill with orange juice, brown chicken stock, honey and rum and season with cinnamon. Glaze portions of the chicken with the sauce and serve garnished with warm segments of orange and watercress.

Pot Roasted Duck with Morello Cherries [***Ente Mit Sauerkirschen*** *Germany*] Pot roast ducks then swill the pan with Madeira, reduce and add jus lié. Add stoned morello cherries to the sauce then finish with kirsch. Serve the duck portions masked with the sauce.

Pot Roasted Duck with Orange [***Caneton Poêlé à l'Orange*** *France*] Pot roast ducks then swill the pan with jus lié. Caramelise orange and lemon juice and sugar, add to the cooking liquid and garnish with blanched julienne of zest of orange and lemon. Coat the carved portions of duck with the sauce and garnish with segments of orange.

Sautéed Poultry

To joint poultry for sauté, remove the legs and cut through the centre of each to give two joints, drumstick and thigh. Remove winglets just before the first bone.

Cut lengthwise on each side of the breast bone to give two joints with the winglet bone attached and divide the remaining breast into two across or along the breast-bone. For Asian, Chinese and Indian dishes, remove and discard the skin from the chicken before cooking it.

Application

Heat oil and/or butter in a shallow pan then add seasoned goujons, cubes or joints of poultry, allow to colour golden then cover with a lid and cook gently without boiling. Moisten with stock, marinade, wine, vinegar or sauce according to recipe, and add herbs and spices as appropriate.

Sauté of Chicken and Oyster Gumbo [*USA*]   Sauté chicken pieces with chopped onion and garlic and diced celery and green pimento. Moisten with jus lié, add flaked dried red chillies, bayleaf and thyme and season with salt, ground cloves and allspice. Finish with poached oysters, chopped parsley and spring onions and Worcester sauce. Serve accompanied by boiled rice.

Sauté of Chicken Bourguignonne [*Poulet Sauté Bourguignonne France*]   Golden sauté a garnish of lardons of bacon, button onions and button mush-rooms in oil, remove and retain. Sauté chicken pieces in oil, add the garnish, cover with a lid and cook. Sauté chopped onion and garlic in oil, moisten with red wine and reduce by half, then add jus lié and simmer for a few min and strain. Serve chicken pieces coated with the sauce, garnished with heart-shaped croûtons and sprinkled with chopped parsley.

Sauté of Chicken Chasseur [*Poulet Sauté Chasseur France*]   Sauté chicken pieces in oil, add sliced mushrooms and chopped shallots, then add tomato concassée, chopped tarragon and white wine. Reduce the liquid by half, add jus lié and season to taste. Coat chicken pieces with the sauce, sprinkle with chopped parsley and serve.

Sauté of Chicken Chikuzen Style [*Chikuzen-ni Japan*]   Sauté chicken pieces in oil then add chunks of konnyaku, sliced shiitake mushrooms, wedges of carrot, bamboo shoots and burdock root. Barely cover with dashi, simmer then add light and dark soy sauces and cook. Add parboiled snow peas and serve.

Sauté of Chicken Country Captain Style [*USA*]   Sauté chicken pieces in oil with chopped onion and garlic and diced pimento and tomato flesh. Add curry pow-der, sugar and thyme, moisten with chicken stock then finish with currants, toasted slivered almonds and chopped parsley.

Sauté of Chicken Creole Style [*Caribbean*]   Sauté chicken pieces with chopped onion, garlic, crushed dried red chillies and tomato concassée. Stir in curry pow-der and moisten with chicken stock; add saffron and finish with coconut cream.

Sauté of Chicken Delhi Style [*Deli Murgh India*]   Sauté chicken pieces with chopped onion and garlic. Season with cinnamon stick, cloves, cardamoms, gin-ger, chillies, coriander, cumin, turmeric and tomato purée. Moisten with stock and lemon juice, cook and serve garnished with chopped coriander leaves.

Sauté of Chicken Domburi [*Jakituri Domburi Japan*]   Marinate goujons of chicken in mirin, soy sauce, garlic, ginger and seasoning. Place dry boiled rice in a dish, arrange the sautéed goujons on top and moisten with chicken stock, the strained marinade and sugar. Finish with chopped spring onions.

Sauté of Chicken Flambé [***Pollo al Ajillo*** *Mexico*]   Sauté chicken pieces in olive oil, add chopped garlic then moisten with brandy and flambé. Cover with a lid and simmer gently until cooked. Sprinkle with coarse salt and chopped garlic, baste for a few minutes and serve.

Sauté of Chicken Hungarian Style [***Csirke Paprika*** *Hungary*]   Sauté chicken pieces, add chopped onion and garlic, stir in paprika, diced tomato flesh and caraway seeds then moisten with chicken stock. When cooked, reduce the liquor by one-third, garnish with julienne of cooked green pimento and finish with soured cream.

Sauté of Chicken in Coconut Milk [***Panaeng Gai*** *Thailand*]   Sauté sliced chicken and retain. Stir-fry curry paste in oil, moisten with thick coconut milk, simmer and reduce by half, then add roasted nibbed peanuts, sugar and nam pla. Replace the chicken and serve garnished with chopped coriander leaves.

Sauté of Chicken in Curry Sauce [***Kari Ajam*** *Indonesia*]   Sauté chicken pieces with chopped onion and garlic. Sprinkle with chilli powder, turmeric and curry powder, add grated ginger then moisten with coconut milk and simmer until tender.

Sauté of Chicken in Madeira with Truffles [***Poulet Sauté Archiduc*** *France*]   Sauté chicken pieces and retain. Swill the pan with brandy, add chicken velouté and Madeira then finish with cream and lemon juice. Serve coated with the sauce garnished with slices of truffle.

Sauté of Chicken in Orange Sauce [*Ajam Berkuah Dan Soya* *Indonesia*]   Sauté chicken pieces, add chopped onion and garlic and sambal ulek then moisten with orange juice and lemon juice and dark soy sauce. Add soft brown sugar and thicken the sauce with cornflour.

Sauté of Chicken in Shrimp Sauce [***Ayam Petis*** *Indonesia*]   Sauté chicken pieces and add chopped onion and garlic, Chinese shrimp paste, sambal trasi and turmeric. Moisten with coconut milk and lemon juice and add soft brown sugar. Serve garnished with shrimps and sprinkled with chopped coriander leaves.

Sauté of Chicken Madras Style [***Murgh Madras*** *India*]   Sauté chicken pieces previously marinated in lemon juice, chilli powder, ground black pepper and salt. Add chopped onion, garlic, grated ginger, ground cumin, coriander and turmeric and crushed dried green chillies to the chicken, moisten with chicken stock and the strained marinade and cook. Finish with garam masala.

Sauté of Chicken Mole Style [*USA*]   Sauté chicken pieces, add chopped onion, deglace with red wine vinegar then add a liquidised paste of green chilli, garlic and tomato flesh. Moisten with tomato juice then add grated unsweetened chocolate; allow to simmer and finish with chopped parsley.

Sauté of Chicken Portuguese Style [***Arroz de Galinha*** *Portugal*]   Sauté chicken pieces in oil with chopped onion and lardons of bacon. Moisten with stock and wine vinegar and half cook. Add short-grain rice and continue cooking. Serve garnished with sliced chorizo sausage.

Sauté of Chicken Teriyaki [***Tori No Teriyaki*** *Japan*]   Sauté chicken pieces, moisten with teriyaki sauce and cook until the sauce is almost completely reduced. Cut into slices and serve sprinkled with sansho pepper.

Sauté of Chicken Vindaloo [*Kholee Vindaloo India*] Blend red and green dried chillies, garlic, ground coriander, cumin, turmeric, cloves, fenugreek, lemon juice, vinegar, peeled cardamom seeds and bayleaves to a paste. Sauté chicken pieces, spread with the paste and continue to cook with chopped onion, chicken stock and garam masala.

Sauté of Chicken with Almonds [*Caribbean*] Sauté chicken pieces, add chopped onion, chopped spring onions, diced cucumber, quartered mushrooms, diced carrot and water chestnuts, bamboo shoots and grated ginger. Moisten with light soy sauce, cook and serve with boiled rice garnished with golden fried flaked almonds.

Sauté of Chicken with Anchovies [*USA*] Rub chicken pieces with garlic and anchovy essence and sauté in hot oil. Swill the pan with lemon juice and add chopped parsley. Arrange in a serving dish, sprinkle with grated Parmesan cheese and butter then gratinate.

Sauté of Chicken with Apple and Cider [*GB*] Sauté chicken pieces with chopped onion and diced apple then moisten with cider and stock and cook. Reduce the liquor and finish with cream. Serve sprinkled with chopped parsley and tarragon.

Sauté of Chicken with Apple Rings [*USA*] Sauté chicken pieces, swill with cider, add grated zest of lemon, reduce the liquor then add cream and chopped parsley. Serve garnished with sautéed apple rings.

Sauté of Chicken with Bacon, Pimento and Tomato [*Pollo Chilindrón Mexico*] Sauté chicken pieces, and add chopped onion, garlic, diced red pimento, lardons of bacon and tomato concassée. Moisten with jus lié, cook and finish with chopped fresh herbs.

Sauté of Chicken with Chestnuts [*Gai Gup Kao Lad Thailand*] Blend to a paste garlic, coriander root and black peppercorns. Cook the paste in oil then add the chicken pieces and sauté. Moisten with stock then add water chestnuts and palm sugar and cook gently.

Sauté of Chicken with Chillies [*Ajam Panggang Thailand*] Sauté chicken pieces with grated ginger in ghee. Moisten with stock and lime juice then stir in turmeric and diced green chillies and cook.

Sauté of Chicken with Coconut [*Kozhi Thali India*] Rub chicken pieces with ground turmeric and salt then sauté without colour. Blend to a paste oven-dried desiccated coconut, dried green chillies, garlic, ginger, coriander, cumin, cloves, cinnamon and coriander leaves. Golden fry chopped onion, add the paste and cook for a few minutes. Add the chicken and cook. When cooked finish with vinegar, tomato purée and yogurt.

Sauté of Chicken with Coconut Milk [*Caribbean*] Sauté chicken pieces and add chopped onion, curry powder, paprika and fresh red chillies. Moisten with chicken stock and coconut milk, thicken with arrowroot and cook. Finish with chopped coriander leaves and serve with boiled rice.

Sauté of Chicken with Coriander and Coconut Milk [*Gaeng Ped Gai Thailand*] Blend dried red chillies, shallots, garlic, ginger, lemon grass, coriander root, mace, nutmeg, zest of lime, coriander seeds, cumin, shrimp paste and seasoning to a paste. Stir-fry the paste in oil then add chicken pieces and shredded bamboo shoots and moisten with thick coconut milk. Serve sprinkled with chopped coriander.

Sauté of Chicken with Coriander and Cumin [*Ajam Bumbu Djeruk* *Indonesia*] Sauté chicken pieces with chopped onion and garlic. Sprinkle with ground coriander, cumin, turmeric, chilli powder and soy sauce. Finish with lemon juice and serve garnished with segments of lime.

Sauté of Chicken with Cornmeal Dumplings [*USA*]   Sauté chicken pieces, add chopped onions, garlic and diced carrot, moisten with chicken stock and cook. Reduce the strained liquid by half, add chicken velouté, season with salt, pepper, mace and Tabasco sauce then add cream. Poach tablespoon-sized cornmeal dumplings in the liquor then add the chicken and sautéed sliced button mushrooms.

    Dumplings: mix together cornmeal, flour, baking powder, egg and milk to a fairly firm mixture.

Sauté of Chicken with Crab, Crayfish and Pork Pilau [*Caribbean*]   Cook diced salt pork in water then drain and reserve the liquid. Sauté chicken pieces and add chopped onion, garlic, fresh red chilli and diced tomato flesh. Moisten with stock, dry sherry and Angostura bitters. Add the diced cooked pork, long-grain rice and peas and cook. Arrange white crabmeat, crayfish tails and chopped parsley on top, add lime juice then cover and simmer until liquid is absorbed. Serve garnished with segments of lime.

Sauté of Chicken with Dumplings [*USA*]   Sauté chicken pieces, add chopped onion and celery including the leaves, moisten with white wine and stock, season with salt, pepper and allspice and simmer. Lightly thicken with arrowroot and finish with cream and chopped parsley. Place circles of dumplings on top, cover with a lid and simmer until firm.

    Dumplings: combine flour, baking powder, sugar, butter, milk and salt; roll and cut out 5-cm rounds.

Sauté of Chicken with Garlic [*Pollo al Ajillo* *Spain*]   Sauté chicken pieces with chopped garlic, moisten with stock and sherry and cook, reducing the liquid to a glaze consistency.

Sauté of Chicken with Ginger [*Gai King* *Thailand*]   Sauté chopped onion and garlic, remove and retain. Sauté chicken pieces then add chopped ginger, mint, spring onions, fresh red chillies and steamed and sliced Chinese mushrooms, followed by the onion and garlic. Moisten with soy sauce, rice vinegar and nam pla and simmer gently until cooked.

Sauté of Chicken with Lemon [*Ornitha Lemonáti* *Greece*]   Marinate chicken pieces in lemon juice and chopped parsley. Sauté the chicken in olive oil, add chopped onion and garlic then moisten with the marinade, grated zest of lemon, white wine and stock. Simmer then lightly thicken with arrowroot.

Sauté of Chicken with Lime [*Ling Mung Tse* *China*]   Marinate chicken pieces in saké, light and dark soy sauces, ginger syrup and salt. Sauté the chicken, add grated ginger, garlic and sliced spring onions then moisten with the marinade. Remove the chicken, brush with sesame oil and serve coated with the following sauce: simmer together soft brown sugar, chicken stock, the cooking liquid and grated zest and juice of limes, thickened with arrowroot.

Sauté of Chicken with Lime and Rum [*Caribbean*]   Marinate chicken pieces in soy sauce, white rum, lime juice and chilli powder. Sauté the chicken, moisten with stock and the marinade then thicken with arrowroot and serve garnished with segments of lime.

Sauté of Chicken with Okra [*Kotopoulo me Bamies* Greece] Sauté chicken pieces and add chopped onion and tomato concassée. Moisten with chicken stock, add oregano and okra and cook, then finish with chopped fresh herbs.

Sauté of Chicken with Olives [*Israel*] Rub chicken pieces with garlic and season with a mixture of cayenne, paprika, coriander, pepper and salt. Sauté the chicken in oil, moisten with saffron-infused stock, add stoned olives and slices of pickled lemon then cook. Serve with boiled rice.

Sauté of Chicken with Peas [*Frango com Ervilhas* Portugal] Sauté chicken pieces, add chopped onion and garlic, moisten with white wine and stock then add peas and cook until tender.

Sauté of Chicken with Pigeon Peas Pilau [*Caribbean*] Cut chickens for sauté, remove the skin and place into a bowl with salt beef cut into 2.5-cm cubes; season with salt, rub in cloves of crushed garlic, season with ground black pepper, cover with cling film and set aside for 2 hr. Sauté the chicken pieces and the beef in oil then add chopped onion, diced tomato flesh and a little stock, cover with a lid and cook for approx. 1 hr. Stir in long-grain rice and previously soaked pigeon peas; moisten with stock, cover with a lid and simmer until all the liquid is absorbed and the meats, rice and peas are cooked. Garnish with segments of lime.

Sauté of Chicken with Pimento [*Tábori Csirke* Hungary] Sauté chicken pieces with diced green pimento and tomato flesh then finish by adding beaten egg yolks to form a light scrambled mixture.

Sauté of Chicken with Pimento [*Pollo in Potacchio* Italy] Sauté chicken pieces in olive oil and add chopped onion and garlic and diced red pimento. Moisten with white wine and stock, add tomato purée and rosemary then simmer until cooked.

Sauté of Chicken with Pineapple and Rum [*Caribbean*] Marinate chicken pieces in rum with pineapple pieces, the zest and juice of limes and ground cloves. Sauté the chicken, add chopped onion, garlic, crushed dried red chillies, tomato concassée, raisins and bayleaf. Moisten with chicken stock and the marinade and cook, then thicken with arrowroot and serve garnished with the pineapple pieces.

Sauté of Chicken with Potatoes and Herbs [*Chakhokhbili* Russia] Sauté chicken pieces with onion, garlic and diced tomato flesh. Add small boiled potatoes in their skins, moisten with white wine, and add turmeric, chopped mint, chopped tarragon, coriander leaves and crushed fenugreek.

Sauté of Chicken with Prawns [*Pollastre amb Gambes* Spain] Sauté chicken pieces and prawns in olive oil, remove the prawns and retain. Add chopped onion, garlic and diced carrot, moisten with brandy and flambé, then add white wine and chicken velouté and gently simmer. Transfer the chicken to a serving dish with the prawns and serve coated with the strained sauce.

Sauté of Chicken with Red Wine [*Coq au Vin* France] Sauté chicken pieces and add lardons of bacon, chopped onion and garlic. Moisten with red wine, reduce by half then add jus lié and cook. Garnish with sautéed button onions and mushrooms and heart-shaped croûtons dipped in chopped chervil.

Sauté of Chicken with Rice [*Arroz con Pollo* Spain] Sauté chicken pieces and add chopped onion and garlic, diced green pimento and tomato flesh. Add short-grain rice then stir in paprika and moisten with white wine and stock. Add a few strands of saffron, season and cook until the rice has absorbed the liquid and is tender, and serve.

Sauté of Chicken with Soy Sauce [*Takpokkum* Korea]   Marinate chicken pieces in soy sauce, sesame oil, garlic, ginger, toasted sesame seeds, chopped spring onion and diced pimento. Sauté the chicken pieces then moisten with stock and the marinade and cook.

Sauté of Chicken with Spiced Coconut Milk [*Goelai Ajam Reboneg* Thailand] Season chicken pieces with salt and ground turmeric then sauté in ghee. Add chopped onion, sambal trasi and sugar and moisten with thin and thick coconut milks, add curry leaves and cook. Garnish with bamboo shoots and chopped spring onions.

Sauté of Curried Chicken [*Kari Ayam Kelapa* Thailand]   Blend toasted desiccated coconut and coconut milk to a paste. Blend onion, garlic, blachan, turmeric, coriander, cumin and lemon grass and peanut oil to a paste then fry the mixture to evaporate the moisture. Add the coconut paste, duan salan leaf and laos powder. Sauté the chicken pieces then add the blended paste to form a sauce and simmer until cooked.

Sautéed and Glazed Suprême of Chicken [*Tori No Teriyaki* Japan]   Sauté suprêmes in oil, drain off surplus fat, moisten with soy sauce and mirin, add sugar then reduce the liquid to a glaze. Slice the chicken and serve garnished with sliced cucumber previously marinated in rice vinegar and soy sauce.

Sautéed Chicken Livers [*Torikimo No Tamago-Toji* Japan]   Rinse chicken livers in cold water, drain then cut into quarters. Sauté the livers in oil, moisten with second soup stock, soy sauce and mirin, add sugar and simmer for 1 min. Pour beaten eggs over the surface of the livers, cook for 1 min and serve in bowls.

Sautéed Chicken Livers with Mushrooms [*Kyckling Lever med Svamp* Scandinavia]   Sauté chicken livers and mushrooms in oil, remove and retain. Swill the pan with sherry then add cream. Replace the livers and mushrooms, season to taste and serve.

Sautéed Duck with Banana and Mandarins [*Pato Guisado à Ribatejana* Portugal]   Sauté duck pieces in oil with chopped onion and brunoise of carrot; moisten with Madeira, white wine and jus lié. Serve garnished with sliced banana and segments of mandarin oranges.

Sautéed Goujons of Chicken in Coconut Cream [*Opor Ajam* Indonesia]   Sauté goujons of chicken with chopped onion, garlic, shredded fresh chillies, grated ginger and coriander. Add grated coconut then finish with coconut cream.

Sautéed Goujons of Chicken in Coconut Shells [*Ajam Disadjikam Dalam Kelapa* Indonesia]   Sauté goujons of chicken with chopped onion and garlic, diced green pimento and tomato flesh, and grated coconut. Moisten with coconut milk then thicken with cornflour. Place the mixture into coconut shells, cover with kitchen foil then bake. Serve sprinkled with white rum.

Sautéed Goujons of Chicken with Ginger [*Chow Tse Shan* China]   Sauté goujons of chicken in groundnut oil with garlic and grated ginger, moisten with chicken stock, saké and light and dark soy sauces, then thicken with cornflour and add soft brown sugar.

Sautéed Goujons of Chicken with Paw-paw [*Chou Tse* China]   Marinate goujons of chicken in saké, light and dark soy sauces, grated ginger, soft brown sugar, egg whites and salt. Sauté the goujons in groundnut oil and add strips of paw-paw and chopped spring onions. Moisten with the marinade, add chicken stock and sesame oil and thicken with cornflour. Garnish with slices of paw-paw and spring onions.

Sautéed Goujons of Chicken with Walnuts [*Cerkez Tavagu Middle East*]   Cook carrots, onion, red pimento and garlic in stock then purée the vegetables and combine with ground walnuts, breadcrumbs, cream cheese, paprika and walnut oil to form a sauce. Sauté goujons of chicken in oil then add the sauce and serve with rice.

Sautéed Goujons of Duck with Mandarins [*Joe Tsjoe Ja Roe China*]   Marinate goujons of duck in sesame oil, mandarin juice, lemon juice, honey, five-spice powder, cornflour and seasoning. Shallow fry the goujons in groundnut oil and add chopped spring onions. Moisten with the marinade and chicken stock and add lumps of sugar rubbed on mandarin rind. Garnish with segments of mandarin.

Sautéed Goujons of Duck with Mangos [*Manggoeo Tsjoe Japiean China*]   Marinate goujons of duck in oil, light and dark soy sauces, hoisin sauce, lightly beaten egg whites and five-spice powder. Shallow fry the goujons in groundnut oil, add chopped spring onions and moisten with the marinade, chicken stock, lime juice and honey. Garnish with sliced raw mangos.

Sautéed Goujons of Turkey with Lemon and Saffron [*Pavo en Pepitoria Spain*]   Blend golden fried breadcrumbs, garlic, parsley, lemon juice, saffron, stock, bayleaf, cinnamon, cloves and paprika to a sauce consistency. Sauté goujons of turkey with chopped onion then moisten with the sauce.

Sautéed Pigeons [*Pichones a la Toledana Spain*]   Sauté pigeon pieces with chopped onion and unskinned cloves of garlic. Moisten with sherry and simmer while reducing the liquid to a glaze.

Sautéed Quail with Parsley and Garlic [*Codornices a la Bilbaína Spain*]   Sauté halved quail in butter, remove and retain. Golden fry breadcrumbs in butter with chopped garlic and parsley, thyme and seasoning, then sprinkle the birds with the mixture.

Suprêmes of Chicken in Cream with Mushrooms [*Suprêmes de Volaille à la Crème et Champignons France*]   Sauté suprêmes in oil and butter, remove and retain. Add sliced button mushrooms to the pan and sauté for a few minutes, moisten with sherry then add chicken velouté and finish with cream. Serve suprêmes coated with the sauce.

Suprêmes of Chicken with Asparagus [*Suprêmes de Volaille Maréchale France*]   Coat suprêmes with flour, eggwash and breadcrumbs then shallow fry. Serve garnished with sprue asparagus and a slice of truffle on each, surrounded with a cordon of jus lié.

Suprêmes of Duck in Honey Sauce [*GB*]   Sauté breasts of duck with chopped onion, moisten with white wine, stir in honey, sprigs of thyme, lemon juice and cream.

Suprêmes of Duck Vindaloo [*Vaathoo Vindaloo India*]   Sauté suprêmes of duck in ghee. Fry chopped onion, crushed garlic, dried red and green chillies, cloves, cardamoms, turmeric, coriander seed, poppy seed, black pepper and cumin and cook for 3–4 min. Moisten with vinegar and chicken stock. Replace the suprêmes, add desiccated coconut and simmer.

Suprêmes of Duck with Curry Sauce [*Vaathoo India*]   Sauté suprêmes in ghee. Fry chopped onion, crushed garlic, strips of fresh green chillies and ginger, then add ground coriander, cumin, turmeric, chillies, black pepper and tomato purée. Moisten with desiccated coconut liquidised with chicken stock, vinegar and salt. Replace the duck and simmer then finish with lemon juice.

Suprêmes of Duck with Orange Liqueur [*Caribbean*]   Marinate suprêmes of
duck in zest and juice of lemons, rum, Grand Marnier and ground cloves. Sauté
the duck in oil then add and fry chopped onion, crushed garlic, tomato concassée and tomato purée. Moisten with red wine, brown chicken stock and the
marinade, simmer and thicken the liquid with arrowroot. Garnish with warm
orange segments.

Suprêmes of Duck with Oranges [*Pato à la Sevillana Spain*]   Sauté suprêmes
of duck in olive oil and sprinkle with ground cinnamon, cloves and chopped
garlic. Moisten with dry white wine, orange juice and honey, add stoned green
olives then allow to simmer and thicken the liquid with arrowroot. Garnish with
warm orange segments.

Shallow-fried Poultry

Application

Coat suprêmes or goujons of chicken with either flour, breadcrumbs or matzo meal
and golden shallow fry in oil, butter or other fat. In some cases no coating is necessary.

Chicken Suprêmes in the Maryland Style [*USA*]   Coat suprêmes with flour, eggwash and breadcrumbs then shallow fry. Serve garnished with shallow-fried
bananas, sweetcorn fritters, rashers of streaky bacon and grilled tomatoes,
accompanied by horseradish sauce.

Chicken Suprêmes with Cream Cheese and Parma Ham [*Pollo alla Valdostano
Italy*]   Spread flattened boneless suprêmes of chicken with cream cheese mixed
with grated Parmesan cheese and chopped chives. Place a slice of Parma ham on
top, fold over, pass through flour, eggwash and breadcrumbs then shallow fry.
Serve surrounded with a thread of jus lié.

Chicken Suprêmes with Sesame Seeds [*Oaf Sum-Sum Israel*]   Coat suprêmes
with a mixture of flour, paprika and sesame seeds, then pass through beaten
eggs and again through the flour mix. Shallow fry and serve on a bed of boiled
rice garnished with black olives.

Chicken Suprêmes with Smoked Ham [*Pollo alla Bolognese Italy*]   Sauté
floured suprêmes in butter then place a slice of smoked ham on top of each,
sprinkle with grated Parmesan cheese and cook until the cheese melts.

Chicken Viennese Style [*Weiner Backbendl Germany*]   Marinate chicken pieces
in lemon juice seasoned with paprika. Pass through flour, eggwash and breadcrumbs and shallow fry.

Shallow-fried Chicken Galettes [*Kotlety Pozharskie Russia*]   Soak breadcrumbs
in milk then squeeze dry and combine with finely minced chicken and butter
and season with salt, pepper and nutmeg. Form the mixture into small galettes,
pass through seasoned flour, eggwash and breadcrumbs and mark trellis-fashion.
Shallow fry in oil and butter and serve garnished with picked parsley.

Shallow-fried Goujons of Chicken with Mushrooms [*Tori Goban Japan*]   Sauté
sliced button mushrooms, chopped onion and spring onions and grated ginger.
Moisten with chicken stock and soy sauce and add peas. Serve dry-cooked, short-

grain rice in bowls then place shallow-fried breadcrumbed goujons of chicken on top together with the mushroom mixture and slices of Japanese omelette.

Shallow-fried Shanghai Duck [*Shanghai Yu Yian Ya China*]   Marinate duck pieces in saké, light and dark soy sauces, sugar, grated ginger, garlic and five-spice powder. Steam the duck then shallow fry in sunflower oil and remove. Add the marinade to the pan together with lime juice, strain and serve the duck coated with the sauce.

Shallow-fried Spatchcock Russian Style [*Kotlety Tabaka Russia*]   Split birds as for spatchcock, shallow fry in oil and serve accompanied by tabaka sauce.

  Tabaka sauce: simmer damsons in water for approx. 5 min, drain and pass through a sieve. Cook fruit purée for approx. 20 min with the addition of crushed cloves of garlic and chopped tarragon.

Shallow-fried Stuffed Goose Neck [*Gefüllteer Gänsehals Germany*]   Combine minced pork and bacon, sautéed chopped onion, marjoram and parsley, soaked and squeezed breadcrumbs, chopped truffle and Madeira. Stuff the necks with the mixture then shallow fry in butter.

Turkey Schnitzel [*Israel*]   Coat turkey escalopes with flour, eggwash and matzo meal then shallow fry and serve with segments of lemon and picked parsley.

Steamed Poultry

Application

Cook the item in a pressure steamer or in a Chinese steamer.

Steamed Chicken with Basil [*Haw Mok Gai Thailand*]   Marinate chicken pieces in thick coconut milk. Blend dried red chillies, zest of lime, shallots, garlic, shrimp paste, lemon grass, coriander root and salt to a paste. Add this paste to the marinade and cook to make a sauce. Encase the chicken pieces and the sauce in foil lined with lettuce and basil leaves then steam.

Steamed Chicken with Ham [*Pai Cheng Tse Hwo China*]   Sprinkle chicken pieces with diced ham, moisten with light and dark soy sauces, saké, grated ginger, crushed peppercorns and soft brown sugar. Steam then serve sprinkled with chopped spring onions.

Steamed Chicken with Saké [*Tori No Sakamushi Japan*]   Marinate boned chicken pieces in soy sauce and saké for 30 min. Blend spring onions and root ginger to a paste, spread the mixture on top of the chicken and steam with the marinade. Cut the chicken into slices and serve in bowls with some of the cooking liquid, garnished with pieces of deseeded cucumber and mustard.

Steamed Chicken with Squid [*Mushidori To Ika No Gomazu Japan*]   Sprinkle boned chicken pieces with salt and saké then steam; when cooked slice the chicken and retain in the cooking liquid. Marinate blanched squares of squid in rice vinegar with salt. Serve the chicken and squid garnished with blanched and sliced seaweed, julienne of spring onion, carrot and cucumber. Serve accompanied by sesame dipping sauce.

  Sesame dipping sauce: blend garlic, toasted white sesame seeds, soy sauce and mirin to a paste then add to mayonnaise.

Stewed Poultry

Application

Jointed poultry pieces are simmered in a liquid with vegetables, herbs and spices, covered with a lid.

Chicken Korma [*Korma* *India*] Blend cashew nuts, ginger, garlic, green chillies and water to a coarse paste. Golden fry chopped onion in ghee with whole green cardamoms, cloves, cassia bark, coriander and white cumin seeds, then add the spice paste and yogurt. Add chicken pieces and allow to stew. Finish with saffron infused in milk, double cream, chopped coriander and parsley.

Chicken Stew [*Dak Jim* *Korea*] Marinate chicken pieces in light soy sauce, sesame oil, garlic, chilli powder and chopped spring onions. Stew the chicken in the marinade mixture with chicken stock and serve with boiled rice.

Chicken Stew Mexican Style [*Pollo à la Mexicana* *Mexico*] Sweat chopped onion and garlic in oil, add sliced mushrooms, diced celery and tomato flesh, bayleaf and oregano then add chicken pieces to the sauce and stew until they are tender.

Chicken Stew with Almonds [*Pollo Almendrado* *Mexico*] Sweat chopped onion, moisten with stock and vinegar, add chilli powder, chopped almonds, sugar and cinnamon, cook then liquidise. Stew chicken pieces in this sauce and serve sprinkled with slivered almonds.

Chicken Stew with Dates and Honey [*Tagine Djej Bil Tamar Wa Assal* *Middle East*] Fry chopped onion, garlic, cumin seeds and la kama spice; moisten with stock and reduce by half. Add goujons of chicken and stew. Add stoned dates, slivered almonds and honey then serve with couscous or rice.

Chicken Stew with Dried Mushrooms [*Dak Busut Jim* *Korea*] Marinate chicken pieces in light soy sauce, sesame oil, garlic and cayenne pepper. Sauté the chicken in oil, add the marinade and sliced dried mushrooms and stew. Finish by adding wedges of onion, sliced bamboo shoots and spring onions. Serve sprinkled with toasted sesame seeds, accompanied by boiled rice.

Chicken Stew with Mangos and Cashew Nuts [*Caribbean*] Cut chickens for sauté. Blend together rum, lemon juice, Angostura bitters, white wine, thyme, crushed cloves of garlic, tamarind juice, allspice, a few threads of saffron and seasoning of salt and ground black pepper. Marinate the chicken in the spiced mixture for 3 hr. Place the chicken with the marinade in a pan, add unsalted cashew nuts and gently simmer for approx. 20 min. Layer with peeled and sliced mango, sprinkle with a little allspice and ground black pepper and cook for a further 10 min.

Chicken and Pumpkin Stew [*Caribbean*] Cut salted pork into cubes, place into a pan, cover with water and simmer until tender, drain and retain the meat. Cut chickens for sauté and remove the skin. Place the chicken into a pan, cover with cold water and bring to the boil, then add whole cloves, crushed cloves of garlic, chopped onion, batons of celery, tannias cut into halves, sliced green bananas, pieces of white yam, pieces of dasheen, a sprig of thyme, lime juice, chopped pumpkin, seasoning and the cooked pork. Place fresh red chillies on top and simmer until the chicken and vegetables are cooked. Remove the whole chillies and serve garnished with segments of lime.

Chicken and Rice [*Frango com Arroz* Portugal] Sauté chicken pieces, diced pork fat, chopped onion and garlic in olive oil, moisten with white wine and stock and half cook, then add rice and continue to cook until all is tender.

Chicken in Mole Sauce [*Mole Poblano* Mexico] Cook chilli powder in lard, moisten with stock then add chopped onion, garlic, pimentos, almonds, raisins, sesame, anise and pumpkin seeds, peanut butter, oregano, cocoa, ground cinnamon, cloves, nutmeg, allspice, ginger and cumin. Allow to simmer for 1 hr, liquidise the mixture then add chicken pieces and stew until tender.

Chicken Fricassée with Brown and Green Lentils [*Murgh Dhansak* India] Sauté chopped garlic and ginger, cloves, cardamoms, cinnamon stick, bayleaves, coriander seeds, fenugreek, cumin, mustard seeds and ground black pepper, then blend to a paste. Stew chicken pieces in water with brown and green lentils, diced eggplant, potato and onion and shredded spinach. Liquidise the vegetables then add the spice paste and serve the chicken sprinkled with chopped coriander leaves.

Chicken Fricassée with Button Onions and Mushrooms [*Hühnerfrikassee* Germany] Stiffen chicken pieces in oil, sprinkle with flour then moisten with stock, add a bouquet garni and stew. Finish with a liaison of egg yolks, cream and lemon juice and serve garnished with sautéed mushrooms and peas.

Curried Chicken [*Gaeng Ped Gai* Thailand] Blend dried red chillies, shallots, garlic, kha, lemon grass, mace, nutmeg, zest of lime, coriander and cumin seeds, shrimp paste and salt and pepper to a paste. Stir-fry the paste in oil then add chicken pieces and strips of bamboo shoots and moisten with thick coconut milk. Sprinkle with fresh coriander leaves.

Fricassée of Pigeon [*Galambbecsált* Hungary] Seal halves of pigeons in butter, sprinkle with flour, moisten with white wine and stock and cook. Add quarters of sautéed mushrooms and finish with soured cream.

Green Curry of Duck [*Gaeng Keo Wan Pet* Thailand] Simmer thick coconut milk with oil and reduce by a quarter, then add green curry paste. Add duck pieces, thick and thin coconut milks, nam pla, slivers of fresh red chillies, chopped basil leaves and coriander and stew until cooked.

Stewed Chicken with Spices [Israel] Sauté chicken pieces with sliced onion, add cinnamon stick, cloves, cardamom, bayleaves, garam masala, grated ginger, crushed garlic and turmeric then moisten with stock and allow to stew until tender.

Stewed Partridge [*Perdizes Estufadas* Portugal] Stew partridges in white wine vinegar, white wine and olive oil with chopped shallots and garlic, diced tomato flesh and tomato purée until tender.

Stewed Pheasant with Truffle [*Salmis de Faisan* France] Roast pheasant, cut into portions and place in an earthenware cocotte with sautéed button mushrooms, a little meat glaze and brandy. Coat pheasant with jus lié flavoured with red wine, decorate each portion with slices of truffle and serve.

Stir-Fried Poultry

Application

Heat a minimum amount of oil in a wok or frying pan, then add seasoned poultry which has previously been cut into small pieces and fry very quickly, tossing continuously until evenly coloured and cooked.

Stir-fried Chicken Chikuzen Style [*Chikuzen-Ni* Japan]   Stir-fry cubes of chicken, wedges of konnyaku and carrots, sliced shiitake mushrooms, bamboo shoots and burdock in oil. Flavour with dashi, sugar and light and dark soy sauces, reduce the liquid by one-third then add mangetout, cook and serve.

Stir-fried Chicken with Almonds [*Sien Gu Lu To Yan* China]   Pass goujons of chicken through cornflour, five-spice powder and soft brown sugar then marinate in light and dark soy sauces and saké. Golden fry blanched almonds and the goujons in sesame oil and remove. Add grated ginger and julienne of green pepper, leek and beansprouts. Replace the goujons, moisten with the marinade, season and serve sprinkled with the almonds.

Stir-fried Chicken with Ginger [*Kai Phat Khing* Thailand]   Stir-fry chopped onion and garlic, add goujons of chicken and grated ginger, moisten with soy sauce, nam pla, saké and vinegar then simmer. Serve sprinkled with chopped spring onions and coriander.

Stir-fried Chicken in Peanut Sauce [*Gai Tua* Thailand]   Blend ginger, garlic, curry paste and thick coconut milk to a paste then marinate goujons of chicken in the paste. Stir-fry chopped onion then add the goujons and the marinade. Add peanut butter, nam pla, sugar and chilli powder and finish with thick coconut milk. Serve on a bed of boiled broccoli and spring onions.

Stir-fried Chicken with Vegetables [*Chow Tse Shan* China]   Pass goujons of chicken through cornflour and five-spice powder and marinate in light soy sauce. Stir-fry the goujons in sesame oil, remove then add grated ginger, chopped garlic, sections of spring onions, diced red and green pimento, carrots, snow peas and bean sprouts. Replace the goujons, moisten with saké, and add tomato purée, the marinade and seasoning. Serve sprinkled with toasted sesame seeds accompanied by plain boiled rice.

Stir-fried Goujons of Chicken with Peanuts [*Gung Bao Ding Tse* China]   Marinate goujons of chicken in diluted cornflour with light and dark soy sauces, beaten egg whites and salt. Stir-fry peanuts and the goujons in groundnut oil, add sliced fresh red chillies, crushed garlic, grated ginger and chopped onion then moisten with saké. Combine the marinade liquid with Chinese rice vinegar, soft brown sugar and light soy sauce, stir into the preparation and cook for 1 min.

Chapter Eleven

Vegetables, Samosas, Stuffings, Potatoes and Sweet Potatoes

This chapter is divided into 14 main categories:

❖ Baked Vegetables ❖

❖ Boiled Vegetables ❖

❖ Braised Vegetables ❖

❖ Deep-fried Vegetables ❖

❖ Grilled Vegetables ❖

❖ Shallow-fried Vegetables ❖

❖ Steamed Vegetables ❖

❖ Stewed Vegetables ❖

❖ Stir-fried Vegetables ❖

❖ Pulses ❖

❖ Couscous ❖

❖ Samosas ❖

❖ Stuffings ❖

❖ Potatoes and Sweet Potatoes ❖

Allow the following amounts of prepared raw vegetables and potatoes per average 10 × 100 g portions:

1.5–2 kg vegetables
1.5–2 kg potatoes

Baked Vegetables

Application

May be referred to as gratinated vegetables, which are cooked vegetables placed in an earthenware dish, sprinkled with breadcrumbs and oil and coloured golden in an oven at 200 °C.

Baked Carrots [*Morot Ringa* Scandinavia]   Mix together onion and brunoise of carrot, and add light béchamel sauce, beaten eggs and seasoning. Pour the mixture into a buttered earthenware dish and bake.

Baked Cauliflower [*Coliflor con Queso* Mexico]   Sauté sliced onion, green pimento and jalapeño pepper in oil then add diced tomato flesh, chopped garlic, sliced green olives, parsley and capers. Arrange blanched cauliflower florets in a shallow dish, mask with the savoury mixture, sprinkle with breadcrumbs, grated cheese and oil and bake.

Baked Chayotes [*Chayotes* Mexico]   Sauté chopped onion and garlic in oil, add diced tomato flesh and chopped oregano, flavour with nutmeg then add crisply fried lardons of bacon. Coat quartered and boiled chayotes with the sauce, sprinkle with grated cheese and oil and gratinate.

Baked Corn on the Cob [USA]   Rub corn on the cob with butter, sprinkle with water, wrap in kitchen foil and bake.

Baked Courgette [*Calabacín al Horno* Spain]   Place sliced courgettes into a shallow dish, sprinkle with olive oil, season then bake. When almost cooked sprinkle with breadcrumbs mixed with chopped garlic and parsley and melted butter and gratinate until golden.

Baked Courgette [*Tök au Gratin* Hungary]   Place cooked courgettes into a shallow dish, cover with soured cream mixed with beaten eggs, sprinkle with breadcrumbs mixed with herbs, dot with butter then bake.

Baked Courgette with Coconut [*Urap Panggang Sayur* Thailand]   Sauté chopped onion, garlic and dried red chillies, stir in ground coriander then add shrimp paste, desiccated coconut and tomato purée and moisten with water. Place prepared courgettes into a shallow dish, coat with the sauce and bake.

Baked Eggplant [*Polypikilo* Greece]   Brush the bottom of a shallow dish with corn oil and sprinkle with chopped garlic, parsley and breadcrumbs. Place in alternate layers of sliced tomato, eggplant, potato and courgette. Moisten with oil and water, sprinkle with breadcrumbs and bake.

Baked Eggplant and Banana [USA]   Arrange slices of lightly fried eggplant, halved bananas and tomato concassée in an earthenware dish, sprinkle with breadcrumbs and oil and gratinate.

Baked Eggplant with Cheese and Almonds [*Berengena con Queso* Spain]
Simmer sliced eggplant and onion in stock until just cooked then transfer the
vegetables to a dish. Blend almonds with the cooking liquor until smooth, cover
the eggplant with the mixture, layer with sliced Munster cheese, sprinkle with
grated Parmesan cheese, nutmeg and melted butter and bake.

Baked Eggplant in Coconut Cream [*Caribbean*]   Place sliced eggplant into a
dish, add chopped onion and sprinkle with crushed dried red chilli and
seasoning. Moisten with coconut cream and bake.

Baked Eggplant with Lemon and Cheese [*Hunkar Begendi* Turkey]   Cut eggplants in halves lengthways, bake until soft then remove the flesh and mix with
lemon juice, béchamel sauce, breadcrumbs, grated Kâskaval or Kasseri cheese
and seasoning. Replace the mixture into the skins, sprinkle with breadcrumbs
and vegetable oil and gratinate.

Baked Eggplant and Mixed Vegetables [*Güvec* Turkey]   Place alternate layers
of sliced shallow-fried eggplant, onion and garlic, sliced courgettes and green
pimento, cooked French beans, tomato concassée and chopped parsley into a
dish. Top with blanched sliced okras and tomato concassée. Moisten with vegetable stock and bake.

Baked Eggplant with Tomato [*Aubergine Imam Bayaldi* Middle East]   Cover
halves of eggplants with a mixture of sweated chopped onion and garlic,
tomato concassée and chopped parsley. Moisten with vegetable stock, sprinkle
with oil and bake.

Baked Eggplant with Yogurt [*Baigan Dahi* India]   Cut eggplants in halves
lengthways, bake until soft then remove the flesh. Fry chopped onion and garlic in ghee and add grated ginger and ground coriander, cumin, turmeric, chilli
powder and salt. Add the chopped flesh of the eggplant and garam masala and
finish with yogurt. Fill the mixture into the skins and gratinate.

Baked Oyster Mushrooms [*Setas al Horno* Spain]   Sprinkle oyster mushrooms
with dry sherry then with breadcrumbs combined with crushed garlic and
chopped parsley. Moisten with a little olive oil and bake.

Baked Parsnips [*Palsternacka Koppa* Scandinavia]   Mix together cooked,
mashed parsnips, a light béchamel sauce, beaten eggs and seasoning. Pour the
mixture into buttered seasoned ramekins and bake au bain-marie.

Baked Paw-paw [*Caribbean*]   Scoop out the flesh of boiled paw-paws and
coarsely chop. Sweat chopped onion in oil, and add tomato concassée and the
chopped paw-paw. Fill the shells with the mixture, sprinkle with breadcrumbs,
grated Parmesan cheese and peanut oil and bake.

Baked Pimentos and Tomato [*Asadillo* Spain]   Place alternate layers of sliced
tomato and strips of skinned, deseeded pimentos into a shallow dish, season
and sprinkle with marjoram and olive oil and bake.

Baked Pumpkin [*Zapekanka iz Tykvy* Russia]   Place boiled cubes of pumpkin
in a shallow dish, coat with cheese sauce, sprinkle with grated cheese and
melted butter and gratinate.

Baked Spinach Triangles [*Spanakotrigona* Greece]   Combine sweated chopped
onion with shredded spinach, cover and cook. Add chopped dill and crumbled
Féta cheese and seasoning. Make triangular filo pastry parcels with the mixture,
brush with oil then bake.

Baked Spinach and Almond Filo Triangles [*Bourekas* Israel] Sweat shredded spinach in oil and combine with sautéed slivered almonds, beaten egg, lemon juice, grated nutmeg, salt and pepper. Make filo pastry triangles filled with the mixture, sprinkle with sesame seeds and butter and bake.

Baked Spinach and Féta Cheese Filo Triangles [*Bourekas* Israel] Sweat shredded spinach in oil and combine with crumbled Féta cheese, beaten egg, lemon juice and chopped parsley. Make filo pastry triangles filled with the mixture, sprinkle with sesame seeds and butter and bake.

Baked Squash [*USA*] Sprinkle a halved squash with sugar and butter then bake.

Baked Stuffed Artichokes [*Anginares Yemistes* Greece] Remove choke from boiled globe artichokes and fill with cooked minced meat combined with grated Parmesan cheese. Mask with cream sauce, sprinkle with breadcrumbs and oil and gratinate.

Baked Stuffed Artichokes [*Cuori di Carciofi con Spinaci* Italy] Remove choke from boiled globe artichokes and fill with chopped cooked spinach combined with sautéed chopped onion, garlic and anchovies, stiffened with breadcrumbs. Sprinkle with grated Parmesan cheese, butter and breadcrumbs and bake.

Baked Stuffed Cabbage [*Erdélyi Tötött Tavaszi Kàposzta* Hungary] Form parcels of blanched cabbage leaves filled with a mixture of cooked rice, chopped onion and minced pork and veal. Place into a shallow dish, moisten with jus lié finished with lemon juice and soured cream and bake.

Baked Stuffed Celeriac [*Töltött Zeller* Hungary] Scoop out the centres of boiled celeriac and fill with a duxelle of mushrooms combined with chopped celeriac and grated cheese. Sprinkle with soured cream and butter and bake.

Baked Stuffed Chayote [*Caribbean*] Cut boiled chayotes in half lengthways, remove the centres including the seeds and mash. Lightly fry chopped onion in peanut oil, add the mashed pulp, season and add grated Parmesan cheese. Fill the shells with the mixture, sprinkle with grated cheese and peanut oil and bake.

Baked Stuffed Courgettes [*Kossa Mashiya bil Kibbeh* Middle East] Stuff courgettes with a mixture of cooked cracked wheat combined with minced cooked lamb seasoned with baharat. Bake in the oven.

Baked Stuffed Courgettes [*Zucchini Ripieni* Italy] Cut boiled courgettes in half lengthways and remove the centre flesh. Combine the flesh with breadcrumbs soaked in milk and squeezed dry, oregano, grated Parmesan cheese, diced prosciutto and egg to bind. Stuff the courgettes with the mixture, sprinkle with grated cheese and butter and gratinate.

Baked Stuffed Mushrooms [*Töltött Gomba Bécsi Módra* Hungary] Fill mushroom caps with a mixture of duxelle of mushrooms combined with chopped ham, mashed potato and beaten eggs. Place the mushrooms in a shallow dish, moisten with soured cream, sprinkle with grated cheese and bake.

Baked Stuffed Onions [*GB*] Blanch onions then remove the centre from each. Chop the centre pieces and combine with veal forcemeat. Fill the hollowed out onions with the forcemeat, brush with oil and bake.

Baked Stuffed Onions [*Cipolle Farcite* Italy] Cook onions in boiling salted water then remove the centres, chop and combine with grated Parmesan cheese and butter. Fill the hollowed out centres with the mixture, sprinkle with butter and brandy and bake.

Baked Stuffed Paw-paw [*Caribbean*]   Cut paw-paws in half lengthways, discard the seeds and cook in boiling salted water. Sweat chopped onion, garlic and crushed dried green chillies in oil, and add minced beef and tomato concassée. Fill the shells with the mixture, sprinkle with breadcrumbs, grated Parmesan cheese and peanut oil and bake.

Baked Stuffed Tomatoes [***Domates Yemistes Horis Kreas*** *Greece*]   Fill the centres of hollowed out tomatoes with boiled rice mixed with chopped onion and garlic lightly sweated in olive oil, chopped mint, the tomato pulp from the centres, currants, sugar and a pinch of cinnamon. Replace the tops, sprinkle with breadcrumbs, chopped parsley and olive oil and bake.

Baked Stuffed Tomatoes [***Domates Yemistes Millomenes*** *Greece*]   Combine lightly fried minced meat and chopped onion, tomato purée and Parmesan cheese. Fill hollowed out tomatoes with the mixture, sprinkle with oil and bake.

Baked Stuffed Tomatoes with Ham and Basil [***Tomates Rellenos*** *Mexico*]   Sauté chopped onion and garlic in oil, moisten with white wine then stir in the pulp from hollowed out tomatoes; add chopped fillets of anchovy, oregano and basil then bind the mixture with breadcrumbs. Fill the tomatoes, sprinkle with cheese and oil and bake.

Baked Stuffed Tomatoes with Pasta [***Tésztával Töltött Paradicsom*** *Hungary*]   Fill the centres of hollowed out tomatoes with a mixture of cooked vermicelli combined with soured cream and grated cheese, then bake.

Baked Stuffed Tomato with Pine Nuts [***Tomates Rellenos con Piñones*** *Spain*]   Lightly fry pine nuts in olive oil, add chopped onion and garlic, diced tomato flesh, oregano and seasoning then stir in breadcrumbs. Fill the centres of hollowed out tomatoes with the mixture, sprinkle with oil and bake.

Baked Stuffed Turnips [***Taytetyt Nauriit*** *Scandinavia*]   Boil baby turnips in salted water. When half cooked drain and scoop out the centres. Combine the chopped centre flesh with golden fried breadcrumbs, chopped almonds, chopped dill and seasoning. Fill the turnips with the mixture, place into an earthenware dish, sprinkle with breadcrumbs and melted butter and bake.

Baked Sweetcorn [***Korn i Eldfast Form*** *Scandinavia*]   Heat cooked sweetcorn kernels in butter, and add light béchamel sauce, beaten eggs and seasoning. Pour the mixture into a buttered earthenware dish and bake.

Baked Yams [*Caribbean*]   Cook peeled and roughly cut white yams in salted water with a little lemon juice, drain and mash them. Combine with butter and cream, mix in chopped chives and season with salt, pepper and nutmeg. Place into a buttered and seasoned earthenware dish, sprinkle the surface with white breadcrumbs, grated zest of lemon and melted butter and gratinate in the oven until golden.

French Bean Bake [***Rakott Zöldbab*** *Hungary*]   Place layers of cooked French beans and diced tomato flesh into a shallow dish. Moisten with soured cream mixed with egg yolks, sprinkle with cheese and butter and bake.

Globe Artichoke Tart [*GB*]   Line a flan ring with short pastry, add sliced cooked artichoke bottoms and sautéed chopped onion and sprinkle with chopped tarragon, parsley and basil. Pour in savoury egg custard, sprinkle with grated nutmeg and bake.

Leek and Potato Bake [*Israel*]   Combine mashed potato, julienne of boiled white of leek, sautéed sliced onion and grated Kâskaval cheese. Layer the bottom and sides of a shallow dish with softened matzos, fill with the potato mixture, sprinkle with grated cheese, beaten eggs with yogurt, matzo meal and oil, then gratinate.

Mixed Vegetable Casserole [***Türlü-Türlü*** *Turkey*]   Fry diced eggplant in olive oil with sliced onion, garlic and okra, and add diced potato, French beans, green pimento and courgettes. Add tomato concassée, tomato purée, chopped oregano, parsley, seasoning and sugar. Place in a dish, moisten with vegetable stock and bake.

Mushroom Bake [***Sült Gombapuding*** *Hungary*]   Dip sliced fried bread croûtons in milk and place in a shallow dish; add a thick layer of duxelle of mushrooms, cover with another layer of croûtons, moisten with soured cream and bake.

Spinach Filo Parcels [***Spanakopites Apo Ti Samos*** *Greece*]   Cook spinach in a minimum of salted water, drain and coarsely chop. Lightly fry chopped spring onions in olive oil, add the spinach, crumbled Féta cheese, chopped dill and grated nutmeg and mix together. Envelop the mixture in sheets of filo pastry to form individual parcels. Brush with oil and bake.

Boiled Vegetables

Application

Green vegetables are plunged into salted boiling water, brought back to the boil, the lid is removed and the vegetables are cooked quickly, leaving them slightly firm. Root vegetables are barely covered with cold water to which salt is added, covered with a lid and boiled steadily until they are cooked.

Asparagus Milanese [***Asparagi alla Milanese*** *Italy*]   Arrange boiled and drained asparagus on a dish. Shallow fry small eggs in nut-brown butter and arrange them on top of the asparagus, sprinkle with grated Parmesan cheese and butter and serve.

Asparagus with Smoked Ham [***Schwetzinger Stangenspargel*** *Germany*] Season the boiled and drained asparagus with nutmeg and garnish with diced raw Westphalian ham.

Bamboo Shoots, Mushrooms and Sweetcorn [***Hung Shiu Say Saw*** *China*]   Stir-fry soaked and sliced Chinese mushrooms in peanut oil, add bamboo shoots and cooked baby sweetcorn, moisten with the soaking liquid, stock, sesame oil, soy sauce and seasoning, simmer for 5 min and serve on a base of boiled rice.

Bean Curd with Crabmeat and Ginger [***Hai Yook Par Dau Fu*** *China*]   Lightly sauté chopped spring onions and grated ginger in oil, moisten with fish stock, add crabmeat then thicken with diluted cornflour to a light sauce consistency. Remove from the heat and add squares of bean curd, season to taste and serve on a bed of boiled rice.

Bean Curd with Ginger [***Chu Hau Jeung Mun Dau Fu*** *China*]   Lightly fry portions of bean curd with chopped garlic in sesame oil, add grated ginger then moisten with light soy sauce, saké and a little honey, season with five-spice powder and simmer for 2 min. Add peas and chopped spring onions and serve on a base of boiled rice.

Beets Harvard Style [*USA*]   Boil cider vinegar, water and sugar then thicken with cornflour. Add diced cooked beetroot and knobs of butter.

Beetroot in Cream Sauce with Cumin [*Betterave au Beurre à la Crème au Cumin France*]   Lightly toss batons of boiled beetroot in butter, and moisten with cream sauce flavoured with cumin seeds.

Broad Beans in Bacon Sauce [*Dicke Bohnen in Specksobe Germany*]   Combine cooked broad beans with cream sauce containing fried lardons of bacon and chopped cooked savoy cabbage.

Broad Beans in Egg Sauce [*Favas com Molho Amarelo Portugal*]   Cook broad beans in salted water flavoured with chopped savory and parsley. Drain then add to cream sauce finished with a liaison of egg yolks.

Broad Beans with Bacon and Sausage [*Favas à Moda de Lisboa Portugal*]   Sauté lardons of bacon and sliced chorizo sausage in lard with chopped onion and coriander. Add broad beans, moisten with stock and simmer until sufficiently cooked.

Broad Beans with Coriander [*Favas com Coentros Portugal*]   Cook broad beans in salted water with chopped coriander and spring onion. Drain then add chopped garlic, chopped coriander, wine vinegar and olive oil.

Brussels Sprouts in Soured Cream [*Kelbimbó Hungary*]   Cook Brussels sprouts in salted water, drain then combine with soured cream, sprinkle with breadcrumbs and butter and gratinate.

Brussels Sprouts with Chestnuts [*Israel*]   Toss together in chicken fat equal quantities of boiled Brussels sprouts and chestnuts.

Carrots and Grapes in Soured Cream Sauce [*Zanahorias con Uvas Mexico*]   Cook batons of carrots in salted water with butter and sugar, reducing the liquid to a glaze. Stir in soured cream, chopped tarragon and deseeded grapes.

Carrots in Lemon Sauce [*Karóta Greece*]   Cook batons of carrots in salted water, drain then toss in hot lemon dressing.

Cauliflower Florets with Tahini Sauce [*Karnabit bi Tahini Middle East*]   Liquidise tahini juice, garlic, lemon juice and water and coat cooked cauliflower florets with the sauce.

Cauliflower Polish Style [*Chou-fleur Polonaise France*]   Sauté cooked cauliflower florets in butter and serve coated with fried breadcrumbs, sieved white and yolk of hard-boiled egg and chopped parsley.

Chard Leaves with Vinegar [*Acelgas con Vinagre Spain*]   Boil chard leaves in salted water, drain then toss them into garlic-flavoured olive oil. Serve sprinkled with wine vinegar and fried breadcrumbs.

Chinese Cabbage and Tofu [*Age-dofu Hakusai-ni Japan*]   Simmer shredded Chinese cabbage in dashi, stir in light soy sauce and sugar then add fried tofu and simmer for 2 min.

Chinese Cabbage with Bonito Flakes [*Hakusai No Ohitashi Japan*]   Simmer shredded Chinese cabbage leaves in salted water for 5 min, drain, cool then roll up in a cloth to squeeze out excess moisture. Cut into slices and coat with a mixture of first soup stock flavoured with rice vinegar and soy sauce. Serve sprinkled with bonito flakes.

Courgette Purée with Spices [*Gooda Bartha India*]   Boil courgettes in salt water and pass through a sieve. Fry cumin seeds and mustard seeds in ghee, add chopped onion, sliced fresh green chillies, the mashed courgette and chilli powder. Cook until the moisture has evaporated.

Creamed Breadfruit [*Caribbean*]   Cook peeled and roughly cut breadfruit in salted water, drain and mash. Lightly sauté chopped onion in oil, add the mashed breadfruit, combine with cream and season with salt, pepper and nutmeg.

Creamed Dasheen [*Caribbean*]   Cook peeled and roughly cut dasheen in salted water, drain and mash. Lightly sauté chopped onion in oil, add the mashed dasheen and combine with cream and season with salt, pepper and nutmeg.

Creamed Kohlrabi [*Kalrabbi i Vit Sas Scandinavia*]   Cook diced kohlrabi in salted water and drain. Toss in butter, moisten with cream and season with salt, pepper and nutmeg.

Daikon Radish [*Daikon Fukume-ni Japan*]   Simmer dashi, salt, light soy sauce and mirin. Place boiled daikon into dishes, pour on the liquid and garnish with sprigs of kiname.

Daikon Radish with Miso Sauce [*Furofuki Japan*]   Cut daikon into slices then make a cross on each side, arrange a single layer in a shallow pan, cover with water, add 10-cm squares of kelp, season with salt and simmer until cooked. Serve the daikon with a little of the cooking liquor. Mask with miso sauce and serve garnished with v-shaped slices of lime peel.

Miso sauce: combine finely ground toasted black sesame seeds, red miso, second soup stock, sugar and mirin, stir and gently heat to combine.

Eggplant with Bean Paste [*Nasu No Misoni Japan*]   Cut peeled eggplants into slices, soak in cold salted water for 20 min, drain and dry. Sauté the eggplant in oil with chopped ginger, moisten with saké, add white bean paste mixed with second soup stock and cook until all the liquid has evaporated. Serve sprinkled with toasted white sesame seeds.

French Beans and Mushrooms in Cream Sauce [*Crön Bönor med Svamp Scandinavia*]   Cook French beans in salted water, drain and retain. Sauté button mushrooms in oil, toss in the beans, moisten with cream and season with salt, pepper and nutmeg.

French Beans with Cured Ham [*Judías Verdes 'Bárcena' Spain*]   Cook French beans in salted water for 10 min, refresh and drain. Toss beans in oil, add chopped onion and garlic and cook until lightly browned; add strips of cured ham, cover with a lid and cook for a further 2 min.

French Beans with Spiced Almonds [*Judías Verdes con Almendras Spain*]   Fry flaked almonds in olive oil, toss in the cooked French beans, sprinkle with lemon juice and season with salt and paprika.

Glazed Mushrooms [*Hung Shiu Doong Gwoo China*]   Stir-fry soaked and sliced Chinese mushrooms in sesame oil, moisten with the soaking liquid, soy sauce and a little sugar, and cook until the liquid has reduced to a glaze.

Glazed Vegetables [*Yachaejorim Korea*]   Cook diced sweet potato, carrots and Korean radish in salted water. Add soy sauce, sugar and grated ginger, cook and reduce the liquid to a glaze.

Green Beans in Soy Sauce [*Saya-Ingen No Shoyuni Japan*]   Cut beans into 5-cm pieces, simmer in second soup stock flavoured with mirin, soy sauce and monosodium glutamate and when cooked, serve in bowls.

Green Beans with Bean Paste [*Saya-Ingen No Miso-Ae Japan*]   Cook beans in salted water for 6 min, drain, cool, cut into diamond shapes and retain. Combine red bean paste, sugar and mirin, cook until smooth but do not boil, then allow to cool. Mix the beans with the bean paste mixture and serve.

Green Beans with Peanuts [*Saya-Ingen No Peanuts-Ae Japan*] Cook beans in salted water for 6 min, drain, cool, cut into diamond shapes and retain. Blend peanuts with soy sauce and sugar to a paste. Toss the beans in the peanut mixture and serve in bowls, sprinkled with bonito flakes.

Green Beans with Sesame Seeds [*Saya-Ingen No Goma-Ae Japan*] Cook beans in salted water for 6 min, drain, cool, cut into diamond shapes and retain. Blend toasted white sesame seeds with soy sauce and sugar to a paste. Toss the beans in the sesame mixture and serve in bowls, sprinkled with bonito flakes.

Lettuce with Ginger [*Chow Sahng Choy China*] Stir-fry small sections of lettuce in peanut oil with chopped garlic and grated ginger. Moisten with stock, soy sauce, a little sugar and seasoning and cook for 2 min. Thicken the liquid with diluted cornflour to form a light sauce and serve.

Mixed Vegetables with Oyster Sauce [*Par Say Saw China*] Stir-fry sliced mixed vegetables in sesame oil with chopped garlic and grated ginger for 2 min, moisten with stock, light soy sauce and oyster sauce and simmer for 3 min. Lightly thicken the liquid with diluted cornflour to form a light sauce and serve on a base of boiled rice.

Okras and Corn Meal [*Coo-Coo Caribbean*] Cook sliced okras in salted water then pour corn meal into the boiling liquid and cook on low heat, stirring steadily. Serve coated with melted butter.

Okras with Rice Vinegar Dressing [*Okura No Sanbaizu Japan*] Cook okra in salted water for 5 min, refresh and drain. Cut into 1-cm slices then toss in vinegar dressing.

Vinegar dressing: mix together rice vinegar, first soup stock and soy sauce and flavour with sugar and salt.

Onions with Chicken and Sesame Seed Sauce [*Tamanegi No Goma Ankake Japan*] Place onions into a pan, barely cover with water and simmer for 3 min, add second soup stock and mirin and simmer until cooked. Stir-fry finely diced chicken in oil, moisten with some of the onion cooking liquor, add soy sauce, season with monosodium glutamate and lightly thicken with diluted potato flour, then add toasted sesame seeds. Serve the onions masked with the sauce.

Peas and Chorizo Sausage [*Ervilhas à Portuguesa Portugal*] Sauté chopped onion and garlic in oil, and add diced tomato flesh, thyme and chopped parsley. Serve boiled peas with fried eggs on top, garnish with sliced chorizo sausage and strips of smoked ham and surround with the tomato mixture.

Peas in Parsley Sauce [*Petrezselymes Zöldborsófozelék Hungary*] Melt butter, add sugar then cooked peas and chopped parsley. Moisten with stock and simmer to reduce the liquor and finish with soured cream.

Peas in Soup Stock [*Endo No Aoni Japan*] Cook peas in salted water for 10 min, drain and retain them. Simmer second soup stock flavoured with soy sauce and mirin, add the peas then chill them in the liquid by standing on ice. Serve the chilled peas with some of the liquid in bowls.

Peas with Chicken and Eggs [*Endo No Nataneni Japan*] Cook peas in boiling salted water for 10 min, drain, refresh and retain. Simmer diced chicken breast in second soup stock flavoured with light soy sauce, mirin, sugar and salt. Add the peas then pour in beaten eggs to form threads over the whole surface, cook for 1 min and serve.

Peas with Cured Ham [*Guisantes à la Espagñole* Spain] Lightly sauté chopped onion, garlic and diced carrot in oil. Add peas and strips of cured ham and cook until the peas are tender.

Peas with Dill [*Pizélia Aspra* Greece] Cook peas in chicken velouté with chopped spring onions and dill.

Plantains in Cheese Sauce [Caribbean] Coat cooked plantains with cheese sauce flavoured with nutmeg and gratinate.

Pumpkin with Minced Chicken [*Kabocha No Ankake* Japan] Simmer small cubes of peeled pumpkin in water flavoured with sugar, soy sauce, salt and monosodium glutamate; remove and retain. Reduce the liquid and lightly thicken with potato flour, add cooked minced chicken and serve with the pumpkin pieces.

Purée of Carrots and Potatoes [*Puré de Zanahoria y Papa* Mexico] Cook carrots and potatoes in chicken stock, purée them then add butter and season with cumin seeds, ground cinnamon and nutmeg.

Purée of Onion and Rice [*Puré de Cebola* Portugal] Combine a purée of boiled rice and onion, add milk, butter and seasoning.

Salsify in Cream Sauce [*Salsifis à la Crème* France] Cook 5-cm lengths of salsify in salted water and lemon juice for approx. 15 min. Drain the salsify, toss in butter, season with salt and pepper then add cream sauce and combine.

Sauerkraut with Bacon [*Szalonnás Savanyú Káposzta* Hungary] Boil sauerkraut in salted water with a piece of bacon then add paprika and simmer. Combine the sauerkraut with a velouté made from the liquor and finish with soured cream. Serve the sauerkraut with slices of bacon on top.

Savoy Cabbage and Potato with Caraway [*Majorannás Kelkáposzta-Fozelék* Hungary] Boil shredded Savoy cabbage and diced potato in salted water with caraway seeds, drain then combine with jus lié flavoured with marjoram.

Sorrel with Raisins [*Sauerampfer mit Rosinen* Germany] Purée blanched sorrel, heat to remove excess moisture then add blanched raisins and season with salt, pepper and nutmeg.

Spiced Cabbage [GB] Toss cooked shredded cabbage, shallow fried sliced onion and apple together in butter and season with ground cinnamon.

Spinach with Almonds and Raisins [*Espinacas a la Catalana* Spain] Soak stoned raisins in orange juice. Golden fry slivered almonds in olive oil, fork in cooked spinach and add grated nutmeg, ground cinnamon, the raisins and the juice and zest of oranges.

Spinach with Rice [*Spanakórizo* Greece] Sauté chopped spring onions in olive oil, stir in rice then moisten with chicken stock, season with oregano, salt and pepper and cook. Place a layer of spinach on top of the rice, cover and continue to cook. Stir the spinach and rice together and serve sprinkled with grated Kefalotíri cheese.

Spinach with Sesame [*Sigumchi Namul* Korea] Coarsely grind toasted sesame seeds, and add soy sauce, sugar and sesame oil. Serve blanched and drained spinach coated with the sesame mixture.

Spinach with Sweet Peppers [Caribbean] Boil spinach in minimum salted water with sweated chopped onion and chopped green pimento, drain and serve.

Swiss Chard with Croûtons [*Séfklo Xerosímisis* Greece] Boil chard in boiling salted water. Drain and serve garnished with golden fried, diced bread croûtons and sprinkled with lemon juice.

Swiss Chard with Croûtons [*Acelgas Salteadas con Migas* Spain]   Cook chard in boiling salted water for 5 min, drain, re-cover with water, add salt and olive oil and cook until tender. Drain, coarsely chop then lightly sauté in oil, add vinegar and seasoning then toss in golden fried, diced bread croûtons.

Taro with Chicken and Vegetables [*Sato-Imo To Toriniku No Umani* Japan]   Rub small taro with salt to remove the skin, wash then layer in a shallow-sided pan and moisten with second soup stock flavoured with saké, sugar and salt. Cover with a cloth and cook until the liquid has reduced by one-third, add soy sauce and mirin, simmer for 1 min and retain. Cook sliced chicken breast in saké, mirin, soy sauce and ginger juice. Serve the taro garnished with the chicken, glazed fluted slices of carrot and cooked sliced green beans, and sprinkled with grated lime peel.

Vegetables in Coconut Milk [*Paag Tom Gathi* Thailand]   Boil bamboo shoots, baby sweetcorn, shredded cabbage and spinach in sweetened coconut milk. Serve the drained vegetables topped with coconut cream.

Braised Vegetables

Application

Place prepared vegetables into a braising pan, barely cover with stock or water, cover with buttered greaseproof paper and a lid and braise in the oven at 200 °C.

Artichoke Hearts in Cider [*Fonds d'Artichaut à la Bretonne* France]   Braise blanched quartered globe artichoke hearts in cider with sweated chopped onion. Reduce the liquor with lemon juice to a glaze, finish with herb butter then mask the artichoke hearts with the sauce.

Artichokes in Oil [*Anginares ala Polita* Greece]   Braise small whole globe artichokes in stock and olive oil with whole shallots, new potatoes, whole new carrots, dill and quarters of fennel.

Artichokes with Broad Beans [*Anginares me Koukia* Greece]   Braise small artichokes in lemon juice and water with sautéed broad beans, chopped spring onions and dill or fennel.

Artichokes with Pine Nuts [*Alcachofas Estofadas con Pinones* Spain]   Braise blanched globe artichokes in lemon juice and water with sautéed chopped onion and garlic. Serve sprinkled with toasted pine nuts.

Belgian Endives Wrapped in Ham [*Chicorée in Schinkenhemd* Germany]   Braise endives with lemon juice. Wrap each endive in a slice of ham then place in an oiled shallow dish. Coat with cheese sauce, sprinkle with grated Emmenthal cheese and butter and gratinate.

Braised Cabbage with Bacon and Dill [*Kal med Flesk og Dill* Scandinavia]   Sauté lardons of bacon in oil and add julienne of leek and shredded cabbage. Moisten with a little stock, add chopped dill and seasoning and braise.

Braised Celery with Apple [GB]   Line a shallow pan with rashers of bacon, spread with apple purée then arrange blanched lengths of celery on top. Moisten with a minimum amount of stock and lemon juice, cover with a lid and braise.

Braised Celery Italian Style [*Céleri Braisé Italienne* France]   Braise blanched celery in white stock for approx. 1.5 hr. Arrange lengths of celery in a serving dish moistened with a little of the cooking liquor. Sprinkle with grated Parmesan cheese, heat knobs of butter in a frying pan until golden and pour over the vegetables and serve.

Braised Courgette with Rice [*Kolokythia Yemista me Avgolemone Saltsa* Greece]   Stuff hollowed out courgettes with boiled rice mixed with chopped onion, tomato concassée, chopped garlic, dill and parsley, plus the chopped pulp from the courgettes; season with salt, sugar and cinnamon and braise. Thicken the liquor with egg yolks, cornflour and lemon juice.

Braised Red Cabbage with Apple and Potato [*Lombarda de San Isidro* Spain]   Sauté sliced onion and lardons of bacon in oil then add shredded red cabbage, quartered apples, bayleaf and seasoning. Moisten with vinegar and braise.

Braised Red Cabbage with Stuffed Apples [*Rotkraut mit Speckäpfeln* Germany]   Sweat shredded red cabbage in oil or goose fat. Moisten with red wine, add red-currant jelly, vinegar, cinnamon stick, cloves, coriander seeds, peppercorns and juniper berries and braise. Fill the centres of hollowed out small apples with fried chopped onion mixed with lardons of bacon and diced ham. Place on top of the cabbage and continue cooking until they are tender.

Braised Soured Cabbage [*Surkal* Scandinavia]   Place shredded cabbage into an earthenware dish, moisten with a little stock, add caraway seeds and seasoning and braise. When almost cooked add vinegar and sugar then finish cooking.

Braised Stuffed Cabbage [*Kaldolmar* Scandinavia]   Blanch cabbage leaves and refresh them, lay leaves onto a cloth and fill with a mixture of finely minced beef, veal, cooked rice, breadcrumbs and seasoning of allspice, nutmeg, salt and pepper. Form into balls and place into a deep-sided pan on a bed of root vegetables, thyme and bayleaf. Moisten with stock and braise. Serve with a little of the cooking liquor, garnished with the root vegetables.

Braised Stuffed Cabbage [*Golubtsy* Russia]   Combine sautéed minced beef and chopped onion, cooked rice, chopped dill and seasoning. Fill blanched cabbage leaves with the mixture and form into parcels. Sauté the parcels then moisten with tomato sauce and braise. Serve with a whirl of smetana on top.

Braised Stuffed Marrow [GB]   Peel and remove the centre seeds from a marrow and fill with veal forcemeat. Lightly fry the marrow in oil, moisten with stock, season, cover with a lid and braise.

Braised Stuffed Vegetables [*Dolmadhes or Ghemistá* Greece]   Combine lightly fried minced meat and chopped onion with cooked rice, diced tomato flesh and chopped parsley. Stuff any of the following vegetables with the mixture and braise in chicken stock: courgettes, tomatoes, Spanish onions, marrow flowers, artichokes, eggplants, green peppers and potatoes.

Braised Turnip Tops [*Pot Likker* USA]   Braise blanched turnip tops with a smoked hock of bacon.

Peas French Style [*Petis Pois à la Française* France]   Place peas, shredded lettuce, button onions, a few knobs of butter, sugar and salt into a pan, barely cover with stock, cover with a lid and cook in the oven for approx. 1 hr. When cooked lightly thicken the liquid with a mixture of flour and butter and serve.

Peas with Bacon and Onions [***Petits Pois Bonne Femme*** *France*]   Place peas, blanched lardons of bacon and button onions into a pan, season with salt, barely cover with stock, cover with a lid and cook in the oven for approx. 1 hr. When cooked lightly thicken the liquid with a mixture of flour and butter and serve.
Sauerkraut [*Germany*]   Melt goose or pork fat in a pan, place in the sauerkraut and cover with boiling water. Add quartered apples, season with caraway seeds and black pepper and braise.

Deep-fried Vegetables

Application

Items that are boiled or steamed before deep frying may be coated in batter. Those that are deep fried without prior cooking are generally passed through milk and then seasoned flour, or through seasoned flour, eggwash and breadcrumbs.

Breaded Chanterelle Mushrooms [***Kirántott Vargánya*** *Hungary*]   Pass raw mushrooms through flour, eggwash and breadcrumbs and deep fry.
Carrot Fritters [***Havuc Kizartmasi*** *Turkey*]   Pass cooked roundels of carrot through a frying batter and deep fry. Serve accompanied by yogurt salcasi.
Cauliflower Fritters [***Karnibabar Kizartmasi*** *Turkey*]   Pass cooked florets through eggwash and breadcrumbs and deep fry. Serve accompanied by yogurt salcasi.
Celeriac Fritters [***Zella Palacsintatésztàban*** *Hungary*]   Pass slices of cooked celeriac through batter and deep fry.
Eggplant Fritters [***Berinjelas à Orly*** *Portugal*]   Pass sliced eggplant through massa vinhe batter and deep fry.
Eggplant Fritters [***Fruituras de Berenjena*** *Mexico*]   Combine slices of eggplant, flour, baking powder and beaten eggs, flavour with nutmeg then deep fry teaspoonsful in olive oil. Serve sprinkled with chopped spring onions.
Eggplant Fritters [***Patlican Kizartmasi*** *Turkey*]   Pass sliced eggplant through batter and deep fry. Serve accompanied by chilled yogurt salcasi.
French Bean Fritters [***Zöldbab Palacsintatésztàban*** *Hungary*]   Pass cooked French beans through batter and deep fry.
Fried Okra [*USA*]   Coat sliced okras with cornflour and deep fry.
Fried Plantains [*Caribbean*]   Peel plantains then slice lengthways. Pass through eggwash and breadcrumbs and deep fry.
Fried Pumpkin [***Zharenaia Tykva*** *Russia*]   Coat slices of pumpkin with flour and deep fry. Serve sprinkled with chopped dill.
Fried Rice Cakes in Broth [***Agemochi Iridashi*** *Japan*]   Deep fry rice cakes and serve pyramid fashion, moistened with dashi flavoured with mirin and dark soy sauce and topped with grated daikon and chopped green onion.
Fried Tofu with Ginger [***Köri-döfu Age-ni*** *Japan*]   Golden fry portion squares of tofu cakes then simmer them in dashi flavoured with sugar, salt, light soy sauce and grated ginger. Serve coated with the liquid, topped with grated ginger.
Mushroom Fritters [***Ràntott Gomba*** *Hungary*]   Pass whole raw mushrooms through beer batter and deep fry. Serve accompanied by sauce tartare with chopped chives.

Okra Fritters [*Caribbean*]   Pass sliced okras through eggwash and breadcrumbs and deep fry.

Onion Bhajias [*India*]   Sieve together gram flour, turmeric, ground cumin and garam masala; moisten with water to form a firm paste then add finely sliced onion and salt. Drop tablespoonsful of the mixture into hot corn oil and fry.

Spring Rolls with Beef [*Martabak* *Thailand*]   Sauté chopped onion, garlic and ginger in olive oil, stir in ground coriander, cumin and turmeric and chopped lemon grass. Add minced beef and continue to cook. Allow mixture to cool, combine with beaten eggs then add chopped spring onions. Fill wonton wrappers with the filling then fry them in oil.

Sweetcorn Fritters [*Pergedel Jagung* *Thailand*]   Mix together drained sweetcorn kernels, chopped onion, garlic and spring onions, ground coriander, chilli powder, rice flour, baking powder and beaten eggs to form a dropping consistency. Fry spoonfuls of the mixture in oil.

Sweetcorn Fritters [*USA*]   Mix together drained sweetcorn kernels, flour, baking powder and beaten eggs to form a dropping consistency. Golden fry spoonfuls of the mixture in oil.

Tomato Fritters [*Ràntott Paradicsom* *Hungary*]   Fill centres of hollowed out tomatoes with a macédoine of cooked vegetables, pass through batter and deep fry.

Grilled Vegetables

Application

Vegetables may be grilled on or under a grill. Items are brushed with oil then grilled, being turned as they become cooked.

Grilled Bean Curd with Bean Paste [*Dengaku* *Japan*]   Rinse bean curd in cold water, wrap in a cloth and place under a weight for 30 min to extract the moisture, then cut to form triangular-shaped slices and steam for 10 min. Heat white bean paste and red bean paste in separate pans and flavour each with sugar, mirin and saké. Skewer the bean curd pieces and lightly grill them. Coat half with the white and half with the red bean paste mixtures, sprinkle with poppy seeds and serve.

Grilled Eggplant [*Nasu No Shigiyaki* *Japan*]   Brush slices of eggplant with oil, thread them onto skewers and grill. Serve sprinkled with toasted sesame seeds and moistened with second soup stock mixed with red bean paste and sugar.

Grilled Mushrooms with Rosemary [*Champiñones a la Partilla* *Spain*]   Sprinkle mushrooms with chopped garlic, rosemary, olive oil and seasoning and grill.

Grilled Radicchio [*Radicchio alla Trevisana* *Italy*]   Sprinkle quartered radicchio lettuce with olive oil and seasoning and grill.

Grilled Spring Onions with Lime [*Cebollitas Asadas* *Mexico*]   Brush spring onions with olive oil and grill; sprinkle with lime juice and serve.

Shallow-fried Vegetables

Application

Raw vegetables such as sliced onion and courgettes may be shallow fried in oil or butter. Vegetables that have been previously steamed or boiled, such as florets of cauliflower and Brussels sprouts, may be shallow fried in oil or butter until slightly coloured. Such items may also be given a coating of breadcrumbs and then golden shallow fried in oil or butter.

Bean Curd [***Tububuchim*** *Korea*]   Cut bean curd into 6-mm slices, dredge with flour then shallow fry in a minimum of sesame oil. Serve accompanied by chojang vinegar dipping sauce.

Bean Curd and Bean Sprouts [***Taukwa Dan Taugeh*** *Thailand*]   Sauté garlic in oil then add sliced bean curd, bean sprouts and seasoning.

Broad Beans with Ham [***Habas con Jambón*** *Spain*]   Sauté lardons of bacon in olive oil then toss in cooked and skinned broad beans, chopped parsley and seasoning.

Broccoli Sautéed in Oil [***Brocolos Salteados*** *Portugal*]   Sauté boiled florets of broccoli in olive oil with chopped garlic.

Broccoli with Garlic [***Broccolo Strascinato*** *Italy*]   Sauté florets of cooked broccoli in garlic-flavoured olive oil.

Brussels Sprouts with Garlic and Wine Vinegar [***Coles de Bruselas Salteados*** *Spain*]   Heat garlic-flavoured olive oil, add cooked Brussels sprouts, sprinkle with red wine vinegar, season and serve.

Bubble and Squeak [*GB*]   Combine coarsely chopped cooked cabbage, mashed potato and seasoning. Heat an omelette pan with clarified butter, place in the mixture and fry until golden on each side.

Cauliflower with Garlic and Paprika Sauce [***Coliflor al Ajo Arriero*** *Spain*]   Blend cloves of garlic, parsley, olive oil, a little vinegar and stock to a smooth paste. Stir paprika into garlic-flavoured oil and add the blended mixture to form a sauce. Lightly sauté cooked cauliflower in oil and serve coated with the sauce.

Courgette with Garlic and Lime [***Calabacitas al Mojo de Ajo*** *Mexico*]   Golden fry sliced courgettes in garlic-flavoured oil. Serve sprinkled with lime juice and chopped oregano.

Eggplant Fans [***Beringelas em Leque*** *Portugal*]   Cut eggplants into fan shapes then pass through flour and beaten egg and shallow fry in olive oil.

Eggplant Fried with Dipping Sauce [***Terong Coloh-Coloh Agus*** *Indonesia*]   Marinate sliced eggplant in lemon juice and salt then golden fry in oil. Serve garnished with fresh red chillies accompanied by a dipping sauce.

Eggplant Fried with Turmeric and Chillies [***Badhapu Vambotu Sambola*** *India*]   Sprinkle sliced eggplant with salt and turmeric and drain in a colander. Shallow fry the eggplant in ghee, and sprinkle with lemon juice and chopped fresh chillies. Serve garnished with fried onion rings.

Eggplant Fritters [***Berejenas Fritas*** *Spain*]   Pass sliced eggplant through milk and flour seasoned with paprika and shallow fry in olive oil.

Fried Artichokes [***Carciofi alla Giudea*** *Italy*]   Golden fry cooked prepared globe artichokes in olive oil, turning them frequently during cooking.

Fried Green Pimentos [*Pimientos Fritos* Spain]   Fry strips of green pimentos in olive oil, cover and cook until soft.

Fried Green Tomatoes [*USA*]   Coat halves of green tomatoes with eggwash containing Tabasco sauce then with breadcrumbs. Golden fry in oil.

Fried Pimentos [*Pimentos Verdes ou Encarnados* Portugal]   Sauté whole green pimentos in olive oil for approx. 1 hr.

Fried Pimento Strips with Garlic [*Fatias de Pimentos Encarnados Fritas* Portugal]   Sauté strips of pimento in olive oil with chopped garlic for 30 min.

Fried Plantains [*Caribbean*]   Shallow fry slices of black plantains in peanut oil.

Fried Stuffed Chayotes [*Chayotas Rellenas* Spain]   Boil chayotes in salted water. Combine chopped olives, garlic, parsley, cooked minced beef, breadcrumbs and beaten egg. Fill the chayotes with the mixture, pass through flour and beaten egg and sauté in olive oil. Serve coated with tomato and pimento sauce.

Fried Stuffed Chillies [*Kochujon* Korea]   Combine cooked minced beef, chopped spring onions and garlic, ginger, soy sauce and toasted sesame seeds. Fill halves of chillies with the mixture, pass through flour and beaten egg then fry in oil.

Fried Stuffed Courgettes [*Hobakmuchim* Korea]   Combine cooked minced beef, chopped onion and garlic, toasted sesame seeds and soy sauce. Sandwich the mixture between slices of courgette then shallow fry in oil. Serve accompanied by chojang vinegar dipping sauce.

Fried Stuffed Eggplant [*Kajijon* Korea]   Combine crumbled bean curd, minced cooked beef, chopped onion and garlic, toasted sesame seeds and soy sauce. Sandwich the mixture between slices of eggplant then shallow fry in oil.

Fried Tofu with Ginger [*Köri-döfu Age-ni* Japan]   Shallow golden fry portion squares of tofu then simmer in dashi flavoured with sugar, salt, light soy sauce and grated ginger. Serve coated with the liquid and sprinkled with grated ginger.

Mixed Vegetables in Oil and Garlic [*Hervido con All-i-oli* Spain]   Boil diced turnips, florets of cauliflower, diamonds of French beans and diced potato in chicken stock. Drain then toss them in garlic-flavoured olive oil.

Puréed Eggplant [*Pez de Tierra* Spain]   Sauté cubes of eggplant in olive oil with garlic; season with salt and cumin and cook until soft. Blend to a purée and serve with fried bread croûtons.

Sautéed Broccoli Florets in Oyster Sauce [*Paad Paag Naam Mun Hoy* Thailand]   Crisp fry garlic in oil, add cooked broccoli florets and fry, then moisten with oyster sauce.

Sautéed Cauliflower in Garlic [*Coliflor Salteado* Spain]   Boil cauliflower florets in salted water, drain then golden fry in garlic-flavoured olive oil.

Sautéed Celery [*Karafsi Magaali* Middle East]   Sauté blanched diced celery in samneh; add thyme, marjoram and toasted sesame seeds and season with aromatic salt and lemon juice.

Sautéed Green Pimento [*Pimientos Fritos* Spain]   Sauté whole green pimentos in olive oil until cooked. Serve sprinkled with coarse salt.

Sautéed Leeks [*Korrat bi Zayt* Middle East]   Sauté chopped garlic in olive oil then add diced tomato flesh, brown sugar, sliced spring onions and chilli powder. Add 5-cm lengths of leek and sauté, then moisten with stock and allow to cook.

Sautéed Mushrooms [*Hongos en Mantequilla* Mexico]   Sauté sliced onion in oil, and add chopped garlic, sliced mushrooms, lemon juice and nutmeg.

Sautéed Mushrooms in Sherry Sauce [*Champiñones al Jerez* Spain] Lightly sauté chopped onion and garlic in olive oil, add mushrooms, sprinkle with lemon juice, season and cook. Remove the mushrooms and retain. Swill the pan with sherry, add velouté sauce, simmer, season to taste and finish with a little cream. Place the mushrooms into the sauce and serve sprinkled with chopped fresh herbs.

Sautéed Parsnips [*USA*] Sauté small boiled parsnips in butter with brown sugar. Serve sprinkled with cider vinegar and chopped parsley.

Sautéed Pimento in Soured Cream [*Chiles en Crema* Mexico] Sauté strips of green, red and yellow pimento and sliced onion in oil; add diced tomato flesh, oregano and seasoning. Moisten with soured cream then add crisp fried lardons of bacon.

Sautéed Pumpkin in Breadcrumbs [*Zucca alla Parmigiana* Italy] Coat slices of pumpkin with flour, eggwash and breadcrumbs, then shallow fry them. Mask with tomato sauce, sprinkle with chopped basil, grated Parmesan cheese and butter and gratinate.

Spinach Galette [*Spenótkrokett* Hungary] Combine stiff spinach purée with breadcrumbs and shape into small cakes. Pass through flour, eggwash and breadcrumbs and shallow fry.

Spinach with Raisins and Pine Nuts [*Spinaci alla Romana* Italy] Sauté coarsely chopped boiled spinach in garlic-flavoured oil with raisins and pine nuts.

Steamed Vegetables

Application

Cook in a chinese steamer or a pressure steamer, according to the manufacturer's guide for cooking times.

Steamed Stuffed Chinese Cabbage [*Mushi Hakusai* Japan] Blanch Chinese cabbage leaves in salted water containing a little oil then drain. Stuff the leaves with a mixture of cooked minced pork and beef, sautéed chopped onion, grated ginger, breadcrumbs and beaten eggs. Steam the stuffed cabbage balls for 20 min and serve masked with mirin sauce and sprinkled with grated lime peel.
    Mirin sauce: simmer second soup stock, mirin and soy sauce and lightly thicken with potato flour.

Steamed Stuffed Turnips [*Kabu No Tsumemushi* Japan] Remove the tops from baby turnips and scoop out the centres. Combine diced turnip flesh, sliced mushrooms, cooked gingko nuts and thinly sliced red snapper, and season with salt. Stuff the turnips with the mixture, replace the tops to form lids and steam for 20 min. Boil second soup stock flavoured with soy sauce and mirin and thicken with diluted arrowroot to serve with the turnips.

Steamed Turnip, Prawn and Chicken [*Kabu No Oroshimushi* Japan] Marinate prawns and cooked diced breast of chicken in soy sauce for 4 min. Grate peeled turnips then squeeze out excess moisture. Add the turnip, sliced mushroom, drained prawns, chicken and cooked peas to lightly beaten eggs; flavour with mirin, sugar and salt, fill into bowls and steam for 15 min. Flavour second soup stock with soy sauce and mirin and thicken with diluted arrowroot. Fill the bowls with some of the sauce and place a cooked top of a turnip at the side of each.

Steamed Vegetable Parcels with Coconut Milk [*Urap Indonesia*]   Blend onion, garlic, sambal ulek and laos powder to a paste and combine with blanched cuts of French beans and bean sprouts, shredded spinach and cabbage, strips of cucumber, grated coconut flesh and seasoning. Enrobe portions of the mixture in lettuce leaves to form parcels and steam them.

Stewed Vegetables

Application

Vegetables are cooked under a lid either in their own juices or barely covered with a liquid and gently simmered.

Artichokes in Brandy and Mustard Sauce [*Corazones de Alcachofa à la Mostaza Mexico*]   Sweat chopped onion and garlic in oil, swill with brandy then moisten with cream. Add mustard, cumin and chopped parsley then add artichoke bottoms and allow to stew.

Artichokes in Lemon Sauce [*Anginares Lemonates Greece*]   Lightly fry cooked globe artichokes in olive oil, mask with velouté made from the artichoke water and lemon juice and allow to stew gently.

Artichokes in Montilla [*Alcachofas a la Montillana Spain*]   Sweat chopped garlic in oil, add cooked artichoke bottoms, a sprig of mint, diced cooked pork and saffron then moisten with Montilla wine and jus lié and allow to stew gently.

Artichokes in Oil [*Carciofi alla Giuda Italy*]   Sauté globe artichoke bottoms in olive oil, season, cover with a lid and cook, adding a little water if necessary.

Artichokes with Cured Ham [*Alcachofas Salteadas con Jamón Spain*]   Sauté cooked artichoke bottoms in olive oil, toss in strips of cured ham, season and serve.

Asparagus Casserole [*Cazuela de Espárragos Trigueros Spain*]   Place cooked asparagus into a shallow dish and sprinkle with breadcrumbs fried in garlic-flavoured oil, then sprinkle with paprika and wine vinegar. Break eggs on top and place in the oven to cook.

Beetroot with Smetana [*Svyokla so Smetanoi Russia*]   Stew grated raw beetroot in butter and lemon juice and finish with smetana or yogurt.

Broad Beans with Mortadella [*Fave Stufata Italy*]   Sweat chopped onion in oil then add broad beans and diced Mortadella, moisten with stock and cook. Serve on slices of fried bread.

Broad Beans with Sesame oil [*Shengbian Candou China*]   Toss broad beans in sesame oil and season with salt and sugar. Moisten with chicken stock and cook, reducing the liquid completely, then add chopped spring onions and sesame oil.

Broad Beans with Sherry and Lemon [*Habas à la Rondeña Spain*]   Sauté chopped onion and garlic in olive oil. Add young broad beans, lardons of bacon and a bouquet garni and moisten with dry sherry and stock. Stew until the cooking liquid has reduced, then stir in breadcrumbs, chopped marjoram and zest of lemon.

Broad Beans with Tomato [*Koukia Yiachni* Greece] Sweat chopped spring onions in olive oil, add tomato concassée, chopped dill, mint, and parsley, sugar and seasoning. Moisten with stock, add shelled beans or whole young beans and stew until tender.

Broad Beans with Tomato [*Fagioli alla Uccelletto* Italy] Sauté chopped garlic and sprigs of sage in oil, add broad beans and diced tomato flesh and a little stock, cover and cook.

Cabbage with Bacon [*Verza Affogata* Italy] Golden fry blanched lardons of bacon with garlic and rosemary in oil. Add shredded Savoy cabbage, moisten with stock and stew.

Cabbage with Coconut Milk [*Sayur Kol* Indonesia] Fry curry leaves in peanut oil, add chopped onion and garlic, crushed dried red chillies and dried shrimp paste and cook until the mixture turns brown. Moisten with coconut milk, add zest of lemon and shredded cabbage and stew. Finally stir in tamarind liquid.

Cabbage with Milk [GB] Simmer shredded cabbage in a minimum amount of seasoned milk, drain keeping the milk and toss in butter. Thicken the milk with a liaison of egg yolks and pour over the cabbage.

Cabbage with Spices [*Cobi Foogath* India] Golden fry chopped onion, dried crushed chillies, garlic and ginger in oil then stir in turmeric. Add shredded cabbage, season and stew.

Carrots Glazed with Honey [Israel] Cook turned carrots in a minimum amount of water with lemon juice, honey and salt, reducing the liquid by half. Combine fine matzo meal and butter then mix into the carrots to lightly thicken.

Carrots Glazed with Lemon [*Havuç Plakisi* Turkey] Sweat chopped onion in olive oil, add sliced carrots and moisten with vegetable stock and lemon juice. Add chopped parsley and sugar and stew until the liquid has reduced to a glaze.

Cauliflower and Tomato Stew [*Kounoupíthi Yahnistó* Greece] Lightly sauté chopped onion in oil then add garlic, diced tomato flesh, tomato sauce and chopped parsley. Place cauliflower florets into the mixture and cook.

Cauliflower with Chillies [*Sambal Goreng Kembang* Thailand] Golden fry chopped fresh red chillies and chopped onion and garlic in peanut oil. Add dried shrimp paste, salt and cauliflower florets, moisten with water and stew.

Cauliflower with Creamed Coconut [*Sayur Masak Lemak* Thailand] Blend shallots, blanched almonds, ground coriander, cumin, white pepper, turmeric, groundnut oil, water and salt to a paste. Sauté the paste in oil, add bayleaf, creamed coconut, water, blanched cauliflower florets and sliced cooked new potatoes, and stew.

Courgettes with Dill and Tomato [*Kolokythia Yiachni* Greece] Sweat chopped onion and garlic in olive oil, and add tomato concassée and chopped dill and mint. Add sliced courgettes and a little water and stew.

Creamed Beetroot [Israel] Lightly sauté diced cooked beetroots in butter, sprinkle with vinegar then add cream and mix together.

Curly Kale with Sausage [*Grünkohl Bremer Atr* Germany] Sauté chopped onion in goose fat then add finely chopped, blanched kale; add streaky bacon and brühwurst pork sausage and flavour with allspice and sugar. Moisten with water, cover and cook then slightly thicken the liquid with oatmeal.

Eggplant in Lime Juice [*Berenjenas Sancochadas* Mexico]   Sauté chopped onion and garlic in oil, and add diced tomato flesh and chopped oregano. Moisten with lime juice then toss in golden fried slices of eggplant.

Eggplant in Sweet and Sour Sauce [*Pacheri Terong* Thailand]   Blend cumin, ground coriander, dried chillies, cloves and cinnamon to a fine powder. Sauté chopped onion, garlic and grated ginger in oil then stir in the spices. Moisten with water, add paprika, tamarind liquid, sugar and salt then the diced eggplant, and allow to stew gently.

Eggplant with Curry Sauce [*Terong* Thailand]   Sauté chopped onion and garlic in peanut oil, stir in the curry powder then add diced eggplant. Add sliced green pimentos and pounded dried chillies, moisten with coconut milk and stew.

Eggplant with Tomato [*Melitzanes Stifatho* Greece]   Stew diced eggplant with whole cloves of garlic, small whole shallots, peeled and sliced tomatoes, olive oil, red wine, basil, bayleaf, sugar and seasoning. Moisten with water and stew.

Forest Mushrooms German Style [*Steinpilze Försterinart* Germany]   Sauté chopped onion and garlic and lardons of bacon in oil. Add sliced field mushrooms and cook then add chopped parsley. Reduce the cooking liquid and finish it with cream.

French Beans and Spinach in Peanut Sauce [*Pecel* Indonesia]   Sauté sliced onion and garlic in oil, stir in sambal ulek, sugar, tamarind paste, laos powder and peanut butter, moisten with stock and cook to a sauce consistency. Finish with soy sauce then add boiled French beans and spinach to the mixture.

French Beans in Sour Cream [*Sure Wälschbauna* Germany]   Cook French beans in salted water, drain and thicken the cooking liquor with arrowroot. Add a little vinegar, strain it onto the beans and serve.

French Beans with Chorizo Sausage and Eggs [*Feijao Verde à Provinciana* Portugal]   Sauté chopped onion and garlic in pork fat, stir in diced tomato flesh and the prepared beans then barely cover with water. Add sliced chorizo sausage and fried lardons of bacon, season and cook. Break eggs into hollows in the vegetables and poach them.

French Beans with Lemon and Oregano [*Ejotes* Mexico]   Sauté sliced onion in bacon fat, and add diced tomato flesh, garlic, oregano and seasoning. Stir in cooked French beans and serve sprinkled with lemon juice.

French Beans with Spices [*Bean Sajoer* Indonesia]   Sauté sliced onion and garlic in oil, stir in sambal ulek, add the French beans, moisten with chicken stock and cook.

French Beans with Spices [*Tumis Pedas Kacang Panjang* Thailand]   Blend shallots, ginger, shrimp paste, dried red chillies and tamarind liquid to a paste. Simmer the paste then add French beans, moisten with water and cook.

French Beans with Tomato [*Fagiolini di Sant'Anna* Italy]   Sauté chopped garlic in oil, and stir in diced tomato flesh and French beans. Cover with water, season and cook, reducing the liquor to a sauce consistency.

French Beans with Tomato and Cumin [*Fosoulákia Frésca Yahnistá* Greece]   Lightly sauté chopped onion and garlic in olive oil then add diced tomato flesh, chopped parsley and seasoning. Place the cooked French beans into the mixture and cook, allowing the liquid to reduce completely. Flavour with cumin and serve.

Glazed Leeks with Rice [*Prassorizo* Greece]   Sweat lengths of white of leek in olive oil, and add tomato purée, sugar and ground cinnamon. Barely cover with water, rain in rice and stew until the cooking liquor is completely absorbed.

Kohlrabi Stewed in Lard [*Pàrolt Karalàbé* *Hungary*]   Lightly caramelise sugar in lard, moisten with stock then add diced kohlrabi and chopped parsley and stew until tender.

Kohlrabi in Soured Cream [*Petrezelymes Karalàbéfozelék* *Hungary*]   Stew diced kohlrabi in butter, moisten with velouté sauce and finish with soured cream and chopped herbs.

Maquechoux [*USA*]   Sauté chopped onion, add diced green pimento, tomato flesh and sugar then stir in equal quantities of cooked whole sweetcorn kernels and cooked pulped sweetcorn. Sprinkle with crisp lardons of bacon.

Mixed Spiced Vegetables [*Sajoer Lodeb* *Indonesia*]   Sweat sliced onion and garlic in oil, and stir in sambal ulek and ground macadamia nuts. Add cauliflower and broccoli florets, French beans, diced carrots and potatoes, laos powder and sugar. Moisten with chicken stock and coconut milk and cook.

Mixed Vegetables in Yogurt [*Aviyal* *India*]   Blend desiccated coconut, garlic, crushed dried green chillies, cumin seeds, sesame oil and salt to a paste. Boil macédoine of vegetables in a minimum amount of salted water and when half cooked, add the paste, diced mango, curry leaves and yogurt and stew.

Mixed Vegetables Tamil Style [*Kuttu* *India*]   Cook red lentils in water with turmeric. Fry cumin seed and desiccated coconut in oil, add macédoine of vegetables, moisten with water and stew, then add the drained lentils. Stir-fry mustard seed in oil then add ground asafoetida, crushed dried red chillies and curry leaves. Add to the vegetables and cover with a lid to retain the flavours.

Mushrooms, Potatoes and Peas with Spices [*Tazzi Kbumben alu Mattarkari* *India*]   Sauté chopped onion in ghee, and add crushed garlic, grated ginger, chopped coriander leaves, turmeric, chilli powder, quartered button mushrooms, new potatoes, peas and water. Stew then add garam masala and finish cooking.

Mushrooms with Marjoram [*Fungbi al Fungbetto* *Italy*]   Sauté chopped garlic in garlic-flavoured oil then add chopped marjoram, sliced mushrooms, tomato purée and seasoning and cook.

Mushrooms with Paprika [*Gombapaprikàs* *Hungary*]   Sauté chopped onion in oil, add strips of green pimento and quartered mushrooms, stir in paprika and stew. Moisten with soured cream and serve sprinkled with chopped fresh herbs.

Mushrooms with Smetana [*Griby v Smetane* *Russia*]   Stew quartered ceps in oil. Sauté chopped onion and the chopped cep stalks in oil, add chopped dill and stew. Add the cooked ceps then finish with smetana.

Okra in Tomato Sauce [*Caribbean*]   Fry small okras in peanut oil, add chopped onion, garlic, fresh green chillies and diced tomato flesh and stew.

Okra with Chillies and Ginger [*Bhendi Kari* *India*]   Sauté chopped onion and sliced fresh green chillies in ghee then add sliced garlic, grated ginger and turmeric. Add small okras, flavour with ground coriander and cumin, moisten with buttermilk and stew.

Okra with Tomato [*Israel*]   Sauté chopped onion in oil then add diced tomato flesh and cook. Add sliced okras and lemon juice and stew.

Peas with Panir Cheese [*Mattar Panir* *India*]   Golden fry cubes of Panir cheese in ghee. Sauté chopped onion and garlic, stir in grated ginger, ground coriander, cumin, turmeric, chilli powder and salt then add tomato concassée and garam masala. Add peas and allow to stew, then finish with grated cheese, chopped mint and coriander leaves.

Peas with Smoked Ham [*Piselli alla Prosciutto* Italy]   Sweat chopped onion in olive oil and add peas. Moisten with stock and stew then add strips of prosciutto.

Pimento and Tomato [*Peperonata* Italy]   Sauté chopped onion and garlic in olive oil, stir in strips of red pimento and stew. Add diced tomato flesh, basil and seasoning and stew.

Ratatouille [*Ratatouille Niçoise* France]   Sauté sliced onion and crushed garlic in olive oil then add diced eggplant, strips of red and green pimento, diced courgette and tomato flesh, coriander seeds and chopped fresh basil, and stew.

Red Cabbage and Smoked Ham [*Cavolo Rosso alla Bolzanese* Italy]   Sauté chopped onion and garlic in olive oil then add shredded red cabbage. Moisten with dry white wine, add blanched diced smoked ham and seasoning, and stew.

Runner Beans with Tomatoes [*Fassolia Yiachni* Greece]   Sweat chopped onion and garlic in olive oil, add tomato concassée and cook. Add sliced runner beans, barely cover with water and stew. When cooked allow to stand before serving.

Runner Beans with Tomatoes in Oil [*Lubyi bi Zayt* Middle East]   Sweat chopped onion and crushed garlic in olive oil, and add tomato concassée, tomato purée and sugar. Moisten with stock, add sliced runner beans and stew.

Spiced Cabbage [*Gobi Foogath* India]   Fry chopped onion, crushed dried chillies, garlic and ginger in ghee. Stir in turmeric, add shredded cabbage, moisten with stock and stew.

Spiced French Beans [*Tumis Pedas Kacang Panjang* Thailand]   Blend shallots, garlic, ginger, chilli powder, kapi, lemon juice, groundnut oil and salt to a paste. Boil the paste then add water and French beans and stew.

Spiced Okras [*Bhendi Bhaji* India]   Lightly fry panch phora in ghee. Add chopped onion, turmeric, chilli powder, garam masala and salt. Add okras and stew.

Spiced Spinach [*Palak Bhaji* India]   Golden fry chopped onion, crushed garlic and grated ginger in ghee then stir in mixed ground cumin, coriander, turmeric, chilli powder and salt. Add spinach and a little water and stew.

Spiced Spinach [*Bajem Sajoer Toemis* Indonesia]   Sauté chopped onion and garlic in oil, and stir in sambal ulek, shredded spinach and laos powder. Moisten with chicken stock and stew. Finish with a sprinkling of soy sauce.

Spiced Spinach and Turnip [*Sagg* India]   Cook spinach and diced turnip in salted water. Lightly fry black mustard seeds in ghee, and add chopped onion, grated ginger, chilli powder, turmeric and salt. Add the coarsely chopped spinach and the turnips and sprinkle with garam masala and lemon juice.

Spinach and Pine Nuts [*Espinacas a la Catalana* Spain]   Cook spinach in salted water. Sauté chopped garlic in olive oil, and add the coarsely chopped spinach, soaked raisins and pine nuts and allow to stew.

Spinach and Rice [*Spanakorizo* Greece]   Sweat chopped spring onions in olive oil, and add chopped dill and spinach and salt. Moisten with chicken stock, rain in short-grain rice and cook. When cooked the liquor should have been completely absorbed by the rice.

Spinach in Lime Juice [*Espinaca en Mantequilla* Mexico]   Sauté chopped onion and garlic in oil, add spinach and cook for a few moments. Season with nutmeg and serve sprinkled with lime juice and fried lardons of bacon.

Squash Georgia Style [*USA*]   Combine sliced marrow and onion, season with salt, pepper and mace then moisten with chicken stock and boil until cooked and the liquid completely reduced. Serve sprinkled with fried lardons of bacon.

Stewed Lettuce [***Savanyúsalàta-Fozelék*** *Hungary*]   Stew quarters of lettuce in lard, and moisten with soured cream and a reduction of wine vinegar and chopped dill.

Stewed Vegetables in Tomato Sauce [***Yachni*** *Greece*]   Sweat chopped onion in olive oil, add diced tomato flesh, moisten with tomato juice and cook. Add prepared vegetables to the mixture and cook on a low heat. (Runner beans, peas, artichokes, cauliflower and eggplant may be used for this dish.)

Stuffed Grape Vine Leaves [***Dereve Pattoug*** *Middle East*]   Cook a short-grain rice pilaff with pine nuts, currants, allspice and chopped dill. Enrobe portions of rice in blanched vine leaves and arrange in an oiled and seasoned pan lined with more leaves. Cover with slices of lemon and moisten with stock. Cover with a lid and stew. Serve warm or chilled, garnished with segments of lemon and accompanied by yogurt.

Stuffed Grape Vine Leaves [***Koupepia*** *Greece*]   Sauté chopped onion in corn oil, and add minced cooked lamb and veal, cooked rice, chopped parsley and mint. Enrobe portions of the mixture in blanched vine leaves. Arrange in an oiled and seasoned pan lined with more vine leaves, cover with slices of lemon and moisten with stock. Cover with a lid and stew. Serve accompanied by lemon and egg sauce.

Sweet and Sour Cabbage [***Cavolo in Agrodolce*** *Italy*]   Sweat chopped onion in olive oil, stir in shredded cabbage and cook, then add diced tomato flesh. Moisten with white wine vinegar, add sugar and stew.

Tomatoes in Curry Sauce [***Tamatarka Cut*** *India*]   Blend roasted desiccated coconut, poppy, coriander and sesame seeds and oil to a paste. Place tomato concassée in a pan, add the paste, gram flour, grated ginger, crushed garlic and chilli powder, moisten with water and cook. Sieve the mixture, reboil and cook to a pulp. Heat sesame and sunflower oils and fast fry cumin seeds, dried whole red chillies, crushed garlic, asafoetida and crushed curry leaves until the chillies are almost black. Pour the mixture over the tomato pulp and serve garnished with sliced hard-boiled eggs and sprinkled with chopped coriander leaves.

Tomatoes with Coconut Milk [***Sambal Goreng Tomat*** *Indonesia*]   Sauté chopped onion and garlic in oil then stir in sambal ulek, laos powder, sugar and lemon juice; moisten with coconut milk and simmer. Add quarters of tomato flesh to the mixture and cook for 1 min.

Vegetable Curry [***Sayur Masak Lemak*** *Thailand*]   Cook chopped onion, garlic and fresh green chillies in thin coconut milk, then add diced potato, shredded cabbage and thick coconut milk and cook. Finish with lemon juice.

Vegetable Paella [***Paella Huertana de Murcia*** *Spain*]   Blend together parsley, garlic and chicken stock. Sauté chopped onion and diced pimento in oil, and add diced tomato flesh. Stir in short-grain rice, diamonds of French beans, lima beans and diced carrot; moisten with the blended stock, a few strands of saffron and seasoning and simmer for 10 min. Transfer to a shallow dish and bake until the rice is almost cooked. Serve decorated with cooked artichoke bottoms and wedges of hard-boiled egg.

Vegetable Stew [*Chakchouka Middle East*]   Sauté chopped garlic and chopped onion in oil then add diced pimentos and tomato flesh and cumin seeds and simmer. Add blanched sliced courgettes, cooked haricot beans and a little of their cooking liquor, season and stew. Stir in beaten eggs, cook and serve sprinkled with chopped herbs.

Vegetable Stew [***Pisto Manchego** Spain*]   Lightly fry sliced onion, garlic and green pimentos in olive oil then add sliced courgettes, diced tomato flesh and chopped fresh herbs and stew.

Yale Beets [*USA*]   Place raw sliced beetroots in an oiled shallow dish, and moisten with a mixture of orange and lemon juices, sugar and salt. Stew until soft then serve sprinkled with blanched shredded orange and lemon peels.

Stir-fried Vegetables

Application

Heat a minimum amount of oil in a wok, balti pan or frying pan then add the vegetables, previously cut into small pieces; fry very quickly, tossing continuously until evenly coloured and cooked.

Cauliflower Balti Style [***Balti Gobi** India*]   Stir-fry sesame seeds, black mustard seeds and turmeric in oil for 1 min then add chopped ginger and chopped onion and cook for 3 min. Add cooked cauliflower florets to the mixture, moisten with a little water, add shredded spinach, chopped coriander and saffron, cook together for 3 min, season with balti spice mix and serve.

Eggplant Balti Style [***Balti Begun** India*]   Stir-fry mustard, sesame and wild onion seeds in oil, add chopped garlic and chopped onion and cook for a few min. Add the sliced cooked eggplant, moisten with a little water then add chopped coriander leaves, oregano and balti spice mixture to taste. Simmer for a few moments and serve.

Okra Balti Style [***Balti Bhindi** India*]   Stir-fry fennel seeds in oil, add chopped garlic then add sliced okra, whole cherry tomatoes and a little tomato purée and cook for 3–4 min. Season with balti spice mix, sprinkle with chopped basil and coriander leaves then serve.

Stir-fried Bean Sprouts and Bean Curd [***Thua Ngok Paad Tao Hoo** Thailand*]   Golden fry cloves of garlic in oil, add bean sprouts and bean curd then moisten with oyster sauce.

Stir-fried Beans and Carrots with Ginger [***Tumis Bunchis** Indonesia*]   Stir-fry sliced fresh green chillies and ginger and chopped shallots, galingale, garlic and curry leaves in oil. Add French beans and diced carrot, moisten with water and simmer for 5 min.

Stir-fried Beans, Chillies and Pork [***Moo Pad Prik Sai Tua Fak Yao** Thailand*]   Stir-fry garlic and sliced fresh green chillies in oil then add minced pork. Add French beans and season with paprika and sugar; add nam pla, moisten with water and simmer until the beans are cooked and the liquid reduced.

Stir-fried Cabbage with Oyster Sauce [***Pak Bung Loy Fa** Thailand*]   Golden stir-fry garlic in oil then add blanched shredded cabbage. Moisten with stock, oyster sauce and yellow bean sauce and simmer for 2 min. Serve the sauce in the dish with the drained cabbage on top.

Stir-fried Cabbage with Red Pepper Paste [*Sala Lobak* Indonesia] Blend shallots, garlic, red pimento, nam pla and water to a paste. Stir-fry the paste in oil and add shredded spring greens; season, cover and cook.

Stir-fried Carrots [*Ninjin* Japan] Stir-fry julienne of carrot and strips of burdock root in oil; moisten with saké, stir in dark soy sauce and sugar, cook to reduce the liquid and season with seven-spice powder.

Stir-fried Courgettes with Sesame Seeds [*Hobak Namul* Korea] Stir-fry garlic in sesame oil then add diced courgette. When almost cooked season with salt and add chopped spring onions, sesame oil and toasted sesame seeds.

Stir-fried Curried Mushrooms [*Dhingri Kari* India] Stir-fry chopped spring onions, crushed garlic, grated ginger and curry leaves in ghee. Stir in curry powder, add button mushrooms and cook then sprinkle with garam masala, coconut milk and lemon juice.

Stir-fried Eggplant [*Nasu Itame-ni* Japan] Stir-fry halved and scored small eggplant in oil with diced red pimento. Moisten with dashi, mirin and dark soy sauce and cook until the liquid has reduced.

Stir-fried Mixed Green Vegetables [*Pat Pak Ruam Mitr* Thailand] Stir-fry sliced garlic and grated ginger in groundnut oil. Add an assortment of vegetables, e.g. French beans, broccoli, courgettes. Add nam pla and oyster sauce.

Stir-fried Mixed Vegetables [*Sabzi Bhaji* India] Stir-fry mustard seeds, curry leaves and crushed garlic in ghee. Stir in grated ginger, turmeric, sliced fresh chillies and salt. Add a julienne of carrot, cauliflower florets, diamonds of French beans and shredded cabbage one by one.

Stir-fried Okras [*Bamiya B'Zayt* Middle East] Stir-fry chopped garlic in oil, add ground coriander then add chopped onion and diced tomato flesh and simmer. Stir-fry the okras in oil, add the tomato mixture and finish with lemon juice, sugar and chopped coriander.

Stir-fried Spiced Onions [*Piaz Bhaji* India] Stir-fry cumin seeds in ghee, stir in grated ginger, turmeric and thickly sliced onions then sprinkle with garam masala and cook quickly.

Stir-fried Spinach [*Paag Boong Paad* Thailand] Golden fry cloves of garlic and soya beans in oil then add spinach, season and serve garnished with sliced fresh red chillies.

Pulses

Application

Pulses with an outer shell require soaking in cold water for 12 hours before cooking; they are then washed in cold water ready for cooking. Pulses with no outer shell do not require soaking. Simmer in water with onion, carrot and a bouquet garni.

Black Beans Mexican Style [*Frijoles de la Olla* Mexico] Cook beans with bacon trimmings and epazote.

Black Beans with Cider [*Caribbean*]   Cook beans with bacon trimmings. Drain and add chopped onion, crushed garlic, diced red pimento and crushed dried green chillies previously fried in peanut oil. Add oregano and ground cumin and sugar. Moisten with cider and stew together. Serve with chilli sauce.

Black Beans with Green Peppers [*Caribbean*]   Cook beans then add fried chopped salt pork, chopped onion, crushed garlic and diced green pimento.

Black Beans with Rice [***Moros y Cristianos*** *Spain*]   Cook black beans with lardons of bacon. Mould rice pilaff mixed with nutmeg, zest of lemon and grated Parmesan cheese in a savarin mould. Turn onto a dish, fill the centre with the beans and mask with sofrito.

Sofrito: sweat chopped onion and crushed garlic in oil. Stir in paprika, tomato concassée and chopped fresh herbs and cook.

Black-eyed Beans with Spinach [***Salq bi Loubia*** *Middle East*]   Cook black-eyed beans then combine with chopped onion and shredded spinach sweated in olive oil.

Boiled Soy Beans [***Nimame*** *Japan*]   Simmer soy beans in water for 10 min, refresh and drain. Parboil rounds of carrot, refresh and drain. Combine the beans, carrots, kombu flakes, dashi flavoured with light and dark soy sauces, salt and sugar and simmer until cooked.

Boston Baked Beans [*USA*]   Combine chopped onion, sugar, molasses, mustard, rum and water and pour over soaked and drained navy beans. Cover with strips of salt pork and bake until tender.

Brown Lentils ['*Ads bi Gibba** *Middle East*]   Cook lentils in water. Golden stir-fry strips of garlic and onion in olive oil then add the lentils, season with salt, cumin and coriander and chopped parsley, and toss to mix. Serve with wedges of lemon.

Brown Lentils with Noodles [***Rishta bi Ads*** *Middle East*]   Cook lentils in water. Combine lentils with chopped onion and garlic previously fried in oil with ground cumin and coriander and boiled noodles.

Chickpea Galettes [***Revithokeftéthes*** *Greece*]   Mince cooked chickpeas with chopped onion and combine with dry mashed potato, chopped parsley and beaten egg. Mould into small cakes and golden shallow fry in olive oil.

Chickpeas Kofta [***Topig*** *Middle East*]   Soak chickpeas, remove the skins and blend the peas to a paste. Combine the paste with an equal quantity of dry mashed potatoes. Boil sliced onion, reduce the liquid completely, and add allspice, cumin, pine nuts, currants and tahini. Spread the onion mixture on a cloth, cover with the pea mixture, enclose and tie at each end. Simmer in stock. Cut into slices, brush with oil, sprinkle with cinnamon and serve with segments of lemon.

Chickpeas with Fresh Coriander [***Frijoles Charros*** *Mexico*]   Cook chickpeas in water with sliced shoulder of pork. Crisp fry lardons of bacon, sliced onion and crushed dried green chillies then add tomato concassée. Add to the peas and finish with chopped coriander leaves.

Chickpeas with Spinach [***Nivik*** *Middle East*]   Cook chickpeas in water. Combine the peas with chopped onion and shredded spinach sweated in olive oil to which tomato purée has been added.

Chickpeas with Spinach and Spices [***Humus wa Sabenekh*** *Middle East*]   Cook chickpeas in water. Add strips of golden fried garlic and cooked shredded spinach to the peas; season with roasted cumin seeds, sprinkle with samneh and chopped herbs and serve with wedges of lemon.

Chuckwagon Beans [*USA*]   Sauté chopped onion in oil with garlic. Moisten with beer, tomato juice and Worcester sauce, and add brown sugar, Dijon mustard, paprika, ground chillies, red pepper flakes and thyme. Place soaked and drained pink pinto or kidney beans in an oven dish, add strips of salt pork on top and moisten with the first mixture. Bake, replenishing with tomato juice as necessary to prevent drying out.

Falafel [*Israel*]   Grind soaked chickpeas to a smooth paste. Combine the paste with soaked and squeezed bread, crushed garlic and chopped parsley and season with salt, cumin, coriander and cayenne. Deep fry small balls of the mixture until golden.

Haricot Beans in Cream Sauce [*Haricots Blanc à la Crème* *France*]   Cook haricot beans in water, drain and combine with fried lardons of bacon, melted chicken glaze, cream, fresh herb butter and lemon juice.

Haricot Beans in Onion Sauce [*Hagymàs Babfozelék* *Hungary*]   Cook haricot beans in water. Combine the beans with onion sauce flavoured with paprika and finished with soured cream.

Haricot Beans with Black Pudding [*Fabada Asturiana* *Spain*]   Cook beans with lardons of bacon, crushed garlic, crushed peppercorns, saffron and salted pig's trotters. Serve with the diced flesh of the trotters and sliced fried black pudding.

Haricot Beans with Cabbage [*Fagioli con le Verze* *Italy*]   Cook haricot beans in water with chopped fennel and onion, shredded cabbage, tomato purée and seasoning. Finish by adding fried lardons of bacon and garlic.

Haricot Beans with Spices [*Fassoolia Baydah* *Middle East*]   Sauté chopped garlic and onion in oil, add powdered cardamom, cinnamon and chilli powder and diced tomato flesh. Moisten with stock, add cooked drained haricot beans and finish with lemon juice and chopped herbs.

Hopping John [*USA*]   Cook black-eyed peas in water. Fry lardons of bacon with chopped onion and garlic, stir in long-grain rice, moisten with red wine vinegar and the pea cooking liquid and cook. Combine the rice with the cooked peas and serve sprinkled with chopped chives and parsley.

Kidney Beans with Cumin [*Ful Medamis* *Middle East*]   Sauté strips of garlic and onion in olive oil, add to cooked kidney beans and season with salt, cumin and chopped parsley. Serve with wedges of lemon.

Lentil Stew [*Israel*]   Sauté chopped onion and garlic in oil, add shredded raw spinach and chopped coriander, cover with a lid and stew. Add sliced cooked potatoes, cooked lentils and some of their liquor. Stew together until thick then finish with grated zest and juice of lemon.

Lentils with Noodles [*Fakómatso* *Greece*]   Cook lentils with onion, tomato purée, garlic and olive oil. Add prepared noodles to the lentils then drain and serve.

Lentils with Turmeric and Cumin [*Caribbean*]   Cook lentils with turmeric then add chopped cooked onion. Fry cloves of garlic and cumin seeds in peanut oil and when the garlic is dark brown strain the oil into the cooked lentils.

Pea Beans with Macaroni [*Fasoulomakàrouna* *Greece*]   Cook beans with tomato purée and savory. Sauté chopped onion and garlic in olive oil then stir into the beans. Add short cut macaroni to the beans and simmer together until cooked.

Pease Pudding [*GB*]   Cook yellow split peas with a studded onion, whole carrot, bacon trimmings and water in the oven. Discard the vegetables and the bacon, drain and pass through a sieve, then add butter to give a firm, smooth purée.

Pinto Beans [***Frijoles*** *Mexico*]   Cook beans in water with chopped onion and garlic, bacon trimmings and cumin seeds.

Pinto Beans with Green Chillies [***Frijoles Charros*** *Mexico*]   Combine cooked beans with fried lardons of bacon and chopped fresh chillies, tomato flesh and coriander leaves.

Red Lentils with Spinach [***Palak Dal*** *India*]   Cook red lentils with sliced onion, sliced garlic, ground ginger and chilli powder. When cooked combine with cooked chopped spinach and yogurt.

Refried Pinto Beans [***Frijoles Refritos*** *Mexico*]   Fry cooked pinto beans in oil then mash them and season with chilli powder and ground cumin.

Succotash [*USA*]   Simmer together cooked lima beans and sweetcorn kernels in cream sauce.

Sweet and Sour Kidney Beans [***Söt Sur Bruna Bönar*** *Scandinavia*]   Cook beans with carrot, onion, bacon trimmings and herbs. Discard the vegetables and bacon then add vinegar and brown sugar; thicken the liquid with arrowroot.

Yellow Split Peas in Spiced Sauce [***Parpu*** *Thailand*]   Cook peas in water with cinnamon, dried red chillies and turmeric. When almost cooked add diced potatoes, strips of garlic, grated ginger and salt; finish with thin coconut milk. Sauté sliced onion in oil, add mustard and fennel seeds and dried red chillies then add to the cooked peas.

Couscous

Couscous [*Middle East/North Africa*]   Fry diced onion, carrot and celery, crushed garlic, ground ginger and cumin in oil and moisten with water. Place coarsely ground millet (couscous) in a basin and work in the liquid. Place the millet on a dampened cloth-lined steaming colander and cover with the cloth. Steam then fork in butter, ground ginger, cumin, cayenne and paprika and continue to steam. To serve, pile the couscous in a serving dish and fork in knobs of butter. Arrange meat and vegetables on top and add some of the cooking liquid. Alternatively, serve the couscous, meat and vegetables and liquid in three separate bowls.

Samosas [India]

Application

Sift equal quantities of wholemeal and strong flour with salt, rub in butter and knead to a dough with boiling water. Roll out very thinly and divide into 13-cm diameter circles; cut each in half and form into cornets, sealing with water. Fill with the cooked mixture, fold over the tops to seal then deep fry at 190 °C.

Cauliflower and Green Pea Samosa [*Gobbi Hari Matar Samosa*] Dry-fry cumin seeds, coriander seeds, cloves and cinnamon then finely grind in a blender. Fry asafoetida in ghee for a few seconds then add cooked cauliflower florets, cooked peas and turmeric and stir-fry. Season the mixture and allow to cool then fill into prepared samosas and proceed in the normal manner.

Cauliflower and Potato Samosa [*Gobbi Aloo Samosa*] Fry grated ginger, chopped fresh green chillies and mustard seeds in ghee until the seeds pop. Add diced tomato flesh, ground coriander, turmeric and garam masala and cook until the mixture begins to thicken to a pulp. Add cooked cauliflower florets, small diced and cooked potatoes, chopped fresh herbs and lemon juice. Allow the filling to cool and proceed in the normal way.

Lamb and Curry Samosa Sweat chopped onion and grated ginger in ghee. Add sautéed minced lamb, stir in curry powder, moisten with stock and white wine vinegar and add seasoning. Cook until tender. Finish with garam masala, chopped mint and coriander. Fill into prepared samosas and proceed in the normal manner.

Potato Samosa Filling [*Aloo Samosa*] Flavour boiled diced potato with chilli powder, panch phora, cumin and salt and moisten with lemon juice.

Spicy Beef Samosa Filling Sweat chopped onion and garlic and grated ginger in ghee. Add and sauté minced beef, stir in garam masala, coriander powder, chilli powder and ground ginger, moisten with stock and cook.

Vegetable Samosa Filling [*Samm-bahr Samosa*] Mash boiled potatoes and season with black pepper, chilli powder, coriander powder, cumin and dried fenugreek leaves, then add cooked peas.

Stuffings

Apple and Cardamom Stuffing Combine bread soaked in milk and squeezed out with diced apple, rum and beaten eggs; season with ground cloves and cardamom.

Apple and Chestnut Stuffing Combine chopped cooked chestnuts, raisins marinated in brandy, coarsely chopped apple with the skin left on, sweated chopped onion, and seasoning.

Basil, Lemon and Nutmeg Stuffing Combine soaked breadcrumbs with eggs, zest and juice of lemon, chopped parsley, chopped basil, salt, pepper, nutmeg and creamed butter.

Chicken Liver, Mushroom and Basil Stuffing Combine lightly fried chopped chicken liver, onion and mushrooms with cream, chopped basil, breadcrumbs, eggs and seasoning.

Duxelle of Mushrooms Lightly sauté chopped shallots in oil then add chopped mushrooms and stew until cooked; finish by adding chopped parsley and seasoning.

Fruit and Nut Stuffing Poach prunes in white wine and poach dried apricots in orange juice. Cut the prunes and apricots into small pieces and combine with diced apple, chopped dates and walnuts, grated zest of lemon and cinnamon. Moisten with port.

Liver and Marjoram Stuffing   Combine minced raw calf's liver, chopped bacon, mushrooms, parsley, marjoram, soaked bread, egg yolks and seasoning.

Orange Stuffing   Combine butter, cubes of bread, diced celery, orange segments, thyme and tarragon with stock to moisten.

Orange and Pork Stuffing   Combine raw minced pork, bacon and chicken livers, onion and garlic with oregano, zest and juice of oranges, melted butter and seasoning.

Potato Stuffing   Combine diced boiled potatoes, chopped onion, chopped chicken livers, chopped parsley, marjoram and seasoning.

Rice, Almond, Sultana and Liver Stuffing   Mix rice pilaff with white wine and stock, add diced and sautéed chicken livers, chopped almonds and raisins and season with cinnamon.

Rice and Pine Nut Stuffing   Chop chicken giblets and sauté them in olive oil then add chopped spring onions and minced beef and cook until coloured. Stir in rice, tomato purée, chopped parsley, rubbed thyme and pine nuts. Moisten with chicken stock and cook until tender.

Sage, Sultana and Apple Stuffing   Combine sweated chopped onion, rubbed sage, breadcrumbs, chopped parsley, lightly fried sultanas, fried diced apple and seasoning.

Spiced Meat Stuffing   Golden fry chopped onion, add minced beef, brown stock, seasoning, cinnamon and allspice. Simmer until the liquid has evaporated. Moisten with pomegranate and lemon juices and add a little sugar.

Walnut, Ginger, Sultana and Onion Stuffing   Combine chopped onion, chopped hard-boiled egg, chopped walnuts, grated raw ginger, sultanas and chopped fresh green chillies.

Potatoes and Sweet Potatoes

Baked Potatoes

Application

This is the cooking of raw sliced potatoes in a mould or sliced or turned potatoes in the oven with the addition of white stock, milk or cream. The potatoes are brushed with oil or butter and cooked at 180 °C. When cooked they should have absorbed most of the liquid and have a light golden surface. There are also variations on baked jacket potatoes.

Anna Potatoes [*Pommes Anna* France]   Heat a little oil an anna mould, neatly arrange a layer of sliced potatoes then fill the mould with seasoned sliced potatoes, brush with butter and bake for approx. 45 min. When cooked remove from the mould, cut into portions and serve.

Baked Potatoes and Rice [*Israel*]   Place chopped onion and short- or long-grain rice in a shallow dish, add barrel-shaped potatoes and moisten with white stock. Brush the top of the potatoes with oil then bake.

Baked Potatoes in Egg [*Kartofelnaya Zapekanka* Russia]   Combine sliced potato, sliced onion, chopped parsley, beaten eggs and seasoning. Place into an oiled shallow dish and arrange overlapping sliced potato on top. Brush the surface with oil and bake. Cut into wedges and serve sprinkled with chopped dill.

Baked Potatoes in Soured Cream with Anchovies [*Janssons Frestelse Scandinavia*] Combine sliced potatoes with soured cream, chopped anchovy fillets and onion. Place into oiled shallow dishes and arrange overlapping sliced potatoes on top. Brush the surface with anchovy oil and bake.

Baked Potatoes in Soured Cream with Dill [*Kartofel so Smetanoi Russia*] Lightly shallow fry diced potatoes in oil, mix with soured cream, chopped dill and a little flour then transfer to shallow dishes and bake.

Baked Potato Kugel [*Israel*] Combine dry mashed potato, eggs, sweated chopped onion, baking powder, salt, pepper and nutmeg. Place into a shallow dish, sprinkle with matzo meal and butter and gratinate.

Baked Potatoes with Bacon [*Döbbekoche Germany*] Drain grated raw potatoes on a sieve then combine with grated onion, beaten eggs, fried lardons of smoked bacon and nutmeg. Bake the mixture in anna moulds. May be served with plum sauce, plum jelly or fruit compote.

Baked Potatoes with Curd Cheese [*Gul'bishnik Russia*] Bake potatoes in their jackets. Remove the pulp from the skins and crush it with a fork. Add butter, curd cheese, soured cream, grated onion and caraway seeds or dill. Bake the mixture in anna moulds until golden and crisp.

Baked Potatoes with Cured Ham [*Patatas Asadas Rellenas Spain*] Bake potatoes in their jackets. Remove the pulp from the skins and crush it with a fork. Add butter, diced jambón serrano and seasoning. Pile back into the shells, sprinkle with breadcrumbs and melted butter then gratinate.

Baked Potatoes with Dill [*Israel*] Lightly golden fry diced potatoes with chopped onion, then place into shallow dishes and moisten with stock. Add chopped parsley and dill, caraway seeds and bayleaf. Brush the surface with oil and bake.

Baked Potatoes with Egg and Chive [*Gefülite Ofenkartoffeln Germany*] Bake potatoes in their jackets. Make an indentation in the centre of each and break an egg into it, then return to the oven to cook the eggs. Serve sprinkled with chopped chives.

Baked Potatoes with Oil and Onion [*Patatas con Cebolla Spain*] Bake potatoes in their jackets, incise and fold back the skin and fill the centres with chopped onion sautéed in olive oil.

Baked Potatoes with Paprika [*Patatas Bravas Spain*] Arrange barrel-shaped potatoes in hot oil and bake. Serve sprinkled with paprika and cayenne.

Baked Stuffed Potatoes [*Farshirovannii Kartofel Russia*] Bake potatoes in their jackets, cut in half and scoop out a spoonful from the centre of each. Combine crème fraîche, egg yolks, breadcrumbs and the scooped out potato then replace dome shaped. Sprinkle with grated cheese and melted butter then gratinate.

Baked Stuffed Potatoes [*USA*] Bake potatoes in their jackets, scoop out the pulp, mash and add butter, soured cream and chives. Pile back into the shells, sprinkle with lardons of bacon and butter then gratinate.

Baked Stuffed Potatoes [*Töltött Burgonya Hungary*] Bake potatoes in their jackets, scoop out the centres and fill with a mixture of the mashed potato, cooked minced meat, soured cream and butter, then bake.

Baked Sweet Potatoes with Chestnuts [***Batata Doce Recheada com Castanhas*** *Portugal*]   Bake sweet potatoes in their jackets, scoop out the pulp, mash it and combine with chestnut purée. Fill back into the shells, sprinkle with grated cheese and butter then gratinate.

Baked Sweet Potato with Chives [*Caribbean*]   Cook peeled sweet potatoes in salted water, drain and mash. Stir in flour, baking powder, chopped chives, diced tomato flesh and cloves of crushed garlic and flavour with allspice. Divide the mixture into 2-cm medallions, place onto baking sheets, sprinkle with melted butter and bake in the oven until golden.

Boulangère Potatoes [***Pommes Boulangère*** *France*]   Combine sliced potato, sliced onion and chopped parsley in a colander and season with salt. Place into an earthenware dish, arrange sliced potatoes overlapping on top, moisten with stock, sprinkle with butter and bake until golden and the liquid almost evaporated.

Delmonico Potatoes [***Pommes Delmonico*** *France*]   Cook 1·5-cm cubes of potato in milk. Place into an earthenware dish with some of the milk, sprinkle with breadcrumbs and butter and gratinate in the oven.

Fondant Potatoes [***Pommes Fondantes*** *France*]   Place barrel-shaped potatoes into a shallow dish, moisten with stock, season with salt, brush the surface with butter and bake in the oven until golden and the liquid almost evaporated.

Moulded Potatoes with Artichokes and Truffle [***Pommes Mireille*** *France*]   Heat a little oil in an anna mould, and combine julienne strips of potato, quarters of artichoke bottoms, small pieces of truffle and seasoning. Fill the mould with the potato mixture, brush with butter and bake for approx. 45 min. When cooked remove from the mould, cut into portions and serve.

Savoyarde Potatoes [***Pommes Savoyarde*** *France*]   Combine sliced potato, sliced onion, blanched lardons of bacon and chopped parsley in a colander and season with salt. Place into an earthenware dish, arrange sliced potatoes overlapping on top, moisten with stock, sprinkle with grated cheese and butter and bake until golden and the liquid almost evaporated.

Scalloped Potatoes with Pimento [*USA*]   Combine sliced potatoes with milk, cream, garlic, skinned and diced red pimento and chopped fresh green chilli and parsley. Place the mixture into shallow dishes, sprinkle with Gruyère and Parmesan cheeses and bake.

Boiled Potatoes

Application

Potatoes are covered with cold water, salt is added and the potatoes brought to the boil and gently simmered until cooked.

Boiled New Potatoes in Red Wine with Coriander [*Afelia* *Greece*]   Lightly fry new potatoes in their skins in corn oil, moisten with red wine, add coriander seeds and simmer. Serve in the liquid sprinkled with chopped coriander leaves.

Boiled Candied Potatoes [*Israel*]   Boil new potatoes in their skins then peel. Lightly caramelise sugar and butter and roll and glaze the potatoes in the caramel mixture.

Boiled Glazed Sweet Potatoes [*Caribbean*] Boil sliced sweet potatoes and drain. Brush earthenware dishes with oil, season and arrange the potato in layers, neatly overlapping. Sprinkle with oil, white rum and demerara sugar and glaze in the oven.

Boiled New Potatoes with Cinnamon and Caraway [*Caribbean*] Boil new potatoes in their skins then cut into slices. Lightly fry chopped garlic and grated ginger in corn oil, add the potatoes and sauté until golden, then flavour with ground cinnamon and caraway seeds and season with salt and cayenne pepper. Sprinkle with chopped coriander and serve.

Boiled New Potatoes with Cottage Cheese [*Caribbean*] Marinate onion rings with salt, cayenne pepper and lemon juice. Lightly fry sliced fresh green chillies in olive oil. Blend cottage cheese with turmeric, the chillies and their pan juices, add halves of boiled new potatoes and serve garnished with the marinated onion rings.

Boiled New Potatoes with Dill and Crème Fraîche [***Kartofel s Kremom*** *Russia*] Boil peeled new potatoes, drain then roll them in crème fraîche and chopped dill.

Boiled New Potatoes with Turmeric [***Patatas Frescas en Ajopollo*** *Spain*] Golden fry garlic, almonds and breadcrumbs in olive oil then liquidise with parsley, turmeric and water. Boil and reduce the mixture to a sauce consistency, add peeled new potatoes and cook gently.

Boiled Potatoes in Miso [***Jaga-imo Miso-ni*** *Japan*] Parboil quartered pieces of potato in salted water and drain. Soften miso in dashi and strain. Cover the potatoes with the dashi, bring to simmering then add the miso and cook. Serve the potatoes coated with some of the liquid and garnish with blanched sliced okra.

Boiled Potatoes in Soured Cream [***Savanyúburgonya-fozelék*** *Hungary*] Flavour velouté sauce with paprika and a reduction of vinegar and bayleaves then add sliced cooked potatoes and finish with soured cream.

Boiled Potatoes in Tomato Sauce [***Paradicsomos Burgonya*** *Hungary*] To tomato sauce add lardons of bacon and sliced cooked potatoes; finish with soured cream.

Boiled Potato Tumble [***Jaga-imo Nikkorogashi*** *Japan*] Parboil quartered pieces of potato in salt water and drain. Parboil konnyaku for 1 min, drain and chop. Stir-fry the potatoes with shiitake mushrooms, grated burdock root, strips of pork and small chicken drumsticks. Moisten with dashi and dark soy sauce, add konnyaku and sugar and cook until the liquid is completely reduced.

Boiled Potatoes with Almonds [***Patatas en Ajopollo*** *Spain*] Golden fry sliced French bread, almonds, garlic and parsley in oil. Blend the mixture with stock, a few strands of saffron and seasoning. Cook diced potatoes in the almond mixture until tender and serve sprinkled with chopped fresh herbs.

Boiled Potatoes with Belly of Pork [***Batatas à Alentejana*** *Portugal*] Golden fry lardons of belly of pork then add new potatoes, cover with water and boil; serve sprinkled with chopped parsley.

Boiled Potatoes with Marjoram [***Majorannàs Burgonyafozelék*** *Hungary*] Flavour jus lié with marjoram, add sliced cooked potatoes and finish with soured cream.

Boiled Potatoes with Pimento [***Batatas à Colombina*** *Portugal*] Boil potatoes, drain and mix them with a julienne of cooked red pimento.

Boiled Potatoes with Tomato and Pimento [*Papas Viudas* Spain]   Sauté chopped onion and garlic, diced green pimento and tomato flesh in oil, add bayleaves and thyme and cook, then toss sliced boiled potatoes in the mixture.

Boiled Savoury Potatoes in Yogurt [*Palak Alu* India]   Boil potatoes in their skins, and when half cooked remove the skins and cut into cubes. Fry dried crushed red chillies and black mustard seeds in ghee then add the potatoes and golden fry. Stir-fry grated ginger in ghee, add chopped spinach, stir in natural yogurt, then add the potatoes and season. Serve sprinkled with chopped coriander leaves.

Boiled Savoury Potatoes with Tomatoes [*Alu Tariwale* India]   Boil potatoes in their skins, and when half cooked peel and cut into slices. Fry cumin, coriander and mustard seeds in ghee then add ground turmeric and chilli, tomato concassée and water; add the sliced potatoes and simmer until the liquid has completely reduced. Serve sprinkled with chopped onion.

Maître d'Hotel Potatoes [*Pommes Maître d'Hotel* France]   Place sliced steamed potatoes into a shallow pan, moisten with milk, season with salt, pepper and nutmeg and simmer until cooked. Finish by adding a little cream to the potatoes.

Mashed Potatoes [GB]   Boil potatoes in salted water, drain, dry, pass through a sieve, add butter and warm milk and season with salt, pepper and nutmeg.

Mashed Potatoes with Poppy Seeds [Israel]   Soak poppy seeds in boiling water, drain and repeat the process; drain then blend to a fine paste. Boil potatoes in their skins then peel and mash them. Mix with boiling milk, the poppy seed paste and seasoning.

Minted New Potatoes [GB]   Boil new potatoes in water with mint, drain, brush with butter and serve garnished with blanched mint leaves.

Parsley Potatoes [GB]   Boil new or trimmed potatoes in salted water, drain and roll in melted butter with chopped parsley

Spiced Mashed Potatoes [*Alu Bartha* India]   Boil potatoes in their skins, then peel and mash them. Fry mustard seeds in ghee, then add and golden fry sliced fresh green chillies and chopped onion. Add turmeric, garam masala, salt, chilli powder and lemon juice. Add and combine the mashed potato and serve sprinkled with chopped coriander leaves.

Deep-fried Potatoes

Application

Raw shaped or moulded mashed potatoes are cooked until crisp and golden in a deep amount of oil at a temperature of 160–190 °C.

Chips [GB]   Cut potatoes 6 cm × 1 cm × 1 cm, wash and dry. Blanch in deep fat at 170 °C until soft but not coloured. Increase temperature of fat to 190 °C and fry until golden and crisp.

Dauphine Potatoes [*Pommes Dauphine* France]   Combine dry mashed potato, egg yolks and chou paste, and season with salt, pepper and nutmeg. Mould cork- or egg-shaped and deep fry until golden.

Florentin Potatoes [*Pommes Florentin* France]   Combine dry mashed potato, butter, egg yolks and diced ham. Mould into flat oblong shapes, pass through seasoned flour, eggwash and broken vermicelli then deep fry until golden.

Fried Potatoes with Almonds [*Alu Badam* India]   Deep fry small new potatoes and combine them with grilled flaked almonds and garam masala.

Fried Sweet Potato [*Caribbean*]   Slice sweet potato and soak in cold salted water. Drain and deep fry in groundnut oil.

Fried Sweet Potato Balls [*Pilus* Indonesia]   Boil sweet potato then mash. Add palm sugar and rice flour to form a firm mixture. Roll into marble-sized pieces, deep fry and serve them plain or accompanied by grated fresh coconut.

Potato Fritters [*Burgonyatekercs* Hungary]   Make a stiff dough mixture with dry mashed potato, flour, eggs and egg yolks. Roll out, spread with a mixture of minced ham and soured cream and roll as a Swiss roll. Cut into slices, pass through breadcrumbs and deep fry.

Spiced Matchstick Potatoes [*Alu Lachche* India]   Cut peeled potatoes matchstick shape, deep fry and season with salt, chilli powder, ground cumin and garam masala.

Sweet Potato Fritters [*Caribbean*]   Pass slices of sweet potato through batter and deep fry in groundnut oil.

Shallow-fried Potatoes

Application

Raw or partially boiled or steamed potatoes, either cut into slices or barrel-shaped, are cooked in a small amount of fat or oil in a frying pan on top of the stove.

Farmhouse Potato Cakes [*Bauernfrühstück* Germany]   Golden fry small diced potato in oil with sliced onion and gherkins, diced smoked ham and red pimento. Whisk together eggs and milk, season with salt, nutmeg and caraway seeds then pour onto the cooked potato mixture and cook to form a golden cake. Serve garnished with chopped chives and sliced tomato.

Fried Sweet Potato [*Kentang Coloh-Coloh* Indonesia]   Blend onion, garlic, sambal ulek, sweet soy sauce and soft brown sugar to a paste then fry in oil for 1 min. Peel and slice steamed sweet potatoes, sprinkle with lemon juice and salt then golden shallow fry in oil. Serve sprinkled with sautéed diced tomato flesh, red pimento and chopped coriander, accompanied by the paste.

Galette Potatoes [*Pommes Galette* France]   Combine dry mashed potato with egg yolks and butter, and season with salt, pepper and nutmeg. Mould into small flat cakes, mark trellis-fashion then shallow fry in a minimum amount of oil until golden.

Hashed Brown Potatoes [*USA*]   Grate potatoes then drain in a sieve. Combine with beaten eggs, flour and baking powder. Shape into small cakes or mould with a spoon and golden shallow fry.

Parisienne Potatoes [*Pommes Parisienne* France]   Scoop out balls of potato using a special ball cutter. Shallow fry potato balls in oil until golden and soft, season with salt and serve sprinkled with chopped parsley.

Potato Cakes [*Burgonyakotlett* Hungary]   Soak white breadcrumbs in milk then bring the mixture to boiling point; squeeze in a muslin to remove excess moisture. Combine grated raw potato with the bread and add beaten eggs, flour and nutmeg. Spoon the mixture into hot oil and golden shallow fry.

Potato Cakes [*Kamjabuchim* Korea]   Grate raw potatoes, squeeze out excess moisture then combine with chopped spring onions and fresh chillies. Bind the potato mixture with flour and eggs to form a batter. Spoon the mixture into hot oil and golden shallow fry. Serve accompanied by chojang vinegar dipping sauce.

Potato Cakes German Style [*Kartoffelkroketten* Germany]   Boil potatoes then mash and combine with butter, eggs and flour and season with nutmeg. Mould into oval cakes and shallow fry.

Potato and Burghul Cakes with Cinnamon [*Kibbet Batata Bi Sanieh* Middle East]   Boil potatoes in their skins, peel and mash. Combine the mashed potato with soaked burghul, grated onion, chopped mint and parsley and season with cinnamon. Knead the mixture until firm then cool in a shallow tray. Cut into diamond shapes and golden shallow fry.

Potato and Mushroom Crescents [*Kartofelnye Kotlety* Russia]   Boil potatoes then mash them and combine with butter, eggs and cooked sliced mushrooms and season with nutmeg. Mould into crescents, coat with flour, eggwash and breadcrumbs then shallow fry. Serve accompanied by soured cream.

Potatoes in Herb Sauce [*Patatas en Salsa Verde* Spain]   Sauté sliced potato in garlic-flavoured olive oil with chopped onion; when almost cooked, drain off the oil and transfer the potatoes and onion to a shallow pan. Moisten with chicken stock, add fried and crushed garlic, mixed chopped fresh herbs and seasoning and simmer until cooked.

Potato Latkes [Israel]   Grate raw potatoes then drain on a sieve. Combine the potato with beaten eggs, flour and baking powder. Shape into small cakes or mould with a spoon and shallow fry.

Potato Latkes Russian Style [*Pampushki* Russia]   Grate raw potatoes then drain on a sieve. Combine the potato with beaten eggs, flour and baking powder. Shape into small cakes and fill the centres with either: cooked minced beef, onion and chopped fresh herbs; cottage or curd cheese and chopped fresh herbs; or smetana and chopped fresh herbs. Shallow fry in hot oil until golden.

Potato Pancakes [*Kartoffelpfannkuchen* Germany]   Grate raw potatoes then drain on a sieve. Combine the potato with grated onion, beaten eggs and flour to the consistency of a batter. Fry spoonfuls of the mixture in the form of pancakes until golden on each side.

Potato Pancakes Korean Style [*Ganja Buchin* Korea]   Grate raw potatoes to a pulp and combine with grated onion, beaten egg and cornflour. Fry scone-sized spoonfuls of the mixture in oil and serve accompanied by hot fermented bean paste.

Potato Pancakes Russian Style [*Olad'i* Russia]   Grate raw potatoes to a pulp and drain on a sieve. Dissolve yeast in warm water, stir into flour and combine with the potato; add beaten eggs, nutmeg and chopped herbs. Allow to prove. Fry scone-sized pieces in oil, drain and serve accompanied by smetana.

Potato Puris [*Alu Puri* India]   Boil potatoes then mash them and combine with flour to form a firm dough. Mould into small balls and shallow fry in ghee.

Sautéed Potatoes in Egg Custard [*Zharennyi Kartofel* *Russia*] Sauté sliced potato in butter, and when the edges become crisp, moisten with a mixture of beaten eggs, milk and seasoning. Allow the egg custard to set, turn out and serve sprinkled with chopped dill.

Sautéed Potatoes with Turmeric [*Israel*] Parboil new potatoes in salted water flavoured with turmeric. Drain then sauté them in grapeseed oil and serve sprinkled with chopped coriander.

Spicy Sautéed Potatoes [*Patatas à La Brava* *Spain*] Sauté diced potato in olive oil; sauté chopped onion and garlic then add to the cooked potatoes. Drain, season and serve the potatoes accompanied by tomato sauce flavoured with white wine, Tabasco sauce and diced dried red chilli pepper.

Stuffed Potato Medallions [*Alu Chap* *India*] Combine dry mashed potato with chopped mint, spring onions and fresh green chillies. Shape into medallions and fill the centres with cooked minced meat. Pass through flour, eggwash and breadcrumbs and fry in ghee.

Filling: fry chopped onion, garlic, grated ginger and minced beef in ghee. Stir in curry powder, lemon juice and stock. When cooked sprinkle with garam masala and chopped coriander leaves.

Roast Potatoes

Roast Potatoes [*GB*] Trim potatoes barrel-shaped, place into shallow hot fat, season with salt and cook in the oven at 200 °C until golden.

Chapter Twelve

Desserts, Sweetmeats and Breads

This chapter is divided into six main areas:

✧ Basic Preparations ✧

✧ Tortes, gâteaux, strudels, cakes, flans and tartlets ✧

✧ Cold Sweets ✧

✧ Hot Sweets ✧

✧ Sweetmeats ✧

✧ Breads and flour products ✧

Basic Preparations

Pastry

Cheesecake Pastry [*Israel*]   Cream together 75 g icing sugar, 150 g butter, 2 yolks of egg and vanilla essence. Mix in 225 g soft flour and 12 g baking powder to form a basic pastry.

Chou Pastry (makes 1¼ l)   Boil 600 ml water, ¼ tsp salt, 2 tsp sugar and 225 g butter. Stir in 275 g strong flour then gradually beat in 8 beaten eggs.

Filo Pastry [*Greece and Middle East*]   Add 450 ml warm water and 75 ml olive oil to 675 g strong flour and 1 tsp salt to form a dough. Allow to rest then roll out very thinly, ideally using a rolling machine.

Pain de Gênes [*France*]   Mix 100 g ground almonds and 75 g sugar. Mix 125 g butter and 75 g sugar until fluffy. Add the almond mixture and 3 beaten eggs, one by one; then fold in 50 g cornflour and 75 ml kirsch. Bake in an 18-cm square cake tin at 180 °C for 45 min.

Pastry Cream [*Crème Pâtissière France*]   Mix 3 eggs, 5 egg yolks, 250 g caster sugar and 150 g flour. Heat 1 l milk with vanilla essence, pour onto the egg mixture whisking well, then return to the saucepan and boil to thicken.

Puff Pastry (makes 650 g)   To 225 g strong flour add 75 ml cold water and 25 ml lemon juice and knead to form a smooth dough. Cut the top of the dough, pull out the corners and roll out flat to form a star. Place 225 g slightly softened butter in the centre, enclose the star ends and roll out to 20 × 50 cm. Give four double turns, wrapping and resting the pastry between each double turn.

Samosa Basic Recipe   Rub 50 g butter into 100 g each strong white and wholemeal flours and 1 tsp salt and mix to a dough with 75 ml boiling water.

Savarin Paste (makes 650 g)   Dilute 30 g yeast in 50 ml warm milk and pour into 450 g warmed strong flour, then add 8 beaten eggs and form a paste. Place 225 g softened butter pieces on top and prove until doubled in volume. Beat in the butter to form a smooth elastic dough and allow to rest for 10 min before use.

Short Pastry (makes 650 g)   Rub in 100 g butter and 100 g lard into 450 g flour and ¼ tsp salt; add 50 ml cold water and mix to form a smooth pastry.

Strudel Pastry (makes 400 g)   Mix together 30 ml olive oil, 125 ml tepid water, 50 g caster sugar and 1 yolk of egg then pour into a bay made in 225 g strong flour to form a dough; knead until smooth and silky.

Suet Pastry (makes 1 kg)   Combine 500 g flour, 2 tsp baking powder, ¼ tsp salt and 300 g suet and mix in 250 ml cold water to form a pastry.

Sweet Pastry (makes 1 kg)   Sift 450 g soft flour with ¼ tsp salt, rub in 275 g butter then add 2 beaten eggs and 125 g caster sugar and mix with 1 tbs water to form a pastry.

Biscuits and Sponges

Genoese Sponge   Whisk together 5 eggs and 150 g caster sugar until it is thick and creamy, then gently fold in 150 g soft flour and 75 ml melted butter. Pour into a 23-cm diameter greased and floured tin and bake at 195 °C for 30 min.

Chocolate Genoese Sponge   Proceed as for Genoese Sponge, replacing 25 g of the flour with cocoa powder.

Lady's Finger Biscuits [*Biscuits à la Cuillère* France]   Whisk 5 egg yolks and 125 g caster sugar until thick then fold in 4 stiffly beaten egg whites and 125 g flour. Pipe 9-cm lengths, sprinkle with caster sugar and bake at 220 °C for 10 min.

Batters

Flour Batter [*Kourkoúti-Salangoúta* Greece]   Warm 450 g flour, whisk in 500 ml warm water to form a batter then add 50 ml olive oil, 2 beaten eggs and seasoning, and strain.

Frying Batter   Whisk 225 ml light ale into 100 g flour to form a batter, season, add 25 ml oil and $\frac{1}{4}$ tsp sugar, strain then fold in 2 stiffly beaten egg whites.

Massa Vinhe Batter [*Portugal*]   Combine 450 g flour, a pinch of salt, 100 ml olive oil, 100 ml beer and 4 egg yolks to form a batter, strain then fold in 3 stiffly beaten egg whites.

Pakora Batter [*India*]   Add 1 tsp each of chilli powder, garam masala and ajowan powder and $\frac{1}{4}$ tsp dried mint to 175 g flour and 1 tsp salt, then whisk in 450 ml water to form a batter. Strain the batter and use as required.

Pancake Batter   Whisk 3 eggs, 30 g sugar and 725 ml milk into 350 g flour with $\frac{1}{4}$ tsp salt to form a smooth batter, then strain.

Tempura Batter [*Japan*]   Combine 2 beaten eggs and 225 ml chilled water and whisk into 225 g flour, then strain.

Yeast Batter   Dissolve 12 g yeast in 600 ml warm water and whisk in 2 eggs and 50 ml corn oil. Sift 450 g plain flour with $\frac{1}{2}$ tsp salt and 1 tsp sugar, and add the prepared liquid slowly whilst whisking briskly to make a smooth batter. Allow to rise then whisk again before using.

Yorkshire Pudding Batter [*GB*]   Combine 2 beaten eggs and 400 ml milk and whisk into 225 g flour and $\frac{1}{2}$ tsp salt to form a batter. Strain the batter and allow to rest before using.

Sweet Sauces

Apricot Glaze   Boil 450 g apricot jam, 250 g sugar and 150 ml water to thread stage (103 °C) then strain.

Coconut Cream Sauce   Heat 400 ml coconut cream and simmer until it thickens.

Custard Sauce   Dilute 100 g custard powder with 275 g milk and 100 g sugar. Boil 850 ml milk, pour onto the custard, return to the pan and bring to the boil.

Gula Malacca Sauce   Cut 200 g palm sugar into pieces, add to 200 ml boiling water and simmer until it thickens.

Lemon Sauce   Heat 125 ml water, 150 g sugar, 3 egg yolks, 100 g butter and the grated zest and juice of 1 lemon until it thickens, but do not allow it to boil.

Stock Syrup   Boil together 1 l water with 750 g sugar until the sugar is dissolved.

Vanilla Custard   Heat 500 ml milk; whisk together 5 yolks of egg, 125 g sugar and vanilla essence, pour on the milk and cook until it thickens, but do not allow it to boil.

Tortes, Gâteaux, Strudels, Cakes and Flans

Almond Flan [*Tarte de Amendoa* Portugal]   Whisk together 6 eggs and 225 g caster sugar then add 225 g ground almonds, 150 g flour and 20 ml brandy. Pour into a flan case and bake at 180 °C for 30 min. Decorate with meringue and bake until golden.

Almond Torte [*Linzertorte* Germany]   Make a paste with 150 g sugar, 150 g ground almonds, ½ tsp ground cinnamon, cloves and nutmeg and mix in 150 g butter, 3 yolks of egg and the grated zest and juice of half a lemon. Spread ¾ of the paste in a 23-cm diameter sponge tin and cover it with raspberry jam. Arrange strips of the same paste lattice-fashion on top and bake at 180 °C for 40 min.

Apfel Strudel [*Israel*]   Stretch strudel pastry very thinly indeed, brush with melted butter then sprinkle with 100 g fried breadcrumbs and cover with 1.5 kg sliced cooking apples, 150 g caster sugar, 175 g sultanas, cinnamon, slivered almonds and the zest and juice of 1 lemon. Sprinkle with butter then fold in the sides and roll up lengthwise. Brush with butter and bake at 190 °C for 40 min, then dredge with icing sugar.

Apple Flan [*Flan aux Pommes Caramelisé* France]   Line a flan ring with sweet pastry and bake blind. Caramelise 100 g butter and 100 g sugar, add 750 g sliced cooking apples and 100 g chopped hazelnuts, cook, then add the juice of 1 lemon or lime and cool. Fill the flan with the mixture and arrange overlapping slices of apple on top. Bake at 200 °C for 25 min and brush with apricot glaze.

Apple Meringue [*Fransk Äppelkakka* Scandinavia]   Poach halves of cooking apples and place in dishes, cut sides downwards. Whisk yolks of egg and sugar to the ribbon stage, add ground almonds and fold in stiffly beaten whites. Coat the apples and bake for 20 min.

Apple Pandowdy [*USA*]   Mix 2 kg sliced apples with 75 g sugar, 50 ml dark molasses and mixed spice, and place into a flan dish. Arrange overlapping 5-cm circles of pastry on top and bake at 200 °C for 45 min. Serve accompanied by lemon sauce.

Pastry: mix 150 ml double cream into 450 g self-raising flour with 30 g caster sugar and 1 tsp salt to form a dough.

Apple and Cheese Pie [*GB*]   Combine 1 kg sliced apple, 150 g grated Wensleydale cheese, 100 g caster sugar, 4 cloves and 50 ml water and fill a baking tin lined with short pastry. Cover with a lid of pastry and bake at 200 °C for 15 min, then reduce the temperature to 180 °C and bake for 30 min.

Apple and Tapioca Bake [*Appel Sagogryn* Scandinavia]   Cook 100 g tapioca in water. Place 1.5 kg peeled and quartered apples into an oiled baking dish, sprinkle with 175 g soft brown sugar or honey, coat with the drained tapioca, sprinkle with ground nutmeg and bake at 180 °C for 1 hr.

Baklava [*Greece*]   Combine 450 g chopped walnuts and 225 g almonds, 50 g caster sugar and ground cinnamon and cloves. Line a dish with buttered sheets of filo pastry. Layer with half the nut mixture, cover with filo pastry, layer with the rest of the nut mixture and top with layers of filo pastry. Brush with butter and sprinkle with water. Bake at 160 °C for 1 hr. Boil to small thread (104 °C) 600 ml water, 50 ml lemon juice, 350 g sugar, 50 g honey, 3 cloves and cinnamon; strain and cool. Cut the baklava into diamond shapes, and ladle over with the syrup.

Black Forest Gâteau [*Schwarzwalden Kuchen* Germany]   Cut a chocolate Genoese into three layers, sprinkle with kirsch-flavoured stock syrup and spread the bottom and middle layers with kirsch-flavoured whipped cream. Arrange stoned black cherries all over and re-form the cake. Coat with the same cream, cover the sides with chocolate shavings and decorate the top with piped cream, glazed black cherries and chocolate shavings.

Blueberry Pie [*USA*]   Line a 23-cm pie dish with sweet pastry, and fill with 675 g blueberries combined with 75 g caster sugar, 50 g flour and 50 ml lemon juice; sprinkle with 12 g butter. Cover the fruit with pastry and bake at 180 °C for 40 min.

Cherry Clafoutis [*Clafoutis* France]   Place 450 g stoned black cherries into a buttered 20-cm dish. Whisk together 50 g flour, 50 g caster sugar and 2 eggs, then add 400 ml hot milk and 75 ml kirsch or cognac. Strain over the cherries and cook at 180 °C for 45 min. When cooked sprinkle with caster sugar.

Cherry Kreplach [*Israel*]   Whisk 4 eggs and 300 ml water then add to 675 g flour to form a dough. Make 8-cm diameter turnovers filled with 2–3 stoned poached cherries. Poach the kreplach in simmering water for 5 min then drain. Serve accompanied by soured cream mixed with sugar and cinnamon.

Cherry Strudel [*Kirschen Strüdel* Germany]   Poach 1.5 kg black or morello cherries in stock syrup, thicken the liquid with arrowroot and allow to cool. Stretch 450 g strudel pastry, sprinkle with fried breadcrumbs, then cover with the cherries. Sprinkle with butter then fold in the sides and roll up lengthwise. Brush with butter and bake at 190 °C for 40 min. Dredge with icing sugar.

Curd Cheese Flan [*Tarte au Fromage Blanc* France]   Line a flan ring with puff pastry. Crumble 450 g unsalted curd cheese, stir in 100 g caster sugar, 25 g flour, 2 egg yolks, 50 g melted butter and $\frac{1}{4}$ tsp salt, then fold in 2 stiffly beaten egg whites. Fill the flan with this mixture and bake at 230 °C for 10 min, then at 190 °C for 35 min. Sprinkle with icing sugar and glaze.

Dutch Apple Tart [*GB*]   Line a flan ring with sweet pastry and fill it with apple purée mixed with a few sultanas. Cover with pastry and bake at 210 °C for 35 min.

Fruit Kugel [*Israel*]   Combine 300 g cake crumbs moistened with 100 ml water, 150 ml red wine, 2 beaten eggs, 100 g each of diced apple, pear, raisins, plums or prunes, grated zest and juice of 1 lemon, $\frac{1}{4}$ tsp each of ground cinnamon, allspice, cloves and salt and 150 g chicken fat or shortening. Bake in a shallow dish au bain-marie at 150 °C for 4 hr.

Glazed Apple and Hazelnut Tartlets [*Pommes Bulgarienne* France]   Poach small peeled and cored apples in stock syrup and red wine. Fill the centres of the apples with pastry cream mixed with hazelnuts and raisins and place each in a pastry tartlet. Glaze the filled tartlets with the thickened syrup.

Honey Pie [*Melopita* *Greece*]   Combine 450 g Mitzithra or Ricotta cheese, 100 g honey, 25 g caster sugar, salt, 3 eggs, 50 ml lemon juice and 1 tsp ground cinnamon. Line a 20-cm flan ring with sweet pastry, pour in the filling and bake at 200 °C for 45 min. Dust with cinnamon and icing sugar and glaze.

Lemon Yogurt Flan [*GB*]   Line a flan ring with sweet pastry and bake blind. Boil 125 g plain yogurt, 175 g sugar, 75 ml lemon juice and salt in a double pan and thicken with 45 g cornflour. Pour into the flan case, cover with 3 whites of meringue and bake at 175 °C for 15 min.

Orange Roll [*Torta de Laranja* *Portugal*]   Dissolve 50 g cornflour in 300 ml orange juice then mix in 400 g caster sugar, grated zest of orange and 10 beaten eggs. Bake at 180 °C for 15 min and roll up Swiss-roll fashion.

Pumpkin Pie [*USA*]   Combine 450 g stiff pumpkin purée, 75 g brown sugar, 50 ml melted butter, 3 eggs and ½ tsp mixed spice, then fold in 300 ml whipped double cream. Line a 20-cm flan ring with sweet pastry and bake blind for 10 min, then fill with the pumpkin mixture and bake at 180 °C for 30 min.

Rum Babas [*Babas au Rhum* *France*]   Fill dariole moulds with savarin paste containing 50 g currants, prove until the moulds are full then bake at 220 °C for 15 min. Soak in stock syrup, sprinkle with rum and brush with apricot glaze.

Sachertorte [*Germany*]   Cream 150 g butter and 150 g icing sugar, add 6 yolks of egg then add 150 g melted plain chocolate. Whisk 6 whites of egg with 40 g icing sugar to a peak and fold into the creamed mixture together with 150 g soft flour. Fill into a 23-cm sponge tin and bake at 180 °C for 1 hr. Brush the top and sides with apricot glaze and coat with chocolate icing. Pipe the word 'Sacher' on top.

Spiced Semolina Pie [*Galatoboureko* *Greece*]   Boil 1 l milk with ¼ tsp salt, 175 g sugar, grated zest of 1 lemon, 50 g butter and cinnamon stick. Rain in 175 g fine semolina and cook for 5 min. Cool, then stir in 5 beaten eggs and a few drops of vanilla essence. Line a shallow dish with 4 sheets of filo pastry, pour in the semolina mixture, cover with 4 more sheets of filo pastry, brush with butter, score and bake at 180 °C for 45 min. Remove and cool. Boil 225 g sugar, 275 ml water, 50 ml lemon juice and a cinnamon stick to small thread (104 °C). Strain the syrup, pour over the pie and serve chilled.

Sweet Potato Pie [*Batata Pie* *Middle East*]   Cook 675 g peeled sweet potato in water, mash and add 50 g butter, 25 ml honey and seasoning of ground nutmeg and ginger. Stir in 150 ml milk and 2 beaten eggs. Pour the mixture into a shallow dish, sprinkle with chopped dates and butter and bake at 180 °C for 45 min.

Sweet Potato and Coconut Pie [*Caribbean*]   Peel and boil 1 kg sweet potato in water with the juice and rind of 2 limes; drain, cool and mash. Combine with 450 g grated coconut, 2 egg yolks, 350 g caster sugar, ½ tsp ground cinnamon and a few drops of vanilla essence. Place the mixture into an oiled pie dish and bake at 180 °C for 1¼ hr.

Hot and Cold Sweets

Charlottes

Apple Charlotte [*GB*]   Slice 2 kg apples, add 200 g melted butter, cinnamon and sugar and cook to a firm purée. Arrange buttered bread fingers overlapping around the insides and bottoms of moulds. Fill the moulds with the apple and top with bread fingers. Bake at 210°C for 40 min. Serve accompanied by hot apricot sauce.

Charlotte Russe [*Sharlotka* *Russia*]   Make a Crème Anglaise with 5 egg yolks, 150 g sugar, 600 ml milk and a vanilla pod. Add 25 g soaked leaf gelatine, allow to cool then whisk in 600 ml whipped cream. Pour into moulds lined with lady's finger biscuits and allow to set. Turn out of the moulds onto a dish, tie a red ribbon around the centre and serve accompanied by raspberry coulis flavoured with kirsch.

Matzos Shalet [*Israel*]   Beat 6 egg yolks then add 4 matzos softened with hot water, 225 g butter pieces, 225 g brown sugar, 100 g nibbed almonds, 100 g raisins and 1 tsp cinnamon. Fold in 6 stiffly beaten egg whites then pour into prepared moulds and bake at 180 °C for 45 min.

Pear Dessert [*Arinal* *Middle East*]   Poach pear halves in stock syrup flavoured with blackcurrant liqueur. Mix 500 g crushed macaroons into 750 ml soured cream; add 10 yolks of egg, 200 g sugar and 50 ml blackcurrant liqueur then fold in 10 whisked whites of egg. Fill dariole moulds with the mixture and cook au bain-marie at 180 °C for 35 min. Serve the soufflés with the pears, coated with the reduced and thickened syrup and sprinkled with slivered almonds.

Cheesecakes

Cheesecake [*Melopita* *Greece*]   Line a 22-cm dish with pastry made with 175 g flour, salt, 125 g lard, 60 g sesame seeds and 1 egg. Sieve 750 g cottage cheese, add 175 g honey, 4 eggs, 25 g toasted sesame seeds and 1 tsp cinnamon. Fill into the dish, sprinkle with sesame seeds and bake at 175 °C for 45 min.

Cheesecake [*Israel*]   Line a flan ring with cheesecake pastry. Blend together 250 g curd cheese, 25 g ground almonds, grated zest and juice of lemon, vanilla essence and 75 g blanched currants. Whisk 3 egg whites to a stiff peak, whisk in 50 g caster sugar then fold into the curd mixture. Fill the flan case with the curd mixture, arrange pastry lattice-fashion on top and brush with egg white. Sprinkle with granulated sugar and bake at 180 °C for 40 min.

Cheesecake Russian Style [*Paskha* *Russia*]   To 1 kg cream cheese add salt and 50 g each of chopped almonds, raisins and candied peel. Cream 150 g butter and 250 g sugar, mix in 1 egg and 5 yolks, and add the cream cheese mixture. Fold in 250 ml whipped cream and vanilla essence and heat until it thickens. Pour into a pyramid-shaped mould lined with gauze, place a weight on top and chill. De-mould and serve accompanied by cream.

Chocolate and Orange Cheesecake [*Cassata Italiana* *Italy*]   Beat together 1 kg Ricotta cheese, 125 g caster sugar, vanilla essence and the grated zest of 2 oranges; fold in 275 g mixed crystallised fruit and 100 g grated bitter chocolate. Line a 23-cm flan ring with sponge fingers then sprinkle with 50 ml rum; fill the flan with the cheese mixture, pressing it down firmly, and place into the refrigerator. De-mould and decorate with crystallised fruit, then dredge with icing sugar.

Egg Custard-based Desserts

Bread and Butter and Cherry Pudding [*Kirschenmichel* Germany] Sprinkle 100 g stoned cherries into shallow pie dishes, cover with 5 slices of buttered bread, crusts removed and cut into triangles, then sprinkle with rum. Whisk together 1.5 l milk, 9 eggs, 180 g sugar and vanilla essence. Pour the mixture over the bread, sprinkle with caster sugar and bake au bain-marie in the oven at 170 °C.

Burnt Sugar Pudding [*Brulepudding* Scandinavia] Boil 225 g sugar and 125 ml water to a light caramel; add 225 g chopped almonds and line the sides and bottoms of charlotte moulds with the mixture. Heat 1.75 l milk and whisk onto 6 beaten eggs, 25 g cornflour, salt and almond essence. Strain the mixture into the moulds and cook au bain-marie in an oven at 165 °C for 1 hr. Serve hot or chilled.

Coconut Custard [*Vattalappam* India] Warm 850 ml coconut milk, 300 ml evaporated milk, 150 ml water, ½ tsp ground cardamom, ¼ tsp ground mace, 3 cloves and 25 ml rose-water and whisk onto 6 beaten eggs and 100 g palm sugar. Strain the mixture, pour into dariole moulds and cook au bain-marie in the oven at 165 °C for 40 min. Chill, then turn out of the moulds and serve.

Orange Caramel Pudding [GB] Line dariole moulds with caramelised sugar. Warm 1 l milk and whisk onto 6 whole eggs, 4 yolks, 125 g sugar and the grated zest of 4 oranges previously mixed together. Strain the mixture into the moulds and cook au bain-marie in the oven at 165 °C for 40 min. Decorate with segments of orange.

Tansy [GB] Whisk 5 whole eggs and 5 whites of egg with 150 g sugar, and add 400 ml warmed milk and 200 ml boiled cream. Cook until it thickens, then mix in 225 g crushed sweet biscuits, 50 g butter, 50 ml sherry, 50 ml orange-flower water, a pinch of salt, 50 g chopped tansy leaves and green colour. Pour into a greased pie dish and bake au bain-marie at 150 °C for 45 min. Turn out and cover with slices of orange.

Zuppa Inglese [Italy] Sprinkle 18 lady's finger biscuits with strong black coffee, 18 with brandy and 18 with Sambuca liqueur. Arrange the biscuits in layers in glass bowls, divided by sweetened whipped cream and cover with cool vanilla custard. Serve cold.

Egg-based Sweets

Floating Islands [*Farófias* Portugal] Whisk 6 egg whites to a peak then fold in 50 g sugar. Using 6 egg yolks, 100 g sugar and 600 ml milk make an English custard. Poach moulded tablespoonsful of meringue mixture in the custard then drain them. Pour the custard into bowls, place the poached meringues on top and serve dusted with cinnamon.

Zabaglione Gritti Palace [Italy] Whisk 12 egg yolks, 400 g sugar and 300 ml Marsala over heat until it becomes thick, light and aerated. Add 6 sheets of soaked and melted gelatine and whisk until cold. Fill into glasses and serve decorated with whipped cream.

Zabaglione with Marsala [*Zabaglione alla Marsala* Italy] Whisk 8 egg yolks, 225 g sugar and 125 ml Marsala over hot water until trebled in volume. Pour into glass goblets and serve warm accompanied by lady's finger biscuits.

Note: the grated zest and juice of 2 oranges may be substituted for the wine, when the dish should be named Orange Zabaglione. The mixture may also be served chilled.

Hot and Cold Fruits

Baked Apples [*Bratäpfel* Germany] Combine some marzipan, apricot liqueur and soft brown sugar. Fill the centres of cored apples with the mixture, sprinkle with white wine, dot with butter and bake.

Baked Apples with Almonds [*Stekta Fyllda Applen* Scandinavia] Brush cored apples with melted butter and roll them in brown sugar. Fill the centres of the cored apples with marzipan, dot with butter and bake.

Bananas Flambé [*Plátanos Flambé* Mexico] Cook sliced bananas in butter, stir in sugar, add a little banana liqueur and cinnamon then flambé with Spanish brandy.

Bananas in Coconut and Turmeric Sauce [Caribbean] Boil 275 ml thick coconut milk, and add 100 g soft brown sugar, $\frac{1}{2}$ tsp turmeric and $\frac{1}{4}$ tsp salt. Remove from the heat and stir in 50 ml lemon or lime juice. Steam bananas in their skins, peel them and serve coated with the sauce.

Compote of Figs [*Incir Compostu* Turkey] Soak dried figs then insert a blanched almond into each fruit and poach in stock syrup with honey and lemon juice. Serve chilled, sprinkled with chopped nuts.

Compote of Fruits [*Khoshaf* Middle East] Poach soaked dried apricots, figs, prunes and seedless raisins in stock syrup then add a little orange-flower water. Serve either hot or chilled, sprinkled with pine nuts or slivered almonds.

Cranberry Fool [*Kisel Klyukvennyi* Russia] Boil cranberries with sugar, lemon juice and water. Once the fruit has disintegrated, liquidise, strain and reboil, then thicken with potato flour, strain and cool. Pour into coupes and chill before serving.

Cranberry Parfait [*Karpalojäädyke* Scandinavia] Whisk yolks of egg and sugar to the ribbon stage, flavour with cranberry purée and fold in whipped cream. Fill into a parfait mould and freeze for 4 hr.

Figs and Dates in White Wine [*Higos y Datiles en Vino Blanco* Spain] Poach dried figs and stoned dried dates in white wine with a little eau de vie and lemon juice, flavoured with cinnamon and cloves.

Flambéd Bananas [*Plátanos con Coñac* Spain] Cook bananas in a mixture of 450 g honey and 175 ml orange juice. Flambé the bananas with Spanish brandy and serve with some of the liquid.

Flambéd Fruit Salad [GB] Caramelise 450 g sugar and 450 ml water, then add 150 ml orange juice and reboil. Place fruit salad into a shallow pan, moisten with the hot caramel liquid and heat through. Flambé it with 125 ml brandy.

Fruit Salad au Gratin [*Gratinado de Frutas* Spain] Whisk together egg yolks and sugar then stir in heated cream and cook to thicken. Pour it over prepared liqueur-flavoured fruits then gratinate under a salamander.

Grapefruit, Orange and Ginger Salad [*Caribbean*]   Add 100 g grated ginger to an ordinary stock syrup and reduce it until it is thick, add the zest of grapefruits and oranges and finish with some kirsch. Place segments of grapefruit and orange in a bowl, moisten with the syrup and serve.

Hot Compote of Fruit [***Arrope*** *Spain*]   Poach stoned quinces and plums in stock syrup until tender, then drain. Poach halved peaches, apples and pears in the liquid from the quinces with 300 ml fresh grape juice and sufficient sugar. Place the fruits into dishes, reduce the liquor until it is fairly thick then pour over the fruit and serve.

Juice Fool [***Mehukisseli*** *Scandinavia*]   Bring sweetened berry juice to the boil, add diluted potato flour and reboil. Pour into moulds, allow to set and serve with whipped cream.

Mango Fool [*Caribbean*]   Add 1-cm pieces of mango flesh to 225 ml thick coconut milk with 100 g soft brown sugar and 125 ml lemon or lime juice. Pour into coupes or into the mango skins, chill and serve.

Mango with Glutinous Rice [***Mamuang Kuo Nieo*** *Thailand*]   Cook glutinous rice in thin coconut milk then flavour with salt and sugar. Pour the mixture into moulds, chill and serve decorated with sliced mango.

Oranges with Coconut [***Naranjas à la Canela*** *Mexico*]   Arrange peeled and sliced oranges on crushed ice and sprinkle with cinnamon, grated fresh coconut and orange liqueur.

Oranges in Caramel [***Aranci Caramellizzati*** *Italy*]   Prepare caramel with 450 ml water and 450 g sugar and a stick of cinnamon; as the mixture begins to turn golden remove the cinnamon then add 150 ml water and reboil. Cook strips of zest of orange in the caramel until candied, cool then pour the caramel sauce over sliced oranges.

Pears Poached in Red Wine [***Poires au Vin Rouge*** *France*]   Poach peeled whole pears in a syrup made with 1 bottle of red wine, 150 ml water, 175 g sugar and a cinnamon stick.

Pears Stuffed with Dates [***Peras Rellenas*** *Mexico*]   Macerate fresh stoned dates in brandy for 12 hr. Poach peeled and cored whole pears in stock syrup. Reduce the syrup then add some grenadine and lime juice. Stuff the pears with the dates and mask with the syrup.

Pineapple in Rum Sauce [*Caribbean*]   Macerate thin slices of pineapple in rum for 30 min. Heat 300 g butter, 200 g sugar, the rum from the pineapple and 5 yolks of egg to a coating consistency. Mask the pineapple with the sauce and sprinkle with slivered almonds.

Poached Figs [***Pàrolt Füge*** *Hungary*]   Wash dried figs in warm water then poach them in stock syrup made with white wine instead of water.

Pomegranate and Almond Coupes [*Israel*]   Combine pomegranate seeds and juice, chopped blanched almonds, sugar and orange-flower water or rosewater. Serve in coupes sprinkled with rosebuds or rose petals.

Pumpkin with Coconut Custard [***Fug Thong Sung-Khaya*** *Thailand*]   Whisk together eggs, thick coconut milk and palm sugar. Remove the seeds from a hollowed-out pumpkin then pour in the cream mixture and steam until tender.

Redcurrant and Raspberry Coupes [*Rod Grog* Scandinavia]   Cook 500 g red-currants and 250 g raspberries in a little water, then blend to a purée, reboil, add 350 g sugar and thicken with 30 g fine sago and 30 g potato flour diluted with 200 ml red wine. Boil then pour into dampened moulds and set in the refrigerator. De-mould and serve with soured cream or fromage frais.

Red Fruit Pudding [*Rodgrod* Scandinavia]   Cook a mixture of berries with sugar to a purée and thicken it with diluted arrowroot. Pour into serving dishes, allow to set and decorate with toasted almonds.

Strawberries in Rhône Wine [*Fraises au Châteauneuf-du-Pape* France]   Place 1 kg strawberries into a bowl, sprinkle with 75 g caster sugar, cover with red Rhône wine and allow to macerate for about 1 hr before serving.

Strawberry Kisel [*Kisel iz Klubniki* Russia]   Cook 1 kg strawberries in 1 l water then strain under light pressure. Add 250 g sugar to the juice, boil and thicken with 50g cornflour. Pour into an oiled mould and allow to set.

Strawberries Russian Style [*Fraises Romanov* Russia]   Macerate 1 kg strawberries in 100 ml Curaçao or Grand Marnier and 100 g sugar. Arrange level in dishes and pipe trellis-fashion on top with sweetened whipped cream.

Strawberries Sautéed with Orange Liqueur [*Fresas al Coñac* Mexico]   Lightly sauté strawberries in butter, stir in sugar, orange liqueur and zest of lime then flambé with brandy.

Summer Pudding [*GB*]   Lightly cook 450 g each of raspberries, redcurrants, black-currants and blackberries with 75 ml lemon juice and 450 g sugar. Line the bot-tom and sides of pudding basins with fingers of stale bread. Fill the moulds with the fruit mixture and cover the tops with fingers of bread. Cover and press under weight and refrigerate. Serve accompanied by cream.

Veiled Country Lass [*Bondepige met Slor* Scandinavia]   Melt butter in a shal-low pan and stir and fry white breadcrumbs and sugar until golden brown, crisp and dry; add grated plain chocolate and allow to cool slightly. Arrange layers of the crumb mixture and sieved stewed apple in pie dishes, finishing with the crumbs. Dot with butter and bake. Serve with whipped cream.

Soufflés

Banana Soufflé [*Caribbean*]   Heat 75 ml oil or butter, add the mashed pulp of 14 bananas, 100 g sugar and 25 ml rum and cook until stiff. Add the yolks of 3 eggs then fold in 3 stiffly whisked whites. Pipe back into 10 of the banana skins and bake at 200 °C for 8 min.

Chestnut Soufflé [*Soufflé de Castanhas* Portugal]   Combine 60 g caster sugar, 60 g butter and 2 eggs, add 200 g sweetened chestnut purée then fold in 3 stiffly whisked whites. Fill into buttered soufflé dishes and bake at 190 °C for 30 min.

Orange and Almond Soufflé [*Tortada de Naranja* Spain]   Whisk 6 egg yolks with 100 g sugar au bain-marie; when thick allow to cool slightly, beat in 175 g ground almonds and whisk until cold. Finally fold in 6 stiffly beaten egg whites, pour into prepared soufflé moulds and cook au bain-marie in the oven at 200 °C for 30 min. Thicken 225 ml orange juice and 100 g sugar with arrowroot. Turn out the soufflés, decorate with warmed segments of oranges then mask with the orange sauce.

Poached Pear Soufflé with Blackcurrant Liqueur [*Armal Middle East*]   Poach 10 halves of pears in stock syrup made with the addition of 50 ml blackcurrant liqueur. Combine 500 g crushed macaroons, 725 ml soured cream, 200 g caster sugar, 10 egg yolks and 50 ml blackcurrant liqueur then fold in 10 whisked whites of egg. Pour into prepared dariole moulds and cook au bain-marie in the oven at 190 °C for 35 min. De-mould and serve with poached pears, coated with the reduced and lightly thickened syrup and sprinkled with toasted slivered almonds.

Rum Pudding Soufflé [*Sufle Romovoe Russia*]   Cream 100 g butter with 100 g sugar then mix in 50 g flour. Add 50 ml rum then whisk in 200 ml boiling milk and almond flavouring and cook. Cool, add 100 g ground almonds and 6 egg yolks then fold in 8 stiffly beaten egg whites. Pour into prepared moulds and bake au bain-marie at 210 °C for 25 min. Dredge with icing sugar and glaze, sprinkle with rum and serve.

Strawberry Soufflé [*Strawberry Auflauf Israel*]   Whisk 6 egg yolks and 275 g caster sugar until creamy then combine with 450 g strawberry purée and fold in 6 stiffly beaten egg whites and 100 g cracker crumbs or coarse matzo meal. Pour the mixture into prepared moulds and bake au bain-marie at 220 °C for 30 min.

Vanilla Pudding Soufflés [*GB*]   Cream 100 g butter and 100 g sugar then add 100 g flour and mix to a paste. Whisk the paste into 425 ml boiling milk with a few drops of vanilla essence and stir until the mixture thickens; allow to cool. Beat in 5 egg yolks then fold in 5 stiffly beaten egg whites. Pour the mixture into prepared dariole moulds and bake au bain-marie at 200 °C for 15 min. Turn out and serve accompanied by English custard sauce.

Ice-cream

Cassata Napolitana [*Italy*]   Place a layer each of vanilla ice-cream and strawberry ice-cream in a bombe mould and chill. Boil 150 g sugar in 125 ml water to the soft ball (115 °C), pour onto 3 stiffly beaten whites of egg and whisk until cool. Add 150 ml whipped cream and 225 g chopped glacé fruits. Fill into the mould, chill until set then cover with a second layer each of strawberry ice-cream and vanilla ice-cream. Freeze until set, de-mould and serve cut into sections.

Omelette Norvégienne [*France*]   Trim a sponge cake to an oval shape, hollow out the centre, fill dome-shaped with 1 l vanilla ice-cream and chill. Mask over the ice-cream and sponge with stiff meringue then pipe the top with a fancy tube and decorate with glacé cherries and angelica. Dredge well with icing sugar and place in an oven at 240 °C for a few min.

Steamed Puddings

Chocolate Pudding [*GB*]   Cream 250 g butter and 250 g sugar until light and white and add 4 beaten eggs. Sift 275 g flour, 50 g cocoa powder, 12 g baking powder and $\frac{1}{4}$ tsp salt and fold into the creamed mixture, then add 50 ml milk. Place the mixture into 2 × 1 l buttered and sugared pudding basins, cover with grease-proof paper, tie a cloth on top and steam for $1\frac{1}{2}$ hr, or 40 min for individual moulds. Serve with chocolate sauce.

Golden Syrup Pudding [*GB*]   Sift together 450 g flour, $\frac{1}{4}$ tsp salt and 2 tsp baking powder, then mix in 250 g chopped suet and the grated zest of 2 lemons. Add 2 beaten eggs mixed with 300 ml milk. Pour 125 ml golden syrup or treacle into 2 well buttered pudding basins, fill with the mixture, cover with greaseproof paper and a cloth, tie with string then steam for 2 hr. Serve accompanied by warm syrup containing lemon juice.

Reina Pudding [*GB*]   Mix together 225 g flour, 12 g baking powder, 150 g white breadcrumbs, 225 g demerara sugar, 250 g seedless raisins and 200 g chopped suet. Dissolve 12 g bicarbonate of soda in a little hot water and add to 600 ml milk, then add the liquid to the dry ingredients and combine. Pour the mixture into 2 × 1 l buttered basins, cover with buttered greaseproof paper and a cloth and tie with string. Steam for 4 hr, and serve accompanied by custard sauce.

Scottish Cloutie Dumpling [*GB*]   Mix together 175 g self-raising flour, 175 g brown breadcrumbs, 175 g chopped suet, 100 g soft brown sugar, 100 g currants, 175 g sultanas, 2 tsp mixed spice, 1 tsp bicarbonate of soda, 75 g treacle and 300 ml milk. Scald a pudding cloth in boiling water. Lay out the cloth and dust liberally with flour. Place the mixture onto the cloth, form into a large round dumpling shape and tie into a traditional pudding. Place the pudding into simmering water and cook for approx. $2\frac{1}{2}$ – 3 hr. When cooked, remove the cloth, transfer the pudding to a plate and allow the outer surface to dry off in the oven. Cut into slices and serve with custard sauce.

Spotted Dick [*GB*]   Sift together 500 g flour, 12 g baking powder and $\frac{1}{4}$ tsp salt, then mix in 300 g chopped beef suet, 150 g caster sugar and 100 g currants. Moisten with 350 ml water to form a fairly firm paste. Divide the paste into two, mould into rolls, then wrap each in buttered greaseproof paper and tie in a pudding cloth, or place in greased pudding sleeves. Steam for 2 hr. Dredge with caster sugar and serve with custard sauce.

Milk and Cereal Puddings

Bread, Saffron and Nut Pudding [*Shahi Tukra India*]   Boil 425 ml milk with 8 cardamom pods, then remove from the heat and add 75 g sugar and a few strands of saffron. Boil and reduce by half 1.75 l milk. Golden fry 30 10 × 5-cm rectangles of bread in 50 ml ghee; drain, arrange in a suitable dish, pour in the saffron milk and stand for 5 min. Add the reduced milk and 50 g sugar and cook au bain-marie in the oven for 10 min. Serve chilled, garnished with pistachios and slivered almonds.

Caramel Rice Pudding [*Riskaramel Scandinavia*]   Bring 850 ml milk to the boil with a vanilla pod, add 75 g short-grain rice and simmer for 30 min. Remove the pod, add 75 g sugar, stir in 4 egg yolks and fold in 4 stiffly beaten whites. Line the bottom of moulds with caramel, pour in the rice preparation and cook au bain-marie for approx. 35 min. Serve accompanied by whipped cream flavoured with caramelised sugar and sherry.

Caramel: heat 25 ml corn oil then add 300 g sugar and 300 ml water, stir and cook to the crack stage (132–143 °C) then add a little water.

Carrot and Raisin Pudding [*Gajar-Ka-Halva India*]   Simmer 850 ml milk and 1 kg finely grated carrot with 2 cardamom pods until all the liquid has completely reduced. Add 75 ml oil, continue cooking and when reddish brown add 75 g sugar. Lightly fry 450 g raisins and 450 g slivered almonds in oil and add to the mixture. Serve warm or chilled.

Cream Cheese Balls in Syrup [*Ras Gula India*]   Curdle 3 l boiling milk by adding 125 ml warm lemon juice. Drain through a muslin then add 25 g fine semolina to the curds and knead until smooth. Mould walnut-sized pieces around a sugar cube. Boil 450 g sugar and 600 ml water to the small thread stage (104 °C), add 12 cardamom pods and the moulded ras gula and simmer gently for 1 hr until light and spongy; cool and add 125 ml rose-water. Serve warm with some of the cooking liquid.

Indian Milk Pudding [*Khir India*]   Cook 150 g short-grain rice in 1.5 l milk with a pinch of salt until nearly tender, then add 150 g ground almonds, 100 g desiccated coconut, 75 g chopped pistachios and 1 tsp each of cinnamon and orange-flower water. When cooked, stir in 200 g diced crystallised fruit, pour into coupes and chill. Serve with coconut cream sauce or gula malacca sauce.

Lokshen Kugel [*Israel*]   Combine 3 egg yolks, 1 tsp cinnamon, 1 tsp nutmeg, 200 g raisins and 125 g sugar, add 225 g cooked noodles and 75 g butter then fold in 3 stiffly beaten egg whites. Pour into prepared moulds, bake at 180 °C for 45 min then sprinkle with brown sugar.

Orange and Cinnamon Junket [*Cuajada a la Manera de Burgos Spain*]   Pour 600 ml warm goat's milk into a dish, add 25 g caster sugar and 2 tsp rennet, gently stir then chill for 3 hr. When set, cover with segments of orange, sprinkle with cinnamon, mask with honey and sprinkle with chopped walnuts.

Oven Pancakes [*Alvenanmaar Pannukakka Scandinavia*]   Cook semolina in boiling milk to a pouring consistency; add egg yolks, sugar, flour and cardamom powder. Heat butter in 13-cm pans, pour in a layer of the mixture and cook in the oven until brown on both sides. Serve spread with a berry jam and a swirl of whipped cream in the centre.

Rice Moulds [*Persian Purim Halva Israel*]   Golden fry 500 g short-grain rice in 50 ml oil, moisten with 1 l water, add 75 g sugar, 1 tsp cinnamon and 1 tsp ground cardamom and simmer until the rice is soft and smooth. Add a few strands of infused saffron and 50 g sugar and cook for 10 min. Pour into moulds, chill and decorate with pomegranate seeds.

Rice and Almond Coupes [*Riz à l'Amande France*]   Bring to the boil 850 ml milk with a vanilla pod, add 75 g short-grain rice and simmer for 30 min. Remove the pod and add 75 g sugar, 25 ml sweet sherry and 50 g chopped almonds. Stir in 25 g soaked leaf gelatine and cool, then fold in 175 ml whipped cream and mould on a dish or in coupes, then refrigerate. Serve garnished with slivered almonds.

Rice and Almond Pudding [*Kheer India*]   Boil 1 l milk, add 175 g blanched short-grain rice and 5 cardamom pods and simmer for 1 hr, then remove the pods. Add 125 g sugar, 75 g slivered almonds and 50 ml rose-water. Mould and serve sprinkled with ground cardamom or grated nutmeg.

Rice and Peach Pudding [*Peach and Rice Auflauf Israel*]   Boil 1.5 l milk with a vanilla pod, rain in 200 g long-grain rice and cook. Stir in 100 g sugar, $\frac{1}{2}$ tsp ground cloves, $\frac{1}{2}$ tsp grated nutmeg, 3 egg yolks and 100 g each of raisins, diced pineapple and diced peaches, then fold in 3 stiffly beaten egg whites. Bake in the oven at 180 °C for 40 min.

Rice and Sweetcorn Pudding [*Khow Niaw Piag* *Thailand*]   Combine fluffy boiled rice with corn kernels and sugar, pour into moulds then mask with thick coconut milk and garnish with sweet basil leaves.

Semolina and Redcurrant Moulds [*Flamri* *France*]   Boil 350 ml white wine and 350 ml water and rain in 175 g semolina, whisking well. Add 150 g sugar and a few drops of vanilla essence. Cook for 3 min, cool, then whisk in 2 yolks of egg. Fold in 5 stiffly beaten whites of egg and 50 g caster sugar. Pour into dariole moulds and cook au bain-marie in the oven at 190 °C for 35 min. De-mould and serve surrounded with redcurrant coulis or melted redcurrant jelly flavoured with kirsch.

Semolina Cakes [*Soojee Halwa* *India*]   Golden fry 350 g fine semolina in 150 ml ghee. Boil 725 ml water, 150 ml milk, a few strands of saffron and 2 tsp ground cardamom. Add the semolina and stir until the mixture leaves the sides of the pan, add 175 g sultanas and 175 g slivered almonds and pour into a shallow dish to set. Cut into diamond shapes and serve garnished with almonds. May be served warm or chilled.

Vermicelli and Fruit Pudding [*Seviyan* *India*]   Golden fry 225 g broken fine vermicelli in 125 ml ghee. Moisten with 850 ml water infused with a few strands of saffron and simmer for 5 min. Add 225 g sugar and 175 g sultanas and cook until the liquid is absorbed. Stir in 175 g slivered almonds and $\frac{1}{4}$ tsp ground cardamom. Serve warm accompanied by cream.

Fritters

Apricot Fritters [*Sonhos de Alperce* *Portugal*]   Marinate apricot halves in brandy, sugar and lemon juice. Coat them with massa vinhe batter and fry in olive oil. Serve dusted with icing sugar.

Banana Fritters [*Caribbean*]   Make a batter of 400 g flour, salt, sugar, 200 ml red wine and 200 ml water, then fold in 2 whisked whites of egg. Deep fry pieces of banana dipped in the batter and serve sprinkled with cinnamon and sugar.

Banana Fritters [*Pisang Goreng* *Thailand*]   Combine thin coconut milk, thick coconut milk, rice flour and butter to form a batter. Coat halves of banana with the batter and fry in clarified butter; sprinkle with icing sugar and serve.

Bread Fritters [*Rabanadas com Mel* *Portugal*]   Remove the crusts and soak slices of bread in milk, then dip them into beaten egg and fry in olive oil. Serve dusted with icing sugar and cinnamon.

Bread Fritters with Honey [*Rabanadas* *Portugal*]   Remove the crusts and soak slices of bread in milk, then dip them into beaten egg and fry in olive oil. Serve dusted with icing sugar and cinnamon and coated with a mixture of honey and port.

Bread and Loganberry Fritters [*Köyhät Ritarit* *Scandinavia*]   Whisk together 6 eggs, 300 ml milk, salt and a little sugar. Dip finger slices of bread in the batter and golden fry in butter. Serve with loganberry coulis on top.

Caramelised Apple and Banana Fritters [*Chah Ping Gwo, Chah Heung Jiu* *China*]   Golden fry yeast-battered apple rings and banana pieces, then plunge them into caramel then into iced water and serve.

Caramel: heat 25 ml corn oil then add 300 g sugar and 300 ml water, stir and cook to the crack stage (132–143 °C), then stir in sesame seeds.

Copra Samosas [*India*]   Make a pastry with 300 g flour, 100 g ghee, salt and approx. 100 ml plain yogurt. Roll out and make triangular turnovers with the following filling and deep fry. Dip into jabelis syrup and serve sprinkled with slivered pistachios.

Filling: combine 750 g grated coconut, 150 g ground almonds, 200 g sugar, 100 g raisins and 10 crushed cardamoms and make into a paste.

Jabelis syrup: dissolve 500 g sugar in 100 ml water with 1 tsp jabelis powder and cook until it thickens to a syrupy consistency.

Frimsel [*Israel*]   Combine 225 g chopped walnuts, 225 g diced apple, 100 ml oil, 150 ml honey, 75 g sugar, 225 g raisins, 6 eggs and 10 matzos softened with hot water and squeezed. Deep fry tablespoonfuls of the mixture in oil.

Golden Batter Fries in Syrup [*Boondi India*]   Heat 300 ml milk and a few strands of saffron to 30 °C then whisk onto 450 g besan (chickpea flour). Scoop perforated spoonfuls of this batter and tap droplets of it into hot oil, golden fry and drain. Place in the following syrup and mix in 75 g chopped pistachios. Serve chilled.

Syrup: boil 450 g sugar and 600 ml water to the small thread (104 °C); cool, and add $\frac{1}{2}$ tsp ground cardamom and a few drops of infused saffron.

Golden Pastry Fries [*Foguette India*]   Rub 50 g butter into 450 g flour and add 25 g icing sugar and $\frac{1}{4}$ tsp salt. Whisk together 2 eggs, 2 egg yolks, 50 ml water and $\frac{1}{4}$ tsp vanilla essence. Add to the flour and knead to a dough. Roll the pastry thinly to a rectangle, cut into strips and roll loosely around dowelling to form a spiral effect. Golden fry in oil, drain and dust with icing sugar. Fill the centres of the spirals with a mixture of chopped pineapple, cashew nuts and raisins.

Milk Fritters [*Creme Frito Portugal*]   Whisk together 300 ml milk, 150 g caster sugar, 60 g flour, 60 g rice flour and 3 egg yolks. Heat 300 ml milk with a vanilla pod, the grated zest of 1 orange and a pinch of salt, then beat into the flour and egg mixture and simmer until it thickens. Transfer to a shallow buttered dish and cool. Cut into triangles, pass through beaten egg and breadcrumbs then fry in olive oil; serve sprinkled with cinnamon.

Prune Fritters [*Beignets Scandinavia*]   Blanch prunes, remove stones and replace with blanched almonds. Dip the prunes in batter and golden fry. Serve accompanied by a fruit coulis.

Strawberry Fritters [*Sonhos de Morangos Portugal*]   Marinate strawberries in Madeira or port and lemon juice. Dip each into massa vinhe batter and deep fry in olive oil. Serve dusted with icing sugar.

Sweet Fritters [*Ausgezogene-Knieküchle Germany*]   Make a yeast dough with 500 g flour, 25 g yeast, 1 tsp sugar, 250 ml milk, 100 ml oil, 100 g caster sugar, 2 beaten eggs and grated zest of 1 lemon. Shape into flat doughnut pieces with an indentation in the centre of each and deep fry. Serve sprinkled with caster sugar and cinnamon.

Sweet Wontons [*Jar Wonton China*]   Combine 225 g chopped dates, 100 g chopped cashews, walnuts or almonds and the grated zest and juice of 1 lemon. Fill 40 wonton wrappers with the filling, twisting the ends to seal them. Golden fry, drain, dust with icing sugar and glaze.

Pancakes

American Pancakes [*USA*]   Combine 3 beaten eggs with 350 ml milk and whisk onto 350 g flour, 4 tsp baking powder, 3 tsp caster sugar and salt to form a batter. Pour sufficient batter into hot butter to form 7.5-cm pancakes. Serve with melted butter and maple syrup.

Cheese Blintzes [*Israel*]   Whisk together 4 eggs, 300 ml milk, 225 g flour and ½ tsp salt to form a batter. Make blintzes (pancakes) with the mixture. Combine 225 g cottage cheese, 1 lightly beaten egg yolk, 50 g sugar, 50 g raisins and the grated zest and juice of 1 lemon. Spread the blintzes with the mixture, roll up then lightly fry in butter. Serve accompanied by soured cream mixed with sugar and cinnamon.

Portuguese Pancakes [*Crêpes à Portuguesa Portugal*]   Heat 60 g butter, 60 g sugar, 20 ml orange juice, grated zest of 1 lemon and 60 ml port. Make pancakes in the usual way using banha (pork fat) then pour the sauce over them and flambé with brandy.

Turkish Pancakes with Cream Cheese [*Rakott Turos Palacsinta Turkey*] Combine 450 g cream cheese, 25 g flour, 4 eggs, 25 ml oil and 150 g sugar. Line a greased baking tray with pancakes and spread with jam then the cheese mixture, making several layers and finishing with pancakes. Sprinkle with butter and bake in the oven at 175 °C for 30 min. Decorate with meringue made with 3 whites of egg and 175 g caster sugar, dredge with icing sugar and glaze.

Baked Sweets

Apple Brown Betty [*USA*]   Fill a buttered dish with layers of 250 g toasted white breadcrumbs, 1.3 kg sliced apples, 225 g brown sugar and the grated zest and juice of 1 lemon, sprinkling each layer with a little cinnamon and nutmeg. Bake in the oven at 190 °C for 40 min. Serve accompanied by cream.

Pineapple Upside-down Cake [*USA*]   Line the base of a shallow cake tin with 75 g butter mixed with 150 g brown sugar and cover with overlapping slices of pineapple. Mix 5 yolks with 50 g softened butter and fold in 5 stiffly beaten egg whites with 100 g sugar and 150 g self-raising flour. Pour the mixture into the cake tin and bake in the oven at 180 °C for 30 min. Serve accompanied by cream.

Sweetmeats

Arlesiennes [*France*]   Roll out 500 g puff pastry to a rectangle 30 cm wide × 3 mm thick; cut into 10-cm wide strips, brush with water and sprinkle with caster sugar. Cut into 1-cm wide strips and twist each twice before laying on a dampened baking sheet, sticking the ends to the sheet. Allow to rest for 20 min before baking at 190 °C for approx. 15 min.

Banana Sweetmeats [*Kela Halwa India*]   Lightly fry 5 ripe bananas in oil or ghee, mash them and return to the stove. Sprinkle in 175 g sugar and moisten with 300 ml water, and simmer for approx. 15 min. When the mixture begins to leave the sides of the pan stir in ½ tsp ground cardamom and ¼ tsp rose-water. Spread the mixture onto a dish approx. 1 cm thick and cool. Cut into small diamond or square shapes, garnish with pistachio nuts and serve.

Battenburg Slices [*GB*]   Bake two genoese sponges, one coloured yellow and one chocolate, in square tins. Cut into 1.5-cm square lengths and stick together in pairs, one yellow and one chocolate, with hot apricot glaze. Then place two pairs together to give a chessboard pattern and place in the centre of a length of marzipan rolled 3 mm thick and 12 cm wide, previously spread with apricot glaze. Fold to enclose firmly then cut into 1-cm slices and brush the surface with glaze.

Biscuits Champagne [*France*]   Whisk 4 whole eggs, 3 yolks of egg and 300 g caster sugar over heat until it reaches the ribbon stage. Remove from the heat and continue to whisk until it is cold, then gently fold in 300 g soft flour and a few drops of vanilla essence. Pipe the mixture into 2-cm diameter bulbs onto a greased and floured baking sheet and sprinkle them well with caster sugar. Shake off surplus sugar and leave the biscuits in a warm place for 12 hr to form a crust before baking at 160 °C until pale in colour.

Carrot Sweetmeats [***Gajjar Halwa*** *India*]   Sweat 450 g grated carrot in 50 ml oil or ghee then boil to reduce any liquid. Prepare a syrup by gently boiling 150 ml water and 275 g sugar with 1 tsp ground cardamom, and when the mixture reaches small thread (104 °C) remove from the heat and add a few drops of rose-water. Pour the syrup onto the carrot, then stir in 300 ml cream, 100 g milk powder and 50 g chopped pistachio nuts. Spread the mixture in a dish approx. 1 cm thick, place a weight on top and allow to cool. Cut into small diamond or square shapes, garnish with pistachio nuts and serve.

Chickpea and Almond Sweetmeats [***Mysore Pak*** *India*]   Prepare a syrup by gently boiling 150 ml water and 75 g sugar with 1 tsp ground cardamom; when the mixture reaches small thread (104 °C) remove from the heat and add a few drops of vanilla essence. Heat 100 g oil or ghee then sprinkle in 50 g besan (chickpea flour) and cook for 5 min, pour in the syrup, continue cooking then add 50 g oil or ghee and continue cooking for a further 10 min. Transfer the mixture to a shallow dish 2 cm thick and cool. Cut into diamond or square shapes, garnish with slivered almonds and store in a dry place for a few hours to allow the sweetmeats to harden.

Congress Tartlets [*GB*]   Line small tartlet moulds with sweet pastry cut with a fancy cutter and pipe a spot of raspberry jam in the bottom. Fill with a mixture made by mixing 250 g ground almonds and 500 g caster sugar with 5 whites of egg and a few drops of almond essence, place two thin strips of sweet pastry on top in the form of a cross and bake at 175 °C for approx. 15 min.

Fondant Fancies [*GB*]   Cut a slab of genoese sponge in half horizontally and sandwich together with jam and buttercream. Cut into small oblong, oval, round or square shapes, dip into hot apricot glaze, allow to dry then dip into warm coloured and flavoured fondant and place on a cake rack to drain. When set, decorate with other colours of fondant, glacé cherries, angelica or chocolate decorations then place in small cake papers. If desired, a small bulb of buttercream, ganache or marzipan may be placed on top before glazing.

Fried Sweetmeats [***Gulabjaman*** *India*]   Sift 250 g flour, 175 g milk powder and 1 tsp baking powder, then rub in 50 g butter and moisten with 275 ml milk to form an elastic dough. Divide and mould the dough into 20 balls and golden shallow fry in oil or ghee. Prepare a syrup by gently boiling 600 ml water and 350 g sugar with a stick of cinnamon; when the mixture reaches small thread stage (104 °C) remove the cinnamon and add 50 ml rose-water. Place the fried sweetmeats into the syrup and allow to cool. The balls will become soft and spongy and should be served chilled.

Gitanes [*France*]   Cut rounds of genoese sponge 1 cm thick × 5 cm diameter and pipe dome-shaped with strawberry-flavoured buttercream. Chill then coat with strawberry-flavoured and coloured fondant. When set, cut across in the top and press open.

Macaroons [*France*]   Mix 250 g ground almonds with 400 g caster sugar and 30 g ground rice. Add 5–6 whites of egg and a few drops of almond essence to form a piping consistency. Pipe small balls 4 cm in diameter onto a sheet of rice paper on a baking sheet, using a plain tube. Brush with water, place a split almond on each and bake at 180 °C until pale golden in colour.

Scotch Gingerbreads [*GB*]   Cream 250 g butter then add 125 g fine oatmeal, 30 g ginger and 350 g flour. Now mix in 350 ml treacle or syrup and 125 g finely chopped candied peel. Pipe into greased madeleine moulds and bake at 190 °C for approx. 12 min.

Scotch Macaroons [*GB*]   Cut 5 cm rounds of puff pastry, prick and allow to rest for 30 min, then pipe with a ring made of 250 g ground almonds and 500 g caster sugar mixed with 5 whites of egg and a few drops of almond essence. Bake at 175 °C for approx. 12 min.

Turkish Delight [***Loukoum** Turkey*]   Heat 500 ml water and 750 g sugar to 113 °C (soft ball). Dilute 50 g cornflour in 75 ml grape juice, add to the syrup and mix in 1 tsp cream of tartar, 1 tablespoon rose-water and 50 g chopped pistachios. Cook until thick, divide into two and colour one part light pink. Pour each into an oiled shallow tray and leave to set. Cut into small squares and dust liberally with icing sugar.

Zürcher Leckerli [*Germany*]   Make a fairly stiff paste with 300 g ground almonds, 350 g icing sugar and approx. 2 whites of egg. Roll out 7 mm thick using icing sugar to prevent it sticking, and cut into 2.5 cm × 3.5 cm oblongs. Leave to dry out for 12 hr then place on a greased tray and bake at 250 °C for a few min. Glaze with gum arabic immediately they come out of the oven.

Gum arabic glaze: place 20 g powdered gum arabic into 120 ml cold water and bring to the boil, stirring until dissolved.

Breads and Other Flour Products

Aberdeen Butteries [*GB*] (makes 15–20)   Make a bread dough using 450 g strong flour, 2 tsp salt, 25 g yeast and 300 ml warm water, then cut in 250 g diced, chilled pieces of lard. Roll out 45 × 20 cm then give four folds. Roll out 1 cm thick and cut into 10-cm squares, then prove before baking at 220 °C for 18 min.

Baguette [*France*]   This is the name given to a loaf of bread in France, usually the small size French loaf (q.v.).

Baps [*GB*] (makes 12)   Make a soft dough using 450 g strong flour, 2 tsp salt and 25 g yeast dissolved in 300 ml warm milk and water. Mould 12 round flattened pieces and allow to prove. Dust with flour and make a small indentation with the thumb, then bake at 220 °C for 15 min.

Bath Oliver [*GB*]   This is a well-known biscuit for serving with cheese. Named after the inventor and the place where initiated. Plain, pale coloured and savoury. Sold ready to eat.

Blinis [*Russia*] (makes 12)   Make a batter using 25 g yeast dissolved in 100 ml warm milk and 50 g strong flour, and place to prove. Whisk 4 egg yolks with 300 ml warm milk, add to the yeast mixture with 250 g strong flour and 1 tsp salt and mix to a batter. Prove again then fold in 4 stiffly beaten whites of egg. Make into 50-ml individual blinis using 10–12-cm pans.

Breakfast Rolls [*GB*] (makes 18)   Make a dough using 450 g strong flour and 1 tsp salt and 25 g white fat, and add 25 g yeast dissolved in 300 ml warm milk and water. Mould round or oval then prove and bake at 240 °C for 15 min. When baked brush with warm milk.

Bridge Rolls [*GB*] (makes 24)   Make a soft dough using 500 g strong flour, 1 tsp salt, 50 g white fat, and 25 g yeast dissolved in 300 ml warm water with 1 small egg, 12 g milk powder and 1 tsp caster sugar. Prove then mould into oval-shaped 25-g pieces; eggwash, then bake at 240 °C.

Challah [*Israel*]   Mix to a dough 450 g strong flour with 1 tsp salt and 25 g yeast and 1 tsp sugar dissolved in 300 ml warm water, whisked with 1 egg and 50 ml oil. Prove, then plait four pieces for each of two challahs. Brush with eggwash, sprinkle with poppy seeds (optional) and bake at 200 °C for approx. 10 min, then reduce the heat to 180 °C for a further 30 min.

Chapatis [*India*] (makes 24)   Mix 250 g wholemeal flour, 125 g strong white flour and 1 tsp salt with 250 ml warm water to make a soft, sticky dough. Allow it to relax then knead again and mould into 24 balls. Lightly flatten and roll out 20 cm in diameter, stretching well. Cook on a griddle until brown spots appear, turn and cook the other side.

   Note: chapati flour, which is finely milled wholemeal flour, may be used instead of ordinary wholemeal flour.

Cheese Loaf [*GB*]   Make a soft dough using 450 g strong flour, 1 tsp salt, 12 g white fat, 25 g yeast and 12 g sugar dissolved in 300 ml warm milk, and 75 g finely grated Cheddar cheese or 50 g bakers' cheese. Prove and mould into two loaves then bake at 240 °C for 35 min.

Ciabatta [*Italy*]   Pour 500 ml warm water into a bowl and dissolve 25 g yeast in it. Add 450 g strong flour and mix to a sticky dough. Oil a basin, put the dough in it, cover and prove for 4 hr in a cool place. Knock back, add 50 ml olive oil, 1 tsp salt and 285 g strong flour and mix to an elastic dough. Prove again for several hours. Cut into two pieces and press each piece into a greased shallow tin 20 cm in length. Cover and allow to prove, then place into an oven at 250 °C with a dish of boiling water in it. Bake for approx. 25 min. It should be a light and feathery loaf which sounds hollow when tapped.

Coburg Loaf [*GB*]   Make a white bread dough, mould round and coat the surface with ground rice. Cover, allow to prove then place on a hot baking tray dusted with ground rice, cut a cross on top and bake at 240 °C for 40 min.

Croissants [*France*]   Make a dough with 450 g strong flour, 12 g salt, 25 g caster sugar, 25 g yeast and 300 ml warm milk. Roll out 50 cm square, spread with 250 g butter and fold the four corners to the centre to seal in the butter. Roll out 30 × 15 cm and fold in three, and give six similar turns. Roll out 4 mm thick and cut into triangles with 15-cm sides. Form a crescent shape, eggwash, prove in a cool place then bake at 230 °C for 15 min.

Crumpets, also called Pikelets [*GB*]   Make a batter with 450 g strong flour, 1 tsp salt, 12 g yeast, 12 g each of honey and oil and 650 ml water or milk. Allow to rise then stir before pouring portions into 8–10-cm greased rings placed on a hot griddle plate. When set, remove the rings, turn over to finish cooking and allow to cool.

Dinner Rolls [*GB*]   Mix 500 g strong flour, 12 g milk powder, 2 tsp salt, 50 g white fat, and 25 g yeast dissolved in 275 ml warm water to form a dough. Mould into 24 pieces to shape, eggwash and bake at 230 °C for 15 min. Other types of roll include bakestone (re-cut pieces of dough cooked on a griddle), Dorset knob (roughly shaped pieces of dough baked in the normal way), farl, hoggie (large size wholemeal finger roll sprinkled with malted cracked wheat), and Italian (flatten the ends of a piece of dough and roll up tightly towards the centre and join alongside each other).

Energen Rolls [*GB*]   These are starch-reduced rolls used as an aid for slimming diets and for diabetics, sold ready to eat. Starch can be washed from a made dough or extra protein added to flour in the form of dry or wet gluten to give a lower starch content than ordinary rolls.

Farmhouse Bread [*GB*]   Make a soft dough using 450 g strong flour with 1 tsp salt, 25 g lard, and 25 g yeast and 25 g honey dissolved in 300 ml warm milk with 1 egg. Mould into two loaves, press flat into two shallow baking tins, allow to prove, cut a deep groove down the centre of each, dust with flour and bake at 230 °C for 40 min.

Festival Bread [*GB*]   Make a fairly stiff dough using 1 kg strong flour with 2 tsp salt and 15 g yeast and 2 tsp sugar dissolved in 600 ml cold milk and water. Roll out the dough, cut to shape for a base, place on a cold, greased tray and decorate, e.g. in the form of a wheatsheaf with ears and stems and a plaited band across the middle. Eggwash well and bake at 185 °C for 1 hr.

Focaccia [*Italy*]   Sift 400 g strong flour with $\frac{1}{2}$ tsp salt; add 25 g yeast dissolved in 250 ml warm water and 75 ml olive oil and mix to a smooth dough. Allow to prove, knock back, divide into 12 pieces, mould and roll out into 15-cm rounds. Place on a greased tray, allow to prove and bake at 200 °C for 20 min. Focaccia are usually covered before baking with ingredients similar to pizzas, or with sweet toppings. The dough may also be flavoured with herbs, cheese, etc. They should be eaten as soon as they come from the oven.

French Loaf or Stick [*France*]   This should be made with imported French flour or ordinary strong flour. Make a fairly tight dough with 450 g flour, 1 tsp salt, 25 g yeast, 1 tsp sugar and approx. 300 ml warm water. Prove slowly then knead on the table, flattening and folding it over to incorporate air several times over a period of 2 hr. Divide in two and mould from the centre outwards into two 90-cm lengths using ground rice to prevent sticking. Prove then cut diagonally along the surface and bake at 240 °C, with a container of boiling water in the oven, for 20 min.

Griddle Scones [*GB*]   Mix 450 g flour and 1 tsp each of bicarbonate of soda, cream of tartar, baking powder and sugar, and rub in 25 g butter. Mix to a fairly stiff consistency with 2 tsp golden syrup dissolved in 250 ml milk. Roll out 2 cm thick, cut out 6 cm plain rounds and cook on a greased griddle until golden on both sides.

Grissini [*Italy*]   Make a fairly stiff dough using 450 g strong flour with 1 tsp salt, 75 g lard and 25 g yeast and 1 tsp sugar dissolved in 250 ml warm water. Prove then knock back and cut into 25-g pieces. Roll 15 cm in length, place on a greased baking tray, eggwash, prove and bake at 240 °C until firm.

Gugelhopf or Kugelhopf [*Germany*]   Make a dough with 350 g strong flour, 1 tsp salt, and 25 g yeast and 25 g sugar dissolved in 200 ml warm milk whisked together with 3 eggs and 100 g melted butter; then add 100 g raisins. Line two fluted moulds with shredded almonds and dust with sugar; half fill with the dough, prove until full up then bake at 190 °C for 45 min.

Hamburger Buns [*USA*]   Mix 450 g strong flour, 1 tsp salt, 25 g lard and 25 g yeast and 1 tsp sugar dissolved in 300 ml warm milk to a soft dough. Prove then mould into 80 g round pieces; prove again then bake at 240 °C; when cooked brush with milk.

Irish Bread [*GB*]   Make a white bread dough and mould into two oblongs 18 × 4.5 cm. Brush the sides and ends with melted lard and place side by side in an oblong baking tin with their sides touching so that during baking they will be forced upwards to give fairly tall loaves with soft and pale sides.

Italian Feather Bread [*Italy*]   Make a soft dough using 450 g strong flour with 2 tsp salt, 25 g yeast and 25 g sugar dissolved in 225 ml warm water with 75 g melted butter. Prove, knock back and knead well. Cut in half, roll each piece to a rectangle 30 × 20 cm and roll up tightly. Prove then brush with beaten white of egg and bake at 220 °C for 35–40 min.

Lefse [*Scandinavia*]   Mix 50 g sugar, 100 ml corn syrup and 225 ml sour milk. Sift 450 g flour with 1½ tsp baking powder and a pinch of cardamom powder then add the liquid and mix well to form a pliable dough. Flatten fairly thinly and cut out 12 circles or squares. Cook on a hot, greased griddle for approx. 8 min on each side.

Malt Loaf [*GB*]   Add 150 g sultanas (optional) and 1 tsp salt to 450 g strong white flour. Melt 25 g black treacle and 100 g malt extract and cool. Dissolve 25 g yeast in 200 ml warm water and pour with the malt mixture into a well in the flour. Mix to a soft dough, knead well then prove. Knock back, cut into two pieces and mould to shape for small oblong loaf tins. Allow to prove then bake at 200 °C for 45 min. Boil together 25 ml milk and 25 g sugar for two min and brush over the tops of the loaves on taking from the oven.

Mannaeesh [*Middle East*]   Dissolve 15 g yeast in 300 ml warm water with 1 tsp sugar and 50 ml olive oil. Add 450 g strong flour and mix to a smooth dough. Allow to prove, divide into 10 pieces and roll out into rounds 5 mm thick. Place on a greased tray and cover with thyme, marjoram and sesame seeds mixed with oil. Allow to prove then bake at 230 °C for 10 min.

Matzo or Matzot [*Israel*]   This is a dry biscuit made of flour and water only in squares of approx. 17 cm for use by Jewish people, particularly during the Passover, instead of ordinary bread. It is bought in packets ready made.

Milk Loaf [*GB*]   Dissolve 25 g yeast and 12 g sugar in 300 ml warm milk, then whisk in 300 g strong flour and a pinch of nutmeg. Cover and allow to ferment slowly for 1 hr. Separately mix 175 g flour with 1 tsp salt and rub in 12 g butter; add the fermented mixture to make a soft dough. Knead, cut into two and mould to fit small loaf tins. Prove in a moist atmosphere and bake at 230 °C for 35 min. Brush with warm milk on taking from the oven.

Muffins [*GB*]   Make a soft dough with 450 g strong flour, 1 tsp salt, 12 g sugar, 12 g yeast diluted with 300 ml warm water and $\frac{1}{2}$ tablespoon oil. Knead well then prove slowly, then knock back and cut into 75 g pieces. Mould in the hands and prove on a tray sprinkled with ground rice, taking care that they do not get dry. Cook on a greased griddle plate until well coloured and baked right through.

Nan [*India*]   This is sometimes called tandoori bread because it is served with most tandoori dishes. Sift 450 g each of strong flour and self-raising flour. Dissolve 12 g yeast in 50 ml warm water and allow to ferment, then add to the flour together with 100 ml plain yogurt and 350 ml warm water to make a soft pliable dough. Refrigerate for 12 hr, remove and prove then knock back and divide into four pieces. Mould teardrop-shape about 6 mm thick. Prick all over, brush with oil and cook under the grill for $1\frac{1}{2}$ – 2 min, then turn over, sprinkle with sesame seeds and cook the second side. Alternatively, bake in a tandoori oven.

Norwegian Wholemeal Bread [*Scandinavia*]   Mix 500 g wholemeal flour and 125 g each of rye flour and strong white flour with 1 tsp salt and 25 g yeast dissolved in 425 ml warm milk to a soft dough. Prove then knock back, knead again, cut into two and mould round. Place on a greased baking tray, cover and prove until doubled in size. Bake at 190 °C for 50 min.

Oatbread [*GB*]   Mix 300 g strong flour with 175 g medium oatmeal and 1 tsp salt, then rub in 12 g white fat. Dissolve 25 g yeast and 1 tablespoon golden syrup in 300 ml warm water, add to the flour mixture and mix to a dough. Prove, knock back and cut into two pieces. Mould round, brush the tops with warm water and dip into oatmeal, and flatten slightly. Place on a greased baking tray, prove then bake at 230 °C for 30 min.

Paratha [*India*]   Mix 250 g wholemeal flour, 150 g strong white flour, 1 tsp salt and 225 ml warm water mixed with 50 ml oil to a soft dough. Knead well then allow to relax for 30 min. Knead once more, cut into 16 pieces, then roll into 15-cm thin discs. Brush with oil then fold over or seal another disc on top and roll and fold again, doing this several times, keeping them from getting dry and finishing as 20-cm circles or 15-cm triangles. Cook on a griddle.

Phulka [*India*]   Sift 375 g wholemeal flour and 125 g strong white flour and mix in 250 ml warm water to make a fairly soft dough. Knead for 15 min then leave to relax for 30 min. Knead again, mould into balls and flatten, then roll out into 15-cm rounds, stretching them well. Cook quickly on both sides on a hot griddle.

Pide [*Turkey*]   Dissolve 25 g yeast and 1 tsp sugar in 250 ml warm water. Melt 50 g butter in 175 ml warm milk. Sift 675 g strong flour with 1 tsp salt, add the two liquids and mix to a smooth dough. Allow to prove, knock back and mould to fit a 30-cm diameter greased tin. Brush with eggwash, sprinkle with sesame and fennel seeds, allow to prove then bake at 195 °C for 40 min.

Pitta Bread [*Middle East*]   Make 450 g strong flour, 1 tsp salt and 12 g yeast dissolved in 300 ml warm water with 3 tsp oil and 12 g malt extract into a dough. Mould 50-g round pieces and roll out oval shape 12.5 cm long. Dust with flour, prove for 10 min then bake at 240 °C for 8 min.

Poori or Puri [*India*] (makes 10)   Rub 50 g ghee into 225 g wholemeal flour and mix with 150 ml warm water. Knead well, relax for 15 min, mould into 20 balls then roll out into 10-cm circles. Deep fry at 200 °C until puffed up and golden.

Poori [*Alternative*]   Mix 55 g each of chickpea flour, strong flour and wholemeal flour; add 125 ml water, 1 tablespoon oil and a pinch of salt and mix well for 5 min. Allow to rest for 1 hr then divide into 12 pieces. Roll out into 12-cm circles and deep fry on both sides until puffy.

Poppadums [*India*]   Poppadums are made by grinding white split gram beans to a paste, which is then made into a smooth dough with baking soda and seasoning. The paste is made into paper-thin 17.5 cm circles and dried, then deep fried at 180 °C keeping submerged under the fat to make it expand. They may also be cooked under a grill.

Potato Dough Rolls and Bread [*GB*]   Dissolve 25 g yeast and ½ tsp sugar in 300 ml warm water and leave to ferment. Sift 450 g strong flour with 2 tsp salt and rub in 125 g cool, dry mashed potato. Add the liquid, mix to a dough and knead. Prove, knock back and mould either into 16 rolls or as one loaf to fit a 1-kg loaf tin. Prove then bake at 230 °C, the rolls for 15 min, the loaf for 40 min. They may be sprinkled with poppy seeds or sesame seeds before baking.

Pumpernickel [*Germany*]   Dilute 100 g cornflour in 350 ml water, add to 350 ml boiling water and cook until thick. Place in a bowl, add 25 g caraway seeds, 1 tsp salt and 50 g butter and cool. Add 350 g dry mashed potato and 25 g yeast dissolved in 125 ml warm water with 25 g sugar. Mix well and gradually work in 250 g rye flour and 250 g strong flour previously sieved together. Knead well, adding further flour to make a fairly firm dough. Prove, knock back and mould to fit 450-g greased loaf tins; prove and bake in the oven at 220 °C for 10 min then reduce to 180 °C for a further 30 min.

Roti [*India*]   Pour 125 ml cold water onto 450 g maize flour and mix to a fairly firm dough. Mould into 16 round pieces then roll out to 12 cm in diameter. Dry fry on one side, remove and cook the other side under a grill.

Rye Bread [*European*]   Mix 100 g rye flour with 50 ml cold water and incorporate, if available, 25 g dough left to go sour from a previous mixing; cover and leave in a warm place for 24 hr. Sift 175 g each of rye flour and strong white flour with 1 tsp salt. Dissolve 25 g yeast in 300 ml warm water and mix into the flour together with the sour dough mixture and 25 g caraway seeds. Knead well, prove then knock back and divide in two, then mould into 30-cm lengths. Prove until double their size. Cut slits along the top and bake at 220 °C with a container of very hot water in the oven for 40 min. If desired the loaves may be sprinkled with caraway seeds or poppy seeds halfway through the baking period.

Scottish Baps [*GB*]   Sift 450 g strong flour with 1 tsp salt and rub in 50 g lard. Dissolve 25 g yeast and 1 tsp sugar in 300 ml warm milk and water, allow it to ferment then add to the flour and mix to a soft dough. Knead well, prove, knock back and cut into 75-g pieces. Mould oval in shape and slightly flatten; then prove. Dust with flour and bake at 240 °C for 10 min.

Scottish Oatcakes [*GB*]   Mix 250 g medium oatmeal with 1 tsp bicarbonate of soda and ½ tsp salt; add 25 g melted dripping or lard and 75 ml hot water to make a stiff dough. Knead well, using oatmeal, then roll out 0.5-cm thick and cut out four rounds, divide in quarters and cook on a griddle.

Singing Hinny [*GB*]   Mix together 350 g flour, 50 g ground rice, 50 g sugar, ½ tsp salt and 12 g baking powder. Rub in 25 g lard, add 75 g currants and mix to a paste with 250 ml cream and milk. Roll out 7 mm thick, cut 18-cm circles and divide into quarters. Prick all over and cook on a greased griddle plate.

Soda Bread [*GB*]   Sift 450 g plain flour with 1 tsp each of sugar, salt, bicarbonate of soda and cream of tartar. Mix in 350 ml butter milk to make a smooth dough, kneading lightly. Mould round and fit into a greased 20-cm diameter sponge tin; cut a deep cross from the centre to the edges, allow to relax for 10 min then bake at 230 °C for 15 min, then reduce to 200 °C for another 30 min.

Soya Bread [*USA*]   Sift 150 g soya flour with 500 g strong flour and 12 g salt and rub in 25 g white fat. Dissolve 25 g yeast and 25 g sugar in 425 ml warm water, add to the flour and mix to a dough. Prove, then shape into three 400-g loaves and bake at 230 °C for 30 min.

Tandoori Bread [*India*]   See **Nan**.

Tortillas [*Mexico*]   Mix 550 g maize flour and 100 g ordinary flour and add 600 ml hot water to make a soft dough. Knead then mould into 40-g round pieces and place in a tortilla press on waxed paper discs to make 1-mm thick circles. Cook on a greased griddle for 30 seconds, turn over and press while cooking the second sides.

Note: tortillas can be made with all white or with all wholemeal flour, but it is advisable to rub in 75 g white fat per 450 g flour.

Tsoureki [*Greece*]   Sift 450 g strong flour and 1 tsp salt into a basin which has 2 eggs mixed with 150 ml warm milk, 1 tsp sugar, 2 tsp water, 100 g melted butter and 15 g yeast. Add the flour with $\frac{1}{2}$ tsp mastic, which is powdered resin, and mix to a dough. Allow to prove and divide into two, then divide each piece into 3 strands. Twist into plaits, place on a greased tray, brush with eggwash and sprinkle with sesame seeds. Allow to prove then bake at 180 °C for approx. 30 min.

Vienna Bread and Rolls [*Germany*]   Dissolve 25 g yeast and 1$\frac{1}{2}$ tsp sugar in 300 ml lukewarm milk and water, add to 450 g strong flour and 1 tsp salt and work to a dough. Flatten out and fold on itself several times so as to incorporate as much air as possible, keeping the dough covered between times. Divide into two then mould tightly into short rolls, allow to relax then roll out to 45-cm lengths. Dust with ground rice, place on a baking tray, prove then cut slits along the top. Bake at 240 °C with a container of boiling water in the oven or in an oven with a steam jet. The loaves should have a glossy appearance.

Note: to make Vienna rolls, cut the dough into 15 × 40 g pieces and mould into various shapes including round, oval, baton, double scroll, twists, plait, coil, crescent, cannon, turn, rocker, serpent, rose ring, blitz, kaiser, etc.

Viennese Croissants [*Hungary*]   Mix together 100 g each of ground almonds and caster sugar, and work in 50 g butter to a stiff paste. Place a strip of this mixture onto croissant dough (see page 262) before commencing to roll each croissant.

Waffles [*USA*]   Make a batter with 300 g flour, 2 tsp baking powder, $\frac{1}{2}$ tsp salt, 2 egg yolks, 75 g melted fat and 275 ml milk. Allow to stand for 30 min then fold in 2 stiffly beaten egg whites and cook on a hot greased waffle iron.

Welsh Fruit Loaf [*Bara-Brith GB*]   Make a dough with 450 g strong flour and 25 g yeast and 50 g sugar dissolved in 150 ml each of warm milk and water and 1 beaten egg. Knead, prove then add 50 g melted lard, 50 g each of currants, mixed peel and sultanas all shredded, and $\frac{1}{2}$ tsp mixed spice. Mix together then mould into loaves, place in greased tins, prove and bake at 200 °C for 30 min.

West Indian Bread [*Caribbean*]   To 450 g bread dough work in 50 g cornflour and 12 g each of white fat and sugar. Roll out, fold in the centre and repeat several times, then mould and place in greased bread tins. Allow to prove and bake at 220 °C for 30 min.

White Bread [*GB*]   Make a dough with 450 g strong flour, 1 tsp salt and 25 g white fat. Add 25 g yeast and 12 g sugar dissolved in 300 ml warm water. Knead, prove for 40 min then knock back, mould into a roll and place in a greased 800 g bread tin, or use 2 × 400 g tins. Prove and bake at 240 °C for 40 min for the large loaf or 30 min for the smaller ones, with a container of hot water in the oven.

Wholemeal Bread [*GB*]   Sift 450 g wholemeal flour with 1 tsp salt and rub in 25 g white fat. Dissolve 25 g yeast and 12 g honey in 300 ml warm milk, add to the flour and mix to a soft dough. Knead well, prove, knock back and prove again. Mould to fit baking tins, then prove and bake at 250 °C for 40 min with a container of hot water in the oven.

Chapter Thirteen

Beverages

This chapter is divided into four main categories:

✧ Non-alcoholic Drinks ✧

✧ Non-alcoholic Cocktails ✧

✧ Alcoholic Drinks ✧

✧ Alcoholic Cocktails ✧

Non-alcoholic Drinks

Coffee

Brulot   Place a few cloves, a small piece each of vanilla pod and cinnamon stick, 1 strip each of lemon and orange peel, sugar to taste and 50 ml brandy in a pan, stir over heat, allow to catch alight and immediately add sufficient black coffee, strain and serve.

Café Viennoise   Hot, black, sweetened coffee served in a tall glass and topped with a whirl of whipped cream.

Cappuccino   Heat sufficient milk on the nozzle of a coffee making machine, pour into a cup half full of black coffee and sprinkle the surface with cocoa powder or ground cinnamon.

Coffee-chocolate   To 600 ml white coffee add 125 g chocolate melted in 600 ml sweetened milk with a few drops of vanilla essence. Whisk well until cold and frothy and serve topped with whipped cream.

Espresso   Strong black coffee made and served in small portions in a special machine which heats water and sprays it as steam through finely ground coffee.

Frappé   This is iced coffee made by adding crushed ice to strong, hot black coffee and sugar and cream to taste.

Iced Coffee   Double strength chilled coffee to which milk and sugar are added as required, served in a tall glass.

Turkish Coffee   Using a Turkish coffee pot, place a small cupful of cold water and sugar to taste and boil; add a heaped teaspoonful of finely ground coffee and bring back to the boil. Remove from the heat, stir to dissolve the frothy head then reboil and immediately pour into a warmed cup, shaking the pot to keep the coffee grounds dispersed. A pinch of ground cloves or crushed cardamom seeds may be added.

Coffees made with liqueurs

Black coffee is poured into a warmed glass, sweetened with sugar and a measure of liqueur is stirred in well. Then double cream or lightly whipped cream is poured on over the back of a teaspoon so that it stays on the surface and swirls around with the coffee. The following are some of the names given to these speciality coffees:

Alsatian (Kirsch)	Italian (Strega)
Calypso (Tia Maria)	Monk's (Bénédictine)
Don Juan (Kahlùa)	Seville (Cointreau)
Highland (Scotch whisky)	Yorkshire (Brontë liqueur)

Coffees made with the addition of a spirit include:

Black Russian (Vodka)	Gaelic (Irish whiskey)
Cobra (Kirsch and whisky)	Napoleon (Brandy)
Dutch (Genever gin)	Royale (Brandy)
French (Cognac)	

Tea

In addition to the normal pot of tea made with a proprietary blend of tea leaves there are many speciality teas, as described below.

Assam A strongly flavoured tea.

Breakfast A blend of teas from India and Sri Lanka especially suitable for reviving the spirits as the first cup of the day.

Ceylon High quality teas grown at great altitudes in Sri Lanka, which are delicate to the taste and fragrant in aroma.

Darjeeling High quality Indian tea from the slopes of the Himalayas, with a deep colour and delicate fragrance.

Earl Grey Strongly flavoured tea made of China tea with the addition of other fine quality teas and oil of bergamot, a fragrant herb with a relaxing quality.

Herbal Teas These are soothing and relaxing teas with the aroma of the herb used and its therapeutic qualities; they should be freshly brewed and drunk without milk, and can be served hot or cold. Some of the varieties available include bergamot, chamomile, elderflower, lime, peppermint, rose hip and valerian (made with valerian roots).

Lapsang Souchong Has a smoky flavour with a light colour, and is made from fermented tea.

Lemon or Lime Tea The delicate flavour is obtained from the dried rind of the fruits.

Maté A South American tea prepared from the leaves of a holly-type bush; it has a bitter flavour but stimulating qualities.

Oolong A China tea of choice quality made of partially fermented leaves.

Orange Pekoe A quality grade of tea of pale colour and excellent taste.

Orange Tea The delicate flavour is obtained from the dried rind of the fruit.

Russian Tea grown in Caucasia for brewing in a samovar and serving with a slice of lemon rather than milk.

Flavoured Teas

Cinnamon Tea [*Dartchinov Tey* Middle East] Gently boil water with cinnamon stick for 15 min. Remove the cinnamon, pour into cups and drink accompanied by sugar.

Iced Tea Make double strength tea and strain over ice cubes. Serve with thin slices of lemon and orange.

Mint Tea Tea which is made with either spearmint or peppermint.

Other Non-alcoholic Drinks

Barley Water Blanch 50 g pearl barley, place in a pan and add 1 l water and a thin strip of lemon peel. Allow to simmer very gently for 2 hr, sweeten if desired with 100 g sugar, and strain.

Bavaroise A hot, frothy drink made by whisking egg yolks and sugar to the ribbon stage then adding a little stock syrup, freshly brewed tea and hot milk; may be flavoured with coffee, chocolate, vanilla, kirsch, etc.

Beef Tea   A healthy drink for an invalid or person convalescing. Make by cooking chopped or minced lean beef in water until all the goodness has been extracted; a little salt may be added. Serve hot.

Chocolate   A hot chocolate drink is usually made with a proprietary brand of drinking chocolate powder. (See also Mexican Hot Chocolate.)

Cocoa   For each mug mix 1 tsp cocoa powder with sugar to taste and a little cold milk from 300 ml; boil the rest of the milk, add the diluted cocoa, reboil and serve.

Coconut and Pineapple Punch [*Caribbean*]   Blend together coconut milk, diced pineapple, caster sugar and almond essence, strain and refrigerate. Serve chilled, with or without ice.

Coconut Milk-shake [*Asia*]   Simmer the following for approx. 10 min: 200 ml thin coconut milk, 100 g sugar, a few drops of vanilla essence and 1 cinnamon stick. Allow to cool then remove the cinnamon. Pour the mixture onto crushed ice and briskly mix in 200 ml thick coconut milk. Serve in tall milk-shake glasses.

Egg Flip   Boil 300 ml milk and pour onto 1 yolk of egg mixed with 2 tsp sugar; beat the white of egg to a foam and fold into the hot milk. One tsp of sherry or brandy may be added.

Honey and Spice Punch [*Sbiten' Russia*]   Boil and skim honey and water. In a second pan, boil sugar and water. In a third pan, simmer water with cloves, peppercorns, cinnamon stick and grated root ginger for approx. 20 min, allow to stand for a further 15 min then strain. Combine the three liquids, heat to just below boiling point and serve in tea glasses.

Lemonade   Add boiling water to the pared rind and juice of lemons and sugar, cover and allow to cool. Strain and serve cold.

Mexican Hot Chocolate   Grate plain chocolate and dissolve over heat in milk with sugar and vanilla essence. When nearly boiling thicken with cornflour diluted in cold water. Whisk well until thick and serve sprinkled with ground cinnamon.

Milk-shakes   Using a cocktail shaker or milk-shake machine, shake sufficient cold milk, ice cubes and a flavoured syrup such as coffee, chocolate or raspberry (or use two scoops of flavoured ice-cream) until blended; may be served with whipped cream on top.

Mint Sherbet [*Podina Ka Sbarbat India*]   Dissolve sugar in boiling water flavoured with cinnamon stick. Pour the sugared water onto coarsely chopped mint leaves and aniseed and allow to infuse for approx. 2 hr. Strain the liquid into a pan, add a little green food colouring, boil and reduce by half and allow to cool. Serve chilled.

Peanut Punch [*Caribbean*]   Boil milk then add peanut butter and sugar and thicken with cornflour diluted with water. Serve chilled, with or without ice.

Pomegranate and Rose-water [*Aseer Romman Middle East*]   Liquidise the seeds of pomegranates with water, rose-water, the juice of a lemon and sugar to taste. Strain the liquid, chill and serve.

Raisin Tea [*Middle East*]   Soak raisins in cold water for approx. 12 hr then transfer the whole to a pan and simmer for 30 min until soft. Flavour with ground cinnamon then liquidise. Serve chilled.

Rose Sherbet [*Sbarbat Gulab India*]   Dissolve sugar in hot water and allow to cool. Add 1 tsp rose-water, red colouring and tulsi previously soaked in cold water, then chill in a refrigerator. Strain through a fine muslin and serve in a glass, diluted to taste with iced water or crushed ice and garnished with a small amount of the tulsi seeds.

Sherbet [*Sharbat* *India*] Boil water, sugar, cinnamon stick, cloves and cardamoms to a thick syrup, then add rose-water and colouring of choice to form a brightly coloured sherbet. Strain and serve chilled.

Soumatha [*Greece*] Blanch almonds, drain and skin then grind them to a fine powder. Boil water, caster sugar, almond essence and the ground almonds for approx. 10 min or until the mixture thickens. Press through a fine strainer or muslin and retain in a refrigerator until required. Serve in glasses, diluted with water.

Tamarind Juice [*Zeera Pani* *India*] To tamarind juice add dried mint, toasted and ground cumin seeds, garam masala, chilli powder and 1 tsp salt; chill and serve.

Tamarind with Cumin Drink [*Zeera Pani* *India*] To tamarind juice add grated root ginger, ground cumin, garam masala and sugar, and allow to stand for approx. 1 hr in a refrigerator. Strain through a fine muslin and serve in glasses diluted to taste with iced water or crushed ice.

Yogurt and Lemon Drink [*Lassi Meeta* *India*] Liquidise yogurt, milk, lemon juice, sugar and rose-water and some ice cubes. Serve in chilled glasses.

Yogurt on Ice [*Tan* *Russia*] Blend together yogurt, water, a little salt and freshly ground black pepper. Chill and serve in glasses with crushed ice. May also be sweetened with sugar or honey, omitting the salt and pepper.

Yogurt with Rose-water [*Lassi Meethi* *India*] Blend together yogurt, water, sugar and rose-water until the mixture begins to froth. Chill and serve in glasses with crushed ice.

Non-alcoholic cocktails

Cinderella Mix equal quantities of pineapple juice and orange juice together with a small quantity of lime juice.

Pussyfoot Shake yolk of egg with lemon, lime and orange juices and a few drops of Angostura bitters, then fill the glass with soda water.

Nursery Fizz Mix equal quantities of orange juice and American dry ginger ale and serve in a champagne glass.

Shirley Temple Add several dashes of grenadine syrup to dry ginger ale.

Alcoholic Drinks

Absinthe (aniseed) and Wormwood Flavoured spirit drunk as an aperitif or digestive, usually laced with water; pastis and Pernod are similar products. Can be used to flavour certain savoury and sweet dishes giving them a hint of aniseed.

Angostura bitters Flavouring and colouring essence made to a secret formula from herbs, barks and aromates, for use mainly in drinks, e.g. pink gin, but also to flavour sauces, salad dressings and sweets. This type of essence is known as a bitter; Underberg is a German version.

Anisette The herb aniseed is used to make liqueurs under several brand names, one of the most popular being that of Marie Brizard 1775.

Aperitif A drink taken before a meal to stimulate the appetite; can be sour or sweet and includes cocktails, sparkling or still wines, sherry, vermouth, white port, spirits, liqueurs or proprietary aperitifs such as Dubonnet, Campari, etc.

Aquavit Distilled spirit made from grain or potato with or without flavouring, e.g. caraway, dill or a spice; served very cold in a small quantity to be swallowed in one gulp, often as an aperitif or with a smorgasbord.

Armagnac Quality brandy made in a distinct area of France with a flavour which is slightly less pronounced than that of cognac (q.v.). It has a nice delicate aroma. Used in clear soups, sauces, meat dishes and for flambé work.

Arrak White spirit distilled from such things as rice, dates, sugar cane or palm tree sap; usually very coarse and fiery.

Brandy General name given to the spirit distilled from wine, regardless of where it is made. Its quality comes from ageing, as denoted by the letters VO (very old), VSO (very superior old), XO (extra old), or 3 star, etc. Brandy can be used to flavour foods by the method of flambéing, when it is set alight so as to leave only the very essence of the spirit in the food, and it has many other uses in cooking.

Cider The fermented liquid from pressed apples made as still or sparkling, dry or sweet, mild or strong; used as a liquid in which to cook foods as well as a drink. Calvados and Applejack are brandies distilled from apples. Perry is made from pears.

Cognac Name given to brandy distilled in a defined part of western France, generally acknowledged to be the world's finest. The wines are distilled twice before the spirit is stored in wooden casks for several years, then blended to produce a certain style; it does not mature once it has been bottled. The term fine champagne is often used to describe cognac and indicates that it was produced in the best area, the Grand Champagne of the definitive Cognac region.

Crème de Menthe Sweet liqueur flavoured with mint to help the digestion, available as green or white in colour.

Curaçao Orange-flavoured liqueur which takes its name from the island of Curacao near Venezuela. Made in various colours including blue, green, orange and white, it is used as a digestive, an after-dinner liqueur and as a flavouring in foods, especially sweets.

Digestives Sweet or bitter drinks which have the capability of calming the digestion, usually made in the form of a liqueur to be drunk at the end of a meal, e.g. kümmel (flavour of caraway), galliano (herbs), anis (aniseed), fernet branca (various herbals).

Gin Spirit distilled from the liquor of grains and flavoured with various aromates including coriander seeds and juniper berries; used to make cocktails, with tonic water or ginger ale, and also in cooking such as game, pork or veal, without being flambéd.

Grand Marnier Orange-flavoured liqueur made with cognac brandy, available as cordon jaune and cordon rouge, both suitable for flavouring all kinds of sweet dishes, and with duck and pork.

Kirin Japanese beer made from rice.

Koumis Fermented mare's milk made with yeast, honey and flour to produce a low alcohol, effervescent drink.

Kvass (also spelt Quass) Mild, refreshing kind of beer, often home-brewed from a mash of malt, rye bread and water made in the form of a dough which starts to ferment. It can be flavoured with apple, lemon, pear, raspberry, etc. and spiced with ginger or with mint to make a low alcohol, refreshing drink. Popular in Russia.

Madeira Fortified wine from the Atlantic island of that name, usually served as an aperitif, ranging in taste from dry to sweet; also used in clear soups, sauces, stews and sweet dishes.

Mahia Spirit distilled from figs. Served as an aperitif and as an after-dinner liqueur.

Maraschino Spirit made from maraschino cherries, used as a liqueur and to flavour various sweet dishes.

Marsala Fortified wine from Sicily, usually sweet, for use in the pastry department, also in sauces and as a dessert wine. Marsala al' uovo is very rich to the taste. Dry Marsala is sometimes served as an aperitif.

Mead Alcoholic drink made from honey, served as a dessert wine. It is also called hydromel, and the herb and spice-flavoured version is known as metheglin.

Mirin [*Asia*] Sweet cooking wine made from rice.

Noilly Prat Proprietary name of a French vermouth which is usually assumed to be dry and therefore used in cooking, especially for fish.

Noyau Liqueur flavoured with kernels of apricot and peach stones.

Ouzo Aniseed-flavoured drink served very cold accompanied with iced water, which turns it cloudy when added, as an aperitif.

Pernod Aniseed liqueur, clear yellow in colour, which turns cloudy when diluted with iced water.

Port Fortified wine from Portugal matured in oak casks as ruby, tawny, crusted and vintage, and also as white port. White port is often drunk as an aperitif, whereas the darker ones are usually drunk at the end of a meal. Can be used in cooking, e.g. with beef, game, duck, etc.

Raki Another name for arrak, a strong spirit distilled from rice, etc. and not from wine; used in oriental cookery.

Rice Wines This includes mirin and saké wines, which are made by fermenting rice. Their alcohol content of around 17% is equal to sherry and port.

Rum Spirit distilled from sugar cane syrup or molasses in the West Indies and used in cooking and as a flavouring in puddings, sauces and ice-cream.

Saké Rice wine used in Chinese and Japanese cookery and as a drink, usually served warm and in small cups.

Schnapps Similar to aquavit, a strong spirit much used in Germany and Scandinavia.

Sherry Fortified wine made in Spain from wine grown in the locality on the solera system, by which it is matured and blended into several types: fino (light colour, dry, nutty, penetrating aroma), manzanilla (matured near the sea, dry and fresh), amontillado (an aged sherry, medium dry), oloroso (heavy and dark, mellow aroma), amoroso (lighter version of oloroso, sweet), cream (very sweet and light), or brown (very dark and sweet). Used as a flavouring in soups, sauces and sweets.

Vermouth   Fortified wine flavoured with barks, herbs, spices and flowers, made mainly in Italy as bianco (white and sweet), rosso (red and sweet), premium (fine wines, bitter-sweet, spicy), secco (dry, in what is called the French style). Vermouth can be drunk neat, diluted and in cocktails, and can be used for cooking (see also Noilly Prat). Chambéry vermouth is flavoured with alpine strawberries.

Alcoholic Cocktails

Bloody Mary   In a cocktail shaker combine 1 part vodka, 2 dashes lemon juice, 2 dashes Worcester sauce, 2 parts tomato juice and celery salt and pepper to taste. Serve in a medium-sized glass.

Harvey Wallbanger   Shake 1 part vodka and 1 part Galliano liqueur with crushed ice and 2 parts orange juice and serve garnished with a slice of orange and a maraschino cherry.

Manhattan   Stir 1 part sweet vermouth, 2 parts bourbon or Canadian whisky and 1 dash Angostura bitters with ice, then strain into a cocktail glass and garnish with a maraschino cherry.

Piña Colada   In a cocktail shaker combine 2 parts pineapple juice, 1 part coconut milk and 1 part white rum. Serve on crushed ice in two highball glasses, garnished with pineapple and maraschino cherries.

Screwdriver   In a cocktail shaker combine 2 parts vodka, 1 part orange juice and 1 part powdered sugar; a few drops of Angostura bitters may be added.

Tequila   In a cocktail shaker vigorously shake the juice of $\frac{1}{4}$ lemon, 4 dashes grenadine, tequila and 1 dash egg white with ice. Strain into a cocktail glass and garnish with a twist of lemon.

Chapter Fourteen

Cheeses

This chapter describes well-known and lesser-known cheeses from most countries dealt with in this book.

Cheeses can be classified in several ways: they can be categorised according to the kind of milk they are made from, e.g. buffalo, ewe, goat or cow, because each kind tastes different; they can be classed according to the process of production as freshly made or fermented; by their consistency, as soft, semi-hard, hard or processed; and, of course, whether plain or blue-veined. Customers may choose a cheese according to its taste as being mild, medium, or strong (mature). In this chapter cheeses are listed in alphabetical order rather than under any of the above classifications.

Abazar Peynir [*Turkey*]   Small, round, flat cheese weighing 500g, plastic-curd type, made from any kind of milk or a mixture of milks; also available as smoked.

Akkawi [*Middle East*]   High quality cow's milk cheese that is unfortunately in short supply.

Allgäuer Gaiskäse [*Germany*]   Allgäu is famous as a dairy region where several different kinds of cheese are made. This one is made as a soft, yellow-coloured cheese from raw goat's milk and cow's milk and has a strong smell; also made as a white kind with an odour of mushroom and a very mild flavour.

Allgäuer Ziegenkäse [*Germany*]   Strong smelling and tasting, soft, creamy-yellow cheese made from cow's and goat's milk, flavoured with kümmel, in the shape of a 250-g flat disc.

Anejo [*Mexico*]   Dry, white-coloured, goat's milk cheese with a crumbly texture.

Aragón [*Spain*]   Soft to semi-hard with a fat content of 54%, made from goat's and sheep's milk in the form of an indented ball of up to 1.3 kg in weight.

Asadero [*Mexico*]   Freshly made with a plastic curd from whole cow's milk, in various weights up to 1.3 kg; the fat content is 26%.

Asiago [*Italy*]   Hard cheese available in two qualities – one is semi-fat with 36% fat, named Asagio d'Allievo and used mainly for grating because of its piquancy; the other is known as Asagio Grasso di Monte and has a smooth texture that resembles Pecorino.

Baladi [*Middle East*]   White, crumbly cheese made in salted and unsalted versions from sheep's and cow's milk; one of the region's most popular cheeses.

Balaton [*Hungary*]   Firm and heavily pressed, light yellow in colour with an unusual rancid flavour; 45% fat content.

Bandal [*India*]   Soft cream cheese with a mellow flavour and 45% fat content, made from the top of the milk.

Barberey [*France*]   Similar to Camembert in taste and size, sometimes sold in unripened form.

Beaufort [*France*]   Large size, rich butter-flavoured cheese similar to Gruyère but without the holes; made in the Savoy mountains with 50% fat content.

Bedar [*Middle East*]   Made with the skimmed milk of the water buffalo supplemented with pasteurised cow's milk; eaten fresh after curing in the boiled whey.

Bel Paese [*Italy*]   Mild tasting, soft cheese with 50% fat from Lombardy, made in a round, flat shape, up to 1 kg in weight.

Beynaz Peynir [*Turkey*]   Made of fresh sheep's milk curdled with rennet, pressed and cut into small cubes, brined and dried then ripened for several months in a very salty brine.

Bleu d'Auvergne [*France*]   From the mountainous Massif Central area, made from high quality cow's milk which is treated with a penicillin mould; the cheeses weigh about 2 kg and are rubbed with salt and pricked with needles to encourage growth of the mould. Several other blue cheeses are made in this area and are considered to be the best in France; they include Bleu de Laqueville and Bleu de Thiézac.

Bleu de Bresse [*France*]   Similar in taste to a mild Gorgonzola but much smaller in size; very stable and keeps well.

Blue Vinny [*GB*]   Cylindrical-shaped cheese of 6–7 kg with varying fat content, made in Dorset; dry and crumbly and not in abundant supply.

Boursin [*France*]   Fresh cream cheese with a light taste, usually flavoured with garlic, herbs, etc. or coated with crushed peppercorns for spreading; 70% fat content.

Brick [*USA*]   Ivory-coloured cheese of American origin with reddish-brown, dried-out skin; mellow to sweet taste and notable aroma, not as sharp as Cheddar; often packed in slices. 50% fat content; some small holes.

Brie [*France*]   World famous and called the 'king of cheeses'. Flat discs up to 3 kg in weight. A soft paste cheese available in mild to strong flavours, though not so noticeably strong as Camembert. Brie de Meux is the original cheese from the Seine-et-Marne département. Brie de Melun and Brie de Coulommiers have a mild, delicate flavour, and are made in 450-g weights. Cendré de Brie has a grey-black ash rind. Also made in England, Germany and Denmark.

Brinzâ [*Israel*]   Of Eastern European origin, small rectangular cheese of 300 g in weight, made from sheep's milk with the addition of goat's or cow's milk; good quality with 45% fat content.

Bryndza [*Hungary*]   Sheep's milk cheese made by processing Hrudkovy cheese which is made in the mountainous pastures and crumbled to produce a slightly sour, salty and spreadable paste.

Burgas [*Spain*]   Fresh sheep's milk cheese made as flat discs of 1–2 kg in weight, rindless and with a delicate taste typical of ewe's cheese; 54% fat content.

Butterkäse [*Germany*]   Made as flat rounds of 0.5–1.5 kg and in sausage shapes of 2 kg; yellow-brown rind, slightly firm but elastic texture.

Buttermilk [*all countries*]   This is the residue from the churning of soured cream and is often cultured with acid-producing streptococci added to the skimmed milk.

Cabecou [*France*]   Popular goat's milk cheese made in individual portions for early consumption. Fairly mild, with the characteristic taste and aroma of goat's cheese.

Caboc [*GB*]   Full cream, cylindrical-shaped, coated with rolled oats. It has a slightly sour taste with crunchiness from the oats.

Cabra [*Spain*]   Fresh goat's milk cheese made for early consumption. Also Queso de Cabra, a Venezuelan goat's milk cheese made in a pear shape.

Cabreiro [*Portugal*]   Similar to Ricotta (q.v.) as a flat disc, ripened in brine for several months.

Caciocavallo [*Italy*]   Hard cheese from cow's milk matured for up to four months for ordinary eating or 12 months for grating and cooking; tastes somewhat similar to Gruyère.

Caerphilly [*GB*]   Soft and fairly mild cheese with a sourish taste; crumbly and early to mature; made as low cylinders of 3.5 kg with 48% fat content, in South Wales.

Caithness [*GB*]   Small, distinguished full fat soft cheese from the north of Scotland.

Cambrai [*France*]   Known as Boulette de Cambrai because of its shape, a fairly strong, sharp-tasting cheese flavoured with herbs and spices, eaten fresh.

Camembert [*France*]   A real, good Camembert should taste slightly of mushrooms and be fairly strong smelling, though not of ammonia, and have a supple consistency. Made in traditional small round moulds of 200–300 g each, it becomes covered with a pure white mould. Over 20% of cheese production in France is of Camembert.

Cantal [*France*]   Very large drum-shaped cheese of 35–45 kg in weight, made from cow's milk with a greyish-white rind and smooth texture.

Caprino [*Italy*]   Goat's milk soft cheese sold by weight from bulk, fresh, slightly sour taste.

Carré de l'Est [*France*]   Made as rectangular shapes of 100–200 g, each with a white skin and the flavour of a slightly salty Camembert.

Cebrero [*Spain*]   Has the appearance of a mushroom with an open cap, up to 40 cm wide with a pale yellow rind. Slightly sharp to the taste, soft, creamy consistency with a shallow blue veining.

Cecil [*Russia*]   Cow's or sheep's milk, low fat cheese from Armenia, made in spiral or ball shapes.

Chabichou [*France*]   Goat's milk cheese for early consumption from Poitou, made in the form of a truncated pyramid.

Cheddar [*GB*]   Britain's most popular cheese, available as farmhouse, which is matured for up to 12 months to improve the strength of flavour, and as factory Cheddar which is matured for a few months only and has a mild, nutty flavour and smooth, elastic texture with a pale yellow colour. Keeps well, melts easily in cooking, and has a 40% fat content. Made in many other countries and with many variations, e.g. spiced, smoked. Imported to the UK from Australia, Canada, France, Germany, Ireland and New Zealand. Also available in the form of vegetarian cheese.

Cheshire [*GB*]   Made from the milk of Shorthorn cows grazing in Cheshire meadows, it has a high salt content, a mild, nutty flavour and 48% fat content. Made in three varieties: red, which is dyed with anatto to give an orange colour; white, which is pale cream in colour and becomes acidy and does not keep very well; and blue Cheshire, rated one of the world's finest blue cheeses with its soft, buttery texture and excellent flavour – it is however, rare, and expensive.

Colby [*USA*]   Soft, granular texture, mild flavour and light to deep yellow colour; useful in salads; 50% fat content.

Comté [*France*]   A Gruyère-type cheese often called Gruyère de Comté; moist and crumbly rind and firm consistency with large holes and a pronounced smell.

Cottage Cheese [*many countries*]   Has approx. 4% or less fat content and only 106 kcal per 100 g; widely used in many countries. It is made by coagulating skimmed milk by heating gently with rennet or an acid then straining out the whey, thus yielding a granular curd which is very mild and without much taste. Also available in flavoured versions, e.g. with chives, pineapple, etc., packed in cartons.

Cream Cheese [*many countries*]   Often made by adding whipped cream to sieved cottage cheese or by adding lactic acid cultures to single or double cream.

Crowdie [*GB*]   Full-cream, freshly made Curd cheese mixed with cream and seasoned with salt.

Dacca [*India*]   Clotted milk is broken up then pressed into small wicker baskets to dry and mature, then smoked over cow dung or wood shavings.

Danablu [*Scandinavia*]   Very popular blue-veined cheese made in rectangular, square or cylindrical shapes of 2.5–3 kg in weight. Its soft texture makes it easy to cut and its pungent taste adds to its prestige.

Danbo [*Scandinavia*]   Full-cream cheese, pale yellow in colour and of a firm texture, made square in shape at 6 kg in weight.

Demisel [*France*]   Fresh full-cream cheese from Normandy with 40% fat content, sold in small containers, similar to Petit Suisse (q.v.).

Derby [*GB*]   Similar to Cheddar though not in so great a production; mild to the taste, solid in texture and best when fully ripened. Made in cartwheel shape up to 14 kg in weight. Sage Derby is marbled with ground leaves of sage and spinach.

Domiati [*Middle East*]   From skimmed buffalo or cow's milk made as a soft, mild cheese with adequate salt, sold either fresh or cured in brine for several months. One of the region's most popular cheeses.

Double Gloucester [*GB*]   Large, cylindrical cheese of 28 kg, of full but mild flavour that is never sharp and has very good keeping qualities. Ripened for 6–12 months before use; 48% fat content.

Dunlop [*GB*]   Similar to Cheddar but bland to the taste even when mature, so usually sold while young; pale to deep cream in colour.

Elbo [*Scandinavia*]   Cow's milk cheese made in loaf shape up to 6 kg in weight; mild but aromatic taste, 20–40% fat content, with a few holes in it.

Emmenthal [*Switzerland*]   The most famous Swiss cheese, from Berne, made as large cartwheels of up to 100 kg with 15–48% fat content. Hard golden-yellow rind, fine aroma and flavour and lots of large holes. Copies are made in many other countries.

Esrom [*Scandinavia*]   Full-cream cheese with yellow paste, dotted with small holes; has a sweet taste and an edible rind. Made in small loaf shapes of up to 1·5 kg.

Evora [*Portugal*]   Small flat discs of 100 g or 150 g weight, made from goat's milk with a dry, salty taste; sold rindless.

Féta [*Greece*]   Made of sheep's milk or as a mixture with cow's milk and allowed to ripen in its own whey and brine, which makes it quite salty to the taste. It has a piquant and slightly sour eating characteristic. Very white in colour, made in rectangular shape without a rind and with 45–60% fat content. Also made in other countries.

Fontainbleau [*France*]   Similar to Petit Suisse (q.v.), a light, spongy, full-cream cheese that can also be used with sugar as a dessert.

Fontina [*Italy*]   Considered to be one of the world's finest cheeses, made in Piedmont of cow's milk in 10–20-kg low cylinder shapes; semi-hard but smooth in texture, whitish-yellow in colour with a brownish rind; slightly nutty and sweet on the palate.

Frisco [*USA*]   Name of a brand of Cottage cheese, a very popular type with only 0.4% fat content.

Fromage du Curé [*France*]   Also known as Fromage Nantais, a small square of approx. 300 g with 40% fat content.

Fromage Frais [*France*]   Very low fat with only 47 kcal per 100g; white, tasteless, slightly grainy but fairly smooth consistency. Used mainly in cooking, in place of cream. Also available in fruit-flavoured form.

Fynbo [*Scandinavia*]   Similar to Samso (q.v.), cartwheel shapes of 7–8 kg and 30–45% fat content, with holes in the rubbery texture and very mild in flavour.

Gammelost [*Scandinavia*]   Soft, smooth texture and sharp, aromatic flavour; though eaten while fresh it has long keeping qualities. The mould that forms is pressed back into the cheese. It has only up to 3% fat content.

Getost [*Scandinavia*]   Goat's milk cheese, eaten very fresh, made in 300–500 g packs, without a rind.

Gorgonzola [*Italy*]   Very popular blue-veined cheese of white to pale straw colour with blue-green veins; it is quite mild to the taste, made of pasteurised cow's milk with *Penicillia gorgonzola* added. Made in the shape of low cylinders of 6–12 kg in weight; 48% fat content. Also made in other countries.

Grana Padana [*Italy*]   Similar to Parmesan but matures more quickly; granular of structure and lighter in taste; used mainly for cooking and with pastas.

Graviera [*Greece*]   An imitation of Gruyère.

Gruyère [*Switzerland*]   Often compared with Emmenthal but more moist and more highly flavoured; made in smaller weights of 30–40 kg. The holes in it are smaller and it is creamier in texture. It is excellent for the table and for cooking.

Halloum [*Middle East*]   Made of sheep's milk, this is Bedouin in origin and is tough, quite salty, good for cooking and can even be used on a kebab. Also made in other countries.

Haloumi [*Middle East*]   Sheep's milk cheese, rather salty in taste with a string-like texture.

Havarti [*Scandinavia*]   Very popular cheese similar to Tilsit (q.v.), made in cylindrical or loaf shape and 4–5 kg in weight. Sharper to the taste as it matures.

Jarlsberg [*Scandinavia*]   Mild-tasting, full-cream cheese, firm and with holes; nutty flavour and slightly sweet; made in cylinders of 10 kg in weight.

Jerevansky [*Russia*]   From Armenia, a semi-hard cheese of 4–6 kg in weight which is ripened in tins sealed with a plug.

Jupneh [*Middle East*]   Made of sheep's or goat's milk with a piece of salted sheep's stomach to curdle it; pressed into shape as a flat disc ready to eat or for boiling in brine before eating.

Kâskaval [*Middle East and Turkey*]   Hard cheese with good keeping qualities made in two kinds. One is made from unpasteurised sheep's milk and follows the Cheddar style of manufacture in the form of a ball of 9 kg in weight which is rubbed with salt and stored for approx. 8 weeks and used within the year. It has a sourish, salty taste and is fairly aromatic. The second kind has a higher moisture content and weighs 7 kg. There is also a cow's milk Kâskaval with a nice amber colour but less taste and aroma.

Kasseri [*Greece*]   A plastic consistency cheese with good keeping qualities made by cutting Kefalotíri cheese (q.v.) into strips and immersing in hot water to render it plasticised.

Kefalotíri [*Greece*]   Hard cheese from goat's or sheep's milk made in cylindrical shapes of 9–10 kg in weight; needs to be grated for use.

Kopanisti [*Greece*]   Blue-veined with high salt content and a peppery flavour; the mould which grows on the cheese is kneaded back into it and it is then ripened for up to two months.

Kugelkäse [*Germany*]   A quark cheese (q.v.) with added spices, kümmel and paprika, hardened by heating for keeping; used mainly in grated form.

Kutunjuusto [*Scandinavia*]   A small rectangular cheese of 200 g and 30% fat content from the town of Tampere; made from goat's milk.

Labaneh [*Scandinavia*]   Made in the form of a flat disc with a fat content of 10%, from skimmed cow's milk.

Lajta [*Hungary*]   Full-cream, semi-hard cheese that is pale in colour with a fresh, slightly sharp taste; made in 1-kg bars with a 45% fat content.

Lancashire [*GB*]   Mild, becoming mellow as it matures and with more flavour than Cheddar; does not travel or keep well. Very white and usually crumbly, but softens when mature. 48% fat content; made in small and large sizes.

Lebbene [*Israel*]   Similar to yogurt, drained and formed into small balls ready to eat; made from a mixture of milks.

Leicester [*GB*]   Made in cylinders of 13–18 kg in weight, very mild and fairly flavourful with a loose, slightly crumbly texture; stands out on the cheese board because of its deep orange colour from the added anatto colouring.

Liederkranz [*USA*]   Mild-tasting Limburger-type (q.v.) with a creamy texture and golden-yellow colour; made in small rectangular shapes weighing 175 g.

Limburg [*Germany*]   This used to be one of Belgium's most famous cheeses but is now made in Germany and copied in many other countries. Very pungent flavour in all the several varieties made, but the consistency varies according to kind and the fat content, which ranges from 20–50%; made in weights from 175 g–1 kg.

Liptauer [*Hungary*]   Also made in several other countries bordering the river Danube; made of sheep's or cow's milk and often flavoured with paprika.

Livarot [*France*]   From the département of Pays d'Auge, a full-cream, soft and mild cheese with a strong smell and small holes, packeted in 300-g and 500-g flat discs.

Maribo [*Scandinavia*]   Made in cartwheel shape and as a square, up to 15 kg in weight with varying fat content of 20%, 30% and 45%; it has a red rind and light reddish-yellow colour flesh with lots of small holes in it; the flavour is distinctive.

Maroilles [*France*]   Soft, pale cheese with reddish-coloured rind and very good flavour, being slightly salty, strong but not too sharp. Usually made square at 800 g and a mignon size of 100 g. There is also a Maroilles Gris which is more mature with a slight smell of ammonia.

Mascarpone [*Italy*]   Soft, fresh cream cheese with a delicious flavour which makes it ideal for use with desserts. Sold in 100–125 g muslin bags with 70% fat content.

Meira [*Middle East*]   Popular sheep's milk cheese, stored in sheep skins to mature for up to 12 months until quite hard.

Mesost [*Scandinavia*]   A goat's milk cheese which is brown in colour with a caramel taste, made in 1·5-kg loaf shapes and with fat content of 10–30%.

Mimolette [*France*]   Cow's milk cheese made in the shape of a ball of 2.5–4 kg in weight with 40% fat content. Has orange-coloured flesh, a mild taste and grey skin, rather similar to Edam. The Dutch called their export grade Edam cheese Mimolette.

Minnesota Blue [*USA*]   A copy of Roquefort (q.v.), made with cow's milk.

Misch [*Middle East*]   Made from skimmed buffalo's milk and cured in salted milk, then ripened for a year or more to give a strong taste similar to Roquefort; it is often spiced.

Mitzithra [*Greece*]   Made in 1-kg baskets from the whey left from the manufacture of Féta, for eating while still fresh and warm; otherwise moulded into balls for storage until ready for grating.

Monterey [*USA*]   Made as small cheeses of 200 g and 500 g, and as cartwheels of 3–4 kg in weight in the same way as Cheddar, from pasteurised whole or skimmed cow's milk.

Monuri [*Greece*]   This is another name for Mitzithra (q.v.).

Mozzarella [*Italy*]   Authentic Mozzarella is made from buffalo milk and is very moist and delicate, but such is the demand for it as an ingredient for pizzas that it is mostly made from cow's milk with perhaps a small percentage of water buffalo milk. Made in balls of 500 g and upwards, with a fat content of 44%.

Munster [*France and Germany*]   In France it is made in the Alsace region bordering Germany, from cow's milk in flat discs varying from 300 g to 1·5 kg, with 40–50% fat content. It has a soft consistency and a tangy flavour with orange-reddish rind. The German version is made in flat discs of 125 g to 1 kg.

Mycella [*Scandinavia*]   Mild, bluey-green veined and yellow flesh, made in cylinders of 5–9 kg in weight with 50% fat content.

Mysost [*Scandinavia*]   Medium flavour, originally made with goat's milk which is still available as Ekte Gjetost (genuine goat's cheese); now made from cow's milk whey. Good for cooking purposes. Norway's most popular cheese.

Neufchatel [*France*]   Soft, slightly salty, fresh in flavour, made square, round, heart-shaped, etc. in 100-g weights.

Nieheimer Hopfenkäse [*Germany*]   A sour-milk cheese of the quark type (q.v.) made mainly from coagulated whey in small balls of 100 g, and sometimes flavoured with kümmel and packed in hop leaves.

Panir Kisei [*Middle East*]   Sheep's or goat's milk cheese packed into pots which are sealed for several months, often kept in sand until matured and hardened.

Parmesan [*Italy*]   Full-cream cheese, salted for up to three weeks and cured for two or three years; after the first year it is coated with a mixture of earth and oil to give a solid crust. Very hard cheese of straw colour, mainly for use grated in cookery and for sprinkling over pastas; spicy rather than sharp in flavour, it is made as giovane (young), tipico (4–5 years old) and stravecchio (very old). Made in cylinders of 22–36 kg in weight with a fat content of 32%.

Parmigiano Reggiano   The Italian name for Parmesan.

Pecorino [*Italy*]   Ewe's milk hard cheese, mainly used grated but may be served on a cheeseboard; made as cylinders weighing 6–22 kg. Also made with peppercorns, when it is labelled Pecorino Pepato.

Petit Suisse [*France*]   Soft, creamy cheese made by the Gervais company in small paper or plastic containers of 25 g, with a fat content of 60–75%; slightly sour, nutty, fresh taste which makes it suitable for use as a dessert. Also made in Switzerland.

Pommel [*France*]   Similar to Petit Suisse, a soft cream cheese wrapped in a paper collar.

Pont l'Evêque [*France*]   Sold in small square chipwood boxes of approx. 300 g; made in the Vallée d'Auge and similar to Camembert, with a distinctive flavour and 45% fat content.

Port-Salut [*France*]   Made by Trappist monks for 180 years, flat cylindrical shapes of 1.3–2 kg in weight. A semi-hard, mild flavoured cheese.

Processed Cheese [*many countries*]   Made from poor quality hard or semi-hard cheeses by emulsifying and heating to 85 °C with added milk powder. Usually moist and plastic.

Provolone [*Italy*]   Mild, firm texture and delicate taste, made in several shapes, e.g. pear, melon, sausage and cone, tied with a cord to suspend them, weighing from 1–6 kg each.

Pultost [*Scandinavia*]   Soft cheese made from skimmed milk, though some have cream added; eaten fresh. Some are flavoured with caraway seeds.

Quark [*Germany*]   Fresh soft cheeses of which there are several kinds, made of pasteurised milk or from milk powder; little taste, sourish, packed in tubs, with varying fat content from 10–85%.

Queijo de Serra [*Portugal*]   Comes in several versions, from semi-hard to very hard according to the farm where made; also in several weights and shapes from 800 g to 1.5 kg. Often curdled with cultures from a wild thistle rather than rennet; 40–55% fat content.

Reblochon [*France*]   Semi-hard, similar to Port-Salut (q.v.), a round, flat cheese of 600 g and 45% fat content; mild, fragrant flavour, ripened in mountain caves.

Red Windsor [*GB*]   A Cheddar cheese impregnated with red wine, which makes it look different on a cheese board.

Requeijao [*Portugal*]   A Ricotta-type cheese (q.v.), also made in Brazil.

Ricotta [*Italy*]   Made from either sheep's or cow's milk. Eaten fresh it is similar to cottage cheese and called tipo dolce, slightly firmer and drier it is called tipo moliterno, and occasionally it is eaten as tipo forte which is more mature. All are round in shape with a white, crumbly texture and slightly sweet taste, with 20–30% fat content.

Romadur [*Germany*]   Small cheeses of 75–175 g in weight, similar to Limburg (q.v.); soft, mild aroma and fat content of 20–60%. Also made in Switzerland.

Roquefort [*France*]   One of the greatest cheeses of the world, a delicately flavoured blue-green veined cheese from the village of the same name in the Massif Central, made in cylinders of 2.7 kg from ewe's milk; has a unique flavour.

Saint-Marcellin [*France*]   Fresh small discs of 75 g each for immediate consumption, some flavoured with mixed herbs or ripened in chestnut leaves.

Saint-Nectaire [*France*]   There is only a small production of this delicious cheese from the Auvergne; cylindrical, supple of texture and mild in flavour, and at its best after six months storage.

Saint-Paulin [*France*]   Very similar to Port-Salut (q.v.), made in many parts of the country in cylinders of 1.3–2 kg in weight. It tastes the same as Port-Salut.

Samso [*Scandinavia*]   Cow's milk cheese, firm, yellow in colour, tastes like strong Cheddar cheese, aged for six months – sometimes has holes in it.

Secretpenir [*Middle East*]   A cheese made by nomads using camel's, donkey's or horse's milks, in the form of sun-dried small balls which are then beeswaxed to mature.

Sicille [*Middle East*]   Sheep's milk with added goat's and cow's milk pressed in baskets and cured in a cellar to give an elastic texture with small holes which hardens with maturity; has a rancid taste; paprika is sometimes added.

Snow Brand [*Japan*]   Brand name of many different kinds of cheeses of European origin as made for Japanese consumption.

Spreads [*several countries*]   Made from inferior cheeses by emulsification with salts, flavours and colours, wrapped in metal foil in triangular or other shapes. They keep well and are very soft and moist.

Stilton [*GB*]   One of the greatest cheeses in the world, made of rich cow's milk in tall cylindrical shapes of 6.5–8.2 kg in weight. The blue mould is injected and the cheeses ripen under careful control for up to six months to maturity, giving a smooth yellow colour and even moulding; the flavour is mellow. Fresh white stilton, which is crumbly, is also available.

Stracchino [*Italy*]   White to pale yellow, mild cheese of compact consistency yet which almost melts in the mouth. Stracchino Crescenza is the best quality with either a soft creamy texture or a harder consistency; made in loaf shapes of 500 g to 4 kg in weight.

Taleggio [*Italy*]   Compact, slightly brittle cheese, white to pale yellow and with a mild fruity flavour; made with 48% fat content in loaf shapes of 1.7–2 kg in weight.

Tilsit [*Germany*]   Cows' milk cheese matured for up to six months to give a mildly pungent flavour; light yellow in colour with some small holes; sometimes made with added caraway seeds.

Tomme [*France*]   There are several kinds of Tomme cheeses, one example being Tomme au Raisin, which is well known because of its rind made of grape pips and skins left after grapes have been pressed for their juice. White to yellow, fairly solid and waxy and with a slightly sour or bitter taste; some have a low fat content of 10%, others up to 45%.

Trappistenkäse [*Germany, Austria and the Balkans*]   A popular cheese originally made by monks in France; a semi-soft cheese resembling Port-Salut (q.v.).

Turunmaa [*Scandinavia*]   Soft, creamy cheese made of goat's milk.

Vegetarian Cheese [*GB*]   This kind of cheese is made with non-animal rennet and tastes exactly like ordinary cheese made from calf's rennet. It is available as Cheddar, Cheshire, Double Gloucester, Leicester and Stilton, and also as Edam from Holland, which is covered with a yellow wax coating instead of the usual red. The cheese is made from milk so is not permissible for vegans.

Vendome [*France*]   Small, flat discs weighing 250 g, a soft cheese made in the Loire valley.

Villalon [*Spain*]   Ewe's milk cheese from Valladolid made fresh in small, elongated cylindrical shapes.

Wensleydale [*GB*]   Known mainly as a white, young cheese with a sour flavour reminiscent of Caerphilly; also available as a blue-veined cheese, though this is somewhat rare; similar to Stilton but with a greyish-white rind, made in cylinders of 4.5–5.5 kg in weight.

Appendix One

Menu Planner

This menu planner is designed to give easy access to the recipes of each country. Dishes are aligned to country of origin and listed alphabetically according to type, e.g. soups, egg dishes, cheese dishes, Italian pastes, noodle dishes, savoury rice dishes, fish dishes, etc. Countries are featured in alphabetical order as follows:

✧ Caribbean ✧   ✧ Japan ✧

✧ China ✧   ✧ Mexico ✧

✧ France ✧   ✧ Middle East ✧

✧ Germany ✧   ✧ Portugal ✧

✧ Great Britain ✧   ✧ Russia ✧

✧ Greece and Turkey ✧   ✧ Scandinavia

✧ Hungary ✧   ✧ South Korea ✧

✧ India   ✧ Spain ✧

✧ Indonesia ✧   ✧ Thailand ✧

✧ Israel ✧   ✧ United States of America ✧

✧ Italy ✧

Caribbean

Desserts and Breads

Banana Fritters
Bananas in Coconut and Turmeric
    Sauce
Banana Soufflé
Grapefruit, Orange and Ginger Salad
Mango Fool
Pineapple in Rum Sauce
Sweet Potato and Coconut Pie
West Indian Bread

Fish Dishes

Pickled Fish
Prawn and Potato Balls
Shallow-fried Salt Codfish and Ackee
Shallow-fried Salt Codfish with
    Tomatoes and Lime
Soused Red Snapper
Stewed Shark Suprêmes Creole Style
Stewed Tuna Steaks Caribbean Style

Meat Dishes

Beef Stew Creole Style
Beef Stew with Christophene
Boiled Beef with Red Kidney Beans
Boiled Loin of Pork with Eggplant
Boiled Pigs' Tails with Rice and
    Cabbage
Boiled Smoked Hock with Red Beans
Grilled Steak Flambéd with Rum
Pepperpot
Pork and Tuna Stew
Pork Stew with Eggplant
Rabbit in Peanut Sauce
Sautéed Pork Chops in Watercress
    Sauce

Potato Dishes

Baked Sweet Potato with Chives
Boiled New Potatoes with Cottage
    Cheese
Boiled New Potatoes with Cinnamon
    and Caraway
Boiled Glazed Sweet Potatoes
Fried Sweet Potato
Sweet Potato Fritters

Poultry Dishes

Chicken Stew with Mangos and
    Cashew Nuts
Chicken and Pumpkin Stew
Pot Roast Chicken with Pork and
    Orange Stuffing
Sauté of Chicken Creole Style
Sauté of Chicken with Almonds
Sauté of Chicken with Coconut Milk
Sauté of Chicken with Crab, Crayfish
    and Pork Pelau
Sauté of Chicken with Pigeon Peas
    Pelau
Sauté of Chicken with Lime and Rum
Sauté of Chicken with Pineapple and
    Rum
Suprêmes of Duck with Orange
    Liqueur

Rice Dishes

Caribbean-style Boiled Rice
Rice Calypso
Rice Creole
Rice with Pigeon Peas
Rice with Red Kidney Beans
Risotto with Mushrooms
Risotto with Prawns

Salads

Banana Salad
Fruit and Vegetable Salad
Mango Salad
Orange and Banana Salad

Sauces, Relishes and Dressings

Chilli Mayonnaise
Chilli Sauce
Coconut Dressing
Coconut Sauce
Cream Dressing
Mango Relish
Orange Dressing
Paw-paw Dip
Pomegranate Sauce
Red Chilli Relish
Roasted Garlic Dressing

Soups

Callaloo
Cream of Avocado and Crab Soup
Cream of Cucumber and Coconut Soup
Cream of Peanut Soup
Cream of Sweetcorn and Prawn Soup
Chilled Breadfruit Soup with Chives
Chilled Orange Soup
Fish Soup
Pork and Tannis Soup
Purée of Pumpkin Soup Creole Style

Vegetable Dishes

Baked Eggplant in Coconut Cream
Baked Paw-paw
Baked Stuffed Chayote
Baked Stuffed Paw-paw
Baked Yams
Black Beans with Cider
Black Beans with Green Peppers
Creamed Dasheen
Creamed Breadfruit
Fried Plantains (Deep-fried)
Fried Plantains (Shallow-fried)
Lentils with Turmeric and Cumin
Okra Fritters
Okra in Tomato Sauce
Okras and Cornmeal
Plantains in Cheese Sauce
Spinach with Sweet Peppers

China

Desserts

Caramelised Apple and Banana Fritters
Sweet Wontons

Dumplings

Mushroom, Pork and Prawn
  Dumplings
Pork Dumplings
Steamed Pork Dumplings
Steamed Pork and Chestnut Dumplings
Steamed Pork and Prawn Dumplings
Wonton Savoury Dumplings

Fish Dishes

Fried Fish with Sweet and Sour Sauce
Fried Lobster with Pineapple
Lobster with Ginger
Lobster with Pimento and Ginger
Poached Bass with Ginger Sauce
Prawn Butterflies
Prawn and Sesame Toasts
Shallow-fried Lobster with Rice
  Noodles
Shallow-fried Scallops and Mussels
  with Snow Peas
Shallow-fried Whiting Szechwan Style
Spring Scallop Rolls

Meat Dishes

Barbecued Spare Ribs
Beef with Oyster Sauce
Braised Beef with Lotus Roots and
  Ginger
Sautéed Beef with Five-spice Powder
Steamed Beef and Pork Balls
Steamed Pork and Prawn Balls
Stir-fried Beef in Black Bean Sauce
Stir-fried Beef with Asparagus
Stir-fried Beef with Ginger
Stir-fried Beef with Mushrooms
Stir-fried Beef with Sugar Peas
Stir-fried Sweet and Sour Pork
Sweet and Sour Pork

Noodle Dishes

Cellophane or Bran Starch Noodles
Crisp Fried Noodles
Crispy Egg Noodles with Chicken and
  Bamboo Shoots
Egg Noodles with Lobster and
  Vegetables
Fried Egg Noodles
Rice Vermicelli Noodles
Rice Vermicelli with Prawns

Omelettes

Ham and Bean Sprout Omelette
Spring Onion and Ginger Omelette

Poultry and Game Birds

Fried Duck Chinese Style
Peking Duck and Mandarin Pancakes
Poached Chicken with Spiced Sauce
Poached Duck with Cabbage and
  Mushrooms
Poached Duck with Chilli Oil
Roast Chicken Cantonese Style

Sauté of Chicken with Lime
Sautéed Goujons of Chicken with
  Ginger
Sautéed Goujons of Chicken with
  Paw-paw
Sautéed Goujons of Duck with
  Mandarins
Sautéed Goujons of Duck with Mangos
Shallow-fried Shanghai Duck
Steamed Chicken with Ham
Stir-fried Goujons of Chicken with
  Peanuts
Stir-fried Chicken with Almonds
Stir-fried Chicken with Vegetables

Rice Dishes

Boiled Rice with Spring Onions
Boiled Rice with Vegetables
Most Precious Rice

Sauces

Ginger Sauce
Lemon and Coriander Sauce
Mandarin Sauce
Pineapple Sauce
Plum Sauce
Sweet and Sour Sauce
Tomato Sauce

Soups

Bird's Nest Soup
Chicken and Egg Soup
Chicken and Mushroom Soup
Chicken and Sweetcorn Soup
Chicken, Prawn and Noodle Soup
Chicken Soup with Crabmeat
Egg Soup
Melon Soup
Shark's Fin Soup

Vegetable Dishes

Bamboo Shoots, Mushrooms and
  Babycorn
Bean Curd with Crabmeat and Ginger
Bean Curd with Ginger

Broad Beans with Sesame Oil
Glazed Vegetables
Lettuce with Ginger
Mixed Vegetables with Oyster Sauce
Steamed Mushrooms with Pork
Stir-fried French Beans

France

Cold Items

Chicken Mousse
Fish Pâté in Brioche Pastry
Game Pâté
Pâté Maison
Potted Goose

Cheese Dishes

Camembert Fritters
Cheese Fritters
Cheese Kebabs
Cheese Straws
Cottage Cheese Quiche
Croque Monsieur
Galette au Fromage

Desserts, Sweetmeats and Breads

Apple Flan
Arlesiennes
Baguette
Biscuits Champagne
Cherry Clafoutis
Croissants
Curd Cheese Flan
French Loaf or Stick
Gitanes
Glazed Apple

Hazelnut Tartlets
Lady's Finger Biscuits
Macaroons
Omelette Norvégienne
Pain de Gênes
Pastry Cream
Pears Poached in Red Wine
Rice and Almond Coupes
Rum Babas
Semolina and Redcurrant Moulds
Strawberries in Rhône Wine

Dumplings

Gnocchi with Cream Sauce
Gnocchi with Potatoes

Egg Dishes

Carrot and Herb Omelette
Eggplant Omelette
Fried Eggs French Style
Moulded Eggs with Chicken
Moulded Eggs with Kidney
Moulded Eggs with Tomato
Scrambled Eggs with Lobster
Shirred Eggs Bercy
Sorrel Omelette
Stuffed Eggs with Mushrooms and
  Cheese Sauce

Fish Dishes

Baked Fillet of Salmon-trout in Ham
Baked Mussels
Baked Stuffed Pike
Bouillabaisse
Poached Eels with Sorrel
Poached Fillets of Sole in White Wine
    Sauce with Mushrooms, Tarragon
    and Tomato
Poached Fillets of Sole with Grapes
Shallow-fried Goujons of Sole with
    Artichokes
Shallow-fried Fillet of Sole with
    Mushrooms and Prawns
Shallow-fried Trout in Cream
Skate with Capers and Black Butter
Snails Burgundy Style

Meat, Game and Offal Dishes

Boiled Beef French Style
Braised Calf's Sweetbreads
Calf's Cheek with Vinaigrette Sauce
Loin of Veal Baked in Pastry
Peppered Sirloin Steaks
Pork Noisettes with Prunes
Pot Roasted Saddle of Venison
Sauté of Chicken with Red Wine
Sautéed Sirloin Steak in Red Wine
    Sauce
Sirloin Steaks in Red Wine
Tournedos Rossini
Veal Cutlets in Cider
Veal Cutlets in Parcels

Potato Dishes

Anna Potatoes
Boulangère Potatoes
Dauphine Potatoes
Delmonico Potatoes
Florentin Potatoes
Fondant Potatoes
Galette Potatoes
Maître d'Hotel Potatoes

Moulded Potatoes with Artichokes and
    Truffle
Parisienne Potatoes
Savoyarde Potatoes

Poultry and Game Birds

Braised Pigeon with Olives
Poached Chicken Burgundy Style
Poached Chicken with Truffles and
    Mushrooms
Pot Roasted Chicken with Mushrooms
Pot Roasted Duck with Orange
Pot Roasted Pigeon with Onions,
    Olives, Potatoes and Truffle
Pheasant with Madeira and Truffles
Sauté of Chicken Bourguignonne
Sauté of Chicken Chasseur
Sauté of Chicken in Madeira with
    Truffles
Stewed Pheasant with Truffle
Suprêmes of Chicken with Asparagus
Suprêmes of Chicken in Cream with
    Mushrooms

Rice Dishes

Pilaff with Saffron
Pilaff with Saffron and Tomato
Risotto with Ham, Tongue and
    Mushrooms

Salads

Fennel and Orange Salad
Tomato and Anchovy Salad

Sauces, Dips and Dressings

Béchamel Sauce
Chasseur Sauce
Cheese Sauce
Cherry Sauce
Chicken Suprême Sauce
Cream Sauce

Devilled Sauce
French Dressing
Garlic Mayonnaise
Green Mayonnaise
Gribiche
Horseradish Sauce
Jus Lié
Mayonnaise
Mushroom Sauce
Olive and Caper Dip
Paprika Sauce
Parsley Sauce
Tartar sauce
Tomato Sauce
Velouté
White Wine Fish Sauce

Soups

Cabbage Soup
Consommé Crecy
Consommé Longchamps

Consommé Madelèine
Consommé Madrilène
Consommé Portugaise
Cream of Chestnut Soup
Cream of Sorrel Soup
Croûtes-au-pot
Fish Soup
Petite Marmite
Vichyssoise

Vegetable Dishes

Artichoke Hearts in Cider
Beetroot in Cream Sauce with Cumin
Braised Celery Italian Style
Cauliflower Polish Style
Glazed Carrots
Haricot Beans in Cream Sauce
Peas French Style
Peas with Bacon and Onions
Ratatouille
Salsify in Cream Sauce

Germany

Desserts and Breads

Almond Torte
Baked Apples
Black Forest Gâteau
Bread and Butter and Cherry Pudding
Cherry Strudel
Gugelhopf or Kugelhopf
Pumpernickel
Sachertorte
Sweet Fritters
Vienna Bread and Rolls
Zürcher Leckerli

Dumplings

Bread Dumplings
Cheese Dumplings
Potato Dumplings

Raw Potato Dumplings
Semolina Dumplings
Steamed Savoury Pudding

Egg Dishes

Boiled Eggs with Soured Cream and
  Herbs
Boiled Eggs with Sweet and Sour
  Sauce
Farmer's Omelette
Leek and Bacon Omelette
Scrambled Eggs with Buckling Herring
Scrambled Eggs with Mushrooms
Scrambled Eggs with Prawns
Scrambled Eggs with Smoked Eel

Fish Dishes

Baked Fillet of Cod with Sauerkraut
Baked Skate with Sauerkraut
Baked Suprême of Halibut
Blue Eel
Lobster in Beer
Poached Darne of Carp in Brandy and
    Fruit Sauce
Poached Eel in Dill Sauce
Stewed Suprême of Halibut with
    Cabbage and Caraway
Poached Suprême of Turbot with
    Cauliflower

Meat and Offal Dishes

Boiled Hand of Pork with Beer
Boiled Knuckle of Pork
Boiled Soured Pork
Braised Beef Olives with Gherkins
Braised Knuckles of Pork with
    Sauerkraut
Braised Loin of Pork with Soured
    Cream
Braised Steaks in Beer
Braised Stuffed Shoulder of Veal
    Hanover Style
Breaded Veal Escalopes
Fried Calves' Feet
Fried Liver in Wine Sauce
Fried Liver with Apple and Onion
Pot Roasted Shoulder of Pork
Veal Cutlets with Soured Cream and
    Paprika
Veal Escalope Holstein
Veal Escalope Vienna Style

Noodle Dishes

German Swabian Noodles

Potato Dishes

Baked Potatoes with Bacon
Baked Potatoes with Egg and Chive
Farmhouse Potato Cakes
Potato Cakes German Style
Potato Pancakes

Poultry and Game Birds

Braised Duck and Cabbage
Braised Partridge with Raisins
Braised Pheasant with Sauerkraut
Braised Stuffed Pigeon
Chicken Fricassée with Button Onions
    and Mushrooms
Chicken Viennese Style
Pot Roast Chicken Hamburg Style
Pot Roasted Duck with Morello
    Cherries
Shallow-fried Stuffed Goose Neck

Salads

Beetroot Salad
Cabbage and Bacon Salad
Cabbage and Cumin Salad
Celeriac Salad
Dandelion Salad
Lamb's Lettuce and Orange Salad
Potato Salad
Red Cabbage Salad
Warm Potato Salad

Sauces

Apple and Horseradish Sauce
Maltese Sauce

Soups

Brown Chicken and Beef Soup
Chilled Beer Soup
Chocolate Soup
Cream of Cheese Soup
Cream of Pea Soup
Cream of Potato Soup
Mixed Vegetable Soup
Pumpkin Soup
Purée of Elderberry Soup with
    Dumplings

Purée of Plum Soup with Dumplings
Rye Bread Soup
Vegetable Soup with Dumplings

Vegetable Dishes

Asparagus with Smoked Ham
Belgian Endives Wrapped in Ham

Braised Red Cabbage with Stuffed
    Apples
Broad Beans in Bacon Sauce
Curly Kale with Sausage
French Beans in Sour Cream
Forest Mushrooms German Style
Sauerkraut
Sorrel with Raisins

Great Britain

Breads

Aberdeen Butteries
Baps
Bath Oliver
Battenberg Slices
Bridge Rolls
Cheese Loaf
Coburg Loaf
Crumpets, also called Pikelets
Dinner Rolls
Energen Rolls
Farmhouse Bread
Festival Bread
Griddle Scones
Irish Bread
Malt Loaf
Milk Loaf
Muffins
Oatbread
Potato Dough Rolls and Bread
Scotch Ginger Breads
Scottish Baps
Soda Bread
Welsh Fruit Loaf
White Bread
Wholemeal Bread

Cheese Dishes

Bread and Butter and Cheese Pudding
Buck Rarebit
Cheese Bakewell Tart
Cheese Fritters

Cheese Soufflé
Macaroni Cheese
Roulettes
Welsh Rarebit

Cold Items

Chicken Liver Mousse
Game Terrine or Aylesbury Game Pie
Potted Avocado
Potted Beef
Potted Bloater
Potted Char
Potted Duck
Potted Grouse
Potted Hare
Potted Hough
Potted Oysters
Potted Pigeon
Potted Pigeon and Walnuts
Potted Salmon
Potted Shrimps
Potted Smoked Cod Roe
Potted Smoked Salmon
Potted Smoked Trout

Desserts and Sweetmeats

Apple and Cheese Pie
Apple Charlotte
Chocolate Pudding
Congress Tartlets
Dutch Apple Tart

Flambéd Fruit Salad
Fondant Fancies
Golden Syrup Pudding
Lemon Yogurt Flan
Orange Caramel Pudding
Reina Pudding
Scotch Ginger Breads
Scotch Macaroons
Scottish Cloutie Dumpling
Singing Hinny
Spotted Dick
Summer Pudding
Tansy
Vanilla Pudding Soufflés
Yorkshire Pudding Batter

Dressings and Relishes

Blackberry Relish
Blue Stilton Dressing
Herb Dressing
Mustard Dressing
Tarragon Dressing

Egg Dishes

Boiled Eggs with Tripe
Chicken Soufflé
Courgette Soufflé
Crab Soufflé
Moulded Eggs with Tripe
Shirred Eggs with Bacon
Spinach Soufflé

Fish Dishes

Baked Fillet of Mackerel in Cider with
    Gooseberry Sauce
Baked Goujons of Cod in Cider
Baked Stuffed Trout
Baked Suprême of Salmon with Cream
    and Cucumber
Eel Pudding or Pulborough Eels
Fried Fillet of Herring Norfolk Style
Fried Scallops
Grilled Cod Steaks

Grilled Skewered Scallops
Jellied Eels
Kedgeree
Poached Herring
Poached Red Mullet with Fennel
Poached Skate with Sorrel and Lovage
    Sauce
Poached Suprême of Turbot with
    Pickled Walnuts and Watercress
Shallow-fried Fillet of Mackerel with
    Piccalilli Sauce
Shallow-fried Fillet of Red Mullet in
    Vinaigrette Sauce
Shallow-fried Herring in Oatmeal
Shirred Scallops
Sole and Oyster Custard
Spatchcocked Eel

Meat Dishes, Game and Offal

Beef, Leek and Potato Pie
Beef, Onion and Mushroom Pie or
    London Double Crust Pie
Boiled Leg of Lamb with Parsley
    Dumplings
Boiled Leg of Pork with Broad Beans
Boiled Salt Pork with Pease Pudding
Boiled Silverside and Dumplings
Boiled Silverside with Pease Pudding
Braised Beef Olives with Veal
    Forcemeat
Braised Ox Tail with Haricot Beans
Cornish Pasties
Egg and Bacon Pie
Game Stew
Grilled Sweetbreads
Hare and Grouse Pie
Haricot of Mutton
Irish Stew
Jugged Hare
Lamb and Sage Cobbler
Lamb Cutlets Reform
Lancashire Hot Pot
Mutton Patties
Noisettes of Lamb with Redcurrant
    Sauce
Pork Chops in Beer Sauce

Pork Cobbler
Rabbit Pie
Rabbit Stew with Fruit or Elizabethan
  Rabbit
Raised Beef and Egg Pie
Raised Mutton Pie or Cumberland Pie
Raised Veal and Ham Pie
Roast Leg of Lamb with Rosemary
  Sauce
Roast Loin of Pork with Apricots
Roast Loin of Pork with Prunes
Roast Sirloin of Beef with Yorkshire
  Pudding
Steak, Kidney and Mushroom Pudding
Steak and Kidney Pie
Steamed Bacon and Potato Roll or
  Bacon Badger
Steamed Bacon Roll or Quorn Bacon
  Roll
Steamed Ham and Pork Roll
Steamed Minced Beef Pudding or
  Farmhouse Pudding
Steamed Pork and Chestnut Pudding
  or Oxford Pudding
Steamed Pork and Leek Pudding
Steamed Rabbit and Mushroom Pudding
Tattie Pot
Toad in the Hole
Tripe and Onion
Veal Cutlets with Lemon
Veal Forcemeat
Veal Plum Pie
Veal and Pork Pot Pie
Venison Pie

Potato Dishes

Chips
Mashed Potatoes
Minted New Potatoes
Parsley Potatoes
Roast Potatoes

Poultry and Game Birds

Chicken, Bacon and Leek Pie
Chicken Casserole with Vegetables

Chicken and Veal Forcemeat Pie or
  Queen's Pie
Grilled Devilled Chicken
Partridge Casserole
Pheasant Casserole
Pigeon and Mutton Pie or Squab Pie
Poached Duck with Onion Sauce
Poached Pigeons and Bacon
Poached Turkey with Celery Sauce
Roast Duck with Honey, Lemon and
  Mint
Roast Duck with Port Wine Sauce
Roast Stuffed Pigeons or Pigeons in
  Pimlico
Sauté of Chicken with Apple and Cider
Suprêmes of Duck in Honey Sauce

Salads

Cucumber and Yogurt Salad
Spinach and Bacon Salad

Sauces

Bread Sauce
Cambridge Sauce
Lemon Sauce
Lobster Sauce
Mayonnaise with Soured Cream and
  Dill
Reform Club Sauce
Soured Cream and Tomato Sauce

Soups

Brown Windsor Soup
Chicken Broth
Cock-a-Leekie
Cream of Almond Soup
Cream of Brussels Sprout Soup
Cream of Cucumber Soup
Cream of Jerusalem Artichoke Soup
Cream of Marrow and Ginger Soup
Cream of Mussel Soup or Billy-Bye
Cream of Potato and Saffron Soup
Cream of Rabbit Soup

Cullen Skink
Game Soup
Leek Soup
Leek and Caraway Soup
Oyster Soup
Mock Turtle Soup
Mulligatawny
Purée of Parsnip and Apple Soup
Purée of Pheasant Soup
Scotch Broth
Watercress Soup

Vegetable Dishes

Baked Stuffed Onions
Braised Celery with Apple
Braised Stuffed Marrow
Bubble and Squeak
Cabbage with Milk
Globe Artichoke Tart
Pease Pudding
Spiced Cabbage

Greece and Turkey

Cheese Dishes

Beurrecks
Fried Cheese
Fried Cheese Puffs

Desserts and Sweetmeats

Baklava
Cheesecake
Compote of Figs
Filo Pastry
Flour Batter
Honey Pie
Pide
Spiced Semolina Pie
Tsoureki
Turkish Delight
Turkish Pancakes with Cream Cheese

Dips and Dressings

Eggplant Dip
Garlic Sauce
Garlic and Egg Sauce
Hoummus
Lemon Dressing
Lemon and Egg Sauce
Lime and Féta Cheese Dressing
Pine Nut Sauce
Red Chilli Dressing
Taramasalata

Egg Dishes

Poached Eggs in Yogurt
Scrambled Eggs with Peppers

Fish Dishes

Baked Lobster
Baked Sardines
Casserole of Salt Codfish
Fried Codfish with Garlic Sauce
Fried Salt Codfish with Garlic Sauce
Golden Fried Baby Squid
Grilled Skewered Swordfish
Sautéed Eel
Shallow-fried Suprême of Turbot in
    Lemon Sauce
Soused Anchovies
Squid Stewed in Red Wine
Stewed Eel
Stewed Octopus in Red Wine

Meat Dishes, Game and Offal

Baked Lamb
Baked Lamb with Onions
Baked Leg of Lamb with Potatoes
Beef and Macaroni Bake
Beef and Onions in Red Wine
Beef Rissoles
Fricassée of Lamb
Grilled Meatballs

Lamb Casserole with Apricots
Lamb Casserole with Cannellini Beans
Lamb Casserole with Fresh Peas
Lamb, Féta and Mitzithra Cheese Pie
Lamb Kebabs
Lamb Kebabs with Yogurt Sauce
Lamb Steak with Rosemary
Lamb Sweetbread, Liver and Heart
   Kebabs
Minced Lamb Balls
Minced Lamb with Saffron Rice
Moussaka
Poached Veal Meatballs in Egg and
   Lemon Sauce
Pork in Red Wine with Coriander
Pork Stew
Pot Roasted Shoulder of Lamb with
   Lemon
Pot Roasted Sirloin of Beef Greek Style
Roast Leg of Lamb with Savoury
   Potatoes
Sautéed Escalopes of Pork with Red
   Wine and Coriander
Sautéed Fillet of Lamb with Peas
Tripe Stew
Veal Escalope Rolls

Potato Dishes

Boiled New Potatoes in Red Wine with
   Coriander

Poultry

Braised Chicken Stuffed with Rice and
   Pine Nuts
Chicken Pie with Filo Pastry
Chicken and Mushroom Filo Parcels
Pot Roast Chicken Greek Style
Roast Chicken Stuffed with Rice and
   Pine Nuts
Sauté of Chicken with Lemon
Sauté of Chicken with Okra

Rice Dishes and Cracked Wheat

Cracked Wheat Pilaff
Pilaff with Orange
Pilaff with Spinach
Risotto with Lentils and Pine Nuts
Risotto with Pistachio Nuts
Risotto with Spinach
Risotto with Tomato

Sauces

Garlic Sauce
Garlic and Egg Sauce
Lemon and Egg Sauce
Pine Nut Sauce

Salads

Cabbage Salad
Cucumber in Yogurt Salad
Cucumber, Tomato and Féta Cheese
   Salad
Eggplant Salad
Orange Salad

Soups

Cream of Egg and Lemon Soup
   Garnished with Meatballs
Fish Soup
Fish Soup with Egg and Lemon
Vermicelli Soup
Yellow Split Pea Soup with Lemon

Vegetable Dishes

Artichokes in Lemon Sauce
Artichokes in Oil
Artichokes with Broad Beans
Baked Eggplant
Baked Eggplant with Lemon and
   Cheese

Baked Eggplant and Mixed Vegetables
Baked Spinach Triangles
Baked Stuffed Artichokes
Baked Stuffed Tomatoes
Braised Courgettes with Rice
Braised Stuffed Vegetables
Broad Beans with Tomatoes
Carrot Fritters
Carrots Glazed with Lemon
Carrots in Lemon Sauce
Cauliflower Fritters
Cauliflower and Tomato Stew
Chickpea Galettes
Courgettes with Dill and Tomato

Eggplant Fritters
Eggplant with Tomato
French Beans with Tomato and Cumin
Glazed Leeks with Rice
Lentils with Noodles
Mixed Vegetable Casserole
Pea Beans with Macaroni
Peas with Dill
Runner Beans with Tomatoes
Spinach Filo Parcels
Spinach with Rice
Stewed Vegetables in Tomato Sauce
Stuffed Grape Vine Leaves
Swiss Chard with Croûtons

Hungary

Desserts and Breads

Poached Figs
Viennese Croissants

Dumplings

Butter Dumplings
Cabbage Dumplings
Cheese Dumplings
Cottage Cheese Dumplings
Semolina Dumplings

Egg Dishes

Boiled Eggs with Soured Cream
Boiled Eggs with Paprika Sauce
Chive and Soured Cream Diamonds
Fried Stuffed Eggs
Poached Eggs in Cheese Sauce
Poached Eggs in Lemon Sauce
Poached Eggs in Sorrel Sauce
Potato and Soured Cream Soufflé
    Omelette
Shirred Eggs with Sorrel

Fish Dishes

Baked Pike with Soured Cabbage
Fish Ratatouille
Grilled Fillet of Carp
Poached Fillet of Perch

Meat Dishes and Offal

Beef Steak with Paprika Sauce
Boiled Ox Tongue in Mushroom Sauce
Boiled Shoulder of Mutton with
    Cabbage and Caraway
Braised Beef Olives with Mushrooms
Braised Beef Olives with Vegetables
Braised Beef, Bacon and Veal Olives
Braised Fillets of Veal with Vegetables
    and Soured Cream
Braised Paprika Steaks with Soured
    Cream
Braised Steaks Hungarian Style
Braised Topside of Beef with Savoy
    Cabbage
Calf's Liver with Onion and Paprika
Goujons of Beef with Marjoram
Goulash of Beef
Grilled Marinated Steak with Fried Egg

Hungarian Hot Pot
Medallions of Fillet of Beef with White
Wine
Mixed Grill
Pork Gulyàs
Potted Veal
Roast Leg of Lamb with Tarragon and
Orange
Roast Leg of Lamb with Vegetables
Roast Loin of Pork with Caraway Seeds
Roast Loin of Veal with Tarragon
Roast Ox Tongue in Wine Sauce
Soured Tokàny
Veal Pörkölt

Noodle Dishes

Hungarian Noodle Paste
Noodles with Cottage Cheese
Noodles with Eggs
Noodles with Ham

Potato Dishes

Baked Stuffed Potatoes
Boiled Potatoes in Soured Cream
Boiled Potatoes in Tomato Sauce
Boiled Potatoes with Marjoram
Potato Cakes
Potato Fritters

Poultry and Game Birds

Baked Chicken with Potato
Braised Duck with Sauerkraut and
Dumplings
Braised Pigeon
Braised Pigeon with Mushrooms
Chicken Casserole in Lemon Sauce
Fricassée of Pigeon
Poached Chicken with Capers and
Mushrooms
Roast Chicken with Liver and Marjoram
Stuffing
Roast Stuffed Goose
Roast Stuffed Goose Neck

Sauté of Chicken Hungarian Style
Sauté of Chicken with Pimento

Sauces

Dill and Soured Cream Sauce
Gherkin and Soured Cream Sauce
Tarragon and Soured Cream Sauce

Savoury Pancakes

Cabbage and Caraway Pancakes
Goose Liver Pancakes

Soups

Beef and Chicken Broth
Beef and Paprika Soup
Beef and Vegetable Broth
Cream of Asparagus and Mushroom
Soup
Cream of Caraway Soup
Cream of Cheese and Pork Soup
Cream of Haricot Bean Soup
Cream of Lamb and Tarragon Soup
Cream of Macaroni Soup
Cream of Rice and Mushroom Soup
Cream of Veal and Vegetable Soup
Mutton and Dill Soup
Soured Cream of Rice and Sorrel Soup
Soured Cream Soup

Vegetables

Baked Celeriac
Baked Courgette
Baked Stuffed Cabbage
Baked Stuffed Mushrooms
Baked Stuffed Tomatoes with Pasta
Breaded Chanterelle Mushrooms
Brussels Sprouts in Soured Cream
Celeriac Fritters
French Bean Bake
French Bean Fritters
Haricot Beans in Onion Sauce

Kohlrabi Stewed in Lard
Kohlrabi in Soured Cream
Mushroom Bake
Mushroom Fritters
Mushrooms in Paprika
Peas in Parsley Sauce

Sauerkraut with Bacon
Savoy Cabbage and Potato with
   Caraway
Spinach Galette
Stewed Lettuce
Tomato Fritters

India

Desserts, Sweetmeats and Breads

Banana Sweetmeats
Bread, Saffron and Nut Pudding
Carrot and Raisin Pudding
Carrot Sweetmeats
Chapatis
Chickpea and Almond Sweetmeats
Cream Cheese Balls in Syrup
Coconut Custard
Copra Samosas
Fried Sweetmeats
Golden Batter Fried in Syrup
Golden Pastry Fries
Indian Milk Pudding
Nan
Pakora Batter
Paratha
Phulka
Poori or Puri
Poori (Alternative)
Poppadums
Rice and Almond Pudding
Roti
Semolina Cakes
Tandoori Bread
Vermicelli and Fruit Pudding

Dips, Relishes and Sauces

Banana and Yogurt Dip
Coconut Relish
Coconut and Fenugreek Sauce
Coriander Relish
Coriander and Yogurt Dip

Cucumber, Coconut and Yogurt Dip
Eggplant and Yogurt Dip
Ginger Relish
Madras Sauce
Spinach and Yogurt Dip

Egg Dishes

Curried Eggs
Egg Fritters
Scrambled Eggs with Chicken
Scrambled Eggs with Coriander

Fish Dishes

Baked Goujons of Cod with Vegetables
Baked Spiced Mackerel Parcels
Balti Prawns
Shallow-fried Curried Fish Cakes
Shallow-fried Fillet of Coley in Curry
   Sauce
Stewed Snapper in Curry Sauce

Meat Dishes

Curried Mutton
Lamb Biriani
Lamb Stew with Saffron and Almonds
Lamb Tikka Kebab
Mutton or Lamb Kebabs Indian Style
Noisette of Lamb in Spiced Batter
Pot Roasted Leg of Lamb Kashmiri
   Style

Potato Dishes

Boiled Savoury Potatoes in Yogurt
Boiled Savoury Potatoes with
    Tomatoes
Fried Potatoes with Almonds
Potato Puris
Spiced Mashed Potatoes
Spiced Matchstick Potatoes
Stuffed Potato Medallions

Poultry Dishes

Chicken Fricassée with Brown and
    Green Lentils
Chicken Korma
Chicken Tikka
Chicken Tikka 2
Duck Casserole with Cabbage and
    Potatoes
Duck Casserole with Pistachio Nuts
Grilled Chicken Tandoori
Grilled Marinated Chicken
Poached Chicken with Yogurt and
    Almonds
Roast Spiced and Stuffed Chicken
Sauté of Chicken Delhi Style
Sauté of Chicken Madras Style
Sauté of Chicken Vindaloo
Sauté of Chicken with Coconut
Suprêmes of Duck with Curry Sauce
Suprêmes of Duck Vindaloo
Tandoori Chicken

Rice Dishes

Boiled Rice with Lemon and Saffron
Boiled Rice with Spices
Pilaff with Spices

Salads

Cucumber and Yogurt Salad
Onion and Coriander Salad
Onion Salad Parsi Style
Onion, Tomato and Ginger Salad
Spinach and Spiced Yogurt Salad
Tomato and Mint Salad
Tomato and Onion Salad

Samosas

Cauliflower and Green Pea Samosa
Cauliflower and Potato Samosa
Lamb and Curry Samosa
Potato Samosa Filling
Spicy Beef Samosa Filling
Vegetable Samosa Filling

Vegetables

Baked Eggplant with Yogurt
Cabbage with Spices
Cauliflower Balti Style
Courgette Purée with Spices
Eggplant Balti Style
Eggplant Fried with Turmeric and
    Chillies
Mixed Vegetables in Yogurt
Mixed Vegetables Tamil Style
Mushrooms, Potatoes and Peas with
    Spices
Okra Balti Style
Okra with Chillies and Ginger
Onion Bhajias
Peas with Panir Cheese
Red Lentils with Spinach
Spiced Cabbage
Spiced Okras
Spiced Spinach
Spiced Spinach and Turnip
Stir-fried Curried Mushrooms
Stir-fried Mixed Vegetables
Stir-fried Spiced Onions
Tomatoes in Curry Sauce

Indonesia

Egg Dishes

Balinese Omelette
Bean Curd and Tomato Omelette
Crab Omelette

Fish Dishes

Baked Snapper Parcels
Curried Squid
Grilled Marinated Turbot Steak
Grilled Skewered Prawns
Grilled Sour and Spiced Trout
Poached Darne of Cod with Coconut
    Milk
Poached Fillet of Mackerel in Coconut
    Milk
Prawns in Coconut Cream
Prawns in Piquant Sauce
Red Mullet in Parcels
Shallow-fried Cod Steaks with Peanut
    Sauce
Shallow-fried Fillet of Red Mullet in
    Coconut Sauce
Shallow-fried Halibut Steak Balinese
    Style

Rice Dishes

Boiled Glutinous Yellow Rice
Boiled Rice with Chicken
Boiled Rice with Ginger
Boiled Rice with Turmeric
Boiled Spiced Rice with Coconut Milk
Fried Rice with Pork and Chicken

Salads

Cabbage Salad with Coconut
Cauliflower Salad
French Bean and Coriander Salad
Mushroom, Sweetcorn and Pimento
    Salad
Pineapple Salad
Pineapple and Pimento Salad
Spinach Salad

Meat Dishes

Boiled Beef with Red Chillies
Boiled Beef with Spiced Beans
Rabbit with Mango
Stir-fried Beef with Peanuts
Stir-fried Goujons of Pork Sambal
Stir-fried Goujons of Pork with
    Oranges
Stir-fried Goujons of Pork with
    Pimento and Tomato
Stir-fried Goujons of Pork with
    Pineapple
Veal Saté

Noodle Dishes

Fried Egg Noodles with Crab and
    Vegetables
Fried Noodles Indonesian Style

Potato Dishes

Fried Sweet Potato Balls
Fried Sweet Potato

Poultry Dishes

Chicken Saté
Grilled Chicken Brochettes with
    Spices
Poached Chicken with Chinese
    Vermicelli
Sauté of Chicken in Curry Sauce
Sauté of Chicken in Orange Sauce
Sauté of Chicken in Shrimp Sauce
Sauté of Chicken with Coriander and
    Cumin

Sautéed Goujons of Chicken in
Coconut Cream
Sautéed Goujons of Chicken in
Coconut Shells

Sauces

Peanut Sauce
Peanut and Tamarind Sauce
Saté Sauce with Oil
Saté Sauce without Oil

Soups

Cauliflower and Noodle Soup
Cream of Chicken and Vegetable Soup
Mandura Beef Soup

Spicy Chicken Soup
Vegetable Soup with Prawns

Vegetable Dishes

Cabbage with Coconut Milk
Eggplant Fried with Dipping Sauce
French Beans and Spinach in Peanut
Sauce
French Beans with Spices
Mixed Spiced Vegetables
Spiced Spinach
Steamed Vegetable Parcels with
Coconut Milk
Stir-fried Beans and Carrots with Ginger
Stir-fried Cabbage with Red Pepper
Paste
Tomatoes with Coconut Milk

Israel

Cold Items and Salads

Cabbage Salad
Chopped Herring
Chopped Liver
Cucumber Salad
Cucumber, Yogurt and Dill Salad
Orange and Carrot Salad
Potted Smoked Salmon
Radishes in Soured Cream
Sweet and Sour Eggs

Desserts and Breads

Apfel Strudel
Challah
Cheese Blintzes
Cheesecake
Cheesecake Pastry
Cherry Kreplach
Frimsel
Fruit Kugel
Lokshen Kugel
Matzo or Matzot

Matzos Shalet
Pomegranate and Almond Coupes
Rice Moulds
Rice and Peach Pudding
Strawberry Soufflé

Dips, Dressings and Relishes

Apple and Almond Dip
Avocado Dressing
Beetroot and Honey Dip
Chickpea and Tahina Dip
Date, Fig and Walnut Dip
Horseradish and Beetroot Relish
Hot Tomato Relish
Sesame Dip
Sweet Beetroot Relish

Dumplings and Savoury Pancakes

Dill and Coriander Pancakes
Fish Liver Dumplings

Kugel
Matzo Dumplings
Nockerel
Potato and Mushroom Pancakes

Egg and Cheese Dishes

Boiled Eggs with Onion
Cheese Blintzes
Kreplach
Matzo Omellete
Savoury Cheese Cakes
Savoury Egg Custard Sephardi Fashion
Scrambled Eggs with Tomato

Fish Dishes

Baked Trout
Boiled Carp
Curried Suprême of Halibut
Gefillte Fish
Pickled Herring – Rollmops or
    Bismarcks
Poached Darne of Carp
Shallow-fried Gefillte Fish
Soused Herring
Stewed Suprême of Halibut with Fish
    Liver Dumplings

Meat Dishes

Baked Minced Beef with Pine Nuts
Boiled Beef with Farfel and Prunes
Boiled Beef with Honey
Boiled Ox Tongue with Sweet and
    Sour Sauce
Braised Calf's Liver Cholent Style
Meat Loaf
Savoury Meat Balls

Potato Dishes

Baked Potatoes and Rice
Baked Potatoes with Dill

Baked Potato Kugel
Boiled Candied Potatoes
Mashed Potatoes with Poppy Seeds
Potato Latkes
Sautéed Potatoes with Turmeric

Poultry Dishes

Braised Goose with Apples
Chicken Suprêmes with Sesame
    Seeds
Grilled Chicken Hearts
Poached Chicken with Egg and Lemon
    Sauce
Pot Roast Chicken Georgian Style
Roast Chicken Stuffed with Oranges
Roast Stuffed Neck of Chicken
Sauté of Chicken with Olives
Stewed Chicken with Spices
Turkey Schnitzel

Rice Dishes

Risotto with Chicken Livers

Soups

Beef Soup with Kasha
Beetroot and Potato Soup
Bortsch
Chicken, Mushroom and Dill
    Dumpling Soup
Chicken Soup
Chicken Soup with Farfel
Chicken Soup with Kreplach
Chilled Bortsch
Chilled Sorrel and Watercress Soup
Cream of Chicken and Almond Soup
Meatball Soup
Peas and Kleis
Sweet and Sour Cabbage Soup
Vegetable Soup with Matzo Balls
Yemenite Beef Soup
Yemenite Chicken Soup

Vegetable Dishes

Baked Spinach and Almond Filo
  Triangles
Baked Spinach and Féta Cheese Filo
  Triangles
Brussels Sprouts with Chestnuts

Carrots Glazed with Honey
Creamed Beetroot
Falafel
Leek and Potato Bake
Lentil Stew
Okra with Tomato

Italy

Cold Items and Salads

Cauliflower and Anchovy Salad
Chopped Chicken Liver and Salami
Mushroom Salad
Orange Salad

Desserts and Breads

Cassata Napolitana
Chocolate and Orange Cheesecake
Ciabatta
Focaccia
Grissini
Italian Feather Bread
Oranges in Caramel
Zabaglione Gritti Palace
Zabaglione with Marsala
Zuppa Inglese

Dressings, Dips and Sauces

Anchovy, Garlic and Truffle Dip
Basil and Pine Nut Pesto
Basil and Wine Dressing
Black Olive, Tomato and Basil
  Dressing
Chilli and Tomato Sauce
Green Dressing
Pesto

Dumplings

Gnocchi with Potatoes
Gnocchi with Semolina

Gnocchi with Spinach and Ricotta
  Cheese
Polenta
Polenta with Fontina Cheese
Polenta with Mushrooms
Polenta with Mushrooms and Ham
Salami Dumplings
Spinach Dumplings

Egg and Cheese Dishes

Calgore
Globe Artichoke Omelette
Mozzarella in Carozza

Fish Dishes

Baked Fillet of Hake with Anchovies
  and Rosemary
Baked Fillet of Swordfish with Tomato
  and Olives
Baked Stuffed Sardines
Baked Stuffed Squid
Casserole of Goujons of Fish
Fillet of Red Mullet in Tomato
Fish Stew Italian Style
Grilled Marinated Fillet of Red Mullet
Grilled Suprême of Tuna Fish
Grilled Tuna Fish Steaks
Mussels with Lemon
Octopus in Tomato and Basil Sauce
Poached Eels in Tomato and Basil Sauce
Shallow-fried Suprême of Salted Cod
  Florentine Style
Stewed Eel in Tomato

Italian Pastes

Cannelloni
Cannelloni Piacentini
Fillings for Pasta Dishes:
  Beef, Pork, Rabbit or Veal
  Chicken and Ham
  Fontina Cheese and Chive
  Spinach and Ricotta Cheese
Fresh Noodle Paste
Lasagne
Pasta Rossa
Ravioli
Ravioli Calzoni di Ricotta alla Molisana
Ravioli Colignione
Spaghetti Bolognaise
Spaghetti with Baby Clams
Spaghetti with Baby Marrow
Spaghetti with Bacon, Egg and Cream
Spaghetti with Bacon and Onion
Spaghetti with Basil Sauce
Spaghetti with Cheese and Pepper
Spaghetti with Chilli Sauce
Spaghetti with Garlic, Oil and Chilli
  Peppers
Spaghetti with Ham and Mushroom
Spaghetti with Mussels and Garlic
Spaghetti with Peas
Spaghetti with Tomatoes
Spaghetti with Tomatoes and Basil
Wholemeal Pasta

Meat Dishes

Beef Rissoles Florentine Style
Braised Steaks California
Calf's Liver with Tomatoes
Escalope of Veal with Ham, Cheese
  and Tomato
Escalope of Veal Milanese
Escalope of Veal Marsala
Escalope of Veal Proscuitto
Fricassée of Lamb Italian Style
Fritto Misto
Lamb, Pork and Veal Kebabs with
  Polenta
Osso Bucco

Roast Leg of Lamb Roman Style
Sirloin Steak Pizzaiola
Veal Cutlets with Fontina Cheese
Veal Cutlets with Sage and Rosemary
Veal and Apple Rissoles
Veal and Fennel Casserole

Pizzas

Pizza Dough
Pizza Tomato Topping – Passata
Pizzas with a Tomato (Passata) and
  Cheese Topping:
  Pizza ai Funghi
  Pizza ai Quattro Formaggi
  Pizza ai Sardine
  Pizza al Tonno
  Pizza alla Gorgonzola
  Pizza Capricciosa
  Pizza con Salami
  Pizza Lazio
  Pizza Marinara
  Pizza Margherita
  Pizza Napoletana
  Pizza Piccola Roma
  Pizza Quattro Stagione
  Pizza Romana
  Pizza Sardegniara
  Pizza Tropicale
Pizzas without a Tomato and Cheese
  Topping
  Pizza Andréa
  Pizza Calabrese
  Pizza Cincemilli
  Pizza Fitascetta
  Pizza Francesco
  Pizza Gardiniera
  Pizza Religioso
  Pizza Vesuvio

Poultry Dishes

Chicken Casserole with Mushrooms
  and Cheese
Chicken Suprêmes with Cream Cheese
  and Parma Ham

Chicken Suprêmes with Smoked Ham
Roast Chicken Stuffed with Cheese
Roast Chicken Stuffed with Ham
Sauté of Chicken with Pimento

Rice Dishes

Risotto with Fennel
Risotto with Saffron

Soups

Borage and Lettuce Soup
Cabbage and Bean Soup
Cabbage and Cheese Soup
Chicken and Pasta Broth
Chicken Liver Soup
Chickpea and Chestnut Soup
Consommé with Eggs
Fish Soup
Minestrone
Mussel Soup
Rice and Turnip Soup
Whitebait Soup

Vegetable Dishes

Artichokes in Oil
Asparagus Milanese
Baked Stuffed Artichokes
Baked Stuffed Courgettes
Baked Stuffed Onions
Broad Beans with Mortadella
Broad Beans with Tomato
Broccoli with Garlic
Cabbage with Bacon
Eggplant with Tomato and Olives
French Beans with Tomato
Fried Artichokes
Grilled Radicchio
Haricot Beans with Cabbage
Mushrooms with Marjoram
Peas with Smoked Ham
Pimento and Tomato
Red Cabbage and Smoked Ham
Sautéed Pumpkin in Breadcrumbs
Spinach with Raisins and Pine Nuts
Sweet and Soured Cabbage

Japan

Batter

Tempura Batter

Dressings and Sauces

Mustard Dressing
Mustard and Egg Dressing
Plum Sauce
Ponzu Dressing
Sea Urchin Dressing
Sesame Dressing
Silver Sauce
Sweet Vinegar Dressing
Tempura Sauce
Teriyaki Sauce
Three Vinegar Dressing

Two Vinegar Dressing
White Miso Dressing
Yakitori Sauce

Egg Dishes

Omelette with Chicken
Omelette with Mirin and Daikon
Omelette with Mushrooms
Omelette with Mushrooms and Prawns
Omelette with Prawns
Omelette with Soup Stock
Omelette with Spinach
Savoury Egg Custard with Mushrooms
    and Prawns

Fish Dishes

Baked Mackerel in Prawn Parcels
Fillets of Herring in Saké
Fried Oysters
Fried Plaice
Glazed Fillet of Mackerel
Glazed Smelt with Ginger
Glazed Suprême of Salmon
Goujons of Cod in Broth
Goujons of Sole with Bean Curd and
    Mushrooms
Grilled Fillet of Mackerel
Grilled Scallops
Grilled Suprême of Salmon
Noodle-coated Prawns
Poached Fillet of Herring in Saké
Poached Fillet of Mackerel with
    Daikon
Poached Sole in Saké with Chillies
Prawns and Vegetables in Batter
Prawns Sushi
Seafood and Vegetables in Batter
Shallow-fried Rainbow Trout
Sliced Raw Fish
Steamed Suprême of Salmon with
    Bean Curd

Meat Dishes

Beef and Vegetable Sukiyaki
Boiled Loin of Pork with Mustard
    Sauce
Breaded Pork Escalopes
Fried Beef Kebabs
Ginger Glazed Escalopes of Pork
Glazed Escalopes of Pork
Grilled Marinated Fillet of Beef
Medallions of Pork with Ginger
Mixed Grill Japanese Style
One-pot Bean Curd
One-pot Chicken, Seafood and
    Vegetables
One-pot Chicken with Vegetables
One-pot Oysters with Bean Paste
One-pot Simmered Beef with
    Vegetables
One-pot Red Snapper with Vegetables

Poached Beef with Ginger
Sautéed Escalopes of Pork with
    Sesame Seeds
Stir-fried Beef or Beef Bowl
Stir-fried Beef Sukiyaki
Stir-fried Glazed Goujons of Pork

Noodle Dishes

Buckwheat Noodles with Chicken
Chilled Buckwheat Noodles on
    Bamboo
Chilled Noodles with Eggs
Chilled Noodles with Prawns
Fresh Noodles
Fried Noodles
Noodle Broth
Noodles in Dashi with Poached Egg
Noodles in the Pot
Noodles with Bean Curd
Noodles with Bean Paste
Noodles with Cucumber
Noodles with Eggs and Chicken
Noodles with Poached Egg
Noodles with Pork

Potato Dishes

Boiled Potatoes in Miso
Boiled Potato Tumble

Rice Dishes

Boiled Rice in Stock
Boiled Rice Japanese Style
Boiled Rice with Beef
Boiled Rice with Beef and Eggs
Boiled Rice with Chestnuts
Boiled Rice with Chicken and Bamboo
    Shoots
Boiled Rice with Chicken and Eggs
Boiled Rice with Chicken and
    Mangetouts
Boiled Rice with Mushrooms
Boiled Rice with Oysters
Boiled Rice with Peas

Boiled Rice with Prawns and French
　Beans
Boiled Rice with Prawns, Chicken and
　Mushrooms
Boiled Rice with Seaweed
Boiled Rice with Vegetables and Prawns
Rice Balls
Rice with Chicken and Bamboo Shoots
Rice with Mushrooms
Steamed Pink Rice with Red Beans
Sushi Vinegared Rice
Sushi Vinegared Rice Squares with
　Crab
Sushi Vinegared Rice with Bean Curd
Sushi Vinegared Rice with Vegetables

Poultry Dishes

Fried Chicken
Fried Chicken Goujons Japanese Style
Fried Marinated Chicken
Fried Sesame Chicken
Fried Skewered Chicken
Grilled Chicken Yuan Style
Grilled Chicken with Chicken Livers
Grilled Chicken with Green Peppers
Poached Chicken with Eggs
Poached Chicken with Vegetables
Sauté of Chicken Chikuzen Style
Sautéed Chicken Livers
Sautéed and Glazed Suprême of
　Chicken
Shallow-fried Goujons of Chicken with
　Mushrooms
Steamed Chicken with Saké
Steamed Chicken with Squid
Stir-fried Chicken

Salads

Asparagus with Mustard Dressing
Asparagus with Mustard and Egg
　Dressing
Bean and Sesame Salad
Chicken and Vegetable Salad
Cucumber Salad (Warm)
Cucumber Salad

Five Salad
French Bean and Sesame Salad
Grapes in Mustard Dressing
Onion Salad
Spinach with Sesame Dressing

Soups

Clam Soup
Clear Chicken Soup
Clear Egg Drop Soup
Clear Egg Soup
Clear Fish Soup
Clear Soup with Bean Curd and
　Seaweed
Clear Soup with Okra and Ginger
Fresh Noodle Soup with Eggs and
　Chicken
Fresh Noodle Soup with Poached Egg
Fresh Noodle and Pork Soup
Miso Soup with Bean Curd and
　Seaweed
Miso Soup with Mixed Vegetables
Oyster and Bean Curd Soup
Red Bean Paste Soup
Vegetable and Fried Bean Curd Soup

Vegetables

Boiled Soy Beans
Chinese Cabbage and Tofu
Chinese Cabbage with Bonito Flakes
Daikon Radish
Daikon Radish with Miso Sauce
Eggplant with Bean Paste
Fried Rice Cakes in Broth
Fried Tofu with Ginger
Green Beans in Soy Sauce
Green Beans with Bean Paste
Green Beans with Peanuts
Green Beans with Sesame Seeds
Grilled Bean Curd with Bean Paste
Grilled Eggplant
Okras with Rice Vinegar Dressing
Onions with Chicken and Sesame Seed
　Sauce
Peas in Soup Stock

Peas with Chicken and Eggs
Pumpkin with Minced Chicken
Steamed Stuffed Chinese Cabbage
Steamed Stuffed Turnips

Steamed Turnip, Prawn and Chicken
Stir-fried Carrots
Stir-fried Eggplant
Taro with Chicken and Vegetables

Mexico

Desserts and Breads

Banana Flambé
Oranges with Coconut
Pears Stuffed with Dates
Strawberries Sautéed with Orange
   Liqueur
Tortillas

Dips, Relishes and Sauces

Avocado Dip and Tomato
Chilli Sauce
Courgette and Lime Relish
Hot Pepper Sauce
Radish and Cilantro Relish
Red Sauce
Tomato and Chilli Dressing

Egg Dishes

Fried Eggs Yucatan Style
Poached Eggs with Pinto Beans
Poached Eggs Yucatan Style
Scrambled Eggs Mexican Fashion

Fish Dishes

Baked Stuffed Rainbow Trout
Baked Suprême of Swordfish, Tomato
   and Herbs
Grilled Suprême of Cod with Garlic
Grilled Suprême of Halibut with
   Orange Sauce
Poached Tail-end of Hake with
   Hazelnuts

Seafood with Rice and Dried Peppers
Shallow-fried Fillet of Sole with Pine
   Nuts

Meat Dishes

Beef and Polenta Pie
Beef Stew in Tequila
Beef Stew with Plantains
Chilli con Carne
Grilled Marinated Steak Mexican Style
Pork and Chicken Stew
Pork in Orange Juice with Cumin
Roast Loin of Pork with Herbs

Poultry Dishes

Chicken Casserole with Almonds and
   Saffron
Chicken in Mole Sauce
Chicken Stew Mexican Style
Chicken Stew with Almonds
Flautas
Grilled Spiced Chicken with Coriander
Roast Chicken with Cumin
Sauté of Chicken with Bacon, Pimento
   and Tomato

Rice Dishes

Boiled Rice Mexican Style
Pilaff with Pimento and Coriander
Pilaff with Tomato
Risotto with Cream Cheese and
   Pimento

Salads

Avocado and Beef Salad
Cauliflower and Avocado Salad
Mushroom and Vegetable Salad
Orange Salad with Pecan Dressing
Pinto Bean Salad
Romaine Salad
Vegetable and Lime Salad

Soups

Black Bean Soup
Chicken, Courgette and Sweetcorn Soup
Corn Soup
Cream of Garlic Soup
Cream of Vegetable and Beer Soup
Cream of Vegetable and Citrus Fruit
  Soup
Beef Soup
Purée of Avocado Pear Soup
Tripe Soup
Vegetable Soup with Chicken and
  Avocado Pear
Vermicelli Soup

Vegetable Dishes

Artichokes in Brandy and Mustard
  Sauce
Baked Cauliflower
Baked Chayotes
Baked Stuffed Tomatoes with Ham and
  Basil
Black Beans Mexican Style
Carrots and Grapes in Soured Cream
  Sauce
Chickpeas with Fresh Coriander
Courgette with Garlic and Lime
Eggplant Fritters
Eggplant in Lime Juice
French Beans with Lemon and
  Oregano
Grilled Spring Onions with Lime
Pinto Beans
Pinto Beans with Green Chillies
Purée of Carrots and Potatoes
Refried Pinto Beans
Sautéed Mushrooms
Sautéed Pimento in Soured Cream
Spinach in Lime Juice

Middle East

Desserts

Filo Pastry
Mannaeesh
Pear Dessert
Sweet Potato Pie

Dips and Sauces

Chickpea and Sesame Dip
Eggplant Dip with Sesame Oil
Eggplant and Sesame Dip
Garlic and Tahina Sauce
Hazelnut Sauce

Dumplings

Cracked Wheat Pilaf
Cracked Wheat Pilau

Egg Dishes

Fish Omelette
Herb Omelette
Herb and Walnut Omelette
Leek Omelette
Onion Omelette
Potato Omelette
Pumpkin Omelette
Savoury Egg Custard with Eggplant
Savoury Egg Custard with Goujonettes
  of Fish
Savoury Egg Custard with Mint
Spiced Potato Omelette
Spinach Omelette
Walnut and Chive Omelette

Fish Dishes

Baked Fillet of Cod with Vegetables
Baked Red Mullet Parcels
Baked Stuffed Monkfish
Baked Suprême of Halibut with Tahina
    and Walnuts
Grilled Cod Kebabs
Poached Suprême of Turbot with Rice
Shallow-fried Red Mullet Stuffed with
    Spices
Stir-fried Spiced Prawns

Meat Dishes and Offal

Couscous
Lamb and Yogurt Stew with Pilau
Lamb Casserole with Fruit
Lamb Stew with Cumin
Roast Marinated Rabbit
Sautéed Calf's Liver, Heart and Kidney
    in Spiced Sauce
Steamed Beef and Vegetables
Stir-fried Spiced Minced Meat
Veal and Apricot Stew
Veal Stew with Cherries

Potato Dishes

Potato and Burghul Cakes with
    Cinnamon

Poultry Dishes

Baked Chicken with Sesame Seeds
Chicken Stew with Dates and Honey
Fried Chicken Meat Balls
Roast Chicken Algerian Style
Roast Chicken Stuffed with Couscous
Roast Duck
Sautéed Goujons of Chicken with
    Walnuts

Rice Dishes

Boiled Rice with Lentils and Macaroni
Middle Eastern-style Boiled Rice

Rice with Honey
Rice with Lamb and Cherries
Risotto with Saffron and Almonds

Salads

Bean Salad
Cracked Wheat Salad
Fish Salad
Mushroom and Yogurt Salad

Soups

Cream of Courgette Soup
Cream of Peanut Soup
Cream of Walnut and Grape Soup
Mutton Soup
Onion and Mint Soup
Prune, Apricot and Peach Soup
Yogurt and Raisin Soup
Yogurt and Spinach Soup

Vegetable Dishes

Baked Eggplant with Tomato
Baked Stuffed Courgettes
Black-eyed Beans with Spinach
Brown Lentils
Brown Lentils with Noodles
Cauliflower Florets with Tahini Sauce
Chickpeas Kofta
Chickpeas with Spinach and Spices
Haricot Beans with Spices
Kidney Beans with Cumin
Runner Beans with Tomatoes in Oil
Sautéed Celery
Sautéed Leeks
Stir-fried Okras
Stuffed Grape Vine Leaves
Vegetable Stew

Portugal

Desserts

Apricot Fritters
Bread Fritters
Bread Fritters with Honey
Chestnut Soufflé
Floating Islands
Massa Vinhe Batter
Milk Fritters
Orange Roll
Portuguese Pancakes
Strawberry Fritters

Dressings and Sauces

Andalusian Sauce
Beirao-style Sauce
Caper and Onion Dressing
Villian Sauce
Vinegar Sauce

Egg Dishes

Savoury Egg Custard with Tomato
Scrambled Eggs with Vegetable Purée
Tomato and Rice Omelette

Fish Dishes

Baked Fillet of Bream and Cod
Baked Salt Codfish with Tomato and
    Pimento
Clams in White Wine
Fried Clams
Fried Sardines
Poached Cuttlefish with Ink
Poached Octopus with Rice
Shallow-fried Salt Codfish
Shallow-fried Sardines with Tomato
Shallow-fried Suprême of Tuna with
    Saffron

Meat and Offal Dishes

Beef Steak in Cream Sauce
Boiled Beef, Chicken and Pork with
    Vegetables
Boiled Tripe Oporto Style
Butter Bean and Chorizo Stew
Calves' Kidneys in Port
Goat Stew
Goujons of Pork in White Wine Sauce
Goujons of Pork with Cockles
Goujons of Pork with Cumin
Lamb Cutlet Portuguese Style
Marinated Calf's Liver
Pork Chops in Port and Rosemary
    Sauce
Pork Medallions
Rabbit Stew with Wine and Port
Roast Kid

Potato Dishes

Baked Sweet Potatoes with Chestnuts
Boiled Potatoes with Belly of Pork
Boiled Potatoes with Pimento

Poultry and Game Birds

Braised Partridge with Grapes and
    Oranges
Chicken Casserole Portuguese Style
Chicken Casserole with Rice
Chicken Patties
Chicken Pie
Chicken and Rice
Poached Duck with Orange
Poached Duck with Rice
Sauté of Chicken Portuguese Style
Sauté of Chicken with Peas
Sautéed Duck with Banana and
    Mandarins
Stewed Partridge

Soups

Beef Broth
Beef Soup
Chestnut Soup
Cream of Rice Soup
Dried Chestnut Soup
Dry Soup Minho Fashion
Game Soup
Garlic and Coriander Soup
Haricot Bean and Saffron Soup
Spring Green Soup
Stone Soup
Tomato and Egg Soup

Vegetable Dishes

Broad Beans in Egg Sauce
Broad Beans with Bacon and Sausage
Broad Beans with Coriander
Broccoli Sautéed in Oil
Eggplant Fans
Eggplant Fritters
French Beans with Chorizo Sausage
   and Eggs
Fried Pimentos
Fried Pimento Strips with Garlic
Peas and Chorizo Sausage
Purée of Onion and Rice

Russia

Desserts and Breads

Blinis
Charlotte Russe
Cheesecake Russian Style
Cranberry Fool
Rum Pudding Soufflé
Strawberries Russian Style
Strawberry Kisel

Dumplings and Savoury Pancakes

Buckwheat and Garlic Dumplings
Caraway Dumplings
Curd Cheese Dumplings
Dill and Cabbage Pancakes

Fish Dishes

Baked Carp in Cider
Baked Herring in Cream
Baked Stuffed Bream
Boiled Herring with Dill and
   Horseradish Dressing
Coulibiac of Salmon
Fried Stuffed Fillet of Plaice
Herrings Stewed in Milk with Dill

Sautéed Eel in Cream Sauce
Stewed Marinated Hake Steaks

Meat Dishes

Beef Steak Stroganoff
Beef Stroganoff
Boiled Beef Russian Style
Fried Liver with Cream
Lamb and Rice Stew
Mutton or Lamb Kebabs Armenian
   Style
Pork Stew with Cabbage and Apples
Pork and Beetroot Stew
Pot Roasted Rabbit with Vegetables
Pozharshie Cutlets
Roast Stuffed Breast of Veal
Shashliks with Pomegranate

Potato Dishes

Baked Potatoes in Egg
Baked Potatoes in Soured Cream with
   Dill
Baked Potatoes with Curd Cheese
Baked Stuffed Potato
Boiled New Potatoes with Dill and
   Crème Fraîche

Potato and Mushroom Crescents
Potato Latkes Russian Style
Potato Pancakes Russian Style
Sautéed Potatoes in Egg Custard

Poultry Dishes

Chicken and Rice Pie
Chicken Galettes
Chicken Suprêmes Kiev
Chicken with Walnut Sauce
Duck Casserole with Apples
Roast Chicken Stuffed with Rice
Roast Duck and Kasha
Roast Goose Stuffed with Apples
Sauté of Chicken with Potatoes and
    Herbs
Shallow-fried Spatchcock Russian Style

Salads and Dressings

Beetroot and Horseradish Salad
Beetroot, Walnut and Yogurt Salad
Cabbage and Celery Salad
Cole Slaw Salad
Cucumber and Dill Salad
Eggplant 'Caviar' Salad
Potato and Dill Salad

Radishes and Dill in Soured Cream
Russian Dressing
Tomato and Dill Salad

Soups

Beetroot Soup
Beetroot Soup Ukrainian Style
Cabbage Soup
Chicken Soup with Vegetables and
    Noodles
Chilled Cider and Herb Soup
Chilled Horseradish and Kvas Soup
Chilled Potato and Vegetable Soup
Chilled Spinach and Fish Soup
Chilled Spinach, Sorrel and Cider Soup
Duck and Barley Soup
Green Bortsch
Nettle Soup
Purée of Cabbage and Nettle Soup

Vegetable Dishes

Baked Pumpkin
Beetroot with Smetana
Braised Stuffed Cabbage
Fried Pumpkin
Mushrooms with Smetana

Scandinavia

Desserts and Breads

Apple Meringue
Apple and Tapioca Bake
Baked Apples with Almonds
Bread and Loganberry Fritters
Burnt Sugar Pudding
Caramel Rice Pudding
Cranberry Parfait
Juice Fool
Lefse
Norwegian Wholemeal Bread
Oven Pancakes

Prune Fritters
Redcurrant and Raspberry Coupes
Red Fruit Pudding
Veiled Country Lass

Dressings and Sauces

Dill Dressing
Gravlax Sauce
Lime, Dill and Yogurt Sauce
Russian Dressing

Egg Dishes, Cheese Dishes and Savoury Pancakes

Bacon and Chive Pancakes
Cheese Pancake Fritters
Curd Cheese Dumplings
Fried Cheese Crescents
Fried Eggs in Madeira Sauce
Shellfish, Mushroom and Cheese
   Pancakes

Fish Dishes

Baked Fillet of Plaice with Spinach
Baked Fish Terrine
Baked Lumpenfish and Dill Moulds
Baked Stuffed Mackerel Parcels
Fried Fish Balls
Fried Smelts in Pickle
Gravlax
Herrings in Cream
Jellied Salmon
Shallow-fried Goujons of Plaice with
   Onion Rings

Meat and Game Dishes

Baked Meat Pie
Baked Venison Steaks
Boiled Beef with Horseradish Sauce
Boiled Beef and Pork with Vegetables
Boiled Leg of Lamb with Dill sauce
Braised Calf's Liver with Soured Cream
Broiled Lamb Chops with Dill
Escalope of Veal with Cream Sauce
Pot Roasted Saddle of Hare
Roast Saddle of Hare
Roast Saddle of Hare with Cream Sauce
Sautéed Belly of Pork with Apples
Veal and Pork Balls
Veal and Potato Galettes

Poultry and Game Birds

Braised Partridge with Mushrooms
Boiled Salted Goose
Roast Goose with Apples and Prunes
Roast Pheasant with Grapes
Sautéed Chicken Livers with
   Mushrooms

Salads

Banana and Nut Salad
Beetroot, Nut, Olive and Egg Salad
Carrot and Apple Salad
Christmas Salad
Herring Salad
Herring, Beetroot and Apple Salad
Herring, Potato and Dill Pickle Salad
Horseradish and Macaroni Salad
Kohlrabi Salad
Mushroom Salad
Salat
Warm Potato Salad

Soups

Chilled Apple Soup
Chilled Rosehip Soup
Cream of Chervil Soup
Cream of Lemon Soup
Cream of Potato Soup with Cheese
Cream of Spinach Soup
Cream of Summer Vegetable Soup with
   Prawns
Fish Soup
Herring Soup

Vegetable and Potato Dishes

Baked Carrots
Baked Parsnips
Baked Potatoes in Soured Cream with
   Anchovies
Baked Stuffed Turnips
Baked Sweetcorn
Braised Cabbage with Bacon and Dill
Braised Soured Cabbage
Braised Stuffed Cabbage
Creamed Kohlrabi
French Beans and Mushrooms in
   Cream Sauce
Sweet and Sour Kidney Beans

South Korea

Dips

Bulkoki Dip
Vinegar Dip

Egg Dishes

Fried Egg Garnish
Savoury Egg Custard with Mushrooms,
    Prawns and Sesame Seeds

Fish Dishes

Barbecued Trout
Fried Prawns
Goujons of Whiting in Sesame Seeds
Grilled Fillet of Whiting with Ginger
Grilled Goujonettes of Fish and Beef
Grilled Marinated Scallops
Grilled Suprême of Turbot with
    Sesame and Ginger
Seafood Chongol
Shallow-fried Red Mullet with Salted
    Black Beans
Shallow-fried Suprême of Halibut with
    Sesame Seeds
Spicy Fish Stew
Stir-fried Octopus

Meat and Offal Dishes

Barbecued Spare Ribs
Beef Kebabs
Beef and Mushroom Kebabs
Beef and Soya Bean Curd Medallions
Beef and Vegetable Stew
Boiled Beef, Chicken and Calf's Liver
Boiled Beef with Chillies and Carrots
Boiled Beef with Rice Vermicelli
Boiled Brisket of Beef
Boiled Short Rib of Beef
Boiled Spiced Beef
Calf's Liver Fritters

Grilled Marinated Steak Korean Style
Korean Shinsollo
Minute Steak with Tabasco
Pork and Bean Curd Stew
Sin Sul Lo
Steak Fritters
Stir-fried Goujons of Pork and Kimichi
Stir-fried Pork with Pimento

Noodle Dishes

Buckwheat Noodles with Chilli Sauce
Chicken and Bean Curd Dumplings
Chilled Buckwheat Noodles
Chilled Son Myon Noodles with
    Vegetables

Poultry Dishes

Barbecued Chicken
Chicken Stew
Chicken Stew with Dried Mushrooms
Poached Chicken and Mushrooms
Poached Chicken with Carrots and
    Potatoes
Sauté of Chicken with Soy Sauce

Rice Dishes

Boiled Rice with Abalone
Boiled Rice with Barley
Boiled Rice with Chestnuts
Boiled Rice with Mushrooms and Beef

Salads

Bellflower Salad
Cucumber Salad
Eggplant Salad
Mung Bean Salad
Radish Salad
Seaweed Salad

Soy Bean Sprout Salad
Spinach Salad
Watercress Salad

Fish Soup
Spinach Soup
Vegetable Soup

Soups

Beef Broth
Beef and Bean Curd Soup
Beef and Bean Paste Soup
Beef and Bean Sprout Soup
Beef and Turnip Soup
Beef and Vegetable Soup
Beef Dumpling Soup
Beef Rib Soup
Beef Soup with Meatballs
Chicken Soup with Meat Dumplings
Chicken Soup with Shredded Egg
Chilled Cucumber Soup
Clam Soup

Vegetable and Potato Dishes

Bean Curd
Fried Stuffed Chillies
Fried Stuffed Courgettes
Fried Stuffed Eggplant
Fried Sweet Potato
Glazed Vegetables
Potato Cakes
Potato Pancakes Korean Style
Spinach with Sesame
Stir-fried Cabbage with Red Pepper
    Paste
Stir-fried Courgettes with Sesame Seeds

Spain

Desserts

Figs and Dates in White Wine
Flambéd Bananas
Fruit Salad au Gratin
Hot Compote of Fruit
Orange and Almond Soufflé
Orange and Cinnamon Junket

Dressings and Sauces

Almond Dressing
Cheese and Herb Dressing
Chilli Sauce
Green Sauce
Tomato and Cumin Dressing

Egg Dishes

Artichoke Omelette
Boiled Eggs with Peppers and Tomato
Chickpea Omelette

Cod Omelette
Country Omelette
Date, Shrimp and Ham Omelette
Fried Eggs with Garlic and Paprika
Fried Quail's Eggs
Lima Bean Omelette
Moulded Eggs with Ham, Sausage and
    Asparagus
Scrambled Eggs with Bacon and
    Chorizo
Scrambled Eggs with Shrimps and
    Spinach
Scrambled Eggs with Tomato and
    Pimento
Scrambled Eggs with Vegetables
Shirred Eggs à la Flamenca
Shirred Eggs with Mushrooms
Shirred Eggs with Tomato and Sausage
Spanish Potato Omelette
Spanish Vegetable Omelette
Spiced Omelette
Spinach and Pine Nut Omelette
Stuffed Eggs with Shrimps

Fish Dishes

Assortment of Fried Fish
Baked Fillet of Flounder with Almonds
Baked Fillet of Hake with Asparagus
Baked Fillet of Hake with Potatoes and
  Cider
Fried Squid
Monkfish Kebabs
Mussels in Sherry
Paella
Pickled Fish
Prawns in Beer Batter
Sautéed Frogs' Legs
Shallow-fried Fish Fans
Shallow-fried Prawns in Garlic
Shallow-fried Prawns in Garlic with
  Chillies
Shallow-fried Trout with Cured Ham
Snails in Tomato and Herb Sauce
Snails with Ham and Chorizo
Stewed Squid in Ink

Meat Dishes, Game and Offal

Beef Stew Spanish Style
Braised Leg of Lamb Castilian Style
Braised Venison in Red Wine
Breaded Beef Steak
Breaded Pork Steaks
Escalope of Pork with Marjoram
Grilled Lamb Cutlets with Garlic
  Mayonnaise
Lamb Stew with Red Peppers
Meatballs in Tomato Sauce
Meatballs in Brandy Sauce
Pork Pie
Pot Roasted Sirloin of Beef in Garlic
  Sauce
Potted Pork
Rabbit Paella
Roast Loin of Pork with Pimentos and
  Eggplant
Sautéed Grenadines of Veal with Wild
  Mushrooms
Sautéed Lamb's Kidneys with Sherry
Tripe with Chickpeas

Veal Cutlets with Cured Ham and
  Pimento
Veal Cutlets with Ham, Mushrooms
  and Pimento
Veal Cutlets with Paprika

Potato Dishes

Baked Potatoes with Cured Ham
Baked Potatoes with Oil and Onion
Baked Potatoes with Paprika
Boiled New Potatoes with Turmeric
Boiled Potatoes with Almonds
Boiled Potatoes with Tomato and
  Pimento
Potatoes in Herb Sauce
Spice Sautéed Potatoes

Poultry and Game Birds

Braised Partridge with Savoy Cabbage
Braised Quail with Grapes
Chicken Casserole with Figs
Duck Casserole with Olives
Fried Quails
Roast Chicken with Orange Sauce
Roast Goose with Pears
Sauté of Chicken with Garlic
Sautéed Goujons of Turkey with
  Lemon and Saffron
Sautéed Pigeons
Sautéed Quail with Parsley and
  Garlic

Salads

Artichoke, Eggplant, Pimento and
  Tomato Salad
Asparagus Salad
Chickpea Salad
Codfish Salad
Endive with Blue Cheese Salad
Pimento and Tomato Salad
Potato and Orange Salad
Rice Salad

Soups

Cabbage, Bean and Pimento Soup
Chicken Soup with Grated Potato
Chickpea and Chorizo Soup
Chilled Almond and Grape Soup
Clear Egg Soup
Courgette and Pumpkin Soup
Cream of Pumpkin and Sweet Potato
  Soup
Fish Soup Seville Style
Fish Soup with Noodles
Garlic Soup
Gazpacho
Gazpacho with White Grapes
Lentil Soup
Onion and Almond Soup
Seakale and Chickpea Soup
Spinach and Chickpea Soup
Watercress and Haricot Bean Soup

Vegetable Dishes

Artichokes in Montilla
Artichokes with Cured Ham
Artichokes with Pine Nuts
Asparagus Casserole
Baked Courgettes
Baked Eggplant with Cheese and
  Almonds
Baked Oyster Mushrooms

Baked Pimento and Tomato
Baked Stuffed Tomato with Pine Nuts
Black Beans with Rice
Braised Red Cabbage with Apple and
  Potato
Broad Beans with Ham
Broad Beans with Sherry and Lemon
Brussels Sprouts with Garlic and Wine
  Vinegar
Cauliflower with Garlic and Paprika
  Sauce
Chard Leaves with Vinegar
Eggplant Fritters
French Beans with Cured Ham
French Beans with Spiced Almonds
Fried Green Pimentos
Fried Stuffed Chayotes
Grilled Mushrooms with Rosemary
Haricot Beans with Black Pudding
Mixed Vegetables in Oil and Garlic
Peas with Cured Ham
Puréed Eggplant
Sautéed Cauliflower in Garlic
Sautéed Green Pimento
Sautéed Mushrooms in Sherry Sauce
Spinach and Pine Nuts
Spinach with Almonds and Raisins
Swiss Chard with Croûtons
Vegetable Paella
Vegetable Stew

Thailand

Desserts

Banana Fritters
Mango with Glutinous Rice
Pumpkin with Coconut Custard
Rice and Sweetcorn Pudding

Dumplings

Steamed Prawn and Chicken Wonton
  Dumplings
Wonton Wrappers with Beef

Fish Dishes

Crab in Curry Sauce
Curried Fish
Fried Fillet of Plaice with Sweet and
  Sour Sauce
Grilled Crabmeat and Pork Rolls
Poached Darne of Cod in Green Curry
  Sauce
Prawn and Cucumber Curry
Prawns in Coconut Cream
Sautéed Squid in Chilli and Garlic Sauce

Shallow-fried Sole with Ginger Sauce
Shallow-fried Trout with Turmeric
Shrimps in Sweet and Sour Sauce
Squid in Black Bean Sauce
Steamed Fillet of Red Snapper
Steamed Suprême Cod with Turmeric
and Coriander
Steamed Suprême of Halibut with
Lemon Grass

Meat Dishes

Beef Curry
Beef Satés
Curried Beef
Fried Pork Balls
Lamb and Lentil Rissoles
Mutton Curry
Sautéed Meat Balls
Sautéed Steak in Soured Cream
Stir-fried Beef in Green Curry
Stir-fried Goujons of Pork with Beans
and Prawns

Noodle Dishes

Crisp Fried Vermicelli Noodles
Egg Noodles with Prawns
Fried Crisp Noodles
Fried Noodles
Fried Rice Noodles with Pork
Rice Noodles Thai Style

Poultry Dishes

Barbecued Chicken
Braised Duck with Vegetables
Chicken Casserole with Mushrooms
and Ginger
Chicken Suprêmes with Water
Chestnuts
Curried Chicken
Fried Chicken Goujons with Yellow
Bean Sauce
Green Curry of Duck
Grilled Chicken with Garlic

Poached Chicken in Coconut Milk
Sauté of Chicken with Chestnuts
Sauté of Curried Chicken
Steamed Chicken with Basil
Stir-fried Chicken with Ginger
Stir-fried Chicken in Peanut Sauce

Rice Dishes

Boiled Rice with Crabmeat and Prawns
Boiled Rice with Pineapple
Boiled Spiced Rice
Steamed Rice Thai Method
Steamed Rice with Crab, Prawns and
Pork
Stir-fried Rice

Salads

Bamboo Shoots and Pork Salad
Beef and Coriander Salad
Cabbage, Coconut Milk and Prawn
Salad
Fruit and Herb Salad
Fruit and Prawn Salad
Mango Salad
Orange and Prawn Salad
Paw-paw Salad
Water Chestnut and Prawn Salad

Sauces and Relishes

Chilli Relish
Chilli and Eggplant Sauce
Chilli and Tamarind Sauce
Egg and Chilli Sauce
Sweet Fish Sauce

Soups

Babycorn Soup and Tofu
Chicken Soup
Chicken Soup with Rice Vermicelli
Chicken Soup with Stuffed Mushrooms
and Water Melon

Chicken and Galingale Soup
Chicken and Melon Soup
Chicken and Mushroom Soup
Chicken and Pumpkin Soup
Cream of Chicken and Rice Soup
Pork and Chicken Soup
Prawn Soup
Prawn Soup with Lily Buds
Pumpkin and Basil Soup
Soured Fish Soup
Soured Soup with Prawns

Vegetable Dishes

Baked Courgette with Coconut
Bean Curd and Bean Sprouts

Cauliflower with Chillies
Cauliflower with Creamed Coconut
Eggplant in Sweet and Sour Sauce
Eggplant with Curry Sauce
French Beans with Spices
Sautéed Cauliflower Florets in Oyster
    Sauce
Spiced French Beans
Stir-fried Bean Sprouts and Bean Curd
Stir-fried Beans, Chillies and Pork
Stir-fried Cabbage with Oyster Sauce
Stir-fried Mixed Green Vegetables
Stir-fried Spinach
Sweetcorn Fritters
Vegetable Curry
Vegetables in Coconut Milk
Yellow Split Peas in Spiced Sauce

United States of America

Desserts and Breads

American Pancakes
Apple Brown Betty
Apple Pandowdy
Blueberry Pie
Hamburger Buns
Pineapple Upside-down Cake
Pumpkin Pie
Soya Bread
Waffles

Fish Dishes

Baked Fillet of Cod with Fresh Herbs
Baked Fillet of Haddock
Carolina Shrimp Mousse
Crab Mousse
Crab Turnovers
Fried Shrimp
Grilled Skewered Prawns and Scallops
    with Mango Sauce
Poached Darne of Salmon with Dill
    Sauce
Shallow-fried Salt Codfish Balls

Shallow-fried Scallops in Tarragon
    Sauce

Meat Dishes

Baked Topside of Beef Colorado Style
Boiled Beef, Pork and Lamb with
    Vegetables
Braised Soured Beef
Braised Venison Steaks
Chilled Green Pork
Corned Beef Hash
Fried Gammon Rasher with Redeye
    Gravy
Grilled Butterfly Lamb
Ham Loaf
Jambalaya
Jambalaya Louisiana Style
Meat Loaf
Meat Loaf American Style
Pomey's Head
Pork with Sauerkraut
Pot Roasted Sirloin of Beef Yankee
    Style
Red Flannel Hash

Roast Leg of Lamb with Buttermilk and
  Rosemary
Roast Loin of Pork with Apples

Potato Dishes

Baked Stuffed Potatoes
Hashed Brown Potatoes
Scalloped Potatoes with Pimento

Poultry and Game Birds

Braised Quail with Pimento
Brunswick Stew
Chicken Pot Pie
Chicken Suprêmes in the Maryland
  Style
Fried Chicken Winglets Buffalo Style
Grilled Chicken with Garlic and
  Chillies
Grilled Chicken Ohio Style
Grilled Chicken Texas Style
Roast Chicken with Oranges
Roast Chicken with Vegetables
Roast Goose with Fruit and Nut Stuffing
Roast Pheasant with Wild Rice Stuffing
Sauté of Chicken Country Captain Style
Sauté of Chicken and Oyster Gumbo
Sauté of Chicken with Anchovies
Sauté of Chicken with Apple Rings
Sauté of Chicken with Cornmeal
  Dumplings
Sauté of Chicken with Dumplings
Sauté of Chicken Mole Style
Vermont Chicken Pie

Salads

American Salad
Bean and Potato Salad
Caesar Salad
Carrot and Turnip Escabèche
Cole Slaw Salad
Corn Salad
Goat Cheese Salad
Grapefruit Salad
Wilted Green Salad

Sauces and Dressings

Blue Cheese Dressing
Dill Sauce
Hot Pepper Jelly
Thousand Island Dressing

Soups

Beetroot Top Soup
Black Bean Soup
Chilled Avocado Soup
Chilled Tomato Soup
Clam Soup
Codfish Chowder
Corn Chowder
Cream of Crab Soup
Cream of Pigeon Soup
Cream of Pumpkin Soup
Cream of Spinach and Oyster Soup
Fish Chowder
Purée of Pumpkin Soup
Salmon Chowder
Shrimp and Okra Gumbo
White Bean Soup

Vegetable Dishes

Baked Corn on the Cob
Baked Eggplant and Banana
Baked Squash
Beets Harvard Style
Boston Baked Beans
Braised Turnip Tops
Chuckwagon Beans
Fried Green Tomatoes
Fried Okra
Hopping John
Maquechoux
Sautéed Parsnips
Squash Georgia Style
Succotash
Sweetcorn Fritters
Yale Beets

Appendix Two

Glossary

This Glossary is divided into the following eleven sections:

❖ Herbs ❖

❖ Nuts ❖

❖ Oils ❖

❖ Salad Greens ❖

❖ Salt ❖

❖ Soy Sauce ❖

❖ Seeds ❖

❖ Spices ❖

❖ Vinegars ❖

❖ Glossary of Ingredients and Terms ❖

❖ Equipment and Utensils ❖

Herbs

Basil – very highly scented, used to make pistou and as an ingredient of turtle herbs (q.v.); can also be used in soups, sauces and stews.

Bay – used in dried form in both savoury and sweet dishes, as part of a bouquet garni (q.v.) and for use on kebabs; it must be used with discretion, breaking a leaf into pieces if necessary. Also available in powder form.

Borage – the whole leaves are used to decorate cold drinks such as Pimms'. Young leaves can be coated with batter and deep fried as fritters or finely chopped to sprinkle over salads.

Bouquet garni – general-purpose seasoning mixture for inclusion in stock, sauces, soups and stews, usually made in the form of a faggot and of a size commensurate with the quantity of food to be flavoured. It consists of parsley stalks, celery, a sprig of thyme and bayleaves tied neatly together. Additional items can include crushed garlic and dried orange peel. Can be purchased ready-made in sachets.

Burnet – known also as pimpernelle, it has fleshy leaves with a smell of cucumber that adds distinction to salads.

Chervil – an essential ingredient of fines herbes (q.v.) and used chopped as a delicate flavouring ingredient in stuffings and salads. The whole leaves are known as pluches and are used as a garnish in many soups.

Chives – thin green stems with a flavour of onion. Always use freshly chopped, e.g. in salads.

Coriander – herb of the parsley family. May be fresh or dried or in seed form, the seeds being similar in shape to peppercorns.

Dill – aniseed-flavoured plant much used in Russian and Scandinavian cookery and for pickling fish and gherkins.

Fennel – the bulb is cooked as a vegetable or sliced for salads and the leaves can be used to garnish and flavour salads. It has a flavour of aniseed, useful for flavouring soups and enhancing stuffings.

Fenugreek – tangy in flavour, its fresh leaves are used in the making of salads in Indian cookery.

Fines herbes – this term means a mixture of finely chopped chervil, chives, tarragon and parsley in the proportions of three parts parsley to one part each of the other herbs. It has many uses such as in omelettes, chicken dishes and sauces.

Lemon grass – aromatic lemon-flavoured grass used to flavour salads, soups, fish, meat and poultry dishes. It may be purchased in powdered form as Sareh Powder.

Lovage – aromatic flavour, celery-like plant.

Marjoram – sweet marjoram has a mild sweet and spicy flavour that blends well with meat and vegetarian dishes; wild marjoram is known as oregano (q.v.).

Mint – mainly used as a seasoning for lamb in the form of mint sauce and for cooking in with boiled new potatoes; it makes refreshing drinks and there are several varieties.

Mustard – sold in powder and ready-mixed forms for eating with food as an aid to digestion. English mustard is quite strong and when made up from powder needs to be mixed with water, milk or cream, or with port or Worcester sauce, then allowed to stand for 1 hour. French mustard is always sold ready-made and is available plain, with seeds, with white wine, peppercorns, spices, herbs and vinegars. It is milder than English mustard. American mustard is mild and light in colour. German mustard is usually dark but mild with a sour-sweet taste. Chinese mustard is very hot to the taste.

Oregano – wild marjoram (q.v.), often used in dried form in pizzas.

Parsley – the best-known herb because of its fairly bland flavour and versatility of use. It is available as curled, dark green leaves and as flat-leaved or French parsley. It is used whole or chopped to decorate dishes, especially for finishing dishes at the last moment. It is widely used in omelettes, fish, soufflés, quiches, sauces, soups and stews and can be deep fried for use as a garnish with deep-fried foods.

Purslane – succulent leaves on reddish stems with a sharp flavour, suitable for inclusion in a mixed green salad.

Rosemary – short, tough, pointed leaves with a very aromatic smell that blends well in the mixture of turtle herbs (q.v.) and is eminently suited to lamb and veal dishes.

Sage – greyish downy leaves with a very strong camphor-like smell that is notable when used in stuffings for duck and pork cooked in the English style, with veal in the Italian style and in eastern European cookery in conjunction with paprika.

Sweet basil – similar in appearance and flavour to European basil (q.v.).

Turtle herbs – a mixture composed of three parts basil, two parts each of marjoram and thyme, one part each of fennel and chervil and half a part of rosemary; gives an exotic aroma and flavour to turtle soup and dishes cooked à la Tortue.

Tarragon – widely used herb with a distinctive flavour from its shiny, narrow, dark green leaves, which are useful whole for decorating dishes and chopped for inclusion in fines herbes and in chicken dishes, various cold sauces and salads.

Verbena – very fragrant, long, narrow leaves with a strong smell of lemon; also known as lemon grass. Used mainly in oriental cookery, in salads and in long, refreshing drinks.

Nuts

Nuts play an important part in many ethnic cuisines by adding flavour, texture and stability to both sweet and savoury dishes. They feature prominently in vegetarian cookery and as a replacement for meat. They are a pleasant conclusion to a meal as part of a basket of fruit and nuts and as components of a dish of petits fours.

Almond – sweet almonds are available as whole, halves, chopped, slivers, flaked, nibbed, ground and as an essence, and can play a large part in nearly every course of the menu. They are popular as salted almonds for receptions and buffets. Bitter almonds are used to make essence but can be used with a greater amount of sweet almonds to provide a slight bitterness.

Brazil – has a slightly oily texture and creamy taste.

Candlenut – hard, oily nut used in Indonesian cookery to enhance flavour and to thicken curries.

Cashew – usually served salted at cocktail parties and receptions, and in cakes.

Chestnut – sweet chestnuts can be used in sweet and savoury dishes and contain more starch than other nuts and much less oil. They are used in soups, stuffings, mixed with vegetables, in cakes and desserts and as petits fours. They are available in cans as purée and whole and as dried chestnuts.

Gingko nuts – used in Japanese cookery, may be purchased in bottles and cans.

Groundnut – see peanut.

Hazel – similar to the cob nut and filbert, which are small round nuts with a robust flavour; they are used whole and in ground form in many sweet dishes.

Kemiri nuts – another name for candlenut (q.v.).

Macadamia nut or **Queensland nut** – grown in Australia and Hawaii, usually purchased shelled and roasted. Its main use is at receptions and cocktail parties as roast and salted nuts.

Peanut – also known as groundnut, used as whole roasted and as peanut butter, and also in ground form to thicken soups and sauces. They may also be purchased in nibbed form as a substitute for nibbed almonds.

Pecan – also known as hickory, similar in appearance to a walnut but more oval and with a smooth shell. Used in ground form in cakes and ice-cream, and whole at receptions.

Pine nut – can be eaten raw or roasted, and for cooking in sauces, soups and pesto; they are very small and white in colour.

Pistachio – a green-coloured nut in a purple-grey skin. Much used in stuffings, to decorate cakes and to make very delectable ice-cream.

Walnut – unripe nuts can be pickled, fully ripe ones are served as part of desserts and to garnish cakes and ice-cream.

Oils

Oils play an important part in modern cookery, especially in countries where butter, lard and margarine are not produced nor acceptable. Oil is often preferred to the solid fats both for cooking and for pouring over cooked food at table as part of the cruet. There are dozens of different kinds of oil for use with food: some have their own natural colour, flavour and aroma from the plant or nut they are produced from, others are neutral vegetable oils that take on an essence of a food stored or steeped in them or added during production, e.g. spiced oil, much used in oriental cookery, made by the addition of spice essences. Some oils are blended, others are hydrogenated into soft or solid forms. Some are made for a particular purpose such as longlife deep frying oils, usually under brand names, and as sprays for non-stick frying.

Natural oils include many kinds of olive oil from France, Greece and Cyprus, Italy and Spain, such as Extra Virgin, Virgin, Ordinary and Light. Other natural oils include corn oil, cottonseed oil, groundnut oil (peanut oil), grapeseed oil, palm oil, poppy seed oil, pumpkin seed oil, rapeseed oil, safflower oil, sesame oil, toasted sesame seed oil, sunflower oil, walnut oil and vegetable oils. There are also blended oils, which may include fish oil; soyabean oil is the most widely used. Flavoured oils include spiced oil, stir-fry oil and truffle oil, and the flavouring oils include aniseed, clove and vanilla as well as mixed spice oils.

Salad Greens

Belgian endive – often referred to as chicory, this salad ingredient is kept covered from the light so that it grows white, tinged with green at the tips. Its shape is an elongated oval and it has a slightly bitter taste.

Cabbage lettuce – the most popular kind of lettuce, which is the basis of most green salads. Referred to as coeur de laitue when cut into quarters or wedges on the stem.

Corn salad – also known as lamb's lettuce or mâche, a delicate green, small with no heart.

Cos lettuce – dark green, elongated lettuce often called a romaine.

Dandelion – young leaves picked before the plant flowers can be blanched before use in a salad.

Endive – known as frizzy or curly endive, batavia, escarole and chicory; lettuce-shaped with delicate curled leaves shading from white to pale green, bitter to the taste.

Iceberg lettuce – a crisp head lettuce that keeps fresh and crisp for a long time and has closely packed, light green leaves.

Little gem lettuce – a small lettuce with a good heart, like a small version of a cabbage lettuce.

Lollo rosso – frizzy salad green with the ends of the green leaves tinged with red.

Mustard and cress – small grass-like sprouts more suitable as a garnish than as part of a salad.

Nasturtium – the leaves add a peppery taste to a salad and are a source of iron and vitamin C; the flowers can also be used in a salad.

Oakleaf – leaf or chicken lettuce, a less popular variety comprising a loose head of leaves.

Pok chai – smallish leaves, like spinach, without a heart.

Purslane – the leaves are usually chopped for use in a salad and are valued for their sharp but clean flavour.

Radicchio – small cabbage-type lettuce. The leaves are a distinctive colour of burgundy red with white veins. It is much favoured for its crispness and attractive appearance.

Rocket – a genus of garden herbs which grow wild but are now cultivated as a distinctive salad leaf.

Savory – long, narrow leaves with a delicate spicy flavour and slightly bitter taste; can be used in stuffings and salads and is closely associated with the cooking of broad beans.

Watercress – pungent, peppery taste; dark green, roundish leaves.

Webb's wonder – a large-size crisp and compact lettuce.

Salt

Salt is obtained naturally from subterranean lakes, mines and from the sea. There are many types of salt, some of which are ideal for cooking purposes and others that are harmful to health.

Block salt – or refined rock salt has no additives and is used mainly for pickling or curing meat.

Flavoured salts – available as celery salt, garlic salt, spiced salt and many others.

Freezing salt – coarse crystallised salt traditionally used for reducing the temperature of liquids, e.g. in ice-cream making.

Purified sea salt – produced from tidal pools of concentrated sea-water, ideal for cooking purposes.

Rock salt – crystallised salt produced from crushed mine salt, may be purchased in many degrees of fineness. Ideal for cooking and as a condiment.

Soy Sauce

This is perhaps the most widely used flavouring in most countries of the Far East, in particular in China where it originated, and Japan. As its name implies it is based on soy beans, and a good quality soy sauce will be made by fermenting quality soy beans and wheat, adding only salt and water. It is allowed to mature for up to six months before being bottled. It pays to buy a quality soy sauce as cheap ones are non-fermented, are not brewed and may contain artificial colours and flavours.

Soy Sauce is in effect a liquid spice which is quite pungent and needs to be used sparingly, mainly to bring out the flavour of the ingredients it is added to. One of the best-known brands is Kikkoman, made in Japan as a light soy sauce which gives many shades of flavours. Chinese soy sauce is made as dark, which is slightly viscous, rich in flavour and useful for marinating purposes, and in light form for delicate stir-frying and salad dressings. Sweet soy sauce, flavoured with molasses, is also available.

Soy sauce is used as an ingredient in many oriental sauces, both home made and ready-prepared.

Seeds

Caraway – narrow, black, curved seeds with a subtle taste of anise; used in Hungarian goulash, bread, cakes and in certain cheeses.

Celery – useful for adding to soups, marinades, fish dishes and dips.

Fenugreek – small, flat, brownish-coloured seeds used in making curries.

Lovage seeds – used in Asian cookery to impart their special flavour to food.

Poppy – very small, black seeds used in Near Eastern countries in sweets, pastries, mousses, etc. and in Germanic countries. Often used to cover bread and rolls.

Sesame – used to make halva (q.v.), bread, pastry, houmous (q.v.), as a condiment and for sprinkling on bread and rolls before baking.

Wild onion seeds – small, black and irregular shaped, used in Asian cookery to impart a sweet, nutty flavour to food.

Spices

Allspice – so called because it has the odour of cinnamon, cloves and nutmeg; it is the seed of the pimento tree of the Caribbean, where it is called Jamaica pepper though it is not peppery. Available whole for use as a pickling spice and ground as a flavouring.

Aniseed or anise – pronounced flavouring used mainly in pastries and sweets and in the making of liqueurs and aperitifs (see also star anise).

Artisha – Greek word for cumin (q.v.), it may be added during cooking, or alternatively served as an accompaniment to be sprinkled over the food by those who appreciate its flavour.

Balti cooking spice mixture – a blend of the following dry stir-fried seeds and spices: coriander seeds, white cumin seeds, fennel seeds, cardamoms, cassia bark, ground mace, crushed fenugreek leaves, cloves, curry powder, garlic powder, chilli powder and mustard. This product may be purchased in packets or jars.

Cardamom – grows as green, black or white pods containing small seeds. Available in whole or ground form. Very aromatic and used as an ingredient in curry powder and as a flavouring in coffee. It is one of the most expensive spices.

Cassia – plant similar to cinnamon but without its subtle flavour; used in curry powder, for spicing meat and for making pilaus.

Cayenne – a very pungent form of pepper used in minute amounts to bring out the full flavour of dishes; it is dull red in colour and not as intense as chilli pepper, although it is made from chillies.

Chillies – very hot and spicy, the small, dark, long ones being the hottest the seeds being the hottest part. The jalapeño variety is usually available only in jars and cans and can be eaten whole, though hot to the taste. Dried pods are stronger than fresh, and a crushed one is often part of pickling spices. Chilli powder is also very hot and should be added slowly, e.g. to a stew such as Chilli con Carne.

Cinnamon – available in the form of a stick, which is the curled bark of a tree of the laurel family and is used in mulled wine, stock syrup and in pilaus and biriani. In powder form it is used in cakes, biscuits, Christmas pudding and mincemeat, and is a component of mixed spice.

Cloves – available whole as hard, dried buds used to flavour certain sauces, pickles, marinades and syrups, and in powdered form as a component of mixed spice; cloves are highly flavoured.

Coriander – aromatic seed with a faint smell of oranges, used in stock syrup, for pastry items and in a variety of savoury dishes; much used in dishes of North African and Asian origin.

Cumin – the hot and bitter dried fruit of a herb, used whole or ground as a spice.

Curry leaves – available fresh as shiny, small leaves and in dried form; they do not taste of curry.

Fenugreek – an essential ingredient of curry powder.

Five-spice powder – an essential seasoning condiment in Chinese cookery comprising ground star anise, fennel seeds, cloves, cinnamon and Szechwan peppercorns.

Galingale – also spelt galangal, a reddish-coloured spice with a hot, strong flavour used in exotic dishes; available in root or powder form it has an aroma of cardamom and ginger and faintly of camphor.

Garlic – plant of the lily family with a pronounced flavour that needs to be used with discretion, when it will give a delicate result with no after effects. After parsley this is one of the most widely used spices and of much importance in latin and oriental cookery. It grows as white, dried bulbs consisting of numerous pods called cloves, and can be eaten raw or cooked in stews, soups and vegetables. It is advisable to chop rather than squeeze, by lightly crushing the cloves with the side of a knife to remove the skin then removing the root and any green parts, flattening it and chopping finely. It is available as a powder and as a purée in tubes.

Ginger – available as fresh and dry roots, as a powder and in pickled and crystallised forms, sour and sweet. It has a biting taste and the best quality roots come from India and Jamaica. It is widely used through the menu from melon with ginger to steamed puddings, and especially in the oriental cookery of India and China.

Horseradish – a very strong-flavoured root which can bring tears to the eyes while grating it, though it is usually only available in prepared form as horseradish sauce or cream and as a dried powder. Much used in German, Russian and Scandinavian cookery as an ingredient of dishes and as a dip.

Juniper berries – dried berries with a strong flavour and scent which go well with venison, in cooking sauerkraut, in sausages and with joints of mutton and pork; it is also available in powder form.

Mace – the outer covering of the nutmeg sold as an orange-coloured powder and as blades for use in flavouring pâté, sausages, stuffings, biscuits and small cakes.

Nutmeg – dried seed of the fruit of a tree that grows in South East Asia and the Antilles, with a pleasant flavour that makes it versatile in use in sauces, stuffings, potato dishes, vegetables (especially spinach), milk puddings in the English style and as an ingredient in mixed spice. It blends well with cooked cheese dishes and pastas.

Paprika – although often referred to as paprika pepper it is made from dried and ground sweet pimentos and should have a vivid red colour and soft, pleasant aroma and flavour. It is widely used in Hungarian cookery where it is available in several qualities from sweet to strong; has many uses in sauces, stews, fish dishes, rice and sausages, and for decorative purposes.

Pepper – dried beans of the pepper vine which produce the most widely used spice. It has a very strong taste and smell that helps enhance the flavour of anything it is cooked with or sprinkled on, and it goes with all savoury dishes. Available as peppercorns for use whole and for grinding freshly, or in powdered form. It is available in various forms: **black peppercorns** – unripe berries in their outer skin; **cayenne pepper** – not a true pepper, being made of chilli pods; **mignonette** – name given to coarsely milled white peppercorns; **white pepper** – the strongest pepper, made from ripe peppercorns; **white peppercorns** – the best quality kind; **green peppercorns** – unripe berries; **red-pink peppercorns** – not a true kind of pepper but the berries of a shrub which grows in Brazil and in Florida; **Szechwan peppercorns** – known as Chinese brown peppercorns, need to be dry-fried or roasted before grinding.

Pickling spice – a combination consisting of equal parts of cloves, cinnamon stick, allspice, ginger root and white peppercorns; for a hotter mixture add dry chilli and mustard seed.

Quatre épices – name given to allspice, formerly known as Jamaica pepper; it carries the flavours of cinnamon, clove, nutmeg and pepper.

Saffron – a pungent spice made from the stigma of the crocus, a native of Arabia but now grown in Spain, Italy, Iran, France, Latin America, etc. It provides a wonderful aroma, a golden yellow colour and a delicate taste to many foods, and is a feature of the cookery of many nations.

Sansho pepper – made from leaves of a prickly ash tree.

Seven-flavour spice or pepper – a seasoning comprising ground chilli, black pepper, dried orange peel, sesame seeds, poppy seeds, nori seaweed and hemp seeds ground into a powder.

Star anise – the fruit of a tree of the magnolia family, it grows in the form of a star and has the strong, spicy taste and smell of anise. It is used in Chinese dishes and is very popular in Scandinavian cookery.

Tamarind – taken from the tamarind tree in the form of large pods containing a red pulp and small seeds, usually sold as pulp or as dried for making into juice by soaking in warm water then discarding the pulp. It is used in making curry and chutney. It may also be purchased in concentrated liquid form.

Turmeric – from the rhizomes of a plant of the lily family made into a powder to give a bright yellow colour and hot gingery taste to rice, curry and mustard pickle. A substitute for saffron but does not have much flavour or aroma.

Vinegars

Vinegar is an acid liquid produced through fermentation of malt or grape juice. Quality vinegar is identified by its clarity, aroma and distinctive flavour. Vinegar is used as a preservative for pickling vegetables such as eggs, gherkins, onions, pimentos, walnuts and red cabbage. Rollmops, which are fillets of herring, are pickled in white wine vinegar with the addition of sliced onion and herbs. Vinegar is also used as a condiment to add sharpness and flavour to salad items and other foods. Vinegar is used in marinades to add flavour and to aid tenderisation of meats, poultry and game and sometimes fish. It is used in the making of hors-d'oeuvre, dips, dressings and cold sauces such as mayonnaise. A reduction of vinegar together with herbs and spices is used to give sharpness to sauces such as devilled sauce and Reform Club sauce. The flavour characteristics of some stews are achieved by moistening with vinegar, for example, the classic Greek lamb stew with onions, Tavas.

Balsamic vinegar – a rich, concentrated, sweet and sour vinegar with a slightly acid taste, made from the juice of Trebbiano grapes.

Beer vinegar – yellowish in colour, rather bitter in flavour.

Cider vinegar – yellowish in colour with a mellow flavour.

Champagne wine vinegar – made from champagne and produced in the Epernay region of Reims, it has the appearance of champagne and is mellow in flavour.

Chianti vinegar – two varieties are produced from the wine of that name, from red or white wine.

Chilli vinegar – a white wine vinegar flavoured with chillies.

Citrus vinegar [*Ponzu*] – vinegar made from a lime-type citrus fruit used in Japanese cookery; lemon juice may be used as a substitute.

Distilled vinegars – these are colourless, strong vinegars mainly used for pickling.

Fruit-flavoured vinegars – e.g. raspberry vinegar, are produced by pickling whole fruits in quality wine vinegar for a number of days then straining off the liquid.

Garlic vinegar – a white wine vinegar flavoured with garlic.

Herb-flavoured vinegar – wine vinegar flavoured with a herb, e.g. rosemary, tarragon, dill or chervil.

Herb and spice vinegar – a white wine vinegar in which fresh herbs, e.g. rosemary, tarragon, cinnamon, cloves, garlic and peppercorns, have been steeped.

Malt vinegar – made from malted barley and yeast with the addition of malt.

Orange vinegar – a white wine vinegar, flavoured with oranges, cinnamon, cloves and allspice.

Orleans vinegar – old established fine wine vinegar made in the city of that name in France.

Rice vinegar – can be red, white or black. Rice vinegars are used in Asian cooking to add a special flavour to dishes; made by fermenting rice.

Rose vinegar – produced by macerating red rose petals in wine vinegar for a number of days.

Sherry vinegar – a high quality wine vinegar matured in oak casks.

Substitute vinegar – chemically produced from a solution of acetic acid in water, its main characteristics are a pungent odour and sharpness of flavour.

Wine vinegars – e.g. red and white wine vinegar are produced from poor quality wines.

Verjuice – similar to vinegar produced from acid juice extracted from white grapes.

Glossary of Ingredients and Terms

Abalone – a mollusc sometimes called St Peter's ear, used extensively in Asian and American cookery; usually canned but may be purchased fresh.

Ackee – fruit of West African origin used extensively in Caribbean cookery. A scarlet pod with shiny black seeds. The flesh is light cream in colour with a texture similar to scrambled eggs. May be purchased in cans.

Agar agar – a setting agent produced from seaweed, purchased in powder form.

Ahimsa – the Hindu doctrine of refraining from the slaughter of animals or from being cruel to them.

Ajowan powder – a spice similar in flavour to caraway and cumin, much used in Asian cookery.

Anatto – crushed seeds or prickly pod of a tropical American tree grown in the Caribbean. The deep orange pulp is used as a colouring agent in oils, margarine, ice cream, etc., or it can be used as a spice.

Andouille – French-style sausage made from pork, tripe, chitterlings, etc., served fried or grilled.

Angostura bitters – aromatic flavouring made from the bark of a tree grown in South America and various other aromatics.

Arroz Roja – a naturally coloured red rice.

Asafoetida – dried resin extracted from *Ferula asafoetida*, a plant native to Asia. Purchased in powder form or in pieces, it has a strong acrid and bitter flavour, therefore only minute quantities are necessary.

Asam jawa – tamarind pulp, used to add a tart taste to many oriental dishes, and sold in packets. Needs to be softened in the proportion of 25 g in 150 ml warm water and squeezed to use the liquid only. Must be kept in a cool place.

Asam keping – dried tamarind slices soaked in warm water and the juice only used to add tartness to dishes.

Ata – wholemeal flour, also called chapati flour, used in the making of Indian-style bread.

Avocado leaves [*hojas de aguacate*] – large leaves from the avocado tree used in Mexican cookery to add an aniseed flavour and aroma to food; they may be toasted then ground, or used whole.

Azuki – referred to as adzuki in Chinese; small, dark variety of mung bean which varies in colour from dark red to black, mottled and cream.

Bacalao – salt cod dried until very stiff, much used in Latin countries, especially for lenten dishes.

Bagel – ring-shaped roll that is first lightly poached then baked, which gives it a slightly chewy texture much loved by Jewish people. Can be sprinkled with sesame or poppy seeds.

Bagoong – fermented fish paste made from shrimps and anchovies in a pink sauce-like consistency, often placed on the dining table as an additional condiment.

Baharat – ground spices including black peppercorns, paprika, cinnamon, cloves, cumin seeds, coriander seeds, nutmeg and cardamom seeds.

Balachan – paste made from fermented shrimps and salt for use as a flavouring ingredient in Thailand.

Balti – a Pakistani style of cookery associated with highly spiced curries, cooked and served in a balti pan (q.v.).

Bamboo shoots – peeled pieces of bamboo spears usually sold cooked in cans; creamy-coloured and nutty in texture.

Bamia or **bamya** – the Turkish name for the okra or ladies' finger.

Banana leaves – can be softened by blanching to use as greased wrappings for salpicons, or freshly picked as plates to eat food from.

Barberries – rather sour berries which resemble currants in texture and colour.

Barded – to cover a joint of meat, fish, poultry or game items with thin slices of salt pork fat.

Batons – lengths 1.5 cm × 2 mm of vegetables.

Bean curd – ground soya beans made into a smooth curd, set with gypsum; has little flavour but is high in protein. Sold as fresh, white dried, sheet form, yellow (which is stiffer in texture) and as dried pieces used for flavouring purposes.

Bean paste – soya beans made into a thick paste, used as a flavouring ingredient. Available as Hot – mixed with red chillies; Sweet – a dip or sauce with added spices and garlic which give a dark red purée (also called Hoisin sauce); and as Salted – made as a yellow bean paste also called Miso).

Bean sprouts – young sprouts of mung beans much used in oriental cooking as a stir-fry vegetable and a filling, e.g. in spring rolls or raw as a salad. Can be grown quickly indoors on a damp cloth or cotton wool, covered to exclude the light until ready to pick in 3–4 days.

Bed of root vegetables – sliced carrot, onion, celery, bayleaf and a sprig of thyme, used for braising meat and fish.

Beefeater mushroom – American mushroom that tastes like beef.

Bellflower – toraji (q.v.), rootlets of the edible bellflower used in Korean cookery; may be purchased in dried form.

Bentos no toma – seasoning mixture containing dried seaweed, dried fish, monosodium glutamate and salt; used in Japanese cookery.

Besan – chickpea flour.

Bewit – flattish buff or greyish-buff mushroom with a bright violet stem, white gills and a slight taste of mint.

Bhaji – a savoury fritter, also called a pakora.

Biltong – dried strips of beef for eating as emergency rations, or can be cooked.

Bird's nest – available as black or white, made by the salanganes birds who build their nests by dribbling thick, sticky saliva around and around, so forming a fort-shaped crust. The nests are found high on the rocks and walls of grottos near the sea in Java and on islands off the coast of Malaysia. They need cleaning, soaking and blanching prior to use.

Biriani – a generic term for a highly spiced rice dish which is generally layered with a spicy savoury dish made of beef, chicken, lamb or mutton.

Bitter orange juice – a combination of 2 parts grapefruit juice, 1 part orange juice and the grated zest of the fruits. Used in a wide variety of Mexican dishes.

Blachan – made of small prawns fermented in salt until they form a paste by rotting away, then dried and packed. The strong odour disappears when cooked to give a depth of flavour, and the cooking can be carried out by frying with other pounded ingredients, by grilling, or by holding a little on a piece of wire over a naked gas flame without burning it.

Black beans – also called turtle beans, prized for their distinctive flavour and the thick black sauce they produce during cooking.

Black-eyed beans – white with a yellow or black eye, widely used in the southern states of America and in China.

Blanch – to cover with cold water, bring to the boil, refresh under cold water and drain, to help keep the colour of the food.

Bombay duck – sun-dried fillet of Indian fish flavoured with asafoetida. Served grilled or baked for breaking up on top of a dish of any kind of curry.

Bonito flakes – dried flakes of fish used in Japanese cookery to flavour basic stocks and soups; bonito is a type of tuna fish.

Borlotti beans – pink, speckled beans from Italy; may also be used as a salad item.

Boston beans – the familiar canned baked bean served on toast, etc. and as cooked in cassoulets; small, round and white.

Boudin – French-style black pudding made from pig's blood, or white pudding made with pork or veal.

Breadfruit – a large round or pear-shaped, green-skinned vegetable with creamy yellow flesh and a slight banana smell. Can be sliced and shallow fried or baked.

Bresaola – salted then air-dried beef cut into thin slices to eat as an hors-d'oeuvre.

Brown rice – rice from which only the outer husk has been removed leaving the bran and germ; also called unpolished or whole grain rice.

Brunoise – 1-mm dice of vegetables, etc.

Bruschetta – homemade or French baguette bread cut in half lengthways and heated through at 170 °C until brown and crisp, spread with finely crushed garlic, seasoned with pepper and salt and sprinkled with olive oil. Served hot.

Buah keras – also called macadamia nuts; often served instead of peanuts at cocktail parties and can be crushed for thickening sauces and stews.

Buckwheat – dried seeds of a grass made into groats (q.v.) then milled into flour that is grey/purple in colour.

Bulgar wheat or burghul – the most ancient kind of cereal, called ala; it has to be soaked then cooked and dried before being milled and is an ingredient in couscous.

Bundnerfleisch – air-dried raw beef that is sliced very thinly and served as an hors-d'oeuvre.

Burdock – root of a plant of the aster family, crunchy in texture and rather neutral in flavour so it absorbs the flavours of other foods.

Burghul – cracked wheat; a processed wheat used extensively throughout the eastern Mediterranean and the Middle East. Hulled wheat is steamed, dried and ground. Available in fine and coarse grades.

Buritos (de machaca) – finely minced beef cooked with spices and used as a tortilla filling.

Burritos – these are tortillas (q.v.) folded into small parcels with a filling of beans, shredded lettuce, sliced tomato, spring onion and grated cheese and reheated with guacamole (q.v.).

Butter beans – creamy-coloured, kidney-shaped beans similar to the haricot bean.

Cactus paddles [*nopales*] – paddle-shaped stems from various types of cactus plants used in Mexican cookery; may be purchased fresh or in cans.

Calzare – small, baked savoury made with a small round of pizza dough folded in half with a filling inside.

Cannellini beans – slightly larger than the butter bean, creamy in colour and kidney shaped; known as fasioli, they have a fluffy texture.

Capsicum – also called pimento and bell pepper, the mellow and sweet kind of pepper used as a salad and a vegetable, available as black, green, red and yellow.

Carambola – also called star fruit, a yellow fruit with sharp ribs, usually served cut into slices to show the star shape.

Carob – a sweet pulp that can be used as a substitute for chocolate, made from the pulp of the locust bean, used mainly in pastry and confectionery work.

Carpaccio – fashionable Italian dish served as an antipasto (hors-d'oeuvre) or a main course, consisting of wafer-thin slices of raw chilled fillet of beef on a bed of roccola (a type of watercress) with very thin, small slices of Parmesan cheese and a few drops of olive oil.

Cassareep – made from the cassava root, a thick black syrup used for colouring in Caribbean cookery.

Caviar – salted roe of the sturgeon, available in several qualities, Beluga being the finest.

Cellophane noodles – fine transparent noodles also called gelatine noodles, made from starch extracted from green mung beans; used in Asian cookery.

Cep mushroom – fleshy, spongy-textured mushroom with a bulbous base to the stem.

Ceylon curry – roast the following ingredients until brown then grind to a fine powder: cinnamon stick, cardamom pods with seeds removed, coriander seed, fennel seed, fenugreek seed, cloves.

Chakchouka – made in the same way as a ratatouille with eggplant, onion, pimento and tomato; it is eaten as a course or served as an accompaniment to sausages and fried eggs in Tunisia.

Chanterelle mushroom – funnel-shaped mushroom that narrows into a short stalk; bright egg-yellow colour and apricot-like smell.

Chapatti – flat disc-shaped unleavened bread made from wholemeal or roti flour, ghee and water.

Chayote – also called coo-coo or christophene, a tropical squash, extensively culti-vated in the Caribbean and tropical regions. May be purchased fresh or canned.

Chickpea – large-sized pea available as whole or split and in ground form for use as the thickening agent known as gram. They are the main ingredient of houm-ous (q.v.) and are also known as garbanzos.

Chilli ancho – dried chillies, almost black in colour, used in Mexican cookery.

Chilli mulato – dried, dark skinned, medium hot chillies, used in Mexican cookery.

Chilli pasill – dried, dark skinned, medium hot chillies, used in Mexican cookery.

Chilli serrano – small green chillies grown in the Sierra mountain region of South America.

Chinese black beans – small black-skinned beans which are allowed to ferment with salt before use.

Chinese gooseberry – another name for the kiwi fruit.

Chinese mushroom – known as Shiitake, a tree fungus with a distinctive flavour, available fresh or dried. The latter require to be soaked for approx. 30 min, and the warm water in which they were soaked is used.

Chinese plum sauce – sauce made from plums, chillies and various spices; may be purchased in cans and in jars.

Chipotte sauce – hot Mexican sauce made from smoked dried chilli jalapeño; pur-chased in bottles.

Chojang vinegar dipping sauce – condiment used as a dressing for a range of dishes in Korean cookery, made from cider vinegar, soy sauce, toasted sesame seeds, garlic, sugar and chilli powder.

Chorizo – short, fat sausage flavoured with paprika in sweetish or pungent ver-sions made with pork and cayenne pepper; may be purchased either smoked or fresh.

Christophene – a tropical, pear-shaped vegetable of the squash family, often with a prickly skin, whitish to pale green in colour. May be purchased in vacuum packs or pickled. Also known as chow chow or chayote.

Chrysanthemum leaves – used extensively in Chinese and Japanese cookery as a vegetable dish.

Chrysanthemum turnip – term used for cutting a turnip into a decorative blossom shaped like the chrysanthemum flower.

Cilantro – Mexican parsley, an aromatic herb with a strong, distinctive flavour.

Citrus leaves – the leaves of the kaffir lime used to provide a distinctive flavour to some oriental dishes, particularly fish; they need to be torn to shreds for use.

Clam – bivalve shellfish much used in American cookery, e.g. in a clambake.

Clarified butter – butter melted and cleared of any particles and all sediment.

Cloud ears – black fungus that gives its special flavour to some Chinese dishes; usually dried then soaked prior to use.

Coconut cream – made commercially, it is sold in block form which can be kept for several months and reconstituted by dissolving the required amount in hot water with a pinch of salt. It has a rich and quite sweet taste and flavour. It can be made by soaking 1 part fresh coconut flesh in 2 parts water for 3 hr then squeezing out the liquid through a muslin.

Coconut milk – this is not the natural juice present in coconuts, which is really only a refreshing drink; real coconut milk and coconut cream are purchased in packets, cans and as slabs. To make coconut milk blend 600 ml almost boiling water and 250 g desiccated coconut for 20 seconds, allow to cool then scoop out the coconut, squeezing out the liquid; the coconut can be used for another purpose and the liquid is the coconut milk. For example, the desiccated coconut may be stir-fried until it is golden brown and crisp and added to a curry towards the end of the cooking time.

Colcoassi – a potato-like root vegetable related to the Indian yam used in Greek and Turkish cookery.

Coriander root – root of the coriander plant, used in Asian cookery.

Corn syrup – made from maize kernels and used in American cookery to sweeten and flavour fruit dishes and ice-cream.

Court-bouillon – cooking liquid used for boiling and poaching fish, meat, offal, vegetables, etc.

Crème fraîche – slightly acidulated cream which gives a more pronounced flavour than ordinary cream when added to soups, stews, sauces, etc.

Croûtons – cubes of fried or toasted bread used as an accompaniment, garnish or a base for canapés.

Cultivated mushrooms – always in season as buttons, cups and opens, each with its own uses. Delicate in flavour, they can be eaten raw and require minimum cooking.

Daikon – elongated white radish used in Japanese cookery.

Darne – slice cut from a round fish on the bone, may be referred to as a fish steak.

Dauan pandan – leaf of the screw pine tree used for flavouring certain sweet dishes and in curries and pilaus.

Dauan salan – an aromatic leaf similar to a curry leaf in flavour, used in Indonesian cookery.

Dasheen – also called eddoe, a large tuba root vegetable with a dark brown, coarse skin, used as a potato though slightly bitter, varying in size from that of a small avocado to a large pineapple. The flesh may be white, pale yellow or pale grey in colour; it is used extensively in Caribbean cookery.

Dashi – the basic form of stock used in Japanese cookery, made of dried seaweed, which is called dashi kombu.

Decant – to remove meat from the cooking liquid and place it into a clean pan; the cooking liquid is then strained over the meat to remove any unwanted food items.

Devil's tongue noodles or shirataki – literally 'white waterfall'. Japanese noodles, made from the root of the devil's tongue or snake palm. May be purchased in cans and vacuum-sealed packs.

Devil's tongue root cake – made from tubers known as devil's tongue, a translucent cake-type product used in Japanese cookery.

Dhal – word meaning all the various kinds of lentils – brown, green, red and yellow. Sometimes spelt dal, the word also includes dried peas and beans.

Dim sum – this is the name given to an assortment of small snacks or titbits that can be eaten as a midday meal or as a prelude to a main meal. It is of Cantonese origin, consisting of a range of small delicacies, usually steamed or deep fried. Dumplings are served with fillings such as shrimps, shredded chicken, sesame seeds, mushrooms, coconut, lotus seeds, dates and red bean paste. Other steamed items can include meat balls, spare ribs, spring rolls, etc., some of which may be wrapped in lotus leaves. Fried items can include fish balls, batons of water chestnuts, tofu, yam fritters, etc.

Dolmas – term used to denote a vegetable filled with a stuffing and baked or steamed, e.g. stuffed vine leaves and stuffed eggplant.

Doner kebab – spit-roasted boned lamb in the shape of a large joint from which slices can be shaved off.

Dried shrimp paste – a pungent paste made from fermented and salted shrimps.

Dried sweet red pepper – hot, dried red peppers used extensively in Spanish cookery, may be substituted by crushed red pepper.

Duan panduras leaf – leaf of the screw pine tree used for flavouring certain sweet dishes and in curries and pilaus.

Durum wheat – type of cereal coarsely milled into flour, mainly for use in making pastas.

Eddoe – a tuber vegetable, also called dasheen although slightly smaller.

Empanadas – savoury turnovers made of rough puff pastry with a savoury mince meat filling, much eaten in Mexico.

Enchilada – another name for a tortilla, a Mexican corn pancake with a bean, chicken or meat filling coated with chilli sauce and cheese.

Epazote – a dried, pungent-smelling herb used in Mexican cookery.

Fairy ring mushrooms – small pink to pale buff cap on long firm stem and whitish gills.

Farinaceous items – term used to denote foods made of flour such as Italian pastas, gnocchi, dumplings, etc.

Fava beans – these are dried broad beans and are beige in colour.

Fécule – general term for thickening agents including arrowroot, cornflour, rice flour, potato flour.

Felafel – small, deep-fried balls of chickpea powder, matzo meal, eggs, cumin, coriander and garlic.

Field mushrooms – flat, white cap on short squat stem and pink to purple gills, as gathered wild from fields or cultivated.

Filo pastry – pastry made with a proportion of cornflour and with oil, widely used in Greece and countries in the Middle East; also spelt phyllo.

Fish sauce – there are several kinds of this oriental sauce sold in bottles as a strong fish flavouring, made by macerating fish in salt over a period of months. Nuoc nam is the name for it in South East Asia and is called nam pla in Thai cookery. Purchased in bottles.

Flageolet beans – small green beans like a small haricot bean, of good quality and delicate flavour.

Flambé – to add a spirit such as rum or brandy to a dish for added flavour and set it alight to burn off the alcohol.

Floret – one of the small flowers of the cauliflower or broccoli.

Flower waters – these include orange-flower water and rose-water, and are made of the highly scented petals for use as delicate flavourings in icings and desserts.

Foie gras – the fattened liver from forcefed goose or duck, a very expensive commodity used as an hors-d'oeuvre or main course.

Fortified wine – wine with the addition of brandy to increase its alcoholic strength, including Madeira, Marsala, port and sherry.

Fromage frais – contains less than 8% fat, made from fermented skimmed milk with added cream.

Ful medames – a small, round bean, light brown in colour, much used in Middle Eastern cookery.

Garam masala – ground mixed spices comprising a blend of dried deseeded red and green chillies, root ginger, cloves, mint and coriander leaves, used with a little water to give a smooth paste. Used in Asian and Indian cookery. May be purchased in jars.

Garbanzo bean – another name for the chickpea.

Gari – cassava meal, also called tapioca powder.

Ghee – clarified butter, used in Indian cookery.

Ginger shoots – pickled ginger roots; generally eaten with grilled foods.

Glutinous rice – long-grain variety of rice which is gluten-free, frequently used for dessert dishes; when cooked it becomes very sticky.

Gram flour – flour made from dried split peas; may be substituted with wheatflour or wholemeal flour.

Gratinate – to sprinkle the surface of food with grated cheese, breadcrumbs, vegetable oil or melted butter and colour golden under a salamander grill or in the top of an oven.

Gravlax – fillets of salmon cured with either whisky, gin or aquavit, sea salt, sugar, crushed peppercorns and dill for 2–3 days. Served with lemon, brown bread and butter and dill and mustard sauce. Also called gravad lax.

Griolles mushrooms – another name for chanterelle mushrooms.

Guacamole – a dip or sauce made from purée of avocado, tomato, chillies, coriander, onion and lemon juice.

Guava – strong-smelling tropical fruit containing many seeds, round or pear-shaped and green to yellow in colour. Used to make jelly, ice-cream, etc.

Halal – the ritual slaughtering method for cattle as practised by Muslims.

Haricot bean – large, flat, kidney-shaped bean, creamy-white in colour.

Hijiki – a type of seaweed used as a vegetable in Japanese cookery.

Hoisin sauce – a thick, sweet, spicy, reddish-brown sauce made from soy beans, spices and garlic. May be purchased canned or bottled.

Hominy – prepared maize kernels used in American cookies, also called grits.

Horn of plenty mushroom – tough, horn-shaped cap mushroom with felt-like inner surface, sooty brown to black in colour.

Horse mushroom – large-sized field mushroom approx. 11 cm in diameter, with a white cap and white to brown gills on a tall stalk.

Houmous – puréed chickpeas flavoured with garlic, lemon juice and olive oil; often served in a pitta and can be used as a dip.

Indonesian spice powder – a blend of shallots, garlic, red chillies, thick coconut milk, coriander seeds, nutmeg, turmeric, galingale, lemon grass, oil and a little water made to a smooth paste. The paste is fried in groundnut oil for a few min. May be purchased ready prepared.

Jaggery – compressed round cakes of a sugar taken from the Nippah palm tree, used in making Japanese sweets.

Jalapeño chilli – a very hot variety of Mexican chilli, small, thin and green in colour, usually canned or pickled.

Jalebi – batter made from flour, milk powder and yogurt, deep fried in whirls and served as a sweet in heavy syrup.

Jambón serrano – a cured ham from Spain.

Japanese artichoke – also called crosne or Chinese artichoke, similar to the Jerusalem artichoke but smaller.

Japanese mushrooms – dried mushrooms, also called shiitake (q.v.).

Japanese noodles [*harusame*] – very fine noodles produced from bean starch; they become translucent when soaked and boiled. When deep fried they puff up and become opaque.

Japanese pepper [*sansho*] – used in Japanese cookery as a garnish. The ground leaf, kona sansho, is used as a seasoning.

Jelly mushrooms – dried, greyish-black mushrooms used in Asian cookery, may also be referred to as cloud ear fungus.

Jerked beef – salted tender cuts of beef dried in the air; also known as biltong.

Julienne – garnish-size strips 3 cm in length of vegetables or other ingredients, e.g. chicken, ham, etc.

Kabanos – long, thin, spicy sausage, dried or fresh, for cooking in a cassoulet or as a salad; made in Spain.

Kaffir lime leaves – leaves of a citrus fruit grown in Asia; bayleaf may be used as a substitute.

Kamaboko – fish paste, may be eaten sliced as part of an hors-d'oeuvre or added to a variety of dishes during cooking. Usually purchased in cakes or in rolls.

Kapi – Thai name for dried shrimp paste, which may be purchased ready-made.

Kasha – roasted buckwheat kernels used in Russian cookery; may be eaten as an accompaniment to other dishes or served with a sauce.

Kashrut – Jewish dietary laws as stated in the Book of Leviticus as to which foods can be eaten, showing how meat must be treated and that milk and meat must not be included in the same meal.

Kataifi – a pastry widely used in Greece and Middle Eastern countries, made as long thin strands and usually drenched with syrup.

Katsuobushi – dried bonito fillet used in Japanese cookery for flavouring dashi, which is a Japanese stock, and for garnishing.

Kecap manis – a sweetish, dark-coloured form of soy sauce much used in Indonesian cookery.

Kelp kombu – brown seaweed much used in Japanese cookery.

Kencur powder – also known as galingale or aromatic ginger, used in Asian cookery.

Kha – root of the ginger plant peculiar to Southeast Asia; may be purchased dried.

Khoa – evaporated milk cooked until it becomes even thicker and caramelised, used to make Indian fudge-like sweets.

Kidney bean – the red kidney bean comes in several colours from pink to maroon, has a floury texture and is widely used, e.g. in Chilli con Carne.

Kikurage – one of the jelly fungi, mostly ligneous with a gelatinous texture, much used in Japanese cookery in dried form.

Kimichi – fermented pickle used to accompany a range of Korean dishes.

Kiname – pepper leaf used as a garnish in Japanese cookery. Not always readily available; substitute with kona sansho ground pepper leaf.

Kochujang – red pepper paste made from soy beans, glutinous rice flour and chilli powder, used extensively in Korean cookery.

Kombu – dried seaweed (kelp) used in Asian cookery.

Konnyaku – devil's tongue jelly, a starchy, gelatinous, dark brownish root. Rather neutral in flavour, may be purchased in unrefined and refined forms, in cake form or in cans.

Kosher – food produced and prepared in accordance with strict Jewish religious laws.

Krupuk – prawn-flavoured cracker served as an accompaniment to many Malaysian dishes as a dip; need to be dried before deep frying without colour.

Kvas – a fermented drink made from rye bread and yeast; may be flavoured with mint. Also spelt kvass.

La Kama – a seasoning mixture of ginger, black pepper, nutmeg and turmeric.

Lablat bean – black bean with a hard skin, widely used, especially in Egypt.

Laos powder – woody roots of a member of the ginger family that has a pine smell and flavour, available in powdered form as a spice.

Lap cheong – a savoury Chinese sausage.

Lardons of bacon – small strips of bacon usually blanched and shallow fried.

Laska noodles – Thai name for egg noodles.

Lemon grass – a lemon-scented grass used for flavouring in south-east Asian cookery; may be substituted with zest of lemon. Available fresh and in powder form.

Lily buds – dried golden buds, also referred to as lotus buds, used in Chinese cookery.

Lima bean – pale green in colour, in small and medium sizes, available in dried and canned forms.

Linzer delikatess – small, firm-textured, yellow-skinned potato.

Lobe-leaf seaweed [*wakame*] – a sea vegetable with lengthy fronds; may be purchased dried.

Lotus root – served peeled and sliced in salads or cooked as a vegetable, also available canned and dried; when fresh it must be kept from discolouring.

Lumpfish roe – salted roe of the lumpfish, available as black or orange-red from Iceland and Denmark, used as a substitute for caviar.

Lychee – fruit with translucent white flesh with a scented flavour, usually eaten as it is after discarding the stone; also spelt litchi.

Maatjes herring – raw boned herring cured in the Dutch way with vinegar, spices and sugar.

Macédoine – mixed diced carrot and turnip with peas and diamond shapes of French beans.

Magret – breast of a Rouen duck which has been specially bred for its liver, which is used in the making of foie gras; the magret is red in colour, thick but tender when cooked.

Maldive fish – dried tuna fish, used extensively in Asian cookery; may be purchased in packets.

Mandu – wonton wrapper dumplings poached in chicken stock.

Mango powder – made from sun-dried mango, it has a distinctive and delicate, sour flavour.

Mangosteen – a dark-coloured, leathery-skinned fruit containing five delicately flavoured segments.

Marmite – an earthenware soup bowl made as individual or large size with a lid; also refers to rich beef stock and is the trade name of a vegetarian meat essence.

Mascarpone – a soft, fresh cheese with a delicious flavour made from fresh cream.

Matsutka mushrooms – regarded as the most delicious of all mushrooms, grows on trees, delicate in quality and tastes like meat; widely used in Japanese cookery.

Matzo – unleavened bread made as flat, round or square biscuits, made especially for eating during the Jewish Passover.

Matzo meal – meal of varying coarseness made from matzo.

Melons – used mainly as an hors-d'oeuvre, either small whole, sliced or as melon cocktail cut in small balls; can also be used as a garnish with fish and white meat and as part of a fruit salad. The best-known varieties are cantaloupe, charentais, galia, honeydew, ogen and water melon.

Mesclun – young sprouting mixture of dandelion, burnet, purslane and rocket; grown like mustard and cress for use as a salad stuff.

Mihoen – rice vermicelli.

Mirepoix of vegetables – roughly cut vegetable mixture with herbs comprising carrot, onion, celery, thyme and bayleaf.

Mirin – Japanese rice wine used only in cookery; dry sherry may be used as a substitute.

Miso – red bean paste.

Miyok – fresh or dried seaweed used in Korean cookery, obtainable in dried form.

Monosodium glutamate – a seasoning of white crystals similar to coarse salt made of hydrolysed wheat or beet, used extensively in Chinese and Asian cookery.

Mooli – a parsnip-shaped, white-skinned radish with a bitter taste; also called daiketin.

Moong dal – yellow split peas.

Morcilla – a Spanish blood sausage used in a wide range of dishes; may be purchased in vacuum packs.

Morel mushrooms – conical cap with ridges and pits, grey to yellowy-brown and delicate flavour.

Mortadella – large, oval pork sausage with peppercorns or pistachios.

Mtzutaks mushrooms – large, delicately flavoured mushrooms used in Japanese cookery. May be purchased in cans.

Mung beans – produce the Chinese bean sprout, a small green and white shoot that grows quickly. Also available as whole, split or skinless, the beans can be ground into a flour used for making Chinese noodles called fen tian.

Nam pla – a fish sauce used in Thai cookery.

Nan bread – yeast dough moulded in the shape of a teardrop and baked in a tandoori oven.

Noisette of lamb – a boned-out loin of lamb cut across the joint into small slices and trimmed heart-shape.

Nori – dried lava seaweed used in Korean cookery.

Nuoc nam – fish sauce used in south-east Asian cookery.

Okra – also called ladies' finger or gumbo, a small, green, tapering pod vegetable; young okra are used by preference.

Onion sambal – chopped onion sprinkled with lemon juice and chilli powder served as an accompaniment to curry dishes.

Oyster mushrooms – blue-grey to buff-coloured flat cap, convex in shape, bracket-like stem and whitish gills.

Oyster plant – name given to salsify.

Oyster sauce – a flavouring ingredient and an accompaniment to various dishes, made as a thick brown essence from soya beans, oysters and starches.

Padi-straw – fleshy, conical cap mushroom with white fibrillose gills.

Palm heart – the tender shoot of a palm tree, used as a vegetable.

Palm sugar – dark, strongly flavoured sugar with a bitter flavour. It is obtained from the sap of coconut and palmyrah palm trees.

Pancetta – cured bacon from belly of pork.

Panch phora – combination of five different whole seeds, consisting of black mustard, cumin, black cumin, fenugreek and fennel.

Pandanus – jaggery (q.v.).

Panettone – sweet loaf made with yeast, eggs and dried fruit; a speciality of Milan and a traditional Italian Christmas treat.

Papain – tenderiser obtained from the papaya fruit.

Papeda – kind of porridge made of sago flour which is obtained from the sago palm tree; usually added to soups.

Parasol – mushroom with an umbrella-shaped cap with dark brown scales on a white surface, on a tall stalk which separates easily.

Parma ham – good-quality cured raw ham from the town of that name in Italy.

Passata – tomato sauce flavoured with oregano and basil.

Passion fruit – fruit with a wrinkled, purple-brown skin and yellowy-green flesh with edible black seeds; can be eaten like a boiled egg. Also known as granadilla.

Pastrami – salted and smoked brisket or topside of beef, spiced and served cold as an hors-d'oeuvre, cut into thin slices.

Patum peperium – fancy name given to a brand of anchovy spread; also called Gentleman's Relish.

Paw-paw – oval, deep yellow-coloured fruit which bruises easily, served cut in half with the seeds removed.

Paysanne – garnish-sized small triangles, squares or rounds cut from a mixture of vegetables.

Persimmon – also called Sharon fruit; of a round shape and orange colour, it can be served by cutting off the top to eat with a spoon, or peeled and sliced.

Pigeon beans – sometimes called pigeon peas, these beige-coloured beans are small and round, and much used in Caribbean cookery.

Pinto beans – beige-coloured and dappled with brown, these are kidney-shaped.

Plantain – looks like a giant banana but is peeled, sliced and sautéed as a vegetable or garnish.

Pleurotte mushrooms – originally a wild mushroom but now mainly cultivated; when very fresh they taste of anise, soon developing a strong taste.

Poeroet leaves – aromatic leaf used in Thai cooking, may be substituted with dried curry leaves.

Pomodori secchi – Italian sun-dried tomatoes marinated in a blend·of seasoned virgin olive oil.

Ponze – Japanese dressing of lime juice, rice vinegar, soy sauce, mirin, bonito flakes, kelp and tamarind.

Poppadums – thin wafers of lentil flour dough, grilled, baked or deep fried to accompany a curry.

Poudre de colombo – a rather mild curry powder blend of spices used in Caribbean cookery, consisting of turmeric, coriander seeds, mustard seeds, garlic and ginger, ground to a fine paste.

Pourgouri – Greek name for cracked wheat (see burghul).

Prawn crackers [*Chinese crackers*] – a small, whitish, round, crispy product made from a paste comprising prawn flesh, starch, salt and sugar which is then dried and deep fried.

Prawn powder – shredded dried prawns used in Chinese cookery.

Pretzel – glazed, brittle savoury snack with a salty crust, made in the shape of a loose knot.

Prosciutto crudo – cured raw ham from Italy, e.g. Parma ham.

Pumpkin – orange-coloured gourd; can be served as a vegetable, made into soup or as a filling for pumpkin pie.

Quas chawal – cooked rice shallow fried in ghee and flavoured with saffron.

Quesadillas – hot sandwiches made with two tortillas (q.v.) filled with grated cheese, onion rings and chopped green chillies.

Quince – pear-shaped fruit that turns deep yellow when ripe; very acid flavour, usually cooked with apple as a tart or pie, as on its own it forms a very stiff paste.

Quorma – also spelt korma, a very mild curry dish.

Quorn – artificial protein food which can replace meat in the diet while still giving its texture, taste and nutritional value. Grown from a tiny plant.

Rahat lakoum – Turkish name for Turkish delight.

Rambutan – small, oval-shaped fruit which looks like a hedgehog, with a yellow to purple skin and translucent flesh.

Rassol – liquor in which beetroot or cucumber is preserved in diluted acetic acid.

Red spice paste – bean paste made from azuki beans, used in Japanese cookery; may be also be purchased in powder form.

Rice – grain grown as a grass in water-covered paddy fields, a staple food in the diet of many races; available as unpolished, polished, brown, carolina or pudding, long-grain or patna, basmati, java, easy-cook and as ground rice and rice flour.

Rice bean – grown in oriental countries, these taste like rice and can be served in its place.

Rigani – another name for wild marjoram as used in Greek cookery; may be purchased fresh or dried. Also spelt origani.

Rillette – potted meat made of belly of pork, goose or rabbit, well flavoured with herbs and spices.

Rocambole – a flavouring ingredient with a mild taste of garlic, grows wild on stems resembling a leek with a small, purple, bulbous root.

Rogan josh – a highly spiced dish of lamb braised in yogurt and cream; a Kashmiri speciality.

Rognonnade – boned loin of veal with the whole kidney enclosed in sausage meat, neatly rolled and tied.

Roti flour – creamy in colour and granular in texture, similar to wholemeal flour.

Rowan jelly – made from the fruit of the mountain ash; usually served with venison and can be added to apple sauce.

Sago tuman – pith of the sago palm tree extracted by immersion in water, then squeezed out and dried.

Saké – Chinese and Japanese rice wine.

Salted tarama – the salted roe of the cod or mullet as used for making the well-known Greek dish taramasalata.

Sambals – accompaniments served with curry dishes, a selection of items including banana, coconut, chutney, pimento, etc.

Sambal bajak – fresh red chillies, onion, garlic and trasi ground with a little water to a smooth paste. The mixture is fried in groundnut oil; grated kemiri nuts, laos powder, tamarind liquid and palm sugar are added, and the mixture is then simmered until reddish-brown in colour and the oil shows signs of separating from the mixture. Used in Asian and in particular, Indonesian cookery. May be purchased ready prepared.

Sambal rojak – a side dish for serving with broth-type soups, made of soy paste and fermented shrimps.

Sambal trasi – a flavouring combination of red chillies, sea salt and trasi (dried shrimp paste). May be purchased in cans or as a cake.

Sambal ulek – dried red chillies, tamarind liquid and salt ground to a paste. Used in Indonesian cookery, it may be purchased ready prepared.

Sambalan – soaked dried chillies, onion, garlic, trasi, groundnut oil, tamarind juice, salt and palm sugar ground to a smooth paste. The mixture is fried in groundnut oil until dark in colour and the oil separates around the edges, then cooled and bottled. Used in Indonesian cookery, it may be purchased ready prepared.

Samneh – clarified butter used in Middle Eastern cookery.

Samosas – deep-fried, oval or triangular-shaped spiced vegetable or meat pasty; can also contain baked or curried beans, cottage cheese, tuna fish or rice.

Sareh powder – Indonesian name for an aromatic flavouring powder made from lemon grass.

Satay – an Asian dish of skewered spiced meat or chicken.

Scorzonera – the black-skinned salsify, prepared and served as for that vegetable.

Sesame paste – roasted and ground sesame seeds mixed to a paste with sesame oil. Sesame seeds become sweet and nutty when roasted or dry fried.

Seto fuumi – seasoning mixture made from dried tuna fish.

Shaohsing wine – fermented liquid made from glutinous rice and yeast, yellow in colour with a golden sheen, named after Shenyang, an eastern province of China. A medium-dry sherry may be used as a substitute.

Shichimi-togarashi – a mixture of spices, poppy and sesame seeds, kemp and rape plus tangerine peel and pepper leaf.

Shiitake mushrooms – Japanese mushroom with a slight taste of garlic.

Shiitaki – Japanese-style vermicelli made from yam flour and water.

Shirataki noodles – made from the devil's tongue root and translucent in appearance, these noodles are used extensively in Japanese cookery; they may be purchased in cans and in packets.

Shoyu sauce – similar to soy sauce but less salty and lighter in colour, used in Japanese cookery.

Shrimp paste – a pungent paste made from dried shrimps with a distinctive flavour; may be purchased in jars and cans.

Smetana – soured cream or equal quantities of natural yogurt and double cream, used extensively in Russian cookery.

Soba – very fine noodles made from buckwheat flour.

Somen – very fine noodles made from white wheatflour; vermicelli may be used as a substitute.

Soya bean – the most nutritious of all beans because they contain all the eight essential amino acids; they are small, oval-shaped and grow as black, green, red and yellow varieties. Can be cooked and eaten on their own or used to make tofu (q.v.), soy sauce, tamari sauce (q.v.), soya milk in powder or long-life form, soya oil and flour made of cooked beans, and also as textured vegetable protein, a meat substitute.

Soy sauce – made of salted soya beans, gives a meaty taste to dishes. Made as white sauce which is thin, and black which is thick. Shoyu is the name given to Japanese soy sauce.

Spring roll wrappers – also known as wonton or won ton wrappers, thin white sheets of pastry used in Chinese cookery; they are fragile and need to be handled carefully. Usually purchased frozen; once thawed, separate and cover with a damp cloth to prevent drying.

St George's mushroom – shallow, convex, white to buff cap on a short stalk with white gills and a strong smell.

Steinpilze mushrooms – a wild, forest mushroom.

Studded onion – an onion with a bayleaf and a clove inserted into it, used as a flavouring for sauces, soups, stocks and when cooking pulses.

Suprême – i. fillet of large fish cut on the slant into portion-sized pieces; ii. a chicken breast with the end of the wingbone attached.

Sweat – i. to cook vegetables without colour in a covered saucepan with fat or oil; ii. to cook vegetables without colour in their own juices in a covered saucepan.

Sweet potato – has white to orange-coloured flesh and a chestnut-like taste.

Swiss chard – also known as seakale beet, the white stems are used as a vegetable and cooked in similar ways to spinach or seakale.

Tabasco – the proprietary brand name of a flavouring liquid made by macerating hot red pimentos and ageing them in salt and vinegar.

Tabbouleh – fine bulgar wheat soaked and squeezed, mixed with chopped parsley, mint and tomato and a lemon and oil dressing. It is served as a salad on young vine leaves or cos lettuce. A Lebanese speciality.

Taco shells – these are deep-fried tortillas (q.v.) made horseshoe shape by holding against the side of the fat fryer, served filled with a mixture of chicken, lettuce and guacamole (q.v.).

Tahina or tahini paste – an oily paste made from sesame seeds and lemon. May be purchased ready made.

Tamara – salted roe of cod or mullet used in the making of taramasalata.

Tamari sauce – made from soya beans and sea salt only and used as an alternative to soy sauce.

Tamarind – an acid-tasting tropical fruit, similar to a large broad bean.

Tamarind liquid – liquid of the tamarind fruit. May be purchased in condensed liquid form in jars or in dried form to be reconstituted by soaking in water.

Tandoori – Pakistani type of cooking using charcoal; meat is first marinated then cooked in a clay oven called a tandoor.

Tannias – similar to the dasheen or eddoe but smaller in size and drier in texture. The flesh is either white, pale yellow, creamy or pale violet in colour. May be purchased in cans.

Tapas – selection of titbits such as prawns, squid, chorizo sausage, chickpea purée, pieces of various flavoured omelettes with pine nuts, olives, garlic, etc.

Taro – starchy tuber also known as eddoe and tannias, the flesh becomes slimy when boiled.

Tempe – soya bean paste made by soaking and skinning soya beans; they are then steamed until tender with a culture and incubated at 30 °C for approximately 24 hrs to produce slabs ready to eat. Much used in Japanese cooking.

Teriyaki – cooking of pieces of marinated fish, meat and poultry on a charcoal grill.

Tikki – brochettes of seafood, meat or chicken previously marinated before cooking in a tandoori oven.

Tiramisu – finger biscuits flavoured with coffee, Marsala, rum, brandy, etc. with mascarpone cheese, dusted with cocoa. May also be made with crème anglaise and mascarpone.

Tofu – soybean curd much used by the Japanese and by vegetarians.

Tomatillos – small, plum-sized, light green, tart-flavoured fruit used for many green-type sauces in Mexican cookery.

Tomato concassée – blanched, peeled, depipped and diced tomato.

Toraji – rootlets of the edible bellflower (q.v.) used in Korean cookery.

Tortillas – unleavened dough made of ground maize and hot water, pressed flat and cooked on a griddle plate.

Trasi – Indonesian name for dried shrimp paste.

Truffle – a fungus that grows in clusters near the roots of young oak trees; there are two main varieties – black and white. There is also a red-grained black truffle. All are rare, much in demand and very expensive.

Tzatziki – mixture of thick, plain yogurt, chopped cucumber, garlic and herbs, served as a dip for crudités or a filling in a pitta.

Udon noodles – thickish noodles made from white wheatflour; tagliatelli may be used as a substitute.

Vésiga – dried spinal cord of sturgeon used mainly in the Russian dish Coulibiac.

Vindaloo – very hot Goanese curry originally of pork marinated in vinegar.

Wasabi powder – pungent green horseradish used in Japanese cookery to accompany raw fish dishes. May be purchased in cans.

Water chestnuts – tuber grown in water, an Asian delicacy used mainly in salads. Available fresh and may be also be purchased in cans or jars.

Wonton wrappers – small squares of pastry used in Chinese and Japanese cookery for making savoury and sweet dishes; usually purchased frozen.

Yam – starchy tuber which quickly discolours when peeled; not the same as the sweet potato.

Yellow bean sauce – used extensively in Chinese cookery; made from fermented beans with the addition of various spices. May be purchased in cans and in jars.

Yogurt – produced from whole, partially skimmed or skimmed dried evaporated milk in many flavours. Made with a culture bacteria which is permitted to multiply at a controlled temperature. When made with cow's milk, yogurt curdles when heated; it therefore needs to be stabilised with cornflour or arrowroot using 2 tsp to 600 ml of milk.

Yogurt salsa – Turkish dipping sauce made of yogurt, garlic and salt.

Yuzu citron – citrus fruit used mainly for the unique aromatic fragrance of its rind; may be substituted by using lemon or lime.

Zakouskis – a pre-prandial selection of appetizers or hors-d'oeuvre similar to a smörgasbord but in bite-sized pieces, usually served with vodka; also spelt zazuskis.

Zampone – full length pig's trotter boned and stuffed with pork sausage meat, boiled and served cut into slices as a main dish.

Zest – thinly peeled rind of citrus fruits such as oranges, lemons and limes.

Equipment and Utensils

Special items of equipment and utensils used in ethnic cookery.

Avli – traditional Greek beehive-shaped oven used for baking, stewing and roasting, used extensively in Greek and Turkish cookery.

Bain-marie – i. container of water for keeping food hot; ii. a shallow container of water for cooking foods in the oven to ensure even temperature.

Balti pan – made of cast iron, stainless steel, or copper lined with tin; small, versatile wok-shaped pans used extensively in northern India for cooking a variety of dishes in the balti style.

Balti pan (Karahi)

Blini pan – small cast-iron or omelette-type pan used for making traditional Russian blinis or bliny.

Cazuelas – flat-bottomed earthenware pots for baking, stewing and roasting, used extensively in Mexican and Spanish cookery.

Chawan-mushi – Japanese term for the traditional straight-sided soup pot with lid.

Chinese wok cooker or Chinese stove – specially designed stove to accommodate the shape of a wok. Gas jets are set in a shallow water container used for reducing the high temperature required for stir-frying.

Chinese wok cooker

Chopsticks – made of plastic, wood or bamboo, lacquered or unlacquered or of ivory or metal, approximately 30 cm in length. Used for eating and for cooking foods instead of spoons, forks and even whisks.
Comales – Mexican term for a griddle.
Couscous steamer – double lined saucepan for cooking couscous.

Couscous cooker

Degchi – two-handled pan used throughout India, made of brass or aluminium with straight sides and a lid that fits over a horizontal rim. The pan may be sealed with a paste of flour and water, making a type of steam cooker for what

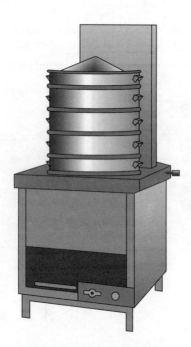

Dim sum steamer

Gas duck oven

is termed dum cooking. Heat is provided by placing hot coals onto the lid providing heat from above as well as from below.

Dim sum or dum steamer – designed for cooking Chinese dumplings and snack items.

Donburi – Japanese term for individual ceramic bowls which are used for serving rice and noodle dishes.

Gas duck oven – oven specially designed for roasting the traditional Peking duck by hanging them on hooks at the top.

Hashi – Japanese term for chopsticks (q.v.).

Idra or degh – traditional earthenware pot with a wide base and narrow opening used for cooking rice in Middle Eastern countries.

Jezve – long-handled coffee pot used for making Greek/Turkish coffee.

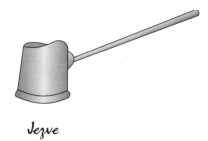

Jezve

Karahi – another name for balti pan (q.v.).

Mushiki – a stacking steamer of several sections made of bamboo or of metal, used in Japanese cookery.

Ollas – Mexican earthenware pot used for cooking beans and soups; larger types are used for brewing coffee.

Paellera – special two-handled, shallow pan made for the cooking of paella.

Paellera

Parfait mould – oblong-shaped moulds 20 cm in length × 10 cm wide × 8 cm high, with a false bottom.

Puchero – a bulbous-shaped earthenware pot used in Spanish cookery, traditionally having two sets of handles, one pair placed at the shoulder the second lower down.

Ramekin or ramequin – individual porcelain dish used for potted foods and egg dishes.

Ravier – an hors-d'oeuvre dish made in oval or oblong shape.

Saganaki – a two-handled frying pan used in Greek cookery.

Shin seol ro – name given to a Korean receptacle in which food is cooked and served from at table. Ornate versions are generally made of brass or a less expensive type of anodised aluminium. They are manufactured in various sizes with a central chimney for holding hot charcoal. Food is placed into a surrounding moat, moistened with stock and cooked to completion.

Shin seol ro

Sudare – a mat made of thin slats of bamboo, used when making traditional Japanese omelettes, sushi and vegetable dishes.

Sushioke – shallow, round bamboo dish for serving the traditional Japanese dish of sushi.

Tabaka – a cast-iron sauté pan with a ridged base and heavy lid to seal in the cooking juices, widely used for traditional Russian dishes.

Tannour – beehive-shaped clay oven used in Indian cookery.

Tamago-yaki nabe – rectangular frying pan used to make traditional Japanese rolled omelettes.

Tamago-yaki nabe

Tandoori oven or cooking pot – made of clay, used extensively in Indian cookery for the slow cooking of bread, meat, fish and poultry dishes.

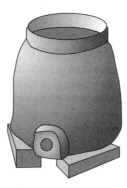

Tandoori oven

Tawa – Caribbean name for a type of griddle plate on which chapatti or paratha are cooked.

Tempura pan – a round iron pan with a built-in draining grid, used for deep-fried items in Japanese cookery.

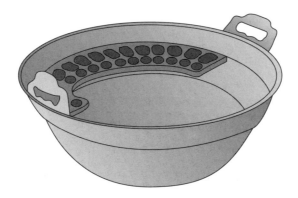

Tempura pan

Tepan-yaki – iron plate grill with cast-iron inset upon which food is cooked in front of customers in speciality Japanese restaurants.

Terrine – an earthenware dish for cooking and presenting pâté.

Wajan – Indonesian name given to a wok.

Wok – a curved-based metal pan used extensively in Asian cookery; available in many sizes, it may be manufactured of stainless steel or iron and is designed to give the fast heat so necessary in the stir-fry method of cookery.

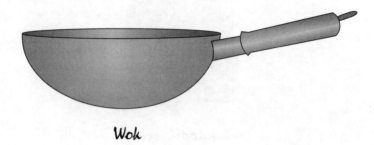

Wok

Wok chan – Chinese ladles and frying spoons which are made of finely twisted wire and available in many sizes.

Yabba pot – glazed clay cooking pot used in Caribbean cookery.

Zaru – plate-sized bamboo strainer or serving dish used in Japanese cookery.

Abbreviations and Conversion Tables

Abbreviations

g   = gram
kg = kilogram
l   = litre
mm = milimeter
cm = centimetre

°C = degrees Celsius (Centigrade)
tsp = teaspoonful(s)
tbs = tablespoonful(s)
min = minutes
hr = hours

Weight Conversions

Imperial		Metric	Imperial		Metric
$\frac{1}{4}$ tsp	=	1.75 g	12 oz	=	350 g
$\frac{1}{2}$ tsp	=	2.5 g	13 oz	=	375 g
1 tsp	=	5 g	14 oz	=	400 g
1 tbs	=	15 g	15 oz	=	425 g
$\frac{1}{4}$ oz	=	6 g	16 oz	=	450 g
$\frac{1}{2}$ oz	=	12 g	1 lb 2 oz	=	500 g
1 oz	=	25 g	$1\frac{1}{4}$ lb	=	550 g
2 oz	=	50 g	$1\frac{1}{2}$ lb	=	675 g
$2\frac{1}{2}$ oz	=	60 g	1 lb 10 oz	=	750 g
3 oz	=	75 g	$1\frac{3}{4}$ lb	=	800 g
$3\frac{1}{4}$ oz	=	90 g	$2\frac{1}{4}$ lb	=	1 kg (1000 g)
4 oz	=	100 g	$2\frac{1}{2}$ lb	=	1.25 kg
$4\frac{1}{2}$ oz	=	125 g	3 lb	=	1.3 kg
5 oz	=	150 g	$4\frac{1}{4}$ lb	=	2 kg
6 oz	=	175 g			
7 oz	=	200 g	1 cup butter	=	8 oz, 225 g
8 oz	=	225 g	1 cup flour	=	5 oz, 125 g
9 oz	=	250 g	1 cup sugar	=	7 oz, 200 g
10 oz	=	275 g	1 qut = 4 cups	=	1 lb, 450 g
11 oz	=	300 g	1 cup water	=	$\frac{1}{2}$ pint

Length Conversions

Imperial		Metric	Imperial		Metric
$\frac{1}{5}$ inch	=	4 mm	7 inches	=	17.5 cm
$\frac{1}{4}$ inch	=	0.5 cm	8 inches	=	20 cm
$\frac{1}{2}$ inch	=	1 cm	9 inches	=	22.5 cm
1 inch	=	2.5 cm	10 inches	=	25 cm
2 inches	=	5 cm	12 inches	=	30 cm
3 inches	=	7.5 cm	20 inches	=	50 cm
4 inches	=	10 cm	$3\frac{1}{4}$ feet	=	1 m
5 inches	=	12.5 cm	1 yard	=	93 cm
ches	=	15 cm			

Liquid Measurements

Imperial		Metric	Imperial		Metric
$\frac{1}{4}$ tsp	=	1.25 ml	12 fl oz	=	350 ml
$\frac{1}{2}$ tsp	=	2.5 ml	13 fl oz	=	375 ml
1 tsp	=	5 ml	14 fl oz	=	400 ml
1 tbs	=	15 ml	15 fl oz	=	425 ml = ($\frac{3}{4}$ pint)
1 fl oz	=	25 ml	16 fl oz	=	450 ml
2 fl oz	=	50 ml	18 fl oz	=	500 ml = ($\frac{1}{2}$ litre)
3 fl oz	=	75 ml	20 fl oz	=	600 ml = (1 pint)
$3\frac{1}{2}$ fl oz	=	100 ml	1 pint	=	600 ml
4 fl oz	=	125 ml	$1\frac{1}{2}$ pints	=	725 ml
5 fl oz	=	150 ml	$1\frac{3}{4}$ pints	=	850 ml
6 fl oz	=	175 ml	2 pints	=	1 litre
7 fl oz	=	200 ml	3 pints	=	1.75 litres
8 fl oz	=	225 ml	9 pints	=	5 litres
9 fl oz	=	250 ml	1 gallon	=	4.5 litres
10 fl oz	=	275 ml = ($\frac{1}{2}$ pint)	$2\frac{3}{16}$ gallons	=	10 litres
11 fl oz	=	300 ml			

Oven Temperatures

° Fahrenheit	° Centigrade	Gas Regulo
150	70	
175	80	
200	100	
225	110	$\frac{1}{4}$
250	130	$\frac{1}{2}$
275	140	1
300	150	2
325	160	3
350	180	4
375	190	5
400	200	6
425	220	7
450	230	8
475	240	9
500	250	
525	270	
550	290	

Index